Reading-for-Men

NELSON DOUBLEDAY, INC.
Garden City   New York

12

Reading-for-Men

The Trouble With
LAZY ETHEL

Ernest K. Gann

EDITOR'S NOTE

Ernest K. Gann is one of America's top storytellers. In recent years he has written hit after hit; it is almost impossible to scan the best-seller lists and movie marquees without encountering one of his smash successes such as *The High and the Mighty, Twilight for the Gods, Soldier of Fortune,* or *Blaze of Noon.*

Now Mr. Gann has written another compelling and highly entertaining story, *The Trouble with Lazy Ethel.* Lazy Ethel is a hurricane that starts as a mere imaginative scrawl on a harassed weatherman's map. But she is to prove an overwhelming storm of destiny for the party of assorted Americans who have come to a South Pacific atoll for a major weapons test.

The Trouble with Lazy Ethel is a warm, human, often highly comic novel. To quote the *New York Herald Tribune:* "The book can be read as a portrait of Americans in a home away from home . . . a remarkably clear one . . . Best of all, it is at all times a good story. Ernest Gann has the precious gift of narrative skill, and he exercises it to the fullest."

1

ON THE FIRST DAY the freighter anchored just outside the narrow channel which led into the lagoon. In the morning the people of the construction company unloaded enough amphibious equipment so that the dynamiting and pile-driving could proceed. A new wharf was completed before darkness, and moving in cautiously, the freighter became a temporary part of Nikki atoll. Then there was night.

On the second day the cargo booms worked with monotonous regularity depositing all manner of equipment upon the new wharf. There were set down tractors, earth-moving machines, diesel generators, pumps, fuel tanks, pipes of many sizes, and great clanging squares of corrugated steel. There were sacks of cement, racks of lumber, stacks of wallboard, toilets and stoves, huge spools of wire, boxes of nuts, bolts, screws, tools, barrels of tar and nails, steel girders with numbers painted on each end, cases of crockery, valves, medicines, candy bars, mattresses, and bedsprings.

Upon all this the natives of Nikki gazed in awe. They stood patiently in the blinding sun on the opposite side of the channel. They kept their backs to their own village and were silent. They stood so until it was night again.

On the third day one hundred and thirty-seven skilled men, most of them stripped to the waist, dispersed among the coconut palms which from the opposite side of the channel seemed to grow out of the freighter. And all of this third day the equipment roared and snorted and screeched at the bidding of these men. By nightfall a principal street had been crushed into the coral, four auxiliary streets traversed it at right angles, three miles of drainage ditches had been dug, stakes covered with hieroglyphics had been methodically set out along the streets, and one mile of heavy pipe had been laid.

On the fourth day, while the grunting earth-movers leveled an airstrip and transported the fill to obliterate a swamp, the carpenters, fitters, joiners, plumbers, sheet-metal men, masons, roofers, electricians, and crane operators moved across the staked area beyond the freighter. Before the trade wind subsided in the late afternoon they had erected thirteen structures of wood, steel, and wire screen. Each was almost exactly like the other.

Upon all this the natives gazed in amazement, for they had barely time to split the husk of a coconut and drink of its milk before another building met their eyes.

On the fifth day eleven additional buildings were completed, as was the airstrip. A seventy-foot control tower was bolted together and the radio equipment installed. The pumping station was set in operation and seventy-six toilet bowls flushed at the press of a handle. The diesel stove was installed in the mess hall. Four radioteletype machines were placed in the small prefabricated building which would serve as the communications center, but there was as yet no electricity to operate them. The foundation boss said he wanted to let the cement set another day before he subjected it to the vibrations of the main generator.

The natives on the opposite side of the channel were unaware of this minor delay. Now surfeited with miracles, they found it a relief to study the swift six-knot current as the ocean spewed through the channel toward the vast lagoon.

On the sixth day there was less noise from the settlement area as most of the workmen were engaged within the buildings. Minor frustrations caused a certain amount of cursing and some laughter, which echoed clearly between the empty buildings and could sometimes even be heard by the natives on the opposite side of the channel. Yet by noon the main generator was started and there were lights in the buildings and on the airstrip and on the new wharf—a development which left the natives aghast, since the sun was bright. The refrigerators which were just behind the mess hall were started, and so was the water evaporation plant. The X-ray equipment in the hospital was tested and approved. Radioteletype communication was established with the control island of Tuamani, which was three hundred miles to the northeast. The lathes in the machine shop and the power saws in the carpenter shop were pronounced ready for such efforts as the future might require. Thirty-eight small ice-boxes scattered throughout the settlement began making ice cubes. Eight Coco-Cola vending machines were filled and began to vibrate slightly with the life of their compressors. The line of six automatic washing machines in the laundry churned their water with busy efficiency, although they were empty of apparel.

A crew of three men passed from building to building in a jeep. They nailed stenciled signs over the doors of certain buildings—PHOTO LAB—WEATHER—SERVICE PERSONNEL—HOSPITAL—COMMUNICATIONS—SCHOOL. In time they paused before a building set apart from the rest. They took a moment to admire its favored location, which was between the sea and a row of coconut palms; then they nailed a more carefully lettered sign over the door—HERBERT ZEBULON PIKE. Along the bottom of the sign in much smaller letters were these symbols: Brig. Gen. U.S.A. Ret.

And again there was night. One of the last men to leave the settlement tested the electric barber-shop clippers on his sideburns.

At the end of the sixth day the ship employed the swift current in the channel to swing out from the wharf and at once proceeded to sea. She did not bother to blow her whistle.

The natives watched her mast lights mingle with the stars and were lost in wonder. This night in their two churches they sang the familiar hymns without enthusiasm. Both the Mormon elders in their church and the Catholic priest in his church had difficulty in capturing their attention. There was so much else to think about—on the other side of the channel.

On the seventh day, just as the bells of both churches proclaimed the Sabbath, a second vessel crept slowly toward the newly created wharf. It was smaller than the first and her decks were lined with passengers.

Herbert Zebulon Pike stood on the bridge wing behind the Captain and watched the approach to Nikki through a pair of massive binoculars. And he said to himself, It is good. He breathed deeply of the fresh morning air, and he thought that he would feel even better if there had been time to take his morning calisthenics. But there wasn't time, dammit! Innumerable problems had assailed him since before dawn. He had twice cut himself during the process of shaving in his cabin. Five teeth were missing from his comb, and for a man of sixty who still had use for a comb and liked to see each hair aligned with mathematical precision, this was enough to merit some comment upon the dubious qualities of plastic and why the hell didn't they still make steel combs like they did during World War One?

It was just then that his wife, Sue-Anne, rose up in her bunk and threw a slipper at him. The slipper had a heel and the hit was direct and the back of his neck was still sore from the impact.

She said in a voice that must have been heard all over the ship or at least in the adjacent cabins, "For criminy sakes, Zebulon! Will you stop splashin' around like a water buffalo and yellin' like you been wounded? You goin' to make every morning of my life just as downright miserable as you can? It's not even light yet and you have to be milling around and primping as if you was agoing to stand dress parade! Well, you ain't, honey. No more parades of any kind for you, so forget about them. Nobody's going to salute you 'cause from now on you're just plain Mister Pike and you better get used to it! So stop thrashin' around like a battery of horse-drawn and leave me get some sleep before I have to look at your silly island!"

Of course Sue-Anne was still a little confused from her energetic celebration of the last night aboard. It was also true that her speech contained certain elements of fact which her husband preferred to ignore. Pike had completed his toilet in such silence as he could manage, put on fresh khakis, and made his way to the dining saloon where he hastily swallowed a glass of tomato juice and a cup of Sanka. Customarily this would have rendered him capable of facing the day, but past experience had never prepared him for the problems which arose even before he had time for what he affectionately referred to as his "morning's morning." Albright, who was his aide and who would have appeared quite at home in a brokerage house, began the day by asking, "What about personnel gear, General? Do you want that unloaded before the dry stores or the other way around?"

"I suppose our people will be happier if they get their own stuff ashore first. I want to start our people off smiling."

Regardless of his past command, Pike had always referred to his soldiers as "our people" and he saw no reason to change now.

"If we do that the stores may not get up to the mess in time for dinner. The kids are bound to be pretty excited and tired and will probably set up an awful howl."

"Unload the stores first then."

"What about all that movie equipment in number three hold? Do you want it ashore so we can have a movie tonight, or can it wait?"

Pike's eyes lit up, for if he had one passion in life, it was the movies. He identified himself with every male star since the silent days, he read the credit titles, and when he could do so without being observed, he read the fan magazines. He particularly liked war movies, perhaps because he had never seen actual combat.

"We ought to have a movie tonight if we can," he said as if he really didn't care. "Starts things off right. Builds morale."

"General, what about the natives on Nikki? I suggest we establish some kind of a policy now before we get there and while everybody is together in one place. It might avoid trouble later on. You could use the ship's loud-speaker system and tell them right after breakfast."

"Good idea. Set it up with the Captain. And, incidentally, I think you better call me Governor instead of General. It sounds better under the circumstances, and I've observed that civilians are touchy about such things. Same thing as when I was in the Army. Never used the Herbert part of my name. Sounded better."

"Right, sir."

By the time the sun rose the ship hummed with activity. And Zebulon Pike found all of it bothersome and confusing. Things were vastly different than he had imagined they would be. Why, sir, on a troopship everything ran like clockwork. This, he thought, as he searched his memory for an exact military simile, was more like the Italian mess at Caporetto. Well, sir, things would fall into line soon enough. Human beings, in or out of uniform, required and were most content with a firm leader.

Later, on the bridge, Pike stepped smartly to the microphone which the Captain held out to him. Those passengers who bothered to make their way to the well deck forward looked up to see a husky man with thick gray hair and deeply tanned face. His eyes were small and set too close together, perhaps, but there was certainly no suggestion of weakness about his mouth or lack of determination in his chin. He held his shoulders well back, so much so that the buttons on his shirt seemed in immediate peril of popping their moorings. The hand which seized the microphone was large and square. Before he spoke he smiled benignly down upon the small cluster of people. Then he covered the microphone with his hand and asked the Captain where everybody was.

"Most of them are still eating breakfast or getting packed. Go right ahead, General, the system goes all through the ship. They'll hear you wherever they are, whether they want to or not."

A flash frown passed across Pike's face. Ah, the Navy, he thought. You could spot a Navy man whether he stood on the bridge of a battleship in full uniform or chose to disguise himself as a merchant skipper. The pompous bastards were all alike. Utterly spoiled ice-cream eaters.

Pike caressed his West Point ring. His confident smile returned and in a carefully modulated voice, with, he thought, just the proper hint of authority, he began to speak.

"Ladies and gentlemen. May I have your attention, please? This is your Governor speaking . . . and the children, of course, too . . . we mustn't forget the little ones. Perhaps I should say citizens of Nikki, for that is what you will be for the next year. . . ."

He paused to let his opening take effect and pretended to clear his throat. Then suddenly an approach occurred to him which he fondled mentally for such a long time that several of the men on the foredeck sat down, lit cigarettes, and gazed off toward the horizon. Pike ignored them. Patton must have felt the same before the Bulge, he decided. Or Eisenhower before Omaha Beach.

He began again, more slowly, and his smile vanished as quickly as it had come.

"I am not Moses leading you to the promised land. But there, just on the horizon, is your new home. Nikki atoll. It is sixteen miles in diameter and the highest land on it is one hundred and fifty feet. It's a long way from anywhere. . . . About all we can say about it is it's in the Pacific Ocean. . . . Ho, ho!"

Pike waited for a responding laugh. There was none.

"There is a lagoon inside that coral reef where we're going to live. . . . I don't mean we're going to live in the lagoon. . . . It's just there, that's all. Anyway, it's a big lagoon, more than ten miles wide from one end to the other . . . and I understand the fishing is pretty good. Unfortunately, there isn't much more to do on Nikki except work. . . . Which is what we came for. There's good quarters for all, plenty of food, water, plumbing, recreation facilities, and even a movie. The Atlas Construction people do things right, and who couldn't if they had a couple of million dollars to throw around. Ho . . . Ho!"

Pike had once read that Teddy Roosevelt had inspired his Rough Riders with a boisterous laugh and he thought that his own must be very akin to it. This time Pike detected a faint titter among his audience, and he saw with satisfaction that several additional men and women had found their way to the foredeck.

"Maybe I'm not Moses, but you are all chosen people . . . chosen by the Commission because of your various skills . . . and believe me we have everything from bankers and bakers to astronomers. All kinds of talent and brains in this outfit! Let me briefly restate our mission . . . the reason we are here . . . the reason the A.E.C. pays us to be here. I have been authorized at this time to inform you of certain additional details because now we are all officially a part of Operation Zeus. On or about February tenth of next year a thermonuclear explosion will take place to the north of us. This will not be a little firecracker like past bombs, but an explosion of such proportions not even the big brains know what the effect will be."

Pike quickly held up his hand. It was almost a gesture of benediction. "Now, tut, tut . . . you mothers. And all the rest of you. We have nothing to worry about on Nikki. No one really has except the enemies of our country. The actual explosion will be a very long ways from here. Our job is to serve as an auxiliary base to the island of Tuamani. As you all know, most of the project will be directed from Tuamani and I should say we're pretty lucky to be out here more or less on our own. Our job is to get ready for what happens later this year because Operation Zeus will spread over several thousand miles, and it takes a lot of doing the ordinary person just never thinks about. And maybe that's a good thing . . . if he's a taxpayer. Ho. . . . Ho!"

On this Pike obtained a very recognizable laugh, but it was spoiled for him almost instantly. He became aware that his wife had somehow found her way to the bridge. She leaned against the pilothouse, lit a cigarette, and blew the smoke toward him. The wind whipped the smoke away, but her eyes and the hopeless way she shook her head caused him to cover the microphone.

She said, "Go on, blowhard. Don't let me stop you."

Pike smiled sheepishly at the Captain and set his jaw. He brought his hands together and his West Point class ring scraped along the microphone. It made a hideous scratching noise out of all proportion to his movement. His face reddened and his voice boomed unnaturally as he spoke again.

"Our mission here is to supply and service such auxiliary guard ships, research ships and project aircraft as may come to Nikki. In addition we will house and service a complement of scientists and foreign observers. Now there's just one thing more . . ."

Herbert Zebulon Pike's wife said, "Thank God for that!"

"Just this. Nikki atoll has been leased from the French government under certain conditions. The main condition was this, and I don't want you to forget it. The natives will be left strictly alone. They have been living here a long time and we're not supposed to louse them up. They aren't cannibals and they don't wear grass skirts. So you younger fellows just forget what may come to your minds. They're all Mormons or Catholics anyway and they don't smoke or drink. Their village is separated from us by a deep-water channel and I'm told that anyone who tries to swim that pass is just about committing suicide. The current runs six knots through here . . . so I say to you again, just forget about it. Let the natives go their way and we'll go ours. Okay? So much for that. . . ."

Pike's wife said, "That's what *you* think."

"A few last details. We should dock in about thirty minutes. Go ashore as soon as you wish. My aide, Mr. Albright, will be standing at the bottom of the gangplank. He will give you the quarters assignments . . . and I want to ask you bachelors to let the married men and their families get set up first. . . . They've got kids and all. Which reminds me that Miss Summer, our schoolteacher, rings the ol' bell at eight tomorrow morning . . . so at least the kids will be off to a flying start. Readin' and writin' and 'rithmetic . . ."

Pike almost sang his last words; then his manner changed abruptly and his voice became husky with emotion.

"We have a big job to do, my friends. Operation Zeus will be a monument in the history of mankind. It is a new shield for democracy. Good luck to you."

Pike waved his hand and lowered the microphone. His wife said, "What's the trouble, honey? You run out of wind?"

When Pike disappeared from the bridge rail, most of the people on the deck split into groups of three and four and watched the black line of Nikki atoll on the horizon. They saw it first as two islands. The more knowing explained that the illusion was caused by the channel which cut through to the lagoon. In a few minutes they were able to distinguish individual palms and on one side of the channel a splatter of faded red roofs among the trees. Someone pointed out a red church spire, and listening, they could hear a bell tolling.

One man ignored the approaching land. He was slim and very tall. He was not handsome; in fact he had often been told that he bore a remarkable resemblance to the young Abe Lincoln. While the similarity was lessened by his short-cut hair, there remained a certain quiet dignity which successfully preserved the illusion. Now he appeared entirely absorbed in the sky. He stood with his hands in his pockets and studied the quickly changing cloud formations, and on his face there lingered a smile of appreciation, as if he alone shared a secret with the variety of cumulus and cumulo-nimbus and the wisps of cirrus far above them. After a while he took a short pipe from his shirt pocket and sucked on it thoughtfully. Since he stood as far apart from the others as the foredeck would permit, his reverie was undisturbed until the ship slowed to approach the wharf. Then Albright, the Governor's aide, came to him.

"You're Adam Smith, aren't you?"

"What?"

Albright's diction was not easy to follow. His voice was peculiarly resonant and he puckered his lips into a small rosette as he spoke. And so the effect was a mixture of a lisp and also that of a man who had just severely burned his tongue. He spoke so rapidly there was almost no separation between his words and thus his question emerged as a fuzzy outburst deep within his throat. He waited with one eyebrow cocked expectantly. He stood with his feet placed closely together, holding a snap board and wavering slightly, which was intended to suggest jauntiness but instead created the impression he was in danger of losing his balance.

"I said you're Adam Smith."

"Well, yes . . . I am."

"Right. I'm Albright, the Governor's aide."

"Pleased to meet you, Mr. Albright."

Adam automatically extended his hand. He withdrew it when he saw that Albright had not the slightest intention of clasping it.

"Right. The Governor would like to know if it will rain tonight."

Adam smiled and shook his head in disbelief. Finally he said, "Well now . . . I just couldn't say one way or . . ."

"You're our weather chap, aren't you?"

"Well . . . yeah. But, golly . . . I'm not a fortuneteller."

"The Governor is extremely anxious about the movies tonight. It's an open-air theater, you know, wooden benches, no roof . . . that sort of thing, and the Governor is most anxious that our first evening go off without a hitch."

"Well, golly! I just got here . . . I'm not even there yet. I have no map and I don't know the local conditions and even if I did, forecasting weather is a complicated . . ."

"Look, old fellow. The Governor wants an answer. And in case you're not aware of it, Governor Pike does not like equivocations. Is it going to rain or is it not?"

Adam said slowly, "I just don't know."

"I can't tell him that. Come along. Give me some kind of an answer."

"All right. You tell the Governor that I don't think it's going to rain . . . but anybody who's going to the movies had better take their raincoats."

"I doubt if the Governor will appreciate that report."

"Well, it's the only one I have. By the way . . . You happen to know where I'll be living?"

Albright ruffled the papers on his snap board.

"Building C with the other bachelors. You chaps should have some jolly times in there."

"Thanks a lot."

"Right."

Albright turned on his heel and was gone as suddenly as he had appeared.

Now, with the ship barely moving toward the wharf, Adam looked away from the sky and found interest in the land. He saw that the shore shelved up from an outer reef in the manner of most coral atolls, and he saw how the channel split the land and led directly to a further expanse of water which would be the lagoon. He could not perceive any sign of land beyond the lagoon; in fact, it appeared as limitless as another sea. As the ship approached the wharf, he looked down at the water and watched a multitude of fishes moving effortlessly against the channel current, and he saw that the violent colors which he had admired in the sky were exactly duplicated in the clear depths.

He was surprised and unaccountably disappointed in the native village, now fully revealed behind the palms which stretched along the shore. It was much smaller and much neater than he had anticipated. It appeared deserted and only the occasional cry of a rooster gave any indication of life. Then he remembered it was Sunday morning.

Crossing to the opposite side of the deck he looked out upon the village created by the Atlas Construction Company. And he was neither disappointed nor pleased. It was exactly as he had thought it would be with the same old barracks-like buildings arranged according to a master plan that never varied. Heritage from the Second World War, he thought, and then he wondered how he had conceived the idea since he had been some five years too young to have any part of that war.

When the ship came to rest alongside the wharf, Adam went down to the cramped cabin he shared with two other men and picked up his suitcase and a duffel bag. Then he made his way to the deck again, excusing himself several times as he collided with other passengers, all of whom, he thought, appeared to be in a near panic to get ashore.

A Marine sergeant with whom Adam had struck up a nodding acquaintance during the two-day voyage down from Tuamani was trying to herd the women and children into some semblance of order. Adam knew that his name was Doolan, and now he appeared to be dangerously harassed. So when Doolan passed close to him, breathing short as if to contain his frustration, Adam smiled. Doolan accepted the smile as a signal of sympathy. He halted and mopped his dripping face. Scowling at the people milling around him, he said, "I'm a diamond-shaped son of a bitch. You'd think the Governor really was leading them to the promised land. We only got just so much transport and everybody wants to get settled down with their grandmaw's picture over the mantel in sixteen seconds!"

Sgt. Doolan passed on and Adam sat down on his duffel bag. The separate sounds of confusion about him melted into each other and became a monotonous hum. He had almost dozed off when he felt a small and very moist hand touch his own. Adam opened his eyes and saw a scrawny boy standing before him. The boy's eyes were filled with tears. He caught at his breath, but he made no audible sound.

"You see my mother, mister?"

"I'm not sure I know your mother."

"She's purty."

"Most mothers are. What's the matter? Lost her?"

The boy nodded his head.

"She'll turn up. They always do. What's your name?"

"Floyd Dunbar."

Adam held out his hand. Sitting on his duffel bag his head was just slightly above the boy's. The boy squeezed his hand more firmly and Adam managed to maintain his smile though he saw their clasp was sealed with the drippings of a candy bar. He said that his name was Adam.

"That's the name of the first man ever invented, ain't it?"

"That's right."

Adam got up from his duffel bag and, holding the boy's hand, he made his way through the crowd around the gangway entrance until they emerged upon the deck. There were several women on the fringes of the crowd. None of them displayed the slightest interest in the boy. When they reached a free place along the rail, Adam hoisted him to his shoulder so he could look down upon the wharf. Below, Adam recognized Albright and saw that he was surrounded by a huddle of men and women.

"Any of those people belong to your family, Floyd?"

"Nope."

"Let's just wait here till they do show up."

"I have to go pee-pee."

"Right this minute?"

"Pretty soon."

Adam heard a woman's voice behind him call Floyd's name. He turned and was surprised to see that the woman was very young. She wore a simple cotton dress over a figure which already suggested dumpiness.

"Floyd! Where you been?"

"Just lookin' around at things. Me and Adam here."

Adam said, "Floyd and I have had a nice talk."

The woman shot him a harried look. She brushed aside a lock of blond hair which had fallen over one eye. As Adam set the boy down she took his hand.

"Thanks, mister. My husband had to go ashore right away and fix some piece of machinery that already busted down. He left me with all the baggage and the kids and all, and I got stuff stacked all over the boat. Just like pioneer times, ain't it? I feel like we should be riding in a covered wagon. Come see us when we get settled in. Our name's Dunbar."

"Sure."

They melted at once into the crowd at the gangway. Adam was about to return to the comfort of his duffel bag when Carlos Raveza joined him at the rail. Carlos was fat and just now he was very hot and his shirt was already sopping with moisture. He touched his wisp of mustache and belched. Adam had never known a man who belched so often. He thought that Carlos must look very much like a hippopotamus suffering from gastric distress.

Carlos said, "I think they keep us here all day, maybe, no?"

"Seems like there's some tie-up in transportation."

Carlos pushed his belly against the rail until it resembled a punctured tire. He shoved his battered straw hat defiantly over one eye and peered down at the wharf.

"That Mr. Albright. His English no comprendo."

"I had a little trouble myself. But then I think he must be an Easterner and they talk funny . . . or a lot of them do."

"He speaks in the manner of a Limey."

"I guess he's just trying to earn a living."

Carlos belched again and seemed enormously satisfied with his effort. Then suddenly a sadness came to his eyes.

"This place looks some little like Mexico. . . . Tampico, you would say. But, naturally, not so gay. In Tampico no person gets excited . . . ever. Positively never. It is, how you say, against the law."

"You mean against custom."

"However you desire it. *I* was born in Tampico."

Poking a fat finger into the upper roll of his belly, Carlos made the announcement as if it were an historic occasion. Then he added, "You can see by my teeth that I was born in Tampico."

"Your teeth?"

"In Tampico there is not one single dentist. It has something to do with the water."

Parting his lips, Carlos displayed his teeth. "Regard! Not so much as one single excavation!"

"They look pretty good."

"They are perfect! In the same way is my liver. Superb! I am sorry you cannot examine my kidneys also. Not so much as a stone. Not even a small pebble!" He made a pinching gesture with his fingers.

"You're lucky. Nothing like a healthy liver."

"In the same way are all of the parts of my body. Whores adore me. They say I am fantástico!"

"Congratulations."

"The secret is never to become excited. Life is like electricity. You must allow it to flow freely, and do not overload. If you do, you blow a fuse. It is as simple as that."

Carlos turned the palms of his hands upward and moved them apart slowly. Then he said, "I have turned my most excellent ear to the Governor and his speech. Simpático, señor . . . very simpático . . . and also full of horse manure."

"It struck me as sort of a pep talk."

"It commence with manure and end with manure. . . . Especially the part about chosen people. I observe only a collection of how you say— misfits and miswits—of which I am the most."

"I dunno. Most of them seem to be pretty nice people."

"To *you,* señor! Ah! But what do you know about these creatures in special? Have you inquired of yourself, for example . . . how in the world did I ever get the job as chief electrician?"

Adam laughed. "Why not? Aren't you a good electrician?"

"Christ no! If I knew my business I would not be here. Naturally I was not so honest when I made application. Not so much as a single one of these people would be here if they could make a good living back in the United States. This includes Carlos Raveza."

"It just so happens that I can."

"Then may I ask just what the hell you are doing here, or did you commit rape or rob a bank or kick opium?"

Adam hesitated. Yes, why was he here on Nikki? Certainly not because he was interested in a nuclear explosion! Or even because of any special interest in the Pacific weather. He took a moment to search his mind for a logical reason and found none that would provide a satisfactory answer. Finally he said, "It beats me."

"Exactly! Now you have say a thing of intelligence. The Governor also say one thing of intelligence, but he forget the main thing. Yes, this must be a big affair . . . very grand, as who but men with very large brains could think up such a big firecracker and have the braveness to light the fuse? But the Governor forget to say that children should not play with dynamite."

"I guess the scientists know what they're doing."

"They do . . . but *we* don't. And we, my friend, happen to be you and I, the little brains in this big world. And it is the little brains not the big ones, who are really going to use this firecracker . . . which is why we will wake up some day and God or the devil will ask us how we got where we are and the only intelligent thing to say will be 'It beats me.'"

2

TRILLIONS OF ORGANISMS which united and perished together so that Nikki atoll might project above the surface of the sea were thus engaged for, some said, a thousand years. Others said five thousand years and others said five hundred years. It depended on who held forth upon its creation; whether it was Yip Kee, the young Chinese merchant; or Fat Sue, the old Chinese merchant; or André, the Mormon elder; or Father Louis, the Catholic priest. Or you might listen to the soft explanation of Tanni, the native chief who had little respect for the theory of coral organisms; or his wife Lua, who had even less; or M. DeLage, who ran the post office and the atoll's feeble wireless that was supposed to maintain contact with the outside world. M. DeLage, who had found his way to Nikki all the way from Lyons via America and consequently knew a great many things, said that Nikki was only partially built by coral polyps and offered as proof the fifty-meter hill which rose on the southerly side of the formation. No other atoll in the whole Pacific had such a hill. Therefore, according to M. DeLage, some volcanic disturbance must have been involved at the birth of Nikki. DeLage proposed that Nikki was a poor relative of Tuamani which had heaved itself frothing toward the sky and left a jagged pyramid which could be seen for a hundred miles. Tuamani was brooding and cloud-covered and thick with jungle. Even in the finest weather its appearance was as savage as the fierce people who once dwelt in its valleys and dined upon each other as often as possible.

Life had always been more tranquil on Nikki atoll, and some gave credit to the easy topography. Nikki was shaped like a flat doughnut. The organisms apparently had become exhausted from their efforts just before they completed the gigantic circle and so failed to meet by a few hundred yards. Some of the older inhabitants who kept faith with the ancient beliefs maintained that a hungry sea monster took a bite out of the atoll and thus formed the pass which led into the lagoon. They said, "Ahwei! You can see it yourself!"

Even the climate on Nikki was different from Tuamani. Except for a month of almost continuous rain during December it was relatively dry and the nearly constant trade winds gave an illusion of vigor to the air. Storms were rare and there had not been a hurricane for a very long time. There were relatively few flies. No one had ever seen a snake. The fish were abundant, mostly nonpoisonous, and co-operative. The coconut palms were healthy and bore well enough so that the gathering and drying of copra had long been the chief source of income for the inhabitants. A second source was found in the lagoon, where the clear bottom provided enough mother-of-pearl shell to keep the divers busy three months of every year. This was just enough to pay off their debts at the two Chinese stores. Many things ran in pairs on Nikki, and now there were two settlements.

Certain unpleasantnesses prevented Nikki from becoming a paradise. The rat population was large and bold. There were countless land crabs for which no one had ever been able to discover the slightest use. There were sharks in the lagoon, most of which were considered harmless, but those which lurked in and about the channel were known to be extremely antagonistic. And so the native divers avoided the channel, and even when the sharks showed an interest in their work in the lagoon, they climbed aboard their outriggers and moved to another area. There were a few cases of elephantiasis on Nikki, but these were regarded as a part of life and those who suffered from it flatly refused to go to the clinic in Tahiti. And there had always been the "No-nu" fish which concealed itself in the sand along the inner and outer reefs.

This fish terrified the natives. For the No-nu was cleverly camouflaged and almost invisible. Its venom apparatus was efficient and complicated; the dorsal, anal, and ventral spines containing poison sacs fed from the glands through lateral grooves. If a man was so unfortunate as to step on one he instantly discovered true agony. It was so that a No-nu's spine contained such vicious poison that the victim was invariably driven mad with pain and, frothing of the mouth, usually welcomed death within a few hours.

Thus the combination of evils and blessings on Nikki atoll was reflected in the temperaments of the people, who had dwelt there long before the first missionaries arrived to confuse them. Because of their isolation they were healthier than most Polynesians. Impetigo, yaws, pneumonia, and malaria were nonexistent. They were also more industrious. Poverty was unknown and so was crime. Authority was vested in the chief, who was elected every six years, and the candidate was invariably chosen for his wisdom, gentility, and good nature.

Three days after the ship had disembarked her passengers, Tanni, the Chief of Nikki, stood on the opposite side of the channel and waited for an approaching motor launch. He was dressed in his best for the occasion: white shirt with tails hanging out, and immaculately laundered shorts. He wore his wrist watch although it had not functioned for some time. Beside him stood Terry Mack, who was a Melanesian instead of a Polynesian and was therefore hirsute and was therefore constantly in need of a shave. Terry Mack was a Cook Islander who had wandered as far as Nikki looking for a place to settle down. He was very small and blind in one eye. He was not regarded as a first citizen of Nikki, but since he hailed from British-mandated territory he did speak English, which accounted for his present position of honor. The entire population of Nikki village including several squalling babies was dispersed loosely behind the pair.

When the motor launch bounced against the old wharf, Herbert Zebulon Pike was the first occupant to step ashore. He was followed by five men, all of them unnaturally solemn, for Pike had said, "All right now, gentlemen. Let's watch our behavior. This is important. We must get off on the right foot with the locals. I've always found getting on with the locals of the utmost value in any operation."

All of the men with the exception of Sgt. Doolan, who had been warned to leave his side arms in his quarters, made a clumsy departure from the launch. Albright's sun helmet fell forward and temporarily blinded him when he reached out for the wharf. Dr. Case, to whom Pike had said, "You just might have a look at the medical situation over there . . . probably find all kinds of weird diseases . . . our own protection, you know," became so entranced with the fishes beneath the wharf he almost fell between the pilings and the launch. Capt. Michaud, the handsome French observer assigned to Operation Zeus, was equally taken with a group of maidens behind the Chief and missed his footing twice. However, one of the many press relations men assigned to Zeus required Doolan's assistance in leaving the launch. He had already discovered that he was the one man on Nikki whom Pike feared, and consequently he could get as drunk as he pleased any time he felt like it. He finally staggered into the informal line which had formed behind Pike.

Pike covered the distance which separated him from the Chief in three forceful strides. There was a faint click from the vicinity of his heels as he came to a halt. His hand started involuntarily toward his right eye as if he would salute and then shot forward. And for a moment he seemed at loss for a greeting. Finally he said, "How do you do, sir."

Tanni took his hand most gently in the Polynesian fashion, which was far more of a caress than a contest of strength. Pike managed to conceal his displeasure.

"Pike's the name. I bring you greetings from your new neighbors across the channel."

It was an opening Pike had rehearsed several times in the privacy of his bathroom. Now, he thought, it sounded just right for the occasion and he was pleased until he realized that Tanni had not understood a word.

The Chief turned to Terry Mack and they conversed quietly in Tahitian. Finally Terry Mack focused his good eye on Pike and said, "The Chief thanks you jolly much, m'lad. 'E sez 'e's glad to see you lookin' so fat."

Pike instantly sucked in his stomach. His lips worked impatiently as Terry Mack continued.

"The Chief sez 'e 'opes you and all yer people are 'appy and if yer want any washin' done 'is women will do it."

Pike looked down upon Terry Mack with disapproval. The little man was not his idea of a dignified interpreter.

"Tell the Chief thanks very much but we have our own laundry. Also tell him I would like to know the disease situation on Nikki."

"The disease situation?"

Terry Mack was openly bewildered. His good eye sought the sky for a suitable answer.

"Yes. I want to know about typhoid, any fevers, and are the women infected?"

Pike glanced significantly at the group of young women who had gathered at a respectable distance behind Tanni. They met Pike's eyes frankly, and then they giggled. Hanover, the press representative, caught up their giggle and started forward. Mumbling vaguely about starting a party, he was restrained and towed back into position by Sgt. Doolan.

Albright said, "If I might suggest, Governor, your question might be rephrased more delicately."

Terry Mack said, "I caught the Guv'nor quite all right. 'E wants to know 'ave the women got the clap."

Pike snorted and his face turned the color of the new coral beneath the wharf. But his forbidding stare failed to affect the little man. He only displayed more of his rotten teeth in a knowing smile.

"The answer is no, m'lad. And if they do get it we'll know where it come from."

Pike's face became redder. The veins in his powerful neck enlarged and his lips became a tight, thin line.

"So much for your delicate approach, Mr. Albright. I'll thank you to stay out of this from now on. Captain Michaud. Would you mind lending a hand as interpreter? If I could communicate with the Chief in French we could get rid of this renegade. I can't say I care for his attitude."

Terry Mack stood his ground. He said, "The Chief don't savvy French, m'lad."

"Then let me straighten you out on a few things. . . . In the first place I am not your lad. I am the duly appointed Governor of our settlement on Nikki and as such I am the senior representative of the United States Government. You will address me with the respect that position deserves."

"Righto, Guv'nor."

Terry Mack seemed honestly contrite. He wiped his nose on the back of his hand, scratched at his beard, and seemed delighted with Pike's rebuke.

"In the second place your duty as an interpreter is to faithfully translate the remarks of the two parties involved and not insert your own opinions. Now is that clear?"

"Clear as the sky, Guv'nor. But I've seen you Yank blokes before and you bring a lot more trouble than you take away."

Pike exploded.

"I don't give a damn what you happen to think! You stick to your business and tell the Chief this is not in any sense a military operation—"

"Then what is that soldier 'angin' about with you?"

"He's *not* a soldier, dammit! He's a marine! He and four of his men merely have the duty of keeping order in our colony."

"Knowing Yanks I should think that's 'ardly enough . . . ."

"Shut up!"

Pike swerved and looked at Albright. "This is impossible! This impudent clown is deliberately insulting us."

"You instructed me to stay out of this, sir. But if I am free to make an observation, I would suggest patience."

"Maybe he's a Russian spy," Hanover mumbled.

Pike turned back and tried to split a smile at the Chief and a glare at Terry Mack. The result was confusing. After a moment he managed to continue although his words came with ominous slowness.

"You tell the Chief that we are normal, law-abiding people. Our population includes several married couples and their children. We have as well some of the most distinguished scientists in the world and the representatives of France, England, and Japan. This is merely a courtesy visit. We have not the slightest desire to interfere with the Chief's village or his people in any way, shape, or form. I have given the strictest orders that no one shall cross the channel, although if the Chief or any of his people wish to visit us, they will be most welcome. Now is that all clear? Do you think you can get it across without making a botch of it?"

Terry Mack shrugged his shoulders and said innocently, "Why not?"

Then while Pike fidgeted he turned to Tanni and spoke with many gestures in the Polynesian manner.

When Terry Mack concluded his speech there was silence while Tanni thoughtfully examined the face of each man in Pike's party. There was no emotion in his large brown eyes. He seemed to be looking into the men rather than at them, neither approving nor disapproving. Pike clasped his hands uncertainly behind his back and assumed an at-ease posture. Capt. Michaud reached for a pack of cigarettes in his shirt pocket and then, thinking better of it, dropped his hand. Dr. Case, suddenly uncomfortable beneath Tanni's searching look, tried a half-smile and abandoned it almost instantly. Albright experimented with his balance as was his habit. Hanover, suddenly sobered, wiped the perspiration from the pouches beneath his eyes and worked his dry tongue across his lips. Doolan alone appeared unaffected by the Chief's examination. He stood rigidly at attention and stared at a red tin roof he had selected as a target at the end of the village street.

At last Tanni seemed satisfied with what he had seen. He beckoned lazily toward one of the women who moved quickly forward and held out a large, cardboard box. Tanni reached into the box and drew out a necklace of sea shells. The shells were a mottled brown and highly polished, so much so they glittered in the sunlight as he placed the necklace around Pike's neck. Then he moved solemnly among his visitors and presented each one with a necklace from the box. When he had finished, he returned to his position and spoke briefly to Terry Mack.

"The Chief sez yer welcome to Nikki, and 'e 'opes yer women will like the shells. You ought to. It takes a long time to get that particular kind."

"Tell the Chief we deeply appreciate his gifts. Albright! Why the hell didn't you tell me this sort of thing was goin' to happen? We should have brought something for these people."

"I'll see that a launch brings over something appropriate this afternoon."

"The Chief sez would you like to see the village?"

"We would be honored," Pike said.

And so Tanni and Pike, with Terry Mack trotting along between them, led the procession along the sun-baked street which was the only one in Nikki. They saw the Mormon church and admired its crudely painted glass windows; and they entered the Catholic church, which was smaller but more serene beneath a cluster of palms. Dr. Case observed that the Atlas Construction Company seemed to have remembered everything but a church in their own establishment, and Pike said yes, that was wrong and that he would do something about it. They saw the Chinese store of Fat Sue, whose wares consisted of canned goods, fishhooks, and needles and thread, and they saw the store of Charlie Yip Kee who sold exactly the same thing. They saw the post office and pretended to admire M. DeLage's antiquated wireless equipment. They inspected a line of sheds in which copra was drying, and Tanni ordered two boys to open enough coconuts so they could each have a drink of the milk. Hanover tried bravely to swallow the liquid but was almost immediately forced to retire behind a tree, where he gagged noisily for such a long time that Pike ventured a frown of disapproval when he finally returned.

The tour of the village took less than an hour in spite of Hanover's lagging, and the re-embarkation into the launch went off without incident. As the launch pulled away from the wharf, Pike stood erect in the stern and waved his hand at the assembled crowd. He reserved a final salute for Tanni. The departure was robbed of some dignity by Terry Mack, who called after them with the maximum effort of his lungs, "Keep yer friggin' nose clean, Guv'nor!"

The question of a name for their settlement troubled the people who now occupied the buildings set up by the Atlas Construction Company. They could not call the place Nikki because that was already the name of the native village across the channel and, furthermore, it identified the entire atoll. Yet everyone seemed to feel the need of a name suitable to their new home. Debates on the subject flourished in the mess hall and at times almost led to violence. There were innumerable suggestions and no one from Pike to little Floyd Dunbar hesitated to voice his opinion. Sue-Anne Pike, who managed to be present at the closing of the bar each night, said she didn't give a hollerin' hoot in hell what the place was finally named if they didn't call it "Bourbonville." Her selection won some support among the more carefree settlers who waited for the bar to open at five each day and were invariably present when it closed at ten.

Others were inclined to be more conservative. Professor Tasamachi, the Japanese observer, suggested "Babylon" because, as he pointed out, it would not be in existence for long. Pete Walsacki, the boss plumber, liked "Little Toledo." He was able to persuade Barney Dunbar, the boss carpenter, Pinkey Riley, the baker, and Ellsworth Tompkins, the chief of mechanical maintenance, to his way of thinking. This was a powerful coalition.

There were independents particularly among the scientific team now resident on Nikki. Dr. H. P. V. Callandar, the physicist, inserted the problem in his IBM-machine brain and after several days of almost audible clicking came up with "Station Sixty-One." His choice aroused so little enthusiasm he never had an opportunity to explain why the number so appealed to him. Dr. Herman Keim, the astronomer, said why not just call the place Nikki and let confusion reign; it was always stimulating. He could enlist no support whatever and brooded for several days on what he called the "human yearning for special identity."

The matter was settled for everyone by a mandate which came down from Tuamani. The message danced across the Pacific sky and found its way down to the prefabricated shack which served as the communications center. It was Sunnie Mandel who saw it first on the number three radioteletype machine.

"Well, whaddya know. We got a name!"

She turned to Margaret Trumpey, who shared the work in the center and pointed at the still-clacking machine. Sunnie blew out her cheeks and said, "Wait until Herbert Zebulon Pike gets a load of this! One of those big brains on Tuamani has fractured a cell! Ya just gotta be dippy to think up such stuff. . . ."

Margaret joined her before the machine. Standing side by side, the two became as much a contrast as Nikki atoll and the island of Tuamani, where the message had originated. Sunnie Mandel was so thin that in certain lights her skin gave the impression of being translucent, and only the lively sparkle in her eyes rescued her from appearing sickly.

Margaret would have made two of Sunnie. Her facial features were lovely, her eyes wide-set and intelligent, her mouth well formed and inviting. And when she smiled it was impossible not to admire her perfect teeth. Her complexion was a striking heritage, and when struck by sunlight, her tawny hair became like well-polished gold.

Unfortunately, Margaret's beauty ended abruptly at her neck, which was all too sturdy. Her neck matched her body and her powerful legs. She would have fitted perfectly into a nineteenth-century landscape stacking grain or crushing grapes with her bare feet. An artist who had once dined at Margaret's home in Beloit, Wisconsin, said that Margaret had not been born like other girls, but had really escaped from a Rubens painting. The next day Margaret went to the library and spent almost an hour studying Rubens. She was both embarrassed and sad. For the artist had been right. He only neglected to mention that fashions in the female figure had changed and that to people who were not artists, and especially to the young men of Beloit, Margaret Trumpey was just overweight. This was untrue. She could not have lost a pound if she tried. She was simply peasant-husky. Yet few young men in Beloit, conditioned by a generation which believed the deliberate malformation of the female figure to be a supreme social duty, understood or appreciated Margaret's honest and graceful proportions. Which was why she was not very unhappy to find herself so far away from home.

Now standing beside Sunnie Mandel, a quiet smile crept along her lips as she watched the last stutters of the machine.

DIRECT URGENT PIKE

FOR CONVENIENCE COMMUNICATIONS YOU NOW CLASSIFIED CODE NAME PISTOL TWO PERIOD OA TITIA ATOLL WILL BE DESIGNATED OA AND EXPLOSION SITE TRIGGER PERIOD COMPLY IMMEDIATELY AND FROM NOW ON SO DESIGNATE PERIOD ALL CONCERNED AIRCRAFT AND SHIPS ADVISED PERIOD SIGNED KEATING

The machine paused and then clacked off EOM, for end of message. Sunnie pulled the yellow paper upward and tore it off below the signature name. She said, "Which one of us is going to risk her life delivering this to His Majesty? Last I heard the Governor was bound and determined to name us Pike City just in case somebody might forget who's boss."

Margaret said, "I'll take it over. I have to pick up the weather map anyway."

"Lucky you."

Margaret paused as she folded the message into an envelope.

"How do you mean?"

"That weather guy. He's pretty cute . . . for a jerk. That is, his face is kind of cute, you know, sort of Abraham Lincoln-y without the beard, you know, sort of the kind that shoulda been a minister, or could be if he turned his collar around. But he's so quiet! He don't talk. Maybe because he's living with an important secret . . . like he was in the Foreign Legion, or he has a wife who is in a T.B. sanatorium, or maybe really he's a counterintelligence man . . . or, you know . . . Cripes, I never met anybody like him either back in Nyack or none of the other projects I worked on. Like NATO . . . Well, there was a few fellows in Frankfort who used to come down and sniff around the machines and keep their mouths shut until they got around to sex, and when I was in Japan with the WAC's there was this lieutenant who never said much either, but he danced like a wild man, which was kind of strange until we found out he used to be in a Broadway show and was as queer as a thirteen-dollar bill. . . . But this weather guy is a character, believe me. Maybe he was tortured by the Chinese or something and they cut out his tongue."

At the door Margaret said, "He talks to me every time I go for the map."

"Yeah? What's he say?"

"Hello. Sometimes he even says good-by."

"He must be in love with you. Maybe that's it. He made some kind of a oath with himself which keeps him Silent Sam until he meets the woman he will love. She will wear some kind of a special sign, like a chrysanthemum or a pearl in her right ear or . . ."

Margaret laughed. "Sunnie, if I had your imagination!"

Sunnie's face saddened and the expression was so rare, Margaret waited at the door.

"You don't have to make with the compliment talk, Margaret. I don't really have any imagination. I'm just repeating the kind of talk that's pretty standard in the Ree-Jay Club. I'm sort of a charter member and it seems like now that smart-aleck yak has become a part of me. But then, I can see from your face you never heard of the Ree-Jay Club."

"I've never been much of a joiner."

"Well, don't ever join the Ree-Jays. There's too many of us now. It's sort of a poor girl's Junior League. I can spot a member a mile off. To qualify you got to be just naturally ugly."

Sunnie glanced at Margaret's legs and then she looked quickly at her face again. Their eyes met, understood, and turned away. Sunnie started to talk again, but she now spoke uncertainly as if she were seeking a convenient exit from what she had begun.

"Well, mainly, there's got to be something about your personality men don't like and which all the Listerine in the world won't help. Maybe the girl has a little mustache on her upper lip, or happens to be eight feet tall, or maybe she's all skin and bones like me. The funny thing is some of the nicest gals in the world belong to the Ree-Jays, only I guess it isn't really very funny. Because no one but ourselves ever bothers to find that out."

"I'm beginning to feel like I'm missing something worth while."

"Oh no, you're not. Don't go and get ideas like that, for heaven's sake! Ree-Jay is our laugh-clown-laugh way of saying *reject*. These government projects are full of us. The best training ground is the WAC's, where you learn to lie in your bunk at night in the dark and cry inside and know that every other girl in the room will know just how you feel. Sometimes it gets to be a regular and sympathetic chorus and in your heart you can hear it as plain and loud as the Salt Lake Tabernacle Choir. I've known Ree-Jays who were thirty years old and never had a date in their lives. They never even had a chance to louse one up. Nobody wants them hanging around home if they ever had a home to begin with, and the competition is too rough in the average business firm. So what does a Ree-Jay do? She signs up to go overseas with some outfit and the good old government is usually the only outfit who'll take her. Overseas, see, things are supposed to be different, and maybe the men aren't so particular because they're supposed to be lonely. Malarkey! The men get with the native girls whether they're slant-eyed, brown-skinned, or what. The men know a reject when they see one, and if they're going to marry anybody, it's Little Nell back home, or Fräulein Schmeercase in Europe, or Madame Butterfly if they get real good and desperate in the Far East. One thing is good about being a Ree-Jay. You get a lot of readin' done and you go to lots of movies . . . by yourself. Which is how I get all those crazy ideas I just spouted about that weather guy. And if you think I'm feeling sorry for myself, well, I am. I do it every once in a while. It's purifying."

Margaret looked at Sunnie and saw that there was not a trace of bitterness in her eyes. Then she said, "I'm awfully glad you're here, Sunnie. I have a lot to learn."

The weather office was housed in the same building as the photo lab and was situated diagonally across the main street from the communications center. Margaret was still squinting from the brilliant sunshine when she opened the screen door. She saw Adam Smith standing before his drafting board, and for a moment she watched in silence as he marked down a series of arrows and numbers on the large chart. Finally she said, "It's eleven o'clock, Mr. Smith."

He raised his head a moment, glanced at the Navy clock on the wall as if to confirm her statement, and then signed his name along the bottom of the chart. He rolled it carefully and handed it to Margaret. Then he smiled and said, "Good-by."

On her way out of the office Margaret said, "Think it will snow today?"

"Nope."

"See you around."

"Sure."

Margaret stepped into the sunlight and began walking down the main street, which had now been labeled Broadway. She walked slowly because she wanted to think . . . mostly about Nikki and a lot about what Sunnie Mandel had said. So? Ree-Jay. At least that was a new way of putting it. Back in Beloit no one had ever heard of a Ree-Jay. A girl who failed to conform to a rigid set of physical standards was known in Beloit as a "dog." She might be a "nice dog" or a "good-head dog" or at worst could be an "awesome dog," but once classified in the canine status a dog remained a dog until she either moved away or enough time passed so that all interest in her was lost. Not, Margaret supposed, that Beloit was any different than other places. She could remember now that the young and eligible men in Beloit had actually been kind to her. Overly kind in one instance. Her mouth twisted into a little smile when she remembered Luther Kidd, who was thirty-two and already owned half of a lumber yard. No one had ever questioned the activities of Luther Kidd. He was the most eligible young man in Beloit, yet he had the grace and intelligence not to show that he knew it. The Junior Chamber of Commerce held an annual picnic which was a lot more than just potato salad and sandwiches and beer and singing. It was an ancient rite in Beloit, as fixed in routine, Margaret thought, as a black mass. The young wives who were already mothers remained in one cluster and talked about their babies and what a relief it was, oh dear, to get away for an afternoon. The young wives who were not yet mothers, but soon would be, or even hoped to be, were allowed to pass through this cluster; in and out without pausing too long, like needles on a loom. If they were obviously pregnant they were permitted to remain in the cluster for as long as they wished, the supposition being that by mere exposure to the chatter, because they were never encouraged to speak, they might absorb the wisdom of those who knew their potties and pablum.

All of the wives at these picnics were still attractive to look upon although a few showed signs of early deterioration. They were the more sophisticated young matrons, who laughed long and loudly about their roles as mothers. They pretended openly and without blushing that their most recent conception had been an accident and that they would just have soon waited a few more years. Most of these wives read the *New Yorker* and were very keen on progressive jazz. If there was enough sex in it, they would actually read a best seller. They were all deeply involved in various charity drives, often at considerable pain to their immediate families, who wound up with peanut-butter sandwiches for dinner because there just wasn't time to make anything else. There was, however, always time to pose for promotional photographs which inevitably found their way into the newspapers wherein the young matrons were identified as Mesdames.

Now, walking slowly down the sunlit street on Nikki, Margaret could almost hear the feminine laughter at the picnic, and hear it echoed by the husbands who stood nearby in their own cluster with their sleeves rolled up to remind everyone and also themselves that their muscles were still hard; well, fairly so, considering. They would laugh about that and suck in their stomachs unnaturally because their waistlines were not often so publicly exposed. And they would be looking down into their glasses pretty solemnly while they talked about the high cost of building even a modest house, and ho-ho-hoing just a little louder than the next man when some wit reminded all of them that it really hadn't been so long since they attended these picnics as free men.

Yes indeedy, she thought, remembering she had better stop daydreaming and get on to General Pike's house. Yes indeedy, there was always an invisible dividing line at those picnics even though almost everyone knew everyone else. To cross that line was asking for trouble. It separated the mated from the not yet mated, or the never-would-be mated, as surely as an electrically charged fence.

There were no dogs among the young mothers and wives. Junior Chamber of Commerce men did not marry dogs. They married the best, and a great many so-called lifetime partnerships had begun on the picnics. If a bachelor just wanted a date, regardless of his design or intentions, he did *not* take her to the Junior Chamber Picnic. There were too many inquisitive eyes focused on both the young man and the girl, and a lot of those eyes could make things tough or easy in a business way.

Then why, everybody wanted to know, did a good catch like Luther Kidd bring Margaret Trumpey?

Now, so far from the sound of any music, she tried to separate just a few of the parties at which she had sat as an unpaid entertainer and played the piano. Those parties were now ancient history, and here on Nikki each melted into the other until they seemed a single affair. The keyboards of all pianos looked very much the same and so did the faces which hung over the piano nursing their drinks, half-screened by cigarette smoke, and their voices were the same, saying, "That's for me, Marge. Play it again," or, "Can you do tum-tum-dee-dee-dum," or, "Why don't you rest a minute, finish your drink and then maybe you'd feel like playing something we could *all* dance to, huh?" The "all" never included Margaret Trumpey. Some of the men leaned far enough over the piano so they could more openly study her breasts. A drunk once said he would like to walk across them in his bare feet. Everybody around the piano laughed.

But it was fun being at the parties anyway. It was fun watching people have a good time, or think they were having a good time, and it was sort of satisfying to think they maybe wouldn't have quite such a good time if you weren't there.

She was thinking about the picnic and why Luther Kidd had taken her when she passed the building which quartered the scientific team and which was already known as "Brains Bungalow." Dr. Herman Keim, the astronomer assigned to Nikki, sat on the concrete stoop which led to the door. Margaret had sat beside him twice in the mess hall and found him delightfully grumpy. He reminded her of a Humpty Dumpty illustration in one of her children's books, and his vast belly sagged in such a way she thought it most nearly resembled a kangaroo's pouch. Since his arrival on Nikki he had grown a walrus mustache which well suited his heavy jowls. Smiling at him, Margaret thought that in the brilliant sunlight his nose was almost as red as his hair.

"Good morning, Dr. Keim."

"What's good about it?"

"Didn't all the stars behave themselves last night?"

"They continue to twinkle. Why do you trot past here with that roll of paper every morning?"

"A girl has to earn a living."

"Come on. What is it?"

"This is a weather map prepared daily for God."

Dr. Keim glanced significantly down the street toward the row of palms which nearly surrounded the Governor's house.

"I thought you ran the radioteletypes."

"We double as messengers. There are times when I could use a horse."

"Would it be violating your security oath to tell me what the weather is going to be like today? I thought I might snoop around the east side of the lagoon and catch a fish."

"The forecaster does not discuss the weather with me in detail. Nor does he discuss anything else. He's the silent type."

"If I were younger I would discuss a great many things with you."

Margaret smiled at the sun and said, "That's the age-old excuse of a mature man who's afraid he will be caught talking to a younger girl."

"Pretty smart, aren't you? But you're wrong. I lost my chances thirty years ago when I fell in love with the stars. I could not see then that the stars would never do anything for me."

"They made you famous, didn't they?"

"Romance with a star has it limitations."

Dr. Keim scowled at the sky, patted his belly; and then as if Margaret had suddenly ceased to exist, he rose abruptly and went into the bungalow.

Margaret continued along Broadway toward Pike's house. She passed the area which had been leveled for a baseball diamond at the intersection of a narrower street labeled Second Avenue. Here, on one corner, stood the small building which housed the Marine detachment. Two marines, Peterson and Randall, labored without enthusiasm on the path which led to the door of their quarters. They were trimming each side of the path with large sea shells. They were stripped to the waist and the sun had already provoked a menacing burn on their backs. Peterson said, "Here comes that Western Union babe again. Get a load of them knockers!"

Randall did not look up from the problem which had occupied him for nearly an hour. Squatting before a pile of shells, he was trying to select a duplicate pair for each side of the doorway. That's the way Doolan wanted it and God-damned if that wasn't the way he was going to get it. Now Randall grumbled, "So what. She's old enough to be your mother. I'll bet she's thirty. What you want to do, wrestle with a Sherman tank?"

"She looks comfortable."

"Comfortable, hell. It would take a chain hoist to get her on a bed."

"Well, Jesus! A guy's got to do *somethin'!*"

"Don't get that desperate. You know what Doolan said. Lay off the local talent."

"What we supposed to do? Lay off the locals and don't go across the channel. What we supposed to do? *Starve?*"

"Affirmative."

"Anyway, her name is Trumpey. I found it out from Aubrey, the barber. He knows everything that gives in this whole godforsaken base."

"How come you're talkin' to that pansy?"

"I got to get my hair cut, don't I? Besides, how you know he's a pansy?"

"Such ideas come to me when I see a guy lift his little finger higher than his coffee cup, and when I see him sashay along with his balloon butt, and when I hear him use words like sensational and très chic. I know."

Still watching Margaret, Peterson smiled and waved a shell in salute. She answered his wave with the roll of paper, but kept on walking. Peterson said, "Even if she is as old as thirty, even if that was so . . . I got a feeling that six months from now she'll look pretty damn good to me."

"Six months from now even Aubrey will look good to you."

Margaret passed the mess hall, which was opposite the Marine quarters.

Now, almost a year later, it was very plain why Luther Kidd had taken her to the J.C.C. picnic. And it wasn't very complimentary, no matter how you switched it around. One of the young wives made no attempt to conceal her fascination with Luther whenever she laid eyes on him. The husband was one of Luther's best customers and, furthermore, so very much liked that he had been elected president of the Chamber three times. Luther didn't dare wander loose about that picnic; and he certainly didn't want to announce his engagement to any girl officially or unofficially. So he invited Margaret Trumpey. He might be on the receiving end of a few laughs from the boys, but she made a hell of a fine shield! So be it. It was fun protecting Luther, even for that one night. It was the only genuine, dyed-in-the-wool, beginning-middle-and-end date she could remember.

Just beyond the mess hall she turned into a much smaller building which housed the establishment Pike had insisted be called the store instead of the post exchange. It also contained the post office and the barber shop. Lillian Strock, who served as clerk in the store and also as postmistress, was still sorting the mail which had arrived on the morning plane from Tuamani. Mrs. Strock was a faded blonde who had lost her husband some ten years previously, a personal calamity which had left her with a constant air of martyrdom. All things in Mrs. Strock's life were verbally dated as before she lost her husband or after she lost her husband. Once begun, her adventures and trials of the before and after were difficult to silence. She only neglected to report that her husband was lost to another woman.

Now when she saw Margaret, she nodded and said, "Mornin'."

"What's for His Imperial Highness?"

Mrs. Strock handed her a large manila envelope and two smaller ones. Then she said, "What's this Pistol Two business? All the official stuff is addressed that way."

"It's our new name."

"To think I'd ever have to live in a place called Pistol Two! Why couldn't they pick a pretty name?"

"I just work here. See you, Mrs. Strock."

On her way out of the post office Margaret paused by the open door which led to the barber shop. She called a cheerful good morning to Aubrey Tinsman, who, as often as the occasion permitted, referred to his place as the beauty parlor and himself as a fashion stylist.

Aubrey said, "Good morning, my dear."

Below the waist Aubrey was considerably wider than about his shoulders, and as a result, his figure most nearly resembled a milk bottle. Now he left his barber chair, where he had been yawning over a movie magazine, and came toward her. Clasping his hands primly before him he smiled and said, "Off on your appointed rounds, my dear?"

"Through hail and sleet, nothing will stop me unless a coconut falls on my head."

Aubrey put one thin finger to his lips and looked at her appraisingly. Then he said, "I should like you to know that the sight of your statuesque beauty at this time every morning starts my day off sensationally."

"Aubrey, this is so sudden!"

Margaret laughed and raised her hand in a mock salute and went out into the street again. She walked rapidly toward the one group of palms which had been left standing in the area. She turned into the circular driveway of crushed coral, followed its course around a flagpole, and knocked on the screen door of Pike's house. She heard him bark something unintelligible from the interior shadows and entered.

The Atlas Construction Company had done well by Herbert Zebulon Pike. Although the house was prefabricated, it managed an air of permanence, and the veranda which surrounded it on three sides was cool and spacious. Part of the veranda was designed to serve as a waiting room for those who might attend on the Governor. Here there were two benches and several chairs set about a round wicker table. Someone had already placed an array of American magazines on the table. This area, which might have been the introduction to any dentist's office, was separated from the rest of the veranda by a bamboo screen. Beyond the screen the furniture was less formally arranged and the veranda overlooked the sea.

Although she went to the Governor's house at least once every day, Margaret had seen nothing of the interior except Pike's office, which was just off the hallway to the right. This was a large room with only two attempts at decoration. An American flag stood in one corner, and on the wall opposite the veranda there was an enormous map of the Pacific. The room appealed to Pike's Spartan tastes. It reminded him of his office at Fort Sill, where he had briefly commanded a battalion of artillery. And when he thought about it, he could still hear the chink of spur chains on the bare floor as his officers reported to him. Those were good times then . . . between the big wars. There weren't a lot of damned reservists around taking all the gravy commands. It was a *regular* army then and if you weren't *regular* army you didn't stand a chance. Those were the days, he often told himself, when soldiers were soldiers. Artillery officers wore boots polished so you could see the sun in them, and they were careful that the only break in these boots was just above the ankle. They wore perfectly tailored whipcord breeches with a chamois patch inside the knee, and they wore spurs and chains even when they weren't mounted. And always there was about those men an agreeable and proper masculine aroma of whisky and horse manure. Now, in Pike's opinion, most soldiers, man and officer, smelled like garage mechanics and they looked like a bunch of God-damned civilians. In short, Pike did not know what the military was coming to.

It did not improve Pike's disposition to know that unless he declared a state of emergency, the Marine detachment on Nikki was for most purposes unavailable to him. Or that his only courier was a mere girl who slipped into his office wearing tennis shoes. He thought wistfully that his courier should be a properly booted young second lieutenant. And so now he looked up unhappily from his desk when he allowed himself to realize that Margaret stood waiting in the center of the room.

"Miss Trumpey . . . do you suppose you could knock before you enter this office?"

"I knocked at the door, sir. I thought that was enough. And you said come in."

"Never mind what I said. I don't like people creeping up on me."

"I'm sorry."

Pike extended his hand and she gave him the rolled weather map. Then she placed the three envelopes which were marked "Official" on his desk and held out the radioteletype. She turned to leave as Pike tore open the envelope.

"Just a minute, Miss Trumpey. I may want to send off a reply to this."

"I . . . doubt it . . . sir."

Displaying elaborate patience, Pike said, "Let me be the judge of that."

Then as Margaret waited in penitent silence, he read the message. And the veins in his neck stood out as she knew they would. While she tried to concentrate on the trade winds brushing the palms outside the window, she heard a low cry escape from Pike's throat. She had just time to think that it sounded like the bleat of a sick lamb back in Wisconsin when he said, "We'll see about *this!*"

"Do you want to send a reply, sir?"

Pike hesitated, and then slowly, as if the muscular effort were almost more than he could bear, his shoulders straightened. He laid the teletype down and aligned its edges with his desk blotter as carefully as if it were a directive to bombard Moscow.

"No. Go down to the carpenter shop and tell Dunbar to stop work on the two signs I ordered for the wharf. 'Welcome to Pike City' is one thing. 'Welcome to Pistol Two' is ridiculous."

"Yessir."

As Margaret crossed the veranda a man who had been waiting on one of the benches called to her.

"Miss?"

She turned in surprise to see a little man whom she vaguely remembered as a fellow passenger on the ship from Tuamani. He peered at her from beneath the brim of an enormous straw hat. He wore a brilliantly patterned hula shirt which was much too large for him and a pair of new khaki shorts long enough and wide enough to accommodate a man twice his size. Yet it was his eyes that held Margaret, for they were of a remarkable blue and now they sparkled mischievously as he smiled. He said, "Did you just leave the Governor?"

"Yes."

"What kind of a mood was he in?"

"Not good."

"Ah. That is going to make things rough."

The little man stared unhappily at the floor a moment and then the life returned to his eyes. He removed his hat and said, "I saw you on the ship and we've passed each other in the mess hall, but I never had a chance to say hello."

He bowed slightly and touched his banana-like nose as if the gesture was a part of his salute.

"The name is Pete Hildebrandt. And you are—"

"Margaret Trumpey. Hi! I work in communications."

"So? If you receive any mail for me would you return it to the sender marked 'addressee deceased'?"

Margaret laughed. "I don't have anything to do with the mail. I work in the radioteletype shack."

"Oh? Well, the same would apply to telegrams. Don't get the wrong idea. I'm not a fugitive from justice. . . . Just from my wife's family. You have no idea."

"Is that what brings you to Nikki?"

"Partly. It's as good a place to hide as any. I'm your sanitation expert. I'll bet you never knew there was the need for such a person."

"I really hadn't given it much thought."

"Few people do. Everybody knows we have to have supplies in a community like ours, but disposing of those supplies is rarely considered. So it's always easier to identify myself as your garbage man."

Again he bowed and then returned the straw hat to his head with a flourish. "I intended to discuss all that with the Governor, and if I could get a line on his mood maybe I could get some action in there. Is he alone now?"

"He was when I left."

"Then I'll take a chance. A thousand thanks for the information. If I can ever do anything for you, you'll find me in Building C. I share a room with our weatherman."

"Doesn't it get a little lonely for you sometimes?"

"He's a man of few words, all right. But sometimes we discuss music. As soon as another flute arrives I'm going to try and talk him into playing duets."

"Does he play a flute?"

Margaret tried very hard to match the little man's serious expression, but she found it almost impossible.

"No. I do. And I intend to teach Adam. You have to come by for our first recital."

"Just give me an invitation."

Pike was not prepared for Peter Hildebrandt. He was still brooding over the directive from Tuamani and trying to reconcile himself to the fact that a place named Pike City would never go down in history, when he saw Peter standing meekly in his doorway. Now, he thought, who is this clown? That shirt looks like a collapsed parachute. Oh God, what next?

"Good morning, Your Honor."

Pike answered him more crossly than he intended. It was the loss of Pike City as a name, he thought afterward. It had him all upset. He said to Peter, "I'm not a judge, sir, so the term 'Your Honor' is out of place here. Out of respect to the meaning of this office you should address me as Governor."

"Then good morning again, Governor. Can I have a few words with you about an important matter?"

"Of course," Pike said, regretting his harshness. "I'm available for grievances at any reasonable time. What's yours?"

There, Pike thought. Go right to the core of things before the petitioner had a chance to beat around the bush. In so doing, you put subordinates on the defensive before they had a chance to justify themselves. "What is it, man? And I'd appreciate your being quick about it because I have a very busy morning scheduled."

This, Pike knew, was a considerable exaggeration, for after he had examined the weather map, which took only a few minutes, he had nothing whatever to do until lunchtime.

Peter Hildebrandt fiddled with the brim of his large hat, turning it around and around. Finally he said, "Governor, you have over two hundred people in this new community."

"I am well aware of that."

Who the hell, Pike wondered, was this fellow? He had seen him on the ship but could not place him now. Where the hell was Albright? He ought to be around at a time like this to identify visitors. Make a note. Set up regular visiting hours every morning and have Albright around to run things. "Go on," Pike said, finding it extremely difficult to give the little man his full attention. God, what a pair of shorts! Made the man look like an observation balloon. "Go on. . . ."

"These more than two hundred people are eating and drinking and opening boxes and cans several times a day. They are also defecating and urinating and washing and sweeping and, well . . . I tell you it's a problem."

"What's a problem?"

"Doing away with it all."

Pike was not certain he had heard the little man correctly. What the Sam Hill was he talking about? Was this some nut who had slipped through the Commission's screening? Make a note. Have Albright send immediately for a strait jacket. And make sure Doc Case had plenty of sedatives. Out of two hundred people someone was bound to go cuckoo sooner or later. Including myself, Pike thought ruefully. Between that fresh girl and her teletype about Pistol Two, and Sue-Anne groaning out her latest hangover down the hall . . . and now this fumbling fool . . .

"Go on, go on," Pike said impatiently.

"I want another dump, Governor."

"You what?"

"I want another dump. It's necessary."

"Sir, you are taking up a good deal of valuable time. Whatever your problem is, go see Mr. Albright."

"I did. He wasn't interested. If I may say so, Mr. Albright is not the type to explore this matter."

"Mr. Albright is my aide. He takes care of all the minor problems here."

"This is not a minor problem. If you would only listen to me . . ."

"I have been listening."

"I don't think you even know who I am."

Pike's voice rose. "And I am beginning not to care!"

Pike thought he would have to get some kind of directive from Tuamani allowing him more of a free hand with the marines. There ought to be one of them on duty outside the Governor's office. Cranks like this little man could be dangerous. His kind planted bombs and all sorts of things. There was, indeed, a mad glint in his eye. Now, without a marine in sight, the best thing to do was humor him.

Pike glanced at his wrist watch. "I am going to give you fifteen more seconds, mister. Then you must excuse me."

"I need a lot more than fifteen seconds, Governor. This here matter will take a lot of figuring if it's going to be done right. Now . . ."

Pike was horrified to see his wife appear in the doorway. She still wore only a nightgown and her flesh was plainly visible through the filmy material. A cigarette hung from her lips and she held an ice bag in one hand. Her hair was matted on one side where she had apparently pressed the bag.

"Where'd you put the aspirin, Zebulon?"

"In the medicine chest where it belongs."

"That bottle's empty."

"Then there aren't any more. Can't you see I'm busy, Precious?"

Sue-Anne Pike looked at Peter Hildebrandt as if he were a creature just arrived from another planet. She moved across the doorway so that the light from the veranda was behind her, and Pike thought that she might just as well be naked. She cocked her head to one side, then moved very close to Peter until she was looking almost down upon him. She shook her head in disbelief, then passed her hand slowly across her eyes as if they had betrayed her. She made a pistol with her hand, raised it carefully to one eye, and pointed it at Peter. She worked her lips experimentally and swayed slightly when she said, "You look like a goblin to me. *Are* you a goblin?"

Peter made a quick little bow and in doing so contrived to step back far enough so that he would inhale a lesser concentration of bourbon.

"No, madame. I am your sanitation expert."

"Would you like to be a goblin?"

"I think maybe I would."

Sue-Anne slapped him triumphantly on the shoulder. "Good! I'll fix it up for you! I know a lot of goblins. A whole delegation came to call on me this morning."

Pike said, "If you will excuse us now, dear. Mister . . . er . . . this gentleman and I were discussing quite an important matter. Weren't we, sir?"

"Oh yes, indeed."

Peter's little eyes sparkled as he added, "This here we were talking about is something that's got to be taken care of right now. It's sort of an emergency."

"Well, I have an emergency, too. I damn well need some aspirin right now, Zebulon. How about you going down to the store and getting me some soon as you all are through talking? I got the willies."

Pike tried briefly and unsuccessfully to remember the time when Sue-Anne did not have the willies. Then he saw that Peter was watching him with open sympathy, and suddenly he was glad that he had come.

He said to Sue-Anne, "I'll see you get some aspirin in just a little while, Precious. Now if you'll excuse us . . ."

"Thank you, Zebulon. Beneath yoah stout chest beats a heart o' gold."

Moving with elaborate care she advanced on Peter. She bent down and took the lobe of his ear between her fingers. He felt the warm moisture of her breath as she whispered, "You can't fool me, mister. Don' you know you can't fool ol' Sue-Anne? I know. You're already a goblin!"

She swayed backward, took a moment to re-establish her bearings and veered off down the hall.

When she was gone, Pike sighed heavily. He was both surprised and pleased to hear Peter emit the same woeful sound.

Peter said, "You know, Governor, I've just got a hunch you'd feel better if I took a few minutes of your valuable time to tell you about my wife's family."

"Go ahead," Pike said. "Tell me."

Thus it was that Peter Hildebrandt and Herbert Zebulon Pike came to understand each other more than either one of them would ever have thought possible. It took Peter the better part of an hour to describe his wife's family. It took less than five minutes for Pike to authorize the location of a new refuse-disposal area exactly where Peter desired it.

"Peter, you just drop in and see me any time," Pike said warmly as he escorted him to the veranda.

"A cross borne by two is always lighter," Peter said.

Then he walked down the coral driveway whistling merrily. He would, he thought, create the most efficient and beautiful dump Herbert Zebulon Pike had ever seen.

3

NOW THAT THE PEOPLE of Pistol Two had been in residence for nearly a month, their first enthusiasm waned and boredom settled like a heavy mist upon the colony. All activity concerned with Operation Zeus was still confined to Tuamani, and the people of Pistol Two waited their cue as minor actors forgotten by the director. Gossip provided a stimulant for many of the inhabitants, but the majority were left with a discussion of the nightly movie, complaining of the food in the mess hall, and rather apathetic fishing expeditions to the lagoon.

In Building C, Peter Hildebrandt began his first letter to his wife since his departure from the United States. Letters to Rose were always difficult, and now Peter frequently wet the stub of his pencil and paused for a considerable time between sentences. He wrote down, "Dear Rose . . ." and then he gazed out the screen window over his bunk until he had at last achieved a state of near hypnosis. It helped when writing to Rose.

Well, here I am on Nikki and I'm glad you're not here too. . . .

Astonished at the force of his subconscious, he erased the last part and substituted a wish that Rose could be with him.

but I guess you can't leave Helen who I guess is still ailing and after all she is your sister and probably you wouldn't be satisfied knowing that Eugene didn't have a place to eat where he could get home cooking. After all Eugene is your brother as you always point out. Just don't feed him steaks too often even if he does love them—unless he should just happen to pick one up from the grocery store and bring it back to the house at his own expense. I don't think it would be fair to Eugene if he became too accustomed to steaks because some day he might get married even if he is nearly forty-eight and with his income it might be difficult to buy steaks for two. Give my regards to your father and wish him a happy eighty-fifth birthday when it comes which I think is soon—but tell him I suggest he doesn't try to drink a whole fifth of my Scotch like he did last year to celebrate because #1—I doubt if there's any Scotch left if Eugene is still there and #2—your father is getting on and I don't care what the doctors say about Scotch being good for his circulation. #3—It would be better if he took such medical treatment in his own home and why doesn't he try it just once?

Also give my regards to your Aunt Grace. Tell her she can play any of my records she wants but please not my Brandenburg Concertos. Those are the ones I bought after she let her cat play with my other albums.

Regards to your cousins, India and also Bessie. When India borrows my Ford again to go to the Gray Ladies will you remind her to put a few gallons of gas in the tank? I know about India's war with the oil companies and all about how the officials stay up nights figuring out ways especially to get her just because she sold Sinclair short in 1930 and how she wouldn't buy another drop of any oil product no matter what, *but the car won't run without it.* Tell her to charge the few gallons to me. It's cheaper than a push which cost sixty-six dollars for a new fender like last time.

And regards to all the rest of your family who were pretty nice about coming over to the house and saying good-by. I forget how many stayed for drinks and dinner but I vaguely remember there were eleven. Oh, and thanks to Max for bringing back my overcoat he borrowed last year. Of course, I really don't need it out here. And special thanks to your Uncle Stanley who brought along that pint of peach brandy as a bon voyage gift. I broke it out on the ship and it made me sicker than a dog but I know he didn't intend it that way. Like he said, "One drink deserves another and if I can drink your Scotch it's only right you should have some of my brew."

Peter's pencil now required sharpening and he spent as long as he could in the process. It was almost five o'clock and soon his roommate would return from the showers.

When he had brought his pencil to a needle-like point, Peter carefully picked up the shavings and threw them into the metal wastebasket. Then he returned to the window, where he stood for several minutes admiring his new dump which he could see in the distance at the end of the airstrip. At first Peter had been dubious about placing the dump so near the airstrip. The smoke, he thought, might interfere with landing airplanes. But he had talked with Dana Wood, who flew down with the mail every day from Tuamani, and he had said that the dump was no hindrance at all. Actually he claimed that since the control tower was not yet manned, the smoke was a great aid in determining the wind force and direction, and, said Dana, he could often see it miles away.

Peter was pleased about that. It was sort of satisfying to know the dump served a dual purpose and that a lonely airman over the sea might first become aware of Nikki through Peter Hildebrandt's work. Sort of a lighthouse, he mused. People just didn't know all the things that went into shooting off one single bomb like Zeus.

Peter left the window reluctantly and sat down on his bunk. He fiddled with his pencil a moment and then wrote rapidly.

Well Rose, I guess that's about it for now. This is a nice island and all of the people who came down here at the same time I did seem very nice indeed. In a way you could say it's a typical American community. Not very big maybe, but we have all the same problems except parking.

I live with a nice young fellow named Adam Smith. He's the weatherman here. I'm still not sure whether he's just shy or what, but he certainly is a great one for keeping to himself. He's from some place in Vermont. I sort of feel sorry for him because most of the time he's alone and when he does sit down with a bunch of the fellows in the mess hall they give him a terrible kidding about the weather. Just seems that when he says it's going to rain it doesn't and if he says it will be a nice night for the movies it rains cats and dogs. Of course these tropical rains never last more than a few minutes but it's enough to soak everybody. I've sent for another flute, (Sears Roebuck) and he says he's willing to try learning to play it. Maybe it will loosen him up a bit, like joining in music sometimes does. Shyness doesn't last long if there's good music around.

Enough for now. I guess winter has pretty well set in back there. Don't forget to drain the toilet in the garage. If the pipes bust you'll have to hire a plumber and even with the fancy pay I get out here you know we can't afford luxuries like plumbers.

I'll write again soon.

Knowing that he would not, Peter scrawled a "Love to all" across the bottom of his writing pad, signed his name, and slipped the paper in an envelope. He was licking the flap when Adam Smith entered the room.

Adam wore only a bath towel and turned his back when he slipped into his pants.

"Good shower?"

"Yup."

"How about a flute session? I could sort of break you in on mine until yours gets here."

"I . . . don't have the time tonight."

Puzzled, Peter watched him take a fresh khaki shirt from his locker. What was this no-time business? When he was through with his nightly forecast Adam should have all the time in the world. So did everybody else on Nikki until Zeus really started cranking up. Now Peter saw that he buttoned his shirt with unusual care and brushed his short hair as if it actually made a difference. Peter was disappointed. He had been looking forward to giving a flute lesson.

"Out on the town tonight, friend?"

"Sort of."

"I don't wear this long nose for nothing. My wife calls it my radar because it's always poking into other people's business. So I'm obliged to ask you . . . what's her name, or rather, since I assume you're not mixed up with the Governor's wife . . . which one is it?"

"You wouldn't know her."

"But I would. A talented scavenger can't help knowing a lot of things. People throw away their immediate past you might say. And I pick it up. You'd be surprised at the things I knew about people back home when I was supervisor of fourteen trucks. Why, I knew who was drinking too much, and who was trying to meet their household budget and who just had a new baby, and who was on a diet and so on and so on. Lots of people think being a scavenger is disgusting. I always thought it was very interesting if you kept your eyes open. By the time you reach my age, keeping your eyes open gets to be a habit . . . which is why I'm ninety-five per cent sure I know the young lady you have in mind."

Adam smiled, but he remained silent as he bent over and tied his shoes.

"It would be that girl who works in communications . . . the one with the bowling pin legs . . . the one who's got sense enough to know she doesn't need make-up. I met her at the Governor's house one day. Nice kid. But you aren't going to get very far with her."

Adam paused in lacing his shoes. His hands remained still for a moment, but he did not look up. Then slowly he resumed his lacing. He said, "Oh?"

"No sir, you won't get anywhere and I'll tell you why if you'll just listen to an old man for a minute."

Adam straightened and, looking at Peter, he forced a half-smile. Then he turned his back and began transferring matches, pipe, and tobacco pouch to his new pants.

"I haven't the slightest desire to *get* anywhere with her."

"What're you taking her out for then . . . a political discussion? You need a button sewed on or something? Next thing you're going to tell me is that there are other things besides sex."

"There are."

"Don't you believe it. That idea was invented by people who can't get it. What are you going to talk about—Zeus?"

"Maybe."

"If you do it will be the last you'll see of her. That girl's got a sense of humor and you better develop one quick."

"I'll see what I can do."

"And wipe that sad look off your face. You look like a pallbearer."

"I've had a bad day."

"Tell your troubles to me. Then you won't to her."

"Our Governor Pike."

"What's his strain . . . besides his wife?"

"He has a very low opinion of all meteorologists . . . especially me. . . ."

Adam paused and for a moment Peter saw a flash of true anger in his eyes. This, he thought, was encouraging. Deep within Adam there was spirit then, and something was eating at that spirit. Just now he reminded Peter of a young man whose house he had once serviced. He had been a quiet young man held in complete domination by his wife. And it was he who meekly lined the garbage pails with paper every morning before he went to the office. And Peter had several times heard him give what he was sure was a standard answer to his wife, "Yes, dear." Then one day Peter read about the young man and knew he had lost an account. His customer had embezzled fifty-thousand dollars from his firm and run off with what the newspapers called a honey-haired matron . . . who just happened to be his boss's wife. So you never knew. And what's more, Peter thought with strange satisfaction, they never caught the young man, either. He was probably having a hell of a time. His mind drifted back to Adam.

"Why let Pike's opinion bother you?"

"In the beginning I didn't. But he keeps needling me. He says he would rather depend on his neuritis than my maps. All this because he happened to get rained on twice in the movies! Golly, I can't tell when one of these tropical cumulus is going to let go. Nobody can! It's a matter of dew point and temperature for each individual cloud and I can't fly around like a sea gull taking readings on every cloud. He won't even read my forecasts any more."

"Can't you just say, possible showers? That's what the experts always say back home. Either way, they're right."

"Not with Pike. He damn well wants to know exactly what's going to happen and I'm tired of telling him only God knows that. You'd think the whole of Operation Zeus depended on my daily weather analysis for this one little stinking atoll."

"It does *not* stink. I've seen to that. And yet I can't say I've received any fan mail for my efforts."

Adam's sudden anger subsided as he lit his pipe. He glanced at his watch, then strode to the window, where he stood silently watching the trade-wind clouds flow past the edge of the roof. Then as if he were speaking to the clouds rather than to Peter, he said slowly, "I dunno . . . I don't care what a man does, he likes to be proud of it; and if he tries hard he likes to be at least respected for trying. Meteorology is supposed to be a science, which it is, but no science will prove itself out consistently unless you know the exact behavior of all the elements involved. So a lot of times meteorology becomes a guessing game and that's where the trouble comes with people like Pike. For that matter there are more jokes about the weatherman than any other profession I can think of. . . ."

"I don't suppose you've ever heard a joke about the garbage man?"

"You don't hear jokes about chemists, engineers, musicians, or, let's say, architects . . . at least not as direct insults to their professional ability. That's what finally gets you down. . . ."

"You're working in futures. That always gives someone else a chance at hindsight."

"If Pike tosses my forecast in the wastebasket once more or sends over a message like 'Tell that fumbling wizard to get himself a new crystal ball,' or says that the whole weather setup here ought to be eliminated to save the taxpayers' money and he ought to get his forecasts teletyped down from Tuamani, where they know their business . . . if he keeps on like that I'm going to blow my top."

"Good. It's long past time. Maybe it will make you more of a human being."

"Just what do you mean by that?"

"I never saw a young fellow with so damn many complexes! Where the hell did you acquire them all? Keep on the way you are and someday you'll bust wide open."

"I'm doing all right."

Peter snorted. He would have been happier, he thought, if the whole conversation had never started. But it was too late to retreat now.

"*Sure,* you're doing all right! You don't say six words to anybody on this whole atoll all day. You work alone and you walk to the mess hall alone unless I deliberately tag along, and you might as well be eating alone because you sit there like a Sing Sing prisoner. It doesn't cost anything to be pleasant to people. They won't bite if you say good morning or good night or even go to hell."

"I haven't anything especially to say."

"Well, find something! You must have said something to make a date with that communications girl."

"No. . . ."

"Well, then will you kindly explain to this ignorant old man how you managed to arrange a rendezvous? Or did you employ sign language?"

"I don't really have a date with her. It's just your idea that I have."

Peter regarded him solemnly for a moment. Finally he said, "I see. You aren't going to be a complete damn fool and try to cross the channel, are you? I somehow don't picture you as swimming the Hellespont."

"No. Nothing like that. I take walks down to the wharf occasionally. I like it down there. You get a good view of the sea. Can I help it if she seems to like it down there, too?"

"So you just sort of *happen* to run into each other down there. Is that it?"

"That's it. That's all there is to it."

"Do you hold a small conversation?"

"Not so far."

"Try it. Pass the time of day and send the bill to me. Try something original like, 'It sure is a nice evening,' as an opener."

When Adam left, Peter stood in the middle of the room and stared at the floor for a long time. And he was not, to his surprise, very lonely, because he was so involved in thinking about Adam. What a dull fellow! What a nothing! And then he remembered the young man who had stolen the wife and the fifty-thousand dollars . . . also, Peter recalled, an astonishingly dull fellow.

He stepped to the metal cabinet at the foot of Adam's bed. It was exactly like his own and served as a combination clothes locker and dresser. He opened the two top drawers and peered hopefully inside. He was disappointed for he could find nothing of any interest. The blindest man could go through my locker, he mused, and come away with at least some line on my personality. Among other things he would find a stack of pennies, two boy-scout knives, a compass, foot powder, fishline, two extra pairs of glasses, a red necktie still folded in its gift box, and, of course, my flute.

Yet here, in Adam's locker, there was nothing but clothes—neatly folded, if that meant anything. Peter closed the drawers in disgust. The man was a cipher! But then so was that rascal with the fifty-thousand dollars and his boss's wife.

Deep in thought, Peter crossed the room to his own locker and almost automatically took out his flute. He sat down gingerly on the end of his bed and wet his lips. As he raised the flute toward his mouth, his eyebrows and playing fingers also ascended as if they were attached to the instrument. He took a deep breath and poised himself for the opening notes of his favorite movement in the Vivaldi sonata.

He hesitated, and for a moment his mind lost all contact with the music. Wasn't it so that banks were never robbed by forceful men? And corporation officers almost never embezzled; it was always some obscure little clerk? And the reasons were not always financial, for they sometimes confessed they simply didn't understand what it was that compelled them to take the money. Who committed hatchet murders? Big, roaring men with primeval tempers? Never. The pictures in the paper always revealed some mouse of a citizen, previously notorious only for mowing his lawn on the Sabbath.

He decided he would have to do some more thinking about Adam Smith. A cipher was not always a circle with nothing in the middle.

He puckered his lips and changed his mind about the Vivaldi sonata. No! The mood was all wrong. He would stimulate his thinking apparatus with a little Mozart. Much better! He took a deep breath and tootled happily until long after the sun had set.

By increasing his pace slightly Adam managed to arrive in front of the carpenter shop just ahead of Margaret. And when it became obvious they would be the only people walking along the street which led down to the wharf, he said, "Good evening."

And he thought that if she was surprised she certainly didn't show it, nor did she seem to mind when he fell into step beside her. She simply said, "Well, good evening, Mr. Smith. And how are you?"

"You don't have to call me Mr. Smith, do you?"

"I guess not. What should I call you?"

"Adam."

"My name is Margaret."

"I know that."

They walked slowly toward the wharf, and after Adam had cleared his throat experimentally, he finally said that Margaret looked different to him.

"Well, I'm wearing lipstick if that's what's different. And I never wear this dress to work."

Adam said he didn't think it was the lipstick or the dress, but maybe it was the way they were walking along together just like they might as well be strolling down the street of some little town in the States, and in some ways it was sort of surprising to him that they couldn't stop in somewhere and have an ice-cream soda.

And Margaret said that yes, she had the same feeling, and wasn't it strange that here they were five thousand miles from anywhere and doing just what people did at home and that it was hard to believe it would all be over in less than a year, and everything just left to wither away in the trade winds.

Adam thought for a while and finally agreed that was a pretty good way of putting things all right because it was picturesque to think of the whole settlement just completely empty of people and having no purpose any more and the buildings standing there in the evening light just like now and wind whistling through the empty buildings just like she said.

Margaret replied that it was a sure thing Adam hadn't made such a long speech ever since he came to Nikki, and he laughed and agreed that maybe it was, and added that he was sorry he just had to think things out before he said anything and since he was a very slow thinker people sometimes just gave up and departed before they heard what he had to say.

Then they were both silent for a long time and remained so even after they reached the wharf. All the way from the carpenter shop they had walked very slowly, and when they reached the wharf Adam found two boxes near the warehouses and set them upright so they could have something cleaner than the creosoted planks to sit on. As he placed them side by side he saw that Margaret was smiling at him.

"Please," he said, adjusting one of the boxes so that it faced the sea.

"Oh, thank you," Margaret said. She sat down quickly. Adam moved his box a few inches farther away from her and lowered himself to it cautiously. His knees were almost level with his chin.

"You have the longest legs," Margaret said.

"In school they used to call me the stork."

Adam lit his pipe, and again there was a long silence between them.

They watched the sun dip into the sea and listened to the swift water in the channel gurgling among the pilings of the wharf and they heard a bell tolling in the village across the water.

Looking at the sun, Adam finally said, "There may be a green flash tonight."

"What do you mean by that?"

"Sometimes in the tropics when it's a clear evening like this and conditions are just right otherwise, you'll see a bright green flash in the sky just after the sun goes down. But you have to watch carefully. It only lasts a second or so."

"You like the sky, don't you, Adam?"

"I do."

"Where I come from there's a lot of it."

"There's a lot of sky everywhere. The trouble is, people spend most of their time looking down instead of up."

"It does prevent stumbling."

"Yeah. But they miss so much. Now. . . . Watch!"

Adam nodded at the bronze glow on the horizon which lingered after the sun. Then, far above it, the sky suddenly became a vivid green. The coloring endured for so short a time, Margaret was not certain she had actually seen it. Yet, glancing quickly at Adam's face, she saw a look of such genuine pleasure she knew he would be disappointed if she had missed the spectacle. And so she said softly, "I liked it very much."

"Pretty spectacular, huh?"

"I like what it does to you. You communicate with the outside world. You talk to people like me. I was beginning to think you were pretty much of a snob."

Even as she said it Margaret regretted it. For she saw the look of contentment die on Adam's face and he seemed visibly to withdraw within himself. Why had she said it? Why take a crack at Adam Smith, who was just another young man and not a very imposing one at that? In Beloit there were a lot of Adam Smiths and even if they lacked the color of a movie hero, or seemed obsessed by money and sex, there was no reason to spit in their eye. Smart girls sighed and told them they were wonderful. And they lived happily ever after. At least most of them tried to act like they did.

Now watching Adam she was almost certain of what he would say even before he stood up.

"Well," he said, turning his back to the twilight, "I guess that's that."

Trying to hide her disappointment Margaret rose beside him and thought that only Adam's legs justified any comparison with a stork. She looked up into his face, appreciating the bones and the crevices which might have been expected in a much older man, and she was certain she saw great inner strength. She said halfheartedly, "If we're going to get any chow we'd better go now. I guess it'll be pork chops tonight because it's Tuesday."

"Okay."

She thought, Well, it's sure a romantic setting down here on the wharf anyway.

He stepped to the edge of the wharf and looked down at the swirling water. It was almost black now and the eddies and whirlpools melted together until the whole surface of the channel appeared violently disturbed. As he stood watching the water, Margaret realized that he was smiling.

"What's so funny?"

"Nothing. I was just looking at those little whirlpools down there and getting some ideas."

At least, Margaret thought, he's not laughing at me. And she thought, too, that they were both terribly clumsy with each other and so nothing would come of this meeting. But then why should she expect anything to come of it?

Finally, when she was sure he had forgotten her, Adam turned and took a step toward her, and the expression on his face was so strange that for one panic-stricken second she thought he was going to kiss her. And then she saw that it was a trick of the dusk light about his face and that what she had mistaken for lust was only a mischievous grin. She was not sure whether she should feel pleased or sorry.

"When you take my weather map to Pike in the mornings . . . does he ever say anything in particular?"

Margaret was trying to remember the last time she had been kissed and was amazed that she could not. She knew that it had to be in high school, but she could not remember either the boy or the event. And now I am twenty-nine!

"How do you mean, does he say anything in particular?" She heard her own voice echo so softly in the dusk it seemed to come from another person. The thought of standing in Adam's arms caused her whole body to become moist very suddenly and she thought, Well, so this is what it's like and why should I be so affected when I don't even know him?

Adam said, "So you won't talk."

". . . about what?"

"About Pike."

"Oh, he's all right. His bark is just a lot worse than his bite."

Cliché—cliché! Oh, you're a great conversationalist, Margaret! Continue and you will fascinate the man, as you have so many others!

"I didn't ask after his health. He can choke during one of his tantrums for all I care. I just wanted to know if when you take the map to him in the morning does he read it, or change it, or toss it away?"

Is this all we can find to talk about . . . on a wharf? On a tropical evening? Margaret desperately searched her memory. She could remember nothing Pike might have said which would be of the slightest interest. Why did Adam care so much what Pike said? After a moment she was amazed to find herself saying, "Well, one morning he allowed as how there was nothing like having a good weather map around."

Adam placed his hands on her shoulders, and the touch of his fingers on her flesh completely destroyed her surface calm.

"You're not telling the truth."

"No. I'm not. Why is it so important, Adam?"

"One of the most important things about this whole operation is the weather analysis. Conditions have to be just right before the explosion takes place; otherwise, there could be hell to pay. If we get the wind wrong, I hate to think of the damage that godawful firecracker can do for thousands of miles around. It's not the scientists who will decide when Zeus blows its top. It's us . . . the meteorologists."

"I should think that would make you feel quite proud."

"It might, even if this is only an auxiliary station. The trouble is Pike has made up his mind all meteorologists are crazy. He has never even been down to the weather office. He ignores my reports and makes up his own according to the way his neuritis behaves. I'm helpless now and I could be helpless when explosion day rolls around. That just might not be very funny, and Pike could turn out to be the greatest villain in history. Unfortunately, I would be hung with him."

His hands were still on her bare shoulders and she found that she wanted them to stay there. She tipped her head back just a trifle, just enough so that if he did decide to kiss her, well, maybe it wouldn't turn out to be a complete disaster. But he did not move. Instead he said insistently, "Tell me the truth. Have you ever actually seen Pike read one of my forecasts? Does he change the summary I make up for Tuamani?"

She waited. Now his hands seemed cold and she wanted to twist away from them. She sought his eyes, trying to discover in them what she thought she had seen before. But the quick tropical twilight had gone and his face was only a silhouette against the sky.

"Is that why you spoke to me tonight, Adam? Is that why we talked? You just wanted information?"

"Well, partly . . . sure. My neck is long enough now. It doesn't need stretching."

"Good night, Adam."

She turned away from him very suddenly and ran along the wharf until she came to the place where it met the street. The sound of her shoes hitting the crushed coral was easier than it had been on the planks of the wharf, and she was very aware of it and grateful for the softer sound, because now, she thought, I don't sound so much like another husky girl running away from the truth. And I must not sound that way—*ever!*

Adam looked after her, and when she had disappeared he reached for his pipe and clamped down on the stem hard with his teeth. You can see what happens when you open your big mouth, he said to the dark whirlpools in the channel. Now how can I tell her I'm sorry and that she took what I said the wrong way? Or at least not the way I meant it. Because for one thing, I guess I like her a lot more than any girl I've ever met.

He stood watching the dark, swiftly moving water for a long time. Finally from across the channel, he heard the sound of hymn-singing. He found peace in its easygoing rhythm, and so he sat down on the box and looked at the few lights across the channel and listened, and wished Margaret were still sitting beside him.

4

THE MORMON CHURCH was the largest structure in the village of Nikki. It was built of plaster. The roof and gables were of red corrugated iron and the design was straight New England. There was a graveyard behind the church, and a wooden shed. During the daytime the interior of the church was illuminated by windows which had been opaqued in squares with varicolored paints so that they resembled stained glass. When they were pushed open, the sea and the coconut palms, lashing softly in the trade wind, were visible to the congregation. During the evening service the interior of the church was less spirited because the congregation was sleepy and the illumination came from a single bare bulb hanging from the high ceiling. It took energy from a generator powered by a one-cylinder gasoline engine and housed in a wooden shed. The exhaust of the motor had rusted through and now it made a terrible racket, at times overwhelming the soft and lazy hymns which the people of Nikki liked to sing.

"Onward, Christian Soldiers" had never been popular on Nikki. It was too strident, too energetic, and altogether unsuited to the Polynesian way of cherishing a note and letting it develop fully and enthusiastically in the throat until of its own variation it became another note and then another, each melting into the other, until the moment required for breathing became a mystery. The devout on Nikki much preferred the slower hymns, and they further slowed the original rhythms until their voices rose and fell as easily and peacefully as the wind outside the windows. Thus such medium-paced standards as "The Church in the Wildwood" became so lethargic and soothing that both the elders sitting before the altar and the congregation in their pews were often mesmerized. Only the noise of the generator motor kept them alert enough to follow the service.

And so the task of arousing her fellow worshipers often fell upon the woman Huahenga, who was exceedingly well qualified. For when Huahenga lifted her head and almost visibly captured the trade wind beneath her vast bosom, her beginning notes of song could be heard even by the night fishers prowling the coral at the far end of the channel. Huahenga weighed three hundred pounds. She invariably clothed her body in spotless white and the total effect was that of a cumulus cloud which had somehow descended into the church and found itself joyous with voice.

Once Huahenga had shocked the congregation with an introductory note, then assistance flowed toward her from various places among the pews. Karara, who was the star of her Bible class and who braided her pigtails so cleverly the gray hairs were almost invisible, liked to join Huahenga on the second note of the hymn, although she invariably chose an octave lower. Subsequently her friend Apakura would rise and spread her bare feet wide so that the floor breeze could billow the hem of her moo-moo gown and pass easily upward to cool her bottom. And she would tip back her head and shout out a rhythmic counterpoint which never varied, but which seemed to fit every hymn perfectly.

The total effect was satisfying to the elders. For the younger women of Nikki would stop fiddling with their hair and close their French movie magazines and sing, and the children of Nikki would cache the bubble gum they had bought at Yip Kee's and they would sing, and the older men of Nikki would rouse themselves from their dreams and sing, and even the few young men who were in the church because they had cut a toe on the coral, or had a sorry belly from drinking too much soda pop, or were otherwise incapacitated from fishing in the lagoon, would stand up and brace their powerful shoulders, and they would allow their embarrassed voices to make a humming sound beneath the melody.

It was inevitable that the young marines, Randall and Peterson, would first be drawn to the source of so much noise and light. They swam the channel because they had been told not to swim the channel and because they were young and had joined the Marines to see the world and because they were convinced that the relative darkness in the native village only served to conceal certain mysteries in which they would very much like to participate.

"Listen!" Randall said, as they stood gazing across the channel. "Listen to that singing . . . only it ain't singing. It's like you call a chant, and right now I bet they're getting all squared away for one of those orgies where the girls run around naked or maybe just carrying a torch!"

Peterson coughed, trying to conceal the hunger in his voice. Then he said, "Pike claims they don't do things like that."

"To hell with what Pike says! How's he know what goes on over there? You think they tell *him?* Why, I bet they have ancient ceremonies nobody ever seen, and here we stand like a couple of jerks when we could be dancin' and drinkin' and doin' things we could be tellin' people about for the next hundred years!"

Peterson looked down at the swift black current and said that he wouldn't mind at all being the father of some kid who was maybe a little dark-skinned and had a towhead like his own; he would even send money from the United States after he got back there, and also he had heard for damn sure that such an arrangement was exactly what all the natives in the South Seas wanted; in fact, they wanted it so much that sometimes they would actually pay a white man to sleep with one of their daughters, or at least, if they were short of cash, they would feed him and treat him like a king and make him so comfortable he just never wanted to go home. "I read it in a book," he said, to establish his information as a fact.

"Well, then let's get the hell over there! We can wade halfway across if we start farther up by the little point. Then we drift down with the current, only we don't drift, we swim like we never swum before, and we wind up right in front of the village! There ain't really nothin' to it."

"There will be somethin' to it if Doolan catches us," Peterson said mournfully. "Or the sharks like white meat."

"What can Doolan do? Ship us back home. Is that bad?"

"I don't want a dishonorable discharge."

"Who's gonna get a dishonorable? If we do get sent home we can just say Doolan is a friggin' fiend and we was abused. That's all there is to it. But we won't get caught. All we got to do is swim over there, see an orgy, swim back before dawn, and say good mornin', Sergeant Doolan, you dumb son of a bitch and don't you wish you were all unfrustrated like us?"

"It will be better if we keep our mouths shut and don't say nothin'."

Now Peterson and Randall, still breathing heavily from their swim, stood in the shadows outside the Mormon church. They wore only their T shirts and pants, which were soaking wet. They were so cold they had difficulty keeping their teeth from chattering. The water in the channel had proved much colder than they had expected, and the distance to swim was much greater because the current had carried them almost to the mouth of the channel, where it met the ocean. As they made their way slowly toward the church and paused beneath a palm, the wind passing through their garments caused enough evaporation to chill them thoroughly.

And inside the fire of their youth was even colder.

"That," said Peterson, standing on his toes so he could see through the open doorway of the church, "is not exactly what I would call an orgy."

"Well, it *sounded* like it, didn't it? How can anybody tell when they sing like that?"

"Where, Mister Wise Guy, is all the dames running around with no clothes on and carryin' torches? Go ahead. I risked my life gettin' here. Now show me."

"Well," Randall said in a voice that had lost all conviction. "Maybe something will turn up."

"Like a cigrett? You can't even buy a cigrett in this creep town. They probably arrest you if they catch you smokin' a cigrett. I heard about these Mormons. They don't allow anybody to have fun. Not even theirselves."

"I heard a guy can have a hundred wives if he wants. How about that, Pete? How would you like to have a hundred wives?"

Peterson did not answer for a moment. He moved cautiously toward the church door so that he could see more of the interior, and he thought that he would sure as hell feel a lot easier about things if he was wearing his boondockers instead of being barefooted because you never could tell what people like those inside were going to do. They might take a dim view of a guy like Randall doing night patrol on their front lawn wearing just his skivvies and that awful smile he used every time he saw a woman, no matter if she was ten or seventy years old.

Peterson ventured even further toward the doorway until he almost stood in the light. Now he could see the whole interior of the church and the elders sitting before the altar, and he decided that it looked pretty much like a Tuesday evening back in the Methodist church in Elmira, New York, where he wished he was right this minute. Except that the people were dark, of course, and the only organ seemed to be a built-in job which was wearing a white dress. And for a moment, listening to Huahenga's voice soar to the roof and reverberate down again, he forgot his chill. When at last her voice subsided until it became only a delicate overtone to the others, Peterson forgot himself and leaned against the doorway entranced. He remained so, motionless, until a touch on his arm startled him.

He turned quickly and was ready to ask Randall just what the hell he thought he was up to, creeping up on him like that when he was jumpy enough already, and then he saw that it was not Randall at all, but a small man who needed a shave and a new eye. Randall was still back in the shadows, but now he came up quickly.

"Well, m'lads! Having a peep at the show?"

Terry Mack displayed his two remaining front teeth and fixed his good eye at first on Peterson and then on Randall, whose fists had automatically doubled at his side. "Now then yer wet and that's a shame. You'll catch a death."

"We was just lookin' around," Randall said defensively.

"Yeah, that's right . . . just lookin'," Peterson agreed. "We were out fishin' and our boat dumped over, and, well, here we are."

Terry Mack scratched his chest. Now since Peterson and Randall had moved so close together he could survey them both with his good eye. He said, "Balls, m'lads. I see ye swim over here. All ye Yanks is balmy. Lucky ye didn't drown."

Randall relaxed his fists and assumed his most diplomatic air, favoring Terry Mack with the smile he normally reserved for sergeants who had something on him.

"We were hot," he said. "And we just thought we'd cool off by going for a little swim. The current carried us away from the other side."

"If that's the story yer thinkin' of tellin' the Guv'nor, ye better find a fancier one," Terry advised.

"We don't want no trouble," Randall said hastily. "We'll just swim back and suppose you make like you never saw us."

"I wouldn't think of it. My woman wouldn't talk to me for twenty-eight days if I let ye lads try to swim the channel again. I'll take ye back in my canoe."

"Well, say, thanks!" Randall said, greatly relieved. Then he looked more thoughtfully at Terry Mack, surprised that his grand manner seemed to actually increase his size. In the light from the church doorway he could see his frizzy hair and the stubble of his beard and the crudely patched shirt which, with the tails out, hung almost to his knees.

"*You* have a woman?" Randall asked so directly that Peterson wanted to slink into the shadows and hide because, he thought, Randall has no damned manners at all and is always going around sticking his nose in other people's business which is how we got in this bind in the first place and now here he is doing it again.

"Of course I got a woman. Ye can't avoid 'em."

"We seem to be able to," Randall said.

"Ye want to go to church?" Terry Mack asked.

Both Randall and Peterson hesitated, and then at once they uttered unfinished sentences which, jumbled together, somehow came out as flat denials.

"I didn't think so," Terry Mack said. Then he waggled his frizzy head and added, "Not much happens here. So it's good to see you even if ye are Yanks. Come avec moi."

Terry Mack revolved as if he had been standing on a potter's wheel and without looking back set off into the darkness. Randall glanced at Peterson and the hope had returned to his eyes. "This is more like it!"

"I dunno," Peterson said doubtfully. Yet with one long step he was beside Randall, who was already pursuing the diminutive figure down the street.

The custom was easy to establish. After night had descended solidly and dependably upon the atoll, Sue-Anne Pike began to relax. This was not a physical manifestation, but a degree of mental tranquillity, which she reached as soon as she emptied her fourth bourbon. The feeling crept upon her softly, enclosing her brain in a gossamer web which allowed her to see through to the outer world and yet served as a protection. She was not drunk. Nor did she stagger, weave, or display any other evidence of physical uncertainty. Sue-Anne seldom surrendered to the "vapors" state in spite of what certain people in Pistol Two reported. She was normally too skillful a drinker and a vapors condition, during which she might miss a great many things, was very much against her desires. Therefore, she rationed herself carefully after the fourth bourbon had enclosed her consciousness in its gentle webbing.

The fifth and the sixth and the seventh drinks she sipped slowly and cautiously according to the needs of the web; when it threatened to become too finely meshed and reduce her outside visibility, she would allow a considerable time to pass so that the delicate balance might restore itself, or she would move her body, or eat a handful of popcorn, or show her charm bracelet to someone handy, or go to the bathroom, or almost anything to avoid becoming a slob. For she knew very well what she was like when she became a slob and it disgusted her. She swore and she yelled. She used four- and eleven-letter words indiscriminately; and if there was

no one around who cared about restraining her, she had a well-nigh irresistible urge to remove at least part of her clothing. She insulted all
other women present who would stand still long enough to hear her,
accusing them of every conceivable kind of bitchery, and if their men
attempted to defend them, she reviled the men also. All of which had
made life very difficult for officers and wives of all ranks inferior to Pike
during his years of active duty. Nor had she ever spared his superiors
on these disastrous occasions, which was one of the several reasons Pike's
military career had limped to such a prosaic conclusion.

"Wal, now, you and Sue-Anne had jes' better have a lil talk," was an
opening phrase Pike had learned to dread. It was like a first salvo. Sue-
Anne was getting the range, and once she had the target bracketed, she
pounded away without mercy. She was never sorry until the next morning, at which time she loathed herself.

She strove with equal anxiety to avoid the opposite condition, wherein
the mesh of the web widened for some reason and dissolved and she discovered to her horror that, in the middle of her fifth or sixth drink, she was
uncomfortably sober. Then she would recognize the absurdities of others
who had been drinking with her; and far worse, discover a shockingly
clear vision of herself. As if emerging from a cocoon, she saw a faded
blonde wearing too much lipstick and such a collection of bracelets, earrings, pendants, and other odd jewelry that she jangled and bangled with
every movement. She saw eyes that were vague and at the same time
troubled. She beheld a multitude of tiny wrinkles which spiked downward
from her eyes and the corners of her mouth, and no combination of
novelty necklaces and rings could hide the crinkled skin about her neck
and hands. She saw, too, and the revelation was almost more frightening
than any other, that her breasts sagged and that her belly was a distinct
mound. Sucking in her breath helped a little, but was limited in time,
and standing up straight was too difficult to remember. It was much easier
to distract attention from her belly by displaying her legs, which still
merited honest appreciation.

Sue-Anne feared the sober side of the web as much as the opposite,
and when she suspected approaching sobriety she swiftly downed another
drink—straight. Consequently in the bar at Pistol Two she walked a constant tight rope and was not always successful in maintaining the exact
status she preferred. At the same time Peterson and Randall plunged into
the channel, she concluded that she had better have another drink—
quick! She raised one arm and shook her charm bracelet and yelled at
the bartender, who was very lonely because he was the only Filipino on

Nikki and who wished he had never signed on for such a deal, no matter how much he needed the money. "Miguel! What the hell kind of a club you all running around here! Set me up with another bourbon chop-chop and . . ."

She paused and looked down at the end of the bar, where a residue of people not yet ready to start to the mess hall had accumulated. "And set all the rest of these heah clowns up, too! Big night! Charge it to the ol' man!"

Fred Hanover, lost in nostalgic memories of applejack drinking with fellow press representatives in a certain little New York bar, had been trying to satisfy himself with a series of Martinis through most of the afternoon. Now he mumbled, "Big deal, Sue-Anne. Big deal. Mighty generous at two bits a shot. Pretty high off the hog, as they say down your way."

"Shut up, you Yankee bastard. Shut up and sit up and drink up yoah gin like a good boy."

"I love you, Sue-Anne. I love you madly," Hanover said solemnly. "I love you because you are such a thorough disgrace to American womanhood."

"An' that includes both the Noath and the South," Sue-Anne said proudly. She jangled her charm bracelet and pushed her fingers through Hanover's hair until he angrily jerked his head away. The gesture almost capsized both Hanover and his bar stool, but he recovered and said, "I wish you would cut that sort of thing out. There's a time and a place for everything."

"Why not, honey? I laike yoah hair. Anytime. Anyplace. It's so naturally curly."

Looking at him even now when he could barely hold his head up, Sue-Anne thought again that he was probably the prettiest man she had ever seen. Any woman would have envied his eyelashes, and his mouth was sensitive and beautifully formed. Yet there was nothing feminine about him. It took a perceptive person to notice that God had cheated Fred Hanover in only one physical aspect. His chin was anything but firm, and when, as now, he had been drinking, it wobbled. "Cut it out," he said when she reached again for his hair. "People are watching and pretty soon they'll be talking and pretty soon after that the old man will throw me off the island and not long after that I'll get the can. I'll get the can when I get home and that will be that."

"Not you, honey. Zebulon Pike wouldn't throw *you* off this heah island. Yoah a newspaper man an' you have a story comin' up in *Life* magazine and Zebulon just won't do a thing to you no matter what kind of shenanigans you pull off. No, Fred ol' boy, not even if you pull off his wife's dress. It don'—"

"Shut up for the love of Mike!"

Sue-Anne slid off her bar stool and stood very straight before Hanover. She held her shoulders back so her breasts would stand out, and she sucked in her breath and held it for as long as she could. That last drink had done the trick; the web was just the right thickness now and if maybe it was a little too thick all of a sudden, well, the hell with it. She didn't have to care, did she? She could tell Mr. Fred Hanover just where to get off. Humph! Telling me to shut up? Just because he was a newspaper man he thought he could go around whenever he wanted, tellin' people who were minding their own business to shut up?

"Listen, you carpetbaggin' son of a bitch, who do you think you're talking to? And since when do gentlemen go around tellin' ladies to shut up? And you're supposed to be a gentleman, aren't you? You and that stuffed shirt, Albright! You both talk laike you have a mouthful o' mashed potatoes, if you ask me. Noathun intellectuals is what you are. *Noath-eastern* intellectuals and that's the *lowest* form of carpetbagger . . . lower than . . ."

"Sue-Anne. Why don't you stop fighting the Civil War?"

"Because it ain't ovah! That's why, Mr. Fred Hanover. It ain't nevah going to be over until you damn Yankees learn to act laike decent gentlemen."

"You read too many books."

"Quit insultin' me!"

Sue-Anne's voice rose in an offended contralto until it easily dominated the music from the juke box. Hanover turned back to the remains of his Martini and tried to pretend he was alone. Sue-Anne was not pleased. She grabbed a handful of popcorn from the plate on the bar and sprinkled it on his head. And throughout the process she purred softly, "Yo' all don' love me any more. That's it, Fred. Yo' all just don' care any more what happens to ol' Sue-Anne. See? It's snowing. Yoah just pushin' little ol' Sue-Anne out in the snow!"

The web was not yet so thick that Sue-Anne had lost awareness of the considerable audience gathered around the end of the bar. Which was why she reached for the popcorn. If Fred Hanover thought he could ignore Sue-Anne Pike he was mistaken. Not until she was ready anyway. "Ah'm leaving you," she said. "Ah'm leaving you because you bore me.

Ah'm leaving you and taking a long trip down to the other end of the state where the gentlemen live! Jus' laike Liza crossin' the ice."

She filtered another blizzard of popcorn through her fingers and held one arm across her face as if to guard against the cold and wind. Then slanting her body against the wind, which by now she could almost feel, she picked her way carefully over an imaginary ice floe which extended to the end of the bar. She arrived among the spectators breathless and triumphant, and she took a little bow when they laughed.

"Now," she said, peering at the faces surrounding her. "Who's for some real honest-to-God deep-down rootin' and hoggin' drinkin'?"

"I will accept another beer," Carlos Raveza said.

"Yo' all don't have to be so damn condescending about it," Sue-Anne said. Then imitating him perfectly even to the intonations of his Mexican accent, she said, "I will 'ave another beer. Who are you? Pancho Villa?"

Smiling at the others, she resumed her normal voice except for a slight addition of throatiness and said, "How about that? Fatso allows as how he'll break down and have another beer. Why don't you have a man's drink? Bourbon whisky, Fatso! That's a man's drink. Come on. Sue-Anne's payin'! Miguel! . . . On target! . . . Bourbons away!"

While Miguel filled the glasses, Sue-Anne took a moment to survey her new-found companions. There were still great gaps in the web and she knew she had seen all of them before, although the only one she knew by name was Aubrey Tinsman, the barber. With what was intended as a gay gesture she jangled her bracelets in his direction and said, "Aubrey, darling! Introduce me to your friends! Don't just sit there and look wistful!"

The moment Aubrey stepped down from his stool, Sue-Anne knew that the time had come for her to watch the web closely, for a woman sat in the shadows behind him and Sue-Anne had not even seen her. She told herself that she would go very easy with this new bourbon. When people started to appear from nowhere, then you had to start being careful.

Aubrey introduced the woman, who was dark and small and, Sue-Anne noticed with relief, not too young. He said that her name was Crystal Blum and that she was in charge of the laundry. She nodded politely and Sue-Anne wondered if her lovely teeth were real.

Aubrey stepped back to reveal another man. Watch it, girl! How the hell many people were back there in the shadows?

"This is Dana Wood," Aubrey said. "He flies the mail plane."

Sue-Anne looked at him and saw that he was quite short and nearly bald-headed, and she wondered why it was that all the pilots she had ever met always looked pretty much like Dana Wood or even worse and where were the ones who looked like Gary Cooper? The next man captured her interest and her glass arrived just in time to raise it to him.

"Pete Walsacki," Aubrey was saying, and then he added something else which Sue-Anne lost in the web. Something about Mr. Walsacki's appearance caused her lips to part and she lowered her glass instead of drinking from it. Mr. Walsacki was a tall and obviously powerful man and his forearms were covered with black hair. So too, she saw at once, was his head. She resisted the temptation to stand on her tiptoes and run her fingers through it. He was grinning at her rather foolishly and his eyes were embarrassed beneath his heavy eyebrows.

"And what do you do, Mr. Walsacki? Do I have the name right?"

"Yeah. You got it right," Walsacki growled. "I'm the boss plumber on this operation."

"Oh! How nice."

Sue-Anne was confused. The web was changing every which way. One minute I'm the big lady and the next I'm a slob. She took a long pull at her glass, which would at least steady the web, and resolved to keep Mr. Walsacki in mind. What a hunk of man!

Aubrey was introducing the man she had called Fatso. Sue-Anne missed his name entirely because she was still admiring Walsacki's neck and chest, but she did manage to ask what he did.

"I am the master electrician," Carlos Raveza said. "I hope you do not mind," he added, holding up his beer can. "I prefer this."

"Pig swill," Sue-Anne said quietly. Now she was eying Crystal Blum and she was remembering that, while many men might be willing to laugh at a woman who had too much to drink, her own sex had no such tolerance. Crystal Blum was sitting there displaying perfect white teeth in what should pass for a smile. Sue-Anne was certain that in reality it was intended as a snarl. And she thought, I will knock those damned teeth down her throat.

"Is it Miss Blum or Mrs.?" Sue-Anne asked. This moment she would play the patronizing part of the Governor's wife. The web had cleared temporarily and such a question would put Madame Toothy-grin on the defensive in case the web should cloud over again.

"It's *Miss* Blum," the woman said and then, once more displaying her teeth, she repeated, *"Miss* Blum, Your Highness."

"Just what do you mean by that 'Your Highness' stuff?" The more

Sue-Anne stared at the teeth and the surrounding face the less she trusted this female.

"I was only joking, Mrs. Pike. After all you are the Governor's wife."

"Pretty funny, aren't you? You made that crack with malice afore-thought, I'd guess. But Ah'm a big girl an' I fo'give easy. Part of my family tradition. Where's yo' home, *Miss* Blum?"

"Hoboken."

"Hoboken? Where in Gawd's name is that?"

Aubrey Tinsman said hastily, "New York is just to the east of it."

Knowing perfectly well where Hoboken was, Sue-Anne said it again. "Hoboken?"

She mouthed the word carefully, twisting her lips around it, and the second time she said it she separated the syllables so that three distinct positions of her lips were required. She faced Pete Walsacki during this process and made sure that he was watching her mouth. Then she smiled.

"You aren't from Hoboken, are you, Mr. Walsacki?"

"No, ma'am. I'm from Toledo."

"Do all the men up Toledo way have so much hair on their chests?"

Pete Walsacki fumbled with the top button of his shirt and then took a long draw at his bourbon. He was about to say that he had never noticed the hair on other men's chests especially, when Carlos Raveza slammed his empty beer can down on the bar and shouted, "If you no drink up everybody, the mess hall close and so you starve."

"Quiet, Fatso. I was talkin' with Mr. Walsacki."

The net was nicely set now, just thick enough to see without being seen. Whoever drank better than ol' Sue-Anne? It was the other people, the weaklings in this world, who were the slobs. If you planned carefully and knew how to handle the stuff, there was never any problem. Come to think of it, the time had come for a slight booster. Smiling an invitation, she reached out and took Pete Walsacki's empty glass from his hand.

As she turned toward the bar she knew that the web had very suddenly become too thick. She was making a mistake. Something happened to the bar. It sailed upwards and at a slant for several feet, then moved abruptly outward and bumped into her so hard she dropped both Pete Walsacki's glass and her own. There was a double crash of glass, and at the same instant the lights went out and the juke box whined down to silence and she clutched at the bar in terror, crying within herself, biting her lips so that the others would not hear her, I *am* a slob, a slob, a slob! I am a dirty, blind-drunken slob and I can't help it!

Then in amazement, she listened to the voices rising in excitement all around her. She leaned against the bar which was so unsteady and pawed at the darkness, hearing the jangle of her bracelets without being able to see them, and hearing also the voices without being able to identify them. She bit her fist in horror because she was sure they had heard her call herself a slob, and she could not tear away the web which had now brought on total darkness. Now I'm blind, she thought, as well as a slob, and the best thing to do is go jump in the channel if I can find it. Whoa! Where is that channel?

Then gradually, as the confusion eased and the bar steadied down, she understood the other voices. Pete Walsacki was saying, "Now what the hell do you know about that?"

Aubrey Tinsman said, "Oh dear, oh dear! Heaven help the poor sailors on a night like this!"

Crystal Blum began to sing "Two Cigarettes in the Dark."

Dana Wood said, "Power failure! Oh, Carlos, are you going to catch hell! Right in the middle of supper call."

Carlos Raveza's face was revealed as perfectly calm when he lit a match and held it before him.

"Impossible." He chuckled. "Still it is very dark, is it not?"

Dana Wood laughed. "You're just lucky it didn't happen during the movie. Pike would have you shot at dawn."

"I suppose it is necessary I walk over to the powerhouse," Carlos said. He waited hopefully as if by doing so the lights might go on again. When his match went out he sighed and said, "This is extremely inconvenient. I am in a sad mood and that is not the best time for me to tinker with machinery, electrical or otherwise."

He belched once and moved off through the darkness.

Sue-Anne fumbled for a bar stool and, when at last she found one, she sat down upon it. And she was so grateful that it was only a power failure and that she was not a blind slob, she bowed her head and began to weep again.

From the darkness at the end of the bar Fred Hanover sang in a husky whisper, "Light a candle in the winder for my wa-a-andering boy . . . !"

Zebulon Pike was en route from his house to the mess hall when the street lights went out. He came to an abrupt halt, stared for a moment at the nearest light, now so dead against the stars, and snorted.

He waited, tapping his foot and looking up at the light, as if it had personally thwarted him. He stuck his thumbs in his belt and looked all about his domain for any sign of illumination. A few candles began to appear in and between the buildings. He watched them moving about like fireflies. He heard a woman laugh and a man curse as he stumbled over something. The mess hall, vaguely outlined in the starlight and normally the origin of considerable banging and clatter at this hour, was silent.

Pike waited for approximately one minute, damn well time enough, he told himself, for any idiot to start the auxiliary generating equipment. He frowned at the outline of the powerhouse. He could detect no activity either in or near it. He waited another thirty seconds, then set off at forced-march cadence.

When he arrived at the powerhouse door, he was breathing heavily, more as a result of anger than from his exertions. The main generator was still running smoothly although it seemed to be under no strain. Why didn't the idiots turn on the lights then?

He saw a match struck and someone moving about behind the generator.

"Hallo in there!" Pike called and at once set off for the match flame. "Who's in charge here?"

"Me, unfortunately," Carlos Raveza answered.

In his haste and concentration on the match flame, Pike suffered a head-on collision with a heavy tool box and for a moment he was convinced he had broken both shins. Cringing with pain he shouted, "What the hell do you mean by leaving equipment around like that?"

The match went out and Carlos said, "Why the hell to look and mebbe be more careful where you're going?"

"This is Governor Pike speaking, I'll have you know."

"So? This is Carlos Raveza. Is there something I can do for you?" Another match flamed and Carlos held it above his head.

"I want to know exactly when you're going to turn on the God-damned lights!"

"Señor Governor, truly I am a lazy man. If you think I prefer this method of illumination you are loco."

Still rubbing his shins, Pike limped gallantly toward him. By the time he stood facing Carlos he had recovered most of his dignity and managed to stand menacingly erect. Unfortunately, his action coincided with Carlos' burning his fingers. He whipped out the match and the effect of Pike's charge was lost. In the darkness Pike said, "Haven't you got a flashlight? Do you have to stand there lighting matches? What kind of an emergency procedure have you got set up here? Are you in charge? Who's in charge? What did you say your name was and when are we going to have *the God-damned lights!* People are eating in the dark, dammit, and I have no intention of eating in the dark, and later on there's got to be a movie!"

Carlos lit a match and Pike was astounded to see that he was smiling. Barely holding on to himself he said very slowly, *"Where,* my good man, is your flashlight?"

"Over there," Carlos said, waving the match casually toward the end of the building.

"Then why aren't you using it?"

"The batteries. Finish."

"Well, put some *new* batteries in it! Now!"

"Impossible, señor. None exist. I have make inquiries at the warehouse and also the chief of supply. They say it is one of the things forgot. Yes, so many things to forget. So even the Atlas Construction Company is not perfect."

"If I find out that's true, I'll get a boatload of batteries here immediately. If it's a lie, you're going home."

"Hooray! That would be very nice of you, señor. My contract is to be pay for one year and I much prefer not to work for the money. I will take a vacation in Cuba, perhaps go to Santo Domingo, where I have friends, then possibly stay a month or so in Venezuela, where the beer is excellent. Later I will—"

Stabbing his fingers at Carlos' belly, Pike said, *"You* have been drinking!"

"But of course, señor! It is a requirement of the soul!"

"Will you stop standing there and holding matches and talking about your soul and geography in general! Fix the confounded lights!"

"By and by I will, señor . . . with luck, that is. But I do not think it so bad a disaster to get the panic. It is better you calm down. Otherwise and for certain you will have bile in your liver."

As Pike clenched his fists helplessly, Carlos squatted before the large control panel and moved his match slowly along the array of dials and switches.

"Who is responsible for your being on Nikki? Who hired you? Who checked your qualifications for this job?"

"Nobody, señor," Carlos answered without looking up from the panel.

"How could *nobody* hire you? You don't answer my questions!"

"You ask so many at the same time it is very difficult which to prefer to answer."

Bending over the control panel, Carlos grunted, "Ah!"

"Have you found something? What's the trouble?"

"No, señor. I only permit air to escape from the lungs because it happens that I am in a very uncomfortable position. I am no longer young enough to bend over so long."

"Where are your assistants? I seem to remember there were several electricians assigned to Nikki. Where the hell are they right this minute?"

"I have two assistants, not several. At this moment they are probably asleep."

"What are they doing asleep? This is dinnertime!"

"They eat later. They must stand watch all night and relieve each other. Also they must do many other things. For example, to make sure all is well with freezers for the meat and various other machinery. Here we labor all the hours of the day and night. It is a silly arrangement. Often there is not even time for siesta."

"I fail to see what there is to check about the other machinery if the main plant is out."

"Sad but true," Carlos said, lighting another match.

Now Pike lit a match and began peering at the control board. Before it had burned halfway through he said, "What's this?"

"What is what?"

"This switch which says *off*, dammit!"

Carlos brought his match, held it beside Pike's. "Ah," he said. "But of *course!*"

"Of course *what?* Has this switch anything to do with the trouble?"

"Most certainly. Without a question of a doubt. Witness, please."

Carlos held the switch down to the ON position. At once the main generator slowed momentarily and then, as if gathering strength, began to labor with a heavy, solid rhythm. The lights hanging from the powerhouse ceiling took on an amber glow and gradually brightened.

"It is the main circuit-breaker!" Carlos yelled above the new pounding of the motor. "She kick out because of an overload, I am proud to state. Automatic!"

"That's all that was wrong and *I* had to find it?" Pike gasped.

"You are a very intelligent man," Carlos said. "I regret that you were troubled."

Pike shook his head in disbelief when Carlos pointed up at the lights and calmly inquired if they could not be considered both efficient and beautiful. "What kind of an electrician," he said through clenched teeth, "are you?"

Still looking up at the light, Carlos smiled thoughtfully. "Not the best, señor. You may be sure of that."

Pike dropped his match on the floor and made his way slowly to the door. He went out into the night without looking back at Carlos Raveza, and he walked all the way to the mess hall in stunned silence. Those who saw him en route failed at first to recognize him, for his normally alert eyes were glazed and his broad shoulders were slumped as if a cannon ball had struck him in the chest.

When he entered the mess hall, Albright looked up from his plate and wondered if Pike had suffered a heart attack.

It was so that things seemed to come in pairs on Nikki atoll. For on the other side of the channel Peterson and Randall were also engaged in an electrical problem. Terry Mack did not lead them, as Randall had hoped, to a bamboo pavilion inhabited by maidens whose sole purpose in life was to satisfy the desires of men. Instead Terry Mack escorted them to the store of Yip Kee, a simple establishment which matched in every respect that owned by Nikki's other Chinese, Fat Sue.

It was the intention of Yip Kee that the similarity between his own and Fat Sue's store should be brought to an end. In fact it would bring no tears to either Yip Kee or his wife or his six children if Fat Sue went bankrupt and was forced to leave the atoll forever. Nikki was too small and the native inhabitants too prudent to bear the exploitation of two merchants. It had proved to be that rare perch in the broad Pacific where not even a Chinese could make a profit. Yip Kee wanted to join with the thousands of other Chinese in Polynesia, Micronesia, and Melanesia and at least get one of his carefully manicured fingers around the financial neck of the Pacific. In time he realized that the most logical way to begin such an ambitious program was to eliminate his nearest competitor. Since the results of violence were always unpredictable, Yip Kee resolved to employ cunning. Which was the reason Peterson and Randall were guided to his store before they were permitted any deviation. Terry Mack was also using his cunning. He was after a reward of five cans of salmon, a delicacy much preferred to the variety of fresh fish the lagoon offered. Any native of Nikki knew that whatever came in a can must be superior to anything found in its natural state.

Yip Kee greeted Peterson and Randall with considerable warmth. Two wooden chairs were placed in the center of the store for them, and they were handed bottles of orange-colored pop which had been kept in cool water. Peterson held up his pop bottle, and after he had taken a sip and the bubbles stung his tongue with unaccustomed warmth, he pointed the end of the bottle at Randall and said sourly, "Yeah. Let's go drinkin'! We can tell people about this here orgy for a hundred years!"

Randall asked him sotto voce to lay off and added that obviously their hosts were only trying to be nice.

As they sipped without enthusiasm at their pop, Yip Kee set before them two coils of wire and the units of a wind generator. They were part of his scheme to eliminate his business competition, for if his store could furnish electric light, he reasoned that all of Fat Sue's customers would be attracted to him. Yet since its arrival the contrivance had not produced a glimmer of light, though the trade winds blew faithfully and the propeller spun industriously on the roof. After endless experiment the reason for the generator's failure became obvious. The instructions for hooking it up were printed in English, a language not even Terry Mack pretended to read.

"Now, m'lads," Terry Mack said, allowing his good eye to rove along the shelves of canned goods. "Do ye think ye could read the words a bit and make things proper? Ye *can* read, can't ye?"

"Naturally," Peterson said, accepting the sheet of instructions. He was, he thought, willing to do almost anything to stop sipping pop. Randall leaned to read over his shoulder, and Yip Kee hopefully held the kerosene lantern between their heads so that they would enjoy a maximum of light.

When they were finished Randall and Peterson looked at each other and then down at the units of the generator. They set down their pop bottles and rose simultaneously.

"Can ye fix it?" Terry Mack asked eagerly.

Peterson smiled wearily and said, "If you have a screw driver it is so simple your friend will have light in five minutes."

A shiny new screw driver was produced instantly, and like two young Americans lost in the intricacies of a hot rod, Peterson and Randall began connecting the wires to the units. There was a reverent silence as they worked.

The mess hall was the largest single structure in Pistol Two and was also the only building with a rounded roof of corrugated iron. From a distance it resembled an old-fashioned aircraft hangar and hence was not an object of beauty. The Atlas Construction Company had erected many such buildings from the Arctic to the tropics and had at last developed what they considered to be a purely functional design. The semicircle of roof shed heavy rain and snow, the concrete floor could be laid in one day, and the sides could be easily adapted to keep out cold, or, as in the case of Pistol Two, screened and left open to admit cooling breezes without subjecting the occupants to the direct rays of the sun. It was fortunate for the Atlas designers that they were never required to dine in their creations for extended periods. They might have been less satisfied, for the round metal roof and the cement floor combined to produce acoustical pandemonium. A fork dropped at one end of the hall sounded more like a falling anvil at the opposite end. Conversation at meal times among the diners was necessarily keyed in competition with noises from the kitchen, which caused considerable hollering even when two people sat side by side.

The kitchen was at one end of the mess hall behind a cafeteria-style serving counter and was firmly governed by a despot known as Clara to those who ignored the grease in her stew, and as Mrs. Riley to those who were courageous enough to complain about it. Clara was of Swedish descent and had cooked for such projects from Greenland to Texas. She took the name Riley when she married one Pinkey Riley, who now served as Pistol Two's baker. He was a very good baker when he was sober, which was seldom.

There were twenty long tables set in two rows along both sides of the mess hall. Normally only fifteen of these were required. The others had been provided to accommodate casual trade which might become involved on Nikki for several days.

Before the first three meals had been served on Nikki certain amenities came to be observed, and within a few days the social structure at dining time became as fixed as a beehive's. The table directly opposite the door and closest to the ice-water dispensing machine became Pike's private board as surely as if there had been a sign forbidding transgressions upon it. Here he had a solitary breakfast and at noon, lunch with Sue-Anne; and when she was not too long detained in the recreation-building bar so that she missed the meal entirely, they had supper together. No one thought it odd that, while the table could easily accommodate fifteen persons, the only other occupant ever seen at the table was Albright. As Pike's aide his presence there was understood and thought correct, an impression which would not have prevailed had anyone else elected to dine with the Governor.

The next table, which was second both numerically and socially, was almost as firmly established as Pike's. It was occupied by the members of the scientific team and the foreign observers. Dr. Case also sat at this table more or less permanently and sometimes Fred Hanover would bring his tray, although he was likely to wander aimlessly about the mess hall for some time before he found a place which pleased him. Impelled by curiosity a stranger from the masses would occasionally make the mistake of sitting at this table, a stranger in the person of a carpenter, or mechanic, or Crystal Blum. And they were made as welcome as the regular occupants were able, which was of little avail because the conversation invariably branched off into subjects not easily followed by people who were merely hungry. Thus, the few who had tried it never returned, and after a few weeks the faces at this table were always the same.

The complement of the next table was more involved and subject to more change than any other. For here sat those who were independent workers or who, through official directive, held positions of authority. As chief electrician Carlos Raveza found himself comfortable at this table. So did Dana Wood, the mail-plane pilot, when he remained on Nikki for dinner. Peter Hildebrandt sat here as did Sgt. Doolan; and sometimes, to Doolan's disgust, Aubrey Tinsman found it inviting. Adam Smith always ate at this table. When it was possible he chose a seat at the end. In nature this became a bachelor's table, although from time to time it would be invaded by the Chief of Commissary Supplies and his wife, or by Alice Summer, the schoolteacher.

The other tables, which stretched to the end of the hall, were voluntarily occupied by the more ordinary citizens of Pistol Two. They usually dined in family groups although there was, for variety's sake, a considerable interchange of children among the tables. Here sat the boss carpenter, Barney Dunbar, and his family, the Pete Walsackis, the Harry McAdoos, and the Ellsworth Tompkins. Here Margaret Trumpey would also be found, and Sunnie Mandel, the marines, the movie projectionist, the paymaster, the man in charge of sports equipment, the photo-lab technicians, Miguel, who doubled as bartender and librarian, and an assortment of men all of whom were abnormally muscular and copiously tattooed. These last were the straight laborers who were required to do almost anything on Pistol Two from maintaining the streets to moving supplies. Most of these men had been employed on overseas projects from Arabia to Alaska, and many had not spent a full month in the United States for over ten years. Those who had saved their money against the day when they would permanently return to their homeland had formidable bank accounts. Those who did not had equally imposing beer bellies.

The noise level in this section of the mess hall was several hundred decibels above any other.

When Pike left the mess-hall doorway, he moved toward his table as if he had not yet awakened from a heavy sleep. He whipped up his napkin, glanced at the bowl of celery, and sat down with a thump. Albright was so unnerved by his behavior he could only toy with his pork chops. He sensed a crisis in the making, and he hoped that somehow he could finish his meal and depart before Sue-Anne descended upon the table. She was already so late Pike might explode when she eventually walked into the mess hall; and since Sue-Anne performed best before an audience, Albright knew that his chances of leaving would be very slim indeed. *He* would be the audience and he dreaded what the role might do to his sensitive digestion.

Normally when Pike sat down to his meal he smiled expansively and waved at those subjects among the farther tables who might be looking his way. It was a part of his regular now-we-are-just-boys-and-girls-to-gether routine. Then he would pass the time of day or discuss the merits of the actors in the night's movie, and he would sit very straight in his chair and make a point of commenting on the excellence of whatever came out of the kitchen. He would say that people were mighty lucky to enjoy such food at no cost to themselves and that Napoleon was right when he said an army marched on its stomach. This would bring him to a brief review of the responsibilities of the American nation to the world in general and further exploration of his pet theory that, unless a careful checkrein were kept on all Americans, they were sure going to hell just like the Romans did and that very soon a nation accustomed to a more Spartan existence would take over the world and then, by God, you would see. All of which Albright considered nonsense in an electronic age as well as being a frightful bore.

Peering at Pike through the stand of celery, Albright saw that he was sweating profusely and he thought that his face was like a steak broiled very rare. He accepted his plate of pork chops without comment and, seizing his knife and fork, manipulated them with such ferocity Albright was certain the instruments, which were Navy surplus anyway, would bend and collapse beneath the strain.

Pike was a meticulous eater, an observation, Albright thought wistfully, he was most certainly qualified to make since he bore witness to the exhibition three times a day. Normally he marched through a meal with admirable dignity and when he had finished not a crumb remained at his place. In Albright's opinion Pike lacked several important attributes of a true gentleman, but he was willing to admit that at one time in his life his table manners must have been properly supervised. For which Albright was most grateful.

Now, therefore, Pike shocked him. He stuffed enormous chunks of pork chop into his face, splattering his shirt with gravy in the process, and there were lumps on both cheeks as he chewed like a busy squirrel. When he pointed his fork at Albright and began to speak without waiting to swallow, Albright momentarily lost all sense of superiority.

"Look here," Pike said without the slightest regard for the fact that in gesturing at Albright his bare elbow dipped into his butter plate. "There are going to be some changes made around here! Believe you me, there are going to be some changes made and that's starting tomorrow morning!"

"Just what seems to be the trouble, Governor?" Albright asked cautiously.

"I am surrounded by inefficiency! I have never seen such loose, fumbling control since I took over the 326th from poor old Chubby Steel."

The 326th, Albright knew only too well, was an artillery regiment which had fallen on evil days back in 1920, allegedly because the often-mentioned Chubby Steel had been assigned to Armenian relief after World War One. It seemed that he had taken to smoking hashish, a habit which he maintained on his return to America and the 326th, and was eventually found unfit to command. Albright had long hoped that he would never hear another word about the 326th's troubles or Pike's solution of them, but now he wished he would stay with the subject in lieu of an unknown something which threatened to be more immediate. He was disappointed.

"I am surrounded by a pack of idiots," Pike went on. "How in the name of God did some of these people get assigned to Zeus?"

"Just which people are you referring to, sir?"

"To our master electrician for one. I will have you know that *I . . . me,* mind you, had to fix his equipment when the God-damned lights went out a little while ago!"

"Couldn't he fix it?"

"No. He could not. And we would still be stumbling around in the dark if it was up to him. Oh, he was frank enough! He admitted he didn't know what the hell he was doing."

"I'll check up on him in the morning."

Pike shoved an enormous forkful of mashed potatoes into his mouth. Albright studied his nails.

"I want a full report on that man's qualifications . . . how he got the job and why."

"Yessir."

"And furthermore I want a marine stationed outside my office during business hours. In guard uniform and equipment."

"May I ask why, sir? As you know they are an independent unit and I would have to obtain authority from their duty officer on Tuamani. I doubt if Sergeant Doolan would have the authority or would be willing to assume the responsibility. My recollection of the directive was that the Marines functioned as police only . . . except, of course, they would be under your direct command in a state of emergency."

"This *is* an emergency! How do I know what that idiot will do after I practically called him a liar?"

"Did you, sir?"

"He said there was not a flashlight battery to be had on the base. I said if he was lying I would send him home."

"And what was his reaction, sir?"

"He said hooray."

Albright, having thoroughly examined his nails, turned his hands over and stared at his palms.

"If you will permit me to say so, that hardly seems to constitute an emergency. It would be very difficult to put into a teletype to Tuamani. I'll go see Mr. Raveza and smooth things over. If he doesn't seem amenable to reason, I'll let you know at once."

"We might not have had a movie tonight if I hadn't gone to the power-house!"

Albright glanced up at Pike's eyes. He almost took the risk and said that the loss of a movie could certainly be classed an emergency when he noticed that Pike's attention had wandered. Furthermore he had stopped eating and placed his knife and fork carefully in line on his plate.

Mother of God, Albright thought. This will be Sue-Anne coming to dine. Perhaps I *had* better call out the Marines.

Albright turned to follow Pike's eyes and was instantly relieved to discover it was not Sue-Anne, but that weather chap who had so captured Pike's attention. He was bound toward the door and Albright noticed that he held a toothpick between his teeth. It made Albright slightly ill.

"And there goes Jack of the beanstalk, the king of my idiots," Pike said. "Look here, I'll prove something to you."

Then he called out in a voice that easily overcame the clatter of dishes. Albright assumed that such a voice, which he had never heard before, could only have been developed over the roar of a cannon. He found his mind unable to resist quoting the opening stanza of Tennyson's "Light Brigade" and he found it easy to visualize Zebulon Pike leading the charge.

"Mr. Smith! Will you come here a moment!"

Adam Smith halted as if he had been lassoed by Pike's voice. He turned to look at Pike and thoughtfully removed the toothpick from his mouth. He hesitated and then walked slowly toward the table. Nodding to both men, he said good evening in a voice which was barely audible. Pike ignored the greeting.

"Mr. Smith," he said, "I would like to ask you a question."

"Sure," Adam said.

"Did you enjoy your dinner?"

Albright was astonished to observe a crafty gleam in Pike's eyes. Of all the characteristics which Albright had discovered in Pike, he thought that deception or a fondness for guile was most certainly not one of them. In Albright's estimation the man was a great plodding oaf, a military hack who would have been eaten alive in the civilian world. Even in the Army, Albright thought, he would have been a hopelessly lost and confused bull if he had not sprung from the sacred womb of West Point. That class ring on his finger was, and had been, his shield against reality. It was as much a part of his body as his nose. Throughout the major portion of his life, when ordinary men were heavily engaged in open war with economics, that ring had constantly established its owner's seniority, and from seniority all blessings automatically flowed. And so during this period of growth and gestation and final maturity, keenness of mind was superfluous for Pike and might in some cases have been an actual handicap. There was no need for cajoling or gentle persuasion in a military order, written or verbal. Albright was convinced that constant exposure to military directives petrified any natural facility for the subtle approach. And so now he watched Pike in fascination, as though he had suddenly betrayed not only himself, but his kind.

"Why yes, Governor," Adam Smith was saying, "I enjoyed my dinner very much. Something wrong with yours?"

Pike smiled benignly up at him and leaned far back in his chair.

"No, indeed. I was only checking up. The well-being of our people here is part of my job, you know. I want to be sure that even our parasites are content."

"I'm not sure just what you mean by that, Governor."

Pike placed his hands on his broad chest and carefully moved his finger tips together so that they formed an isosceles triangle. He beamed on the structure as if it were a trick not easily mastered.

"I mean nothing by it especially, except that every project of this magnitude is like establishing a separate society. There are the workers and the truly skilled. . . . And then there are the . . . shall we say, drones, and even incompetents who must be carried along with the others. In the Army we counted on such weaknesses and provided for them. In battle the weak elements were sent to the rear, although, of course, we continued to feed them. . . ."

"Just what has all this got to do with my dinner?"

"Another question. Is it going to rain and spoil our movie tonight?"

"It might and it might not."

Pike separated his hands and spread them palm upward in a gesture of hopeless finality. "There you are!"

Though he took on the most forlorn expression, it was obvious to Albright that he was enjoying himself thoroughly. Yet there was no cruelty in his manner; only, Albright thought, a sort of silly flexing of his muscles, the garish performance of an iron-headed bully who was not really a bully because the last thing in the world he would do would be to actually strike anyone. He was certain now that Pike just wanted to roar a little and pace up and down in his cage and perhaps frighten any captive spectators. Albright was also certain that the Governor would retreat whimpering to a neutral corner if anyone so much as went boo at him, but he doubted if Adam Smith knew it.

"Correct me if I'm wrong, Governor, but I don't think you like me," Adam said.

"My dear fellow, I am not permitted any personal likes or dislikes in this community. I must regard each individual in the same light no matter how my personal feelings may be involved. I was merely remarking, and I thought you might do some thinking about it, that one's mere *presence* on this island does not establish one's value. In your case I am beginning to wonder if I haven't been perhaps . . . overly tolerant?"

Albright saw Adam's face redden, and his lips became a thin, hard-pressed line. Whatever the circumstances, he thought Pike had chosen a poor time to chastise this Smith chap even if he deserved it. Albright was framing a soothing interruption when Adam said, "You don't like me, Governor, because you don't like my weather. Has it ever occurred to you that I don't make the weather?"

"You have officially stated on four separate occasions that it was not going to rain. Unfortunately, those statements proved to be one hundred per cent in error."

"Those were *not* official forecasts, Governor. I would never attempt to forecast the occurrence of local rain squalls, particularly in the tropics. A single cloud can open up any time. It's a question of dew point and temperature."

"Don't try to confuse the issue with technicalities, Mr. Smith. The fact remains that you are being fed well and paid well to forecast the weather and in my opinion you are doing a most haphazard job of it. I realize that our nightly enjoyment of a movie is unimportant, or even the fact that our people must walk home soaked to the skin. . . . After all, Project Zeus is far more important than any individual's comfort or enjoyment. But it is exactly Zeus which concerns me. How, when the big time comes, when every detail of this vast enterprise must click like a drill team . . . how can I trust your winds-aloft report when you have twice missed on that?"

"Any meteorologist misses once in a while. It just happens."

"Well, it can't happen here, Mr. Smith. It *must* not happen here, do you understand? As I've mentioned before, my neuritis has proved to be much more reliable than your past reports. Some improvement must be shown in your record very soon or I shall be forced to . . . Well, I think you understand?"

"I understand perfectly."

Adams said it quietly and apparently without anger. Then he turned and walked to the ice-water machine. He bent over the spigot and took a long drink. Without looking back at Pike he passed the back of his hand across his wet lips and went out the door.

Adam stood in the middle of the coral street for several minutes, looking up at the stars and listening to the night sounds of Pistol Two. The banging and clattering of the mess hall formed a solid background for other sounds which he took a strange pleasure in identifying. He could distinctly hear the juke box playing in the recreation building. There was the steady whirring sound from the powerhouse, and somewhere far down the street he heard a small boy fighting off Indians. Adam wondered if it was Floyd Dunbar. Since their first meeting he had seen him only once. Floyd was on his way to school and there was only time for an exchange of "Hi's." By listening carefully Adam could hear the sea brushing along the beach and the intermittent thwacking of the palm fronds in the wind. And finally it seemed to him that he could hear Governor Pike's voice still roaring in the mess hall although he knew the notion was ridiculous.

He walked slowly down the street, thinking first of Pike and then of Margaret Trumpey. Well, it certainly hadn't been a very good night! Golly! Maybe Peter Hildebrandt was right and he should strive to be more pleasant. But how could you come right out and say to a girl like Margaret that things were on the lonesome side and you thought maybe it might be for her, too, and that maybe it would be a good idea if the two of you sort of went places together in Pistol Two like to the movies or even over to the bar in the recreation building for a drink before dinner, and maybe it wouldn't be too obvious if once in a while you sat at the same table and at least had dinner together? How did you get the ball rolling on something like that when probably a girl like Margaret had half the men on Nikki asking her to do this and that all the time, because after all there was a terrible shortage of women, and, well, there you were?

Adam halted at the intersection of the main street and the one which led to his quarters. He was uncertain why he stopped at just that moment and place, but very suddenly in his thinking about Margaret Trumpey, the memory of the channel's black swirling waters returned to him, and it brought on the same wild feeling he had known in the mess hall only a few minutes before. It was like a whirlpool stirring within him and it was so compelling that, when Pike finished his speech, he had almost reached out and seized that thick neck between his two hands.

Now, standing in the street, his hands rose involuntarily and formed into fists which he shook at the night even though he knew it was innocent. How could that ignoramus be appointed Governor! Pike and his crazy neuritis! He didn't understand the first thing about meteorology because he didn't *want* to understand! He wanted someone he could kick around, some handy joker he could make eat humble pie whenever he felt like it because he knew his power was temporary and he had to taste all of it. And the joker was Adam Smith!

Why not put into reality the idea which had flashed across his mind when he stood on the pier with Margaret Trumpey? Who besides Adam Smith would ever know the truth when it was all over? No harm done and it would be Major General Zebulon Pike, or whatever kind of a general he was, quaking in his boots and running around in circles and looking silly instead of Adam Smith.

A smile crept across his face and he favored the night sky with it instead of his fists. He started to walk rapidly toward his office and by the time he had passed "Brains Bungalow" he could hardly refrain from breaking into a run. His thoughts were still far from organized, but they were churning like the black waters of the channel. He would have to calm himself, separate the sudden wild notions which had come to him. The best place to attempt this would be in complete solitude. In the night. In his office. For they were not mere notions. They were inspirations, all the more intriguing because it was possible to base them upon scientific fact.

Beneath the third street light he passed two young men walking in the opposite direction whom he recognized as part of the Marine detachment.

"Hi!" Adam said almost gaily, and he thought it rather remarkable that neither of the marines seemed to sense the exhilarating activity in his mind.

"Hi," Randall said.

"Hi," Peterson said.

He continued on, his mind much too busy to query the disheveled appearance of the normally neat marines. In two days, perhaps three, if he actually had the nerve, Pike just might have something to take his mind off rain at movie time.

SUE-ANNE WAS in a melancholy mood when she left the bar. To hell with it. To hell with everybody. Nobody loved lil ol' Sue-Anne!

She moved through the soft night uncertainly, pausing at times to stare at the lights in the scattered buildings, moving on again when she had seen enough, standing in the dark places between the street lights to look up at the stars. And then, somewhere between the bar and her own house, she lost track of things. She would stand for long periods, either in the light or the dark, weaving as she stood, and trying to focus upon something definite. It was not easy. After a while a sense of peace possessed her and she could not imagine the reason until she discovered that, when she stopped, the bangle and the jangle of her charm bracelets also ceased. So experimenting, she would take a few steps swinging her arms and she would listen to the jangle. Then she would stop. And again there would be silence.

I sound like the lead team of one of Zebulon's batteries, she thought. I chink, chink along . . . no, not like the lead, but more like the wheel team! And suddenly remembering the harmonious clinking of the chains which were so much a part of the horse-drawn artillery, she was young again. The notion so exhilarated her she kicked off her patent-leather pumps and ran along the coral road, not feeling the cuts on her feet. She spread out her arms, embracing the night, seeing not the stars or the lighted buildings which fled past like the sides of a bewildering canyon, but only herself. She was laughing and she wore a tremendous hat to shade her young face against the Oklahoma sun. For it was hot at Fort

Sill. And she wore a print dress and she was sitting in the reviewing stand while Captain Zebulon Pike rode past. The battery of seventy-fives chinked along behind him and the caissons followed, rumbling and chinking, too, with the enlisted men sitting, arms folded smartly, like dolls taken for a ride. Everybody loved Sue-Anne Pike then. She could depend on it. The Colonel loved her and said so, and after the review they went back to his quarters and loaded up on Okalihau which the Colonel had preserved from his Hawaiian service, because, of course, it was Prohibition then. She could depend on the Colonel saying that he adored her right in front of his wife. Who was old. Forty!

Sue-Anne laughed at the night. Forty! It never occurred to her then that one day she would be so old, much less fifty!

Chink, chink. Halt! Who goes there? Sue-Anne Pike, formerly, only two years before, Sue-Anne Spencer. Daughter of the regiment! Really daughter of Orville Spencer, who would have been astounded to learn that according to his little Sue-Anne, he was quite wealthy. He would have been just as surprised to hear how his modest frame dwelling in Memphis had been described as a vast plantation, and as a lifetime foe of alcohol he would have been distressed to know that, according to his daughter, not an evening was allowed to pass without his mint juleps brought by a colored man who had been with the Spencers since birth. Orville Spencer had never in his life spent a morning on his bay mare riding through his cotton fields. He owned neither a mare nor a cotton field. And he did not eat a long luncheon at home off silver preserved in the Spencer family since pre-Revolutionary days. It was all he could do to afford the streetcar fare down to his small hardware store, and he took his lunch along with him in a cigar box.

Sue-Anne had described her father and his plantation so many times that both had long since ceased to be imaginary. So firm was the vision fixed in her mind that, when Zebulon Pike asked her to marry him, she almost suggested the ceremony be held in the formal gardens which surrounded her father's mansion. Her hostess at Fort Sill, who was a highschool friend and who had arranged the meeting with Captain Pike in the first place, suggested that the less said about her background the better. And for once, Sue-Anne listened . . . until the swords crossed over their heads.

Ah, Zebulon! He was so beautiful then! Straight as one of his own shell cases, lean and hard, and his uniform fitted as if it had been plastered on his body. In the polo games he rode like a wild man, coming past her at the end of a chukker with his helmet tipped back just far enough to show his blue eyes. And he would flip her a little salute, or lift his mallet in a very private signal of pleasure when he had played well. Oh fun, with every officer's wife on the Base envying her! Oh fun, as long as they didn't have to spend long hours alone with Captain Zebulon Pike; and slowly, like the creeping of a volcanic ooze, suspect, and then know for certain, that while Zebulon Pike was certainly beautiful, he was also most certainly an absolute dumbbell.

"Alas!" she sighed dramatically. "Alas, alas . . . alas! I am married to an ass!"

With her arms spread wide she twirled along the coral street, jangling and bangling to the music which suddenly swept her being; for now, this moment, she was a long way from Nikki. She was a ballerina of international fame twirling her way homeward through the streets of Vienna. And spinning along the street she sang in waltz tempo, La-tum-ta-ta-tum-ta-ta-tum . . . until suddenly she fell against the porch door of her own house and knocked a section of the wire screening out. Things were very misty for a moment. She drifted helplessly though pleasantly and she could not seem to lift the veil. Then there she was, not in Vienna at all but on Nikki, and Zebulon was holding her about the waist while he disengaged her arm from the screen door.

"Easy now, Precious," he said. "No sense in cutting yourself any more."

The blood did it. She stared at her arm and saw the bloody scratches, and decided it was time to be sick. Good ol' Zebulon! Take me down to the ball game. . . . No, take me down to the flagpole where I can barf.

He held her head and encircled her waist with his arm for solid support while she vomited. And over and over again he said, "Easy, Precious."

At last he led her into the house and cleaned the little cuts on her arm, and he was a long time at it because one of her bracelets proved difficult to remove and he considered it a possible source of infection.

"Why don't you call Dr. Case?" she asked. "You don't have to do this, Zebulon."

"I know I don't. But it isn't serious and I'd just as soon keep Dr. Case out of this case."

"Haw, Zebulon! You made a funny!"

Now that her equilibrium had been restored, she found it was very pleasant to lie back in the big wicker chair on the porch while Zebulon methodically bathed her wounds. He brought a bucket and filled it with a peroxide-and-water solution. He dipped her feet in it and very carefully cleaned the tiny coral cuts with a cotton swab.

"Good ol' Zebulon," she said, looking down the length of her body as he worked over her feet. "Good ol' Zebulon, you are just laike a great big ol' St. Bernard dog. Only one trouble. Yo' come to the rescue but you forgot the rum."

"Why do you do this to yourself, Sue-Anne?"

"Because I laike to. Where else can you get good bourbon at two bits a shot?"

Zebulon nodded his head and for a moment, before he bent over her feet again, she saw his face very clearly. The veil seemed to swing completely away, and there was that same handsome visage which she thought would surely befit a Roman centurion better than it did a general who no longer had any occasion to put on a uniform.

"Zebulon?" she said, lowering her voice until it was hardly more than a whisper.

"Yes, Precious?"

His interruption of her thought was too much for her to surmount just then. The thought became stillborn and she pressed her eyes closed trying to recapture it. But all she could find in her mind was a lingering objection to his familiar "Precious." Why did he always use it, she thought, or almost always, just when he should take me off in the bedroom and beat the living tarnashin out of me? What kind of a man would let his wife in the house when she was stewed to the gills and then get down on his knees and bathe her feet just like he was a plantation slave?

"Zebulon, you are a fool."

She said it very quietly and slowly and flatly. He did not reply, but he looked up at her just for a moment, and then he went back to his swabbing. The light was behind the big chair and she could plainly see down the length of her legs to his iron-gray hair, but she could not see his eyes. She wondered if he cared what she had said, or had even heard her. She turned her head away from the sight of him and looked through the screens at the line of coconut palms along the beach and finally, as if twenty-seven years of resentment demanded the same immediate exit as the whisky beside the flagpole, she spoke again. She wept a little as she rambled on and her words were often slurred and she hated the words which came out of her mouth, but she could not seem to stop them.

"You are the biggest fool in the world, Zebulon. A genuine jerk. Nobody evah tol' you that did they, Zebulon? Because they were scared of you. God only knows what they were scared of because you wouldn't hurt a fly. . . . No siree. Not a fly. We have plenty of flies in this crazy place to hurt, but you wouldn't . . . would you, Zebulon Pike? Par'rm me . . . *General* Pike! Lil ol' Sue-Anne knows. You bet she knows. Maybe you can fool the public by stomping around and making laike a real general but you can't fool lil ol' Sue-Anne. On account I know you haven't got the guts of a feather duster. When you were a platoon commander you were scared of your captain and when you were a captain you were scared of Major Miller, and when you were a major you were scared silly every time ol' Colonel Boyd opened his mouth. No wonder they decided the best place for you to fight a war was runnin' an arsenal. Ol' chicken-on-his-shoulders Zebulon Pike stomping around a bunch of concrete warehouses and brewing up a storm of papers. Ol' Sue-Anne knows. . . . Sue-Anne knows you didn't put in for transfer to combat laike you let everybody think you did. Sue-Anne knows because she got good an' loaded one night in the club with ol' Spang, who if you just happen to remember was Division Commander then, and he said that, hell no, he didn't see any reason why I should look for smaller quarters because no request had ever come in from you to go anywhere. He said he remembered way back when you managed to wheedle out of even foreign service in the Philippines. . . ."

"What did you do with your shoes?" Pike said.

"Tossed them up in the air. Threw them away like I ought to do with a lot of other things."

"We'd better find them before somebody else does. They might recognize those shoes and maybe they might get the wrong idea."

"Oh for Christ's sake, Zebulon! Don't give me that Sherlock Holmes business. I haven't been out in the bushes with anybody. I've been down in the bar gettin' good and drunk laike a lady. You about done with my feet?"

"Yes. You'd better stay off them for a few days. They're going to be very uncomfortable."

"Why don't you order me to bed and order me to stay there, General? What the hell's the matter with you? You can't make your own wife behave! I'll tell you why, Zebulon . . . because you never were a real general. They shoved that star through for you two weeks before you were due to retire, so they weren't taking any chances. And they shoved it through 'cause Frank Hoover really deserved a star and they couldn't very well bang him without including you. Just one trouble out of the whole thing, Zebulon. They made you a general in the wrong service. It should have been the Salvation Army."

"All right," Pike said quietly as he lowered her feet to the floor. "The cuts weren't really deep and they're good and clean now. I'll take another look at them in the morning."

She pushed herself out of the chair and stood up. She kept her feet well apart and managed to remain quite steady until she reached up to brush back a lock of hair that had fallen over one eye. The gesture almost capsized her. Before she fell against the screen Pike caught her, and for a moment she hung limp in his arms. She peered at him thoughtfully, the lids of her eyes almost closed.

"Why do you do this, Zebulon? Why do you take care of me?"

"Come," he said.

He led her to the bedroom and laid her gently on the bed. He pulled the sheet up to her neck because the trades were strong even through the screens, and turned out the light. As he started for the door she called after him.

"Where y'all goin'?"

"To the movies."

"Have a good time, Zebulon."

"Yes."

He closed the door with great care and almost tiptoed down the hall. Before he reached the front door he heard a sound that caused him to halt very suddenly. He listened and his lips gradually tightened. It was raining—hard.

When Fred Hanover had consumed enough Martinis to deaden any errant pangs of conscience he went back to his quarters and sat down before his typewriter. He was already two days late in producing the weekly piece he was supposed to send from Nikki, and he just simply had to put something in Dana Wood's mail pouch before he flew up to Tuamani in the morning.

It was not going to be easy for, as far as Hanover could see, things had come to an absolute standstill. Typing out, "No movie tonight raises Pike's Pique," just wouldn't do. And no matter what he wrote, it had to be siphoned through press relations on Tuamani. When you wrote for or about the colossus A.E.C., you had anywhere from five to fifty editors. Hanover thought that it was worse than his stint on *Time*. Never mind the news, grind the axes and above all mold opinion. And the colossus was so big it was like writing about the Indian rice problem. Only much bigger. Here was an isolated enterprise, only one of many, and the climax of this one would begin and end in less than a second. And would cost at least fifty million dollars. Just the plant investment of the A.E.C. was more than eight billion dollars! How could you put such figures into words and expect comprehension from anyone except Aristotle Onassis?

On *Time* magazine you could take up a cause, or one of the master-minds would throw a cause in your lap, and you could hammer away at it with a lot of smart-aleck phrase inventions until the subject died a natural death, or somebody made a dull Italian movie that would be given the two-page masterpiece treatment, or some idiot made a series of paintings using the lobe of his ear as a brush and attached honeydew melons to his nudes, in which case he would be solemnly given the genius treatment. You could do such things on *Time* according to your depart-mental niche, but, by God, Hanover thought, you could not so blithely monkey around with the Atomic Energy Commission or its endeavors. Presumably Operation Zeus was going to be the most terrifying cataclysm ever conceived by human beings if it was a success, and a simply un-believable waste of talent, energy, and money if it was a failure. "Which," Hanover murmured aloud, "I hope it is."

But you couldn't write that. Tuamani would never pass such opinions if you did write them down. And if it ever did pass, the public would never read the stuff anyway. People did not *like* to read such things; and he, Frederick Payson Hanover, the poor man's Patrick Henry, the Am-herst boy who couldn't even make the grade on *Time* . . . did not blame people in the least.

There was only one solution, and for the past few days he had been working at it with such energy as he could muster. He had even made a few notes. Flipping through them now, he smiled sourly when he noticed that he had unconsciously reverted to *Time* style in making the notes. He was trying the only approach left open to him—the personality angle. On Nikki, with even the lowest-magnitude celebrity far below the horizon, using the personality approach was tricky, and after investigation, showed an alarming tendency to prove a dry well.

. . . Pert, vivacious, piano-playing bachelor girl Margaret Trumpey of Beloit, Wisconsin, may signal the end of mankind with finger tips trained to the delicate cadence of Bach. . . .

Nuts! Margaret Trumpey was anything but pert. She hadn't been par-ticularly vivacious when Hanover talked to her, and she certainly was not going to signal the fate of mankind with her finger tips. She sent out weather reports and could, if authorized, signal for additional cartons of canned milk, but most of the messages were coming her way and they were dull beyond description. The only factual thing about the notes was that Margaret was unwed, which was not exactly surprising, and that she came from Beloit. Beloit papers, if there happened to be more than one, please copy.

So much for Margaret Trumpey. She was a nice girl, *but,* Hanover thought, I am not being paid to write about nice girls. Such material was expertly enough handled by *Cosmopolitan* and *Redbook* writers. Glowering at the rain cascading past his screen window, Hanover remembered that those nice magazine girls were almost invariably in grievous trouble. Which the Trumpey girl was not.

"No!" he muttered at the rain. "My job, if it can be so designated, is to write about the creation of the most vicious, insulting slap in the face that God has ever received from the hand of man! Not really write about it . . . just make it easy to swallow!"

Hanover bent his head and closed his eyes. He discovered to his horror that he was gnawing at his knuckles, and he wished that he had not consumed so many Martinis. Since when, he thought, have I taken off on this religious kick? It is going to get me into trouble because I'm not equipped either by training or inclination to explore spiritual urges and, furthermore, it just will not make good copy. I am thirty-five years old. I smoke too much and I drink too much. I am educated after a fashion and generally conform to certain rules set down by the particular society into which I was born. I do not violate those rules because I am aware that to do so will get me in endless trouble . . . and yet, I am partner to the greatest social violation in known history. I prod my flabby brain, which has only become a hunk of punk, to convince others that this violation is perfectly all right, and there is nothing to get concerned about . . . worse yet, that there will be trouble if we *don't* commit the violation. I must even imply that through some mysterious process, about which I can be as vague as I please, this tragedy is somehow going to benefit society. Holy Mackerel! *This* is making a living? *This* is justifying my existence?

He looked at his notes again.

. . . high-domed scientists and brawny-armed laborers worked feverishly side by side on the flyspeck of an atoll to do their part in making Operation Zeus the biggest, most fantastic firecracker of them all. . . .

Hooey!

No one on Nikki was working up the slightest fever, side by side or in any other position. The laborers spent most of their time lying in their bunks reading comic books when they weren't drinking beer. No one knew what the scientists were up to, but it certainly wasn't much. Maybe, he thought, I ought to fly up to Tuamani, where things are supposed to be happening. But I wasn't assigned to Tuamani. I was assigned to Nikki and I either make something out of it or go home.

. . . Bar-straight, hammer-jawed veteran soldier, General Herbert Zebulon Pike, establishing proper diplomatic relations with Nikki natives, found the presumed savages had outdevoted his model town in the middle of nowhere. Score two to nothing. The native area of his atoll boasts two churches. Pike's pulsing model of American habitation—none. By teletype roared God-fearing Zebulon Pike: URGENT. SEND ONE CHURCH!

Religion section please copy. Otherwise dull stuff.

And Pike would be justifiably mad because the omission of a church wasn't his fault anyway and he shouldn't have the credit of creating Pistol Two, if indeed, any credit was deserved. The whole thing was Atlas Construction. Also it was very possible he sent that wire more out of a sense of being cheated rather than a need for spiritual dedication.

Hanover lit a cigarette and walked to the window. The wind which had first come with the rain was gone now, and the smoke from his cigarette was drawn straight out through the screen. Across and down the street he could see the weather office, and he was surprised to notice that the light was on and that Abraham Lincoln sat over a drawing board. How about that guy? Maybe he was Honest Abe's great grandson, or nephew, or *something?* Maybe there was a piece in him. Jesus, if he even came from Illinois you could sort of work it around!

The rain came down heavier and the weather office became a dull blob of light. What was his name? . . . Smith! Why the hell couldn't it be Lincoln? Maybe he could at least be persuaded to grow a tuft of beard. A photo story on look-alikes maybe? Local contest? Phooey!

Hanover turned around to face his typewriter. He stood motionless, staring at it for a long time. Why didn't the contraption write its own stories? They invented every other kind of a machine. . . . Give enough information to an electronic brain and a machine could translate an income-tax report into Russian in a few minutes. Why not just feed an idea to a machine, go smoke a cigarette, and come back to read the story? Ask one of the boys in "Brains Bungalow" about such a machine in the morning. Make a fortune.

He sighed. All right, admit your brain is dead. Go for a walk in the rain. Get some fresh air. For lack of anything better to do, stop by and see that fellow Smith. At least he seemed to be able to find something to keep him busy nights. Maybe he was rewriting the Gettysburg Address.

Adam had almost forgotten about Pike. For over an hour he had been lost in the large map on his drawing table, and the lines and symbols which he had drawn upon it were now as real as the rain outside. He was working over one of the standard printed weather maps which he used as the basic form for each day's weather analysis. The principal islands and atolls of the area were represented by rough approximations of their shapes in faint brown ink. Nikki atoll was placed a few inches from the bottom of the map; Tuamani was three hundred miles to the northeast; Oa Titia atoll, which like Nikki was an auxiliary to Operation Zeus, was near the very top. One hundred and fifty miles to the west of Tuamani a small atoll was indicated and marked with an X. This, when the time came, would be the actual explosion site. The meridians of longitude and the parallels of latitude were printed in a fine blue overlay and covered the entire map.

Normally, Adam drew in such weather fronts as might be present in the area, basing his drawings on information teletyped from Tuamani and his own observations. Some freedom and imagination were both permissible and necessary in sketching in the isobars and isotherms because it was impossible to obtain a reading from every section of the area. Pressure, temperature, and wind reports from ships, radiosonde balloons, airplanes, Tuamani, and Oa Titia served only as guideposts when plotting on the map. Connecting them produced various line patterns; and, while Adam wished there were more reporting points, yet he saw no reason for Pike or anyone else to question the general accuracy of his work. The area was vast and there were bound to be local disturbances which would never appear on his maps or anyone else's, but the general pattern of the weather and, particularly, the all-important behavior of the winds aloft were based upon a known system which rarely betrayed a trained meteorologist.

So Adam told himself that he was only allowing his thoughts to simmer down when he first began doodling a portrait of his storm. He was just blowing off steam, that was all, and trying to forget about Pike in the mess hall. His pencil moved idly over the map, barely sketching, making what in the beginning appeared to be meaningless circles, one around the other. He was not really concentrating on a storm pattern in the beginning. He was thinking more about Margaret Trumpey and wondering how he could approach her again without sounding like a dunce.

The map was fresh and clean, ready for his next morning's work, when he sat down quietly before it, and it *was* quiet he needed, not Peter Hildebrandt's tootling on his flute. He sat listening to the rain, the arrival of which only proved that Pike had ceased to read his forecasts. He had predicted it as a result of a mild front presently passing to the north of Tuamani.

And then suddenly . . . there it was! Now Adam stared at what he had drawn and for a moment he wondered about the power of the human subconscious. Certainly he remembered drawing it. For that matter his pencil was still poised above the series of concentric circles which, to anyone with the slightest knowledge of weather, would indicate a hurricane. And he had, without too much thought or intention, located the center of his circles about a hundred and fifty miles to the southwest of Nikki . . . actually in the middle of nowhere.

Smiling at his fancy, he started to label the hurricane MARGARET; then he stopped and erased the letters. Just for the hell of it, where would a hurricane go? How would it move if there *really* were one to the southwest of Nikki? There was no reasonable basis for prediction. Maybe the natives on the other side of the channel would know, but that was questionable because it had been a long time since anything of the sort had come anywhere near Nikki. It might, Adam thought, hang around in the vicinity for days, in which case—

Adam moved the pencil slowly in an arc around Nikki; then his hand swept off to the northwest on the map. In which case, he thought, it might reverse its course, make a lazy giant circle and become lost in the umpteen square miles of the Pacific. Cocking his head to one side, he again followed the course of his imaginary monster and decided that as long as he was momentarily in control of the elements he would feel better if the thing moved very slowly. It struck him that he had a fine name for such a slow-moving storm. Where he had erased Margaret's name, he solemnly printed LAZY ETHEL in bold letters.

Now thoroughly absorbed in his fancy he began to write a summary. A summary with a smile, he thought.

"A tropical disturbance of hurricane character is approaching Nikki atoll. Further references this storm will be coded Lazy Ethel. Center is estimated one hundred and fifty miles southwest and moving slowly in a northeasterly direction. . . ."

He hesitated, wondering what Pike's face would look like if he read such an analysis. He might even challenge the rights of the elements to make such a commotion and command them to cease.

Ah, well . . . it had been fun anyway. And he was feeling much better about everything—even General Zebulon Pike. He yawned. Now perhaps he could sleep. He was about to crumple up the summary and throw it on the floor when he heard the screen door slam behind him. He turned to see Fred Hanover standing in two rapidly forming pools of water.

"Hi!"

"Hi!"

Hanover smiled and wiped the water from his face and his hair. "Kind of wet outside," he said.

"Yeah."

"Is this going to last all night?"

"Probably."

Hanover advanced a few paces toward the drawing table and wondered how, with being out in the rain and all, he could still feel those Martinis. He fished in his shirt pocket and brought out a sodden pack of cigarettes.

"Don't happen to have a cigarette, do you? Mine seem to be pretty damp."

"Sorry. I only smoke a pipe."

"Oh."

Hanover hesitated, then placed a limp cigarette between his lips. Adam struck a match and he leaned over the drawing table to accept the light. He puffed for several seconds without success and he wondered later if it was because his mind was, very suddenly, not on smoking. He straightened up finally and said, "The hell with it."

He tossed the cigarette into the wastebasket beneath the drawing board. "I hope you don't mind my barging in on you like this?"

"Nope."

"I've seen you around, but no one ever bothered to introduce us. Hanover . . . Fred Hanover's the name. I'm in press relations, which probably doesn't mean much to you."

"Well, not exactly."

"No matter. I just thought I'd stop by for a talk. . . . Seeing you sort of left a candle in the window."

"I guess I'm not much of a talker, but you're welcome anyway."

Hanover glanced at the drawing board again and then looked carefully at Adam. "What's cooking . . . generally?"

"How do you mean?"

"I mean who, what, and where? You know. People like me have to make a living like everyone else. Nikki is a very easy place to get stuck for a story, I can tell you!"

"I suppose it is."

This fellow, Hanover thought, is like playing badminton with a balloon. You hit the object, swing through the air, and nothing comes back. A very smart character, and who did he think he was kidding? Martinis or no, Fred Hanover had twenty-twenty vision and he had seen that drawing board. He could still see it.

"Nothing special at all, huh?"

"Not as far as I know."

Oh, you lying bastard! I'm looking right *at it!* Are you going to sit there with pie on your face and tell me there isn't anything going on? Not as far as you know? Who the hell *else* would know about a little newsy item which seemed to be labeled Lazy Ethel and which certainly did not appear to be very far from a certain atoll known as Nikki? Except maybe Pike, who must already know about it, which, of course, explained why he was in such a flap when he left the mess hall.

"Not a thing doing, huh?"

"Nope."

"I suppose it does get pretty dull weatherwise around here. The Pacific being the Pacific and all that."

"Occasionally, it is pretty interesting," Adam said matter-of-factly. "You'd be surprised."

"Yes. I guess I would."

Hanover looked about the office and his eyes came to the written summary. He took a step closer to the drawing board and was grateful again for his perfect vision. He could easily read the words Adam had written.

"Could you," he said slowly, "give me some idea what the weather will be like tomorrow? I was thinking I might go fishing in the lagoon."

"It should be very nice."

Hanover pressed his lips together and made a humming sound. He was both uneasy and uncertain. If he told this Class A dullard that he knew very well he was sitting on the best story ever to come out of Nikki, he might get to Pike and manage to stop it. And he could just about guess why Mr. Dullard was being so cagey. Also why he was working nights.

"Well," Hanover said. "Nice to talk to you. If you find out anything that might be of interest newswise . . . let me know, will you? I live over behind Brains Bungalow."

"Sure. Good fishing."

Hanover walked slowly to the door. He opened it, looked back over his shoulder and suppressed a sudden urge to wink at Adam. He said, "This rain doesn't mean anything special . . . is that right?"

"Correct."

"Good night. Thanks for the hospitality."

"You're welcome."

Hanover stepped out into the rain. When he moved away from the glow of light he turned and saw that Adam was again bent over his drawing board. He watched him only a moment, then trotted toward his quarters. He still had plenty of time to crank out a story before Dana Wood flew back to Tuamani. And the chances were very good indeed, what with the hour and all, that his little piece would hit the desks in Tuamani even before Abe Lincoln's technical manifesto found its normal way through the morning teletype.

This, Hanover decided, would put press relations in its proper place where press damn well belonged—at the head of the line. What a flap! The brass on Tuamani getting their first dope on a little item called Lazy Ethel from a mere journalist! A journalist who just happened to be in the doghouse more or less. Yes, sir. A journalist who had been exiled to the bush league island of Project Zeus because he allegedly drank too much, but now by God in heaven they would have to admit that, drunk or sober, one Fred Hanover was very much on the job.

He hummed tunelessly yet happily as the rain spattered on his head. Stories, he thought smiling, are where you find them.

6

PIKE ROSE before the sun as was his custom. He set his wrist watch on the wash basin and spent exactly twenty-one minutes brushing his teeth, shaving, and showering. He brushed his stiff hair vigorously for exactly fifty strokes, then took up his watch again. He glanced at it with considerable satisfaction, then strode into his bedroom. There he stood before the open doorway which led onto the porch and began those ritualistic movements which had, with rare exceptions, officially introduced his day ever since his graduation from the Point. He began, as always, with his push-ups, stiffly executing twenty before he jumped to an erect position again. Pike was methodical and realistic about his push-ups. When he was thirty he had done forty every morning and at forty, in the interest of his heart, he had deliberately cut the effort to thirty. Now, for the past five years twenty push-ups seemed quite enough and he was considering cutting things down to fifteen. The forced reduction did not depress him. He glanced at his watch again before he did twenty bends, touching the palms of his hands to the floor each time. He was also thinking of cutting these bends to fifteen. After all.

Then he rested, red in the face, yet breathing only slightly faster than normal. He rested with his feet together and his hands at his sides in a posture of attention, although on this morning his head was bent in contemplation of his nakedness. His feet were still good and well formed, but lately the veins in his legs were becoming too prominent, standing out like small purple ropes entwining his muscles. Yet his belly was firm and showed no signs of becoming a pot.

Regarding his body with honest curiosity, he began to wonder if he would ever again lose himself in Sue-Anne's passionate embrace. It had been a very long time, so long, in fact, that the preliminary maneuvers which always seemed so necessary, now presented an almost insurmountable wall between them. How, presuming Sue-Anne was in the mood, which she never seemed to be any more; how could he possibly start things off? How could he, without embarrassment, without making a damned fool of himself, without having Sue-Anne burst out laughing and say for criminy sakes Zebulon, *what* in tarnashin you trying to do, how could he begin? Supposing he went through the door and into her room now, right now in the morning when he was so charged with energy? Supposing he slipped into her bed and began, as they had on so many mornings for so many years? Would she welcome him, or submit with bored indifference as she had done the last time, which would now be over two years ago; or would she laugh? And if she laughed that would be the end. Forever.

He decided not to risk it. Certainly not on this morning. The cuts on Sue-Anne's feet were going to hurt and she was going to have a terrible hangover. It would be much smarter to stay out of her way for the rest of the day.

He raised his arms above his head, taking a deep breath as he did so and standing on his tiptoes. He repeated this process fifteen times, staring vacantly straight ahead at the row of palm trees beyond the porch and at the sunrays which were now just touching their tops. As he breathed he thought about Sue-Anne sprawled on the bed in the next room, and he wondered why it was that he had never even considered spending himself within the body of another woman. No. That would never be the answer. Half-smiling at the morning, very much awake now, he murmured, I guess I'm just a one-man dog.

He dressed rapidly and with mechanical efficiency. No old soldier would have been ashamed of Zebulon Pike when he had finished, for somewhere in his career he had mastered the tricks of smartness until every shirt and pair of pants he possessed seemed to be faded just the right amount, and they fitted his torso as if most expensively tailored. His starched khaki shirt hung perfectly on his shoulders. The pockets were creased and always buttoned, his service belt was scrubbed, and the brass buckle shone as if his fingers had never touched it. The jodhpur shoes which he chose to wear on this morning were old and well broken, yet so carefully polished and preserved it was almost impossible to detect any wear.

He made his bed with equal efficiency, turning the top sheet down precisely eight inches and snapping the pillow slip until it was quite smooth. When he tucked in the ends and swept his hand swiftly across the top sheet, there was hardly any evidence that the bed had been occupied. Then he snapped on his wrist watch and saw that the entire operation since his first push-up had taken twelve minutes. As it always did. Holding his shoulders well back so that his shirt and pants appeared to be a sort of secondary skin, he strode out of the room. The time was exactly six-thirty.

He quick-marched to the mess hall and ate his breakfast in solitude. This displeased him, not because he was particularly anxious to talk with anyone over his Sanka, but he thought that Albright, in his position as aide, should be up and about before hoi polloi. The brass, Pike had long been firmly convinced, should be brass in every connotation of the word. They were entitled to certain privileges, but there were also certain penalties attached to those privileges. Brass should lead, in effort as well as time. It was not seemly for those common laborers at the far end of the mess hall to be all through with their breakfast and ready to go to work when the brass, or a part of it in the person of Albright, was still lolly-dollying around in bed. The result of poor training, Pike thought, as he drained the last of his Sanka. Intellectual parents, no doubt, too much money, doting mother, Eastern school, unmarried irresponsibility, no experience with military discipline; all that. Very well, he would speak to Albright about this getting-up business. It would be the second such address and most certainly the last one.

He stood up and carefully patted his mouth with his paper napkin, which had remained unsoiled and folded. He was, as soon as he had revisited his bathroom, ready for what he was determined must be a very busy and fruitful day.

School for the children of Pistol Two began at seven o'clock with a ceremony carefully prescribed by Pike. He considered that he had rather cleverly circumvented an early and primary directive set down by his superiors. Normally Pike had a reverence for any directive which might arrive through channels. He was convinced there was only one way to run an organization and that was by a strict allegiance to tables of organization, plus absolute obedience to any directive worthy of being placed on paper. There was not, there never had been, and there never could be, any other way to control any given number of people from a squad to the entire population of an occupied country. A properly authorized directive was *not* just red tape, whether it covered the invasion of a hostile beach or stated the number of wastebaskets required per square foot of office space. Without directives, in Pike's solemn opinion, any organization of more than two people was automatically doomed to chaos. Furthermore, a good and well-written directive left no opportunity for personal interpretation. It stated bare facts, nothing more. Which was why Pike considered he had not taken undue liberties with that certain directive A-12 which stated, in what he thought were rather ineffectual terms, that "it must be remembered the A.E.C. is in no sense a military organization or even a branch of the military. While we co-operate and in turn receive co-operation from all branches of the armed services and employ ex-service personnel, we function purely as a civilian organization. Direct identity with any branch of the armed services could be detrimental to our authorized functions and could easily result in adverse public reaction to our basic goals. Therefore all those to whom this directive is addressed will avoid any act or procedure which might possibly be considered as of a miltary nature and/or originating from military authority."

Pike almost knew the directive by heart and it had come as a profound shock to him. But it was still a directive, innocently denying its theme by being set down and mimeographed in the best military form with suitable space for acknowledging initials, and it was signed by the Director himself. Therefore Pike had no hesitation in complying. He believed that he was within the bounds of propriety, however, in the business of the flag.

It would, of course, be in direct violation of the directive to have the Marine detachment hoist the American flag over Pistol Two every morning, or take it down at sunset. Yet Pistol Two was as much an outpost as Fort Ticonderoga back in the seventeen hundreds. The thought of beginning or ending a day without the good old Stars and Stripes troubled Pike, and he was determined that any place commanded by himself was going to observe the ceremony.

He believed that he had solved the problem neatly. The school children would raise the flag in the morning and a special honor detail, based upon their grades and behavior, would lower the flag at night. Ho—ho! Who could ever accuse school children of representing the military?

And so every morning before school began the flag was raised and every evening it descended, albeit without bugle or gun, which Pike could not see any way of providing. And every morning the Governor of Pistol Two stood at rigid attention while Alice Summers, the schoolteacher, saw to it that her charges displayed a minimum of restlessness during the ceremony. When the flag was up and the halyard made fast,

Pike beamed on the assemblage gathered about the pole and he watched with enormous satisfaction as they filed into the schoolhouse. Like so many childless men a great yearning welled up within him whenever he saw the issue of others, and when they were particularly well behaved as they always were at this fresh time of day, it was all he could do to refrain from following them into the building and patting the more likable students on the head.

Yessir, he thought, as the last pair of scrawny legs disappeared through the school's screen door. There is nothing like the little ones! Nothing was too good for them and within the physical limits of Pistol Two he had provided well. He had seen to it that the carpenters made teeter-totters from leftover dock planks and had authorized the plumbers to use all excess pipe for Jungle-Jim bars. He had personally designed the six swings now hanging motionless in the morning sunlight and had subjected them to the most strenuous tests himself by swinging nearly to the horizontal and performing a wild "chain snap" fifteen feet off the ground, for which he was resoundingly cheered. Now in the afternoon when school was out, he could hear the distant playground cries and shouts of delight in his office and he found it the most rewarding experience since he first beheld Nikki atoll.

He stood for a moment looking at the playground and regretting the fact that no amount of technical ingenuity had been able to furnish a proper slide or trampolin. If I had more money, he thought, I'd send for a trampolin myself and that would be the end of it. But he didn't have the money, and the two request letters he had sent to Tuamani for such equipment had so far been ignored. He would write again today. Dammit, millions to explode a bomb and the A.E.C. couldn't spare a hundred dollars for a kid's slide! There was no directive to cover such items, or he would long since have allocated the amount out of settlement funds.

He turned away from the school and set off briskly on what he had come to think of as his daily reconnoitering patrol. This consisted of a fast-paced tour throughout the environs of Pistol Two. It took him the better part of an hour. Leaving the school yard he walked through the equipment park, noting as he passed that the tractors, fork lifts, emergency cranes, jeeps and carryalls were properly aligned and covered with tarpaulins. Leaving the park he glanced at the wharf and the warehouse, about which there was rarely any activity at this hour, and then he proceeded down the center of Broadway. He passed the carpenter shop and saw that Barney Dunbar was still tinkering with his power saw, but he did not slow his pace lest Barney again beg him to order another. There was a limit to the equipment even the A.E.C. could provide at this distance from the States, and Pike had heard quite enough whining about that damned saw. He hardly glanced at the weather office as he passed around the corner of it, but he did note that it was still unoccupied. Of course that weather fellow would be lolly-dollying around in bed.

He passed the movie, noting grimly that the benches were still wet from the night's rain. Leaving the road he cut across an open area which would lead him between the laundry and the building which housed the foreign observers. Hanover was quartered in the same building, and the room at the far end was Albright's . . . who would, of course, still be lolly-dollying around in bed.

Pike halted briefly outside Albright's window. He listened for any sound of activity and, hearing none, considered entering the room and hauling Albright out of bed by the ears. Finally he dismissed the project as beneath his dignity. He would handle Mr. Albright later.

He swung off again without a backward glance and turned up the narrow coral road marked Second Avenue. Where it intersected with Broadway he passed the Marine quarters and saw that they were engaged in swabbing down the floor or "deck" as Sgt. Doolan would have put it, and he saw that Doolan himself was in charge. Pike approved, even though Doolan seemed to take a secret pleasure in withholding a salute. He was within his rights, of course. Marines did not salute civilians and Pike was a civilian. But Doolan did throw away his cigarette and assume a posture which at least resembled attention, and he said, "Good morning, Governor," smartly enough. There was neither affection nor resentment in his voice, and if there had been either intonation, Pike would have followed old instinct and stopped to find out what was wrong.

Pike continued up Second Avenue, passing the deserted ball park and the recreation building, which was locked at this hour. On the opposite side of the street he noted that the space between the two buildings which housed the single ladies had again been selected as a place to dry their laundry. He frowned at the two pairs of panties hanging from a line and assured himself that if the buildings had quartered WAC's, he would most certainly have spoken sharply to their lieutenant. Under the circumstances about all he could do was maintain his frown until the thoroughly un-military spectacle was far behind him and he had reached the hospital.

Now, because almost a week had gone by since he had inspected this particular building in his domain, Pike halted again, executed a smart right face, and entered the doorway. Dr. Case, who had his own rather spacious quarters in the rear of the hospital, was brewing a pot of coffee on his sterilizer. He looked up when he heard the door slam and regarded Pike without any sign of welcome. He was still in his pajamas, which Pike thought were not particularly clean for a doctor, and he muttered good morning in such a way Pike wondered if he was still asleep. Probably lolly-dollying around in bed, Pike thought, when he should have been up polishing his instruments, or going over some old X rays, or something since there were not, so far as he knew, any sick to heal in Pistol Two.

"Good morning to you, Doctor!" Pike boomed, aware now that Case was flapping about in his bare feet, which was probably most unsanitary. And he was smoking a cigarette before breakfast, which anyone knew was extremely unhealthy.

"Have a cup of coffee, Governor?" Case offered without enthusiasm.

"No, thank you. Never touch it."

"Why?"

"I don't think stimulants, artificial that is, do the body any good."

"It's possible that, taken in moderation, they don't do any harm, either."

"You're the doctor. Ho. Ho!"

Pike could not understand why Case seemed to wince at this instant. Actually the sentence, which had slipped out of him before he had really thought about it, seemed worthy of an echoing ho-ho from Case. His dour look, now, was disappointing. The man obviously had no sense of humor. As a matter of fact there were a great many things about Dr. Case which were puzzling. Reaching into his file-case mind, Pike clearly recalled their original interview, which had occurred in the ship. He had bluntly asked Case why he had abandoned his practice in Oregon and taken the assignment with Operation Zeus.

"If you'll sit still and listen for a week or so I'll tell you in about a hundred thousand words," Case had said. "It could be because I refused to join a new high priesthood which makes the Spanish inquisitors look like a bunch of amateurs. You must remember, Governor, that in America at least, a doctor is more than a professional man. He is a holy man, an untouchable, of whom one speaks only in whispers, or the most reverent tones. A part of this aura of greatness has been created by the doctors themselves, but for the most part it is the tribute of ordinary citizens who would not so respect the President of the United States or even one of the latter-day saints. The secret hero of every woman over thirty-five is her doctor, and otherwise sensible men often prostrate themselves before these new tin gods. I could not go along with this nonsense. I called some doctors fatheads publicly. I asked and accepted advice from outside the priesthood. I admitted openly that there were times when I didn't know what the hell I was doing. No one could seem to convince me that a code known as 'medical ethics' gave any man license to put those in his care through the torture of the damned. So I took this job because I finally gathered up enough courage to do some thinking, and a Pacific island seemed to be a pretty good place to do it. Frankly, I get too wrapped up in my patients' emotions to make a very good doctor. I found that I was unconsciously looking for gratitude, which is wrong. Jesus cured eleven lepers and only one returned to thank him. You see, a good doctor should never admit to himself that his patient might have recovered from two medicines . . . time and the will to live. If he does, he becomes inept from doubt, or conscience-stricken from sending his bill, or both. Well, sir, that's what was happening to me and that's why I'm here."

Looking at him now in his wrinkled and slightly soiled pajamas, Pike thought the man presented nothing to inspire confidence. All right for cuts and bruises perhaps, but he wouldn't have made buck sergeant in the Medical Corps.

"Don't you like our mess-hall coffee?" Pike asked.

"No, sir, I do not."

"What's the matter with it?"

"It tastes and looks like urine. Sometimes it even smells like it."

"I'll look into the matter."

"Do," Case said, scratching his bald head. "In the meantime what's your trouble?"

"I don't have any troubles . . . physically at least. I just dropped by for a checkup."

"Heart bothering you?"

"No. Not that kind of a checkup. I'm in fine shape. Always have been and intend to stay that way. It's another . . ."

Dr. Case peered at him from beneath his eyebrows, which in contrast to his bald head were as bushy as a mustache. He took a puff at his cigarette, which brought on such a fit of coughing Pike allowed time for it to subside before he continued.

"I just dropped by to check up on you and the hospital. Quite a community we have here, you know, Doctor. I like to look in on everything now and then . . . keep things at my finger tips."

"I suppose it would be too much to ask if you'd schedule your visits a little later in the day. I'm not at my best in the mornings. As a matter of fact I prefer absolute silence. It's better for thinking. That's why my office hours are in the afternoon."

Case engaged in another fit of coughing while he poured himself a cup of coffee. He sipped at it hungrily and said, "However, since you're here, I'll give you a brief run-down on the medical situation in Pistol Two. When it ceases to fascinate you, you are at liberty to stop me. Floyd Dunbar, who is eight years old, was punched in the face by one Herbert Fry, who is nine years old, at approximately sixteen hundred hours yesterday and arrived here with a bloody nose. Patient treated and dismissed after being held thirty minutes for observation and a mild lecture on the folly of picking on people who are bigger than you are. A Mrs. Pickering, I think that's her name, came in and wanted her gall bladder removed. I questioned this patient at some length in an attempt to find out why she considered such an operation necessary and she advised that she had been trying to get said gall bladder removed for some time and this seemed like an ideal opportunity since the government would assume all expense of the operation. Patient was otherwise obscure about her desire to have operation performed except to state that she had previously, and at her own expense, had her tonsils, adenoids, and appendix removed, and since all of those fixtures were hangovers from primeval man, she assumed she could get along very well without her gall bladder as well. Patient dismissed after medication. Two aspirin. A man with the rather interesting name of Jellico came in to complain about his back. It seems he drives one of the bulldozers and they give him such a rough ride he often slips a disc in his spine. After considerable conversation about where in the name of God he inherited a name like Jellico, which incidentally he never explained to my complete satisfaction, I took what turned out to be a pretty good guess and diagnosed his trouble as rheumatoid arthritis. He then admitted to me that he had been under treatment for that disease for several years and had graduated cum laude from courses in traction, physiotherapy, cortisone derivatives, aspirin, and frogs' left ears captured and swallowed only by the light of a full moon. After we got through all that we spent about twenty minutes bemoaning the fact that doctors didn't know a damn thing about arthritis including the two most elementary facts which would be how it's caused, or how to cure it, and we both felt a hell of a lot better. He's an interesting man, that Jellico . . . and a brave one. Care to hear more?"

"No, thanks," Pike said, wishing he had never stopped by the hospital in the first place. Convinced that Dr. Case was "peculiar" if not actually a little crazy, he turned for the door. Then suddenly he faced about and, trying to avoid looking directly into Case's piercing eyes, he said, "By the way, Doctor. I don't suppose they included any strait jackets in your medical equipment?"

Pike forced his attention to remain on the ceiling so as to appear entirely casual, as if the question of strait jackets was only a demonstration of his devotion to detail.

"Strait jackets! What the hell for?"

"You know. Among so many people, and all civilians, there are bound to be a few . . . unfortunates. Perhaps I should say a few who lack stability . . ."

"Is that so?"

"Matter of fact, a man called on me not long ago whom I at first considered as somewhat unbalanced. It turned out that he was perfectly all right . . . matter of fact, very intelligent man . . . but it set me to thinking."

There was a moment's silence while Dr. Case explored the contents of his coffee cup. And again Pike wished he had not stopped by the hospital. Finally Case said, "Well, Governor, there are still a lot of boxes in the storeroom I haven't looked at. Maybe one of them contains a strait jacket. I don't know and I don't much care. But if the need for such a thing arises, there are other methods these days to keep a patient quiet. Medicine hasn't made much progress in the last fifty years, but it has made some."

"Thank you, Doctor. I have complete confidence you could handle any such situation."

"I can always borrow a baseball bat," Dr. Case said and broke into a violent fit of coughing.

Pike retreated two steps to the door and fled. He passed along the side of the hospital as quickly as he could without actually breaking into a run. He had spent entirely too much time in the hospital and it had been wasted time at that. So instead of taking the long way back to his office, which would have permitted at least a cursory inspection of the airstrip, the garage, machine shop, and water-evaporation plant, he cut directly across an open area behind the store and barber shop. He marched with new determination, chin up, shoulders well back, arms swinging to match his full stride; for now the real business of this day would begin and he was more than anxious to begin.

HE PASSED through the grove of palm trees which surrounded his own quarters. On the supposition that any governor and his lady would automatically be sensitive to natural beauty, these had been allowed to stand, but on this morning Pike was not to be diverted by natural beauty. He entered a small building marked PLUMBING SHOP and asked for Pete Walsacki. A thin, yawning youth, who looked so young Pike wondered at once why he was on Nikki instead of in the Army, said that Pete Walsacki had just used up his last hacksaw blade and had gone to the warehouse for a new supply and would be back any minute. Pike also noted that the young man was smoking a cigarette and wondered if he had as yet had breakfast.

"Tell him to come over to my place as soon as he arrives," Pike ordered.

"Something busted?"

Pike hesitated. Nosy young man. Better find out more about him. "My shower," he said. "It needs repair. Tell him to be sure and bring his tools."

"Okay."

"Tell him to come to my office first and I'll explain what's wrong."

"Okay."

"Have you ever been in the Army, young man?"

"Unh-uh."

"A few years wouldn't do you any harm. You might learn that there is an English word commonly used in addressing your elders or those in authority. That word is *sir*."

"Ya, sir."

Pike left the plumbing shop, crossed through the palm grove, where he paused momentarily to pick a single flower, and then continued until he reached his front porch. He took the steps two at a time. He glanced at his watch when he entered his office. It was exactly one minute past eight. Twirling the flower between his fingers, he circled his desk impatiently. Then he went down the hallway and stopped before Sue-Anne's door.

He carefully turned the knob and entered the room on tiptoe. He saw with some disappointment that she was still asleep. And he saw, too, that the morning sun which now shafted through the veranda doors was unkind to her and all that surrounded her sleeping figure. The pillow was smeared with lipstick. An ash tray containing eight cigarette butts was on the floor within easy reach of her hand. Her charm bracelets were strewn about in little piles on the night table. One of them encircled an unopened jar of cold cream. Another had been placed around a glass of water. Her dress was a collapsed oval of Shantung on the opposite side of the bed, and her slip had somehow been tossed onto the porch. Pike remembered her shoes. He would have to retrieve those today and he would have to do it himself. When she awakened she could tell him where to start looking.

Still twirling his flower, he tiptoed to the porch. He picked up the slip and placed it on the bureau. Then he carefully closed the porch shutters. Moving cautiously through the dim light in the room, he picked up the ash trays, emptied them in the wastebasket, and placed the flower in a glass of water. Finally he bent down and gently shook his wife. He said, "Good morning, Precious."

"What the hell do *you* want?"

"I just wanted to tell you that you're going to have plumbing trouble."

"Now, Zebulon! I'm in no mood or condition for yoah bum jokes. Go 'way."

"Just you rest, Precious. But if anyone should ask you, we *did* have plumbing trouble. Shower wouldn't drain. It was fixed this morning. In fact I don't care if you drop that little bit of information when you go to the mess hall or the hairdresser or whatever."

Sue-Anne tried to raise her head, then eased it back to the pillow again. "Zebulon? What in tarnashin you talking about?"

"Pete Walsacki. He's on his way over to fix the shower drain."

"But there's nothing wrong with . . . Wait a second. Did you say Pete Walsacki? That big fellow?"

"Yes. He's the boss plumber."

Some of the glaze removed itself from Sue-Anne's eyes. "Oh ye-yes!" She spoke with an enthusiasm Pike made no attempt to understand. "Of course he really won't fix it. I just wanted you to know about it in case someone asked what he was doing here. . . . Then you would have an explanation that made sense."

"Why won't he fix it? Zebulon, *you* aren't making any sense . . . which only surprises me because I'm not awake yet."

"The shower is perfectly all right."

"Then what . . . ?"

"Never you mind, Precious. Now you know, and you can go back to sleep. I'll see you for lunch."

He left the doorway and returned down the hallway. He did not hear Sue-Anne say that she was certainly not going back to sleep if Pete Walsacki was going to pay a call. And he would have been amazed at the speed with which she left her bed.

Pike sat down at his desk; and, after he had arranged his two pens and several pencils precisely behind the small triangular sign which spelled out ZEBULON PIKE, he tipped back in his chair and waited for Pete Walsacki. How long did it take to get a hacksaw blade, dammit? On this particular morning, time was of the essence.

His fingers moved automatically to his gold class ring and he pushed it slowly around and around, musing on the devices worn almost smooth; the crossed rifles, the sabers, the crest, and the spread eagle. And he saw himself a plebe at the Point again, frightened and terribly anxious to please his upperclassmen. He saw the cold, gray battlement-encrusted buildings with the Hudson flowing beneath them, and he heard the high-pitched cries of day orders echoing down the barrack halls. Swiftly, as though the intervening years were like a moment's sleep, he heard the flat explosion of the reveille cannon outside his barracks window, and the more distant, lilting notes of the day's first bugle. And somehow then, it became a Sunday morning. There he sat on the gray blanket which covered his iron cot, and across his knees was spread the blouse of his dress uniform. There were, including those adorning the sleeves and the claw-hammer tail, forty-eight brass buttons on that blouse, each shaped like a small ball and arranged in lines. He heard the clicking as he slipped the metal "button board" over the first row so the polish would not stain the fabric, and he could smell the peculiar tang of the polish itself as he vigorously massaged the protruding buttons. Cadet H. Zebulon Pike never received a single demerit for neglect of uniform. The device on his shako, the rectangular plate which clipped to the intersection of his white shoulder straps, the insignia on his patent-leather cartridge case, all glistened; not only on Sunday morning, but every morning of every year he had been at the Point. Cadet Pike may have graduated in the lower third of his class and had his troubles with algebra, but no one could ever say he had not been a good soldier.

Then, Pike suddenly found himself asking, what happened? What went wrong between the time he was a second lieutenant and the time he reached his majority? There were a lot of years in between those commissions and they were not nearly as clear as his cadet days. And after he had pinned on a major's leaves, was there anything to remember except a string of posts around the country, all somehow very much alike until it was impossible now to distinguish any feature about them save the difference in climate? Fort Sill, Snelling, Ethan Allen . . . Monmouth, Plattsburg, the remount station at Riley, Funston, Sam Houston, and finally, for an all-too-brief tour of duty, the Presidio. A house, a "dog-robber," prisoners raking leaves in the yard . . . whisky, horses, Sue-Anne talking huskily and endlessly on the telephone to other officers' wives . . . and debts. For what officer above the rank of captain ever managed to live within his income? And all of those years the most dangerous exposure was summertime maneuvers. And when it was all over, a star. No ribbons, no medals, just a star which there had never really been an opportunity to display in active service. Those two weeks before retirement could not honestly be counted. The star was a reward for honest, if not distinguished service, thoughtfully arranged by a few surviving contemporaries who had been at the Point with Zebulon Pike. Seeing that old Pike got his star, which would, of course, increase his retirement pay, was a matter of class honor. There were also certain elements of self-preservation involved since those recommending the star were looking forward to at least equivalent consideration upon their own separation from the service.

So I became a general! Pike grunted audibly at the thought and swung around in his chair to stare at the palm trees beyond the window. Sue-Anne was right. It could just as well have been the Salvation Army.

He heard the screen door slam and heavy steps in the hallway. He whirled around to face his desk again and assumed his most formidable pose. When Pete Walsacki appeared in the doorway, Pike was more than ready for him.

"Close the door," he said quickly. Then he arched one eyebrow and his voice took on a conspiratorial tone. "Good. You look exactly like a plumber."

Walsacki smiled and thoughtfully scratched at the black hair on his powerful forearms. "I am," he said.

"Where are your tools?"

"On the porch. I didn't think you'd want me to lug them in here."

"No. . . . No. Of course not. That wouldn't be really necessary." He pointed to the visitor's chair beside his desk.

"Walsacki," he began gravely, "we have trouble."

Reaching into his desk drawer he pulled out a sheaf of papers. He wet the end of his thumb and flipped through the papers until he came upon one which caused his eyes to narrow until they were mere slits. By God, when Zebulon Pike read a paper he remembered what was on it! Every last word and item!

"Yessir! *There* is the item on the manifest, plain as day . . . item number 2605 dash J . . . flashlight batteries . . . four cases."

He handed the sheaf of papers to Walsacki, who accepted it without the slightest sign of interest.

"What do you make of *that?*" Pike asked.

Walsacki hesitated. "Well . . . it looks like somebody thought of everything and ordered four cases of flashlight batteries."

"Exactly. But there are no batteries in Pistol Two. I was so informed last night. They have disappeared. Gone!"

Beneath the black fibers which covered Walsacki's neck under the open shirt an experimental rumbling occurred as if the man behind the matting had unsuccessfully attempted to start a reciprocating engine. "That's too bad," Walsacki finally said.

"Too bad? It's theft of government property, that's what it is! Therefore it becomes your baby."

"Why mine?"

"You're the F.B.I. agent here, aren't you? Unless I have been misinformed this is a straight F.B.I. matter. Theft of government property is strictly the province of your agency."

Walsacki forced a smile and looked disbelievingly into Pike's eager eyes. He stuck one finger into his ear and wiggled it vigorously as if he would erase the words he had heard. "Look, Governor. You have not been misinformed. Theft of government property is and always has been a function of the Bureau—"

"Then catch the bastard!" Pike broke in triumphantly.

"I was about to say that while you are legally correct, these things sometimes have to be viewed with regard to the overall picture. I am fairly certain that no one on this island but yourself knows I'm with the Bureau. A great deal of my effectiveness, if not all of it, would be lost if it was generally known that I was not just a plumber."

"To hell with the overall picture! I want those flashlight batteries and I especially want the bastard who stole them! Who knows what he'll make off with next?"

"Whatever it might be, may I suggest that he can't go very far? Assuming the batteries were stolen in the first place and not just misplaced or really never arrived, don't you think it would be rather unfortunate to jeopardize my primary function by kicking up a fuss about flashlight batteries? Wouldn't it be a lot easier to just order some more batteries?"

"Your primary function is to protect government property and act as my deputy in so doing. You know as well as I do that I'm charged with every damned thing on this base from toothpicks to dock pilings. I was in the Army too long, Walsacki. Nobody's going to hang Zeb Pike with a paperwork noose."

Walsacki wiggled his finger in his ear again and took a long moment to re-establish his patience.

"Governor," he said finally. "While you are technically correct, the Bureau did not send me here to investigate petty thievery."

"Then what the hell are you here for?"

"If you were not informed, then I must assume you are not supposed to know."

Walsacki kept his voice so controlled and polite he could have been talking to a nun.

Pike pressed his lips together until they vanished. His short-cropped hair seemed to bristle as if it were on the back of an angry dog and the thousands of tiny veins in his face became as suddenly visible as if he had turned an electric switch. It was with some difficulty that he refrained from pounding his fist on the desk.

"I am supposed to know *everything* that goes on here! *Everything,* do you hear?"

"I hear you very well."

"Apparently there is something I do not know. You will tell me at once."

"I am sorry, sir."

Pike rose abruptly and brought his hands together behind him with a loud smack. He paced across the room and did an about-face just before he collided with the flag standard.

"If you were a soldier I'd let you think this over in a stockade!"

"I am sorry, sir, but I am not a soldier."

"Nonsense! We are all soldiers here. We have to be. Only way to get the job done. Perhaps we don't salute or wear uniforms, but by God we are all soldiers in the cause of democracy!"

Liking the sound of what he had said, Pike turned and gave Walsacki his full Sunday-morning-before-chapel-battery-inspection glare.

"Frankly, I don't like your attitude, Walsacki. I will not tolerate any Gestapo-like activities on this base as long as I'm Governor. I will not have you snooping around in other people's business and informing Washington or anywhere else as to their politics. I know you cloak-and-dagger fellows! Ho! Ho! Well, you just remember this is a little bit of America here and I intend to keep it that way."

"The Bureau functions in America, Governor. I don't think anyone except people who prefer another type of government consider us a secret police."

"Dammitall, I didn't call you over here to engage in a political discussion! I want those flashlight batteries and I want to lay my hands on the man who stole them."

Pike clasped his hands before him and cracked his knuckles as if they were the disintegrating vertebrae of a handy battery thief.

Walsacki said, "Well, Governor, about the only suggestion I can make is that you have the marines or somebody like that check over on the other side of the channel. Whoever made off with your batteries might find the trading pretty good over there. There certainly isn't any place to dispose of them here. It would be most unwise at this time . . ."

Walsacki sighed with visible relief when a sharp knock on the door interrupted him. Pike at once brought a precautionary finger to his lips and glanced at the door.

"Yes? Who is it?"

"Teletype, sir."

Recognizing the voice, Pike relaxed slightly. That damned girl. She had a genius for appearing at the wrong moment. She was not due until she brought the weather map.

"Come back with it at your regular time," he said as mildly as he could.

"The message is designated Urgent First Priority, sir. It's from Tuamani."

Pike hesitated uncertainly. Walsacki and the flashlight batteries were important, but this was the first time any such message had come through.

He stalked thoughtfully to the door and yanked it open. Margaret Trumpey handed him a sealed manila envelope.

"Do you want me to wait?" she asked.

"No. Yes . . . maybe you'd better."

Pike tore the envelope open and squinted angrily at the enclosed message. The first time he read it his mind was still on Walsacki and the flashlight batteries, so the words were nearly unintelligible. Then slowly, as he began a second reading, his mind which had never shifted easily from subject to subject, began to assimilate some meaning from the words.

PIKE PISTOL TWO

WE ARE MUCH DISTURBED OVER FAILURE YOUR MET OFFICE TO FILE REPORT ON LAZY ETHEL THROUGH NORMAL CHANNELS PERIOD THIS NOT ONLY EMBARRASSING FOR ALL CONCERNED BUT RENDERS IT IMPOSSIBLE TO PROVIDE YOU AID AND ADVICE PERIOD ARE YOU TAKING MEASURES TO EVACUATE QUESTION MARK WHAT HELP WILL YOU REQUIRE QUESTION MARK WEATHER CHARTS HERE SHOW NO INDICATION ANY SUCH PRESSURE AREA NEAR YOU PERIOD INSTRUCT YOUR METEOROLOGIST ADVISE US IN FULL OF PROGNOSTIC SITUATION PERIOD REPEAT ADVISE IMMEDIATELY AND MAINTAIN COMMUNICATION THIS STATION LONG AS YOU ARE ABLE PERIOD GOOD LUCK PERIOD

KEATING

Shaking his head in honest bewilderment, Pike again read the message, even more slowly this time, trying to forget that Margaret Trumpey and Pete Walsacki were watching him. The girl, the damned girl, knew what was in the message, of course. She must have typed it herself. How many other people knew what was in the message, which, if he had translated it correctly, accused him of withholding information on some kind of storm now threatening Pistol Two; a storm about which he knew absolutely nothing? Lazy Ethel? Good luck? What the hell was going on?

He passed his hand slowly across his forehead, scanned the message once more, then refolded it very carefully. Oh this *was* a morning, all right, and it was already filled with deceit and treachery! So *that* was the way the ball bounced! Ho, ho! Not only were people stealing flashlight batteries and the complete duties of certain staff members were being kept secret from him, but now a minor functionary had contrived to put him on the spot because of a fancied personal insult which any reasonable man would have considered merely a sound suggestion for improvement. That weather fellow! So! This sort of thing was precisely what he had feared when a group of people were required to work together under a system, or lack of system, wherein there was no recognized table of command, reward, or even punishment. It showed exactly what would happen without a proper manual or written regulations. Jealousies, personal animosities, ambition for attention, scheming, undermining of morale. . . . Pike could think of innumerable evils all sparked by a single glaring fault, lack of firm authority and lack of authority to exercise authority, dammit. The result was a restless, inefficient rabble of which one individual now stood out like a blank shell in an otherwise full caisson! Well, sir, Zeb Pike knew how to nip such craftiness in the bud. He glowered at Margaret Trumpey and said, "How fast can you run?"

"Fast enough."

"Then get down to the weather office. Tell that fellow Smith or whatever his name is, to report here on the double."

"On the double?"

"As fast as he can make it."

"Yessir."

"And after you've seen him, find Mr. Albright. Tell him to come here immediately."

"Also on the double?"

"Yes. On the double. And . . ."

Pike seized Margaret's arm before she turned away. He pressed it firmly and lowered his voice so that Walsacki would not hear him.

"Now listen to me, young lady. I want to make sure, *very* sure, that nothing is known of this message anywhere. *You* know what it is, but under no circumstances are you to repeat the contents of this message . . . *to anyone* . . . understand? Forget you ever saw it, do you understand me thoroughly?"

"Yes, General . . . I mean, Governor. I understand."

"Absolutely no one. This is between you and me and that damned teletype machine."

"Yessir."

After Margaret Trumpey had left, Pike turned back to Pete Walsacki. And in the very act of turning he felt a sharp pain in his shoulder. His neuritis again. Ye gods! It was better than any barometer or sad-faced weather experts with all their charts and instruments. He prodded that part of his shoulder where his neuritis seemed to be the worst as he faced Pete Walsacki and said, "Now about those damned flashlight batteries!"

ADAM WAS just taking his first upper-wind observation with his theodolite, and the balloon had gone up so straight he had a crick in his neck from tracking it, when Margaret came to his side and said in a strangely breathless way, "Good morning."

Adam looked down at her, quite willing to let the balloon rise to infinity since there was no wind anyway. Remembering their all-too-short meeting on the wharf, he said, "Well, it's a dull morning, but you brighten it considerably."

Then he locked off his theodolite and cleared his throat nervously, and said, "I didn't really mean the way I sounded last night. I was sorry when you left. So I would like to apologize. I guess that in a lot of ways, I'm a total loss. I seem to have a special way of antagonizing people."

"You sure do," Margaret said. "Pike is about ready to blow his top. He wants to see you on the double."

"What's his trouble now?"

"Don't you know? How cagey can you get?"

Adam looked into her eyes and saw, or thought he saw, a suggestion of mistrust, even accusation, and he wished that he could remember everything he had said on the wharf so that he could apologize in more detail.

She said, very calmly, almost as if she were addressing an inanimate object, "You'd better trot along. There is drool on his chops. It looked to me like heads are going to roll."

"Pike swung his ax my way again last night. I am not exactly his favorite citizen. In fact it's beginning to look like I'm in a lot of people's dog-houses. I'd like to have you know it's not because I want to be."

"Can I make a suggestion?"

"Sure."

"Remember he's got a colony to run. Good or bad, he's the boss and so he has a right to know what's going on."

"I'm not keeping anything from him. Neither is anyone else that I know about."

Again the look. The thing to do was take her back to the wharf and get everything straightened out in the same atmosphere. He said, "Are you going down to the wharf tonight?"

"I might. If it's still there. I should think it might depend on the . . . prognostic situation."

Adam wanted to ask her just exactly what she meant by that, but she was gone before he could say anything more. She was walking, almost running, toward the quarters at the end of Second Avenue. Watching her, Adam thought she moved with particular grace. He was vaguely disappointed when she did not look back. What was this, "If it's still there." He sighed and thought that it was no wonder his success with women was anything but distinguished. How did you ever know where you stood with the creatures? They were more complicated than the adiabatic lapse rate. No matter what you said it turned out to be the wrong thing.

Furthermore, they could with one little change of expression scare hell out of you. Still looking after Margaret, he decided that he wanted very much to be a success with her.

As he mounted the steps of Pike's front porch Adam remembered a phrase which had stayed with him since his school days. "I have often regretted what I have said, but never my silence." He could not recall the originator of the words in spite of the fact that they had long influenced his social behavior. Of all times, he warned himself, he must remember those words now. Otherwise Pike was certain to provoke him into saying things he really didn't want to say, and as Margaret had pointed out, good or bad, he was the boss. He could fire Adam very quickly if he so decided and pack him off on the very next airplane for Tuamani and home. I will not give him that satisfaction, Adam thought. I will leave this job only when it is done and I will leave in good order. I will not let a petty tyrant rattle me and capsize everything I've worked for. No matter what he says, I'm going to hold my peace. It is the greatest weapon ever created when properly used, and almost impossible to conquer. I will co-operate and I will keep my mouth shut. I must.

So armed, Adam crossed the porch in two long strides. He opened the screen door, and waited a moment for his eyes to accustom themselves to the shadowed hallway. Then, uncertain as to which door opened on Pike's office, he took a few cautious steps down the hall. Pike's voice rang out and brought him up as if he had been lassoed.

"In here!"

Adam turned into the office. Now careful, he remembered, be very careful what you say. And say as little as possible. You, not Pike, will be the victor if you can leave this room with your job.

"You wanted to see me?" Adam said, approaching Pike's desk casually, as if a meeting in this office was an everyday event.

Pike tipped back in his chair and, looking steadily at Adam, manipulated his fingers into his favorite isosceles triangle. His voice was much more controlled than Adam had anticipated.

"Does that surprise you?"

"Well, yes . . . sort of."

"You don't think, then, that there is any special reason why I might want to see you on this particular morning?"

"No. . . ."

There was a long silence between them, and Adam could hear the palm fronds softly clicking outside the window as he met Pike's eyes. Then he knew. They were going to go over the fact that the movies had been called off on account of rain again. Ah, well.

"I'm sorry about the rain last night, Governor. As I explained to you before, I just don't make the weather."

He tried to smile, half-hoping Pike might join him.

"I did not think that you did make the weather, Mister Smith. For some reason you seem to believe that I'm not quite bright. Well, sir, I make no claim to being a mental giant or even to being in the same league with some of the scientists we have on this island, but I am not an utter fool, either. In the past I have only questioned your *interpretation* of the weather from time to time, more or less with a view to urging improvement on your part. I have helped a great many younger men in my time and I've long since discovered that in certain men, soft words do more harm than good. In your case I seem to have taken the wrong approach. I have only succeeded in offending you."

"I wouldn't say that."

"You wouldn't?"

Feigning enormous surprise, Pike raised his eyebrows and allowed his isosceles triangle to collapse. He poked one finger experimentally at the neuritis spot on his shoulder and winced.

"What *would* you say then, Mister Smith? Would you say that my efforts, however misguided they may have been, were based on honest concern for the welfare of this community and the successful completion of our project? Would you say that, accepting criticism in the spirit with which it was intended, you have in return made every effort to co-operate with your fellow workers and satisfactorily perform your duties?"

"I've done my job to the best of my ability . . . sir."

"Have you indeed."

Pike said the words not as a question, but as a flat statement. He reached into his desk drawer and pulled out a manila folder. He placed it unopened before him.

"Do you know what is in this folder?"

"No."

"I do. Even though I give you my word that I haven't looked inside of it for more than two months. This happens to be your personal folder, Mister Smith . . . your past record, your application for employment on Project Zeus, comments, letters of recommendation and so forth. Let us see how many of the more vital facts contained in that folder I can recall. Other than a certain vanity, I have a special reason for doing this now, a part of which I hope will become apparent to you as I proceed."

Prodding his neuritis spot as if the pain would stimulate his memory, Pike deliberately looked out the window and recited tonelessly, "You were born Adam Smith . . . no middle name or initial given. In Rollins, Vermont. Mother deceased at time of application. Your brother operates a drug store in Providence. You were attached to Air Transport Command during Korean war. . . . I *suppose* that might be considered military service. Graduated University of Vermont. . . . I won't take this morning's precious time to remember the year, but I assure you I could if I had to. Subsequently took one year post-graduate work at M.I.T. . . . Employed Continental Airlines as meteorologist 1954. . . . Presently on leave of absence. . . . All references good. Loyalty oath signed and political slate clean. Salary according to A.E.C. standard category D-12, at $7200 for year's contract. Have I made any errors so far, Smith?"

"You have a remarkable memory, Governor."

"If it's on paper I'll remember it. I could go on, including the fact that your father's name was Matthew, which, judging from the choice of Biblical names in your family, would suggest to me that you came from a good and God-fearing American family of solid background. Admirable. There is nothing in your file to indicate a rebellious nature or suggest that you might wish to sabotage authority."

"Now just one minute, Governor!" Adam suddenly clamped his lips together. There you go, he thought, squeezing his fists tight lest he continue. There you almost went shooting off your mouth when you didn't know what this was all about yet. Pike was licking his chops, all right. He was clearly just waiting for a chance to pounce.

"Yes, Smith?"

"I was about to say that . . . well, somewhere along the line we just don't seem to understand each other."

"I should say we do not. The reason for my little recitation of your file was to convince you once and for all that I take my duties here very seriously. It is a part of my duty to know the people in my charge and for the key positions, of which yours happens to be one, I can quote their records just as I have yours. Now, Smith, you have very clearly demonstrated, for reasons which you have so far not had the courage to explain . . . demonstrated that you would like to see me placed on a very hot spot and, possibly, if things work out just right, you might even see me removed from this office. You have been clever enough to realize that anything of a major nature which might affect this base is my responsibility and should a real foul-up occur, it would be me and not you who would bear the consequences. And, Mister Smith. . . ."

Pike pronounced the word *Mister* as if an aspirin tablet were dissolving on his tongue. He placed his thumbs in his belt and leaned far forward so that his resolute chin was halfway across his desk. "And, Mister Smith, I'm not going to let you get away with it."

Adam was completely bewildered. I don't care, he thought suddenly. I don't give a damn about the job or what a mess it is going to be back at Continental Airlines trying to explain why I have been given the sack. This man is crazy!

"Get away with *what?* Governor, I just don't know what the hell you're talking about!"

"Lazy Ethel."

"Lazy Ethel? What . . . ?"

Pike jumped to his feet. He was truly angry now and the intricate designs formed by the tiny red veins in his face flowed together until they became heavy splotches.

"Yes, *Mister* Smith! Lazy Ethel. I don't know how long you've known anything about that storm, but you have not seen fit to notify me of its existence, or more important, that it constitutes a threat to the safety of this base!"

"Governor!"

"You have deliberately withheld vital information from me in the hope I would be caught flat-footed. If it's any satisfaction to you, you almost succeeded!"

"Governor! You're away off . . ."

"You obviously had no intention of informing me until it was too late or you would have said something the moment you walked into this room. Oh, I gave you every chance, Smith! You just didn't have the good sense to take it."

"Governor, will you please listen to me?"

Adam was smiling now, a reaction which further infuriated Pike. "Just listen to me a minute, please. There *isn't* any storm. I just dreamed it up. I haven't the faintest idea how anyone found out about it."

"Don't tell me that, Smith! You're just getting yourself in deeper. I know God-damned well there's a storm around here somewhere. Not only is my neuritis killing me, but I have been so advised from Tuamani!"

"This is ridiculous . . . er, sir!"

"Ridiculous, is it? Ridiculous, all right, if I'm caught with my pants down and Lazy Ethel hits this island! I'll be the one who looks ridiculous if that expensive new wharf plus warehouse gets washed out to sea, or if every damned piece of GI property on this island gets blown to hell and gone because we weren't prepared! What was Pike doing when the thing was on its way? Sitting on his ass? Drunk? Gone fishing? Several people hurt or even killed maybe, and what was Pike doing? *You* think up some of the answers to those questions, Smith, because I just might have to answer them! And wipe that smile off your face while you're thinking!"

"Governor, look. I was fooling around on my plotting board last night and for some reason . . ."

Adam knew that he was floundering, but what else was there to say? Talking to Pike under the best of circumstances was not easy and it was very apparent that he was not in a listening mood now. But a lot of things were clear, anyway, especially that peculiar look in Margaret Trumpey's eyes. ". . . I was fooling around. . . . Why I drew in a hurricane I just can't explain, and for some other reason I can't seem to explain I named it Lazy Ethel . . . it's customary to name very low pressure areas, you know, but usually you start a season with an A. Now as to Tuamani finding out about it . . . Well . . ."

Adam's voice faded into indistinctness, for he saw that, though Pike was regarding him with rapt attention, his anger had been replaced by a coldness which was far more ominous, and there was, too, a look of cunning in his eyes. If I suggested that it must have been that press representative . . . ?

"So you still persist? Right to the end, eh? Oh, you're a smart fellow, Smith. You were just fooling around and you just can't explain why. It seems there are a great many things you can't explain and one of them, I have no doubt, includes Tuamani's knowledge of this storm. Amazing, I must say, Mister Smith. Truly, *truly* amazing!"

"I know it sounds sort of strange, but—"

"Not at all! On the contrary. Very logical. The pieces all fit in perfectly, that is, once you've been so obliging as to give me the key. You maintain that the storm is nonexistent. I believe you. I am lulled into a sense of security. My acute neuritic pains are meaningless. Meanwhile you cover yourself by allowing Tuamani to know what I do not know. Then, out of nowhere, the storm which, of course, does not exist, arrives. It is then very much too late for argument. Ho, ho! I'm going to recommend you for Naval Intelligence!"

Accompanying his steps with a series of diminishing ho-ho's, Pike circled his desk. He wagged his head and poked at his neuritic spot and only occasionally glanced at Adam. Then it was a look clearly designed to assure Adam that he was not only overwhelmed by his treachery, but was torn between his bounden duty, which was to exact some kind of penalty, and since he was a man of great wisdom, experience, patience, and intelligence, perhaps a final effort at a peaceful compromise.

At last he halted before Adam and, clasping his hands behind him, assumed parade rest. He would have been much more imposing if he had not had to look up at Adam, yet by remaining absolutely motionless his stature seemed to increase until Adam found himself deliberately slumping. Pike compressed his lips and, recognizing it as a danger signal, Adam was certain that unless he could somehow think of a more logical explanation for Lazy Ethel, his employment on Nikki atoll was as good as finished. Along with a lot of other things, he reminded himself, including an association with a girl named Margaret which was certainly more interesting than any other he had ever known. Then, even before Pike spoke, he saw a possible solution to the whole affair and he became so intrigued with its possibilities he only half-heard the man who stood so challengingly before him.

"No, Mister Smith," Pike was saying, "I refuse to fall into every ambush you set for me. I did not get where I am because I was asleep in my tent all the time. I *know* there is a storm hereabouts. I want full information on that storm, and I want to be kept fully supplied with further information as long as it presents the slightest hazard to this community. If you do not co-operate in the fullest, I will request another meteorologist from Tuamani at once and you may consider yourself discharged. I don't think I need to point out that my report on the reasons for your dismissal will hardly be favorable to you."

Pike rocked back on his heels, then settled into parade rest again. Adam took a deep breath. So the old saw was true and necessity was the mother of invention. You found yourself walking down a path and, if you ever expected to reach the end of it, you had to follow that path regardless of twists and turns. In this case it seemed that no harm could be done and life on Nikki could attain a more peaceful air if you were just willing to make a very slight compromise with your integrity. Maybe, he thought, your father was right when he said that you were often too stubborn. It could be called controlled compromise to give Pike what he wanted, and then in a few days it would all be over. And there was no reason to involve that damned newsman in this jam . . . yet. He might have a wife and kids to support.

"All right, sir," Adam said slowly. "There is a storm. But it doesn't amount to much . . . which is the reason I didn't bother to tell you about it . . . not because I wanted to deceive you or put you on a spot. If it did amount to anything I would have informed you at once. I'm sorry as can be about the confusion. It looks like I was wrong."

Adam was profoundly shocked at how easily the words came to him. Could it be, he wondered, that I am a natural-born liar? And Pike was visibly relieved. It was so easy.

"If the storm is so small, how come you bothered to inform Tuamani about it?" Pike asked.

Adam searched desperately for a plausible explanation. The newsman and his family, if there was one, would have to share his fate. There would have to be *some* elements of truth to support this tottering structure.

"I think I can explain that, sir. Last night when I was fooling around . . . I mean when I was making a plot of the storm . . . a newsman, I think he said his name was Hanover, dropped by the office. It's very possible he made something of it. . . . Yes, I'm sure he must have."

"Hanover? How could he . . . ? I shall have a very serious talk with him at once."

"I really think the less said about this to anyone, the better, sir. You know how people exaggerate. It honestly doesn't amount to a thing and . . . well, I doubt if it will come anywhere near Nikki."

"You're right," Pike snapped. "See that you keep your own mouth shut. In the meantime I want a report on the situation every two hours."

"It wouldn't be practical, sir. I don't have enough reports myself to follow a storm that closely."

"Can't Tuamani help? They have plenty of ships and planes."

This invention could get out of hand, Adam thought, unless I think fast.

"No, sir. You see this storm is to the south of us . . . where there isn't much of anybody. It's . . . well, it's moving very slowly and I should say the chances are very good that in a few days it will disappear altogether."

"How can a storm disappear?"

Pike had his storm. Now Adam saw to his horror that he wanted to play with it.

"It dissipates. It loses force when the pressure pattern begins to equalize. This one will very likely just . . . well, sort of blow itself out down in the so-called Roaring Forties. That's a long way from here."

This was unbelievable! Adam Smith was not only talking like a magpie, which he had sworn not to do, but what he was saying was worse than untrue because it was a lie based upon a hastily assembled collection of scientific facts which were fortunately, or perhaps unfortunately, very solid and true.

Adam stared at the floor. He was confused now, and he found it suddenly difficult to remember that Lazy Ethel did *not* exist. Well, he would get rid of it in a hurry, a process which was beginning to appear much more difficult than its creation. Pike's earliest opinions were very nearly right, Adam thought frantically. I do make the weather!

"How often can you give me the situation?" Pike was asking with the most solemn determination.

Adam hesitated. Invention on top of invention! And it would have to be reasonably believable. He was going to be a very busy man! "Once a day," he said uncertainly.

"Is that all?"

"Yes. There's a lot of work involved. Really, Governor . . . it doesn't amount to a thing. Er . . ."

"We both have our work cut out for us," Pike said with a grim smile. "In the meantime Tuamani demands some satisfaction. You will file a report immediately through regular channels, and along with your technical mishmash you will clearly indicate that you personally did not consider the storm severe enough either to notify me or alarm them. Do you understand me thoroughly, Smith?"

"Yessir, I'm sure I can handle that. And could I suggest again that we keep this more or less quiet, Governor? No use to get people all excited."

"Right. We'll keep it plenty quiet. Maximum security on this. You will prepare two charts. One chart for me, which you'll bring to this office yourself, and your usual chart brought up by that teletype girl. She knows too much already. Took the teletype from Tuamani. I've already cautioned her and will do so again."

"I doubt if she's the type to start rumors," Adam said.

Pike frowned at him. "All women start rumors. They live, eat, and breathe rumors. Very poor security risks as history has often proven. This has got to remain a secret between you and me."

"It certainly has," Adam said with a sigh of relief.

"Get going. Do a good job for me on this and I'll forget our past misunderstandings. I'm that way, Smith."

"Yessir!"

When Adam left the porch and emerged into the brilliant sunlight he glanced up at the sky and was rather surprised not to see telltale streaks of high cirrus clouds which might foretell a storm. There was, of course, nothing of the sort aloft; only the normal little build-ups of fluffy cumulus which always accompanied trades. He paused for a moment to study the now slowly drifting cumulus and found them strangely reassuring. For they promised that he had not entirely lost his wits and that the session with Pike had only been like something out of a meteorological nightmare in which he, Adam Smith, was magically empowered with the ability to create a holocaust. Well, now, in the sunlight, with the very real streets and buildings of Pistol Two about him, it was possible to return to reality and even smile about this little deception.

Moving down the street in his easy, loose-limbed fashion, Adam began to relax. Smiling inwardly, he supposed that there were certain elements of risk involved, but at the worst he could only lose his job, which he had come very near doing anyway. Lazy Ethel! The name itself gave the explanation for its performance. He would place its center to the south in accordance with his lie, and he would allow it to move very slowly toward the east and the open Pacific, until after a few days he would report it as no longer worthy of anyone's attention. But he would have to watch Tuamani. They were far enough away to prevent any exact check on his analysis. But if they sent airplanes to investigate, that might be a very different matter. Their immediate curiosity would have to be satisfied. Just how was still a problem, but there was no reason, as long as Pike was willing to have two charts made, why Tuamani should make any special effort to confirm Lazy Ethel. Not for a few days, anyway.

Again he was surprised at this new and unusual way his mind seemed compelled to work. Maybe, he mused, I am a frustrated criminal at heart! Certainly I am scheming and plotting like one, finding ways to cover my tracks if I should be questioned, fabricating alibis, even planning methods of escape when the deed is done! But what harm? Adam supposed that occasionally the most honest bank tellers surrendered to impulse and stuffed a few thousand dollars in their pockets just to see what it felt like. What harm if they replaced every penny of it after a few minutes, or at least before the daily accounting was done? It could be an exhilarating lift in an otherwise dull day; a tiny episode which could momentarily enliven a job as prosaic as a meteorologist's.

He caught himself. What kind of thinking was this? You are going off your rocker! It was said that some people just could not stand the isolation of a Pacific atoll, yet those people were neurotics who had a record of instability wherever they landed. And most certainly no one had ever accused Adam Smith of instability. On the contrary, your record in college and at Continental Airlines was of such solidness and dependability several people had, in an offhand way, suggested that you break out and live a little.

What happened if the bank teller failed to return the money in time? Suppose, on that particular day, someone chose to do the accounting at an earlier hour, or the vault locks stuck in a closed position? One chance in a million. Just as there was here. And anyway, for all you know, there may very well be a storm to the south. It was, when you came right down to it, almost a certainty. Because the Roaring Forties would not be the Roaring Forties without some kind of disturbance. That's where the name came from. Sailors in the old windjammers running down their easting in the forty-degree latitude had reason to curse that area of the Pacific. For the needs of Lazy Ethel it was not overly important that the Roaring Forties were a long way south of Nikki atoll. Lazy Ethel was an errant spawn of the Forties. She just happened to wander a little far north of the usual track. She could wander right back again . . . after a decent time.

Then if she came from so far, how did you manage to learn of Lazy Ethel? Tuamani would know what Pike would never admit; that storms were not located by a pain in the shoulder. Their extent and nature and probable track were plotted from a series of reports on barometric pressure, temperature, and wind velocity. It was unlikely, in fact nearly impossible, that a single man on a lonely atoll would be able to obtain such information. Yet it had happened. The typhoon which completely devastated Wake Island in 1954 arrived without any official warning whatsoever. And there were not only trained meteorologists on the island at the time, but a vast system of aircraft and ships to supplement and aid their observations. No one had known in advance about that storm. It was very conceivable, then, that Adam Smith would be the only person who knew about Lazy Ethel. How? Stopping in the middle of the street between the teletype shack and his own office, Adam was again surprised at the ease with which he found the answer. One more slight invention. Just a little one, but it had to work.

He turned and went into the teletype office.

ADAM WAS DISAPPOINTED not to find Margaret in the teletype office. Instead, the other girl who occasionally came for his charts and who, Adam vaguely recalled, was known as Smilie or Sunnie, looked up from a movie magazine and said, "Good morning. What can I do for you?"

Adam waited uneasily. Margaret obviously knew about Lazy Ethel, but what about this girl? And would it really make any difference if she did know? There were so many things to be considered, he thought. Quickly, very much too quickly it seemed, the possible reaction of everyone on Nikki had to be anticipated.

"Cat got your tongue?" Sunnie Mandel asked.

"I want to send a message."

"Why not? We got umpteen thousand bucks' worth of equipment and nobody's using it."

She rose from her desk and moved slowly toward Adam. He saw with alarm that her movements were openly inviting, as if she had been waiting breathlessly for his arrival. And then he was sorry for her. She was so frail, so flat in every respect, and now her walk became a pitifully grotesque imitation of any movie star. He wondered that he had never noticed it before.

Looking up at him she said, "I wish more people would come in here with messages. It gets awful lonesome. When Margaret's gone I get babbling to myself . . . like some female hermit who is fabulously rich, has all her money in old tin cans . . . and won't talk to the outside world."

"Where is Margaret?"

"Gone to Aubrey for a haircut. But don't broadcast it. You aren't s'posed to get haircuts on government time. Only coffee breaks. Like I was saying to Margaret last night, it don't make any special difference *where* you're working for the government, the rules and regulations are always the same. There is the kind of rule that is printed down and the kind they put on bulletin boards which everybody has got to initial to prove they read, but those regulations are just made up by people who have to pass the time and they don't mean a thing once you know your way around. No matter where it is, it isn't like private industry with capitalists in gray flannel suits thinking up things for people not to do. You work for the government and you got no worries so long as you live by the regulations which are *not* written down. This produces what I call massive ennui."

"Those are pretty big words," Adam said, still trying to decide if he should give this girl his message or wait for Margaret's return.

"I like to play around with big words," Sunnie said. "You can therefore better express what's on your mind. The idea when you work for the government, and I should know, is to do exactly what you're told and absolutely, positively, do not do one little thing more. Because if you do, you're liable to upset somebody's applecart who is up above your category and who is trying very hard not to do one single thing more than they were told to do. It's a chain reaction and it goes right on up to the President. Nobody hardly ever gets fired for not doing their job right. They get transferred to another agency if their boss has enough influence and energy, or maybe they might be dropped a category if they're low on seniority anyway, but they do not get the can. You get the can when you peel the mildew off your brain and start getting ideas how maybe you could do your job quicker and maybe better. Do I make myself clear?"

"You certainly do," Adam answered with a smile. Peter Hildebrandt was wrong. You got around and talked to a lot of people, or rather they talked to you. Peter should have tagged along on this morning, for example.

"So Margaret won't really get the can because she's having her hair cut on government time. She will, though, if she thinks up some new way of sending a teletype message that maybe goes quicker or don't use so many words."

"My message is very brief."

Sunnie looked into his eyes and sighed. She said, "From you, what else? Look, Silent Sam, I don't care how many words you put in a message.

My job is to punch those keys until I hit EOM, which means end of message. The character who thought up that abbreviation was probably fired just for doing it. And while we're on the subject do you mind if I mention one little thing before I let you out of my clutches?"

"I guess not."

Sunnie laughed. "You couldn't stop me, anyway. Nobody can once I get started. Anyway, I'd just like to go on record that you are the darnedest pebble kicker I ever ran into. There's a certain girl on this lousy little island who wastes a lot of time, including the government's, thinking about you. So why don't you break down and give her the time of day once in a while? Just so you won't be scared to death, the girl isn't me. Now what's your message and where's it going?"

"To Tuamani," Adam said hesitantly. "To the meteorological office."

"That's MET around here. TUA dash MET. Cuckoo, isn't it?"

"If you have a pencil handy I'll write it out; then you can more or less put it in your own style."

"Oh no," Sunnie said, handing him a pad of forms. "I'm part of the massive ennui. Remember? Your words. I send." She tapped her head. "Monkey see. Monkey do. I won't go up a single category if I think."

Twisting his mouth thoughtfully, Adam slowly printed out the words which had come to his mind in the street. As he did so, he found himself wondering again about the temptations of bank tellers and it seemed certain to him now that there was no possible retreat.

He handed the pad to Sunnie Mandel and watched her eyes carefully as she read it aloud.

LAZY ETHEL ANALYSIS BASED ON INCOMPLETE RADIO INFORMATION OBTAINED JAPANESE FISHING BOAT VICINITY PERIOD REGRET DID NOT CONSIDER SOURCE SUFFICIENTLY RELIABLE FILE FORMAL WARNING OR NOTIFY GOVERNOR PIKE UNTIL SITUATION CLARIFIED PERIOD WILL ADVISE IF FURTHER DEVELOPMENT PERIOD

SMITH

Sunnie looked up at him and shrugged her shoulders.

"I suppose I would be wasting my time if I asked you who Lazy Ethel was?"

"Yeah," Adam said. "You would."

"You slay me."

She turned to a teletype machine and sat down before it. Adam experienced a strange, almost triumphant, sensation throughout his body

as her fingers began to play over the keys. He whistled when he went out
the door.

"*Well,* Mister Albright!" Pike said, enunciating the *Mister* with very
little more warmth than he had addressed Adam. He prodded his shoulder
and winced. As Pike's eyes roved over him, Albright was unable to discover the slightest evidence of approval.

He lit a cigarette and waited, swaying slightly in an attempt to maintain at least the appearance of easy confidence. It was not easy these
days, he thought; partly because in Pike's presence he had the damnedest
feeling of inferiority and partly because he found the emotion extraordinarily boring. Yet what else except boredom could one expect of the
military mind? The whole of Nikki, its population, its very purpose, was
boring beyond any sane person's imagination! Who was there on this
godforsaken atoll who might discuss literature, at least elementary music,
or, say, the ballet? Who read the *New Yorker* or ever heard of Henry
James? The migrant clods on Nikki were all devoted to the *Reader's
Digest* and the *Saturday Evening Post,* which hardly put them in a way
to enjoy the *Saturday Review.* Sometimes, like this time, Albright was
certain that on the day he signed up with the A.E.C. he had been either
drunk or bewitched and had somehow mistaken his application for an
income-tax form.

Pike was still looking at him. He said, "Do you always have to wear
shorts, Albright?"

"I find them most comfortable in this climate. Is there something wrong
with them?"

Albright was convinced that Pike would jolly well have trouble finding
anything wrong with his shorts. They were especially designed for his
narrow hips by a Madison Avenue tailor and they cost a comparative
fortune. During an impromptu style preview of his going-away apparel
in Albright's New York apartment, his friends had clapped their hands
and exclaimed at their smartness and they had all enthusiastically agreed
he looked like a British officer long in the desert. Rather like a Sandhurst
man, one of them had said. And, recalling his friends, Albright wished
with all his heart that he was back with them, instead of standing like a
congenital idiot, awaiting the pleasure of a man whose taste and sense of
delicacy must have been nurtured near the rear end of an artillery horse.

"I've always thought shorts took a certain amount of dignity from a
man," Pike was saying. "They look more appropriate on Boy Scouts."

"I'm sorry if they offend you, sir."

"Oh, now don't get uppity with me, Albright. It's not that bad. The matter is of no consequence at the moment because the climate is going to change around here, anyway."

"I'm afraid I don't quite follow you."

Pike prodded his shoulder, then moved his thumb experimentally down his arm. He said, "If you would get up a little earlier in the mornings you might be in a better position to follow a lot of things. For instance, I'm sure it's news to you that we're probably in for a hurricane. Do you know what that means?"

"It sounds a bit grim."

Albright stopped swaying. He remembered two hurricanes in New England, one in 1944 while he was still at Yale, and it had been an absolute ball. At least something might relieve the boredom of Nikki.

With a dramatic sweep of his hand, Pike unrolled a map of Nikki and spread it across his desk. "It means," he continued gravely, "that we've got our work cut out for us whether the storm comes or not. Of course, I'm hoping it doesn't come anywhere near us, but we've got to be prepared in advance regardless. Once it heads this way it will be too late. Our job is to anticipate what we might call the enemy's movements, make every possible defense . . . and, if necessary, even make a strategic retreat."

Pike allowed a slight smile to creep across his mouth. God! Albright thought, as Pike beckoned to him and pointed at the map. Hannibal is now going to cross the Alps. Napoleon is at Austerlitz. This man, so starved for action, was going to bombard a hurricane!

"I've got this all figured out," Pike went on. "It's going to take some organization and a lot of work, but we won't be caught sleeping on our arms. We just can't afford to be, or somebody is liable to get hurt."

He pondered the map a moment, and Albright saw that his blue eyes were alive with determination. Standing beside him, dutifully imitating Pike's examination of the map, Albright considered that they would have made a far more picturesque pair if they had been standing on the summit of a hill overlooking troops in full battle.

"Our intelligence, such as it is, informs us the storm will be most likely to approach from the south. In that case we should move our people somewhere in here . . . to the north side of Nikki so we'll get protection from the southerly reef and also the lagoon itself."

"I see," Albright said as solemnly as he could manage.

"The situation is complicated by the fact that we are dealing with civilians and so we must take every precaution to prevent panic. The only way I know is to maintain absolute secrecy. Our people must not know *why* they are being moved until the fact is accomplished. Once safely encamped on the north side, we can explain matters and prepare for the worst."

"Are you suggesting, sir, that we move everyone on Nikki bag and baggage to the north side?"

"No. Not bag and baggage. Their personal effects must be left behind. We will only take every available tarpaulin for use as shelters . . . our workmen can rig up some kind of tents for the children at least . . . and we'll require at least three days' provisions . . . plus some means of cooking."

"How about the natives across the channel?"

"They'll have to go, too, whether they want to or not. I don't want to be responsible for the loss of a single life . . . or even any injury if we can help it. Doc Case will have to take his medical supplies along, of course."

Slowly, almost as if one of his regular attacks of mess-hall nausea had overcome him, Albright began to appreciate the magnitude of Pike's enterprise. Much more quickly he envisioned a mass of detail exploding in his face, all tedious, all involving endless argument, evasion, and lack of sleep.

"General," he said, "there are an awful lot of people here. To just pick them up and arrange for a mass exodus will be a tremendous undertaking."

"It's got to be done. What's more, we're pressed for time."

"When is the storm supposed to arrive?"

"I don't know exactly. It's maneuvering to the south right now."

"Are you basing this information on that Smith chap?"

"Yes."

"You seem to have renewed your faith in him."

"I have not for a moment done so. Believe me, I am keeping a wary eye on our Mr. Smith. But his prediction has practically been confirmed by Tuamani and, what's more, I've received a few signals of my own."

Pike poked his thumb into his shoulder and, to Albright's astonishment, winked at him. Then he said, "I doubt if even our Mr. Smith would fumble a situation as serious as this. If the storm is coming our way he'll tell me with no *if*'s, *and*'s, or *but*'s about it."

"When do you want to start all this?" Albright asked. He tried to hide the misery in his voice.

"Now. Right now. You will begin by commandeering every boat, launch and canoe on the island. I want them at the wharf manned and ready to load at noon. Earlier if you can make it. This is logistics, Albright. Allow an hour to cross the lagoon and an hour after we get there to settle down. Sergeant Doolan and his men will stand by during the loading and patrol here until the last boat is ready to leave. We don't want any looting. The boss laborer will be in charge of loading the tarpaulins. Mess-hall personnel will prepare three days' rations . . . there doesn't have to be anything fancy . . . and see that those are loaded. You'd better arrange to contact Chief Tanni on the other side and have him get all his people set. They'll have to bring their own rations. Oh . . . those girls in the teletype shack should also be assigned to the last boat. I want to keep communication with Tuamani right up to the last minute."

Pike shot his arm forward and glanced at his wrist watch. He frowned. "It's almost nine-thirty now so you'll have to get cracking. Oh . . . don't forget light. We'll want illumination of some kind. See that electrician fellow. He may have some kind of a stand-by generator . . . one of those little gasoline-powered jobs that are portable. If not, have him make do with something. . . . Maybe he can round up some emergency pressure lamps. I know damn well there aren't any flashlight batteries available . . . and another thing. Absolutely no whisky or spirits of any kind are to be taken except for medicinal use by Doc Case if he says he wants some. We don't want this thing to turn into a brawl. Remember there will be all kinds of types mixed close together under campaign conditions . . . kids and everything. We'll have enough trouble as it is."

Overwhelmed with the trouble he could see, Albright sought momentary consolation in the ceiling. The attempt was a failure, for he saw in the plywood above him only signals of vast confusion and acute discomfort, in which he, Livingston Albright, who preferred to do his camping out amid the better restaurants of New York, was pinioned in the exact center. He could distinctly taste the rancid flavor of woe in his mouth when he found the will to speak again.

"Governor," he began apologetically. "If I start stirring up this hornet's nest, people are going to start asking questions. They are going to want to know what it's all about. The preparations can hardly remain a secret. What am I supposed to tell them?"

"Say as little as you can, although naturally there will be inquiries. Tell them . . . I have it! You tell them this is merely a drill which we always intended to hold anyway . . . at least twice during our stay. A hurricane drill. . . . Nothing more. They should regard it as a relief from their routine duties. . . . An outing, if they please. There is no reason for them not to regard it as sort of a holiday. Let the children think they're going on the biggest picnic of their lives. A real adventure! I want to be very certain they aren't frightened."

"Supposing some of the people refuse to go. Maybe they don't care for picnics."

"Ah!" said Pike as if he had discovered a large and poisonous spider moving across the map of Nikki. "You have a point there which I missed. I just can't get used to dealing with civilians. It's so damn unhandy and this is a perfect example. We'll have to use some persuasion if there should be any firm objections . . . which I very much doubt there will be if you present this thing properly. Put it this way if you have to. Those who refuse to go will find themselves outcasts. The mess hall and all the food will be locked up. There won't be any light and the water-evaporation plant will be shut down. They will be a lot more comfortable with us. Make them understand that thoroughly. Then if there are many holdouts, send them to me. Now get on with it."

"Yessir," Albright said, walking hopelessly toward the doorway. He could see himself challenged by that brute of a man, Barney Dunbar, who headed the carpenter shop. Or worse yet, Mrs. Walsacki or any one of her chattering group would want to know exactly what the children were going to be fed. And when.

"One more thing," Pike called after him. "Smith is going to come here with the latest on Lazy Ethel at noon . . . says he can't follow it any closer. We may postpone, but you proceed anyway unless you get a written cancellation from me."

"Lazy Ethel, did you say?"

"Yes. That's the name of the hurricane."

Albright arched his eyebrows, then shook his head sadly. He was suddenly filled with a mighty weariness.

"Who thought up that name?" he asked.

"Our Mr. Smith."

"So? I hardly thought him capable of such imagination. Sounds like a fat whore."

"She might be just that," Pike said grimly.

Pike was alone for only a moment. He was making a list of the vital papers he should take with him when he heard Sue-Anne's voice. He looked up and saw her posed in the doorway. In spite of his preoccupation he noticed that she was unusually well groomed for so early in the morning. Her hair was combed and, though she wore only a negligee, her face was carefully made up. He thought that, considering the ordeal of the night before, she looked quite beautiful. He waited for her to complain of a hangover.

"Zebulon," she said, "I thought that man was coming to fix the plumbing."

"You misunderstood me, Precious. He wasn't really coming."

"That's what I thought you said, but it didn't make sense."

"A lot of things don't make sense around here. Including the fact that you're going on a picnic."

"A picnic? Now really, Zebulon! You know I don't like picnics. All that sand in my food."

"You won't like this one at all. I want you to pack a few things . . . the regimental bracelet I gave you at Knox, your pearl earrings and that photo of you and me with Mark Clark. Take anything else you think is valuable, but nothing more than you can slip in a handbag."

"What kind of a picnic is this? Zebulon, you've been working too hard."

She advanced toward him and walked around his desk until she could clasp his head in her arms. She pressed it against her bosom and said, "I'm sorry about last night, Zeb. I don't know what gets into me. Forgive me . . . forgive ol' Sue-Anne. I let you down."

"You're forgiven, Precious. How are your feet?"

"All right, thanks to you. Did you find my shoes?"

"I didn't look for them. I don't think we need to worry about little things like shoes this morning."

"Are they finally going to shoot the bomb? What is all this picnic business?"

"Never mind right now. Just be all set to go by noon. Wear as much clothing as you can. It might be chilly."

"Here? In this godawful . . . ?"

"Yes. Here. Now run along. I'm up to my ears in work."

Sue-Anne released him and backed away. She patted his cheek, and when she smiled he thought how magnificent she could be when she felt like it. A real soldier. No prying questions. Just appreciation of the need for orders . . . and obedience.

"Of course, Zebulon," she said. "I'll be ready. You just send up a flare when you want me."

She strolled into the hallway, moving with such grace that Pike in one blazing instant of desire thought of abandoning everything on the desk and lifting her off her feet. He would carry her laughing down the hallway and on this fateful morning they would be together again.

At the door she turned to smile at him. "I really am sorry about last night," she said.

She was gone before he could quite raise himself from behind the desk.

By ten-thirty Adam had his regular map prepared and was waiting for Margaret to call for it. It was a true map, monotonously similar to those he had drawn for weeks. Based on his own observations and the routine sheaf of teletype clips which came in from Tuamani every morning, he had again plotted a mild low-pressure trough to the west of Oa Titia atoll and an occluded front some five hundred miles east of Tuamani. The occluded front was practically stationary, shifting back and forth only a few miles each day, and since it was very near the doldrums area its presumed movements could be as much influenced by cumulative errors in reporting and plotting as any true activity. It was extremely unlikely that it would ever have the slightest effect on the weather at Nikki.

Over the rest of the area covered by his chart, there was nothing remarkable. Nikki lay almost in the middle of a large and easy high-pressure ridge, which the lines of barometric pressure defined more or less in the shape of an egg.

Now, regarding the map with some distaste, Adam knew that for the next few days at least, the winds would be light, the temperature and humidity about normal for the season, and there would very probably be the usual tropical rain squalls during the nights. There was not the slightest evidence of any Lazy Ethel or even a remotely comparative storm. So be it.

His map would not have been considered as wholly accurate or even entirely reliable by an airline operating within the United States itself. None of them ever had been, since they were drawn upon the information offered from a bare minimum of reporting stations. Adam estimated that for the same area in the States he would know the pressure, dew point, temperature, the wind direction and force prevailing at no fewer than fifty stations. Here, he was obliged to rely on only seven stations, Tuamani, Oa Titia, Trigger, the explosion site, a chartered motor vessel two hundred miles to the northwest of Trigger, a Coast Guard cutter two hundred miles to the east of Tuamani, and his own observations on Nikki. These reports had been occasionally supplemented by advice from aircraft and regular merchant ships which came close enough to the area, but Adam had little faith in it. It was almost always incomplete and usually so old by the time it was sent on to Nikki as to render it useless. Later, when Operation Zeus approached explosion date, Adam understood that a considerable number of Navy ships and Air Force planes would be employed to gather weather data and check particularly on the movements of the upper winds. He sincerely hoped so. The winds above thirty thousand feet would govern both the spread and radioactive fallout of Zeus. If they set the damnable thing off while relying on only those scanty reports now available, he believed they would be taking a terrible chance.

Beneath the regular map Adam had spread a blank form ready for the following day. Underneath the form he had concealed Pike's special map which he would personally deliver at noon. He had drawn it with care and considerable forethought. Lighting his pipe he smiled when he recalled how easily he had contrived to place the center of Lazy Ethel just far enough to the southwest of Nikki so that Pike's neuritis would receive full satisfaction. Yet it was not close enough to make anyone, least of all Pike, ask why the climate on Nikki was not being affected.

On a separate paper he had tentatively sketched in the future of Lazy Ethel. Tomorrow morning he would show her as moving well to the southeast of Nikki and on the following morning she would begin to dissipate an obviously safe distance to the east. By the next day he would explain to Pike that Lazy Ethel had completely vanished off his map. As for Tuamani, if they kept their interest and became overly curious, he could say that no further reports had been intercepted from tuna boats and apparently any disturbance had blown itself out. Pike would have had enough excitement to satisfy him and perhaps he would leave Adam Smith alone. A harmless deception at the worst—and, he mused, well deserved.

Now if Margaret would only come. He blew smoke at the clock on the wall and saw that she was already five minutes late.

He was rolling up the map for Margaret when he heard the screen door slam behind him. He turned around on his stool to smile and was instantly disappointed. His visitor was Hanover.

"Well," Hanover said, wiping the ever-present perspiration from the pouches under his eyes. "Well, good morning to you, Abe Lincoln, and what's with the Union Army?"

Hanover's fingers trembled as he lit a cigarette and sauntered from the door to Adam's drawing board. Leaning on the board he said, "I hope you don't mind me calling you Abe. You're a dead ringer, you know."

"I've been kidded about it before. I wish the resemblance went a lot further."

"Good answer. Now I also hope you don't mind if I ask a couple more questions. To begin with, friend, what's new?"

"Nothing that I know."

"Is that so?"

Adam did not like the tone of Hanover's voice. It suggested that they were old friends who met on every morning and perhaps, just now, shared a secret. The way his eyes widened in mock surprise left little doubt that he knew about Lazy Ethel and had been the person who had informed Tuamani of its existence. Adam took his time snapping the rubber bands around the rolled map. This Hanover, unless carefully diverted, could be a banana peel beneath a well-planned walk. He would be the janitor who accidentally fell against the switch and closed the bank vault just as the teller decided to return the money. He could make a lot of trouble.

Adam managed with some difficulty to return Hanover's fixed smile.

"Just the same old thing around here. If anything turns up, I'll let you know."

"Sure you will, friend. You've got my interests at heart. You've thought it all out how I've been going crazy trying to get some kind of a story out of this hunk of coral and you're lying awake nights trying to think up something for me to write about. I want you to know how much I appreciate your efforts. Have a cigarette."

"I just use this," Adam said, tapping his pipe. "Now I'd like to ask *you* a question. Have you got a family?"

"No." Hanover's eyes became questioning and then solemn. "No . . . Is it that bad?"

Adam sighed unhappily. This was, he thought, all he needed.

"Now look here, Abe," Hanover was saying. "Be a good guy. I have to make a living just like you do. How about briefing me on what's going on? I want it from the original. In my business we call it from an informed source . . . or an authoritative spokesman. I'll use either one if you don't want your name mentioned. What's going on?"

"What *is* going on?"

"You know, friend," Hanover said easily, "you missed your calling. You should have been an actor. Right now your eyes are as innocent as a pugilist accused of taking a fall. Don't just sit there and tell me you of all people don't know what's going on."

Adam shrugged his shoulders. The gesture helped him to ignore the sudden queasy feeling in his stomach.

"What have you been doing for the last hour?" Hanover asked.

"My work. Drawing up the daily map."

"Sure, you have. Then *of course* you wouldn't know why all hell has broken loose on this paradise of the Pacific. You wouldn't know that our idyllic little Polynesian refuge has been suddenly turned inside out . . . and when I say *out,* I mean just that. You wouldn't know why our dear General Pike has selected this particular morning for a so-called hurricane drill?"

Adam bit hard into his pipestem. It was already lit, but he reached for a match anyway. When he struck it and applied the flame to his already hot pipe, the resulting cloud of smoke almost smothered Hanover. As Adam had hoped, he moved back from the drawing board. Behind his smoke screen Adam sought frantically to collect his thoughts and find an answer which might subdue his fears.

"A hurricane drill?" he asked.

"Yes, friend Abe. Only I happen to know it's not a drill. All this stuff Albright is passing out about our moving the whole shebang over to the north side of the island . . . just one big happy family on a picnic to end all picnics, is ridiculous. You might have drills—maybe you line up four landing craft, two speedboats, and a barge along the wharf to make things look right and give whoever is responsible for it the practice—but you don't start actually loading them with the essential needs of mankind . . . food, shelter, and light. You may go through the motions, but you don't actually start closing down the normal facilities, and what's more you don't post marines around with real bullets in their guns, or stir up your simple-minded neighbors across the channel until they don't know whether to consult with their priest or a witch doctor. I've been through plenty of lifeboat drills in my time. I know the form, and I know when you're just supposed to go to your station and stand there and look at the boat and when it's for real and the ship is on its way to the bottom. Now come on, Abe. Give! I know about Lazy Ethel. Give with the details. Let me get my story off while there's still time and I'll leave you alone."

Adam barely managed to sit placidly and puff on his pipe. Holy mackerel, he thought, what have I done? And what has Pike done? To cover his confusion he pinched at the bridge of his nose, making a face as he did so. For a moment he wondered whether it was Pike or himself who had gone mad.

"Come on, Abe. Unroll that map and show it to me. Give me the straight dope and I'll get the hell out of here."

Then he said with an honest sincerity which appalled Adam, "I know you're plenty busy even if you don't act like it, and I realize you're going to be a lot busier. If I have a chance I intend to do a piece on you and the discovery of Lazy Ethel. How bad is it, now, really? Tell me, Abe. My life insurance is paid up. I can take it."

"I wouldn't worry," Adam said, hearing his own voice as if it came from a total stranger. "I just wouldn't bother about the whole thing."

"You mean it's that rough? I remember Wake Island. Will it sweep clean across Nikki like the one did there?"

Adam shook his head. There must be some way out of this, or should he confess now? And if he did, would Hanover believe him? He said, "I . . . I doubt it very much."

"Then why all the preparations? I went to see Pike. He claimed he was too busy to talk to me. For once, I believed him."

"Look," Adam said hesitantly. He was about to tell Hanover the full truth, yet he could not for the life of him find an easy or convincing way to begin. He would sound just as he had before Pike, confused and determined to hide something. "Look," he began again. "I don't know what steps Pike has taken . . . he's sort of excitable, you know . . . but I doubt if there's much chance this storm will come anywhere near us. Pike is probably just getting things ready in case there should be a change."

"He's doing more than getting things ready. He's going. Departure is set up for noon. Christ, if I only had a decent camera!"

"I can almost guarantee you any departure will be canceled," Adam said heavily.

Hanover seemed not to hear him.

"When is Lazy Ethel supposed to hit? When will we see the first indications? It's a funny thing, but when I came over here I looked up at the sky and it sure seemed to have a funny color to me. Weird."

"The color of the sky is now perfectly normal," Adam said firmly. "I can't just say when you might see any indications."

"What's the difference between a typhoon and a hurricane?"

"None, really," Adam answered with a momentary sense of relief. It was so much easier to talk about the theories of weather than it was to create it. And far less involved.

"Both hurricanes and typhoons are cyclonic in nature, although as a general rule a typhoon covers a much larger area. The difference is really in terminology. The word *typhoon* is customarily used to describe cyclonic storms in the Western Pacific. The word *hurricane* is normally used in the Carribean and Atlantic area to describe similar disturbances.

I don't know just how or why both terms are used. In the southern hemisphere the winds revolve clockwise . . ."

"Aren't typhoons usually accompanied by a tidal wave?" Hanover interrupted. "For instance, couldn't one follow Lazy Ethel and sweep Nikki clean?"

"Both types of disturbance are frequently followed by a definite rise in the level of the sea along coastal projections or islands, but really . . ."

Adam was shocked to see that Hanover was taking notes. How far could this thing go? He had to stop it right now! There was probably a severe penalty for inventing storms although he could not remember any mention of one in his entire study of air-mass analysis. Did they send you to prison for drawing storms which did not exist? Or did they, when a government project was concerned, shoot you for treason? That girl in the teletype office was absolutely right. It did not pay to think when you worked for the government. Nor anywhere else when you were guilty of thinking this way.

"How hard will the wind blow?" Hanover pressed.

"There's something I want to explain to you . . ."

Adam paused while a truck roared down the street. He looked out the window and was horrified to see it piled high with what were obviously food supplies from the warehouse. The driver and the two men who hung on near the tailgate had a peculiarly grim look about them. Now, looking down the street, he saw that it was alive with activity. Another truck was maneuvering down by the equipment park and a jeep, racing along at high speed, raised a cloud of coral dust near the Marine headquarters. Nikki was usually very quiet at this hour.

Adam was about to start the explanation which he now knew almost by heart, how Lazy Ethel would soon pass harmlessly out of existence, when Margaret came through the screen door. She said in a way that he thought was all too bright for the moment, "Hi. Is the map ready? Oh, hi, Mr. Hanover."

Hanover said, "Hi. You all ready for the big picnic?"

"Sure. But Sunnie and I are bound to miss some of the fun. We're assigned to the last boat."

"Then chivalry is dead on Nikki," Hanover said. "I always thought it was women and children first."

Adam wanted to hide under his drawing board when Margaret replied that the children were getting ready to go any minute. "But it seems we're supposed to stay around with the teletypes."

"That's sensible," Hanover said. "Much to my surprise, Pike seems to be handling this thing right."

"Of course, it's just a drill," Margaret said with a long look at Adam. Once more he put down a desire to crawl under the drawing board. Her expression was a strange mixture of sympathy and what he thought might almost be resentment, as if he should have told her about Lazy Ethel on the wharf. He was amazed when he remembered that just last evening, hardly fifteen hours ago, he had never heard of Lazy Ethel himself. Then he remembered staring down at the whirlpools in the channel after Margaret had left the wharf, and he knew when this troublesome beast had first been conceived. He was going to have to kill it in a hurry.

"Naturally," Hanover was saying to Margaret, "a hurricane drill is the most natural thing in the world around these parts. As far as I can find out after a brief conversation with a man named Terry Mack who lives on the other side of the channel, there hasn't been a storm here since about 1915. He thinks we've all gone crazy and made some fairly pointed remarks about the emotional antics of Americans in general."

"I'm late," Margaret said, looking at the roll of paper beside Adam's hand. "Can I take the map?"

Adam handed it to her and as he did so he wished that Hanover would go away so that he could talk to Margaret alone. He wanted to begin by telling her all about Lazy Ethel from the very beginning. Perhaps, having had as much contact with Pike as any of the lesser mortals on Nikki, she might understand why he had been compelled to create it. And if she did, then that would be a very satisfactory thing in spite of the ultimate disaster which now seemed certain. She had been right when she said that heads would roll. *My own first of all,* he thought.

"Would you come back here for a minute after you've delivered the map?" Adam said to Margaret.

"Sure. If Pike doesn't think up something else for me to do."

"I'll just walk up that way with you," Hanover said, opening the door for Margaret. Then he said, "Thanks, Abe. I'll be back later, too."

"Yeah," Adam answered without the slightest invitation in his voice.

Another truck roared past as they went out the door. Beyond them Adam saw Carlos Raveza sitting on a piece of machinery in the back of the truck. He grinned when he saw Adam, shouted something unintelligible and threw him a careless salute. He looked, Adam thought, all too much like a brave recruit hurrying off to war.

He turned slowly around on his stool and placed his hands over his eyes. He had to think, and he had to think fast. Now he became increasingly aware of the noise outside his office, and he found it almost impossible to concentrate. How could he have got himself into such a jam? What had begun as a harmless fancy seemed to have expanded like a thunderhead until it had become a monstrous thing. It was rapidly threatening to take charge. "I am sitting on a personal Zeus," he murmured.

He opened his fingers far enough so that he could peek between them at the street. It was now well populated. Those people who did not appear to be carrying something, or bound on some urgent mission, were standing in groups talking earnestly. Adam could guess what they were talking about. How many others besides Hanover, he wondered, had made up their minds this was not a drill?

He saw Margaret walking briskly toward Pike's office. Hanover was still beside her. Damn him! Why couldn't he find his stories somewhere else?

He closed his fingers again, blotting out the sight of the street. He yearned for darkness, silence, complete isolation. He must make one last desperate attempt to find an immediate and honorable end for Lazy Ethel. But the bank vault was closed. It had been slammed shut, way ahead of time! How can I get the money back where it belongs? God help me! What have I done? His hands slipped down and around his neck in an involuntary gesture, and he bent his head low.

10

ON THE OPPOSITE SIDE of the channel, Chief Tanni leaned against a coco-nut palm and alternately pondered both the white beach which formed the nearest lip of the lagoon, and the sky. The beach he knew well; almost every granule of coral on it had at one time or another known the weight of his bare feet. It reminded him now of the pearling season when there were always excitement and activity enough to rouse the laziest of his people. Those were the good times on Nikki, and Tanni found it saddening to think that his status as chief forbade him true participation in the pearling. Ahwei! It was not always so.

He could see himself before he was elected chief, that would be five years ago, and the vision pleased him. He was not so fat then, and during the season he had departed from the same beach every day, bound for the pearling grounds near the center of the lagoon. It was a voyage of nearly ten kilometers to the center of the sparkling blue water; and when the wind was faithful they made it in a very short time . . . twenty canoes when the price of pearl was low and only a few divers from the other islands considered it worth while to come to Nikki. As many as seventy canoes when the price was high. Ahwei! They would spend the entire day diving and surfacing and diving again in the water, which was neither too cool nor too warm, shouting to each other across the wavelets and laughing at jokes spewed out along with the water from their mouths. Then, Tanni remembered wistfully, he had thought nothing of diving twenty meters, even twenty-five meters if the bottom looked promising through the glass in his water box. And there were others who were so driven by a mixture of greed and pride that they sometimes dared to dive even farther into the blue lagoon. The results were not always so happy, Tanni recalled. For the bodies of those who had been either too brave or foolhardy, were often carried ashore twisting in agony, or sometimes as limp as a needlefish. Then the priest would come, or one of the Mormon elders. And the young body would never slip beneath the surface of the lagoon again.

But almost always the return to the village was a happy and triumphant affair. When the lowering sun robbed the depths of workable light, then the divers' lungs were sore from the special laboring, anyway. So the canoes would start back laden with shell. And if the wind was just right, there would be a race to arrive on the beach first, and if the wind had dropped dead, then the paddles would flash red in the afternoon sun and there would still be a race.

And the beach, Tanni thought, would sound and appear almost exactly as it did now.

He looked down at his people, knowing every one of them down to the last child screaming its delight, and he saw that they were almost finished with their preparations. Every canoe in the village had been dragged to the edge of the water, even a few which had not been used for years and so were cracked with dryness and leaked, and there were others which had been left awash and were soggy with neglect. Now in a spasm of activity, broken outriggers had been repaired, and a great exchange of paddles had taken place so that even those who had not used their canoes for a long time were properly equipped. Amid much hilarity, both Fat Sue and Yip Kee, who were merchants and had never been in a canoe in their lives, were instructed in the proper ways to handle the craft Tanni himself had lent them. In return they were bringing along a generous assortment of the precious cans from their shelves, both agreeing that when the storm came they would lose all anyway and they might as well use this opportunity to create good will. Tanni saw M. DeLage helping his native wife load their canoe, which had an ancient outboard motor attached to the stern. And since M. DeLage could not paddle any better than the two Chinese, Tanni hoped the motor worked better than his wireless, which after almost the full morning's nursing had failed to establish even momentary contact with Papeete or anywhere else over the horizon.

Evaluating the situation on the beach, Tanni estimated that all would be ready for departure long before the time set by the Americans. His people were working together. . . . The Mormons and the Catholics were assisting each other as if there had never been the slightest division of interests. Terry Mack was, as usual, running about from group to group, chattering like a monkey and making a nuisance of himself, but generally the people were too busy to pay him much attention. . . . Which was good, because the little Melanesian who didn't belong on Nikki anyway and never could, had been the first to bring news of the storm from across the channel. He had been running about ever since on his spindly legs, foretelling the most awful debacle. It was good that his words were not swallowed entirely for there was not going to be any debacle, which was the French word Terry Mack had used over and over again. There was going to be a storm, but not a debacle if the people across the channel, who were very clever to have known of the storm so far in advance, had done the rest of their thinking properly. Tanni was not so sure about that.

He studied the sky for a long time. Ahwei. Yes, the Americans were clever although how they could have known that a storm was on its way before the sky itself showed a certain milkiness, was beyond his understanding. They were clever, too, in denying that any real storm was approaching, which, of course, was an untruth, but if they preferred to start that way Tanni could not see any harm done. Long before the Americans were ready to leave their own settlement, Tanni's people would rendezvous beneath the low scrub which dotted the land on the north side of the lagoon and would have their cooking fires ready. They had been told to settle down and wait at that place which Tanni knew very well since he had often explored there in his youth. Now he thought of it without enthusiasm. It was not, he considered, the best place to seek refuge from any storm which might strike Nikki. It was the flattest part of the atoll and the lowest in respect to the sea. The land offered nothing except the scrub and a few mounds of coral intermixed with small hummocks of sand. None of these elevations were higher than a man's head.

Still enrapt in the sky, Tanni tried to remember the last big storm which had passed across Nikki. But he was only six years old when that had occurred and he found it impossible to recall anything except a vision of his mother singing to him. Thinking back, he was not at all sure the memory did not reflect some other occasion. He had always been under the impression that all storms approached Nikki from the north. Yet whether his belief originated from remembered fact or simply echoed opinions he might have long ago heard from his elders, he could not be sure. He had confirmed his vague opinion by talking with Huahenga's mother and the uncle of Apakura, who were the oldest people on Nikki.

Both had shaken their heads dubiously and said that the north side of Nikki was the wrong place to go. They agreed that much more favorable protection would be found on the south side, where there was a fifty-meter hill if things became really bad.

Tanni rubbed his eyes because staring so long at the sky had made them begin to water. And he was getting a headache, whether from his observation of the sky or the argument within himself, he did not know. If the Americans had learned of the storm so far in advance, he finally decided, then they must know what they were doing. If they said the storm would come from the south, then it would come from the south in spite of Huahenga's mother and Apakura's uncle, who were old and addled anyway. The Americans were modern. They had machinery and they knew. Look how, in so short a time, they had built a village far more comfortable than Nikki. Ahwei!

Pushing himself away from the coconut palm, Tanni strolled slowly down toward the beach. There was no longer any reason to look at the sky, for of its present nature, at least, he was very certain.

As they passed the post office, Margaret told Hanover she would have to leave him and see if there was any mail for the Governor's house. When he said she would be wasting her time because the mail plane hadn't come and probably wouldn't under the circumstances and why shouldn't they stop in the store and he would buy her a Coke, she said she had to make sure about the mail anyway.

Leaving Hanover, she went into the post office and found that it was closed. So, too, was Aubrey Tinsman's beauty salon. She was surprised because less than an hour before Aubrey had given her a haircut. Now he had left a sign on his door, GONE TO PICNIC! She waited a moment, not wanting to rejoin Hanover. All the way from Adam's office he had tried to persuade her to show him the map and it was getting to be a bore refusing him. Hanover had also proven himself to be a fanny pincher, perhaps still in the embryonic stage, but there was no other logical explanation for stumbling twice and reaching to her hip for support . . . not when the street was perfectly smooth coral. Fanny pinching, Margaret thought with a wry smile, was not necessarily confined to older men or, for that matter, to any special time of the day. Hanover should know better.

When she went out into the street he was still waiting for her. "Just like I told you, wasn't it?" he asked.

"Yes. It was closed."

"Everything is closed except I still think we can get that Coke."

"No. Thanks very much," Margaret said, starting out for Pike's house with a firm step. She added, "See you at the picnic."

But obviously Hanover had not chosen to hear her. "About that map," he said, again falling into step beside her. "I don't see how you could possibly get in any trouble if you just let me have a peek at it."

"It isn't a question of my getting into any trouble. I'm just a messenger girl, Mr. Hanover. Why don't you ask Pike if you want to see it?"

"I imagine he's pretty busy right now with all this going on."

He nodded at a group of laborers who were nailing temporary battens across the windows of the water-evaporation plant. He said, "A good newsman picks his time if he possibly can and sees people when they're not up to their necks in something else. So for the last time, how about just a peek?"

"*No,*" Margaret said decisively.

Hanover sighed. "Have it your way, girl. I know what's on the map anyway. Abe Lincoln told me."

"Oh? He did?"

"Regular Gettysburg Address on the nature of hurricanes. He's a smart fellow, but a very poor actor."

They reached the intersection where the narrower road from Pike's house joined the main street. Without slowing her stride Margaret turned into it. Hanover stopped, reached out, and seized her wrist. "You and Abe are making a mistake. It never pays to hide things from the press. We can be very helpful people."

"I said I'm just a messenger girl!" Margaret twisted her arm until her wrist was free and quickly walked away.

Her anger was replaced by complete surprise when she entered Pike's office and he smiled broadly at her. "Good morning to you again, young lady!" he said cheerily.

Not certain she had heard him accurately, Margaret advanced until she could place the map on his desk. She saw that it was littered with papers, some of which were prominently labeled SECRET and others RESTRICTED. A small hand compass and a many-bladed knife had been placed just behind the sign which bore his name, and a pair of binoculars held down a sheaf of papers on one side.

"Good morning to you again, sir," Margaret said hesitantly. "There wasn't any mail."

"Of course not," Pike boomed without the slightest sign of disappointment. "And a good thing, too! We've got enough going on around here without getting lost in a lot of paperwork. *Well!*" he went on, still smiling, "all packed to go on the picnic?"

"I was told I would go in the last boat so I thought I had plenty of time."

"Better get your gear together. I may move the departure up a half-hour or so. No sense in waiting until the stable is on fire before you move the horse. Ho, ho!"

As Pike chuckled to himself, Margaret studied his face in wonder. What in the world had gotten into General Zebulon Pike? He was acting as if he were really going on a picnic and one which he would thoroughly enjoy. His eyes, normally cold and always, she remembered, a little uncertain as if his pride had somehow just been wounded, were now fairly snapping with anticipation. Now, of all things, he carelessly tossed the rolled-up map aside and smiled again at her.

"Here's a message I want sent off right away," he said, ripping a sheet of paper from his note pad. "There may be one or two more, but I doubt it. Better read it to make sure you don't have any trouble putting it on the teletype. My neuritis is giving me the very devil and I'm afraid my penmanship isn't quite up to par."

Margaret read the message which was written in Pike's careful, almost Shakespearean hand. It was perfectly legible, quite beautiful visually, she thought. If Pike apologized for his writing, she mused, he should try to read mine. The message was for Tuamani.

Situation Pistol Two well in hand. All possible measures being taken protect personnel and government property. Classified documents secured. For your information have assumed emergency authority placing Marine detachment under my direct command. We are ready for Lazy Ethel.

Pike.

"It's quite clear," Margaret said. "Anything else, sir?"

"No. Just get it out right away."

Before Margaret started toward the door Pike winked at her. "Better take along some warm clothes," he said. "You just happen to be one of the very few people who knows this isn't a drill. No sense in catching cold."

He looked at her and his voice took on a tender, protective note. "Not a little afraid, are you?"

"No, sir."

"Good. Brave girl. It won't be so bad. Everyone will be taken care of."

When she reached the main street again, Margaret looked carefully down its length to make sure Hanover was not waiting for her. But he was not to be seen. Instead, the street was now almost deserted except where it terminated down by the wharf. There she could see a considerable crowd of people. She had not realized so many lived in Pistol Two, probably, she thought, because they had quickly dispersed after their arrival and had never all been assembled in one place again. As she approached the communications shack she saw that many of the people were already in the boats. Those still waiting to board were laden down with packages and clothes, and the mothers were having a busy time corralling the children.

In spite of herself, Margaret knew a sense of pleasurable excitement. At the very least Lazy Ethel was going to be inconvenient and she supposed that it could be dangerous; but just now with the sun shining and the leisurely, almost festive air with which the people milled about the wharf, it was hard to believe the gathering represented anything more than a picnic. Albright, whom she could see striding anxiously about in the best tradition of a social director, seemed to be the only harassed person on the wharf. Just like the Beloit J.C.C.'s, she thought, only on a considerably larger scale.

She entered the communications shack and found Sunnie Mandel engrossed, as usual, in a movie magazine. Margaret had never been able to understand how her supply of movie magazines seemed so inexhaustible, until one day Sunnie had explained she read each one several times in the belief that careful study would enable her to write for them. "The people who write this stuff have it made," she had explained. "They get paid for yakking with the stars. Imagine!"

Now she did not look up from her magazine, but did acknowledge Margaret's entrance with a throaty hello.

"Hi," Margaret answered and went directly to the number one teletype machine. As she sat down before it and clipped Pike's message to the scanning board she said, "It looks like we're about on our way. Have you done any packing?"

"Unh-uh. They won't let you take enough to make it worth while. I'll be satisfied with a toothbrush."

"We'd better take something to keep us warm, anyway."

"I suppose."

There was a long pause while Margaret's fingers tripped over the teletype keys. She waited for Tuamani's stand-by acknowledgment, then sent Pike's message.

When she had finished, Sunnie said, "Our hero was in this morning."

"Who?"

"Silent Sam, the weatherman. Only he's not so silent lately. We almost had a conversation."

"Fine," Margaret said. "I think he needs someone to talk to."

"He does indeed. Say, what's with him?"

"How do you mean?"

"What's with him? He acts like he's been in the cookie jar . . . like he's sick in the head from something he et."

"I don't understand you, Sunnie."

"We-yell. . . ." Sunnie closed the movie magazine and, doubling her fists, placed them beneath her chin. She leaned forward on her elbows and stared thoughtfully across the street at the weather office. "Well, maybe I know something I shouldn't. For my money, anyway, it just doesn't figure. This is all aside from the fact he's madly in love with you."

"Oh now, come on, Sunnie. You're not making sense."

"I am. But he isn't. My twisted little mind has been working overtime and what it comes up with scares me."

Margaret sighed. There were times when Sunnie Mandel could be anything but a delightful companion. She was often given to long periods of brooding and the most merciless self-analysis. It came, she freely admitted, from wanting a man so badly she sometimes caught herself shivering all over at the mere sight of a likely male. Margaret wondered if she would ever suffer the same affliction. Maybe a few more years of government work would do it. The Ree-Jay Club always had room for new members.

"Get this," Sunnie said. "Out of a clear blue sky this morning comes a message from Tuamani asking about a storm. They don't know a thing about it, see, and we are supposed to cue them. Okay. But, before that, is there any message from us to anybody about said storm? There is not. So how did they find out about it in the first place? They have a crystal ball, maybe?"

Sunnie furrowed her brow and placed a fingernail between her teeth. She was about to start gnawing on the nail when Margaret said sharply, "Stop that!"

It was a habit they were both in league to break and Sunnie lowered her hand in shame.

"So what happens?" she went on. "A little later, Silent Sam comes in here and he's got a message he wants to send to Tuamani. It says he got the dope about the storm from a Jap fishing boat. So okay. I send it.

Now what bothers me is how did Silent Sam hear from this fishing boat? He has a special radio in his room, maybe, which speaks Japanese?"

"I don't see where it really makes any difference."

"It does to me and I'll tell you why in a minute. Or did you receive some click from a fishing boat . . . maybe when I was gone to the biffie?"

"No. I didn't."

"All right, then. Neither did I. Those machines have been silent as a busted-down organ all morning. There wasn't anything yesterday afternoon or last night either. We didn't hear from any boat even if it were possible for them to get on the circuit, which it isn't . . . but I do smell something fishy."

Margaret was touching up her lips before the mirror which hung over the number one machine. She paused now, wondering what strange avenue Sunnie's mind would venture along next.

"You know what I think?" Sunnie said.

"No, I don't know what you think. Frankly, I'm never quite sure."

Margaret knew she was vaguely annoyed and she could not understand why she should be just now. Sunnie was merely chattering along in her standard style. Perhaps, she considered, I am actually a little nervous about going to see Adam Smith without an official reason. But that was silly. Well, anyway, her lips were now all right.

"I think there isn't any storm," Sunnie said flatly.

"What in the world would give you that idea?"

"I think somebody threw a curve at Tuamani just for kicks and they fell for the gag. Now, who would do a thing like that is the next thing I ask myself. And the answer comes through right away clear as if it clicked off number one machine. Silent Sam, it says. Who else?"

"That imagination of yours!" Margaret said, wondering again why she felt so uneasy. "Why would he do a thing like that?"

"That, I can't answer. But like I told you he wasn't himself when he came in here. He was nervous as a witch on Hallowe'en. When he sent that message to Tuamani he was covering for himself."

"I'll tell you what I'll do," Margaret said, trying very firmly to put down her misgivings. "I'm going across to see him right now, anyway, and I'll just mention the fact you don't think there is a real storm. Maybe for once he'll laugh right out loud. Or he would if there was anything funny about a storm."

"Don't!" Sunnie said hastily.

"Why not? He deserves a laugh."

"Just don't. Please. It wouldn't be smart. Especially for you. Men are funny. They don't like suspicious women and he might blame my thoughts on you. I want him to like you."

"I thought you said he was madly in love with me?"

"A figure of speech. That comes later. Now don't go louse anything up. Please."

Because of her tennis shoes, Margaret made no sound as she entered Adam's office. She allowed the door to close very softly behind her and stood waiting for a moment in silence. Adam was bent over his drawing board, his back to her, and at first she thought he was deeply engrossed in his work. Then she saw that his eyes were closed and there was only a blank piece of paper beneath his elbows. His shoulders sagged and his whole body had somehow taken on a posture of utter dejection. She wondered if his work with the storm had kept him up all night.

"Are you just taking a nap?" she said finally. Hanover was right. He did look like Abe Lincoln, and she thought it very strange that she had never really noticed the resemblance before. Only now he looked like a very weary Lincoln, somewhat like the portraits she remembered in her schoolbooks.

He stood looking down at her in silence for so long Margaret began to be uncomfortable; then very suddenly she decided she would wait for him to speak first if it took all day.

"Thanks for coming back," he said at last. "I wanted to apologize for making such a fool of myself on the wharf last night."

"You already did that. Forgiven."

"I like you."

Margaret swallowed hard. When Adam Smith did speak he certainly didn't beat around the bush. "Well . . . good," she said.

There followed another silence, and again Margaret was determined he should do the talking. She stood motionless, her hands clasped behind her, looking up at him almost defiantly. She was no longer uncomfortable.

"There's something I want to tell you," he began. "It isn't easy and, for a little time at least, you will be the only person besides myself who knows it. I want to tell you because someday I would like to see you again . . . maybe under better circumstances. I . . . well, I just never before met anyone who . . . well . . . I want you to believe me now when I try to explain how I feel about you . . . because maybe later on you won't believe me. I'm making an awful bungle of this."

"You are a little vague," she said. For some reason she wanted him to tell her again that he liked her in just the same way he had done before. It should have been embarrassing, but it just wasn't. Yet he was deeply troubled and before he spoke again she knew what he was going to say.

"I've made an even bigger fool of myself. I invented a storm which doesn't exist and I named it Lazy Ethel. The reasons why I did this thing are so childish and complicated there's no sense in trying to explain, but I certainly never dreamed it would cause such an uproar and inconvenience so many people. I just underestimated Pike's craving for action, and what with one thing and another it's a cinch I won't be around here very long. I wanted you to know the truth before I went up and told Pike. Then maybe someday . . . when you come back to the States, I could find you, somehow . . . and when I told you again you'd believe that business about my liking you."

His eyes were so miserable Margaret wanted to reach up and caress them. She would believe Adam Smith, all right. Anywhere.

"I guess that's all I have to say. You can go now."

"What . . . do you think Pike will do?"

"Can me, for sure. Then call the whole thing off. I just wish he hadn't been so hasty or I could have stopped him."

"You'll break his heart. I never saw a man so full of enthusiasm for a project. He's a changed man, too. It's all right up his alley. You've done him more good than harm."

"I doubt if he'll look at it quite that way. I'm sorry. I'm very, very sorry about this whole mess."

"Pike is going to be a lot sorrier. I've got a hunch he has to prove himself. He has the bit in his teeth and he's going to hate dropping it. Isn't there some other way? Couldn't you just let him have his fun?"

"I tried that and it's already out of hand. I still have to live with myself."

He went quickly to his drawing board and after a moment's hesitation scribbled a name and address on a piece of paper. He turned back to Margaret and handed it to her. "Here. Please keep this and write me a card when you get home. It's my brother's address and it will be forwarded to me. I'm not just sure where I'll be after this."

Margaret folded the paper and placed it in her pocket. The silence between them was broken by the sound of the engines in the landing craft. As she listened they roared to full power, then gradually diminished. When it was quiet again, she said, "Anyway, they'll have a fine boat ride at government expense."

Adam went quickly to the door.

"That must only be the first load. I've got to stop the rest. I'd better go see Pike right now."

"Good luck."

"So long . . . Margaret. Thanks for taking my folly the way you have."

She did not leave the weather office immediately. Instead she climbed on Adam's stool. Through the screen window she could see him hurrying up the deserted street toward Pike's house. He looked so very much alone. And she thought, if anyone knew what it was like to feel alone in a hostile world, she did. So she tried very hard to think of some way to help Adam Smith.

11

THERE WERE FORTY-FIVE PEOPLE in the first landing craft to leave the wharf at Pistol Two. As it cleared the channel and entered the calm expanse of the lagoon, the passengers settled down as comfortably as they could manage in the confined space. For many it was their first real view of the lagoon, so the novelty of its clear depths held them entranced for several miles. The children were especially excited, and it was all the mothers could do to keep them from falling overboard as they clambered up and down the high-sided craft and fought for vantage points. There was no complaining, most of the passengers having accepted without question Albright's explanation that it was only a drill. There was even, as Pike had hoped, a festive air about the expedition. This atmosphere would have been easier for all of them to maintain if the diesel engines had made less racket. Because of this noise the majority of the passengers were obliged to settle down and wait in thoughtful silence.

The only place in the craft where it was possible to carry on wholly intelligible conversation was in the bow. When the channel entrance and the buildings of Pistol Two had sunk beneath the horizon, several passengers gathered there who were not attached to any particular family group. So it was that Peter Hildebrandt found a comfortable seat on a box of canned peas which he almost immediately surrendered to Crystal Blum, who ran the laundry.

"Don't thank me," Peter said with a little bow. "I am in your debt for doing such a nice job on my shirts."

"Oh, Mr. Hildebrandt!" Crystal said with a delighted giggle, "you are a true gentleman!"

"The old scoundrel will sully your honor if you give him the chance," Dr. Case said. "I wouldn't trust him."

Dr. Keim, the astronomer, stood looking aft. He rubbed sunburn lotion into his bright-red nose and said, "Look. You can still see the top of the control tower. Just the top of it is sticking up . . . right there. In case any of you are interested there is perfect proof the world is round. Our visibility is much less than you think it is from this height. Not much more than three miles."

"We're out of sight of the land," Aubrey Tinsman said. "I shall pretend I'm cruising on my yacht."

Turning to Carlos Raveza, who had been assigned to the first boat on the theory he would have time to set up his portable light plant, Aubrey said, "Steward, you may bring my bouillon now."

"For a certainty this is absolute foolishness," Carlos Raveza answered. "If we are going to have a drill, why not just go for a boat ride and then when it has been proved no one knows what they are doing . . . we can return to our quarters like sensible people. I have no want to spend the night on some deserted beach. There will be mosquitoes."

"I didn't think there were any mosquitoes on Nikki," Crystal Blum said.

"Pike banished them by directive," Dr. Case said.

"There will be mosquitoes. There will be mosquitoes wherever I go," Carlos sighed. "It is a curse of my family. If there was not so much as a single mosquito before, then there will be swarms of them now. I am one of those people. When I left Tampico forever the mosquitoes soon starved."

Peter Hildebrandt was struck by a thought which suddenly robbed him of further enjoyment on the voyage. He had been brooding on the disposal problem which must attend the dislocation of so many people. Viewing the situation with the confidence and detachment of an experienced professional, he was thus not greatly concerned until he remembered something he was certain no one else had remembered. "Pardon me for bringing up such a delicate subject, but did anyone see any toilet paper put aboard?"

There was a long and embarrassed silence while the entire group surveyed the collection of boxes which now served as seats.

"What about cigarettes?" Aubrey Tinsman said with genuine alarm. "I only brought one pack and it's nearly finished."

"Beer," Carlos Raveza growled. "I don't see any beer. What kind of a picnic is this?"

Dr. Keim was still looking back at the fast-sinking control tower. It had nearly disappeared now, and the two other landing craft following in their distant wake were the only prominent objects on the horizon. "Maybe all that stuff is in the other boats," he said without any real hope in his voice. "If it isn't, then this is a very poorly organized drill."

"What about blankets?" Crystal Blum asked. "We ought to have something to sit on. It isn't very comfortable just sitting on sand. I went on a vacation once at Virginia Beach and—"

"Or sleeping on it," Dr. Case interrupted sourly.

"What do you mean sleeping on it?"

"We are obviously supposed to spend the night or Mr. Raveza would not have been invited to bring along his lighting plant."

"Have no fear," Carlos said. "I will never get it to work. There is no possibility. We will have to go back then."

"Is this trip really necessary?" Aubrey said. Then his attention was captured by a line of dark objects stretching across the cobalt blue of the water ahead. "Look! Cannibals! White man, go no farther!"

Hearing the sound of engines, Tanni looked back over his shoulder and saw the landing craft of the Americans approaching. Instinctively he quickened the rhythm of his paddling although he knew very well that even his enormous arms were little better than useless in a race against machinery. He glanced at his wife and his two children, who sat smiling in his own canoe, and then he looked thoughtfully at the long line of his people's canoes spread out on each side of him. Ahwei! This was good! The people were singing and laughing and joking as if it were Bastille Day. The other men, now aware of the overtaking power craft, were paddling as if a fortune in pearl waited for them only a few meters ahead. The canoes lifted to their efforts and small white wavelets appeared beneath their bows. The paddlers began to shout, urging each other to greater speed, and then they began a chant which Tanni had not heard for a long time. The sound of it, rising rapidly stroke by stroke, caused a tingling of pleasure along the skin of Tanni's bare arms; and though he knew his children had never heard him sing so before, and would wonder what had come over their father, he joined in the chanting. He allowed his heavy voice full expression, not caring for the frowns of the Mormon elders in the nearest canoe. Farther along the line he was delighted to hear the unmistakable voice of Huahenga, penetrating even at a distance. And it was not, he thought with strange satisfaction, a rhythm or a melody she had ever sung in church. There were no formal words to the chant for not even Huahenga's mother was likely to remember them, but the rhythm and proper joyousness soared up from the breasts of all the singers and Tanni found it more deeply moving than anything the elders had ever offered. "Alli, alli, yay! . . . Alli, alli, yay! Ah*wei!*"

Then, without intention, Tanni fell silent. The joy left his face and the tingling subsided beneath his skin. For the chanting had brought him a vision of the lagoon which was so different from what he could see now. He wanted to groan instead of sing. He saw the lagoon as it had once been, as his grandfather and great-grandfather had described it, in voices which even in the telling became vigorous again. The lagoon and the sea around Nikki were dotted by a thousand canoes. This same chant echoed and re-echoed across the lagoon and was carried far over the horizon when the young men paddled and sailed the six hundred kilometers to Tuamani for war. There were villages situated around the entire coral circlet of Nikki, and there was even a large settlement near the very place they were headed now. Ahwei! There was no longer any trace of it, nor of the others. The people of Nikki had vanished, or nearly so. Outsiders had begun to frequent Nikki in his great-grandfather's youth. They appeared more frequently and were welcomed in his grandfather's time, and his father had seen the true beginning of the end. The people died because the outsiders brought disease they could not fight with their clubs or spears. The people died because the old customs upon which they relied were pronounced evil, and this had a way of killing the desire to live. And so, in time, many more of the people simply expired.

Tanni looked over the pitiful fleet about him. There were no more than twenty canoes or, perhaps, twenty-five, and there were less than a hundred people in them. Which was all of the people in the village of Nikki.

He glanced behind him again at the snarling landing craft. They were almost upon the line of canoes and in a few moments they would pass. What were these outsiders bringing? Why had they felt the need to come to Nikki? Why had they left their own villages and traveled so many kilometers only to leave again and vanish as surely and completely as his ancestors? According to Terry Mack they would cause an explosion, not on Nikki, but near Tuamani or Oa Titia, and this would kill all the fishes and the birds which had survived a hundred storms. They were not doing this unexplainable thing on Nikki, because they did not wish to kill people—not even the few on Nikki. Then why, if they did not wish to kill people, did they go to so much trouble about the whole affair? Certainly not just to kill the fishes and the birds, for it was said they would not even touch their dead bodies. Then why?

Tanni felt his headache returning, and just as the first landing craft came abreast of his canoe he decided the hurt between his ears came from utterly useless thinking. He looked up and saw heads appearing like bleached coconuts along the sides of the landing craft. The owners of the heads were shouting and waving, and a few of them were taking his picture with their cameras. Tanni saw very distinctly that they were agreeable and most friendly. Certainly they did not appear to be the kind of people who would devote so much effort to the killing of fishes and birds. He found himself wondering if they would soon begin to vanish like his own people. Or had it already begun? Were there atolls where they had come from, once heavily populated and now almost deserted? Had they, too, somehow lost the desire to live? Ahwei! My head!

Tanni paused long enough to raise his paddle and acknowledge their waving. He saw with approval that his people in the other canoes were doing the same thing. Almost at once their delighted shouts of greeting were drowned out by the exhaust from the engines. The landing craft passed swiftly through the line of canoes, leaving them bouncing wildly in their wakes.

The singing had ceased in the canoes, and for a moment there was only the fast-diminishing roar of the engines. Then, before it was entirely quiet in the lagoon, Tanni raised his voice in the chant again. Looking at the sky, he thought that the sooner they reached land again, the better. So in spite of the terrible ache in his head he gave his voice all the lustiness within him. The others soon joined in the singing and paddled as industriously as before.

Tanni did not know why his skin failed to tingle again or why the chant seemed to have lost zest. Now it seemed to have taken on a melancholy tone. Perhaps it was because the big American craft had left them behind so easily, or perhaps it was because of the color of the sky.

Adam did not bother to knock before he entered Pike's office, so he was neither surprised nor disappointed when he was greeted with a heavy frown.

"Where is the real chart?" Pike asked, looking with disapproval at Adam's empty hands.

"You have the real chart," Adam said firmly. "I sent it up with Miss Trumpey at the regular time."

"Now come on, Smith. There's no storm on that chart. I checked just to make sure."

"No, there is not any storm on it or anywhere else, Governor. There just *isn't* any storm, sir. Lazy Ethel simply does not exist and it never did. You've got to believe me and put a stop to all this nonsense immediately!"

"Nonsense, is it?"

Pike pushed back his chair and stood up. His eyes never left Adam as he slowly circled around his desk. "Just what kind of a shenanigan are you up to now, Mr. Smith? I was under the impression you were all straightened out. I thought you had taken a brace and were going to play honest ball with me."

"I straightened myself out and I am being honest. I know you're going to fire me and I don't blame you, but you have got to believe me. *There is no such thing as Lazy Ethel!* There never was and it is extremely unlikely there ever will be. I dreamed it up just like I told you the last time I was here. Then I lied because it seemed to be easier going along with you than arguing. You aren't an easy man to talk to, Governor."

Pike studied him in silence. After a moment he turned abruptly away and walked over to the flag standard. He remained with his back to Adam, looking alternately at the flag and the line of palm trees beyond the window for a long time.

At last he turned around and Adam was instantly sorry for him. He was like a man who had collided with a tree in the dark. His face bore a crumpled look, as if he were totally incapable of mastering the disappointment and honest bewilderment which fought for supremacy within him. When he spoke his voice was flat and so subdued Adam was not at all certain the sound came from Pike at all.

"You mean this, Smith? You confess that you have deliberately tricked me? This isn't a new deception? There isn't any Lazy Ethel?"

"No, sir. I'm sorry. I really am *very* sorry. I didn't set out to trick you. It just worked that way."

"What would make you do a thing like that?"

"I don't know. I've tried to think it out, but I didn't come up with any very satisfactory answers."

There was another long silence while Pike stared at his boots. Finally he said, "You are discharged, of course."

"You have every right to feel the way you do, sir."

"I won't go into the fact that you have betrayed a trust. Perhaps it's better things turned out the way they have . . . now. God knows what you might have done when explosion date comes around."

Pike returned to his desk, crossing the room very slowly as if the shock of Adam's revelation had somehow brought a stiffness to his joints. "There will be some severance papers for you to sign," he muttered, and now he so deliberately avoided any recognition of Adam's existence he might have been standing out in the road. "I will arrange for transportation to Tuamani for you as quickly as possible. In the meantime I want a full written report from you on this whole matter."

Pike looked directly at Adam, and the hurt in his eyes was such that Adam decided that under no circumstances would he mention Pike's heckling, but would only blame himself. "You realize, of course," Pike said quietly, "that you have succeeded in making me look like a complete damned fool?"

"I'm sorry, sir."

"You will go to your quarters and remain there until further notice. I do not like to use the word *arrest,* but you should realize I have the authority to use it."

Adam turned, grateful that, at least, the whole thing was over. He wondered if there was some gymnastic feat whereby he could kick himself.

Pike called after him, but now there was neither antagonism nor any indication of a military order in his voice.

"Smith. If you are as sorry as you claim to be, then there is one thing you can do for me. I have no intention of striking a bargain with you, but if you will at least try to co-operate, perhaps I can modify some of the opinions which must be in my own report. Our people have been sent off with the impression they are doing a drill . . . fortunately. I don't see where it will have any bearing on this case if that impression is allowed to remain. It will not help their morale if they learn the full details of this unfortunate incident. On the other hand, it will help me considerably if they don't. Therefore I will appreciate it if the matter remains between you and me. We'll think up some logical reason for your departure and that will be the end of it. Is that all right with you?"

"Yessir," Adam said quickly. "I'll be only too happy to keep my mouth shut."

"Good day, Mister Smith."

When Adam had left, Pike spent a long time aligning the pencils behind the little sign which bore his name. Once they were exactly end to end, he carefully restacked a small pile of paper clips until they were also perfectly set one upon the other. And when there no longer remained any convenient preoccupation for his hands, they automatically came together in his comfortable isosceles triangle, the apex of which he employed to support his chin. He sat immobile in his chair, his eyes closed tightly, his mind composing innumerable teletypes for Tuamani, all designed to explain away one Lazy Ethel. None of his compositions offered a reasonable excuse for his action in closing down Pistol Two and sending the entire population over ten miles across the lagoon. None of the messages, forming and re-forming in his mind, suggested that a responsible and, most of all, stable personality was in charge on Nikki atoll.

Gradually, Pike saw the ingredients of a personal disaster creeping across the clutter of teletypes in his thoughts, and he knew only too well that he was poorly armed against high-echelon censure. Whether Adam Smith had originally intended to bring about his final defeat was beside the point. There were nuances of peril of which he could not possibly have been aware.

For example, Smith could not have known of the backstage maneuvering which had brought Zebulon Pike to Nikki in the first place. It had been a very close thing indeed, and there were several times when it had seemed only wistful hoping that the job could be won. Pike knew of at least five retired general officers, three of them with most distinguished war records, who were even now cursing over their peony gardens and protesting to the highest authorities that in the selection of Zebulon Pike, the most flagrant favoritism had been shown. Which was true enough. There was, of course, nothing crooked about it, although the words *scandalous, outrageous, criminal, fantastic,* and *God-damned shame* had all been uttered by the disappointed candidates and their respective families. It was largely a case of nostalgia which had prompted Pike's old polo teammate, "Owlhead" Wheeler, to recommend him. And since "Owlhead" had served through many years of staff assignments, he knew his way around Washington much better than he had ever learned to hit a near-side forward shot, despite his remarkable ability to revolve his head. He had pointed out to the selection board that highly decorated war heroes were ever reluctant to forget their prerogatives. They might be dashing, but they also reveled in friction and trouble. Examination of Pike's record easily proved to the most doubting that none of these things need be feared in his case. He was, one member of the board remarked, as obscure as a titmouse.

Once the Korean war had limped to conclusion, the surplus of formerly high-ranking army officers became appalling. Pike could not imagine where they had all come from and, of course, there was the Navy, too. Every peaceful retreat in the United States suddenly blossomed with discreet signs identifying the modest house behind it as the final residence of General Blank or Admiral Blank or Colonel Dash or Commander Dash. The countryside sprouted with these men puttering in their gardens, raising dogs which did not require too much food, donning tweed coats when they escaped long enough to go for the mail, and serving on as many local committees as they could possibly infiltrate. On the whole they tried to participate as actively as they could in every local enterprise. And they conducted themselves with notable dignity, perhaps too much, Pike thought. They were almost fiercely determined to be good citizens.

It was not easy. The sudden loneliness, for one thing, was chilling. An elderly stranger, hale and handsome to look at, perhaps, but still perforce a stranger, settled amid a community which had grown up together. However small or large, the population was bound to each other by a million invisible ties of background and circumstance. All of these had been established while the military man served out his active life elsewhere; occupied, and at the same time almost totally isolated, in what might just as well have been another world. It was a rare officer who found it either possible or desirable to retire in the vicinity of an Army post or a Naval base. They went out into their native land as children, hopefully, willingly; convinced that at last they would reap some kind of reward. Except for those very fortunate few who had married rich wives, the results were far from spectacular. They soon discovered that their pensions left no provision for that occasional bottle of Scotch which might make entertainment of their new neighbors an easier and more congenial affair. They found it almost impossible to understand or participate in conversations with the younger men who were engaged in the fast-changing business of making a living. Having always known that their own basic needs would be provided for, talking to businessmen of their own age was not much easier. If they were also retired, then those harness-worn men preferred to recall the era in which they had served as executives in some corporation, a world of secretaries, contracts, conventions, and tolerated conniving. They were not even slightly interested in the maneuvering of battalions or who commanded what battleship, unless the tale involved actual combat; and even then it had to be something they remembered reading about in the newspapers. Worst of all, there were those whom Pike and his fellow officers thought of as professional taxpayers. They secretly, and sometimes not so secretly, resented the very existence of any retired military man. They resented his meager pension as if they had just reached into their wallets and paid it directly, and they had a great deal to say about how, by God, no one had ever offered to take care of them from the cradle to the grave. This was the cruelest rebuff of all.

So cruel, in fact, many retired military men set forth once more into the world and tried almost desperately to mitigate their status. Unprepared, they sold real estate or at least tried to; they sold insurance and automobiles, ran motels or gun clubs. There were admirals who had not so long before commanded five thousand sailors and a flotilla of ships, who were now themselves quite familiar with the business end of a mop. There were generals and colonels responsible for the lives of many thousands of their fellow Americans and millions of dollars' worth of material, who became hopelessly lost between the lines of a simple lease. And frequently their wives sold Christmas cards.

There was another category of retired military man who moved in a more rarefied environment. Pike knew that it was unlikely he could join them and so had never given them much thought. For they were specialists of a kind, not mere soldiers or sailors, and their change-over to civilian life had brought them even greater benefits. These men were welcomed and highly paid by large corporations who employed them as "Advisors," or frequently and more specifically, "Advisors to the President." It surprised no one that those firms were heavily engaged in production for or services to the Armed Forces. Or they would like to be. In recent years some Air Force officers had not even found it worth while to await their retirement. They simply resigned, exchanged their uniforms for well-tailored suits, and joined whatever airline or aircraft manufacturer had offered the most enticing bid for their services. Pike did not resent their good fortune. He realized that the large majority were highly trained technicians, as well as very personable men. He was even willing to concede that, had they begun their careers in civilian life, they would probably have done better. Most certainly they were not just old "war horses" . . . especially the kind who had never been very near a war.

So it was not going to be easy . . . this explaining away of Lazy Ethel. There were men on Tuamani who remembered the circumstances of Pike's selection, and at the very least a few of them would begin to wonder if the original objectors were not right. The slightest inefficiency within the vast framework of the A.E.C. met with the most searching appraisal. The whole project, of which Zeus was only a minor adventure, was so vulnerable to criticism, the slightest foul-up shook everyone from top to bottom. Pike and his superiors on Tuamani were well aware that the breath-taking budget of their Commission was nearly impossible to justify no matter how the sabers clanged around the world. As a consequence, the general feeling within the colossus, and particularly among those directly charged with its confused destiny, was that the less said publicly about it the better.

Yes, indeedy, Pike thought. A cog like himself, who might even momentarily attract the spotlight, would be sacrificed instantly. He was at once haunted by three dismal visions, each originating in such a catastrophe. There would be the loss of his twenty-thousand annual pay. There would follow the hopeless prospect of trying to live on his pension, for there was not a dime saved in any bank. And Sue-Anne would seek permanent escape from her sorrows via the bottle. Lovely. And damn that weatherman to hell forever!

Besieged with his thoughts and visions, Pike leaned far back in his chair, clasped his hands behind his head, and broke wind. He was honestly embarrassed when Albright entered his office almost simultaneously. He at once pretended to be engrossed in his papers.

"Your barge awaits, sir," Albright said, swaying somewhat less than usual. "The last landing craft left twenty minutes ago and I think things are pretty well in hand. Everyone reasonably happy and all accounted for except yourself, Mrs. Pike, our weather wizard, and two marines I thought best to hold for the last boat. I presumed you intended that we should all ride along with you?"

"Yes," Pike answered vaguely. "Very good, Albright." Then he fell silent. How the hell was he going to explain this thing even to a nitwit like Albright? Finally he said, "You didn't have any particular trouble?"

"Rather to my surprise, I did not. How goes our affair with Lazy Ethel?"

"The situation has changed somewhat. Did you say there are still two marines here?"

"Yessir. Sergeant Doolan and one of his men. Peterson, I think his name is."

"Tell Doolan I want him to come up here and stand by the porch for possible assignment. Something special may turn up."

"Yessir."

"You'd better leave the other marine here too. Because of certain new developments, er . . . which I haven't time to explain just now, I'm going to change the setup a bit."

Pike prodded his shoulder with a gesture that had already become habit. Dammit, his neuritis was *still* with him. Amazing, he thought, the power of the human mind. Only it seemed the mind could change much more quickly than the symptoms it generated in the body. Nursing his shoulder, he said, "I'm sure you'll be needed at the camp, so you take off right now and you might as well take Mrs. Pike with you. When you get there have a good look around and see if we've omitted anything essential. Then send the boat back for me with any requests."

"What about Smith? Do I take him along?"

"No. He'd better remain here for the time being. I don't think he feels very well."

"Maybe he's been worrying too much about Lazy Ethel. I wish you'd give me the latest poop, sir. I'm naturally interested, and when I get over to the north side I'll have to answer a lot of questions."

"As far as our people are concerned this is still a drill. Let's leave it at that for just now."

Pike knew he was procrastinating and he could see that his indecision was suspect in Albright's eyes, but he was still fishing for some kind of escape. It seemed that every damned road he turned down was barricaded.

"They'll all be wanting to know when they can come back," Albright said.

"Avoid a direct answer to that question."

"Then you just want me to stall?"

"Yes. Just stall them off for a while. Organize a baseball game or something. I'll be along and straighten things out later. But don't let anyone start back until you receive word from me."

"Don't stall too long yourself, sir. Lazy Ethel may suddenly find some energy."

"Ho! Ho!" Pike forced a chuckle and wished that Albright would get the hell out of his office and fetch Sue-Anne, and they would both leave him in peace so he could do some thinking. "Ho! Ho! Don't you worry about old Zeb Pike. I'll clear out long before the advance patrol shows up. You'll find Mrs. Pike on the side porch or possibly in her room. Just give her a call. She's all ready to go."

Albright hesitated. He seemed about to speak, then apparently changed his mind. Pike thought with a strange sadness that his attempt at an about-face was the clumsiest he had ever observed. And the shorts only made matters worse. Also his actions would have been easier to stomach if Albright had not chosen to speak out a crisp and very British "Right!" as he marched away.

To prevent what he knew might become a flood of self-recrimination, Pike stood up. He gathered the papers marked SECRET and CLASSIFIED and began placing them back in the safe.

Adam had no exact idea how long he had lain on his bunk, simply shifting one of his long legs from time to time, mostly just staring at

the unpainted rafters above him. He tried unsuccessfully to sleep, anything to pass the time, and then decided that he might as well get his
packing done.

When he finally sat up and yawned he wondered if he actually had
slept, for certainly a considerable time had passed. The room was much
darker than when he had entered it, as dark as if it were nearly evening.
He glanced at his watch and found that it was only three-thirty. . . .
There was still a lot of this endless day remaining. Then he looked sleepily
out his window and saw that the sky was overcast, a heavy layer of stratus
from the look of things, and he thought, Well, it's going to rain and
for once I won't have to listen to Pike grousing about his movie.

He reached under his bunk and hauled out his duffel bag and, after
it, his small and much-battered suitcase. He crossed the room to his bureau and was about to pull out the top drawer when he saw that two
pocket books had been set pyramid fashion on top of the bureau. On
top of the books was an envelope, and around it someone had wrapped
a piece of white paper. He could not imagine why he had missed the odd
arrangement except that, when he had entered the room after leaving
Pike, he was not noticing much of anything. And when he stretched out
on the bed he had been facing the other way.

He removed the paper from the envelope and unfolded it. Inside he
recognized the bold scribble of his roommate.

Adam—
Sorry missed you in haste of departure. Everybody in a big flap about not
holding the boat up. Will see you later at picnic. Young lady in teletype
asked to leave enclosed for you. Congratulations! You are apparently
making some progress there.

                                                                    Peter

He let the paper fall to the floor and quickly opened the envelope.
It contained another note which was clipped to a long sheet of yellow
teletype paper. He moved quickly to the window for better light and
read eagerly.

Dear Adam,
Thought you might like to have this sheet as a souvenir. It came through
our copy machine after you went to put your head on a Pike. It doesn't
make sense to me, but then I'm not half-bright about these things anyway.
But I *will* write to you. Good luck.

                                                          Hastily,
                                                   Margaret Trumpey
P.S. You certainly cooked up quite a storm!!

Smiling sadly, Adam read the note through twice. Then he removed it from the teletype sheet and folded it carefully. He placed it in his pocket and began, without any real interest, to study the lines of gibberish on the teletype sheet. It was merely an exchange of messages between the other stations which were a part of Operation Zeus; they had automatically been recorded throughout the entire teletype circuit. At first it distressed him to think of himself as the instigator of all these words which clicked so magically through the atmosphere; then as the symbols and abbreviations translated themselves in his mind, his fingers pressed harder on the paper.

Each message was separated by a blank space to avoid any possibility of confusion. He did not study the time of each transmission until he sat down bewildered on his bunk and read the entire series through a second time. The first message was from the northernmost atoll concerned with Zeus, Oa Titia. It was consigned to Tuamani.

OA-TUA

RE OBSERVATION FROM PISTOL TWO BELIEVE LOCATION IN ERROR POSSIBLY DUE FAULTY TRANSMISSION PERIOD WE LOCATE CENTER LAZY ETHEL APPROX ONE HUNDRED MILES SOUTHEAST OF TRIGGER PERIOD MOVING SOUTH SOUTHEAST APPROX 20 KNOTS PERIOD CONFIRM PERIOD EOM

Then Tuamani had followed a few minutes later with an inquiry to the barren bit of coral upon which Zeus would actually be exploded. Adam knew that two very lonely men would be making weather observations there until only a few hours before the actual event.

TUA-TRIGGER

ADVISE YOU HAVE ANY DOPE ON LAZY ETHEL QUESTION MARK EOM

Their answer, Adam thought, was brief and certainly to the point.

TRIGGER-TUA

NEGATIVE PERIOD EOM

Tuamani was not so easily satisfied. The time of their next message was only a few minutes later.

TUA-TRIGGER

ADVISE PRESENT WEATHER YOUR STATION PERIOD EOM

Adam saw that the reply had not been sent for more than thirty minutes.

TRIGGER-TUA
OVERCAST PERIOD LOWER BROKEN STRATUS PERIOD LITE RAIN PERIOD
VISIBILITY TEN PERIOD CEILING 5000 PERIOD TEMP 68 PERIOD DEW
POINT 65 PERIOD WIND WEST TWENTY WITH GUSTS TO THIRTY PERIOD
BAROMETER 29 POINT 90 PERIOD FALLING SLOWLY PERIOD WHAT'S
THIS ALL ABOUT QUESTION MARK EOM

Adam could all too easily imagine the confusion on both Tuamani and Trigger.

TUA-TRIGGER
DUNNO PERIOD IF OA TITIA ANALYSIS CORRECT LAZY ETHEL IS TO THE
SOUTH OF YOU PERIOD EOM

TRIGGER-TUA
WHO IS LAZY ETHEL QUESTION MARK EOM

Adam groaned inwardly. Then he thought, It must surely have been some wag on Tuamani who sent the next transmission.

TUA-TRIGGER
YOU'LL FIND OUT PERIOD CONTINUE SENDING YOUR COMPLETE
WEATHER EVERY HOUR THAT IS IF YOU ARE ABLE PERIOD EOM

Trigger's reply was characteristically brief.

TRIGGER-TUA
WILDO PERIOD EOM

After a month's tour of duty on the explosion site, Adam concluded, the two men had probably lost the art of conversation both with each other and with the outside world.

He wished they had more to say, for . . . just a minute! Just an all-fired whopping damned minute!

Clutching the paper, Adam jumped to his feet. He went quickly to the window and examined it once more. Just an all-fired Jumpin' Judas minute! What was this? Oa Titia did not deny the existence of Lazy

Ethel! They said, or at least that's the way it looked . . . they claimed there *was* a storm and Oa Titia had almost as big a meteorological staff as Tuamani itself. They were only protesting its *location!* Could they have just talked themselves into it? Like Pike? Hell, no! They were technicians on Oa Titia and they knew what they were doing. Then there had to be a storm *somewhere* and they had just assumed it was Lazy Ethel. Their information was doubtless obtained from far more reliable sources than Adam Smith's imaginary fishing boat!

Hardly trusting his eyes, he quickly reviewed what Trigger had to say. Trigger was only a hundred and fifty miles from Nikki. If any real storm was to the south of it, then that distance could easily be halved, or it might put such a disturbance in a direct line to the west.

Glancing again at his watch he found that Trigger's reply with "present weather" was already more than four hours old. Rain? Trigger had been deliberately chosen because it was known to be the driest bit of vacant land in the hemisphere. Overcast, lower broken clouds . . . meaningless. But the wind! West at twenty knots . . . Gusts to *thirty!* He could not recall reading a single report from Trigger with a wind of over ten knots. And it was always from the east in accordance with the trades. It could be, then, that Trigger was feeling the effects of a storm's topside, presuming that a clockwise revolving air mass was to the south of them. The barometer was not especially low at the time the message was sent, but they had reported it as falling.

Adam looked out the window. So? Nikki was also overcast and the layer of clouds appeared to be thickening. Could it be that some genie had decided to give birth to a real Lazy Ethel?

He studied the line of palm trees which bordered Peter's new dump and the airstrip. They were nearly motionless. Only an occasional movement of a frond revealed that they were not painted against the sky. Adam cursed himself for thinking that the very air itself now appeared to be heavy and unusually oppressive. "Oh, cut it out!" he said aloud. "You are worse than Pike!"

But he could no longer tolerate the confines of his room. He hitched up his pants and walked thoughtfully down the corridor to the entrance of his quarters. He stepped outside and saw that Pistol Two was totally deserted. Cautioning himself that he must not allow his imagination to complicate his life again, he looked up at the sky. It was unrewarding. A vacuous, completely inanimate cloud mass blanketed all he could see. Now it did not even appear as if there might be rain. Yet visual observation, Adam knew only too well, was about as reliable as Pike's neuritis.

He had to reassure himself. He had to be sure that he was not going mad.

He started to walk slowly toward his office. To hell with Pike and his confinement to quarters. He was not a soldier. He was not even an employee any longer. I am a nothing, he thought. But there was a triangle and a T square on his drawing board which he had a perfect right to pack since he had paid for them himself. During the first part of his walk he refused to admit that he really wanted a look at his recording barometer. It just might be very interesting. Holy mackerel! Suppose . . .

By the time he was halfway down the empty street, he was running.

12

ADAM'S RECORDING BAROMETER was placed on the spare desk in his office. It was enclosed in a glass case which he removed every eight days to wind the mechanism. The device itself consisted of a clock-driven metal drum around which he secured a strip of paper each time he wound the spring. Vertical lines on the paper divided it into segments of eight days, and it was further marked with parallel horizontal lines representing the divisions of atmospheric pressure. As the drum turned, a scribe filled with red ink recorded the rise and fall of pressure on the paper. The scribe was activated by sensitive metal bellows and so the result was a fine line of red ink tracing the pressure changes. Since the day segments were further divided into hourly intervals, a very accurate history of the atmospheric pressure on Nikki was constantly visible.

The instrument expressed the pressure in inches of mercury, the red line rising or falling accordingly. On Nikki, Adam had never seen any erratic movement of the line. Ever since his arrival it had maintained a remarkably constant pattern, the line undulating in easy wavelets, rising slowly through the day and descending gradually toward evening. This formula had become so monotonous that Adam had occasionally wondered if the barometer was working properly. The peaks of the red line rarely exceeded thirty and three-tenths inches of mercury, and the valleys had never descended below twenty-nine and nine-tenths inches. These readings were normal companions to fine weather in any part of the world.

Now Adam stood aghast before the glass box. The last time he had looked at it was just before he went to see Pike. He saw that the red line had not departed from its habitually innocuous tracing until about an hour after he had left. Then it had begun a gradual descent, leveling off for approximately another hour at twenty-nine and nine-tenths inches of mercury.

The line's behavior during the next two hours caused him to emit a low whistle, the tone matching the descent of the line as if he were reading measures of music. For two successive hours the red line had plunged almost straight down, until now it terminated at an even twenty-nine inches! And apparently it was still descending! The lowest pressure Adam ever remembered hearing or even reading about was twenty-eight and three-tenths. That pressure had produced winds of one hundred and thirty miles an hour. . . . Supposedly the last recording before the anemometer itself was destroyed.

Wherever its center might be, and it could be very near, this storm was evidently not going to be any Lazy Ethel! It was going to be a beast, even if the scribe failed to descend another millimeter.

Adam quickly removed the glass cover from the instrument, and peeled off the paper graph. He wrapped a fresh paper around the drum, replaced the glass cover with hands that were far from steady, and started for the door. Then he paused very briefly for a last glance at the barometer. He was not at all sure he would see it or his office again.

He ran down the street, his long legs striking far out in front of him. By the time he reached Pike's house he was gasping for air and wet with perspiration. He labored up the steps and saw Doolan and one of his marines playing acey-deucy on the magazine table. Neither of the marines bothered to acknowledge his arrival with more than a grunt. They turned back to their cards as he crossed the porch.

It was dark in Pike's office, so dark that Adam was at first uncertain if the figure seated behind the desk was actually the man he sought. The voice reassured him.

"What's on your mind now, Mister Smith?"

"Governor, you've got to listen to me!"

"I thought I told you to stay in your quarters."

"Will you please turn on a light? I've got something to show you. It's extremely important."

"I couldn't turn on a light if I wanted to. The generating plant is shut down and you of all people ought to know why."

Adam fumbled for a moment with the strip of graph paper he had removed from the barometer drum.

"I don't know how I'm going to explain this to you, sir, but there *is* a storm. I have the proof right here. Please, haven't you got a flashlight or something?"

"No, I do not have a flashlight. At least one that works. And the reason that I haven't is because you are not the only idiot on Nikki. We even have our dishonest idiots. Now will you go back to your quarters like a reasonable man and wait until I send for you? Even a man in my position is entitled to some privacy."

Pike's voice came out of the gloom in patiently measured tones as if he were convinced he was dealing with a lunatic. There was also a distinct note of weariness, almost an appeal for understanding, which Adam had certainly never heard before. It was only with the greatest effort that he kept his own voice as calm.

"Governor . . . please. I *know* . . . I admit you have every reason to think I am out of my head. But there *is* a storm! You've just got to believe me. There is one hell of a blow coming and you've just got to do something about it right this minute."

"I believe you," Pike answered with such unctuous patience that Adam wanted to jump around his desk and haul him out of his chair. "I do indeed. If you say there's a storm, then of course there is one. That ends it. Now will you go . . . quietly?"

"No, I will not go. Not until you get those people off the north side of Nikki. I don't know for sure just where this storm is, but I'm convinced it's between us and Trigger, which would bring it in from the north. Those people just couldn't be in a worse position."

"I see. Where do you recommend I ask them to move? Up or down? We are short of both submarines and balloons."

Pike allowed a very taut ho-ho to escape his lips.

"Please, sir. This is a very serious business."

"You are absolutely right."

"If my guess is right, we haven't much time. Those people should be moved down to the south side of Nikki as fast as possible. They should be sent to the highest available ground and stay there. It may mean their lives, sir . . . not to mention our own. This has all been practically confirmed by other stations and even by Tuamani."

"Good old Tuamani," Pike said. "They also confirmed Lazy Ethel. Very agreeable people."

Adam could contain himself no longer. "For Christ's sake, Governor! Will you listen to me with an open mind!"

Then even in the darkness he saw Pike's fingers form themselves into their triangle. "Will you have the good sense to look at *this!*"

He placed the graph paper before the shadowy figure in the chair and after a frantic search through his pockets found his matches. He struck one, and the flare revealed not only the paper but Pike's cold appraisal of Adam's violently shaking hand.

"Just what is this gibberish?" Pike asked. "I'm afraid I am not much interested in stock-market trends at the moment."

"Our barometer readings for the past four hours."

Trying to control his finger, Adam managed to guide it along the red line. "See how it took a dive? Normal . . . that is, standard pressure, is twenty-nine and ninety-two hundredths inches. When I took this off the recorder just a few minutes ago it was already down to twenty-nine. A typhoon like the one that wiped out Wake Island probably didn't go much lower."

The match burned Adam's fingers before Pike spoke again. He had hardly glanced at the paper. "Look here, Smith," he said finally. "You have been under great strain . . . just why, I don't know. Perhaps I am the one to blame for it. Now, young man, I want to help you in any way I can, but if you think I am going to be taken twice for the damned fool and ask our people to move ten miles across a lagoon in the middle of the night, which it would be by the time we got there, you're very much mistaken. I don't want to be any more severe than necessary, but if you persist in annoying me and don't leave this office at once in a quiet and peaceful manner, I shall be forced to call on Sergeant Doolan for assistance."

"Governor! Dammit! *There is a storm!* Won't you recognize scientific fact? This is *not* something I invented! Throw me in irons! Shoot me! Do anything you want, but for the love of God get those people down to the south side of Nikki! *Now!* If you don't you may well be a murderer!"

Adam had not realized that in his anxiety he was shouting. And he was pounding his fist so hard on the desk all of the pencils and paper clips jumped from their positions. Then from the gloom he heard Pike's voice cut through his own and it was the high cry of a professional drill master.

"Sergeant Doolan! On the double!"

"You can't possibly realize what a wind force like this can do . . ."

Adam was not able to finish before he felt Doolan's hand seize his arm.

"Yessir?" Doolan said.

Pike was standing up now and he said coldly, "Sergeant, Mister Smith is unwell. Could you hear him shouting at me from your post on the porch?"

"Yessir."

"Mister Smith is having trouble with hallucinations. You will bear witness that his shouting was violent and of a threatening nature."

Doolan hesitated and glanced unhappily at Adam. "Well . . . it didn't sound too friendly."

"You heard him accuse me of being a murderer?"

"I did not say that!" Adam protested. "I said that if you didn't move those people . . ."

"I think you've said quite enough. Sergeant, for Mister Smith's own protection I think it best that he be placed in protective custody. You will take him to his quarters and see that he remains there until further orders."

"Yessir."

"Dismissed."

As the pressure of Doolan's hand tightened on his arm, Adam jerked away. He faced the dim figure of Pike. He was thoroughly angry now. Pike just had to listen.

"You can't do this to me. I'm a civilian! I demand . . ."

"This island has been declared in a state of emergency for several hours. Under those conditions I have full authority to perform my duty as I see it. Take him away, Sergeant."

As Doolan shoved him toward the door, Adam yelled over his shoulder, "But what about the storm? Sir, this is madness!"

"It certainly is. You will bear witness, Sergeant."

There was no arguing with Doolan. Though he was a good foot shorter than Adam, the Marines had taught him well. He was an expert at escorting a man to a destination which might not be of his own choosing. He did say, "Sorry, fella," as he propelled Adam across the porch and down to the road.

Pike watched them through the window, then returned to his desk and sat down again. Was there anything else that could go wrong? Now he was saddled with a madman, or at least a man who was suffering such mental tribulations he was as much a problem as a squalling baby. It was going to be difficult taking Smith over to the north side when the boat returned. He would undoubtedly start yelling again, accusing everybody of all kinds of things, and at the very least it would be extremely embarrassing. But he couldn't be left behind either. Left alone he might cut his wrists, hang himself, or some such messy thing . . . and Tuamani

would send down investigators on top of investigators. Technically he
was still a government responsibility and his family could bring all kinds
of charges. The thing could snowball and might even become another
Jeanette inquiry. A whole Congressional Committee had been called on
that little episode, and even the best advocates of the United States Navy
couldn't save the reputation of the *Jeanette's* commanding officer. Pike
recalled, with sorrow, that the *Jeanette* affair had also concerned antagonism between a civilian and a military man. Moreover the civilian,
whose name Pike tried desperately to recall, had been assigned to that
expedition as weatherman. Personal persecution was alleged and damn
near proven, even though both parties involved had lost their lives before
the inquiry was held. It made no difference that the affair took place on
a ship locked in Arctic ice. It was a U.S. government ship and it could
just as well have been Nikki.

Pike rose from his chair and began circling his desk very slowly. All
right, what could be done with Smith? God, what a thorn! A complete
pain in the neck ever since the first day he became noticeable, which
would be the very first night on Nikki. Which would be the time he
more or less said the movie was not going to be rained out, and it was.

Reviewing that incident with distaste, Pike recalled that he had said a
few sharp words on the matter, intended more to express his disappointment than anything else. Had it begun then? Had Smith nursed those
statements, allowing them to ferment in an already troubled brain until
everything said to him was taken amiss? If so, Pike was sorry, very sorry,
he mused, for people in mental distress deserved sympathy and understanding. Yes . . . every person involved in a project like Zeus should
be cleared through psychologists *before* they were hired. Then their presence would not present a lot of problems to operational personnel who
had enough troubles without delving into motivations and kindred mysterious manifestations they were not trained to recognize. Much less, offer any cure.

He sat on the edge of his desk and picked up the strip of graphed
paper Adam had left. He studied the red line. Here was a perfect example
of what a tortured mind could produce. A trained medic would know
exactly how to handle it. How to sympathize and satisfy. Smith was a
"Section 8." The army had once issued a complete manual on the treatment of psychos. He should have read it more carefully. His own attempts
at agreement had obviously been all wrong, for he had only succeeded
in making Smith become more violent. Pike did remember reading that
the first step in the pacification of any demented personality, whether

suffering from shell shock or otherwise, was agreement. All right. At first he had deliberately agreed there was a storm. And what happened? More nonsense.

He was about to crumple the strip of paper and throw it into the wastebasket when he thought better of it. No. It should be kept. If there was ever an inquiry, particularly one which might somehow try to advance the proposition that he was a fiend incarnate and had devoted his entire time on Nikki to the persecution of a single innocent civilian, then this reflected the unhappy scrawling of a sick mind possessed by one Smith! What tortures he must suffer, having now apparently convinced himself there really was a Lazy Ethel. The name alone could hardly have been conceived in a totally normal mind. Perhaps he might feel a little better if he had something to eat. That, thought Pike, is the very least I can do.

Then he went to the window and leaned through it until he could survey the length of the porch. As he had hoped, one of Doolan's marines sat with his feet propped up on the magazine table. He appeared to be dozing.

"Marine?"

Peterson jumped to his feet. He made one quick pass at his sleepy eyes before his heels clicked to attention.

"Yessir!"

"Any sign of my boat yet?"

"No, sir."

"It's still a little early although how you could observe it with your eyes closed is beyond me."

"Sorry, sir."

Pike held the keys out to him.

"One of these fits the mess-hall kitchen. I want you to go down there and scrounge up a sandwich or two. There ought to be plenty of things lying around. Take them down to Mister Smith's quarters with my compliments. I believe he's in Building C. If you like, make a sandwich for yourself and Doolan, too."

"Yessir. Thank you very much, sir."

Peterson reached for the keys and stepped back.

"You don't happen to have a workable flashlight, do you?"

"Not with me, sir. But I think Doolan has a couple stashed down to our own quarters."

"Bring them back with you. If my boat is late we might need them."

"Yessir."

"Oh . . . and check around the kitchen for some candles. I recall several birthday cakes since we've been here. The cook just might keep them handy . . . or they could be in the bakeshop."

"Yessir."

"On your way."

To Pike's immense satisfaction, Peterson saluted smartly and executed a perfectly timed about-face. As he marched off the porch Pike shook his head with approval. There were a few left. Yes . . . a very few real soldiers left here and there. Even in the Marines.

He looked up at the heavy sky and his momentary pleasure was destroyed. Poor Smith, indeed. Poor Zeb Pike! Because of the tricks played by his own mind, his shoulder was throbbing unmercifully. And he still had to find some explanation for all the trouble with Lazy Ethel!

After considerable persuasion Doolan allowed Adam to stop by his office long enough to pick up his barometer. Nestling the instrument tenderly in his arms, stepping as lightly as he could so the scribe would not be shaken, Adam carried it to his quarters. He placed it gently on the writing table between his own bunk and Peter Hildebrandt's. Then with Doolan leaning casually against the door jamb, bored almost beyond his richly developed capacity for boredom, the two waited in the gathering darkness.

Adam paced miserably back and forth between Doolan and the window. He halted frequently to peer at the glass box. When he had taken it from his office the scribe had descended to twenty-eight and ninety-five hundredths inches. Now it was down to twenty-eight ninety. Adam saw that it was still slipping downward.

When he paused in his pacing and remained absolutely motionless, listening carefully, he could hear the faint ticking of the clock mechanism which turned the drum. It was so still outside the window. The palm fronds were now dead.

"You hear that?" he said to Doolan. "That's your time running out. And mine, too. Everybody's."

"I don't hear nothin'," Doolan answered with an obliging smile that said if Adam wanted to hear things it was all right with him as long as he didn't start any trouble.

"Listen!" Adam said, waggling his finger at the glass box. "Just listen . . . that's all I ask you."

"I *am* listenin'. You tryin' to tell me you got some time bomb or somethin' there?"

"In a way you might say it is. And the fuse is getting awfully short."

"I wish you wouldn't talk that way, Smith. I almost believe you. You'll have me buckin' for Section 8 if you don't shut up."

"You'd better believe me unless you want to get blown to kingdom come. And everybody on this island with you."

"It don't look like no bomb to me and in case it's any never mind to you I sweated out a whole course in demolition at Camp Pendleton."

"This isn't the same kind of demolition, Doolan. It's going to be total and complete. It might even be as big as Zeus. Maybe bigger."

"Sure. All alone you're going to do better than the U.S. Government who only has to throw a couple of billion bucks around trying."

"I'm not going to do it. God is."

"Oh, brother!"

Doolan shook his head sadly and folded his arms across his chest. Then he sighed and said aloud to himself, "What did I ever do to deserve this?"

Looking at Adam he asked not unkindly, "How do you feel?"

"Terrible."

"Sure you do. Why don't you just calm down and hit your sack for a while? You'll feel better all around when you wake up."

"You think I can sleep with the end of the world coming? Practically right here?"

"Keep on and you'll have me singing Judgment Day right along with you. My aunt from Carolina used to sing it all the damned day long, so I even know the words. Please. Will you lie down?"

Adam had not the slightest intention of lying down. Somehow, some way, he must reach the northern side of Nikki and talk to the people there. Especially one Margaret Trumpey. But there was no getting past Doolan unless he could be convinced. Looking at him now, his face a mask of studied indifference, Adam knew it was not going to be an easy task.

"Doolan. Come here a minute."

"Unh-uh. You stay there, and I stay here."

"Why do you think I'm under arrest?"

"Now look. I don't want to hurt your feelings."

"You think I'm crazy, don't you?"

"Well . . ." Doolan's voice trailed off in embarrassment.

"Do you?"

"Well . . . like Pike said, maybe you ain't been feeling too good. You admitted that yourself. Just now."

"I didn't mean it that way, Doolan. I feel fine . . . physically and mentally."

Adam spoke slowly and distinctly as if he were talking to a very small child. "I'm only deeply concerned about a terrible storm I am sure is coming. This little instrument foretells a storm, do you understand that? I know how to read it. Pike doesn't. The people who went on the so-called picnic are going to be in very great danger if someone doesn't tell them to move to the south side of the island . . . and even then I can't guarantee their safety. I want to warn those people and get them moving while there's still time. Look out the window, Doolan. Have you ever seen it so dark at this hour? If you don't believe me or this instrument, look at that sky. Have you ever seen it look like that before?"

"It looks like we're probably going to have some rain. Too bad. It'll spoil the picnic."

"You bet we're going to have some rain. Tons of it. So much you won't be able to see the end of your nose. And there's a damn good chance the sea will sweep right over Nikki. Are you listening to me, Doolan? If you've got an ounce of heart for those people out there, if you've got half a mind of your own, you'll let me talk to them. I won't try to escape. You can go right along with me if you want. May God strike me dead this minute, Doolan, if I'm not telling you the truth."

There was a long silence. Doolan puckered his brow. He shifted his weight from one foot to the other, and his gun belt squeaked with the movement. He compressed his lips tightly, then blew air through the crease that was his mouth.

"Look at the instrument, Doolan. It's gone down some more. I didn't cause it to do that. You've been right here. You've seen for yourself, I haven't touched it. The *storm* is moving that scribe."

"Pike says you stay here. What you want to do? Get me busted? I like these stripes."

"They won't show up so well on your dead body floating in water."

"Aw, come off it."

He was making progress, Adam thought. Not much, but a little. Doolan was shifting uneasily from one foot to the other now. There was, unless he was being too optimistic, Adam decided, the slightest suggestion of fear in his eyes.

"Doolan, listen to this. If you'll go with me to the north side and a storm *doesn't* come, I'll swear I came up behind you and hit you on the head and escaped. We'll stage things so it looks like you went beyond the call of duty and recaptured me. You'll probably get a medal."

"You don't sneak up behind no good marine and cold-conk him. Especially not a sergeant."

"Then I'll run away from you. I'll run slowly so you can't miss. You can shoot me down deader than a mackerel. How much more can I offer than that?"

Doolan lit a cigarette. He filled his lungs and exhaled with such force the smoke went straight out from his mouth. He repeated the process immediately. "It would look phoney," he said finally. "Besides, I don't want to shoot you or nobody else."

"Doolan. You just heard me stake my life on this. No matter what you think, I'm not that crazy. I'll stay in front of you every minute of the time. All I want to do is talk to those people! Look at that sky, Doolan. It's getting darker and darker. We won't be able to see each other pretty soon!"

Doolan rubbed the end of his nose violently. "How would we get there? There ain't no boats."

"I don't know. There must be a canoe or something that will float in the native village. If there isn't, we'll have to do it the hard way and hike it around the beach."

"You mean swim that channel?"

"Yes, I do. And I'm not much of a swimmer, either. That's how much I believe in this thing. If I drown, you can just say I ran away and committed suicide by jumping in the channel. The main thing is we've got to get going right now."

"Nuts."

Doolan again drew heavily on his cigarette. He closed his eyes for a moment and said through the smoke, "This whole operation is nuts."

"You're an intelligent man, Doolan. You didn't get to be a Marine sergeant for nothing. You can read an instrument, and especially this one, as well as I can. The least you can do is take a look . . . just to satisfy yourself I'm not talking entirely through my hat. Come on. What you'll see on this instrument now is something you can tell your grandchildren about. You'll be looking at history . . . certainly the beginning of one of the biggest storms in history. Go ahead. Look! I'll stand way over at this end of the room if you still don't trust me! I couldn't possibly get within three feet of you!"

Slowly, so slowly Adam hoped he was not just imagining the movement, Doolan rolled his shoulder about the door jamb and looked at the glass box on the table. Adam held his breath as Doolan's hand slipped down to his holster. Then he placed his weight on both feet and faced the table. Adam waited in agonized silence as Doolan took a single hesitant step into the room. He halted, his head cocked suspiciously to one side, looking at Adam and then at the glass box. Another step toward the table. Another. Adam was sure that, if in the next moment he spoke, Doolan would certainly retreat.

Another step and Doolan bent down, placing his powerful hands on his knees. His eyes were level with the instrument.

"I can hear it ticking all right," he whispered.

"Sure you can. Look at that red line. The paper is marked off in hours. See how the line goes down."

Doolan studied the interior of the glass box as if it contained a snake. His underlip shot forward and he twisted it around and around. He scratched his forehead and wrinkled his nose. Then his eyes rolled upward to look at Adam. "It's gone down, all right. I can see that."

"Smart man. Now figure it out for yourself. That's an expensive instrument. *There's something driving that line down and it isn't me!*"

"I don't really see it move."

"Of course you don't. You can't really see the hands of a clock move, either. But if you stood there even half an hour, you'd see the difference."

"Maybe we better take this gadget up to Pike and show it to him."

"I already did that. At least I took the previous paper. That's what our big argument was about. I was yelling at him because he just wouldn't listen. You know Pike. He's a hard-headed man."

"All generals are hard-headed. They got a brass brain."

"You're absolutely right, Doolan. Now can we go while there's maybe still time?"

"I still think we oughta see Pike."

"He'll only stop us, you know that. He'll stop us because, like all generals, he hates to approve anything that isn't his own idea."

"Yeah . . ." Doolan said very slowly. He rose to an erect position and glowered at the sky beyond the window. "Yeah . . . maybe you got somethin' there. It wouldn't be the first time I stuck my neck out."

"Good!" Adam said quietly. "Let's go."

"I'll be right behind you. All the time. And I got every marksmanship medal in the book. Just keep that in mind."

Pike fretted in his office. Now the gloomiest doubts assailed him, as dark as the sky outside his window. He had already envisioned a series of ugly spectacles in which he played a most ignominious role. He had suffered through a preliminary hearing on Tuamani during which he found himself very hard put to account for certain of his decisions; and all too quickly thereafter, he saw himself in Washington, gulping and perspiring before a committee which practically included both houses of Congress. It was an easy mental journey from there to the hard pavement of a used-car lot. He saw himself passing out business cards with the legend ALMOST HONEST JOHN'S SUPER BARGAINS, prominent on the face. His own name was along the bottom not nearly so large. Zebulon Pike—Sales Representative. At least, he thought, the "U.S.A.-Ret." would be neither necessary nor proper.

Ye gods, suppose there really was a storm! Suppose Smith was not crazy at all, but for once in his miserable life had been perfectly sincere. If there was any truth to his story about the barometer he might still be ready for a padded cell and yet, from habit if nothing else, recognize a storm. Oh, no. The case was cut and dried. Pure, unadulterated case of vengeance against imagined injuries. Then why was it so damn dark outside? It was only a little after five. And where *was* everybody? For a terrifying moment he saw himself as entirely alone on Nikki . . . the last man on earth after a number of Zeuses had been exploded. Ye gods, it was Zeb Pike who was about ready for a padded cell!

He wished now that he had not sent Sue-Anne along with Albright. She made very good sense, Sue-Anne. When she was sober, of course. He could have talked this whole thing out with her and she would have settled his mind. She would undoubtedly say the whole business was a tempest in a teapot and what in tarnashin was he worrying about? Forget it, honey, she would say. You're just making a peck of trouble for yourself because you take everything too seriously. She would say you just can't get out of the habit of doing your duty and another man would have sluffed the whole thing off as just one of those things. She would say things like that . . . if she was sober. In the opposite condition she would be more likely to say Zebulon, you bonehead, a trained technician came to you and told you there was going to be a storm and you told him he was crazy. That's just like the time you told one of the world's best armament manufacturers his outfit didn't know how to rifle a gun. It just cost you your only chance at Staff College, that's all. You were still singing the praises of French seventy-fives when the Germans were lining up their eighty-eights, which happened to be very similar to the gun the manufacturer only asked the opportunity to prove. When you were in procurement, and it was a good thing they got you out of there before we lost the war, if a new item didn't come down through channels it was no damn good. Not for your popgun brain, anyway.

Yes, if Sue-Anne was loaded she might say a few things like that.

Brooding on what Sue-Anne might have said, and what she still might have occasion to say, Pike remembered his boat. Where the hell was it? Albright had been lolly-dollying again. And where the hell was that marine? How long did it take to make a sandwich even if you used a bayonet to slice it? And what about those flashlights he was going to bring? Where the hell was everybody!

As if his unspoken demand had a magical power to bring results, he heard footsteps on the porch. The steps approached quickly, and in a moment Peterson snapped to attention before him. His salute was marred by a sandwich in his hand.

"Where the hell have you been?" Pike said, choosing for the moment to ignore the sandwich.

"Looking for Doolan and that other guy, sir."

"What do you mean, looking for them? I told you where they were."

"They ain't there, sir. I looked every place for them, sir. I looked in the quarters you told me and then I looked everywhere else. I even looked down to the wharf."

"And you couldn't find them?" Pike said incredulously.

"No, sir. I didn't see *nobody*. It's kind of scary. Every place is deserted like it was a ghost town or something and most places are locked up. I even looked down to our own quarters thinking maybe Doolan might have gone back there if maybe he forgot something or run out of cigarettes or . . ."

Pike jumped to his feet. "You must be blind, marine. We'll see about this. Did you bring some flashlights?"

"Yessir," Peterson said, reaching into his hip pocket. "I brought two. They were all I could find. One of them, the battery is sort of weak."

Pike reached out and took a flashlight from Peterson's hand.

"Follow me."

"Yessir. Jeez, it's just like we are the last two people in the world out here."

Pike shot a quick frown of disapproval at Peterson and marched out of the office.

By the time they had stomped through the building which contained Adam's room, then doubled back to the Marine quarters, Pike was yelling Doolan's name with such force his voice echoed and re-echoed between the buildings and along the deserted streets of Pistol Two. With Peterson half-trotting along a few paces behind him, Pike challenged each building as they passed, though most of the windows were crossed with boards and the doors were shut tightly. Now as they returned to the main street, Peterson shivered at the sound of Pike's voice, which was becoming increasingly hoarse and eerie in the gloom.

It was so dark that the oval pattern from Pike's flashlight sweeping the street and the buildings was clearly visible. The blob of light revealed nothing which might suggest that Pistol Two had once been an active settlement. A few drops of rain spattered against their faces, and Pike began to divide his attention between the buildings and the sky. His demands also lost concentration, for he began to call out Smith as often as he called the name of Doolan. Peterson wished he would abandon the search. Somehow it was like yelling in a graveyard.

Pike halted before the weather office. Though it was dark and obviously unoccupied, he called out Smith's name with such authority and assurance Peterson would not have been overly surprised if an answer had come through the screen windows. Pike stalked back to the middle of the street, faced about, and glanced at the building as if its very silence was deliberate. Then suddenly he tilted his head to one side and pointed a cautioning finger at Peterson. "Listen!" he said furtively. "Do you hear what I hear?"

Peterson listened obediently, turning his head in imitation of Pike's. He did not at this moment want to hear anything unless it was the comforting growl of Doolan's voice.

"It's in there," Pike said, taking a step toward the communications shack.

"Sounds like a typewriter," Peterson said.

Pike crossed the street quickly and, rising on his toes, peered through the screen window. Immediately afterward he moved around to the door. "It's one of the teletypes. Somebody left the damned thing on."

He tried the door. It was locked. "We'll have to kick it in," he said to Peterson.

Pike's frustration semed to find outlet on the door. He kicked at it so viciously Peterson had little chance to assist him before the door collapsed. Pike charged through the splintered wood and directed his flashlight at the teletype machines. The last one in the line continued to click busily. Then it stopped very suddenly.

Pike approached it warily. How could the machine function if the main power supply was off? As he had ordered! That idiot chief electrician! If he had disobeyed orders he would have to do some fancy answering. Or was he so dumb he had just gone off to the picnic and forgotten about the one thing he was presumably on Nikki to attend?

While Peterson watched, Pike's flashlight swept the office. It came to rest on the cord of the overhead light. He reached out suspiciously and jerked the cord. The light flashed on and both men blinked at the illumination.

"Well, I'll be damned!" Pike said.

"Sure is nice to see some light, sir . . . that is, after stumbling around with flashlights for so long."

"That idiot's idiot!" Pike said. "I'll tell you one thing, young man, giving orders to civilians is a waste of breath."

"Yessir," Peterson said, looking out the window. "You want I should go get us some rain gear, sir? It's beginning to come down pretty good."

"Do that. You'll find mine hanging just inside my office door. Bring Mrs. Pike's, too. It's in the hallway."

"Yessir."

"I'll meet you down at the wharf in five minutes. My boat should be along any minute now."

"Yessir."

"On the double."

At the door Peterson turned as if reluctant to travel the street alone. "I guess this will sort of spoil the picnic, sir."

"Yes. I'm afraid it might," Pike said absently. He was staring at the line of teletype machines and almost appeared to have forgotten Peterson. "Keep your eye out for Doolan and Smith," he said.

"I just got a hunch I won't see them, sir," Peterson said forlornly.

When he was gone Pike crossed the room very slowly until he stood in front of the last teletype machine. He leaned forward and saw the end of a message beneath the glass. The signature was Keating. It would be from Tuamani then.

Hesitantly, almost as if he knew the contents of the message, he reached for the end of the yellow paper which had fallen over the back of the machine. Now he saw that there were several messages. The machine had been busy, all right, apparently working ever since the girls had left. The paper reached nearly to the floor behind the machine.

He carefully pulled it upward, then found the knob on the side of the case. He turned it until the last message was above the glass and tore the whole paper off. He moved beneath the light. Much of the printing was unintelligible to him, but there were parts which caused him to pull back the desk chair and sit down.

TUA-TRIGGER
HOW ABOUT YOUR PRESENT WEATHER QUESTION MARK

TRIGGER-TUA
YES MAN PERIOD WE KNOW WHAT YOU MEAN NOW PERIOD PRESENT
WEATHER HEAVY RAIN PERIOD VISIBILITY NIL PERIOD WIND SOUTH
SIXTY KNOTS GUSTING TO SEVENTY PERIOD LONESOME PERIOD

TUA-TRIGGER
HOW CAN YOU BE LONELY WITH LAZY ETHEL QUESTION MARK BE OF
GOOD HEART PERIOD CENTER OF STORM NOW DEFINITELY LOCATED
MORE THAN HUNDRED MILES SOUTHEAST YOUR STATION PERIOD YOU
ONLY HAVE EDGE PERIOD

TRIGGER-TUA
TAIL END YOU MEAN QUESTION MARK

TUA-TRIGGER
ROGER PERIOD NIKKI WILL GET THE FULL BLAST PERIOD

TRIGGER-TUA
WHEN QUESTION MARK

TUA-TRIGGER
DUNNO FOR CERTAIN PERIOD SOME TIME TONITE PERIOD ALL AT-
TEMPTS CONTACT PISTOL TWO SINCE 13:00 NEGATIVE PERIOD WE ARE
GOING TO SEND BLIND TO THEM AS SOON WE HAVE MORE DOPE PERIOD

TRIGGER-TUA
GLAD TO BE HERE PERIOD

TUA-TRIGGER
CONTINUE TO STAND BY FOR POSSIBLE INTERCEPTION MESSAGE FROM
PISTOL TWO PERIOD CIRCUIT MAY BE LOUSED UP PERIOD EOM

TRIGGER-TUA
WILDO PERIOD

There followed an interchange of messages between Tuamani and Oa
Titia.

TUA-OA
YOU HEARD ANYTHING FROM PISTOL TWO QUESTION MARK

OA-TUA
NEGATIVE PERIOD

TUA-OA
STAND BY FOR POSSIBILITY PERIOD THEY PROBABLY HAVING PLENTY
TROUBLE ALREADY PERIOD

OA-TUA
WILDO PERIOD

Pike noted that the time of the answer from Oa Titia was fifteen hundred. Over two hours ago. There was a blank space, then several lines of X's interspersed with frequent A-A's as if the machine had developed a speech impediment. Finally he came to a long message which caused him to groan audibly. He saw that it had been sent an hour before and was specifically addressed to himself.

TUA-PISTOL TWO PERIOD URGENT PERIOD PIKE
LAZY ETHEL NOW DEFINITELY LOCATED WITH CENTER APPROXIMATELY
SIXTY MILES WEST OF YOU PERIOD SAME MOVING IN GENERAL EAST-
ERLY DIRECTION AT APPROXIMATELY TEN KNOTS PERIOD EXPECT
WINDS POSSIBLY EXCEEDING ONE HUNDRED PLUS HEAVY RAINS PERIOD
STRONGLY RECOMMEND MOVING ALL PERSONNEL TO ANY AVAILABLE
SHELTER SOUTH SIDE REPEAT SOUTH SIDE NIKKI ATOLL AT ONCE PERIOD
RESCUE SHIPS WITH ALL DISASTER SUPPLIES ALREADY ENROUTE YOUR
ASSISTANCE PERIOD AIRPLANES WILL ARRIVE FOR CASUALTY EVACUA-
TION SOON AS CONDITIONS PERMIT PERIOD YOU AND PISTOL TWO
METEOROLOGIST MERIT COMMENDATION FOR BEING ON TOES PERIOD
WITH FEWER FACILITIES YOU SPOTTED LAZY ETHEL LONG BEFORE ANY
OF US PERIOD GOOD LUCK PERIOD

                                                                    KEATING

There were two more messages, the second of which had just been transmitted.

TUA-PISTOL TWO URGENT
IF STILL ABLE TO COMMUNICATE ADVISE YOUR LATEST WEATHER AND
DISPERSAL OF PERSONNEL PERIOD

There was, of course, no answer. Where the reply from Pistol Two should have been, the paper offered only a blank space to Pike's agonized eyes.

TUA-ALL STATIONS-SPECIAL
ASSUME PISTOL TWO EVACUATED PERIOD HOWEVER ALL STATIONS ON
CIRCUIT WILL STAND BY FOR POSSIBLE MESSAGE INTERCEPTION FROM

THERE PERIOD CIRCUIT WILL REMAIN CLOSED TO ALL EXCEPT EMER-
GENCY TRANSMISSION UNTIL LAZY ETHEL LEAVES AREA PERIOD

KEATING

For the first time in his life Zebulon Pike looked down at his strong hands and found himself wishing for a gun. There was, he thought with a mind that had suddenly become remarkably clear, only one answer. His West Point ring glistened in the light and he found it a hideous mockery. Other officers who could not live with themselves had found the answer before . . . and, at least, there was some sympathy for their memory. It was the oldest creed of the true soldier in any country, as ancient and time-honored as the Roman Legions. Yes, he could easily borrow the marine's automatic.

He stood up with the definite intention of appropriating Peterson's gun as soon as they met on the wharf. Nor was it fear which caused him to change his mind as he carefully turned out the light and left the communications shack. Zebulon Pike had been laughed at aplenty since the day he was first commissioned a second lieutenant. Zebulon Pike was a paper warrior with a very few friends who had nursed him through a whole blundering career, and he could think of three times when only near miracles had saved him from earlier disgrace. But no one had ever accused him of not being a soldier. This last time for Zeb Pike was not going to be a failure. He was not going to cover for himself. He would get the people of Pistol Two down to the south side of Nikki, behind the hill. He would do so no matter what difficulties were involved.

He marched calmly through the rain, his shoulders well back, his arms swinging in easy cadence. He knew now that he was not parading before others, but before himself, and he marched proudly. When his people were safe, or at least as safe as they possibly could be under the circumstances, then he would get on with the other business. As befitted Zebulon Pike, General, U.S.A.

When he reached the wharf, Peterson was waiting for him. He was standing beneath the eaves of the warehouse huddled in his poncho. Pike forced an easy smile when he saw him.

"Any sign of our boat yet?"

"Yessir. I saw the lights. They should be here in a minute. You want your rain gear, sir?"

"Yes. Thank you very much. Fine night for a picnic, eh, marine? Ho. Ho!"

Compared to the terrain which now confronted them, Adam and Doolan saw that their swim across the channel might rate as the easiest part of their expedition. They had found the native village completely abandoned. A few minutes' search of the beach area confirmed their fast-growing fears that nothing which might be practical for crossing the lagoon had been left behind. They discovered one ancient canoe beneath a copra-drying shed, but it was badly split along the bottom, the out-rigger was missing, and there were no paddles. So after only a few minutes' hopeless discussion of its suitability they set off along the beach, following the inside rim of the coral ring which formed Nikki.

The first mile along the beach proved easy going. Then, just as the first drops of rain began to fall, they met the first shocking obstacle. They came upon an inlet which could not be circled because of the heavy entanglement of brush surrounding its entire border. This inlet was much wider than the channel between the native village and Pistol Two.

For the first half-mile they were able to wade across the inlet although they stumbled frequently on the uneven bottom and Adam, who was in the lead, stepped off twice into deep holes and floundered wildly before he could find sure footing again. Soon afterward the floor of the lagoon sank abruptly and they were forced to swim the last part of the inlet. At last they reached a slime-covered ledge of coral which lay only a few inches below the surface. Doolan promptly sat down and cursed Adam with monotonous devotion to the details of his ancestry. When he had exhausted his extensive vocabulary and his words had brought no reaction from Adam other than a mild request that he get on his feet so they could move again, Doolan said grudgingly, "You long-legged son of a bitch, you should have been a marine."

"I'm hardly the type, but thank you anyway," Adam answered and started off sploshing through the shallow water.

It was nearly dark. The lagoon was now a deep gray and indefinite mass on their right hand. The rain obscured any horizon. The land was a featureless blob narrowing to a vanishing point as far ahead as they could see. Its existence as part of a giant circle was not apparent in the half-light and the minor configurations were never recognizable until they actually stumbled upon them.

One inlet followed another. They were able to work their way around a few without entering the lagoon, but the majority required wading at least waist deep and several obliged them to swim. Doolan complained they were making less than a mile an hour and stated with profane conviction that they would never reach the north side of Nikki until the following morning . . . if they ever did. Adam remained silent, pausing only occasionally to glance at the fast-darkening sky.

Eventually they came upon a region of the beach where the undergrowth was impenetrable. They turned inland, away from the lagoon, and toward the sea itself. Here, Adam stubbornly refused to pause for a rest and led Doolan through several hundred yards of brambles and cactus-like undergrowth, which sliced at their clothing and left long, deep cuts on their skin. Finally they were able to turn forward again, and with the last light they moved along the narrow strip of land separating the lagoon and the sea.

They found it easier to avoid the beach itself although the terrain consisted of seemingly endless undulations of coral and sand. They panted up the steep sides of hummocks, often sliding backward in the loose sand, and they staggered clumsily across deep pits filled with sea shells and rotting vegetation. It was more than two hours before they saw a glow of light ahead and knew for certain that they were approaching the north side of Nikki. The rain was still spasmodic and much lighter than Adam had dared hope. He was grateful, too, that as yet there was no definite indication of wind.

They paused for only a moment to look at the light. Doolan moved beside Adam and catching his breath said huskily, "Now *I'll* be a red-haired son of a bitch! We almost got it made."

When the boat snorted up to the wharf Pike was astonished to see Sue-Anne standing in the bow. She was the only passenger. She was wet and he knew that she was angry. When she held out her hand for aid to the wharf, Pike ignored it and jumped down beside her.

"What are you doing back here, Sue-Anne?"

"What am I doin'? I came back for some bourbon, that's what. Who but you would think of slinging a picnic without any liquor? Why, there's not a drop up there, as if it wasn't the dullest place I evah been, anyway. What are we supposed to be doing? Working for our Eagle Scout badge?"

"Shut up."

Pike said it quietly, yet very firmly. Then he turned aft to the boat operator. "Shove off," he said. "Get us back to the north side at full speed. Give her everything you've got!"

Peterson slid reluctantly into the boat. "Sir? What about Doolan and that Smith fella? We just leave them here?"

"I'm sure they've gone already. We have a lot more people to worry about."

The operator gunned his engines and the boat slid swiftly away from the dock. Pike turned to Sue-Anne and held out a raincoat. She regarded both the coat and her husband in stunned disbelief.

"Zebulon Pike," she said finally. "You gone right out of your mind?"

"Maybe I found that I had one."

"You told me to shut up," she said accusingly.

"I did. Put this raincoat on."

She hesitated; then without taking her eyes from him she moved into the coat. Something in his manner and his eyes caused her voice to soften.

"What's wrong, Zebulon? What's come over you?"

"Lazy Ethel."

"Who?"

"Lazy Ethel. It's the name of a storm. It's coming this way fast and it isn't going to be any picnic. Because of me you'll all be lucky to get out with your lives."

"What have you got to do with a storm? *You* haven't had a drink, have you, Zebulon? If so, I'll never forgive . . ."

"No. I haven't been drinking although I might just as well have been. I've been blind enough and stupid enough to qualify for a lot of things."

His voice trailed off while he took her hand and held it thoughtfully. Then he said, "I wouldn't admit it to myself, but I've known what you've thought of me all these years. And you were right. You married the dumbest soldier in the American Army."

"Zebulon . . . I don't know you just now! You're tired. You're in trouble."

"I'm not a bit tired."

He turned aft and yelled at the boat operator. "Can't you make this thing go any faster?"

The operator shook his head. Pike gently placed his arm around Sue-Anne. Looking at the black lagoon, he said, "I'm sorry, Precious. This night isn't going to be much fun for anybody . . . especially not for you."

13

THOSE WHO WERE ENCAMPED on the north side of Nikki passed the early part of the afternoon with little complaint or discomfort. The children, shepherded with varying degrees of success by their mothers, found endless, screeching pleasure in their exploration of the sand hummocks. Barney Dunbar and a group of laborers seasoned by years of employment on government projects, and long accustomed to completely incomprehensible deviation from the specific tasks they had been hired to perform, took the opportunity to sleep. Many of them snored with gusto in spite of the squadrons of sand fleas which circled and chandelled about their upturned faces.

Albright was everywhere, mincing and swaying and mashing potatoes with his voice, and yet showing surprising concern for the welfare of his charges. When Aubrey Tinsman decided to go for a swim and cut his foot on a jagged piece of coral and was nearly reduced to tears as a result, Albright acted as a crutch so that he could limp to Dr. Case for treatment. Not long afterward Mrs. Walsacki came to him and complained that something should be done about allotting separate relief areas for the men and women. She had just been surprised by Miguel, the bartender, as she squatted behind one of the low bushes which topped the sand hummocks. She was more angry than embarrassed. Albright sought out Peter Hildebrandt, who at once took the project to his heart. Refusing all outside aid and advice, he erected two remarkably efficient shelters of tarpaulin and sticks.

Albright was less successful in the latter part of the day, shortly after his return from seeing Pike. He knew then that the picnic would continue through at least a part of the night and something had to be done about light. After an extensive search, he found Carlos Raveza slumbering peacefully beneath a bush. A small bird was perched on the rising and falling mound of his stomach. It flew away as Albright approached.

"Wake up, if you please, Mr. Raveza. We're going to need some light eventually."

Carlos opened his eyes, rolled over on his side and regarded Albright with ill-concealed distaste.

"So? Then you have come to the wrong person."

"You're the chief electrician, aren't you, old boy?"

"Yes. But I am not an old boy. I am like a young boy, you might say, in especially when I am dreaming in the manner which you just stop. You broke the film just as it reaches the most interesting part, where the young lady compares me favorably to an Altura bull. I do not like you for this."

" 'Let there be light.' . . . Then you can go back to your dreaming."

Discouraged by the total lack of interest in Carlos' face, Albright reminded himself that perhaps Pike was a more patient man than he had thought.

"You do not comprehend," Carlos said with a mighty yawn. "It is true that I am in charge of light . . . along with the help of God. But I am not mechanic. The machine which makes the light is small and obstinate. It is a gasoline engine and it is complicated. It does not function at all. When someone fixes the machine, then it will make sense for me to hook up the wires. It will not make any sense to do such a thing until the machine works. Even you will understand that it is depressing to look at wires which are dead and lamps which are also dead. So until the machine is fixed, please go away and leave me alone. I would like to close my eyes and say ah this is where I came in. Adios."

It was almost dark before Albright found one of the mechanics and persuaded him to tinker with the portable light plant. In fact, Albright's chief problem in the encampment was the peripatetic tendencies of his flock. They were constantly going off in the two directions which the narrow strip of land afforded, and they were particularly attracted to the area occupied by Tanni and his people. Knowing that Pike would be anything but enthusiastic about fraternization between the two groups, Albright did what he could to keep them apart. Dr. Case proved to be the most consistent offender, having found, as he described it, a soul mate in Terry Mack.

"We share a common lack of respect for authority," he explained after Albright had persuaded him back to his own area for the third time. "That little fellow is a jewel. When he discovered I was a doctor he laughed right in my face. He said to me, 'Well now, blimey, if you haven't got all the earmarks of a doctor. You got yourself a low tone of voice which is supposed to make sick people feel a little sicker than they are, which is your bread and butter. The voice says if you'll listen to me carefully for ten shillin's' worth you'll enjoy whatever is wrong with you much more because you done all you could by just callin' the doctor. The voice says take this pill or that pill and choke it down and the sound of my voice all soothin' and the like, you can either spend ten bob more and get sicker, or be satisfied with what you spent and get well.' "

The last time Albright retrieved Dr. Case he told him about Terry Mack's eye.

"I asked him if he had ever had any treatment for it," Case explained, "and I'm going to think about his answer for a long time. 'No, m'lad,' he said to me. 'Because I don't really miss it so much as you think. When I want to see something I turn my good eye at it and when I don't I turn my head just a little the other way. Convenient, huh? And there's a plenty of things I don't want to see, m'lad. This way I don't have to close both eyes to avoid such things like most people do when they are sad or in trouble. The main reason we got eyes, anyway, is to keep us from stumbling into things or falling down. The real things, the things that count, you see inside yourself and you don't need no eyes at all for it. The blindest man in the world can see something ugly, or if he's of a mind, he can see all kinds of beauty, too.' "

"Please," Albright said without having heard a word. "Please stay over here with us. That's all I ask, Doctor."

There was no marked change in the atmosphere of either encampment until the first droplets of rain fell. Then, as it grew darker and the people were drawn together, those of Pistol Two began to complain. The children cried more frequently and fought out their pettishness in small, unorganized wars which the mothers could not stop. The laborers, slept out, and almost as restless as the children, demanded to know what the hell this was all about. Were they going to spend the whole night in this lousy place which smelled of dead fish? And what about some chow? Why not just take the boats and go back to Pistol Two and gear up the mess hall and at least get something in their bellies before everybody got soaking wet?

Albright temporarily dissuaded them by pointing out the tarpaulins they had brought. If they would just rig those between the boats and perhaps fasten the ends as far up the beach as they could, then everyone would be more comfortable until word came to return.

By the time the portable generator putted to life and Carlos Raveza had managed to connect a line which carried two bare lamps, it was obvious that further amenities would be required to pacify Albright's charges. The rain was creating real anger, and several of the men were muttering that they didn't like the look of things one damned bit. So this was only supposed to be a drill? Well, the weather was sure co-operating. How come Nature knew about it? Pike's name was mentioned with increasing frequency, and since the references were far from complimentary Albright thought it just as well Sue-Anne had demanded transportation back to Pistol Two. The situation further deteriorated when the two pressure camp stoves refused to work in spite of the best efforts of Mrs. Riley, her husband, and various volunteer experts from all departments. They were obliged to imitate the natives, and after a great deal of milling about over the hummocks they found enough suitable wood to build a small fire. As many as could push through the crowd around it stood in angry silence, only forsaking their places when the pungent smoke became unbearable.

At last when the rain steadied to more than isolated showers, a delegation of six men led by Barney Dunbar approached Albright. He found it extremely difficult to maintain a casual air as they gathered before him, and his uneasiness compelled him to sway even more than was his habit.

Barney Dunbar cleared his throat ominously and, placing his gnarled hands on his hips, said, "Look here, Mr. Albright. We been talkin' this thing over and we don't like what we see. You told us this was a drill and, well, we could make it sort of a picnic if we want. . . . Well, we had enough drill and picnic, too. Our kids are hungry and they'll be up past their bedtime pretty soon. And our wives don't like this sittin' around on the wet sand and we don't care much for it neither. So our idea is to get out of here now and go back where we belong."

"I cannot authorize you to leave until I receive word from the Governor," Albright said, wishing that, for this occasion at least, he was not wearing shorts. Laboring people, those who worked with their hands, were necessary creatures, of course, but, after all, emancipation was for politicians. How could you understand what such people were thinking really, and mightn't they consider shorts as a possible object of ridicule? And wasn't ridicule of those in power an early warning of revolution?

Hearing the faint rumble of tumbrels rolling in his direction, Albright added, "I'm dreadfully sorry, really, but we must remain here."

"We just ain't goin' to, Albright. We talked it all out and we're loadin' up our families and takin' the boats. In other words, we're goin' home and Pike can yell all he wants. He can't fire us all."

"I forbid you to go near those boats," Albright said with as much assurance as he could muster. "Really, gentlemen, I must ask you to co-operate."

"You ain't forbiddin' anything. Not that it would do any good, anyway. We got our rights and we're goin'. We done all the co-operatin' we're about to do for one day."

The original delegation had now been augmented by most of the male population of Pistol Two. They formed a gradually closing circle about Albright, and he searched frantically for at least a few sympathetic faces. At the edge of the crowd he saw two marines. Both were avoiding his eyes.

"I should be most reluctant to request aid from the marines," Albright said. "I hope you realize I can do it?"

"Them marines are nice boys and smart ones, too. They won't give us no trouble."

Oh dear God, Albright thought, where is Pike? I did not sign up for martyrdom. Pacifying peasants is not my forte.

"Well . . ." he said uncertainly. "I suppose . . ."

Whatever he had in mind to say Albright gratefully left unfinished. For all attention was suddenly diverted from him when two disheveled men stumbled out of the night and pushed their way through the crowd of people. Albright saw they were Sgt. Doolan and Adam Smith. Perhaps Doolan could do something with the rabble.

When they reached the center of the circle Adam hardly glanced at Albright before he turned to face the people. He held up his hands, and he was so tall that when he stepped quickly on top of a small sand hummock all could easily see him.

"Can I have your attention, please!" he began. "Please . . . Everybody . . . Listen to me! This is very important!"

As Adam waited in the dim light from the two small bulbs, he heard several uncomplimentary remarks about his appearance. His pants were nearly in shreds and there were several cuts on his face. And he seemed very near exhaustion. *"Listen to me, please!"* Adam begged, and such was the appeal in his eyes that their talking subsided momentarily until there was only the sputtering of the light plant to compete with his voice.

"You must believe what I am going to tell you, even though you have every reason to do some wondering . . . about . . . well, about what you've been asked to do. I'm not much at speech making as you can see . . . or hear, I mean. Now what I want you to believe is that your trip up here was not a drill. There was a mix-up which was my fault to begin with. . . ."

Knowing he was doing a very poor job expressing himself, Adam paused a moment to collect his thoughts. Now everyone in the encampment was coming toward him, even those who had held a favorable position beneath the tarpaulins. He was about to begin again when he saw Margaret Trumpey standing near the outer fringe of the crowd. She was looking up at him, and once more the sequence of what he wanted to say fled from his mind. He wiped the rain from his face while he sought words which would impress and yet not alarm the faces around him. He knew his silence was already overlong and was not doing his cause any good, and he was startled when he heard a man say, "What's this guy up to? Looks like he's off his rocker to me."

"No, it is definitely not a drill," Adam said desperately. "There is a real storm coming and it will hit Nikki very soon . . . maybe in a few hours. . . . I can't be sure about that part. But I am sure the winds will be very strong, probably of hurricane force . . . and so you've got to leave right now and go down to the south end of the island, where there is some high ground and you'll have better shelter. You've just got to believe me when I say this could be a matter of life and death for all of you!"

"Just a minute," Barney Dunbar called out. "What's going on around here? First they make us come up here to the north side, and now you're telling us to go down to the south side. I'll tell you right out I don't think much of takin' my family all around the lagoon after dark just to get wet."

"How did *you* get here?" another man demanded.

"I walked. And it wasn't because I enjoyed hiking."

"How come you didn't ride up here in the boats with us? You're the weatherman, aren't you?"

"Yes, I am. And I know what I'm talking about. There's a very good chance the sea could cover this whole part of Nikki because the storm will approach from the northwest. On the south side you'll at least get some protection."

Adam turned to Albright and said, "Please. Can't you help me? They should start out in the boats right now."

Those who were within the inner ring of the crowd listened attentively to Albright's answer.

"Indeed I will not. I just finished telling them they must remain here. Those are Pike's orders."

"To hell with Pike! I know what I am talking about."

"Neither your manner nor your appearance would suggest that you do. Furthermore, I'm having quite enough trouble without your meddling. Sergeant Doolan! Will you please escort Mr. Smith to a less conspicuous place."

"I been escortin' him for the past two hours. I think he means what he says."

"That may very well be true, Sergeant. But Governor Pike is the authority here. Until he arrives we are his representatives. Furthermore, I can personally vouch for the fact that Mr. Smith is very likely to disagree with anything Governor Pike might say."

From the middle of the circle a woman's voice came through the rain. "He looks cuckoo to me. I'm not going to put my children through anything more. I want to go home."

A murmur of approval passed through the crowd. Then another woman yelled at Adam and there was a hint of hysteria in her voice. "If you're telling the truth why weren't we told about this here real storm? What do they mean by sending us up here?"

A man called out, "Where is Pike, anyways? How come he isn't here and hasn't been here? Somebody ought to be in real authority around here and I right now nominate Barney Dunbar."

"We got to have some kind of a leader!" another man said. "You can't do anything right unless somebody says so and so is so!"

Another man said, "Maybe we ought to elect some kind of a committee!"

"The hell with all that! Let's go home and get dried out!"

"I could use a drink!"

A woman's voice cut through the others. "Where's Pike's wife, I'd like to know? I saw her leaving in one of the boats before it got dark. Are they hiding someplace?"

"I second the motion for Barney Dunbar!"

"It's gettin' so you can't trust nobody!"

Adam spread his long arms wide. *"Please! Everybody!* You haven't got time to debate this thing. You must leave right now and you can't go back to your homes. It may be just as bad there as it will be here."

A man said, "I can't figure out just what for, but you and Pike must be

in cahoots about something. I still want to know why you had to hike
it up here?"

"Yeah! And how come Doolan is with you? The only thing I believe
that you've said is that there's been some kind of a mix-up. It looks like
you're the one who's mixed up, mister!"

Now the noise from the crowd became more than a murmur. The
sound multiplied upon itself until the puttering of the light plant dissolved within it. Adam searched the upturned faces anxiously. For the
first time he could feel wind on his face. And though it was still feeble, its
strength was increasing. The wind was coming, as he knew it must, from
the north. Not too far away to the westward, then, swirled the center of
Lazy Ethel.

Again he held up his hands and achieved a measure of attention.

"Maybe you'll believe me if I explain something more to you! It is not
Pike's fault you're here, but mine. I deliberately gave him the wrong
information . . . never mind why now. He thought he was doing the
best thing for you. What I did is unforgivable, I know. I deserve whatever punishment you think up for me. The reason I had to hike here was
because Pike not only fired me, but put me under arrest. I am still under
arrest, which is why Sergeant Doolan is with me. He knows, too, there is
a real storm coming. Ask him how he saw the barometer falling. And
believe me . . . *please,* for your own sakes and the sake of your families,
believe me and go down to the south side right now!"

A stunned silence fell upon the crowd. Again Adam searched their
faces. Only one held his attention and it gave him even less comfort than
the others. For it was Hanover, the press representative, and he was
smiling as if this was exactly what he had been waiting for. Adam looked
beyond him and found Margaret Trumpey again. The girl called Sunnie
now stood beside her and they were both obviously puzzled. Margaret
alone seemed half-convinced, and after a moment he thought he saw her
smile.

Then a man called out from the side of the crowd and his voice was
heavy with mistrust.

"Looks to me like we been lied to. If that's so, somebody ought to
get hung for it!"

"Maybe we could begin with a little tar and featherin' party," another
voice called out. "That is, when we get to where there's some tar and
feathers."

"I've had enough of this! Let's dump him in the lagoon and hold his
head down 'til he gives us the truth!" his companion yelled.

"Shut up!" Dr. Case challenged.

"Nobody's goin' to make me shut up if things are as bad as he says they are. All of us got a right to know what this is all about!"

Beyond the ring of light, somewhere under the tarpaulins, a child began to cry. As if the sound separately inspired each person, the crowd began pressing in more closely around Adam. He watched them hopelessly, appalled at his inability to make his words take effect. Knowing himself, he should have foreseen this. He should have taken time to prepare a speech that would convince, and not just rush blindly at them with a mixed-up relation of mix-ups. But I have never been a speech maker, he thought unhappily. I have never been able to say exactly what should be said, even standing alone with a girl on a wharf.

"*Please!* . . ." he began again, but Hanover's voice rode over his own with chilling assurance. Turning his back to Adam, Hanover faced the crowd and said, "You people have every right to question the behavior of this man. And Pike, too! Why they both deliberately chose to conceal the fact there is a storm coming, I don't know, but I guarantee you, both men have known about it since last night. They even knew its name . . . Lazy Ethel. I think we ought to go back to Pistol Two, find Pike, and make him tell us the best place to go. It looks to me like they outsmarted themselves and now they're trying to cover each other. As a result we're going to get it in the neck!"

"Stay away from those boats!" Albright called to three men who were moving out from the crowd. "You must have some organization or . . ."

A laborer pushed Albright aside before he could finish. The man was nearly as tall as Adam when he stood before him. He was at least fifty pounds heavier and for a moment he merely stood quietly, flexing his fingers into fists. Adam was very sure that in a moment the man was going to take a swing at him, and he saw approval in the faces of the crowd. They waited, glancing at each other and working their mouths in anticipation. Maybe if I just let him hit me and do nothing, they'll believe me, Adam thought. That is, if I can just stay on my feet.

The man stooped slightly and took another step up the sand hummock. He looked back over his shoulder at the crowd as if seeking their support, and as he turned he was suddenly shoved aside. Adam saw that Margaret Trumpey had made her way around the back of the crowd and now stood where the man had been. A laugh of appreciation came from the faces as she usurped his place. She returned the man's glare with a smile and said, "You won't accomplish anything that way, big boy."

Then she spoke to the crowd and Adam marveled at the clarity and confidence in her voice. "I know a lot of you, but for those whom I haven't met, my name is Margaret Trumpey. I work in the radioteletype shack. That's why I feel I have a right to speak now. It is true there have been a series of communications about this storm. It is also true that some of them have been conflicting. But if a man comes to you as Adam Smith has done and openly confesses what perhaps might have been a serious mistake, then we should believe him. Surely you can all see that to come here under the circumstances, and fight to get here in the way he has done . . . then he must be perfectly sincere. Adam has the kind of courage I think we're going to need. I believe him. If he says we should go to the south side of Nikki, then I believe we should leave immediately. Think about it for just a moment, won't you? Think quietly and soundly. And don't be influenced by men who do not know what they are saying."

She glanced at Adam, then turned back to the crowd. "Take a good look at Adam Smith and you'll believe him . . . as I do. Take a good look at a man who was not afraid to come here and tell us he had made a mistake. Ask yourselves if you would have had the courage to do the same thing."

Now a confused babble spread over the dim mosaic of faces. The solidity of the ring was broken as they turned to each other and clustered in groups and argued among themselves. There were those who wanted to stay and those who wanted to return to Pistol Two, and Adam observed with new hope that many were agreeing to leave for the south side. He tried to ignore the few who were still obsessed with the idea of throwing him into the lagoon before anything else was attempted. To Margaret, who had moved nearer to him, he said, "Thanks for doing what I couldn't seem to do."

The rain had plastered her hair against her head; and as she stood watching the crowd Adam wanted to tell her that as far as he was concerned she was the most beautiful drowned rat he had ever seen, but he decided to keep his silence. Drowned rat, no matter how beautiful, didn't seem to be the best term to explain the way he felt about Margaret. He hoped he would have a chance later to think of something more complimentary.

There was still no indication that the crowd would reach any unanimous opinion when a rhythmic chanting came through the rain and darkness. The singing came from the vicinity of the native encampment, and even at a distance the voices were loud enough to be heard over the light plant. At first the chanting was ignored; then gradually the people in the crowd began to listen and their own conversation lost intensity. Finally their talking lapsed altogether and they listened in uneasy silence. When they were quiet a voice rang out across the lagoon. Both Albright and Dr. Case instantly recognized the derisive tones of Terry Mack.

"Cheerio, Yanks! Chief says to tell you we're leavin' whether ye likes it or no. This place ain't fit . . ."

The rest of what Terry Mack yelled was lost in a burst of chanting. Those who turned and sought him in the darkness of the lagoon saw only the occasional glint of a wet paddle reflecting the light. In a moment even the reflections were gone and then the chanting diminished rapidly.

"Come back here! I insist you come back here!" Albright called desolately.

"That's enough for me!" a man in the crowd said firmly, and Adam saw that it was Pete Walsacki.

He took his wife's hand and they ushered their two children toward the black forms of the landing craft. Now only a few were still insisting that something should be done about Adam Smith. A splinter group moved back to huddle beneath the tarpaulins and debate the wisdom of complying with Albright's pleas. The majority began to drift like frightened sheep toward the boats.

With an angry glance at Margaret and Adam, Albright left the hummock and, running to the beach, tried to head off the people. Doolan stood solidly on the hummock ignoring his frustrated cries for assistance. "I got my money on you, Smith," he growled at Adam. "I hope you aren't as nuts as some people think."

Alone, Albright was soon overwhelmed by the sheer mass of people from Pistol Two. Finally, in defeat, he dropped his hands to his sides and let the crowd flow past his dejected figure.

The movement of the crowd was anything but an orderly procession. Herd instinct seemed to lead most of them toward one boat while the others were left nearly unoccupied. Finally a few of the landing-craft operators took their positions and started their engines. Many of the people, still apprehensive and undecided, lingered near the tarpaulins or merely stood along the beach in hopeless silence. Adam saw that, in spite of the Walsackis' example, these were mostly the people with families. Now it appeared certain that unless someone held the boat operators, who were gunning their engines anxiously, a good many people could be easily left behind. And the wind, Adam thought, the wind is no longer a breeze. Whatever influence Albright might have had upon the crowd was now obviously gone. Someone had to take command before it was too late.

It came as a shock to Adam when he suddenly realized that even as a Boy Scout he had always stood in the rear rank. In fact he had never in his life led others anywhere, and the vision of himself trying to order so many people about and see to their safety, was even more terrifying than his conception of what Lazy Ethel might do to Nikki. Why couldn't he be the hero and do something besides standing like a shivering dunce, a hapless mute, while the people waited . . . and Margaret waited? Yet he seemed as rooted to the hummock as if the sand reached to his waist. And he could only think that a coward survived in spite of himself.

He glanced miserably at Doolan, who appeared so completely in charge of himself, and he tried to smile at Margaret before he took his first hesitant step toward the beach. He would probably make a botch of it, but someone, even he, Adam Smith, the young man who vastly preferred to keep his peace, must co-ordinate this now hopeless exodus. Some of the people were already beginning to shove others around as they sought favorable positions in the boats. It was becoming all too obvious that real panic could be fired by a single thoughtless personality.

"I'm going to try and make them go about this sensibly," he said with all the determination he could drag from the depths of his being.

As he left the hummock a landing craft roared out of the darkness and hit the beach with a crunch. Adam saw Pike leap over the side and land ankle-deep in the water. And in spite of his experience with the man, Adam was vastly relieved. For the Pike he could see now was not the Pike he had known. Even at a distance the effect of his arrival was easily apparent. He began at once to move quickly and confidently among the people, directing and encouraging, smiling as Adam had never seen him smile before, and his solid orders rang out crisply across the beach. And best of all, he was explaining that they were bound for the south side of Nikki.

Doolan had gone to him at once and under Pike's commands was posting his four marines before each landing craft. In a few minutes they were counting off the people as they mounted the ramps, and they assisted the women and children as if it was a job they had done every day of their enlistment. While Adam watched, what had threatened to become a dangerous rout was transformed into an orderly retreat.

"I guess we might as well go, too," he said as Margaret came up beside him.

Walking slowly toward the boats, Adam felt the wind on the back of his neck, and he saw that the wavelets fringing the beach were now alive with energy and even beginning to hiss. It could well be too late, he thought, and the passage across the lagoon was certain to be an uncomfortable affair. Yet there was Pike. Pike the bigot, the hard-headed slave to red tape and official decree. There was Pike, the silly and dogmatic bully-boy with his infuriating manner, somehow as transformed as the scene around him. He seemed to know instinctively what was required to get these people on their way safely and speedily and he was getting what was needed. I could never have done so, Adam thought sadly. I am the little man, not Pike. I am a very little man who lost his head and twisted the tail of a tiger. Now it is Pike, of all people, who must slay him.

When Pike saw Adam, he shouted a final order at the operator of the first loaded boat and quickly marched up the beach. Adam instinctively squared his shoulders as he approached. "Here comes my appointment with the firing squad," he said to Margaret as casually as he could manage. "You'd better leave. It isn't always smart to be seen in unpopular company."

"I'm staying right here."

Pike halted before them and stood like a dripping pillar in the rain while he surveyed Adam. His shirt was soaked and the bristles of his gray hair lay flat and wet on his head. Water streamed from the end of his broad nose and dribbled down his hard-set jaw. His eyes, like the man, were new to Adam. Even in the dim light he could see they had lost their cold calculation and were now deeply troubled, which somehow had the effect of making them friendly and warm.

"Smith," he said slowly, "I owe you an apology. A message came through from Tuamani. Your Lazy Ethel is very much alive."

As Pike wiped his face, Adam said nothing for there was nothing to say. He could only guess how difficult it must have been for Pike to come to him, so he glanced up the beach at the tarpaulins, which were beginning to shake in the wind. He had to raise his voice slightly when he finally spoke. "Sir, I wish I'd never heard of Lazy Ethel."

"It would help if I knew how long it will last."

"I can't be sure of that, sir, with what little information I have. But I can make a good guess. The wind is just beginning to come from the north. It will continue to increase until the eye of the storm passes. If we are directly in line with the eye, then it will be calm for a while . . . possibly as much as several hours. Then it will come on again from the south and blow until it's all over. We'll know when that will be without any question . . . that is, if we're still around."

"We will be," Pike said firmly. "When we get down to the south side will you explain that to our people? I think it will be better coming from you."

"Yessir. I will."

"If the wind is eventually going to come from the south, aren't we taking a risk going to the south side?"

"Yes. But I don't see how it can be helped. Our chances of the eye passing directly over Nikki are pretty slim if the storm is not too big in area. The wind itself can't hurt us too much if we stay away from Pistol Two. It's sea water over the whole atoll that we need to worry about most, and the only high ground is to the south. I'm very glad we're leaving."

"And I'm very glad you came to Nikki," Pike said, turning back to the beach.

Striding toward the boats he passed Carlos Raveza, who was ambling through the sand as if he was employed in a leisurely exploration for sea shells.

"I thought I told you to cut off the main power," Pike said so mildly that Carlos turned to him and smiled trustingly.

"It is true. You did."

"I suppose you have some explanation?"

"That I have . . . if you will trouble to listen."

"I'm listening to a lot of things."

"Very good. I did not turn off the power because I like to eat. My belly is always of importance to me. To turn off the power completely was not an order I think you fully think out."

"Why?"

"There are many tons of fresh meat in the freezers. If I turn off the power the meat will spoil, which would be a sin. I was not even a little certain you think of such a thing."

"Thanks. I did not."

"Details," Carlos said, spreading his fat hands to catch the rain. "Leave the details to others and you will sleep as I do."

Sixty-odd miles to the northwest of Nikki, the eye of Lazy Ethel swirled clockwise about itself and moved ponderously through the Pacific night. The air mass which embraced the eye was also circular in form and thus extended in all directions. Near the eye the winds were the most powerful, diminishing gradually toward the outer circumference until the very edge of the mass was merely a full gale. No living thing could see this cyclopean giant, for the albatross and the frigate birds had long ago fled to regions where the membranes in their skin told them it was safe to rest. Even the fishes—the ono, the dolphin, the shark, and the bonito—had left the surface of the sea and dived to colder layers of water which provided almost nothing in the way of food, but offered a less troubled world. The mammals, whales and porpoises, imitated their descent, sounding deeply and remaining below for such periods as their lungs would permit. Even the invertebrates of the sea, the plankton, the tiny purple and silver marine organisms, and the jelly blobs of sub-life descended, driven downward by the fresh-water pollution of their element. For such was the volume and solidity of the rain, the sky seemed to become one with the sea.

Thus over two hundred square miles of the Pacific Ocean was left to the mercies of Lazy Ethel. The surface was a strident pandemonium of sound and furious movement. Even the subterranean depths lost peace. All of this cataclysm moved slowly upon Nikki atoll and sent emissaries forward to warn of its power.

As the landing craft rolled across the black lagoon, the warnings became evident to every person who had lived on Pistol Two. They no longer argued or displayed any resentment against a second crossing of the lagoon. They huddled quietly together in the bottoms of their craft, and the children, sensing the growing fear in their parents, were so afraid only small mewing sounds escaped them.

In a very little time, before the landing craft had wallowed halfway across the lagoon, the wind created formidable waves which frequently threatened to capsize the ungainly vessels. The rain spewed diagonally out of the cloud base, rattling against the metal skin of the landing craft and stinging the faces of those who were foolish enough to turn toward it. The wind swallowed the sound of the engines.

The landing craft moved together in loose formation, and even their bright running lights became frequently invisible. In the lead boat, Sue-Anne shared half of her raincoat with Dr. Case. They had both given up trying to light a cigarette and were looking aft where Pike stood exposed to the full fury of the wind and the rain. He had planted himself on the engine hatch and, peering ahead, gave occasional sharp orders to the helmsman. Somehow he managed to remove all anxiety from his voice and appeared entirely at ease and confident. Dr. Case said, "That's quite a man you have there. I'm beginning to think I've misjudged him."

Sue-Anne shifted her position slightly and pulled her wet skirt down over her knees. Then after a moment she said, "No, you haven't, Doctor. I don't know who that man is, but it isn't my husband."

"He's certainly making the best of what looks to me like a sticky situation."

"You wait. He'll pull a boo-boo yet."

"Mrs. Pike. Because I have a rather nasty disposition myself, I can't help but admire the way you refuse to be convinced."

"Twenty-seven years of experience. You don't change all that in a few hours."

"Is it possible that he's never had a chance to show himself before?"

"Yes . . . I suppose it's possible. But don't be surprised if sooner or later we all don't have to swim for our lives. Say, how badly do I have to be injured before I can apply for some of your medicinal whisky?"

"In your case . . . upon the point of death."

"I like you, Doctor," she said very simply. Then huddling against him she stared thoughtfully at her husband for a long time.

Crossing the lagoon took over an hour, and as the last landing craft reached the south shore the native canoes appeared one by one from the night. They were abandoned immediately, and the paddlers herded their families to the place where Pike stood beckoning with his flashlight. His voice rang out so strongly most of the three-hundred-odd people who now surrounded him could distinctly hear his words in spite of the wind and rain.

"Attention, please! All of you! We should be relatively safe here even if a trifle uncomfortable. Listen to me carefully and for your own sakes do exactly as I say! Is that interpreter here? If so, sing out, please!"

"Right, Guv'nor!" Terry Mack called, and there was a new respect in his voice.

"Are all your canoes here?"

"Right, sir!"

"Good. Advise your chief to have all his people stay closely with us. We will feed and take care of them. Now all of you, that's everybody . . . will follow me around to the south side of this hill. It is of the utmost importance we all stay together. Anyone who wanders off is asking for trouble. We will remain on the south side until the wind shifts. That may be several hours from now. When I give the order we will move around to the north side and remain there until this storm has definitely passed. For your encouragement, assistance is already en route from Tuamani. So we have nothing to be afraid of as long as we keep our heads. Right now, all of you men go back to the boats and pick up everything you can carry—especially boxes of provisions. When we are settled down on the south side of the hill, feel free to come to me with any suggestions, or if you need further help. The main thing is to keep calm, dig a little foxhole for yourselves in the sand if you want when the real wind comes, and remember it won't last forever. Now keep your children close to you and follow me!"

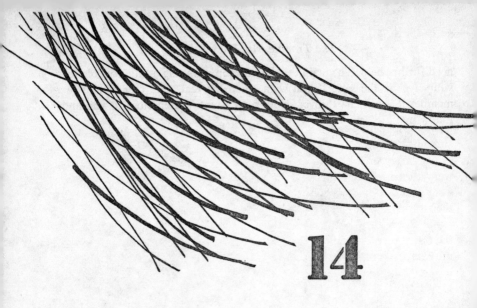

14

ACCORDING TO ADAM'S WATCH Lazy Ethel did not seize Nikki fully within its grasp until nearly midnight. It was the last chance he had to look at his watch, for the true wind did not increase gradually as he had supposed, but seemed to explode and reach its maximum within a very few minutes. It was as if something in the void beyond the lagoon had raised a vast curtain and a penetrating cold was released. Adam was certain the temperature dropped fifteen degrees in as many minutes. Yet to the others, clutching like terrified insects at the safety of their earth, the change in temperature went unnoticed. For even their imagination could not conceive of the wind which pounded against their prone bodies, even though its full force was expended upon the opposite side of the hill.

There was no recognizable sound from the people. All was dissolved in a dual sound; a rumbling moan which became a continuous, unbelievable roaring. There was nothing but the wind. Its blast existed. All else did not exist.

The heavy canoes vanished immediately except for one which was somehow caught up by the wind and propelled end over end up the hill and over the top, where it finally plunged down the opposite slope and skittered over the people as if it were made of papier-mâché. Finally it sailed through the night and also disappeared.

All five landing craft were lifted from their perches on the beach and hurled like toy boats against the north side of the hill. The water level in the lagoon rose more than five feet. Yet to Sue-Anne and Pike and Tanni and Carlos Raveza, and Peter Hildebrandt and Terry Mack and Sgt.

Doolan, and Sunnie Mandel and Albright, all of this was invisible. Like all the others of Pistol Two and the natives of Nikki, they lay face down in the sand, squirming against it as they sought even more protection, and trying desperately to breathe. There was only the wind, all pervading, stunning every sensibility except the primary urge for survival.

Adam lay in a common pit beside Margaret Trumpey. Their heads were buried in their arms to form a barrier against the stinging wet sand. They breathed in quick gasps, half through their nostrils and half through their mouths. They could not open their eyes nor could they even attempt to speak. Only the occasional movement of their bodies assured the presence of the other. They lay shivering in this position until three-thirty in the morning, when the wind eased. Then Adam turned his head, covered his nose with his cupped hand so he could still breathe, and spoke to Margaret.

"Are you all right?"

"Yes."

"I've been doing a lot of thinking."

"So have I. Some praying, too. When I wasn't doing either one, a tune kept going through my head. Do you know *The Sorcerer's Apprentice?*"

"I think I heard it when I was a kid."

"It reminded me of you and Lazy Ethel."

"Yeah. . . ."

He listened to the wind for a moment, assuring himself that it was actually subsiding. He wiggled as close to Margaret as he could, until their heads were almost together.

"Margaret?"

"Yes?"

"Maybe this isn't the best time to tell you, but I'd never get up the nerve anywhere else. . . . I was thinking it would be a lot easier if you didn't have to write to me."

"Is there any chance Pike will let you keep your job?"

"It isn't that . . . and it doesn't really matter. If I do go home though, I was sort of . . . well, maybe you would consider going with me."

"Is that a firm invitation?"

"Yes. It is."

"You have more nerve than you think. You don't know much about me."

"I know enough."

"I can't cook."

"Learn."

"I'm nearly thirty and . . . well, I don't know anything about making love either."

"Learn."

"You'd be getting what lots of men didn't seem to want. I'm almost a fully qualified reject."

"Will you?"

She was silent for a moment; then she said okay very softly.

Adam was trying to wipe the sand from his lips so he could bend across the pit and kiss her when he heard Pike calling. He looked up and saw him a yard away, crouched in the sand.

"The wind is dropping, Smith! Do you think it's time we moved around to the other side of the hill?"

"Yes, sir. I do."

Pike rose stiffly, keeping his back to the wind. He switched on his flashlight and Adam saw that he was smiling. "You'll have to admit," he said, "my neuritis is pretty accurate."

"I'd like to hook it up to an instrument," Adam answered.

As the wind moderated rapidly, Pike moved among his people like a solicitous shepherd. When he had gathered them all together he asked Adam to explain about the eye of the storm, and how the wind might soon return from the opposite direction. Then he led his people around to the lagoon side of the hill, where he ordered the ration boxes opened.

They ate in relative peace. Now the rain had ceased, and for some five minutes a hole appeared in the overcast through which the stars were visible. The phenomenon inspired Chief Tanni's Mormon elders so that they called upon Huahenga to lead a song of gratitude. As her great voice rose from the sand, all of the people joined with her, though those from Pistol Two did not have the faintest idea as to the exact meaning of her words. It made little difference. The two groups were now hopelessly inter-mixed, and the wife of Barney Dunbar was astonished to find herself happily clutching the wet hand of Apakura.

It was just after the singing when the stars again disappeared and Sue-Anne came to Pike. He was standing a little apart from the others and she said, "Zebulon, I want to have a word with you."

He was staring at the blackness of the lagoon and frequently rubbed at his tired eyes. For the first time in twenty-seven years Sue-Anne saw that his shoulders were slumped.

"Yes, Precious?" he said absently.

She was silent for a moment while she thought about the exhaustion in his voice. "I want to tell you something before the wind comes again."

"Maybe it won't."

"I want you to know I think you've done a damn good job."

"I'm afraid that isn't so. We're just lucky no one has been hurt . . . so far."

"I haven't been a very good soldier, Zeb. I've been the fathead. Given the breaks, I think you could be a general in anybody's army. I won't promise anything because I'm a lot weaker than you are . . . but I'm going to try very hard never to get drunk on you again."

Even as he reached for her hand Pike knew that his respite was ended. For the wind swirled around the hill and came upon the back of his neck and it was already picking up sand.

"All right, everybody!" Pike called. "Let's start digging in again!"

He squeezed Sue-Anne's wrist so hard the charm bracelets left small indentations in her skin. He said, "Thanks." Then he walked quickly toward the people and ordered the heavy ration boxes to be buried as quickly as possible.

There was very little rain with the second wind and it was somewhat warmer. Yet, if anything, its strength seemed greater. Here, on the lagoon side, the hill sloped more gradually, which allowed freedom to the wind and so may have accounted for its seeming increase in fury. And the people, both those of Nikki and Pistol Two, were nearly exhausted from the drubbing upon the exposed parts of their bodies by the wind. And while they had survived the original blasting without any obvious dangers, now a new peril terrified those who opened their eyes long enough to observe it.

Each of the landing craft had carried a full fifty-gallon drum of diesel oil. The new wind snatched these from the overturned craft, hurling them up along the hill, dropping them and picking them up again as if they were small tin cans. One landed on Hanover's leg and broke it below the knee. His screams for immediate attention were lost in the wind. Another rolled over the entire Walsacki family, who were huddled in a common pit. Miraculously, they suffered only bruises. The same drum finally came to rest against Huahenga's protruding rump, and later it took three men to extricate her from beneath it. Another drum, tumbling end over end, barely touching its edges as it leaped through the people, cut a deep gash in the back of Albright's head and he was unconscious for several minutes. Yip Kee, the Chinese merchant, had failed to dig far enough into the sand. The wind plucked him upward and carried him straight across the slope of the hill until it plastered him helplessly against a scrub bush. His entire body was covered with bruises and cuts, and he was both blind and speechless until long after dawn.

Only then did the wind subside, very slowly, as if reluctant to abandon its playthings. And in the dawn, which arrived without the encouragement of normal light, the people on the hill picked themselves up from their ordeal singly, and in groups of two or three.

As their enterprise returned, they looked down upon the lagoon which they had known as a blue and delightfully clear body of water. Now it was the color of chocolate and littered with debris. What remained of the wind lashed the surface into foaming whitecaps which pounded voraciously on what was left of the beach.

In many places the beach was gone. From their elevation the people could see where the ocean completely covered the flatter portions of the atoll, making the ring of Nikki a series of islets.

As the pale light grew stronger they saw where the two settlements had been. The area was nearly unrecognizable. The channel could still be identified although it appeared much wider. The wharf was gone and so was the warehouse which had stood upon it. All of the coconut palms which had shaded the native village lay flat, like matches spilled from a box. Only the walls of the Catholic and Mormon churches stood out. There were no dwellings of any kind to be seen, and it took Pike some time to explain through Terry Mack that somehow he would arrange for their replacement. "If it's the last thing I ever do!" he added vehemently. "My government is spending millions to blow up another atoll. They're going to spend a few thousand and put yours back in shape!"

There was even less evidence that Pistol Two had ever existed.

"What the Atlas Construction Company created in seven days," Dr. Case said as he worked in the sand pit which served as an improvised aid station, "God must have had a lot of fun obliterating in maybe seven minutes."

The outlines of the airstrip were still apparent although the whole design shimmered with water. The crisscross of the streets was also distinguishable even though the pattern was frequently interrupted by lakes. There were dun-colored square patches where the buildings had stood, but nothing remained of the structures except scattered heaps of broken lumber.

"We think we have something in Zeus," Dr. Keim said, pulling on his nose, which was very sore and red from contact with the sand. He stared moodily at the devastation and said, "I feel sick . . . and puny."

Shortly after sunrise an airplane appeared. Skimming low over the still-turbulent ocean it circled Pistol Two first and then turned toward the hill. It banked once around the hill, then descended to fly past the happily waving people. They could clearly see the U.S. Navy markings along the fuselage. On the second pass along the hillside a series of parachutes vomited from the plane's door. The people ran toward them and the plane continued on its course. Before the chutes collapsed on the sand it was already a faintly humming insect against the gray northern sky.

Attached to the parachutes were more rations than had ever been contained in the combined stores of Yip Kee and Fat Sue. While the people of Pistol Two engaged themselves in opening the crates and passing out cigarettes and chocolate bars, which met with the most demand, the natives lost all restraint as they fingered the nylon chutes. Led by Huahenga, the ladies of Nikki ignored the stores and were soon parading before each other in hastily fashioned gowns of yellow and white. They screamed with delight at its marvelous texture.

Sgt. Doolan brought Pike a letter which had been attached to one of the packages. Pike sat down in the sand and rubbed the stubble of his beard for several moments before he opened the envelope, though his name was prominently lettered across its face. He was looking at the gun hanging from Doolan's belt as he walked away, and he wondered if Doolan would suspect anything if he asked to borrow it for a little while. Now in the gray morning the promises which he had made to the natives seemed hollow and the leadership which he had tried to display appeared, on looking back, to be the vain strutting and hollering of a petty tyrant lost in his own catastrophe. That it had not been a disaster, he thought, looking across the lagoon at the north side of Nikki, where only a few specks of solid matter protruded above the water, was very little less than a miracle. He, General Zebulon Pike, U.S.A.-Ret. in accordance with the inscription on the envelope, had been, as that fellow Smith predicted, very nearly a murderer; and a mass murderer at that. "Thank God," he murmured as he slowly opened the envelope.

His eyes were almost too tired to read the letter and his brain took some time to absorb its numbered paragraphs and stilted phrasing. It began with a single word: Congratulations! Then it assumed a more normal tone.

1. You and your entire staff are commended for your foresight re the discovery and preparation for tropical Hurricane Lazy Ethel.
2. Upon the arrival rescue fleet you will report at your earliest convenience Tuamani to accept our personal congratulations and discuss immediate

rehabilitation station Pistol Two plus such other recommendations as
you may have.
3. You will advise all personnel that Project Zeus will proceed on schedule.
    Any injured will receive appropriate disability compensation.
4. All personal effects lost or destroyed will be replaced at government
    expense.
5. Rescue fleet will arrive your station approximately 0900. They will
    anchor off present sight of Pistol Two and remain on station until recon-
    struction is completed. There are ample living accommodations for all
    personnel.
6. Atlas Construction Co. is providing crews and material for immediate
    rebuilding. Estimate seven days restoration of complete facilities.

> For the Commission,
> W. A. Keating

Pike refolded the letter and placed it in the envelope, trying not to soil
it with his dirty fingers. He sighed and rubbed his eyes again. It was the
first letter he had received in his entire career which began with a commendation.

He looked down the slope of the hill to where Doolan was standing
near the parachutes, and he thought about his gun. That was one way and
he was certain he was not afraid of it. In fact he could not remember ever
having been much afraid of anything as long as the danger was physical.
It was paper which terrorized him and always had; mountains of paper
and the millions of words upon it had stifled his whole career.

There was a harder way than Doolan's gun, he thought, pressing the
envelope into his shirt pocket. He would take this paper and read the
first part of it to Sue-Anne. Because it was true that drunk or sober, he
loved Sue-Anne. And then he would tell her the truth. Eventually he
would take the paper to Tuamani and read the first part again. Aloud.
And tell them the truth. Then he would see. . . .

By night most of the ocean had receded from Nikki atoll.

On the next day two freighters anchored just outside the narrow channel which led into the lagoon. In the morning the Atlas Construction
people unloaded enough equipment so that the work could proceed. A
new wharf was completed before darkness, and moving cautiously, the
freighter became a temporary part of the land. Then again there was night.

On the second day the cargo booms worked with monotonous regularity, depositing all manner of gear upon the new wharf. Yet to all of
this the natives of Nikki paid little attention. For they were chiefly con-

cerned with the construction of a bridge which, before night had returned again, completely spanned the channel. They crossed the bridge freely and brought to their village such materials for building as they had never seen before.

On the third day the heavy earth-moving equipment roared and snorted and screeched in the hot sun. Guiding the equipment, the men from the freighter sweated and swore and tore and shoved at the confusion of coconut palms and debris. Among other things they caught up a pair of patent-leather pumps.

On the fourth day the airstrip was made serviceable and the first airplane arrived. Those who unloaded it were amazed to find that a large portion of its cargo consisted of flashlight batteries. There were also a number of metal filing cases. And a flute.

On the fifth day . . .

Heinz
Randow

ZOO HUNT
IN CEYLON

TRANSLATED BY CHARLES JOHNSON

ILLUSTRATED BY HEINER ROTHFUCHS

Copyright © 1958 by George G. Harrap & Company, Ltd.
Illustrations Copyright 1950 by Hundt-Verlag
Published by Doubleday & Company, Inc., Garden City, New York

EDITOR'S NOTE

Hunting for animals as a zoo supplier is an uncertain and dangerous business, somewhat more difficult than hunting for food or sport. For one thing, the zoo hunter usually confines himself to the rare and hard-to-find creatures. And often, the problems of care, feeding, and safe shipment of choice specimens are tougher than the hunting itself.

Heinz Randow is an old hand at the zoo game. After the first World War, he built and supervised the great aquarium at the Eberfeld Zoo. From there he went to Columbo, Ceylon, where he headed the Dehiwala Zoo, discovering and shipping to Europe many unusual species of reptiles and fish. And his most recent post is director of the world-famous Hanover zoological gardens.

In *Zoo Hunt in Ceylon* Mr. Randow writes of his adventures as a hunter in the lush, steaming forests off the southern tip of India, where dwell many of the strangest creatures known to man. In the selections that follow, you will read of Randow's handling of the kabaragoya dragon, a variety of amazing monkeys, a rare and poisonous spider, some unusual snakes and fish, and ten hungry bears.

The original edition of this book appeared in German under the title AUF TIERFANG IN CEYLONS DSCHUNGELN UND GEWASSERN published by Hundt-Verlag, Hattingen (Ruhr).

ONE MORNING shortly after sunrise I set off, accompanied by ten boys under the leadership of Anthony, my staunch head coolie, to capture snakes and rare lizards. It had been reported to me that in a swampy region some twelve miles from the compound there was a huge monitor lizard, twelve feet long, which attacked men. Knowing how the natives love to exaggerate, I did not believe the story, but from the various accounts I heard there was little doubt that, so far as the natives at least were concerned, the creature in question was an exceptionally large specimen of the kabaragoya, a giant dragon.

Soon the rainy season would be upon us, but just now the small brooks and the swampy, lagoon-shaped sheets of water in the flood areas were almost dried up. In fact, there were some areas across which one could safely have driven a heavy truck. Wide rifts were everywhere apparent in the parched, clayey soil. The whole countryside was in desperate need of rain, yet there was not a cloud in the sky, only the relentless sun casting its scorching rays down upon us.

At first we walked in single file through prickly undergrowth; then for two hours we made our way through a sparsely wooded region where I found a great variety of trees—coconut palms, betel and fan palms, jak trees, mangoes, rubber trees, and others which were unknown to me. Here and there climbing plants, which sent out a thick, tangled network of tendrils among the trees, were so dense that we had to slash our way through with a hacking knife in order to make progress.

A troop of wanderoo monkeys, swinging from tree to tree, escorted us with subdued chattering as we plodded on. Suddenly a loud whistling noise was heard. The inoffensive wanderoos now began gibbering excitedly and, using their long tails as rudders as they sailed through the air and as grappling hooks as they landed on the next tree or branch, they vanished with great, elegant leaps into the dense foliage of the jungle. In their place appeared a troop of about fifty bonnet monkeys which looked down on us chattering loudly. Bonnet monkeys, sometimes called toque monkeys, are very vicious and dangerous animals, unlike the wanderoos, which are timid in disposition and highly sensitive; they keep out of the way of bonnet monkeys as much as possible. Anyone who makes the mistake of throwing stones or other missiles at bonnet monkeys puts his life in danger, for these insolent little creatures retaliate with a frantic bombardment of branches and coconuts, after which they clamber down the trees and hurl themselves bodily at their attacker. Cases are known where troops of these monkeys have literally torn men to pieces. They possess large eyeteeth which strongly resemble those of beasts of prey and therefore each attacking monkey constitutes a very real danger, especially as a bite from their unclean teeth may produce poisoning which can easily prove fatal. I am a living example of the danger of monkey bites, because even now I still have a slight limp thanks to a bite I received in Sumatra from a macaque monkey, on whose account I came within a hairsbreadth of having my leg amputated. In the tropics every bite wound, however slight, must be treated with the utmost caution, as the consequences may otherwise be very serious.

Not wishing to take any unnecessary risks, and to avoid frightening away any game there might be in the neighborhood, we paused for a rest and waited for the troop of excited and abusive monkeys to continue on their way.

After a long march we came to the banks of a small, winding stream flanked by a native path. This we followed, all the while keeping a watchful eye on the bank and the nearby edge of the forest. The sun stood directly above us, reminding me that we were only five degrees north of the equator. Silently and on a broad front we moved cautiously over the club mosses, which overlaid the ground like thick cushions. Here and there appeared tufts of the sensitive plant, *Mimosa pudica*. These are dwarf mimosas which reach a maximum height of only eight inches and have fine, pinnate leaves which on being touched immediately cling to the stalk. At the water's edge grew huge clumps of alocasia and colocasia with their brightly colored leaves. The wide stretches of water along the river course, which was at a very low level, were covered with waterlily leaves and lotus blossoms. Hereabout there were no crocodiles to be seen, but this certainly afforded no guarantee that these armored lizards were not lurking under the masses of water lilies. Squatting on the waterlily leaves were some half-grown, many-colored turtles which at our approach slid noiselessly into the water. From the slope of the bank a water adder slipped into the stream and streaked out of sight. At that moment even this creature was not worth our attention.

After a sharp bend the river was hemmed in by hills. Giant clumps of bamboo covered the steeply rising slope and formed an impenetrable barrier. We approached this place cautiously to avoid the danger of being surprised by leopards or other beasts of prey. In the reddish-brown laterite, from which grew the aspiring stems of the giant bamboos, there were many holes, probably caused by jungle rats. Cobras have a liking for these subterranean passages, which they use as shelter after they have devoured the inhabitants. As they usually avoid the scorching heat of midday, we were for the moment in no danger of stumbling on poisonous snakes. Cobras, like the highly dangerous Russell's vipers, are creatures of the dusk and the night; in fact, animal life in the tropics in general is more active in the evening and during the night than during the hot hours of the day.

In spite of this, Anthony began prodding about in the holes with a long reed, hoping to bring any inhabitants there might be into the open. For some time he had no luck, but then, suddenly, a big cobra, almost six feet in length, shot out of one of the holes, hissing furiously. In a flash Anthony and his companions had taken to their heels, but almost at once he returned and advanced warily towards the cobra, which had meanwhile coiled itself and was now swaying to and fro with the raised part of its body, ready to strike. It had inflated the skin of its neck so that the hood, which has on it a white design resembling a pair of spectacles, showed quite clearly. I approached with my long snake-pole, threw its running noose over the enraged snake's head, and pulled it tight just behind the jawbone. Immediately the muscular body of the snake wound itself round the pole. Now came the most difficult and most dangerous part of the operation, which was to seize the wildly defiant snake firmly behind the jawbone so that, even when it twisted its upper jaw, its venomous fangs could not bite the hand that gripped it. Cautiously Anthony unwound the snake's body from the pole and heaved the creature into a sack, which in turn was placed in a box. This double precaution was necessary because otherwise the snake might have bitten through the sacking, thereby freeing its poisonous fangs to wound the native carrying it.

No matter how often one experiences such an adventure, the excitement is always the same. This is in no way surprising, for if any member of the party puts a foot wrong, he exposes everyone to the danger of being bitten; and this, in view of the frequent lack of prompt medical attention, usually has fatal consequences.

Speaking of the absence of medical attention, I am reminded of two experiences with cobras in which I myself was involved. Both were highly dramatic but neither, I am glad to say, resulted in tragedy.

The owner of a remote plantation about twenty-five hundred feet up on the slopes of Adam's Peak, not far from Kandy, was sitting one evening in darkness on his veranda. He was smoking a Manila cigar and drinking a whisky and soda; in doing so he must have fallen asleep, for he was suddenly brought to his senses by a noise. The moon, shedding its silvery beams from a sky bright with stars, bathed him in an eerie phosphorescent light. From the distant huts of the coolies the wan glow from paraffin lamps pierced the darkness, and from the forests came the muffled sound of the bush villagers' tom-toms. He lay in a deck chair, barefoot and wearing only a shirt and trousers, as was his custom during the evenings.

Suddenly with a start he leaped to his feet, but immediately recoiled with a horrified shriek and collapsed into his deck chair. The shriek was forced from him by a sudden stabbing pain in the toe of his right foot. He looked and found a drop of blood the size of a pinhead. It now became quite clear to him that he had been bitten by a poisonous snake. He had no serum, nor was there a doctor within easy reach, and the nearest telegraph office was a good four miles away. There was therefore no hope of receiving immediate medical aid.

He realized that he must do something quickly. With his heart pounding in his breast, he snatched the whisky bottle which stood by him, still three-quarters full, and gulped it down in the hope that it would act as an antidote. He drank and drank until his eyes began to start out of his head. Then he bellowed for his boy, who had already gone off to bed. Heavy-eyed, the boy came scurrying along. The planter scribbled a few words on a piece of paper and ordered the boy to send the telegram with-

out delay. Then, feeling at the end of his tether, and soaked in perspiration, he sank back into his deck chair. To make doubly sure, he drained another half-bottle of whisky, and then his senses left him.

As if pursued by Furies, the boy ran to the nearest telegraph office, handed over the message, woke up his master's friends, and called on the doctor. Three hours later, as dawn was breaking, a cavalcade of cars drew up at the scene of the accident. The men found the "patient with the snake bite" sprawled in his deck chair, lost to the world. It was as though he had floated off on a whisky cloud into the land of the blessed. The doctor and the man's friends combined forces in an attempt to revive him, plying him with innumerable cups of strong coffee. Their efforts were rewarded, for slowly the "blessed one" regained consciousness and finally opened his eyes. He stared around him in sheer bewilderment, for he must surely have believed that he had passed beyond, judging by the surprising questions which he put to those present. When the doctor examined the place where he had been bitten there was a further surprise, for it was discovered that the "poor victim of a snake bite" had merely trodden on a common tin tack. The guffaws which followed this medical pronouncement have probably haunted the "patient" ever since. The story had a sequel, however, which was not so funny and which might easily have had serious consequences. The telegram had been sent to England to the mother of the man bitten by a "tin tack cobra" which read: DEAR MOTHER, HAVE BEEN FATALLY BITTEN BY COBRA—LAST GREETINGS—GEORGE. As this telegram could not be intercepted, a second one had to be sent. Fortunately the old lady in England, on receiving the first telegram, did not have a stroke or a nervous breakdown.

Less amusing was the real cobra bite which my wife received. One evening, about ten o'clock, we were sitting on the veranda of our bungalow. The houseboys were already asleep, and except for the occasional distant sound of palaver tom-toms, it had become quiet in the village. The evening air brought no cooling breeze, and it was so hot that sleep was out of the question. We sat in our pajamas half stifled by the heat. I was tormented by a terrible thirst, and asked my wife to fetch me some lemonade from the kitchen. She got up and, as the kitchen was situated in an annex to the bungalow, she was obliged to go through the house and across the stone floor of the veranda at the back to reach it. Because it was pitch-dark—there was a new moon that night—she used an electric torch. After a while she returned, gave me a glass of lemonade, and said to me quite calmly, "As I was coming out of the kitchen a snake bit me." At first I was transfixed with horror; then, with the words sticking in my throat, I asked her where she had been bitten. "Above the instep of my right foot," she replied. We looked and found two small punctures, the edges of which had turned pale violet. I was at my wit's end, as there was no doctor for miles around and I had no antidote at hand. I feared for the life of my wife but did the most foolish thing I could possibly have done: I stood there ranting and raving at her, loading her with reproaches. As so often happens in situations of this kind in the tropics, my nervous agitation, heightened by the dilemma I found myself in, made me frenzied. My wife, however, did not lose her composure—she even laughed, and said, "I think I'll go into the bedroom and lie down for a while, otherwise I shall feel faint; in fact, I'm feeling rather dizzy already." Helpless, I let her have her way, and began chain-smoking cheroots. An hour later she came out on the veranda again; she sat on the arm of my chair, complained that she was having difficulty in breathing, and said without emotion, "I've come out so that you can see me die. . . . I am afraid all by myself . . . and all this because of a silly glass of lemonade!"

Now she broke out in perspiration, and felt a strong impulse to vomit. Two hours later the characteristic symptoms of poisoning had, strange as it may seem, receded so much that she was no longer in any real danger. We breathed a sigh of relief after these hours of torture. Obviously the only explanation for this happy turn of events was that the snake—it was, I suspect, the cobra which we stumbled on the following day in the undergrowth of our garden—had just previously bitten a number of victims while hunting for food, so that its supply of poison had been used up and was no longer sufficient to kill a human being.

This experience showed us that the extreme caution we had been exercising was not enough. There is an unwritten law in the tropics that on no account should one go out into the garden after dusk. The experienced planter will not allow flower beds or climbing plants in the vicinity of his house, because snakes love to use them as hiding places. For the same reason, one should never remove flower pots with one's bare hands or indeed have anything at all to do with them.

After these digressions let us return to our dragon quest. Our encounter with the cobra had delayed us temporarily; now we continued on our way, and soon came upon a landscape in which the hills gave place to low-lying marshland across which the river broadened out. It was here that the dragon had last been sighted. A thorough search was made of all the pools round about to ascertain whether they still contained fish and turtles. As we found no sign of life in them, however, we concluded that the dragon had devoured all their inhabitants. The kabaragoya thrives in marshy ground, across which it moves from pool to pool in search of fish and turtles, to which it is very partial. It will often lie submerged for hours feeding on these creatures, disposing of the animal life in one pool before moving on to another. The marsh palms and other marsh plants, which grew in clumps over the whole region, were searched, but without success. Our search brought us almost to the edge of the jungle, and I had almost decided to abandon the hunt when we heard a rustling noise in a thicket just ahead of us. With long bamboo canes we raked and prodded the thick tangle of plants. At first our efforts were in vain, for no creature showed itself; then suddenly and with a mighty spring, a really enormous kabaragoya lunged out of the thicket. Never before had I seen such a creature as this. Supported by its powerful tail, it ran in a half-upright position, raising the upper part of its body like a kangaroo, with its front legs pressed to its body. In this fashion it pursued its wild flight in a straight line across the marshland, the way into the forest being denied it. We had great difficulty in keeping pace with the giant lizard, but finally succeeded in cornering it. I had no wish to shoot this valuable creature, but was prepared to go to any lengths to take it alive. With jaws gaping and its enormous tail curled in a spiral, it crouched under a marsh palm in an aggressive posture, ready to let fly at us without warning. The power in its tail muscles was more than enough to shatter a man's shinbones, and a single bite from those massive jaws would tear one's wrists to shreds. The claws alone, some of which were as much as four inches long, were capable of tearing great flesh wounds.

The problem was how to approach this creature without exposing ourselves to too much danger. Having given previous thought to all these hazards, I had brought with me a large net, made of strong cord a quarter of an inch thick, in which to ensnare the dragon. With the help of long bamboo poles, we attempted to throw this net over the ten-foot monster. Unfortunately the dragon kept managing to disentangle itself from the meshes; but we dared not come any closer to the creature, which, lashing out furiously with its tail, had already torn up the small bushes around it. Then Anthony hit on the idea of throwing a sack over to it, in the hope that it would vent its savage fury on that. This maneuver was a complete success; the dragon caught hold of the sack in its jaws and shook it as a terrier would a rat, with the intention of rendering its supposed enemy unconscious and powerless. This gave us the opportunity to move closer and throw the large net over the dragon. Immediately it let go of the sack and ferociously snapped at the net, striving to disentangle itself from the meshes with its giant claws; but the more it struggled, the more caught up it became until finally it was completely enmeshed. This was the moment we had been waiting for, as we could now approach the giant lizard in comparative safety. Armed with sacks, the coolies rushed over to the confused lump of netting, sack, and dragon and trussed up the living bundle with ropes. Then we felled a giant bamboo, about thirty feet high, and lashed the enmeshed dragon to the middle of it. I placed coolies at each end of the bamboo, which they hoisted on to their shoulders. In triumph we now began our journey back. On closer inspection the lizard was found to be an old, as well as extraordinarily large, specimen of the kabaragoya monitor, or dragon, which must not be confused with the famous giant Komodo dragon.

Our adventure with the dragon was, however, not yet over. On the following day, having arrived back at the compound without mishap, our first task was to construct a huge crate to house the dragon adequately for shipment to Europe. For this purpose I used planks of teak an inch thick. When finished, the crate measured 2 feet 4 inches in width, 11 feet 6 inches in length, and 2 feet 6 inches in height. This meant that, with tail outstretched, the dragon just fitted it snugly. At one end of the crate there was a vent-hole about a foot wide for breathing. The planks were nailed on to the transverse battens of the framework in such a way that there were air spaces of about an inch between them. This enabled us to swill water over the whole creature, which could lap it up if it felt so inclined; the same method was used to flush out the dragon's excrement. Above the creature's head I had an eight-inch-square trap door fitted, which could be firmly clamped down after the dragon had been fed through it.

There were still two weeks remaining before the next consignment of animals, including the dragon, was due to leave the compound for shipment to Europe. Already some twenty crates containing cobras, smaller species of monitor lizards, and crocodiles were assembled on the shady veranda of my bungalow; now this crate, distinguishable from all the others by its enormous size, was to be added.

When all these preparations had been completed, we were faced with the seemingly impossible task of freeing the dragon from its entanglements and getting it into the crate. However, a method was devised, though it involved sacrificing the net. I cut through part of the net, an operation which required great care to ensure that the dragon was given no scope to bite, to use its claws, or to lash out with its tail. The dragon was released from its meshes, head first, but before any part of it which could have done mischief was disengaged, it was firmly tied to a bamboo pole that stretched from the head along the spine. After it had been completely freed from the net, the creature, trussed to the long bamboo pole, resembled a thick log. The pole was now raised and the dragon, still bound to it, was lowered into the crate. Then, when the heavy lid of the crate had been placed loosely over the pole, we began cutting through the cords which secured the creature to it. Twelve strong men pressed down on the lid as the pole was snatched away and the dragon fell with a heavy thud on to the floor of the crate. Then the lid was nailed down. . . .

For a fortnight all went well. True, the dragon made a terrible fuss for the first few hours, but after that it quieted down completely. As is well known, reptiles can survive without food for months at a time, but it is essential for them to have water. Every morning, therefore, a bucket of water was poured over its head which it dutifully lapped up. Every other day the small trap door was carefully opened and in went a flying fox, which immediately disappeared into the dragon's jaws. Several buckets of water were used during cleaning operations, the water draining away through the air spaces. So far as we could judge, the dragon, which we had christened Fritz, seemed quite happy in his new abode. From time to time natives would pass by and call it names and make scornful remarks about how it had come down in the world.

One day at noon, having drawn the blinds and settled back in my chair, I was just nodding off to sleep when I heard a noise on the veranda which sounded like heavy objects falling. Cursing, I shouted to the houseboy to stop making a din. My words re-echoed, and a deathly silence reigned. There was no sign of the boy. All at once I heard a shuffling noise, as if a heavy object were being dragged along the cement floor of the veranda; then three crashes, accompanied by a loud rumbling sound and shuffling. A few moments later the excited shouts of many natives pierced my ears. I could hear them calling "Loco-Master! Loco-Master!" I sprang to my feet, ran on to the veranda, and saw in a single glance what had happened: the fantastically heavy crate was no longer there! I could see only the marks where it had been dragged across the veranda and down three cement steps leading to the path. About fifteen yards away the dragon was advancing resolutely across the compound, licking the path with its long tongue and dragging the crate behind it as though it were a cardboard box. What had happened was that the dragon had levered the lid of the crate off and had climbed out. As, however, for reasons of security, we had tied a thick cord round its waist, that is to say, just in front of its hind legs, fastening the other end to the crate, it had had no choice but to take its cage with it. Thanks to the cord, we were able to recapture this highly prized creature. When the dragon had been reinstalled in the crate, we did not make the same mistake of securing the lid with nails; this time we screwed down every part with iron clamps.

Later we learned that Fritz, after a long sea voyage, landed safely in Europe, and for years afterwards was the main attraction in a public aquarium.

IN THE COMPOUND we kept many species of monkeys which had been captured in Ceylon, India, and even as far afield as the Malayan Archipelago. Among them was a pair of fully grown pigtailed macaques from Sumatra which had been leading a quiet, contented life in their cage for almost a year. They had a six-weeks-old baby, which was already making amusing attempts to climb up the bars of the cage. One morning Old Marian came running up to me in a fever of excitement and told me in a frightful jumble of Tamil and English that something terrible had happened to the Sumatra monkeys. I hurried over to the cages, where Anthony, Sussa, and many other coolies stood chattering among themselves in a ferment of agitation. As I approached I saw that the baby monkey had got its head stuck between the bars. This was indeed a delicate situation, for whenever one of the natives approached to release the baby's head the father would spring furiously against the bars of the cage, while the mother tried to take the baby into her arms. The way she tugged at the little creature was pitiful to behold; its neck was being stretched so much that we feared its head might be wrenched off at any moment.

As I was on good terms with this family of monkeys, I ordered all the coolies to make themselves scarce and, taking some rice and a few bananas and onions with me, I walked slowly up to the cage, spoke softly to the parents and fed them. But the moment I attempted to get near the baby, its mother snatched at it and tried to tug it away from me. This method of approach was therefore of no avail.

The front of the cage was barred, and the entrance to it was at the back, so that the monkeys could only see what was going on in front of them. I told Anthony and Sussa to go round to the back of the cage, to open the door with a sudden jerk, and to keep the monkeys occupied until I had freed the baby's head.

Everything turned out as I expected. I just had time to stretch the bars and free the young monkey's head before the mother rushed over and clutched the baby to herself. The father had meanwhile hurtled out of the cage and, baring his teeth threateningly, put Sussa to flight. Pursued by the other coolies, the monkey, with amazing speed, climbed a coconut palm, one of an isolated group of five. Thus, though he was free to swing from one to another of these palms, by besieging him from below we could restrict him to these five trees. As we stood looking up among the fronds of the palm trees, we occasionally caught a glimpse of the renegade scowling down at us.

Meanwhile Anthony had made a lasso and clambered up the smooth trunk of the palm tree. When he had reached halfway, the monkey saw the impending danger, picked coconuts as fast as he could lay hands on them and, uttering deep grunts, bombarded us so heavily that we were obliged to seek shelter from these weighty missiles. Undeterred by our warning shouts, Anthony continued climbing, and the monkey, catching sight of him, lowered himself on to one of the fronds and then swung high through the air, landing safely on the next palm tree. There he nestled in the plume, calmly awaiting the next move from those below. Anthony again began climbing, but this time ordered his team to do likewise on the other four palm trees; but, fearing that they would be attacked by the monkey, they refused to obey.

At this point I intervened and gave instructions that everyone should keep well clear of the clump of palms and the monkey cages. I was secretly hoping that, given this opportunity, the monkey would return to his family. I went across to the bungalow and focused my telescope on the palm trees. All at once I noticed that the monkey began to climb down; halfway down, though, he changed his mind and climbed up again.

Until evening there was no change, and we wondered whether the creature would remain in his retreat all night; yet, as it happened, the tree was vacated even before sunset. From footprints I established that he had returned to the cage, no doubt to pay his wife a visit.

Two days later a native woman from the nearby village came to my bungalow, accompanied by a large crowd of men chattering excitedly, and asked permission to speak to me. In her arms she carried her child, who was bleeding badly from a head wound. As I was unable to grasp fully what was being said, I called in my interpreter, Harry, who after a brief conversation with the woman explained to me what had happened. The child, a two-year-old girl, had been playing in the middle of the village street with some bananas when suddenly an enormous monkey—larger than the monkeys of Ceylon—appeared from behind a hut. It approached the child and hesitantly took a banana from her, which it hurriedly skinned and ate; then it snatched at a second banana, but this time the child was unwilling to part with it and raised her hand to shoo the monkey away, whereupon it attacked her, tearing at her hair and head.

By this time some men, attracted by the child's screams, had come running up to the scene and were just in time to see the monkey making off into the forest.

So that was it! I realized that they had come to me because they wanted me to give the child medical aid, for every native here takes it for granted that a European is invariably a doctor. If he is successful in his treatment, then the natives will go through fire and water for him. It is therefore very important—and quite normal—for the European here to have a well-stocked medical chest at his disposal. The little native girl had a sweet face and long black locks; her wound, a seven-inch gash across the top of her skull, looked worse than it really was. On examination I was relieved to find that it was only a surface wound, and that the bones of the skull were not damaged. I took the mother and the little girl into the bungalow to disinfect the wound and stitch it. My job was made more difficult than it need have been by the mother's refusal to sit on a chair while she held the child; instead, she insisted on adopting the squatting posture which is customary to her race. These natives, who are simple in their way of life, have no use for chairs but relax by squatting on their haunches. Even Harry's persuasive powers could not induce the young Sinhalese woman to sit on a chair. In order to be able to treat the child properly, we therefore took her away from her mother and laid her on a table. These natives can bear a great deal of pain without complaining aloud. Even this child hardly uttered a sound during the operation, which was certainly a painful one; only the large tears from her lovely dark eyes coursing down her brown cheeks betrayed the pain she felt. The pretty creature was soon well again, and always came running up to me whenever she caught sight of me in the village.

It was clear to us all that the culprit responsible for this injury could have been no other than our renegade monkey. Extra efforts were therefore made to recapture him, but although we tried for a whole week we had no success.

Another broiling hot day came round. In the village the inhabitants went about their day's work. Some of the men, still half asleep, were lolling about on their bast mats in front of their huts. They were roused by the first traffic of the day; a couple of carts, their large wheels grinding, were being pulled through the village street by teams of oxen. An old Sinhalese, dressed only in a loincloth, was busy taking down the wooden shutters of his shop. I walked past the shop just as the old man was climbing over the counter, which half filled the entrance. As he disappeared into the dim interior, all that could be seen of him were his lean brown legs covered with white hairs. With a cry of terror he collided with a dark figure which was moving about in the half-light and, clearing the counter with a mighty leap, he fled shrieking through the village street. Behind him a well-aimed pineapple came flying through the air, striking him on his bare back and sending him sprawling. From all directions the people of the village came hurrying along and congregated in a broad arc round the shop, inside which a creature with humanlike form could be seen moving about. Grunting with anger, the intruder was kicking up a rare shindy and throwing buckets and bottles all over the shop. The old man was bewailing the damage, and implored the onlookers to seize the offender, but no one was prepared to enter the danger zone of missiles. I had already sent word to my coolies, many of whom had wives and children living in the village. They came running up to assist, and we discussed how best to establish the identity of the intruder. However we were saved this trouble, for he climbed on to the counter and performed a savage war dance: it was our pigtailed monkey!

When sacks, lassos, and stout nets had been fetched to catch the fugitive, I led my men towards the entrance of the hut and tried to throw a net over his head. Skillfully evading it, he withdrew into the shop where he became lost to view among the dark shadows. I was just on the point of pursuing him into the shop with Anthony, who was right alongside me, when a deadly accurate and seemingly endless volley of lemonade bottles and jam jars was unleashed at us, forcing us to beat a hasty retreat. Whenever anyone approached the shop, the barrage was renewed with coconuts, pineapples, papaws, bananas, mangoes, jam jars and bottles. Soon the entire stock of the village shop was scattered higgledy-piggledy up and down the village street. I now divided the besiegers into several groups and placed them at strategic points around the shop so that, at a given signal, a full-scale attack could be launched from all sides. The bombardment had meanwhile ceased, but now the monkey, sensing that he had been surrounded, began tearing away the cadjan thatch to climb out through the roof to safety. At the very moment the monkey thrust his thick skull through the thatch, I gave the signal and we stormed the shop. A lasso was thrown over his neck, followed by a large net which enveloped him completely in its meshes. Then we tugged him away from the tangle of thatch, tied him up in a bundle and, singing a song of triumph, we carried him back to the compound. There we reunited him with his family in the cage, where he had a loving reception from his wife.

The Monkey Paradise

AS I WANTED to keep monkeys in large numbers, I built a so-called monkey paradise similar to those which can be seen in modern zoos. These grounds were so laid out that a broad ditch, surrounded by a ten-foot wall, cut off the monkey island from the outside world. As there was no lack of space or cheap labor for such a project, I was in the happy position of being able to erect a very large monkey island. In the middle of this terrain there was an enormous mango tree with widely spreading branches. At a distance of about twelve feet from the outermost branches of this tree, there was a coconut palm sixty feet high.

Seeing that these grounds were in the tropics, that is to say, in the monkeys' natural habitat, I thought it advisable to extend the width of the ditch to thirty feet and the enclosure wall beyond to twelve feet. I judged that the monkeys, accustomed to the tropical climate here, would be able to jump farther than they could, given the same facilities, in northern latitudes. Later events not only confirmed this opinion but proved that the allowances I had made were inadequate.

One afternoon a shipment of five hundred rhesus monkeys arrived from Calcutta. As soon as they reached the compound, I had the crates, in which they sat huddled together, placed in the center of the grounds, as I wanted all the monkeys to be released at the same time. Before releasing them, though, we watered them liberally, as they had suffered from thirst on their overland journey by oxcarts.

At last the great moment arrived when the doors of the crates could be opened, allowing hundreds of monkeys to swarm onto the plateau and clamber up the coconut palm. Tense with excitement we stood on the enclosure wall to watch this rare spectacle. With great circumspection the first half-dozen monkeys poked their heads out and peered anxiously all around them; but catching sight of the mango tree, they left their crates and with a few giant leaps disappeared into its branches. Others followed, and in the twinkling of an eye a multitude of reddish-brown monkeys, screaming abuse at one another as they all tried to leave the crates at once, swarmed over the grounds. Dozens of them sat in the crown of the palm tree, or hung like ripe fruits among the mango

branches, cramming their cheek-pouches with the fresh, cool leaves of the
mango tree, so that within a few minutes it was stripped bare, its denuded
branches revealing nothing but monkeys.

Suddenly the excited monkeys began a curious chase, unique in my
experience. The horde sitting in the coconut palm climbed down the
smooth trunk at lightning speed and scampered, uttering loud screams
and whoops, across the ground to the already overfull mango tree, which
they straightway climbed, driving the monkeys already in possession into
the highest and farthest branches of the tree. All at once a large male
grasped the end of a branch and swung through the air, landing safely
on the coconut palm. Another followed, then a third, and in next to no
time the scene had changed completely. Scrambling up the mango tree,
they sailed through the air like a living bridge of monkeys, landing in the
crown of the coconut palm. In a seething mass they then slid down the
trunk of the palm tree, and rushed straight back to the mango tree to
rejoin the queue. It looked like a witches' sabbath, this climbing, leaping,
flying, sliding chain of monkeys, until we brought the frantic performance
to an end by throwing maize, bananas, and paddy across to them.
Greedily they pounced on the food; and for the first time peace reigned.

After the monkeys had replenished themselves they relaxed for a while
before making a thorough inspection of their new home. Only now did
they seem to discover that the grounds in which they found such liberty
of movement did not spell freedom for them in the full sense of the word.
Two hundred yards away from them they saw the green, mysterious, and
oh! so tempting fringe of the forest. The call of the jungle was so strong
that they tried to leap over the enclosure wall, but their efforts were in
vain. A few large males, it is true, jumped to an astonishing height, but
even so they failed to clear the wall by about three feet. Proud of our
work, we fondly believed that no monkey could escape, and were just
on the point of leaving our observation post when I noticed quite a dis-

turbance going on among a group of large, old males. Interested to see what the outcome would be, we decided to stay and watch for a while.

As if at a given signal, all the large males raced like mad over to the foot of the wall, which they began to circle at tremendous speed. We could not make head or tail of what the monkeys were up to, but we soon found out. Going full swing, they suddenly flung themselves high into the air, and before we realized what was happening, seven of them had reached the top of the wall. Two or three vanished with long leaps into the jungle; the rest remained perched on top of the wall screaming encouragement at those who had failed and who were now running round the enclosure squealing with frustration. They were not long in deciding to make a second attempt to scale the wall, and this time three more reached the top and disappeared into the dense foliage beyond to join the other fugitives. By the time we left, about seventy males had escaped in this way, but evidently the jumping powers of the females were not so great, since not a single one of them managed to get away.

The monkeys which still remained on the island were fed morning and evening. It was interesting to see that the renegade males, or some of them at least, returned at feeding time to enjoy the benefit of free rations. Soon there was a well-worn monkey path to the spot where the big males scaled the wall when entering and leaving the monkey island. If these escaped monkeys had behaved themselves during their visits, we would not have minded, but as time went by, they became so impudent and unmannerly that we regarded them as a menace. Not only did they prevent the resident monkeys from enjoying their food in peace, but in their importunity they even tried to steal the food from the coolies as it was being taken to the enclosure.

Every day about two o'clock they appeared at the sunny fringe of the jungle. It was delightful to watch them peering out warily from among the dense foliage and from the crowns of the palms. Then, swinging from palm to palm across a stretch of open country, they climbed down the steep bank leading to the lake to bathe. A few of the monkeys actually swam, while others splashed about in the water for a while before climbing on to the rocks to sun-bathe. One quite old male, perched on a rocky pinnacle, acted as look-out and watched unconcernedly as the crocodiles sunned themselves on the surface of the lake. When the monkeys had first gone down to bathe there, the crocodiles had attacked them, but as the monkeys, scolding loudly, had always skillfully eluded them, the crocodiles after a while gave up the chase and paid no further attention to them.

One day a Sinhalese peasant came to me with a heavy sack full of very small, unripe coconuts and told me with much lamentation that the foreign monkeys had raided his plantation and robbed him of his crop, which had just started to ripen. He wanted compensation, and after a good deal of haggling I paid him five rupees for the damage that had been caused. For some time after this, a different native appeared each day with a sackful of "evidence," until it became too much of a good thing and I insisted that they should apprehend the culprits and bring them to me as indisputable evidence. They would then be entitled not only to damages but also to a reward for recapturing the monkeys. I later discovered that the same unripe coconuts had been paid for six times over, having been passed on from one successful applicant to the next, in accordance with that well-known oriental proverb: "He who lies and cheats best in the village becomes headman." The outcome of my stipulation was that no more peasants came to see me.

Meanwhile, the monkey menace was going from bad to worse, especially as they were now becoming positively dangerous. It annoyed us greatly to see them biting and bullying the residents at the rice-feedings so that the lion's share would fall to them. But how were they to be recaptured? Experience had taught them to beware of snares set with bait, but on the other hand, they had such a passion for sweet cooked rice that by exploiting this weakness of theirs, there might yet be some way of outwitting them.

As I turned this problem over in my mind, a story by Wilhelm Busch occurred to me, in which he recounts an old mariner's recipe for catching monkeys. The mariner rows ashore and walks barefoot over to a palm tree, beneath which he sinks down with loud groans and sighs. Watched by a monkey perched in the crown of the tree, he then proceeds to make a great display of putting on a pair of top boots. Noticeably relieved of his pain, he swaggers back to the boat, leaving behind him a miniature pair of top boots, the inside of which he has covered with pitch. Stepping back into his boat, he has scarcely rowed a stroke or two when the inquisitive monkey climbs down from the tree to see whether a pair of top boots will bring the same spectacular benefit to him. Quickly he puts his feet into the boots which the old seadog has left behind, and at this very moment the mariner returns. The monkey tries to escape up the palm tree but with his feet stuck to the pitch in the boots, he cannot move an inch, and the mariner is richer by one monkey.

In the same sort of way, I thought, there must be some means of recapturing my own monkeys; and no sooner said than done.

Near a copse not far from the enclosure wall I had a row of ten bamboo stakes rammed into the ground, spaced at intervals of five yards. In the hollows of these bamboos, which were about five inches in diameter, we set wire loops, the pulling ends of which were led through the stems and extended into the copse. These snares lay out of sight just beneath the hollow tops of the bamboos. In the copse a young, intelligent Sinhalese, whom I had put in charge of the nooses, concealed himself so that he had a clear view of the bamboos and could tighten the nooses at the crucial moment.

The inquisitive monkeys, who were quick to spot this novelty and lost no time in giving it a thorough examination, were left alone for the first few days. Then one day I appeared with a steaming bucket full of sweet milky rice and slowly made my way with it towards the enclosure. Descending on me from all directions, the swarm of renegade monkeys tried to steal the rice from the bucket, but I forestalled them by throwing a few handfuls among them, which they all scrambled for. Then I walked over to the bamboos and busied myself there in an obvious manner, stuffing rice into the hollow stems and inserting my arm into them as I did so. I smeared some of the rice over the top edges of the bamboos, the remainder I threw into the enclosure. Completely ignoring the renegades, who had been following every movement with the utmost curiosity, I walked off.

Everything happened just as I had planned. The monkeys went straight over to the bamboos and inspected them closely. First they ate the rice which I had smeared round the edges; then, plunging their arms into the hollow stems right up to the shoulder, they took the rice which I had put there. This experiment was repeated in the same way four days running, each day at the same time. Invariably the swarm of renegades would be there waiting for me to appear with the rice.

The time was now ripe for putting our plan for recapturing the monkeys into effect. On the morning of the fifth day the young Sinhalese took up his position at the point in the copse to which all the wires led so that he had control of all the snares. At the accustomed hour I went over to the bamboos with the bucket of rice and, after throwing a few handfuls to the renegades who were hankering round me, I used the remainder to bait the bamboos. I had not gone more than twenty paces after completing this operation when I saw one monkey desperately struggling to free his arm from the noose. In next to no time all ten nooses had claimed a victim; at each bamboo a monkey was striving with might and main to free an arm, while the others squatted nearby and impatiently scolded them for taking so long over their turns. My coolies appeared on the scene, loosened the wires and bundled the victims into sacks, and then reset the snares.

By this artful device we recaptured forty-seven monkeys, which we confined in a cage with wire netting to prevent their escaping a second time. The monkeys which still remained at liberty appeared now and then in the vicinity of the compound, but after a while disappeared for good, except for one very strong male, who occasionally returned to have a look round.

The Giant Spider

HARRY TOLD ME one day at breakfast time that there was a Sinhalese at the door with a box in which he had a giant spider he wished to sell, and he wanted to know whether I might be interested in purchasing it.

"No," I replied, "I have no use for spiders; they are not a commercial proposition, and besides, we have enough of them here ourselves, of all sorts, even bird spiders—all we need do is to go over to any corner of a room and we can take our pick. And what with those dark-brown spiders which find their way on to every banana boat bound for Europe from Jamaica and the Canary Islands, there's no market for them. Tell the man I don't want his spider!"

Hesitantly Harry persisted, suggesting that I should at least take a look at the creature as, speaking for himself, he had never in all his born days seen such a spider, silvery-gray with light-brown bands and—incredible though it may sound—a body as big as a man's fist.

"Surely you don't expect me to believe that," I said. "Why, if that is true, then the fellow must have caught a robber spider." This species, which is very rare, lurks near the edge of jungle pools and can run across the surface of the water. I needed no further encouragement from Harry to see the visitor, who on entering warned me in broken English that the spider was "very poison."

Carefully I opened the lid of the box and was struck dumb with amazement: inside was a giant, silvery-gray spider with exquisite golden eyes, a perfect specimen, not damaged in any way. It sat there moving its lethal claws gently to and fro—a wonderful, uncanny creature! In my travels I had seen thousands upon thousands of creatures of all kinds, but never such a one as this. I was so deeply impressed from the moment I set eyes on it that I bought it from the man straight away, giving him half a rupee for it, as I was well aware that he must have set his life in peril to capture it alive.

To house this prize specimen, I had a small, thick wooden box constructed, taking the greatest care that it was so well made that there was no possible means of escape. A square hole, cut out of the lid to allow air into the box, was covered with a piece of fine metal gauze, and a thick pane of glass in front enabled one to observe the giant spider's movements. The interior of the box was laid out to represent a miniature landscape: earth, pebbles, and a dead twig on which grew an orchid. The captive spider seemed quite content in these new surroundings, and spent a good deal of time carrying the pebbles from one corner to another, but made no attempt to weave a web. Every evening I squirted some water over it and the landscape so that the box would retain a certain consistency of humidity. The box was placed on the rear veranda on top of a wooden cage in which I kept four tame Asiatic chipmunks. Once a week this remarkable spider was given a frog or a young lizard, which it immediately seized and sucked dry.

In this way four months passed; as it was winter in Europe, I could not risk sending the rare spider on a long voyage there. To make the transition from tropical to northern climates bearable, creatures born in the tropics are dispatched so that they arrive in Europe from just before Whitsuntide until the end of September at the latest. I therefore had no choice but to wait.

One morning, after I had taken my bath, I went before breakfast on to the veranda to say good morning to my ring-necked parakeets, my tame wanderoo monkeys, and my chipmunks. On such occasions I always visited too a castor oil bush behind the bungalow in which lived a good friend of mine, an enormous praying mantis. Whenever I called on her, I would begin by teasing her a little with a stick so that I could admire her hingelike pincers and her bright round button-eyes; then, using a pair of tweezers, I would feed her with a dragonfly or some other large insect, which she would seize and devour with little attention to etiquette. She had been sitting in the same bush for six weeks, apparently waiting for a love-starved male to come along and be her husband; when he had performed his duty by fertilizing her eggs, she would show her tremendous gratitude by making a hearty meal of him. But so far she had waited in vain.

That morning, after feeding her, I went along to feast my eyes on my pet spider, but as I approached the box, I noticed that the underside of its body, where there should have been flesh, had become a gaping cavity. This in itself did not startle me, for already on a previous occasion I had found what at first glance appeared to be two spiders in the box, the one wearing brand-new apparel and looking very smart in its gleaming new colors, and the other reduced to an empty, almost colorless husk. Like all mollusks and arachnids, and in common with lizards and snakes, spiders must periodically slough their outer coverings, which are not elastic and do not grow with them. This time, however, instead of a second spider in the showcase, there was a countless swarm of tiny ants pouring out of the hollow shell of what had once been my prize spider. An army of these small, well-organized insects had descended in the thousands on the tyrant of the jungle, paralyzing it with their formic acid before cutting into it with their sharp pincers and devouring it. Now hundreds of them were marching out through a minute gap which had remained unnoticed between the joints of the box. Well aware of the potential danger of these ants, I had taken the precaution of placing the table legs on which the box stood in a bowl of water; but disdaining this safeguard, the ants had constructed a bridge of twigs and fragments of plants which, placed across the water barrier, had enabled them to reach their objective.

Angry at having lost my spider, but made wiser by the experience I had gained, I went about my day's work.

WE WERE EXPECTING a shipment of Asiatic black bears and Malayan bears, and to confine them I adopted the same system as for the monkeys, namely, a spacious enclosure with a ditch, rocks, and caves. The bears would therefore not be behind bars, but at liberty to roam the grounds as they pleased.

One morning the long-awaited news reached me that early next day the bears would be arriving from Bombay. This meant coping quickly with all the necessary preparations, and so I had all the available workers called together and allotted tasks to each. Harry and Anthony were made responsible for getting six oxcarts ready, while Marian, Sussa, and Hussein were to assemble all the ropes and cordage. The cook, a woman whom we nicknamed Twinkle-toes, collected from the provisions shed a hundredweight of rice which she took to the cooking-hut to boil over an open fire. Others hurried off to buy supplies of bananas and bread-tree fruit. We could not afford to overlook anything necessary in catering for ten hungry bears—indeed, everything had to be available in generous quantities. By evening all the preparations had been completed and we were ready for the new arrivals.

Having selected Harry to be my traveling companion, I proposed making Small, the head worker, responsible for things while we were away. I therefore summoned him and told him bluntly that he would be laying up trouble for himself if, during my absence, he got drunk, as he did all too often on the native toddy. He swore to me by all his grandmothers that in future he would avoid alcohol like the plague. Although I was not taken in by his lavish assurances, I acted as though I believed him and bade him a gracious farewell. At nightfall I took a quick shower, put on the clothes which the houseboy had laid out ready for me, had some light refreshment, and then we set out for Colombo.

The scene before us was breath-takingly beautiful; in the black heavens hung the full moon, bathing the plumes of the palm trees in silvery light. The great lights of the Southern Cross gleamed brilliantly, and the peace of the night was scarcely disturbed even by the tedious crunching noise made by the high wooden wheels of the oxcarts or the monotonous "Ho!

Ho!"'s of the drivers. The men walked in front of the ox teams holding long, burning palm switches, with which they beat the ground from time to time to frighten away snakes and other creatures. The heat became almost intolerable as we were swallowed up in dark forest, with dense jungle and impenetrable bamboos on either side of us. Hesitantly in the darkness a coolie began to chant, then another, then a whole chorus of voices were heard, chanting the native *Donno Bundunge;* it was fear which wrung from them this invocation to the "Good Moon." According to their philosophy, the forests are peopled with thousands of evil spirits, to whom singing is anathema; and so to drive away these evil spirits as well as their own fear, they sang until we reached the highway and open country.

Now the sinister forest lay behind us, and before us, the sea. Like liquid silver the waves rolled unendingly shoreward, each borne out of the lap of the next, always in sevens, every seventh wave higher than the rest. As they broke on the coral reef some way out from the beach, they sprayed like a fountain, silver against the black night sky, and then sank back into the dark waters. Warm though the sea breeze was, after the stifling, moisture-laden heat of the forest it seemed most refreshing to us as it played around our hot bodies. In a gently curving sweep the palm-fringed coast merged with the sea to where the distant beacon in the harbor of Colombo threw its beam into the vast, empty waters of the Indian Ocean.

We passed on through sleeping villages and small fishing settlements, where picturesque outrigger canoes had been pulled high up on to the white, sandy beach. As we came to the outskirts of Colombo, the fiery sun rose over the mountains, flooding the city with dazzling light.

On arrival at the quayside, I hired a lighter to take me across to the steamer when it anchored so that I could collect my bears. The ship cast anchor at ten o'clock, and by noon, after two hours' strenuous work, the bear crates had been loaded on to the oxcarts. Because the fierce heat of the sun would have endangered the bears' lives, we decided not to begin the return journey until the comparative cool of the evening. We therefore parked under a covered way near the market place and waited for the sun to set.

The return journey was by no means as smooth as the outward one had been, for when we were halfway through the dense forest the draft oxen suddenly stopped and would not go a step farther. Apprehensively my men tugged at the carts, but the oxen only grunted and stubbornly refused to budge. The chirping of the crickets had ceased, and close by

some owls passed overhead, hooting with alarm; a couple of fruit bats left their tree and flew off noiselessly like black specters in the moonlight. Releasing the safety catch of my rifle, I attempted to discover what it was that had startled the owls and bats from the tree by directing the powerful beam of my torch into its tangled foliage. There, about thirty feet above the ground, I saw a pair of greenish-red gleaming points, and found myself gazing into the eyes of a large leopard. I immediately switched off the torch, and at the same moment a dark form, silhouetted against the moonlight, hurtled through the air towards me. Instinctively I sprang to one side and raised my rifle to my shoulder. Very fortunately for me the leopard jumped short, landing five yards ahead of me to my left. Crouching on the moonlit path, its fine speckled coat shining like silk, it snarled viciously, ready to spring again. But for a brief moment it hesitated, as though unable to make up its mind whether to attack the oxen, which stood pawing the ground in terror, or to spring at me as I stood alone in the middle of the path. This hesitation cost the leopard its life, for in that moment I aimed and fired two shots.

The leopard tried to spring again, but jumped only one yard before falling in a heap on its side; for a few moments it tore at the earth with its unsheathed claws and then lay motionless. On my instructions we remained where we were for ten minutes, during which time no one was allowed to approach the leopard. I myself had on frequent occasions had nasty experiences with leopards I had shot, and I know of hunters who have been killed or badly wounded by these big cats, which are very tenacious of life as much as ten minutes after a lethal bullet has penetrated their skulls. There was not a spark of life left in this leopard, however; one bullet had entered its brain from above the right eye, the other had pierced its neck from under the left jawbone and was later found lodged in the left side of the heart.

The coolies loaded this unexpected booty on to one of the carts, and amid loud chanting to the "Good Moon" and the "Ho! Ho!"s of the drivers, we made our way noisily through the sinister forest back to the compound. My Sinhalese and Tamil coolies feared for the safety of their families living in the village, for so large a leopard had never before been sighted in the neighborhood of the compound; but during the weeks

which followed no other big cat made an appearance; in fact not until six months later was another one seen, which put us all on our guard.

At daybreak we put the ten bears into the new enclosure, where they seemed to be at home from the very outset, behaving themselves extremely well. Sussa, to whom I had given the task of looking after them, was able to wander about in the enclosure almost without danger, for he only needed to show them a stout stick and a whip and they would retreat hurriedly into their caves. When they were fed, chiefly with sweet rice, there was generally a free-for-all among them, which sometimes developed into ill-tempered tussles. In spite of these, all went well in the enclosure for the first six months, by the end of which the bears had become almost fully grown. At about this time, however, one of the Asiatic black bears began to adopt a somewhat aggressive attitude towards Sussa, and so one day I decided to accompany him on his bear round. For this visit I took with me a leather whip with which to bring the "revolutionary" to reason, seeing that Sussa was too soft-hearted to do so himself.

The entrance to the bear enclosure was through an iron door, and it was a rule that the keeper should always close the door after him. As we stepped inside, the bears trotted up as usual to Sussa and allowed themselves to be stroked and petted behind the ears, with the exception of the surly fellow, who shuffled about growling. He seemed determined to pick a quarrel with me, and circling round, he suddenly reared up and struck at my face with one of his paws. Side-stepping, I dealt him a smart blow across the body with the whip, making the dust fly from his coat. Growling, the bear turned his back on me and trotted off four or five steps, but all at once he turned round with lightning speed and attacked me again as he reared up on his hind legs. But I was ready for him, and whipped him soundly about the body until he fled to the far end of the enclosure. Taking no notice of Sussa nor of the other bears, which had scurried off in terror, I pursued the rebel and gave him a few more lashes to remember me by; his resistance broken, he slunk off into his cave.

Suddenly I heard shouts, and pandemonium broke loose in the compound. Amid the trumpeting of elephants, the roaring of tigers and leopards, and the gibbering of hundreds of excited monkeys, I could hear Anthony shouting, "Master, the bears are out of the cage!" and Harry calling, "Come quickly, Herr Randow, the bears have escaped!" What had happened, as I discovered later, was that Sussa had taken fright in the enclosure and had run off, forgetting to bolt the door after him. The other nine bears, who had been trotting after him on the assumption that it was feeding time, had as usual pawed at the door and, finding that it opened, had marched out in single file. Seeing Sussa still running, they had trotted after him and tailed him in a game of follow-the-leader. Hussein, riding our largest elephant and leading two smaller elephants, one on either side of him, just happened to be crossing the path at the very moment when the nine bears hurried past. The startled elephant pulled up short, raised its trunk and trumpeted, and then, turning round, it careered back towards its shed, uttering shrill warning cries as it fled.

Hussein lost all control of the beast, and of the two smaller elephants, which copied everything the leading elephant did. The effect of this sudden rampage on the other animals in the compound was electrifying; in a frenzy of excitement they raised their voices in loud and vehement protest. The emus and cassowaries chased round their grounds in wild confusion, the parrots in the aviary screamed and fluttered, and swift action was necessary to prevent the situation getting too much out of hand.

We still held one bear captive, so I posted Anthony at the entrance and impressed upon him that he must open the door without hesitation when I returned with the other nine, but not until. Then I sounded the alarm on the gong, and in next to no time all the coolies had assembled, armed with sticks, ropes, and nets. The chase began, and it was not long before we had some success. With shouts and whoops we herded the nine bears, which stayed closely together, by devious paths back to their enclosure. Anthony opened the door, and they contentedly filed back into their familiar surroundings. We heaved a deep sigh of relief at having recaptured all nine of the runaways so easily.

Our pleasure and relief were short-lived, however, for at the very moment when we drove the nine bears back to where they belonged, the tenth bear, the surly fellow, appeared from nowhere and escaped through the open door, making straight for the forest. It required almost superhuman efforts on our part to head him off, but we just managed to do so before he reached the fringe. This was very fortunate for us, as it would have been virtually impossible to recapture him if he had reached the cover of the forest. In a sweeping arc the bear now struck out in the direction of a small, almost circular lake, which was flanked on three sides by high, steep banks; the bank on the fourth side was level and open,

with a few scattered shrubs and trees. There were no crocodiles in this lake, only water tortoises, fish, and a few mandarin ducks. Reaching the open bank of the lake, the bear ran up and down growling with anger; whenever we approached him, he reared up on his hind legs and flashed out his paws at us aggressively. Our efforts to throw a noose over his head were of no avail, for he skillfully eluded it and even began playing with it until it was torn to shreds. Although it was clear that it was going to be far from easy to recapture the bear, I nevertheless had no wish to shoot this valuable creature.

Summoning the coolies to withdraw and so give the bear a chance to quiet down, I led them a short distance away and watched to see what he would do next. We saw him climb a tall mango tree and eat some fruit, after which he nestled in a fork to rest after his exertions. Seizing this opportunity, I had some of my men bring across a heavy transport crate with a sliding door, and we surrounded the tree. Alarmed, the bear left his comfortable nook and retreated to the outermost branches, which overhung the water. A few stouthearted Tamils, with lanky James leading the way, climbed up after him and tried to noose the bear, who, in a desperate effort to avoid the rope, lurched backwards and toppled into the water, where he began swimming.

Our hopes soared, for we thought that all we need do now was to wait and catch him as he swam ashore. But every time he placed his front paws on the edge of the bank and saw us, he turned tail, shaking his head in anger, and swam off again. All at once he headed for the steep rock face on the opposite bank and making use of a small, jutting piece of rock, he heaved himself up by clutching at some brushwood which grew there in the clefts. Once out of the water, he settled down, apparently determined to remain where he was.

Sussa wanted to swim across the lake and drive the bear out of his niche. Being an impulsive fellow, he ignored my instruction to stay by me and, plunging into the water, struck out towards the spot where the bear had taken refuge. Meanwhile the bear had made himself comfortable and refused to be intimidated by the coolie's approach. Shouting and splashing, Sussa tried to evict him from his stronghold, but he would not budge an inch. Changing his tactics, Sussa clung on to a creeper and attempted to oust the bear, which was reclining by the water's edge, by giving it a kick; but the bear took not the slightest notice. Angered by his indifference, Sussa approached still closer and jabbed him in the side with his right foot.

We saw Sussa fall back into the water and swim out into the middle of the lake, while the bear remained peacefully where he was. Sussa seemed to be swimming very slowly, but we did not suspect that anything was amiss until we heard him cry out in a tremulous voice, "I'm wounded!" and then we saw that the water round him was red with blood. Immediately Anthony and James hurried to his assistance, bringing their wounded friend safely ashore, where he collapsed in a state of exhaustion. The bear had bitten him in the right leg, but with such lightning speed that not one of us who had been watching had seen him do it. The leg was bleeding badly and looked very serious, but fortunately, as I discovered from a quick examination, the bones and sinews were undamaged. I staunched the flow of blood and bandaged the wound. After an hour I loosened the tourniquet, and the following day had Sussa taken to the hospital in Colombo.

As the bear had reduced the situation to a stalemate, all we could do for the moment was to keep him under observation. I therefore posted lookouts with strict instructions that they should report to me without delay if the bear left his stronghold.

Just after sunset the thought occurred to me that it might be worth trying to drive the bear out of his unassailable position by means of fire. On my instructions, some of the coolies heaped up brushwood and straw at a point where the rocks overhung the lake, while others set light to the highly inflammable material and hurled it down at the bear. The rest of us meanwhile made our way over to the flat stretch of shore to prepare a reception for the bear, and as it had become quite dark, we made a fire by the edge of the lake to light up our surroundings. We saw the first few flaming missiles fall short of the mark, but the coolies finally succeeded in reaching their target, as we could tell by the smell of singed hair. After a while we heard a splash, and in the reflected glow of the water we saw the bear make for the bank where we were waiting and climb out on to dry land. Straightway we cut off every escape route and, snatching burning branches from the fire, we drove him into the large crate, where he slunk defeated into a corner. Apart from a few singed hairs he had come to no harm from his escapade.

But the same could not be said of Sussa. After five days in the hospital, he returned to the compound in an oxcart, having decamped because he was afraid that the surgeon was going to amputate his leg, which had swollen to an enormous size. Scolding him for his imprudence, I removed his bandage and saw that the purulent wound was smeared with ointment. The leg was swollen right up to the top of the thigh, and the skin was taut and glassy in appearance. He looked a hopeless case, and it was obvious to me that if extreme measures were not taken without further delay, it would be all up with Sussa. I therefore resorted to a form of treatment which would have made a European doctor gasp with horror.

I filled a large cauldron with water and placed it on a low wood fire in front of the hut in which Sussa lived with his family. The wood was only glowing and the fire was kept up by a coolie blowing on it. Then I gave Sussa, who was moaning and groaning with the pain, a morphia injection and laid him on a bed of branches in such a way that the whole of his suppurated right leg was immersed in the water of the cauldron. I made sure that the water rose slowly in temperature without becoming so hot that he would be scalded. This procedure, which was extremely painful for the patient, was continued for twenty hours. After I had given him a further injection, we carefully laid him on a bast mat and, while several coolies held him down, I massaged the pus and the foul-smelling, lumpy blood out of the wound. I will excuse myself from giving further details, but suffice it to say that I succeeded in saving Sussa's leg and his life. Three months later he was able to use the leg without hindrance, and soon after was even able to run and swim again. This successful treatment greatly enhanced my prestige among the inhabitants in this part of Ceylon.

"Malu-master"

I HAVE ALWAYS HAD A PASSION for reptiles and fish; even as a boy I was a keen collector and reared my own specimens, and later I built the public aquarium in the Wuppertal Zoo and for years was in charge of it. This deep-seated passion impelled me time and again to return to the tropics to add to my knowledge of the behavior of fish in their natural habitats, and to discover new things about the life cycles of reptiles through the changing seasons.

Then one day came the invitation from my doctor friend, who lived on the coast, to install a temporary collecting station at his villa. I felt that as my wife and Harry were now competent to run the compound by themselves for a few weeks, I could accept the invitation with an easy mind.

As I sketched out my plan of campaign, however, I became more and more convinced of the support which my wife, with her technical qualifications, could give me in the work I envisaged, for not only would she be of valuable assistance to me in catching fish, but moreover she would be able to take notes on our observations, an integral part of research work. During our absence Harry would have to take sole charge of the compound, but he would be able to contact me easily if any difficulties arose, since I would be only a day's journey away. When I made these thoughts known to my wife she beamed with joy, for she felt that she had been rather left out of the picture when I had gone off on my expedition to the wild animal reserve without her.

"We'll start out tomorrow," I told her, "and for the next month or so we shall be living in the doctor's new, modern bungalow right by the sea. Anthony and the cook will go with us, and if we find that we need any more helpers when we get there I expect we shall be able to recruit them on the spot. You three will have to go on ahead of me, as I must go to Colombo first to collect some air pumps and filters which are waiting for me there at the customs office. There's a lot to be done, so if you're going to be ready in time, you had better start getting your things together right away."

Next morning, before driving by car to Colombo, I watched Nona, Anthony, and the cook climb on to a bullock cart loaded with everything but the kitchen sink. Perched high on top of the crates and boxes sat Lottie, Nona's tame wanderoo monkey, and Jacko, her ring-necked parakeet. As the cart lurched through the gate of the compound and lumbered off in the direction of the coast, I imagined that this was how it would have looked had Robinson Crusoe and Man Friday moved house.

The doctor was deeply interested in my research work and shortly after my arrival, sitting with him on the veranda of his bungalow, I discussed ways and means of getting the large, iron-framed tanks constructed. We finally reached the conclusion that they would have to be built in Colombo; but when I went there to place my order, I found myself up against a total lack of understanding by the contractors. Despite all my explanations and numerous sketches, they were quite incapable of forming any visual picture of the equipment I required, and could not even grasp that the finished articles were intended to serve a useful purpose. Furthermore, thick glass was essential, and in the tropics this is very scarce. These difficulties were eventually overcome, however, and one day I received news that the tanks were ready for collection. They proved to be satisfactorily built, and after I had had them lined up along the verandas of two adjacent bungalows, I installed the pumps and filters. In addition, I sank circular concrete pipes measuring three feet across in specially prepared pits, the bottoms of which I had spread with a mixture of concrete. In these outdoor aquaria, which were placed under shady papaw trees, the water remained at a constant cool temperature, and they were therefore ideal for the very important process of acclimatizing the fish placed in them.

In the time I could spare from making these arrangements, I went for walks with my wife to spy out the surrounding countryside. Not far from the villa we discovered the bed of a small river, dry during the hot seasons and filling up when the monsoons set in. Its estuary was some thirty yards wide, and dense undergrowth, consisting chiefly of mangroves, grew right down to its banks on either side. A few hundred yards offshore stretched a coral reef which acted as a breakwater.

The bungalow where we were staying was fitted with all those modern conveniences which we had had to do without for so long. In its courtyard I had a snake house erected, and installed a tank for turtles; these, together with the assortment of transport crates lined up there, formed our temporary collecting station.

All these preparations had taken a fortnight, but as yet our collection amounted to very little. This was certainly not due to a shortage of personnel, for I had recruited an ample number of assistants, but they brought me very little; evidently something was amiss. I reflected that in the past there had been periods when things seemed to go wrong because the natives did not bring me the specimens I wanted, and in the course of time I realized that the reason for this lay simply in their lack of understanding of what I required. In spite of their ever ready willingness to co-operate, they failed because they could not grasp the object of the work in which I was engaged. To illustrate the measure of their ignorance of my aims, I will recount an experience which is true in every detail and which occurred shortly before I set out on the fishing expedition.

Before making up my mind to go on this expedition, I had already systematically explored all the streams and rivers in the neighborhood of the compound, and the fish I had caught were placed in tanks two and a half feet long which were kept on the veranda of my bungalow. These searches had yielded some very beautifully colored fish which varied in length from two to six inches. The problem of acclimatizing them to the static water of the tanks proved to be a very difficult one, but as time went by, the tanks became filled with a very impressive assortment, including some species hitherto unknown to science. Every morning I went to make sure that the fish were still alive and to feed them before making my customary tour of inspection round the compound. My collection of ornamental fish afforded me a good deal of pleasure, and my wife, being especially fond of sensitive and delicate creatures, was likewise deeply interested in them.

One morning, as I went over to inspect them, I was struck dumb with horror and dismay at the sight that met my eyes. The covers placed over the tanks to prevent the fish jumping out were in position, but the water was cloudy and in each tank a large creature almost as long as the tank itself was swimming round and round. Peering into the turbulent water I saw that they were snakeheads, eel-like fish about the thickness of a man's wrist. In order to throw some light on this extraordinary mystery, which had destroyed the fruits of many weeks of painstaking efforts, I had Anthony and the cook brought before me. The cook, a meek and placid man from northern India, could only tell me that half an hour previously the village headman had been in the garden with some other villagers and had gone up to him in the kitchen behind the bungalow; with a smile of satisfaction the headman had told him that "loco-master" now need go hungry no longer! I immediately suspected that this sinister statement had something to do with the new occupants of the tanks, and therefore sent Harry into the village to get to the bottom of the matter. When he returned he could at first hardly speak for laughing, but at length I learned that the villagers, incited by my own team of keepers, had come to the conclusion that Nona Randow had not been looking after me properly, as she was in the habit of concocting "undefinable dishes"; they were convinced that "loco-master" did not get enough rice and curry, and most important of all, the fish in his tanks were much too small for fish curry. Out of sheer pity they had therefore thrown away the small fish and replaced them with large ones so that he could have bigger dinners. . . .

This story illustrates the sort of problems with which I was faced in my endeavors to school these simple-minded natives to an understanding of my aims and intentions. I had a most difficult time trying to explain to them the differences, which, it is true, are not always easy to determine, between fresh water, brackish water, and salt water, so that when they returned from their excursions they could give precise details as to the kind of water from which their specimens were taken. This information was of vital importance to me in helping to identify the specimens so that I could place them in the appropriate aquarium to acclimatize them.

In the beginning I was constantly being given wrong information about this decisive biological question, and as a result I lost many valuable fish. Even Anthony, who was more experienced in my methods than any of the other natives, tended to make mistakes; once he brought back a magnificent argus fish two inches long which he maintained he had caught in the river, but this was impossible, for I knew that this fish lives only in sea water. I therefore immediately transferred it from the fresh water aquarium to the salt water aquarium, but it was already too late to save it. I went with Anthony to the exact spot where he had caught the argus fish and, by means of a hydrometer, established that it was pure sea water. The spot was situated at the mouth of the river which I mentioned earlier; at high tide the sea swept in and submerged the estuary with very salty water. In order to show the natives precisely what the difference was between these various kinds of water, I decided to make a three-day expedition upstream which, at the same time, would enable me to ascertain which species of fish lived in which sections of the river.

At first light we set out, taking with us enamel pails, dragnets, hand nets, a large garden hose, watering cans on the spouts of which were fastened pieces of rubber tubing a yard long, small transport crates and sacks, together with a lot of other equipment. I also thought it advisable to take a supply of snake serum and some rifles, for even though our way would take us along the river from one village to another, there was nevertheless a good deal of jungle between the villages. There was no question of driving by car along the riverbanks, which I knew would be marshy in places and overgrown with bush. Now and then a narrow native path would follow the course of the river, but generally speaking we would have to battle our way through tangled masses of climbing plants and thorny undergrowth.

On arrival at the estuary we saw that the sea was at high tide, and the waves, breaking over the sandy shore, had entirely filled it; at ebb tide the waters would recede and the estuary would be dry again. Thus we were able to make our first observations and scientific notes without delay.

As the tide went out, it was interesting to watch the young sea perch, whose parents had penetrated into the upper estuary during the rainy season and had spawned in the brackish water there, now moving down to their true habitat, the salty sea. Varying in length from three to six inches, these fascinating, multicolored perch could be seen making their last despairing efforts to escape from the river to the Indian Ocean; here they would live in the submarine gardens of the coral reef until the monsoon came and filled the river. The resultant mixture of fresh and sea water between the coral reef and the shore would rouse their mating instincts, whereupon they would fight their way against the current to the spawning grounds in the upper reaches. The partly fresh and partly brackish river water of the monsoon period gives rise to huge masses of infusoria and myriads of other microorganisms which turn the water now yellow, now red, and provide food for the millions of fish larvae and young fry. The young fish grow very quickly in these ideal conditions, but as the river gradually dries up they swim off into their true element which Nature has ordained for them, the sea.

Explaining the sea perch's dual life cycle to my simple-minded coolies was no easy task, but fortunately a happy coincidence intervened which made it simpler than it would otherwise have been. Near the estuary there were a number of shabby, windowless fishing huts, and close by the finely carved outrigger canoes of the fishermen lay high and dry in the shade of a cluster of coconut palms. Thin ribbons of smoke curling into the clear morning air wafted the scent of burning wood across in our direction. I suggested to Anthony that we might strike up a conversation with these fishermen, but he strongly opposed the idea, saying that he regarded them as untrustworthy and dangerous people. My doctor friend had also warned me against them; yet it was from just such men, whom everyone decried, that I had on various occasions gained some most useful practical knowledge. While I was still turning over in my mind what I should do in this particular case, Nature herself intervened and made my decision for me.

A small, dark-blue cloud loomed low on the horizon out at sea, growing larger and more foreboding as it drifted towards us. Very soon it would be upon us, bringing a short but violent rainstorm. In the tropics it is dangerous to be caught in a storm because the unbearably humid heat which sets in immediately after the downpour can cause serious attacks of fever. Concerned at the possible consequences for my wife, who was less inured to these climatic extremes than I, I proposed that we should run to take shelter in the fishermen's huts before it was too late. Racing as fast as our legs would carry us, we reached the first hut just in the nick of time.

The fishermen had seen us running, and one of them, a white-haired old man whose skin looked like shriveled leather, was waiting at the entrance of his hut, and with a deep salaam ushered Nona inside. I myself remained outside during the fierce storm, sheltering against the leeside wall of the hut. Resolutely crossing the threshold, my wife disappeared inside the almost dark hut and, exhausted by her sprint, sank into a chair

which the old man offered her. It was an old three-legged chair, on the back of which was carved the flag of a shipping company and the date 1832; it was probably a relic of the old pirate days. The fishermen of Ceylon have always had a bad reputation for piracy which, it would seem, they thoroughly deserve. Even today they occasionally try to lure coasting schooners on to the perilous coral reefs by means of false signals so that they can plunder the wrecks.

The storm lasted barely a quarter of an hour; then the sun came out again and blazed down from a sky which was now quite cloudless. From all the huts fishermen emerged, bringing with them their skinny goats, which had likewise sought shelter from the rain. Their wives and children also appeared, but it was not until Nona had presented them with small coins that they became at all friendly or amenable. Then Anthony, acting as interpreter, told the fishermen about our expedition. At this their faces lit up, and one of the men, who was about thirty and who impressed me with his fine build and physique, seemed particularly interested. He could even speak a little English for, as we learned later, he had formerly been employed as a stoker on European steamers. I explained to the attentive fishermen the difference between salt water and fresh water, and then told them that their assistance in catching rare fish and other creatures for me would be most welcome. They were amazed that, being a foreigner, I should know so much about the fish which lived in their part of the world, for in their simplicity they believed that they alone were aware of such things. I then spoke about various species of fish, and among these I happened to mention puffer fish which, I said, must inhabit these waters, adding that they were poisonous and should therefore not be eaten. These fish were well known to them, but under a different name. The men marveled at my knowledge, and when I showed them a book containing color illustrations of fish, they almost swooned with wonderment. By these means I was able to establish a very friendly contact with the fishermen, who dubbed me "Malu-master" (Fish-master), a nickname which stayed with me throughout the rest of my stay in Ceylon.

The fishermen accompanied us the short distance to the estuary and showed me a spot where I could catch puffer fish. Jumping into the waist-deep water and using our hand nets, they soon returned with a fine catch of fish which they had netted from the hollowed-out sloping banks of the river. Among them I identified young therapons, silver-and-black-striped sea perch, small green and sepia-brown argus fish flecked with black dots like a leopard and, in one variety, with a rich red sash across its head. We also found three varieties of puffer fish, the largest of which was about the size of a child's clenched fist. When they were taken out of the water they pumped themselves full of air till they resembled inflated balloons. Placed on the surface of the water, they floated like bladders for a while; then, gradually releasing the air through their abdominal cavity with a soft hissing sound, they sank to the bottom of the river and darted out of sight. I tried to explain to the natives that this behavior on the part of the puffer fish was due to a natural instinctive reflex action, but I think they failed to grasp what I meant. I invited the English-speaking fisherman, who appeared to be the most useful of the party for my purposes, to join our fishing expedition, and after I had presented the others with a handful of cheroots and a few plugs of tobacco, we parted company.

After a three-hour march upstream, we came upon a stretch of land which was so swampy that it was no longer possible to follow the bank in carefree fashion as we had been doing; instead, we were obliged to make a detour to avoid the worst of the swamp. The water samples which we took from this part of the river still revealed traces of salinity. The marshy terrain was luxuriant with marsh palms and mangroves, which at this point had ousted the coconut palms. Our progress was impeded by hundreds of small pools and channels which shimmered in the hot, sun-drenched air, and over which swarms of mosquitoes hovered. Continually sinking knee-deep in waterholes, we soon looked as though we had just emerged from a mud bath. Jumping from one islet to another, we at length reached the edge of the forest and with it terra firma again.

From time to time, deeply concerned about my wife, I glanced discreetly back at her to see how she was coping with this "walk" through the mangrove swamp. Besides the almost unbearable heat and the mosquitoes, we were plagued by hordes of bloodsucking leeches, and after a while I asked her how she was bearing up to these trying conditions. She replied with calm assurance that she was quite content and that, so far as she was concerned, the leeches and mosquitoes were an integral part of the experience. She added that, unlike the tropical houses in the botanical gardens of Europe, this panorama was genuine down to the last detail. I was pleased that she was disposed to view the situation in such a buoyant manner, and turned again to my observing.

This marshy region harbored many mudskippers of various species, some of which displayed on their heads and backs large skin-combs embellished with hairs. These peculiar fish, which grow to a length of ten inches, live amphibiously, although for the most part they perch on mudbanks in the broiling hot sun looking for all the world like antediluvian salamanders. As I approached one of them, it looked up at me inquisitively with its goggle eyes; then, skillfully using its pectoral fins as legs, it hopped into the water to safety before I had time to stoop and pick it up. Brownish in color with dark, hieroglyphic markings, these mudskippers glow with a shimmering iridescence which at times gives their moist newt-like skin a bluish appearance. In shallow water they wriggle very adeptly with eel-like movements, and they can bury themselves at lightning speed in the mud.

Here and there grew dwarf water lilies and large-leaved cryptocoryne plants, and in the less marshy places multicolored species of colocasia blossomed, looking magnificent with their arrow-shaped, red-and-yellow-veined leaves. A water test revealed a slight acidity in the water, which meant that the organs of the mudskippers and of any other fish living here must be adapted in such a way as to enable them to live in water deficient in oxygen. Nature must also have fitted them with means of overcoming the periods of drought when the region dried up almost completely. I now sought with great interest to establish what other species of fish were to be found living in these conditions.

At the edge of the forest we came upon a piece of raised ground which was dry, and there we pitched camp because I wished to spend the whole of the following day in the region carrying out further research work. That evening we witnessed a uniquely beautiful sunset, which lighted up the sky with every conceivable shade of color, ranging from dark red to midnight blue and tinged with greens and yellows. The landscape of mangroves continuously changed color, and every pool and waterhole gleamed like liquid gold shot through with streaks of quicksilver. Like ghosts the small white herons stood motionless on the islets. In the incredibly short space of half an hour all this splendid array of color vanished as the evening yielded to the tropical night. A fresh sea breeze swept in along the estuary, bringing a certain measure of relief to our scorched bodies. We lit a campfire and fed it with damp wood to make smoke, which we hoped would drive away the hordes of mosquitoes. And then the marshland was filled with the sound of old Vienna melodies and Grieg's soulful music which we coaxed from our gramophone, until the mosquitoes, which became more and more troublesome, drove us back into our tent. There in the fervid heat, I spent a restless night, and as though in a half-dream I heard in the distance the tom-tomming of the palaver drums of the nearby villages.

As the sun came up I set about my work, systematically searching all the pools for fish, while my wife took notes on all the individual species brought up in the nets. These operations were watched attentively by hundreds of herons which waded around us, fishing. Before long they grew bolder and began coming closer and closer until it was almost possible to stretch out one's hand and seize one. Whenever we emptied the contents of a net into a pail and started examining it for new species, these birds came strutting along and with all the impudence in the world robbed us of one fish after another. Vastly amused by their affable impertinence, I refrained from putting a stop to their poaching.

For the most part the specimens consisted of labyrinth fish which, although true fish, are capable of drowning. This may sound incredible but it is a fact. They are very brightly colored fish which are found in marshy regions throughout the tropics and subtropics. They breathe during the first few weeks of their life by means of gills; then a labyrinthlike accessory breathing organ forms on either side of the head, after which, in order to be able to live under water, they have to rise to the surface and take in atmospheric air through their mouths. If they were kept in an aquarium and were prevented from coming to the surface for air, they would suffocate and drown in their own element. Labyrinth fish are very popular ornamental fish much sought after by dealers and collectors because of their splendid colors. When the danger of drought threatens, they bury themselves in mud which, although hard and parched on top, has beneath the surface layer another layer which remains moist; there they pass through a period of torpor until the rainy season stirs them to new life and activity.

Next I searched eagerly for the fabulous climbing perch, with which I was already familiar but specimens of which I had never yet caught. After several futile attempts to explain to the fishermen what it was I wanted, my wife decided that the best way of conveying the idea was by a visual demonstration, and she therefore promptly threw herself into a shallow pool and clambered back unaided on to dry land, flapping her arms as though they were a seal's flippers. That the Sinhalese did understand; they laughed loud and long, beaming and shaking their heads vigorously, which in this part of the world signifies "yes." I too was tickled pink by Nona's demonstration and by her appearance on reaching land; she was striped like a zebra from top to toe.

Knowing now what to look for, my team of men began fishing with flat baskets among the hollowed-out riverbanks, scraping the rims of the baskets along the bed of the river before bringing them up to the surface again. In this way all the fish and other forms of life which were lying concealed among the crevices had no choice but to come out and be trapped in the baskets. By this method we caught some large, nine-inch-long, brackish-water prawns of a kind hitherto unknown, some rare water insects and snails, and finally even several climbing perch with copper-colored scales. The coolies took hold of these creatures with great care warning me not to pick them up with my hands because the spine on the gill-cover is poisonous. Some time later I was to find this out for myself to my own cost when I happened to be taking a climbing perch out of an aquarium with my hand; I pricked my finger on the gill-cover spine and felt a stinging pain run right up my arm to the armpit. The feeling was just like an electric shock, and my arm was completely numb for several hours afterwards.

Towards midday we gathered together all the fish we had caught and returned to our camping site, as it had become quite impossible to continue working in the oppressive heat and moisture-laden atmosphere.

That evening the moon hung like a yellow sickle in the heavens, and lantern cicadas by the hundreds winked out their Morse signals. Nona sprayed her legs, arms, face, and neck with insecticide while I lay back listening to the gramophone and smoking a cheroot. All at once the English-speaking fisherman appeared and asked whether we would care to accompany him on a short walk. Taking my pocket torch I stepped out of the tent, followed by Nona, and together we walked behind the fisherman, who was making in the direction of the river. Just before reaching the first waterhole we noticed several dark creatures the size of a man's fist hopping clumsily through the undergrowth. I discovered that they were toads, the first I had seen hereabouts. We collected a few specimens, and saw that they were dark brown with reddish markings.

Then came a great moment for me, for I saw a climbing perch actually scaling a tree stump! The scene reminded me of a picture which as a boy I had often gazed at with rapture; but never in my wildest dreams had I supposed that one day, in the company of my wife and a native guide, I would see that picture spring to life before my very eyes. At first we saw just one, then we counted up to forty climbing perch skipping across the dewy grass and over the carpets of club mosses in the direction of the river. Everywhere they could be seen climbing out from the pools which were almost dried up, and without hesitation setting off towards the river. Using the muscular, scaly base of their pectoral fins, they made surprisingly good progress, moving in much the same way as a seal does on land. I had discovered that they are night creatures, only venturing from their waterholes when the grass is wet with dew. I was delighted at having seen for myself these remarkable fish, whose instinct was to me quite incomprehensible; they sensed that they must abandon their waterholes and pools, which the high tide had left behind, and find water elsewhere because their pools were drying up. Spurred on by the instinct of self-preservation, they made their way overland towards the river, knowing that there alone was their salvation. This sight of scores of climbing perch was at once a unique experience and a revelation which moved me deeply and made me forget all my troubles and mosquito bites. For the Sinhalese fisherman, on the other hand, it was evidently nothing remarkable, and he was dumbfounded when, as a token of my appreciation, I handed him a rupee.

After skirting two villages, we reached a part of the river where the water was fresh. The banks were high and dry, and the path alongside, hemmed in by giant bamboos and a great variety of trees and shrubs, was very narrow. Here we had to exercise rather more caution, for from now on big game and preying cats might well disrupt our explorations. At this point the river widened into small lake-like expanses, on the banks of which there were occasional clumps of reeds and rushes. In the shallow water giant clusters of lotus blossoms and water lilies grew luxuriantly. Underwater plants impeded us as we laboriously waded through the shallows. The bird world was represented here by numerous species; the region was swarming with rose-colored starlings, mynahs, Brahman starlings, dial birds, shama thrushes, and bulbuls, and flocks of ring-necked parakeets flew to and fro across the river. Mousedeer, like miniature stags, scurried along the edge of the forest, butterflies fluttered through the air, and ahead of us skinks and Calotes lizards streaked by. Over the surface of the water kingfishers hovered for a few moments before suddenly plunging out of sight into the water, reappearing seconds later and flashing off with a fish in their beaks.

On reaching this lake-like widening of the river I called a halt, as I wished to devote a whole day to exploring the region. After making sure that there were no crocodiles lurking under the dense pads of water-lily leaves or elsewhere, we decided to make a thorough search of this stretch of river to see what sort of water life there was here. It was my intention to take the most interesting species back to the villa so that later, after they had been acclimatized to their new life in aquaria, they could be shipped off to Europe. We pitched our tent and made ourselves as comfortable as the limited space allowed. I decided that the day was to be devoted primarily, not to fish, but to reptiles.

We divided up into several groups and each party searched a particular stretch along the edge of the forest or along the riverbanks. We did not have to search long before we had our first success, some fleet-footed Calotes lizards, which we captured with running nooses. Why this agamoid species is called a bloodsucker I have never been able to find out, for it is quite harmless; even the natives have no fear of this fine lizard, which can radiate all the colors of the rainbow. Like the chameleon, it possesses the amazing ability to change color; one moment it is earthy brown, then suddenly its scaly back takes on an olive-green color, its throat changes to azure blue, and its head becomes cherry red. With debonair nods of its head, it sits on branches watching for insects which it catches by leaping through the air. This lizard, one of the two species of Calotes lizards found in Ceylon, grows to a length of twenty inches. It is difficult to capture because it can climb the smooth, whitish-gray trunks of coconut palms at breath-taking speed; then, as soon as it is out of range, it looks down askance, constantly changing color and nodding its head. The changing of color is not a means of camouflage but the expression of its feelings.

My wife drew my attention to another Calotes lizard, emerald green in color and over eighteen inches long, which was perched on a palm trunk some six feet from the ground. This Calotes lizard was a different species from the one which changes color, and is considerably rarer. I tried to catch it with a butterfly net but was unsuccessful, for with a leap the living emerald sprang down from the trunk of the palm tree and, with its body raised, ran like the wind on its hind legs only, using its long, whiplike tail as a support, across to the nearest mango tree where it ran nimbly up the trunk and disappeared from view among the curtain of leaves. In the course of that day, however, we managed to capture several splendid specimens of this fine lizard.

One of my men had caught some skinks, which are smooth-skinned lizards. In the course of their search they discovered a whole nest of young skinks less than an inch long. These lizards have a bronze appearance and grow to a length of twelve inches. They live secure in the vicinity of ant colonies, and sometimes even take up residence in anthills. Skinks have a firm, smooth, polished coat of scales similar to that of the European slowworm which, incidentally, also has a predilection for living in and near anthills. We had already collected rat snakes in sufficient quantities, so I was not interested in the additional specimens which were brought to me.

In her eagerness to discover things for herself, my wife had ventured forth alone. After a while she hurried back to where we were and with an expression of fear on her face, told me that she had started to climb a tree because in one of its forks she had seen a rare orchid growing; when she had climbed halfway up the tree, she had tried to cling to the aerial roots of the climbing plant when they suddenly eluded her and vanished among the tangle of foliage higher up. At first she had thought she was seeing things, but had stopped climbing so that she could recover from the shock. Then, taking a closer look at the leaves and aerial roots around her, she had lost her nerve and scrambled down the tree as quickly as she could.

"It's unnatural," she said. "I've never seen anything like it; just come and take a look! The leaves are alive and run along the branches, and then the aerial roots start moving too, shrivel up and vanish into the thick foliage!"

The fear which had entered into her was still clearly visible. I took this welcome opportunity to warn her sternly against going off to explore by herself. I had a shrewd idea of the cause of this phenomenon, and accompanied my wife to the "bewitched" tree, which had leaves similar to those of our own native oak. The tree itself was almost hidden by the twining stems and leaves of a blossoming arborescent ipomoea. Nona did not show the slightest inclination towards climbing the tree a second time, but I told her that she must. I went up with her, leading the way, until we were close to the leaves which had given her such a fright. The leaves stirred and did in fact move away. This unusual sight might indeed have struck terror into anyone who did not realize that these "moving leaves" were really insects, known as stone crickets. Possessing one of the most perfect forms of mimicry among living creatures, they resemble oak leaves so closely that at first glance one automatically assumes that they are leaves. How many people must have gained that impression when seeing these crickets for the first time in an insect house! Thousands upon thousands of them were here in this tree, the leaves of which provide them with food.

But what had happened to the living aerial roots which had also frightened Nona? We looked everywhere among the tangle of leaves, but could only discover a few brownish climbing tendrils with pale green extremities. I tugged at one of them: it was quite genuine. Then I drew Nona's attention to a thin, grass-green aerial root which was hanging down above our heads, and asked whether it was those she meant; she nodded vigorously that she did. Cautiously I touched the end of this root, whereupon it moved and in next to no time had disappeared among the tangle of leaves further up the tree.

"Do you know now what sort of roots they are?" I asked Nona, who had again begun trembling with fright.

"Yes," she murmured, "they're snakes."

"Yes, snakes," I said, "and you may count yourself lucky that this species is not very poisonous. You might have come across a tree adder instead; then it would have been a different story altogether."

Having solved the riddles of the bewitched tree, we climbed down again and I sent Anthony up to shake the snakes out of it. Before climbing up, he smiled roguishly at my wife, for he was very glad to be one up on Nona for once.

As Anthony shook the tree, those of us standing below witnessed the strange sight of dozens of these tree snakes gliding through the air and landing on bushes several yards away. Now we could understand why their bodies are arched and concave on the underside, and why they are hard and dry in contrast to the soft roundness of most other snakes. The belly revealed a snowy whiteness, the upper body a magnificent gleaming lime green, the small head was needle-shaped, the long snout ran on in a pointed, wormlike continuation, and the eyes were extraordinarily large and expressive. They glided sinuously and at great speed among the branches, which they barely touched, and without exaggeration one could have spoken of "flying snakes." All at once one of them shot like an arrow from the end of a branch horizontally into the air and landed, swinging up and down, on a bush at least five yards away. Some of these tree snakes were almost six feet in length, but only as thick as one's middle finger. The green ones are poisonous, and are known among the English-speaking natives as eyepickers because they strike at the eyes of their enemies. In the course of the afternoon we captured a considerable number of them, together with some brown snakes with gleaming yellow longitudinal stripes on the upper side of their bodies. Nearby we found some small, multicolored monitor lizards, as well as some brown lizards, and specimens of both were placed in sacks and crates. One very large Indian varanus, know by the natives as a *tallagoya,* was caught and cooked in the pot. For our next meal, besides our usual rice and curry, we enjoyed the tender white flesh of this creature, which for flavor and succulence can hold its own with chicken. By the riverbank we found large numbers of various kinds of water adders; these are related to our European ring snake, but their markings are altogether more colorful. A few soft-shelled tortoises, some of them no bigger than a half crown piece, completed our generous haul for the day.

While we were still engaged in accommodating our snakes and lizards, my wife came rushing over to us from the tent.

"There's a snake in the tent," she blurted out, "a thick, brightly colored snake two feet long that was hiding under a shirt. When I disturbed it, it hissed viciously and tried to bite me."

Startled, I ran off as fast as my legs would carry me, with Anthony close behind, to catch or to kill the creature. In the half-dark interior of the tent, we were unable to discover it for some time, but at length we found it half concealed in a fold of the canvas floor. After a great deal of exertion, Anthony succeeded in capturing the aggressive snake without injury to himself, and he put it out of harm's way. The snake was one of Nature's masterpieces; the Sinhalese refer to it with reverence and horror as *tic polonga* (spotted viper), but it more generally is called a Russell's viper. This species is reckoned to be the most dangerous snake in India and indeed throughout the Indian archipelago. It has the appearance of an embroidered pearl girdle and seldom exceeds three feet in length. Unlike the slender, agile cobra, it is a sluggish creature, but always aggressive, and its bite is almost invariably fatal. This incident served as a stern reminder to exercise greater caution, for during the whole day when we had been out exploring we had wandered about in the neighborhood carelessly and with gay abandon, neglecting to look where we were treading.

In spite of our encounter with the viper, we slept very well in our tent that night, for there were fewer mosquitoes than usual, and the exertions of the past few eventful days had made us very tired.

Next day we again set out along the riverbank, but before beginning operations we made a thorough search of the surface of the water and the edges of the banks, paying the closest attention to any objects resembling old tree trunks lying in the water, as they might in fact be crocodiles. We also searched the banks very carefully for cobras and Russell's vipers: the fright we had had the previous evening had put us on our guard. Nevertheless, we discovered quite a number of interesting creatures. Our coolies gathered round and listened as Anthony translated the observations concerning fish and other creatures which I dictated to my wife. They showed keen interest in my remarks, and being men who live their lives in close contact with every kind of wildlife, they frequently asked very intelligent questions, which led to a lively discussion.

My wife pointed to a small shoal of finger-long, cylindrical fish, which from our bird's-eye view of them resembled torpedoes. With their coffee-brown, spindle-shaped bodies they would hardly have been distinguishable had it not been for a bright, opalescent spot on their flat, pikelike heads. They were all stationary facing upstream between the bank and a tangle of reeds. I turned to my coolies and told them that with a single movement of my arm, and without touching the water, I would spirit these fish away and then, after a short while, make them visible again. They all looked at me a little incredulously and supposed that I wanted to have my little joke. Not wishing to disappoint them, I replied in the same spirit, but warned them to keep their eyes on the glowing spots on the heads of the fish, because otherwise the joke would misfire. I then mumbled a few abracadabras and stretched out my arms over the water and—the fish with the opalescent heads vanished! With another incantation, behold, the opalescent spots began, one by one, to reappear, and soon the whole flotilla was there again in exactly the same place, rowing peacefully against the current. My wife looked at me with wide-eyed amazement, while the coolies, uttering subdued murmurs of astonishment, looked shyly askance at me.

What had happened? What had I accomplished? I now tried to explain to them this peculiar phenomenon, but I believe that, with the exception of my wife, they never grasped the explanation which I gave of the mystery. The outcome was, however, that from then on I firmly consolidated my nickname "Fish-master," and night after night palaver drums beat out messages about the "Malu-master" and the strange power he wielded over fish. In order to give the simplest possible explanation of this so-called marvel to these children of Nature, I took a handful of these fish, which were halfbeaks, and placed them in a pail of water where everyone could get a good view of them. After leaving them in peace for a while, the bright opalescent spot appeared on their heads, vanishing the moment an object, such as one's hand, was placed over the pail. I told the coolies that millions of years ago many creatures had three eyes, the third of which was on top of the head. In the case of halfbeaks, it is scientifically termed the occipital eye. With this occipital eye, which is beneath the skin over the crown of the head, these creatures became aware of varying degrees of brightness. If fish-eating birds approach them, they turn off the glowing "third eye" and thereby become invisible, since the color of their backs matches the muddy river bed beneath them. Seen from the side, however, these same fish sport the most splendid colors, iridescent black, red, or green. Their camouflage is, therefore, primarily a protection against enemies attacking them from above. It is, in fact, true of nearly all fish that their backs consist of only one color, usually gray, brown, or black, while their sides often display several varied bright colors.

The coolies then brought out a dragnet and standing in the middle of the river where the water was chest-high, they slowly approached the bank in a half-circle. As they did so, they struck the water with switches and branches to drive the fish in towards the bank. When the net was laid on the bank, it was squirming with thousands of fish of all sorts and sizes, an indescribable array displaying all the colors of the rainbow. Its kaleidoscopic brilliance reminded me of a giant heap of living diamonds. The coolies threw the large fish, or at least those which they did not wish to take home to their wives for cooking, quickly back into the water. They were of no interest to me, for only in the smaller varieties could I expect to find new species. In the catch there were some beautifully colored barbs and rasboras, splendid perch, and strange sheat fish. Most of the species were already known to me, some only by their Latin names, but among this seemingly inexhaustible wealth of fish were two small species of barb which were completely unknown to me. They were given special care and were later transferred to an acclimatization aquarium.

After a peaceful night we broke camp next morning, and retracing our steps to the estuary, we returned with all haste to the villa and transferred our captured specimens to the aquaria.

The
Doctor Business

RICHARD CARTER

EDITOR'S NOTE

Are you getting the best possible medical care? Are you being overcharged? Does your health insurance offer real security? Do you feel the old-fashioned doctor-patient relationship has changed? Are you aware that there are a great variety of economic pressures on the average doctor?

Richard Carter's book, *The Doctor Business,* pulls back the curtain that hides the commercial side of your doctor's practice and of organized medicine in America. It is a frank analysis of the policies and practices of the powerful American Medical Association, of the availability of health services, of the cost of diagnosis and treatment, and of the efficacy of various types of health insurance.

From this startling study we present two outstanding chapters, "Medical Delinquency" and "Group Health". They are of vital, personal importance to everyone who goes to a doctor's office, clinic, or hospital.

Richard Carter is a seasoned reporter and medical writer whose work has appeared in such leading magazines as *Life, The Saturday Evening Post, True,* and *Coronet.* He is a recipient of the George Polk award for journalism. Mr. Carter spent seven years in collecting, sifting, and evaluating the facts and trends revealed in *The Doctor Business.*

Medical Delinquency

Whatsoever house I enter, there will I go for the benefit of the
sick, refraining from all wrongdoing or corruption. . . .

HIPPOCRATIC OATH

Life is short and Art is long; the Crisis is fleeting, Experiment
risky, Decision difficult. Not only must the physician be ready to do
his duty, but the patient, the attendants, and external circumstances
must conduce to the cure.

HIPPOCRATES

ONE of the most extraordinary documents in the recent history of organized medicine was mimeographed in 1954, pushed aside in 1955, and
forgotten in 1956. It was an attempt by the AMA's Special Committee
on Medical Practices to consider some of the financial problems that
tend to corrupt a physician's relations with his patients and colleagues.
The report was unprecedentedly frank. It acknowledged that improper
practices exist and are traceable to competition for fees. It pointed out
that the AMA and the state and county medical societies do little or
nothing to discipline physicians who try to beat the fee system by exploiting patients. It urged the AMA to use its authority in the interest
of reform.

In dealing with the primary responsibility of the medical profession,
which is to render service to humanity, the report made the honest observation that the physician also has responsibilities to himself and his
family. It suggested that, while financial gain is supposed to be a "subordinate consideration"—as codified medical ethics sometimes phrase it
—large and frequent fees are of inescapable importance to a physician
trying to survive in a competitive setting. The committee realized clearly
that conflict between duty to mankind and duty to self underlies most
current problems of the profession.

As an AMA committee responsible to AMA officers and trustees, this group was in no position to seek fundamental solutions. Its function was not to wreck the AMA's cherished fee-for-service system of individual practice, but to find means of propping it up. The committee could not recognize that the way to align altruism with self-interest is to organize medical services so that physicians' incomes can be regularized and their services co-ordinated—as is done in some outstanding hospitals and group-practice clinics. However, the committee could suggest palliatives; and it did.

For example, it proposed palliatives for fee-splitting, a common corruption in which the surgeon or other specialist kicks back part of his fee to the physician who sends him the paying patient. The report declared with justice that one reason for fee-splitting is that general physicians are not now getting an equitable share of the medical dollar from the patient and seek to supplement their incomes by making referrals to surgeons who will kick back. It urged that organized medicine devise a system of evaluating medical services according to their relative worth. While the resultant scale of values would not be binding on physicians in setting their fees, it would tend to reduce some of the grab-bag aspects of medical economics. And, by entitling the general practitioner to a greater than usual share of the surgical patient's total disbursements, the relative value scale would reduce his yen for the kickback.

As to the conflict between altruism and opportunism, the committee naïvely suggested a publicity campaign in which the public would be "informed *at exactly what point* [italics added] the doctor can be expected to subordinate his normal self-interest in order to safeguard the patient's vital interests."

This wrinkle evoked tart comment from Dr. Paul R. Hawley, director of the American College of Surgeons. "Where is the point?" he wrote in the ACS *Bulletin*. "Is it where the patient's vital interests are invaded 50 per cent, 40 per cent, 10 per cent or 5 per cent? Or is it, as we doctors have long boasted, where the patient's vital interests are 100 per cent protected? The fixation of this point will be of the greatest interest to patients."

Dr. Hawley is a gadfly. He fastened on the committee's failure to stress that medical corruption is a scandalous deterrent to health and not merely an embarrassment to the carefree practice of medicine. "The report," he wrote, ". . . is a challenging, thought-provoking document. It deals with medical practice from almost every point of view other than the interests of the patient."

Despite its essential conformity with AMA values, the committee report was too rich for the AMA's blood and was sat upon. Dr. Hawley is also too rich for the AMA's blood but declines to be sat upon. For years he has been leading the College of Surgeons' attempts to interpret AMA ethics literally, combat surgical incompetence and cupidity, and eradicate fee-splitting, unnecessary surgery, and related evils. Because he has not hesitated to seek public support in this campaign and has made the rest of organized medicine look disgraceful by comparison, he has been excoriated in the AMA and in numerous state and county societies. But he keeps talking. Moreover, he keeps talking with the approval of the College and is largely responsible for that group's present eminence as the only important subdivision of organized medicine which is not afraid of change, not resentful of consumer opinion, and not reluctant to discipline any surgical malefactor that it can catch.

Before going any further, I must emphasize that I do not know how many physicians split fees, plunder insurance funds, or accept commissions from drugstores and diagnostic laboratories. Neither will anyone else know until some public agency uses the power of subpoena to find out. But I do know that the medical society functionary who dismisses these problems as confined to "the unethical few" has no basis for that comforting contention. The facts are that medical corruption is common knowledge wherever physicians drink coffee and swap clinical details.

What is most important about these transgressions, I am sure, is that they are not the heart of the matter. They are mere symptoms of a more profound and infinitely more offensive affliction—the jungle-type medical economics perpetuated by organized medicine. The evils assailed by Dr. Hawley are products of, and indivisible from, a fee system which almost propels the physician toward violation of his sworn trust. The thousands upon thousands of fee-for-service physicians who do not succumb to this awful pressure are lucky to have such stern consciences or such rich relatives. But their goodness does not make the fee system good.

Let us now inspect fee-splitting not as an isolated product of abstract evil but as a characteristic of the fee system. Fees are split because the growth of medical science has imposed difficulties on the individual physician. If he is a general practitioner, he frequently encounters cases with which he is less qualified to cope than a specialist would be. Or, if he is a specialist, he gets cases which could be handled more skillfully by another specialist. His consideration of the case is affected by the patient's medical insurance, which usually pays off only for surgery or other in-hospital treatment and ignores nonsurgical services in home and office. The physician has three choices:

1. He can decide that the case will probably respond to the treatment he is able to provide. He will then be able to get the entire fee, including insurance benefits. But, by depriving the patient of the more highly specialized skills available from another physician, his decision may endanger the patient's health.

2. He can decide to send the patient to the most appropriate specialist, thereby doing himself out of the insurance payments and extra fees.

3. He can decide to send the patient to a specialist who may not be the right man for the job but will pay for the referral by splitting the proceeds. Usually, this specialist inflates his charges to compensate for the kickback.

The only decent choice, the second one, works hardship on the physician. Fee-splitting is therefore rampant. Except where the American College of Surgeons or a strong-minded board of hospital trustees has been able to persuade the surgical staff of a local hospital to submit account books to an annual audit, the only obstacle to fee-splitting is the individual conscience.

In April 1956 Dr. Robert S. Myers, assistant director of the College of Surgeons, told the Ohio State Surgical Association: "When the American College of Surgeons decided to take its case against unethical practices directly to the public a few years ago, it did so reluctantly and only after realizing that the help of the public was necessary to curb the evils of fee-splitting . . . It was necessary since no other group in organized medicine was disposed to lend effective aid to eradicate unethical practices. In fact, the inertia of most medical organizations and the outright opposition of a few segments of organized medicine were best expressed by the cries of anguish and outrage which greeted the College's campaign. In almost every instance, these outbursts did not attempt to deny that evil practices were common and undesirable. No! They lamented that the dirty linen of the medical profession should be washed in public and protested piously that the unethical few should be left to their local societies for justice and disciplinary action. To the uninitiated, these protests may have sounded reasonable and promising; to the experienced, they smacked of hypocrisy, a judgment since documented by the report of the AMA's Committee on Medical Practices, which frankly admitted that the present supervision, by county medical societies, of organized medicine over the ethical standards of doctors is not adequate to protect either the public or the reputation of the profession. This did not come as a surprise to the College."

When I visited the AMA, nobody could remember when a physician had been expelled from the association for splitting fees. "Discipline," said Dr. George F. Lull, the AMA secretary, "is a local problem. What good does it do to exclude an unethical man from organized medicine? The expulsion does not bar him from practice. All it does is rule out any further possibility that organized medicine may be able to help him mend his ways."

The College of Surgeons' dedicated campaign against fee-splitting has not been a howling success, except in attracting attention to the problem. Surgeons in Columbus, Ohio; Detroit, Indianapolis; and Lincoln, Nebraska, are known to have adopted a plan of annual financial audits. Under ACS prodding, a few Internal Revenue bureaus have begun to disallow specialists' claims that their kickbacks to other physicians are tax-deductible as business expenses. Twenty-three state governments have made fee-splitting a crime, but prosecution is unheard of.

When it was proposed that the book-inspection plan be adopted in Chicago, the Chicago Medical Society urged its members not to capitulate to "infringement of the rights of the individual." And one eminent Chicago physician got into serious trouble by admitting that fee-splitting was an active problem. Dr. Loyal Davis, a member of the ACS Board of Regents, editor of the scientific journal *Surgery, Gynecology and Obstetrics,* professor of surgery at Northwestern University Medical School, and chief of surgery at Chicago's great Passavant Memorial Hospital, is a man of enormous distinction in his profession. Yet when he told a news conference, "There is no question but that fee-splitting is on the increase in Chicago and surrounding areas," the reaction of the leaders of the Chicago Medical Society was to charge *him* with unethical conduct.

The proceedings against Dr. Davis were not concerned with whether or not he had spoken the truth. The charge was that, in speaking, he had done harm to his profession. The society's Committee on Ethical Relations voted him guilty. He faced expulsion. When Chicago newspapers criticized the society's behavior, the action was rescinded. Meanwhile, the society passed a resolution recommending that medical ethics be revised to permit discreet forms of fee-splitting. Typically, the main concern seemed to be preservation of the fee system, and the public take the hindmost.

Chicago was not unusual. The state associations of New York, Illinois, Iowa, West Virginia, and North Carolina passed similar resolutions, as did large numbers of county societies. At the 1953 convention of the AMA, eleven resolutions of censure were introduced not against fee-splitters but against Paul Hawley, for having discussed fee-splitting in a published interview.

To its credit, the AMA has never adopted a resolution softening its official opposition to fee-splitting. However, its punctilious refusal to "interfere" in the affairs of state and county medical societies which tolerate fee-splitting is in itself a kind of tolerance. When the AMA senses urgency in a situation, it is not always so ceremonious. For example, if some state attorney general were to start trying to enforce his law against fee-splitting, it is unthinkable that the AMA would remain aloof.

A close relative of fee-splitting is unnecessary surgery, an inhuman practice which often takes place whether fees are split or not but seems to depend in part on whether the victim has insurance against surgery bills. The national health insurance survey by the Health Information Foundation and the National Opinion Research Center found that people covered by surgical insurance undergo almost twice as many operations as persons not covered. Appendectomy and tonsillectomy rates are especially compelling: among every 100 persons with hospitalization insurance, the survey turned up 11 appendectomies per year. Yet, among every 100 uninsured people, there were only five appendectomies per year. Among insured children there were more than three times as many tonsillectomies a year as among uninsured children.

Obviously, there can be no causal relationship between ownership of insurance and acute appendicitis or purulent tonsils. Making all allowances for the fact that insured people are more likely to seek medical attention than uninsured people, and conceding that there is a difference between "elective" surgery and "emergency" surgery, it is impossible that all the additional surgical service rendered to holders of insurance is medically necessary or even justifiable. If the extra service to insured persons were necessary, the statistics should mean that thousands of uninsured people perish of appendicitis and its sequelae every year—which is not so.

Dr. Warren F. Draper, former Deputy Surgeon General of the United States who now is medical director of the United Mine Workers Welfare and Retirement Fund, has made frequent complaints to the AMA about unnecessary surgery inflicted on insured miners and their families. "Unnecessary surgery performed by reasonably competent physicians who know better, but want the money, is hard on the patient . . ." he once said. "Closely related are the services performed by physicians who know they are not qualified for certain work but who will attempt almost anything in order to retain the fee. The results are often gruesome."

In the January 31, 1953, issue of *The Journal* of the AMA, Dr. James

C. Doyle reported on a study he had made of hysterectomies performed on 6,248 women. He found that one-third of the operations "seemed to be unwarranted." He added: "An appalling number of the patients aged 20 to 29 who were subjected to [removal of reproductive organs] had no disease whatsoever [30 per cent]." In individual hospitals the percentage of unnecessary hysterectomies has been as high as 66.

Here, as in fee-splitting, the AMA and the state and county societies go morosely through minimum motions while the American College of Surgeons agitates publicly for reform. Since 1918 the College has been trying to raise hospital standards. It originated annual inspections of hospitals to reduce unnecessary surgery and other professional abuses of the public. It insisted that tissue removed by surgery be examined for disease by a physician specializing in pathology. Hospitals whose pathologists reported a high incidence of ill-advised surgery were deprived of College accreditation. Many hospitals did not seek accreditation, however. And among those that did, the relations between surgeons and pathologist were not always conducive to objective evaluations on his part.

For the past several years the hospital accreditation work started by the College has been done by the Joint Commission on Accreditation, representing the AMA, the American Hospital Association, the American College of Physicians (composed of diagnostic specialists), the Canadian Medical Association, and the College of Surgeons. This commission, with its greater resources, is able to cover more ground than the College could on its own. Since only about 3,000 of this country's 7,000 hospitals are accredited, there is much ground to cover.

According to Dr. Hawley, the accreditation process has a dramatic effect on the volume of surgery performed in an institution. He mentions one hospital whose surgery rate fell from 769 operations in one year to 298 the following year. The first year there had been 305 appendectomies; the following year there were only 66. "The patient load was the same in both years," says Dr. Hawley. "The effect of accreditation requirements on that hospital was extreme, but is a clue to the amount of unnecessary surgery performed in the United States."

And a clue to the zeal with which the AMA and the state and county medical societies track down the butchers in their midst was given by the AMA Special Committee on Medical Practices. After reviewing questionnaires answered by 1,100 county societies, the committee wrote about the disciplinary procedures of organized medicine: "This total of 21 doctors expelled in two years seems to us to indicate a lack of vigorous activity on the part of county societies in the supervision of their membership. We feel that because of their close professional and personal ties, members of county societies are unable to exercise the judicial and disciplinary functions."

Among the 21 expellees, the committee found only four expelled for offenses against patients. Ten had been expelled for "unspecified reasons," six for "illegal acts," and one for "an offense against colleagues."

Before moving from what Dr. Hawley calls "the hewers of flesh and drawers of blood" to other forms of medical corruption associated with the quest for fees, it is necessary to mention something called ghost surgery. Here the unqualified physician is not brutal enough to attempt the operation himself, but is anxious to remain a living god in the eyes of his patient. He therefore pretends to the patient that he is going to operate, but he turns the cutlery over to a colleague who does the actual job. The colleague is always a better surgeon, but is at a serious disadvantage, since he has never seen the patient before and has had no opportunity for personal diagnosis. This means that the poor patient is also at a serious disadvantage.

A more prevalent variety of corruption is known in the trade as "overutilization" of hospital facilities and, as usual, is related to the irrational failure of conventional health insurance to provide comprehensive coverage. Since the insurance usually pays off only for services performed in hospitals, it offers a tremendous incentive to use hospital beds when hospitalization is not needed. The patient may require nothing but a diagnostic work-up available in any good clinic. But his insurance does not cover such services. Rather than pay the full cost of the procedure, the patient may prefer to go to the hospital and draw on his hospitalization insurance plus whatever medical insurance is applicable. The physician's desires are equally urgent: unless he is a rare specimen, he lacks the expensive apparatus needed for the work. Unless he puts the patient into the hospital, he has to send him to other physicians, or to a clinic, and lose fees.

In 1952 and 1953 Dr. Harry F. Becker, medical director of the Michigan Hospital Service, studied the clinical records of 12,102 general hospital patients and concluded that "over 28 per cent of all hospital admissions contained some element of faulty use." Suggesting that the problem might be reduced if health insurance covered diagnoses in hospitals' outpatient clinics, Dr. Becker remarked, "One would be very naïve were he not to realize that this particular point treads rather heavily upon some areas that are already a little tender. The doctor, jealous of his roles as entrepreneur and director of the medical team, has traditionally opposed anything he feels could result in an encroachment on his preroga-tives." As you may have noticed by now, "prerogative" is often a medical synonym for "money."

"I must emphasize," wrote Dr. Becker in *Hospitals,* the periodical of the American Hospital Association, "that we did not conclude that the patients who used these unnecessary days did not need the medical, surgi-cal or diagnostic care they received. In most cases they did need it . . . But these patients did not need to occupy a hospital bed in order to re-ceive it."

And there, of course, corruption lies. Misuse of hospital facilities is strictly the responsibility of the profession. Lopsided health insurance may give the patient financial incentive to use a hospital bed that he doesn't need, but he has no way of getting into that bed unless some physician has authorized the hospital to admit him. Every time a physi-cian succumbs to such temptation, Blue Cross or some other hospitali-zation insurance fund is needlessly drained. The inevitable increase in premium rates is a momentous disservice to the public.

Efforts to extend Blue Cross coverage to services performed in the outpatient clinics of hospitals have been frustrated repeatedly by opposi-tion from organized medicine. A fairly typical comment was made in 1957 by Dr. Samuel B. Hadden, president of the Philadelphia County Medical Society. He wrote in the society's periodical, *Philadelphia Medi-cine:* "Blue Cross is now proposing a plan to extend coverage for medical services on a hospital outpatient basis in order to cut down bed occu-pancy. This we oppose as a most discriminatory procedure. Such a plan permits the subsidized, tax-free institution to compete unfairly with the individual physician who provides his own equipment and is subject to many taxes."

A plain answer to this declaration came from C. Rufus Rorem, Ph.D., executive director of the Hospital Council of Philadelphia and former executive officer of the national Blue Cross Commission. "He suggests," wrote Dr. Rorem of Dr. Hadden, "that patients be required to pay pri-vate physicians for such services as X-ray diagnosis, pathological tests, anesthesia services, cardiographic studies, basal metabolism tests, physi-cal therapy treatments, analysis and administration of transfused blood or serum—in short, all those services which differentiate a hospital from a hotel or boarding house.

"Dr. Hadden imputes motives of self-interest to the unpaid trustees and salaried administrators of non-profit voluntary hospitals. He implies that the patients' financial interests would be more adequately safeguarded by the attending physicians who earn their livelihood from private fees charged for professional services at hospitals.

"A hospital is defined by Dr. Hadden as 'the workshop and private domain of the physician.' His discussion of Blue Cross problems is based upon this concept of a community hospital. It seems necessary, therefore, to present certain facts . . . The people provide the hospitals; they support the hospitals; they use the hospitals. It is to their interest that all services furnished at hospitals be co-ordinated financially as well as professionally.

"A hospital without doctors is unthinkable; it would resemble a school without a faculty. But this fact does not make a hospital 'the private domain of the physician.' The hospital is a public workshop, not a private playground."

Some of the better hospitals are understandably strict about needless admissions. Physicians who indulge in the practice have to resort to stratagem to get the patient through the doors. Thus, someone who needs diagnostic tests may be hospitalized under a totally unjustified label of "diabetes" or "mononucleosis." Someone with a nasty case of the grippe may be hospitalized as a "pneumonia" patient. In the September 1955 issue of *The Modern Hospital,* Drs. Robert S. Myers, Vergil N. Slee, and Robert G. Hoffman called on hospital staffs to audit their own work. They illustrated what seemed to be faulty care given 1,109 alleged diabetes patients in 15 representative hospitals. Although any sophomore should know that the test of diabetes is the amount of sugar in the blood, only one of the 15 hospitals was able to report that more than half its "diabetes" patients had been given appropriate blood tests. In seven of the hospitals the tests were given to fewer than 10 per cent of the patients. No matter how you slice this one, the hospital insurance fund and the public are ill used. If the patient does not really have the symptoms of diabetes, the physician has no business saying that he has; if the patient really has diabetes, or is suspected of having it, he should get adequate care.

The same article gave statistics on the percentage of "pneumonia" patients given the chest X-rays considered essential to examination. "Each of these hospitals," wrote the authors, "has available and adequate X-ray diagnostic facilities. Why did 95 per cent of the patients with 'pneumonia' receive at least one X-ray of the chest in Hospital No. 1 as opposed to only 45 per cent of the patients in Hospital No. 15?" Indeed why?

Conventional cash-allowance insurance insures the physician but not the patient. No review of medical delinquency would be complete without examples. Martin E. Segal, insurance expert who serves as consultant to several hundred health insurance funds, is concerned about the alacrity with which fee-for-service physicians adjust their fees upward whenever insurance allowances are increased. The allowances rarely overtake the spiraling fees. "Our company analyzed over ten thousand surgical claims where benefits were paid under a $150 surgical schedule," Segal said in 1955. "We found that this surgical schedule paid only 55 per cent of the surgeons' total charges. A similar analysis, for claims paid under a $225 surgical schedule, showed that such a schedule paid 60 per cent of the surgeons' total charges. And an analysis of claims paid under a $300 surgical schedule showed that such a schedule paid only 69 per cent of the surgeons' total charges. As you can see, a 100 per cent increase in the surgical indemnity schedule served to reduce the patient's share of the bill by only 14 percentage points."

Several years ago the AFL-CIO United Auto Workers studied the bills paid by 20,000 auto workers' families under a surgical insurance plan. The cash allowances averaged $51.52 and the surgeons' fees averaged $80.13. This meant that the average patient's insurance failed by $28.61 to cover the price. On the assumption that a more liberal schedule of cash allowances might be helpful to the policyholder, the union studied a group of members covered by a better plan. In this group allowance for surgical fees averaged $77.08. However, the surgeons' bills presented to the patients averaged $100.07, leaving the average patient with $22.99 to pay out of pocket.

With this kind of thing not only permitted but encouraged by organized medicine's belief that the patient must be responsible for extra payment to the physician, it is perhaps no wonder that things go from bad to indescribable. In 1952 the California Physicians' Service, an aptly named non-profit insurance plan sponsored by the California Medical Association, revealed that at least 200 doctors had been stealing more than a million dollars a year by collecting insurance benefits for services never performed. All the sticky-fingered gentlemen were required by their medical societies to make restitution but only a few suffered other punishment. Actually, what they were doing was only an exaggeration of what takes place practically everywhere else: in most parts of the country, an indeterminate fraction of physicians feels understandably put upon by the need to fill out insurance forms. Fee doctors complain that the labor eats into their valuable time and that, in any event, the insurance benefits are inadequate. To compensate themselves for these hardships, they sandbag the insurance fund for every possible charge, even if it means seeing the patient more often than necessary and performing utterly unnecessary services.

When patients or insurance people become noisy about such depredations, the AMA invariably proclaims that it, too, thinks that avarice is not nice. After the California scandal erupted, Dr. John W. Cline, who then was president of the AMA, wrote in *The Journal:* "Voluntary insurance against sickness has been sold to the American people as a practical means of protecting themselves from unexpected and perhaps overwhelming medical costs. The value of these plans must not be destroyed by the few physicians who view them as an opportunity to collect an increased fee."

At the local level, consumer groups which are not awed by organized medicine find that they can get results if they protest unreasonable fees to the appropriate medical society. To facilitate this, some unions retain physicians as medical advisers and let them carry the ball in negotiation with their colleagues. This technique does not make an idyll of the traditional physician-patient relationship but has an inhibitory effect on scaled-up fees, unnecessary services, and other obvious breaches of common decency.

For some mysterious reason, California always seems to bear the brunt of criticism for corruption which, while marked there, is not necessarily less abundant elsewhere. In 1948, for example, the Los Angeles Better Business Bureau announced that 70 per cent of the county's physicians were accepting financial rebates from drugstores, medical supply houses, opticians, and laboratories. Dr. William H. Leake, president of the Los Angeles County Medical Association, made the customary rejoinder about the practice being confined to a "small but undesirable minority." After seeing the Better Business Bureau's evidence, he admitted that "a substantial number" of doctors were involved.

This was a deadly grave business with hideous implications. Los Angeles County is one of the nation's biggest and is distinguished by some of the highest medical prices to be found anywhere. The AMA Board of Trustees swung into action. It signed a *Journal* editorial reviewing some of the best-known varieties of medical corruption, calling on the subsidiary societies to clean house, giving credit to the Better Business Bureau for its investigative work, and observing in a final shot: "The housecleaning has been too long delayed. Biology has proved that any living organism that tries to maintain itself in the presence of filth invariably dies." Very impressive, those words.

At the AMA convention in Chicago later that year, each delegate was given a letter from the Los Angeles Radiological Society (X-ray specialists), saying: ". . . as yet no effective machinery to stop rebating has been devised by the American Medical Association. The unfortunate facts are that resolutions, broad principles and editorials are not enough to stop the most flagrant medical racketeering since diploma-mill days . . . The public is mystified by the AMA's attitude of taking credit for the actions of honest doctors but dodging responsibility for its unscrupulous members. The question is now whether the AMA will shoulder responsibility . . ."

The convention's answer was to vote that rebating was unethical. Four and a half years later rebating was still unethical, still going on, and the AMA was still calling for a clean house. Dr. Louis H. Bauer, the incumbent president, listed as one of his objectives for 1953 ". . . disciplining those physicians who tarnish the reputation of the whole profession by their unethical acts of overcharging, accepting kickbacks and making commercial arrangements with pharmacists."

That very year the state of New York caught 187 physicians in undercover deals with druggists. Nothing useful was done about it, either by the state government or by the state and county medical societies. In 1954, reacting to pressures from profession and public, the AMA revised its principles of ethics in what it thought was an effort at clarification. Prior to amendment, the principles said: "The acceptance of rebates on prescriptions or appliances, or of commissions from attendants who aid in the care of patients is unethical. An ethical physician does not engage in barter or trade in the appliances, devices or remedies prescribed for patients, but limits the sources of his professional income to professional services rendered the patient." The amended version said: "It is unethical for a physician to participate in the ownership of a drugstore in his medical practice area unless adequate drugstore facilities are otherwise unavailable. This inadequacy must be confirmed by his component medical society. The same principle applies to physicians who dispense drugs or appliances. In both instances, the practice is unethical if secrecy and coercion are employed or if financial interest is placed above the quality of medical care. On the other hand, sometimes it may be advisable and even necessary for physicians to provide certain appliances or remedies without profit which patients cannot procure from other sources."

The revision caused great anguish in the profession. The ethical imperatives were substantially the same in both versions, but some of the new emphases rankled. The explicit reference to ownership of a drug-store was not welcomed by physicians who owned drugstores. The command to seek approval for such commerce from local medical societies caused unease. The line about the occasional desirability of providing drugs and appliances *without profit* was a harpoon. Physicians with the best argument against the amendment were rural practitioners. Many traditionally sell drugs to patients who otherwise would have to travel miles to the nearest pharmacy. Some of these country doctors sell the drugs at cost. Others maintain small dispensaries at a slight profit. Others profiteer. All were distressed by the amendment.

The group of physicians hit hardest by the new formulation were ophthalmologists (eye specialists, sometimes called oculists), who had only just begun to recover from wounds inflicted by the U.S. Department of Justice. Thousands of ophthalmologists—a majority of the specialists in the field—had been implicated in anti-trust actions charging eyeglass-lens manufacturers with fixing prices and paying kickbacks to physicians. The cases had been settled by consent decree, which is essentially a promise to behave, and numerous oculists had begun to sell eyeglasses themselves as a legal alternative to collecting surreptitious rebates from opticians and lens manufacturers.

I am told that no AMA convention has ever attracted so many ophthalmologists as turned up in Atlantic City for the 1955 session of the House of Delegates. Amid all the agitation the House did the democratic thing. It dismantled its amendment of the previous year and gave the boys a free hand. The ethics were now revised to read: "It is not unethical for a physician to prescribe or supply drugs, remedies or appliances as long as there is no exploitation of the patient."

In 1957, as part of a general streamlining of the code, the wording was changed to: "Drugs, remedies or appliances may be dispensed by the physician provided it is in the best interests of the patient." There, with his passport to commercial enterprise signed and sealed by the AMA, is where the practicing physician stands today. That relatively few physicians peddle merchandise is usually evidence of individual good taste. Sometimes it is evidence of reluctance to antagonize the druggist, who may be an excellent source of new patients and other gifts. In any event, the decision on whether to open a small store in the waiting room is an individual one, subject to local realities and the mores of the county medical society.

Secret rebates from druggists and suppliers; open retailing in physicians' offices; organized medicine's increased tolerance of individual commercialism—these phenomena upset anyone who thinks that the physician should be dedicated to human well-being. A physician engaged in drug commerce is under burdens which we wish he did not have. When we buy medicine on a doctor's prescription, we want to be sure that we are buying the best possible medicine at the most reasonable price. A physician with no financial interest in the sale can be presumed to see our illness with greater, more scientific objectivity.

But the problem runs deeper. The conditions of contemporary private medical practice are such that a physician's freedom from financial ties to the drugstore is no guarantee that he will write a proper prescription. The frequent failure of prescriptions to accord with the best interests of the patient has become so noticeable in recent years that leading members of the profession have begun to warn of disaster.

During the June 1957 convention of the AMA, Dr. Harry F. Dowling of the University of Illinois told the Section on Experimental Medicine and Therapeutics, "Within recent years the drug industry has discovered that the techniques that had been used so successfully in the advertising of soaps and toothpastes and of cigarettes, automobiles and whiskey could be used as successfully to advertise drugs to doctors. Advertising to doctors has become flamboyant, as shown by two-page gaily colored spreads in nearly every medical journal. Advertising has become incessant; nearly identical advertisements for a new drug appear in each day's mail for weeks on end. Advertising is without question confusing . . . Most practicing physicians do not see a sufficient number of patients with any one disease to make a critical trial of a new drug themselves . . . The bewildered physician prescribes by suggestion and not from knowledge."

In September 1957 Dr. Joseph Garland, editor of the *New England Journal of Medicine,* which is generally regarded as one of the most distinguished medical publications in the English language, discussed the influence of the pharmaceutical industry at a London meeting of medical journalists. "This untoward effect," he said, "is seen in the recommendations, through the various advertising mediums, of pharmaceutical products in cases where they are not specifically indicated; in the encouragement of unnecessary or even undesirable combinations of agents, and in their exploitation beyond the limits of their usefulness. It is seen in the proffering to and the acceptance by the profession of gratuitous patronage outside the scope of reasonably friendly professional relations. The physician is in danger of surrendering some of his responsibility for the enlightened care of his patients—as well as some of his prestige—in favor of becoming to too great an extent a purveyor of proprietary remedies about which he may sometimes lack sufficient knowledge for their consistently intelligent employment."

The pharmaceutical industry spends at least $300 million a year (four times what it spends on research) to promote prescriptions for its so-called "ethical" products, which are now selling at an annual rate of about $2 billion. The term "ethical" is a loose one: generally, it refers to the supposition that the manufacturer is advertising the product only to the profession, not to the public. Yet the sums spent on sales promotion include several millions devoted to getting news about drugs and their manufacturers into newspapers and magazines and onto television and radio, so that the public will clamor for the latest prescription miracles. It is notoriously true that some patients shop around until they find a physician willing to write them a prescription for the marvel extolled in the magazine. In succumbing to these importunities the physician assumes that, if he doesn't write the prescription, the patient will take his trade elsewhere.

Obviously, medical leaders who oppose the kind of premature publicity that results in demand for overpriced and unproved medicine put themselves in the untenable position of demanding that science news be censored. The real problem, of course, is not science news at all, but the unavoidable preoccupation of competitive, fee-for-service physicians with each other's economic jugular veins. By contrast, a patient who walks into a successful clinic and asks one of its salaried specialists for the wrong medicine can be set straight without the specialist losing one cent of income.

In addition to pressure from patients, the physician receives about as many as 4,000 pieces of pharmaceutical mail every year, including hundreds of dollars in free drug samples, souvenirs, glossily produced leaflets, booklets, and giveaway periodicals. The promotional techniques employed in these mailings vary between the hard and the soft sell and the content ranges from mendacity to the genuinely useful fact, but there is a lavish sameness about the stuff and no physician with a busy practice has time or inclination to read it all. The typical mailing piece is elaborately devised, with flashy artwork, commanding typography, impressively textured paper trickily folded. The cost of all these elegantly aesthetic postal demonstrations of industrial regard for the M.D. is part of the price which the public pays for its medicine.

Pharmaceutical manufacturers also employ about 20,000 field representatives, known as "detail men," who cultivate personal relations with physicians, bringing them new samples, new clinical information, new gossip, and whatever else is needed to replenish good will. Good detail men usually know more about pharmacology than the physicians they visit and are heavily relied on for advice. They are the backbone of pharmaceutical sales, even though they sell nothing. The actual selling, when you get right down to it, is done by the physician, via the drugstore.

The more hectic pharmaceutical companies are remarkably like manufacturers of ladies' dresses and automobiles. To keep the sales curve in attractive upthrust, they feel the need to bring out new models every season. As *The New England Journal of Medicine* commented in a 1957 editorial: "Whereas at one time a new [drug] product could hold its field for five years it is now faced with five or six competitors within a year, with no real benefit to the customer. For the most sanguine physician will hardly believe that last year's product, so highly extolled at the time, can really be as ineffective as it must be if this year's replacement is so much better. There is no millennium—not this year—but each year the public is expected to pay for one."

If the new model is actually a new drug, it gets a tremendous promotional sendoff, often before anyone knows whether it is good. But, since new drugs are hard to come by, the seasonal ballyhoo is most often concentrated on what the trade calls new "dosage forms," which are new packages containing old drugs with new flavors or possibly in ingenious new combinations with each other.

The alacrity with which the profession prescribes the fancy new models has been a source of great gratification to the industry, but not to physicians with expert knowledge of pharmacology.

"When the drugs that are produced so prodigally are tested in the laboratory," said Dr. Dowling, "only those are eliminated that are obviously toxic. Drugs . . . that are of dubious effectiveness are continued in the process and eventually reach the market . . . At the next step in the process, pressure is applied upon investigators to report that all the drugs recently produced are beneficial to patients, that they are better than existing drugs, and that they have fewer side-effects. Since this tremendous multiplication of new drugs exhausts the existing facilities for clinical investigation, inexperienced investigators are cajoled into assessing drugs in patients. Some learn the proper methods . . . most do not but unwittingly call a spade a diamond—to the confusion of the Food and Drug Administration, the exasperation of the experienced and honest investigators, the quick profit of the particular manufacturer, and the loss of prestige of the medical profession and of the pharmaceutical industry as a whole."

In advertising drugs to the profession, the expert testimonial is of central importance. The only meaningful testimonials are those which can be extracted from clinical research findings published in reputable medical journals. Some pharmaceutical companies do not hesitate, however, to cite research published in "tame" journals, or to cite research that is irrelevant, or research that takes place in their own laboratories and proves only that the drug has been tried in test tubes or mice.

To support clinical investigation and obtain the desired testimonials, the companies give financial grants to practicing physicians, supplementing these attentions with well-publicized symposia at which the researchers can make speeches about their findings. It takes a shrewd and knowledgeable individual to distinguish among these symposia and recognize which are scientifically worthwhile.

Lucky physicians whose findings have been particularly appropriate are sometimes flown at company expense to other continents where they participate in *international* symposia. Physicians not fortunate enough to get in on these junkets nevertheless qualify for other forms of entertainment. Nobody legally eligible to write a prescription is neglected. With the possibly naïve co-operation of local medical societies or local chapters of specialists' organizations, the more aggressive drug companies fling social outings, banquets, award presentations, unveilings of memorial portraits, tours of company laboratories, cocktail parties, duck shoots, barbecues, fishing tournaments, bowling tournaments, golf tournaments, picnics, and anything else that the authorities will stand for.

Dr. Garland comments, ". . . we as physicians recognize and appreciate our ancient partnership with our dynamic friends, the manufacturing apothecaries. We admire their scientific foundations and their genuine philanthropies and appreciate their cocktail parties, where our cups runneth over, but we stand a little in awe of the sinews they have acquired . . . Our own first duty is to the public, plainly enough, and so is theirs, for whereas much of modern advertising is designed to create a desire where there is no need, that of the drug business should still be patterned on the principle of responsibility to humankind."

It is probably no accident that Dr. Garland's periodical, though owned by the important Massachusetts Medical Society, carries little advertising by comparison with that found in journals of less distinction. *The Journal* of the AMA publishes $4 million in advertising every year. Assuming that 100,000 of its 185,000 subscribers are in position to write lots of prescriptions (which happens to be the advertising industry's estimate of the situation), *The Journal* is collecting $40 per reader target per year.

This fantastic income may be compared with the appeal to advertisers of our most potent consumer magazine, *Life,* in which about $138 million is spent on ads addressed to about six million purchasers—or $23 per individual target per year.

It can be seen that *The Journal* and the organization whose interests it advances are clearly of huge importance to the pharmaceutical industry. Less evident, but equally true, is the industry's life-and-death importance to the AMA. *The Journal's* advertising revenue has become the largest source of AMA income, roughly 40 per cent of the annual budget, and unavailable from any other quarter.

The impact of this reality on AMA policy must be great, but is clearly less than cynics might expect. Through the years the association's pharmacological experts have maintained a record of probity in their evaluations of new drugs produced by leading advertisers, so there can be no consumer complaint on that score. Furthermore, *The Journal* refuses unacceptable advertising reportedly equal in dollar volume to the advertising it accepts. Yet, if the AMA has not delivered itself lock, stock, and stethoscope to the pharmaceutical companies, neither has it been willing to take uncompromising leadership in protecting patients against all of the industry's enthusiasms. A sample was provided not long ago by the AMA's Dr. David B. Allman, who caroled, "Both the medical profession and pharmacy must shoulder one major public relations objective: to tell the American people over and over that nearly all of today's drugs, especially the antibiotics, are bargains at any price."

It is one thing to be properly appreciative of the pharmaceutical industry's matchless technological accomplishments. It is quite another to believe that the public should confine itself to worship full payment and should be deterred from examining sharp practices.

The Journal published Dr. Dowling's urgently important text in its issue of October 12, 1957, but was unable to accompany the article with a merited, long-overdue attack on the problems he raised. *The Journal* could not even find it in its heart to permit the text to stand alone without comment. Instead, it printed a lengthy editorial which echoed the pharmaceutical industry's insistent self-praise. The editorial also belittled Dr. Dowling's remarks by saying that they pointed "to problems obviously disturbing to the author and presumably also to some of his colleagues . . . there are statements in the article that may cause confusion, even consternation, if they are taken out of context."

In advancing the AMA's own view of the pharmaceutical business, the editorial asserted that "aggressive selling is certain to occur. In a free enterprise system such as exists in the United States where there is competition and a need for some return for shareholders one finds evidence of such selling in any industry whether it be the manufacturing of cars, appliances, clothing or foods." The consumer might have greater difficulty in equating the sale of pharmaceuticals, involving the preservation of human life and human health, with the sale of automobiles, refrigerators, brassières, and dry cereal.

The publication by the AMA of an occasional article such as Dr. Dowling's may rebut charges of indifference, but is no substitute for vigorous medical leadership. With such uninspired guidance from the association which rules private medicine, it is no wonder that confused physicians continue to shill for the drug companies. It is no wonder that they prescribe millions of doses of expensive antibiotic combinations when less expensive doses of single antibiotics or sulfas are usually better. It is no wonder that thousands of doctors persist in selling antibiotics to patients with colds and other ailments in which the drugs are rarely indicated. It is no wonder that physicians without training in psychiatry continue to pass out tranquilizers as if the pills were popcorn.

Physicians make these and other serious mistakes for diverse reasons, few of which are good but not all of which can be blamed on the individual. The entrepreneur physician is a creature of organized medicine. The country and state societies and the AMA never hesitate to write him a letter or call him on the phone when they feel the need. Their failure to whip him into line where prescriptions are concerned is eloquently significant. From the consumer viewpoint, this failure ranks with fee-splitting, overcharging, unnecessary surgery, exploitation of hospital facilities, and other corruptions of the medical oath. Here again the performance of organized medicine is a vivid argument for the acquisition by consumers —and possibly their legislatures—of appropriate control over the economics of medical service.

Group Health

> As we men of medicine grow in learning we more justly appreciate
> our dependence upon each other. . . . It has become necessary to
> develop medicine as a co-operative science, the clinician, the spe-
> cialist and the laboratory workers uniting for the good of the patient.
> . . . The people will demand, the medical profession must supply,
> adequate means for the proper care of patients, which means that
> individualism in medicine can no longer exist.
>
> DR. WILL MAYO (1861–1939)

A SATISFACTORY RELATIONSHIP between patient and physician is an en-
nobling experience for both. The patient is in physical or mental need—
helpless without the physician. The physician has the necessary knowledge
and skill plus the compassion and tenderness on which prompt recovery
so often depends. It is natural for a warmth to grow between the two
human beings. Later the physician looks back with justifiable pride on
his accomplishments in the case, remembers the patient as having been a
deserving person, and may also congratulate himself on being part of a
profession so uniquely equipped to perform vital services. For his part,
the patient will never forget the physician's deft work, keen insights, and
heartening presence. And he will feel somewhat stronger for the assurance
that the physician remains available to him. He need never again feel so
helpless as he did the last time.

In debating social and economic issues with the leaders of organized
medicine, the consumer should not forget that they, too, are physicians
and have had thousands of experiences of the kind just described. When
they invoke what they call "the sacred doctor-patient relationship" as an
argument against innovation, it is well to remember that they are talking
about something important. Aside from their self-interested dread of
economic change, they bespeak everybody else's interests in urging that
nothing hamper the physician's freedom to employ his fullest skills.

Unfortunately, self-interest carries the leaders of organized medicine

past the boundaries of reality. Although they are communicants of a
science and should know that nothing stands still, they believe that the
physician-patient relationship is not only changeless but unadaptable.
They claim that it is susceptible to blemish unless associated with individual fee transactions. They deny that the fee system is obsolescent and that
the physician-patient relationship is being damaged by it. They reject
efforts to enhance the relationship by giving it a more wholesome environment.

One of my favorite illustrations is provided by Dr. John W. Cline,
who was AMA president during the 1951–52 term. In a reference to the
vital relationship, Dr. Cline said that it is "something precious that has
made American medicine the best in the world." A straight answer to this
familiar refrain came from Father Gordon George, S.J., who wrote in
America: "Actually the progress of American medicine, like that of
American industry, stems primarily from the amazing growth of science
and technical know-how. Add to this the efficient organization which
provides corps of nurses, medical technicians and social workers, grouped
around the fabulous technical resources of our modern hospitals and
clinics, and you fill out the story. The 'precious something' in the doctor-
patient relationship had precious little to do with all that . . . For good
or ill, the family doctor of our grandfather's day has succumbed to technological revolution."

As we discovered in the previous chapter, some of the professional
graces of our grandfather's day have also succumbed. We saw that fee-
splitting, unnecessary surgery, ghost surgery, needless use of hospital
beds, and the imposition of extortionate charges on patients were modern
products of an ancient fee system that is inadequate to satisfy either
public or professional needs in an era of medical specialization. We now
turn our attention to forms of medical service in which not a single one
of those corruptions is to be found. These forms of service have not
achieved the levels of spiritual and scientific perfection claimed by
organized medicine for solo, fee-for-service practice, but, for that matter,
neither has solo, fee-for-service practice. The new forms, however, are
free of the worst inhumanities of orthodox practice and have begun to
record medical accomplishments of the greatest significance.

The kind of medicine I have in mind has two features. One is *group
practice* by organized teams of physicians representing the various medical
skills. The other is *group purchase* of service by large numbers of consumers whose aggregate prepayments of money provide the medical

team with financing sufficient to sustain high standards of performance and a professionally acceptable standard of living.

Group practice without group prepayment has achieved a certain respectability in organized medicine. The 1958–59 president of the AMA, Dr. Gunnar Gundersen, heads a celebrated group, the Gundersen Clinic in La Crosse, Wisconsin. The Lahey, Ochsner, Cleveland, and Mayo hospitals and clinics are other well-known examples of fee-oriented group practice without group prepayment.

Group practice is an outgrowth of the technological revolution mentioned by Father George. Its beginnings were in the great hospitals, where adequate application of science's full benefits to any single patient required the teamwork of numerous specialists and technicians. The same technique was employed in the hospitals' outpatient clinics, first with charity patients and later, much to the distress of organized medicine, paying patients. The "unfair competition" offered to the soloist by magnificently equipped, fully staffed outpatient clinics has been lamented, denounced, and sabotaged for decades.

Logic decreed that the proven techniques of group practice be applied at other levels of diagnosis and treatment. There are now believed to be almost 1,000 medical groups, including about 13,000 physicians, rendering private, fee-based service in this way. In big East Coast cities, the word "clinic" still reeks with the depressing, institutional aroma of the old charity dispensary, even though some wonderful group practices are to be found in such cities. But in many smaller towns, particularly in the Midwest, "clinic" is the attractive brick, glass, and steel building with all the equipment, where the best private doctoring is to be had.

The President's Commission on the Health Needs of the Nation reported in 1952: "The patient benefits through having his entire health service concentrated in one place. This gives greater unity and continuity to his care, encourages consultation whenever it is needed and minimizes travel. The patient also gets more service per dollar spent through the economy of group practice. Physicians working together in a group continue the best features of their training period throughout their professional lives—the stimulation to keep up with medical progress through constant appraisal by informed colleagues and ready access to consultations and technical assistance. On the personal side the physician in group practice has greater opportunity to take time off for study and vacation in addition to more stable income throughout his years of practice."

In 1957 *The Journal of Medical Education* published findings made by the Rockefeller Foundation and the University of North Carolina in a study of the quality of care rendered by that state's general practitioners. The researchers said that group physicians practiced medicine of a quality significantly higher than that practiced by soloists. Also, the group physicians read more medical journals, had better equipment, better technical assistance, and, oddly or not, better academic records in medical school.

The AMA, which has never been a partisan of group practice—it seems to be reserved toward any organized activity other than its own—has studied the subject at intervals for years. In July 1957, however, its Committee on Medical and Related Facilities reported in *The Journal* that a large percentage of physicians in group practice "thought they could practice better medicine in a group than separately."

Group medicine also offers its practitioners certain economic advantages, but these cannot be proved. They can only be deduced. Precise comparisons with the economics of solo practice are impossible. Nobody knows how much the solo, fee-for-service physician makes. As one irreverent soloist told me, "It's because we get paid in cash so often. We're not the world's best bookkeepers and we sometimes lose track. There's only one other profession comparable to ours in that respect. It's a much older profession—the oldest." Jokes aside, all national estimates of physicians' "average" incomes are regarded by statistical experts as spectacularly unreliable. Yet authoritative whisperings from health insurance companies and gossip from hospital coffee shops indicate that some urban specialists make in excess of $200,000 a year. Some general practitioners make less than $10,000. Physicians engaged in group practice are usually sure that they fare at least as well as do most soloists of equal experience in the same towns, although not nearly as well as some. In addition, group practitioners prize the regular hours, paid vacations, paid leaves to attend scientific meetings, and the other privileges and amenities that accrue from having colleagues who can mind the store. By sharing overhead expenses, the cost of equipment, and the wages of technicians, they find that they save about ten cents more of every fee dollar than the solo practitioner can, yet they far exceed that practitioner in the scope and caliber of services that they can offer.

By and large, all this has to be good for the patient, yet the AMA manages to resist any urge toward enthusiasm. Its studies stress the difficulties of group practice rather than the advantages. Some of these difficulties are serious—especially the economic controversies which sometimes spring up among individualists trying to achieve a mutually satisfactory formula for sharing group income. In his testimony before a

Congressional inquiry in 1954, the AMA's Dr. Walter B. Martin sounded the customary cool note when he said, "I certainly do not feel . . . that one of the urgent problems of medicine [is] that we establish more group practice."

When group practice is combined with group purchase of service under a prepayment plan, organized medicine becomes hostile. It is only under plans of this kind that the public is assured of reasonably comprehensive medical care, ranging from home and office calls to protracted, hospitalized illness, at a fixed, predetermined, all-inclusive, annual price. For about $200 a year per family, underwritten by wage deductions or employer contributions or a blend of the two, approximately three million people in about 100 American communities are getting this kind of care, including complete hospital service and in some instances drugs, eyeglasses, and dentistry. The best available combinations of conventional health insurance policies cost over 50 per cent more, cover far fewer services, and, almost without exception, require substantial out-of-pocket disbursement by the patient or his family. From a financial standpoint, there simply is no comparison between conventional insurance and the comprehensive prepaid medical service plans.

Both in theory and in practice the patient can also derive marked medical advantages from the comprehensive plans. They offer the aforementioned benefits of group medicine and, through the prepayment feature, eliminate the fee barrier to physical checkups, prompt treatment of potentially dangerous minor ailments, and other preventive service.

I said *"can* derive" by way of indicating that not all patients actually do derive such advantages. Indeed, my rather extensive interviews in the field and some small experience as a patient of two prepaid groups taught me that some of the plans are less uniformly glorious in actuality than in theory. Some patients complain of being rushed, snubbed, regimented, and even of being made to feel that they are imposing on the physicians whose services they have hired. Prepaid group practice, while demonstrably preferable to any other system of medical service yet devised, is not beyond flaw. However, it is perfectible, and its occasional defects are more amenable to public repair than are the evils of solo, fee-for-service practice.

The tendency of some prepaid groups to give the patient short shrift is related to a system of paying the medical team according to the number of patients it undertakes to treat during the year. This method is known as capitation—per capita payment—and in some groups is associated with administrative efforts to enroll as many patients and hire as few physicians as possible. The results are the opposite of the unnecessary services that characterize fee medicine and are just as abhorrent, particularly for any patient who was dubious about the whole thing in the first place and is all too ready to develop fond memories of his old private practitioner— crowded waiting room, unavailability for night calls, failure to keep appointments, strange tendency to prescribe expensive medicines, and all.

Needless to say, county medical societies exploit these weaknesses of prepaid comprehensive service plans to the hilt, when seeking to take patients away from them. Furthermore, they allude to the weaknesses even when the medical group under fire is guilty of none of them. At the top, or AMA, level the criticisms are more general.

Some of organized medicine's more philosophical objections to comprehensive medical service plans have been referred to previously, particularly the dismal idea that freedom from extra charges stifles the patient's sense of responsibility. Another argument, which deserves to be taken a bit more seriously, is organized medicine's categorical distrust of the "third party." As you will recall, this is a reference to the deleterious influences which can be worked on the doctor-patient relationship by outside forces whose financial interests may militate against the health interests of the patient as well as the scientific and economic interests of the physician. To the degree that consumer organizations or other lay forces are influential in the establishment and operation of a comprehensive prepaid service plan, organized medicine's opposition increases, regardless of whether the plan offers good service. The fact that the "third party" may be the patient's own consumer co-operative headed by his own elected representatives does not lessen the opposition, but increases it.

A big argument, and a not very persuasive one, is organized medicine's recurrent complaint that the prepaid plans deprive the patient of "free choice" of physician. We have already examined some pitfalls that typify the more pristine varieties of free choice. Organized medicine finds these preferable to a system in which the patient arranges to purchase a year's medical care from an expertly organized and carefully managed panel of physicians. The patient has chosen the panel without a gun at his head and is free to discontinue the arrangement at the end of the year's time, but these facts cut no ice with organized medicine. To be sure, there have been cases where a minority of union members were outvoted by the majority and found themselves in a prepaid plan rather than with the conventional health insurance that they preferred. Organized medicine has never been able to concede that this kind of group democracy is acceptable, although it claims democratic virtues for its own electoral processes.

In recent years the largest prepaid plans have refuted most arguments of that sort by requiring that full choice be offered to union members. Those who join the prepaid plan now do so entirely of their own choosing: others are free to get their medical care through orthodox channels. But organized medicine continues to say that prepaid plans violate the principle of free choice in providing benefits only to patients who use the plans' own physicians. When it gets vehement enough on this score, organized medicine puts itself in the weird position of denying people the right to choose a prepaid medical group—as if a choice were "free" only when it coincided with organized medicine's own preferences.

Many of the physicians who belong to the prepaid groups work for salaries. This is another thorn in the side of organized medicine, which believes that the physician should be paid directly by the individual patient. Here, of course, is a variant on the third-party theme. County and state medical societies are vigilant in opposing the employment by hospitals of salaried physicians, and in recent years they have caused dreadful fusses over the issue in at least a dozen states. The AMA itself has been constrained to admit that salaried practice is not unethical per se, but makes no bones of its belief that a hospital or clinic physician who works for fees is less likely to be subject to supposedly anti-scientific influences than one who works on salary.

The fact that more than one-third of the active medical profession is now on a salary basis (*The Journal* of August 10, 1957, reports 72,488 such physicians) is disquieting to organized medicine, which can hardly claim that many of these doctors are being forced to violate their oath by the hospitals, government agencies, medical schools, unions, pharmaceutical companies, and entrepreneur physicians that employ them. The percentage of physicians working for salaries continues to rise at a rapid rate, while the percentage in solo, fee-for-service practice declines.

It must be reiterated that the salary is unquestionably a bad business if it undermines medical science. But there is no need to match organized medicine's emphasis of the point. The record shows rather distinctly that the best medicine is practiced by salaried physicians in teaching hospitals, the best research is done by salaried physicians in government, university, hospital, and industrial laboratories, and that salaries are no more dangerous to medicine than to nursing, engineering, soldiering, the courts, or the schools. The level of scientific and economic rectitude discernible in various branches of fee medicine justifies the supposition that salaries are far preferable. To guarantee that a salaried doctor will be free to do his best work in a prepaid service plan, the consumers and physicians who run the plan take pains to see that the work is adequately supervised, that earnings are proportionate to professional status, and that the physician's schedule is not overcrowded.

After the abstract embellishments are removed, we can recognize that organized medicine's reservations about salaries stem not primarily from fears that science will be harmed but that individual gross income may be lessened. It is quite possible that the $200,000-a-year man might take a cut if some miracle resulted in reorganization of the entire profession on a salary basis, but it is unthinkable that the total income of the profession would be diminished. The pressures that are producing a gradual shift from fee to salary are also pressures for more health care, more public and private expenditures. No advocate of comprehensive medical insurance is foolish enough to suggest that it would cost the nation less than the total that is now being spent. If it were applied to the entire population it unquestionably would cost more, but would provide more care and would spread the costs more evenly, making medical care a budgetable expense for service of determinable quality instead of an unforeseeable hardship associated with service of unpredictable quality.

An amusing insight into the physician's attitude toward the salary, as contrasted with organized medicine's attitude, was given in 1954 when C. Rufus Rorem, executive director of the Hospital Council of Philadelphia, wrote in *The Canadian Medical Association Journal:* ". . . medical group practice uses to a relatively high degree the salary principle as the basis of reimbursement. What does this do to the quality of medical service and to professional incentive? Several years ago, I made it a practice to ask every physician whom I met in connection with my work the following question: 'What do you think of the suggestion that all physicians should receive a regular salary?' The replies were always the same, namely, 'What amount of salary did you have in mind?' "

Since group purchase of medical service from organized teams of physicians is a threat to almost every prerogative loved by organized medicine, the prepaid comprehensive service plans have not had smooth sailing. Their physicians have been ostracized socially, barred from membership in medical societies, denied certification as specialists, expelled from hospital staffs. Under prodding from organized medicine, twenty-six state governments have adopted laws which make it either impossible or immensely difficult for consumer-sponsored service plans to be established. The chief provisions of most of these laws are legalization only of plans controlled by the profession itself, such as Blue Shield insurance. Consumer-sponsored service programs are either clearly outlawed or placed in a legally equivocal position. Congressional budget proposals which might have facilitated the initial capitalization of medical-group clinics and the consequent growth of prepaid service plans have been crushed.

Because of all these restrictions, reprisals, and the American public's completely understandable and largely uninformed preference for old-fashioned medicine, the growth of the plans has been painfully slow. It is noteworthy, however, that, whenever they have taken their persecutors into state or federal courts to seek relief against professional boycott, the plans have won. As the court decisions continue to mount in favor of prepaid group practice, organized medicine's opposition becomes less frightening. It is entirely possible that, after years of slow, uncertain growth, the plans may eventually begin to expand at a rate more consonant with their value to the public.

By all odds the most generous, objective, and enlightened statement ever to emanate from AMA headquarters on the subject of lay-sponsored health plans was made by Dr. F. J. L. Blasingame, who took over as the association's general manager in January 1958. In an interview with *The Modern Hospital,* he said: "I believe in a free economy and in a free America and I believe in carrying out medical practice. I think that . . . union and other third-party plans are attempts to approach the solution of medical care problems in a little different way. I think we're too close to these experiments yet to see how they're going to develop . . . If they can do a better job in a particular situation, let them do it! I question whether or not they will be able to survive over a period of time, but let them try . . . Fundamentally, it's a question of motivation. Why are they in the business? Are they in it to make an economic experiment, or are they in it for the care of the sick? Philosophically, the care of the sick individual—to give him the best possible medical care at a reasonable cost—is a laudable desire whether it's done by professional people or lay people. It's difficult in such a technical field as medicine to see how lay people can be motivated over a period of time to carry on an institution that will survive. But let them try, and let's see if they can do a good job, or a better job . . . I cannot see how any plan can long survive if there is impairment of the patient-physician relationship."

Whether the tolerant negativeness of Dr. Blasingame will influence local medical societies to abandon their hostile negativeness, or whether the AMA will even attempt to exert such influence is quite another mat-

ter. In 1949, when the AMA was busily mending fences to prevent federal legislation of compulsory health insurance, some of its leaders got
together with leaders of the Co-operative Health Federation of America
(now known as the Group Health Federation), to work up a statement
of principles under which consumer-sponsored medical-care plans would
qualify for acceptance in organized medicine. Twenty-one principles were
agreed upon. Twenty of these concerned the responsibility of the plans
to remain on a non-profit basis, avoid aggressive salesmanship, maintain
high-quality standards of medicine, refrain from interference in professional and technical matters, give the staff physicians a voice in over-all
policy, encourage fee payments to staff physicians for services not covered by the subscribers' contracts, submit to periodic inspections by the
AMA, and so forth. The twenty-first principle was agreement by the
AMA to effectuate the other twenty principles as bases for truce between
the plans and local and state medical societies.

After the document had been processed by the AMA convention, it
emerged with only twenty points. Missing was the principle that would
have required AMA co-operation in getting the local societies off the
consumer-sponsored plans' necks. The fact that most prepaid medical
groups and the consumer organizations that sustain them had been observing the twenty principles for years, and still do, has not made their
competition more welcome in organized medicine.

We now shall review some prepaid group-practice plans, with an eye
to organized medicine's performance and their own.

Dr. Michael Shadid: In 1929 this Syrian immigrant, who had worked
his way through medical school and achieved great success in private
practice, contributed $20,000 to the Farmers Union Hospital Association,
enabling it to establish the first medical co-operative in the United States,
the Community Hospital-Clinic at Elk City, Oklahoma. Under Dr. Shadid's medical direction, physicians joined the staff as salaried employees.
The subscribing membership grew rapidly, attracted by a wide, if not
fully comprehensive, range of top-quality services at low prices. The
Beckham County Medical Society was outraged. Dr. Shadid had been a
member of the society for twenty years, but in 1931 it expelled him by
the ingenious method of dissolving itself and then reorganizing without
him. At the same time, the society tried to promote boycotts of the medical plan and made legislative efforts to have Dr. Shadid's medical license
revoked. These spiritual endeavors were frustrated by the state's Farmers
Union, a potent political force.

The Community Hospital-Clinic has continued to grow, essentially because it has brought to western Oklahoma a quality of medical service previously unavailable there. It now has about 2,000 dues-paying families whose lifetime membership costs $100, plus about $12 per family member per year. These minuscular charges entitle members to examinations, medical treatments, surgery, obstetrics, and some less important services, all without extra payment. For hospital room, board, and nursing care, members pay around $8 a day. Laboratory tests, X-ray treatments, and dental care are provided to members at discounts ranging from one-third to one-half the hospital's normally low charges.

The hospital and clinic treat non-members of the co-operative on an inexpensive fee basis. The business affairs of what has now become one of the most modern installations in that part of the country are managed by a Board of Directors elected by the subscribing membership. This board, in turn, elects a medical director who has full charge of scientific and professional matters.

In 1950, when harassment from the local medical society showed no signs of letup but the co-operative was in better shape to deal with it, a suit for $300,000 was filed, charging the society with restraint of trade. Two years later the society settled out of court, agreeing to admit the co-operative's salaried physicians to membership. The hospital in turn agreed to admit outside physicians and their patients.

Ross-Loos: In 1929 the employees of the Los Angeles Department of Water and Power contracted to purchase comprehensive medical and hospital care on a prepaid basis from the newly formed Ross-Loos Clinic, an establishment owned by two physicians and employing others in group practice. The members paid $24 a year for all-inclusive services. Their family dependents paid 50 cents for office visits and $1 for house calls. The service was investigated from stem to stern and was found to be of high quality. The group physicians were happy. The patients were happy. The Los Angeles County Medical Association was not, even though Ross-Loos was obviously free of consumer domination. Drs. Ross, Loos, and others were expelled from organized medicine. The action was so blatantly an attempt to wreck formidable competition without due regard for even the surface niceties of human ethics that the Judicial Council of the AMA nullified the expulsions in 1936. This was done on procedural rather than substantive grounds, however, leaving the AMA and its affiliates free to undermine any other prepayment plan they might choose. Meanwhile, Ross-Loos was readmitted to the fold. It stopped enrolling new membership groups that wanted to join and it now functions with the approval of the local society and the California Medical Association.

It has somewhat less than 40,000 subscribing families totaling about 135,000 people, to whom it provides comprehensive medical service. The family premium is $72 a year. Dependents pay small extra fees for service. Hospitalization insurance is purchased through a private carrier, at extra cost. The service continues to be good, by all accounts, but actuarial problems are increasing as the membership grows older and more subject to chronic illness. To reverse this trend, the plan would have to recapture the early dynamism that was so antagonizing to organized medicine.

Group Health Association of Washington, D.C.: In 1937 this non-profit corporation was organized by 1,000 low-income employees of the federal government, using a loan obtained from the New Deal's Home Owners Loan Corporation. Seven physicians were placed on salary and began giving comprehensive medical and hospital care to subscribers for a prepayment of $2.20 per month. The District of Columbia Medical Society made the usual accusations about inferior care and socialized medicine. GHA physicians were expelled from membership in organized medicine or coerced into quitting the group plan. Members of the medical society were provided with a "white list" of approved organizations, with GHA prominently excluded. Hospitals were pressured into denying staff privileges to GHA doctors, who now found it difficult to find other physicians who would even consult with them on medical problems.

All this was quarterbacked by the AMA, in the interests of good medical care and "free choice." An elderly GHA patient who was run over and taken to a hospital was not allowed her own doctor and had to leave. A young woman scheduled for operation by her GHA surgeon was taken to the surgeon's hospital, given morphine, and then, four hours later, forced to go elsewhere, because the hospital was afraid to let the GHA man operate. A man with acute appendicitis was rushed to the hospital late at night, refused the services of his own physician, and forced to submit to the surgery of a doctor acceptable to the medical society.

After a year of this GHA got help from the U.S. Department of Justice. The AMA, the District of Columbia Society, the Washington Academy of Surgery, sixteen Washington physicians, and five AMA executives were indicted for violation of the Sherman Antitrust Act. In announcing the action, Assistant Attorney General Thurman W. Arnold was gracious toward organized medicine. He said he did not want to be punitive, if only the AMA would stop sabotaging competition. "The department does not take the view," he said, "that the offenses committed are crimes which reflect upon the character or high standing of the persons involved. The analogy . . . is that of a prosecution for reckless driving committed by a person of distinction and good will who is in a hurry to meet his legitimate engagements."

The AMA was not charmed. *The Journal* said: "The conclusion seems inescapable that the Department of Justice has embarked on a course of prosecution, if not persecution, of the medical profession in this country with a view to forcing its contentions as to what should be the nature of medical practice in the United States." And, wrote the editorialist: "No doubt those who have been primarily concerned in breaking down established order in the field of medicine and who care little or not whether the high standards of medical service which now prevail are wrecked, are rejoicing in this appeal that the hospitals be opened without restraint to every half-educated medical pretender and charlatan."

In 1943, after much *Sturm und Drang,* the Supreme Court of the United States voted 6 to 0 to uphold the AMA's conviction. Ever since then the AMA has been careful to observe whatever proprieties are necessary to hold it safe from charges of participation in interstate commerce. It stresses the autonomy of the state and local societies and never issues written directives, only "suggestions."

GHA is a success. It provides comprehensive medical and hospital care to more than 20,000 residents of the Washington area. The members control the policy and the business undertakings of the association. Medical technique is, of course, the responsibility of the medical group, which numbered 35 physicians and 11 dentists at last reports. There is also a full complement of nurses, technicians, and other help, and a well-equipped clinic. The subscribers' annual costs are about $200 per family. The association's accomplishments may be measured statistically; in 1954 the medical director announced that his obstetricians had completed 16 successive years of service without a maternal death. The association's infant mortality rate for 1953 was eight per 1,000 live births, compared with a District of Columbia average of 26 deaths per 1,000 infants.

Kaiser-Permanente: This is the largest, best-equipped, and most aggressive of all prepaid group-practice plans. It is an outgrowth of medical services which Henry J. Kaiser made available to his employees in prewar construction projects such as the Grand Coulee Dam. During the war, when he took over the Richmond, California, shipyards and the town population grew from 18,000 to 100,000 in a few weeks, Kaiser again provided group medicine on a prepaid basis, with the funds coming via wage deductions. Essentially, this was industrial medicine and Henry Kaiser was very much a "third party" in arranging for employees and their families to obtain medical care from physicians who otherwise would not have been available to the mushrooming town. Organized medicine did a good deal of grumbling about this during the early days of the war but no meaningful anti-Kaiser campaign was mounted. Through the years fulminations against third-party influence and its alleged effect on the quality of medical care have been directed almost exclusively at plans which compete with private physicians for community trade. Since Richmond did not have nearly enough fee physicians to handle the traffic, it was hard for organized medicine to get exercised about competition from Kaiser.

In 1945, with the closing of the shipyards, the Kaiser-sponsored "Permanente" medical groups were working in two hospitals, one in Richmond, the other in Oakland. The alternative to shutting up shop was to make group practice available to the community at large. Kaiser himself was enthusiastic and financially co-operative. In 1946, therefore, Kaiser-Permanente emerged from the cloister of industrial medicine and offered itself as community competition to solo practitioners and conventional forms of health insurance. At that moment organized medicine recalled that Kaiser-Permanente was bad medicine and was violating all manner of fundamental "principles" and needed to be destroyed.

Kaiser, who enjoys a good fight as much as he enjoys being identified with medical progress, has remained a generous supporter of the groups. Thanks to him, as well as to its own medical accomplishments, the health plan has been able to resist organized medicine's onslaughts. It now serves more than 550,000 people from Vancouver, Washington, to Southern California. There are 12 Kaiser hospitals with more than 2,000 beds. The hospitals not only serve their own health-plan subscribers but are open to other members of the public, including charity patients. Grouped around the hospitals are 37 medical clinics. There also are two rehabilitation centers and a school of nursing. Employees total 4,300, including 500 physicians in every specialty. The younger physicians are full-time salaried employees of the groups, and the senior physicians are full-time partners. Top earnings are around $30,000 a year, plus the usual paid vacations, paid postgraduate education, regular hours, and other advantages of successful group practice.

To avoid collision with various statutes forbidding the corporate practice of medicine and to demonstrate that the Permanente physicians are independent of third-party control, the organizational structure of Kaiser-Permanente is a welter of corporations, foundations, and other legal gimmicks. The Kaiser Foundation is Henry Kaiser's philanthropic trust that owns hospitals, clinics, and other physical properties and leases them to

Kaiser Hospitals, a non-profit corporation engaged in the hospital business. The Permanente Medical Group is a true partnership of physicians engaged in group practice and providing medical care to prepaying subscribers signed up in the Kaiser Health Plan, which sells service contracts to consumer groups and individuals, keeps 10 per cent of the proceeds for overhead and administration, and divides the rest between hospitals and physicians.

Service is comprehensive. It is not unusual for a subscriber to undergo exhaustive diagnostic tests, complicated surgery, days of expensive post-operative treatment, and on departure, after consuming hundreds of dollars in room, board, drugs, and service, get a bill for 10 cents, the price of the telephone call he made. This kind of coverage costs him and/or his employer in the neighborhood of $200 a year, a price which, regardless of all mythology disseminated by organized medicine and the health insurance industry, is actuarially sound. It can be stated without fear of contradiction, furthermore, that the quality of service is excellent.

Differences between the Kaiser plan and coverage provided through conventional insurance are illustrated by the choices offered to San Francisco longshoremen. In presenting the choices, the joint employer-union welfare fund told the longshoremen: "The insured plan provides you with money towards the payment of doctor and hospital bills . . . you go to any doctor or hospital you choose. The amounts allowed . . . pay the bills in full, or may pay them in part. You will have to make up the difference, if any, between the insurance allowance and the amount charged. The Kaiser plan provides you with services . . . you have to secure your medical care from the doctors who practice in Kaiser Foundation medical centers and hospitals."

Hospital care: The cash-allowance insurance provided a maximum of $14 a day, up to 70 days per illness, for room, board, and general nursing. Kaiser: Room, board, and general nursing (private room and special nursing if ordered by physician), for 111 days per illness, without extra charge.

Hospital extras: Conventional insurance paid up to $280 for laboratory tests, X-ray, drugs, physical therapy, and anesthesia. Also up to $50 for ambulance. Kaiser: All services, including ambulance, at no charge.

Surgery: Insurance: A schedule of cash allowances with a maximum of $300. Kaiser: All surgery at no charge except tonsillectomies, $15.

Doctor visits in hospital: Insurance: Up to $5 per day, with a maximum of $155. Kaiser: All doctors' services at no charge, including specialists' consultations.

Home and office visits: Insurance: Up to $5 per home or office visit, one visit per day, starting with the *third* visit per illness or injury. Kaiser: All office visits at no charge. For *first* home call per illness, $2 charge, none thereafter.

Maternity care: Insurance: No benefits. Kaiser: A charge of $60.

Permanente physicians are in solid agreement that their experiment proves the viability of prepaid group practice and comprehensive service. Yet many of them are dismayed by an apparent failure of the plan to make the most of its medical opportunities. One of them told me, "As soon as money accumulates it is put into physical expansion, new clinics, new hospitals. We should be making haste more slowly. The medical staffs in existing clinics and hospitals should be enlarged first, and quality of care should be upgraded to the maximum. The way things are, some of our physicians are rushed to a point where they can't give every patient the time required to satisfy that patient. Some patients become antagonized—less receptive to our efforts. This does not improve the quality of care, but worsens it. And it's grist for the mill of organized medicine."

A pro-Permanente physician engaged in fee-for-service practice in the San Francisco Bay area told me that he gets "dozens" of patients who prefer his services to those of the Kaiser clinic. "It's inexcusable," he said. "They come to us because Permanente has estranged them. If Permanente would only slow down and warm up, this would not happen, because Permanente is the beginning of the greatest thing that has ever developed in American medicine."

An anti-Permanente physician in the same area told me that he, too, gets many Permanente patients. A bulwark of the local medical society, he grinned happily as he said, "Permanente can't do the job. When you've got physicians working on salaries under the sponsorship of an industry whose main concern is industrial relations, you have to run into this kind of trouble. All the physicians want to do is get rid of the patient. They have no other incentive. All the industry wants is more hospitals, more clinics, more publicity. Only when the physician works for a fee has he the greatest incentive to give proper attention to the patient."

The remarkably low frequency with which Permanente patients are hospitalized, as compared with insured patients of fee physicians, is also taken as evidence of neglect. Charges of that sort come perilously close to slander. The facts are that hospital bed utilization is always uniformly lower among persons covered by comprehensive service plans. The main reasons were given in the last chapter: comprehensive service plans provide diagnostic services in outpatient clinics, and neither physician nor patient is under economic pressure to use a hospital bed unless it is really needed. Also, comprehensive plans give preventive service and stop an indeterminate number of illnesses from developing to the hospital stage.

Furthermore, if Permanente service were generally as impersonal and rushed as its severest critics imply, this flaw would combine with organized medicine's excellent public relations facilities to run the Kaiser plan out of business in nothing flat. Criticism of Permanente by its own physicians does not mean that they think Permanente is practicing poorer medicine than is practiced by fee soloists. It means only that Permanente is making the mistake of not surpassing fee medicine by the widest possible margin, a mistake which sometimes involves brusqueness and other bureaucratic behavior toward patients. It is proof of the patients' human dignity, but not of their medical acumen, that they go back to private practitioners who may or may not provide equally sound service but often are nicer about it and always charge more for it.

The most enthusiastic booster of the Kaiser plan whom I have met is Joseph T. De Silva, secretary of Local 770 of the Retail Clerks International Association, Los Angeles. His welfare fund prepays Kaiser $1,200,-000 a year for medical and hospital service to union members and their families.

"I don't know how it is up around San Francisco," he said, "but down here the Kaiser docs are on our side all the way. Once a month we meet with them and iron out any small troubles we have, and we're getting real service. We went into Perm because regular indemnity insurance had too much water in it, even though regular indemnity insurance is easier on union officers. All you have to do with regular insurance is buy a policy and collect your brokerage commission under the table if you're that kind of a skunk, and from then on the members and the doctors are on their own. In Perm it's harder. You're closer to the situation. You are buying service and you have a stake in it.

"About half our members are women," he continued, "and in the beginning they naturally prefer to have their own personal, private physician but you'd be amazed at how they warm up to Perm, and the families with children are completely sold on it. Every year our members choose the kind of insurance to have, and not more than 15 per cent of them decide to go back to regular insurance. At the same time some of those in regular insurance come back to Perm. No extra fees. No running around from Beverly Hills to Santa Monica, chasing your X-ray pictures. No unnecessary surgery. Can't beat it."

From the start Permanente had trouble recruiting enough physicians of the quality it needs. Few local physicians were interested in abandoning their fee practices. Candidates from other parts of the country knew that they would be barred from organized medicine, unable to get certification in their specialties, and otherwise branded. Only in the last few years has the Alameda-Contra Costa Medical Association admitted Permanente physicians working in Oakland and Walnut Creek. Those working in San Francisco and Los Angeles counties were still barred.

I asked the AMA's official spokesman, Dr. George F. Lull, about this shortly after he had told me that fee-gouging, unnecessary surgery, and similar brutalities are best handled at the local level and that it does no good to banish an errant physician from organized medicine because such action does not help him to mend his ways. "Why," I asked, "do medical societies bar Kaiser physicians? Why cut them off from the mainstream of organized medicine? Why not invite them in so that they can be helped?"

"That," he answered patiently, "is the privilege of the local society. It's strictly a matter for local determination. We cannot interfere."

Health Insurance Plan of Greater New York: When Fiorello La-Guardia became mayor of New York he was enraged by the news that many city employees were in debt to usurers or more respectable lending institutions and that the chief reason for the indebtedness was sickness bills. In the early forties he asked experts to devise a plan for comprehensive, prepaid medical care free of extra, unforeseeable bills. In 1947, with loans (since repaid) from philanthropic foundations, HIP began functioning. It had 22 groups of physicians and about 100,000 subscribers, most of them city employees.

By 1958, HIP was serving almost 500,000 enrollees through 32 medical groups which included slightly more than 1,000 physicians. The plan provides full medical care but not hospital care. Subscribers purchase Blue Cross hospitalization insurance. Their total family expenses, including hospitalization, come to the usual $200 or so per year, of which employers usually pay at least half.

HIP gets about $36.36 per year per patient, of which it deducts $4.56 for administration, research, and other pertinent expenses. The medical group chosen by the patient is thus given $31.80 to care for him, and divides the money to suit itself.

The earnings of HIP physicians vary greatly, according to the financial rules of the particular group and the number of patients who have chosen to use the group. In some of the busier groups, a certified specialist may make between $25,000 and $30,000 per year. This figure is not subject to comparison with the earnings of Kaiser-Permanente physicians, because HIP physicians are rarely on a full-time basis. Whereas the Kaiser plan is an integrated, centralized one with its own hospitals, clinics, and full-time medical staffs, HIP is much less highly organized. Only 50 of its physicians are full-timers. The rest combine HIP practice with private fee practice, often in the same office and during the same hours. In some of the groups general practitioners or specialists in internal medicine who serve as the subscribers' family physicians are not even in the same building with the specialists. This deprives the physician and the patient of the prompt consultation and co-ordinated service which is supposed to be the *sine qua non* of group practice. In fact, it conduces to a kind of fragmentation of service which, except for the absence of extra fees, is similar to that found in conventional practice. Because of this, organized medicine charges that HIP is not really group practice at all, but is only "panel" practice. As usual organized medicine exaggerates. Some of the HIP groups practice group medicine of the very highest order.

The consumer complaints leveled against Kaiser-Permanente are echoed by some HIP patients, despite the different settings. Among the most acute problems are those which arise from the physician's ambivalence as both a HIP and a "private" physician. The fee patients sometimes like to think that they are getting more for their money than the HIP patient gets, whereas the HIP patient likes to believe that he is entitled to equally ceremonious and careful treatment. The conflict is bothersome to certain physicians and results in irritation among their patients. Physicians more concerned with the patient than with the kind of dollar he represents are apt to encounter less trouble of that kind.

HIP has always tried to make friends with organized medicine, but the record indicates that it can do so only by liquidating itself. For example, Consolidated Edison, a New York gas and electric utility, provides 23,000 employees with inexpensive, fully comprehensive medical, dental, and hospital services rendered under a group-practice program that dates back to 1902. While organized medicine would prefer the company's employees to be in the open market for medical service, it never complains. The objection to HIP's comprehensive plan, then, is that it is competing with fee physicians for all the patients it can get.

Five anti-HIP bills have been introduced into the state legislature by lawmakers attentive to organized medicine. HIP physicians have been ostracized in hospitals, banned from at least one county medical society, charged falsely with breaches of ethics. In 1954 the same session of the House of Delegates of the Medical Society of the State of New York that adopted a resolution favoring a polite form of fee-splitting adopted another resolution which, if enforced, would have destroyed HIP by coercing its physicians into resigning.

The spurious solicitude for public welfare that underlies the anti-HIP shenanigans of organized medicine is identical with the tenderness displayed during the early days of the Group Health Association in Washington. That the medical societies do not have a scientific leg to stand on was demonstrated in 1958 when new statistics indicated the superiority of HIP medicine to the medicine generally available from competing practitioners and conventional forms of health insurance. A study financed by the U.S. Public Health Service enabled HIP to announce that, among 57,000 HIP patients, the rate of hospitalization during 1955 had been 77.4 per 1,000. Among 53,000 New Yorkers with the identical hospitalization insurance but less comprehensive medical insurance (Blue Shield), the hospitalization rate had been 95.8 per thousand. Less than two weeks before these statistics were published, the *American Journal of Public Health* disclosed that perinatal mortality[1] rates were lower among HIP subscribers than among other New Yorkers. The HIP rate was 23.9 perinatal deaths for each 1,000 deliveries. The rate among other New York patients was 38.1. The article said: "The lower rate in HIP is not due to differences in the kinds of hospitals used . . . The observed number of perinatal deaths among births to HIP women (105) was lower than would have been expected (138), if the rates were the same as among births to other women admitted to the same hospitals by private doctors."

One possible explanation for the superiority of HIP medical service to mothers and newborn babies is the stress HIP places on prenatal care and the fact that such care is given at no extra charge. Also the health plan has one qualified obstetrician for every 1,000 female patients of childbearing age. In New York as a whole the ratio is 1:3,300. Moreover, the plan applies exceedingly high standards not merely in screening the qualifications of physicians but in policing their performance. It is safe to say that in the past ten years more physicians (27) have been dropped from HIP medical groups for unsatisfactory behavior—such as refusal to make night calls or discrimination in favor of non-HIP patients —than have been expelled from all the nation's county medical societies for unnecessary surgery and gross overcharging.

Other Plans: The Group Health Co-operative of Puget Sound (Se-

---

[1] Perinatal mortality is not the same as infant mortality. It refers to deaths among newborns under one week of age, plus fetal deaths after gestation of twenty weeks or more.

attle), which has 42,000 subscribers, and the Community Health Center of Two Harbors, Minnesota, which has 3,500, are now free to provide comprehensive prepaid service after years of struggle against vengeful medical societies. The Seattle plan was unshackled by a Washington Supreme Court decision ordering the King County Medical Society to stop boycotting the competition. The Two Harbors co-operative won an out-of-court settlement which admits its physicians to membership in organized medicine and makes the road easier.

In the field of labor union medical centers, the picture is clouded. Some unions, despairing of getting equitable deals through available forms of health insurance, have sought to establish their own health services. The Labor Health Institute of St. Louis was started in 1945 by a CIO union of warehouse workers that later was absorbed into the International Brotherhood of Teamsters. Its 58 part-time physicians and dentists are paid on an hourly or sometimes a monthly basis under a complex formula that has caused occasional wear and tear, but the facilities are excellent and all medical studies of the center staff's comprehensive service in clinic, home, and hospital have been laudatory. A few other labor health centers offer medical treatment in their own clinics, but not in the patient's home and, unless he is covered by insurance, not in the hospital. Most labor centers confine their services to diagnostic tests, referring the patient to private physicians for treatment. Recent efforts by longshore, clothing, and auto unions in New York, Pennsylvania, and Ohio to expand the scope of health center services have been militantly opposed by medical societies.

The longshore example is eloquent. It involves a Brooklyn waterfront union boss named Anthony "Tough Tony" Anastasia. He is not widely regarded as a do-gooder, but he has visions of empire and, regardless of his checkered past, is interested in accomplishing something for his constituents. In 1957, after collective bargaining left his union with a welfare fund large enough for the purpose, he set about establishing a million-dollar health center through which longshoremen and their families could get comprehensive medical care. The Kings County Medical Society, fervent enemy of HIP and any other medical service that competes with the private practitioner, changed Tough Tony's mind for him. When he tried to get the legislature to pass the enabling act needed to legalize a corporate medical service of this kind, the medical society deluged the state capital with messages of protest. Rather than be defeated in Albany, the union withdrew the bill and crept humbly to the medical society for a private prescription. Generously the society helped draft new legislation which was quickly passed and allows the union center to perform diagnostic tests and certain other rigorously limited services. The center is gorgeously equipped, has a full-time medical director, and about 100 society-approved part-time physicians who are paid from $9 to $15 an hour for diagnostic procedures. In cases of emergency, they also are permitted to render stopgap treatment before referring the sufferer to private care.

Like everything else related to American medical service, the future of prepaid group practice rests in the hands of the public. State laws which hobble the establishment of comprehensive plans under consumer sponsorship usually prove chimerical when tested in court. If not chimerical, they can be repealed or amended. Capital financing, which up to now has come largely from philanthropy and therefore has been limited, can come from government-insured loans or even from government loan or government grant. The reluctance of physicians to join medical-service plans that are opposed by organized medicine is not insuperable. As HIP and Kaiser demonstrate, reluctance diminishes in inverse ratio to the financial stability of the plan, the scientific opportunities it offers, the money it can pay, and, above all, the amount of community loyalty it can command. Regimentation of patients, bureaucracy, discourtesy, and other disappointments which occur in some plans are not unique in prepaid group medicine. They are found wherever the paying customer allows himself to be placed at a psychological disadvantage. In prepaid medicine such abuses are eradicated by vigorous consumer control of the plan's human relations, as exemplified in some of the co-operatives. Or, as shown by the Kaiser plan in Los Angeles, abuses can be limited even where the consumer lacks control but at least has an influential voice.

To narrow the gap between what science can provide in the way of health care and what the private patient is now able to buy, the public will ultimately start negotiating with its physicians and its legislators. It can do this through farm organizations, church organizations, labor organizations, political parties, civic improvement leagues, veterans' associations, and existing affiliates of the Group Health Federation of America.

THE
GREY
SEAS
UNDER

---

by Farley Mowat

EDITOR'S NOTE

The North Atlantic is a hungry ocean. From September to June a perpetual sequence of gales whips its waters into a sullen fury, spurred on by the hurricanes which drive northeastward from the Caribbean. Impenetrable masses of ice, sweeping down on the Greenland current, blockade its coasts and harbors, and the ever-present fog lies over the face of the ocean like a grey shroud.

In *The Grey Seas Under,* Farley Mowat tells the story of a small, ocean-going salvage tug, the *Foundation Franklin,* and the rescue work she did over a period of years to save ships buffeted by wind, storm and sea on these cruel waters.

The story of the indomitable *Franklin* is also the story of her men. Mostly Newfoundlanders, they were born to the sea, and no one could beat them at their perilous trade.

Farley Mowat describes the epic struggle of the *Franklin* and her crew against their ancient enemy, the sea, with a life-and-death intensity reminiscent of Joseph Conrad.

Into the Ice

THE SUMMER AND AUTUMN PASSED and there was very little work for Foundation Maritime, although the two rival companies seemed to keep busy enough. Then, in mid-December *Franklin* was ordered to Halifax for her annual inspection and for the long-overdue alterations which would better suit her to the North Atlantic.

She stayed on the slip for three months. The shipwrights began her transformation by extending the boat-deck forward to her stem, thus adding six feet of freeboard forward. The new belowdeck space resulting from this change was turned into quarters for the crew, and the black hole aft, which had been theirs, was converted into a hold for stowing pumps and other salvage gear. The after mast was strengthened and fitted with an eight-ton boom to handle the big pumps and the ground-tackle anchors. The bridge structure lost its gay, excursion-boat appearance and was completely housed-in, leaving only monkey's island, atop the pilot-house, for would-be promenaders.

The work was well executed. When she again took the waters of Halifax harbor *Franklin* had lost all suggestion of friskiness, and had acquired a singularly resolute, if somewhat strait-laced appearance that was more in keeping with her new name. She looked to be quite capable of seeking out a north-west passage through the arctic ice and, as things turned out, she was soon to be put to a test that bore some similarities to the experiences of Sir John Franklin's doomed but indomitable little ships, the *Erebus* and *Terror*.

Looking extremely fit in her new black paint, her green-and-white funnel markings, and her varnished upperworks, *Franklin* put out from Halifax in the last days of February to take up station at St. John's, Newfoundland, for the balance of the winter. She made a good passage over, despite very heavy weather, and arrived at her new port on March 3, to be received by what amounted to a civic welcome.

Newfoundland was then in dire economic straits. Poverty was the common lot, except amongst the semifeudal merchant class which, for a century and more, had held most of the people in a form of slavery by virtue of the debt system. St. John's one major industry—shipbuilding—

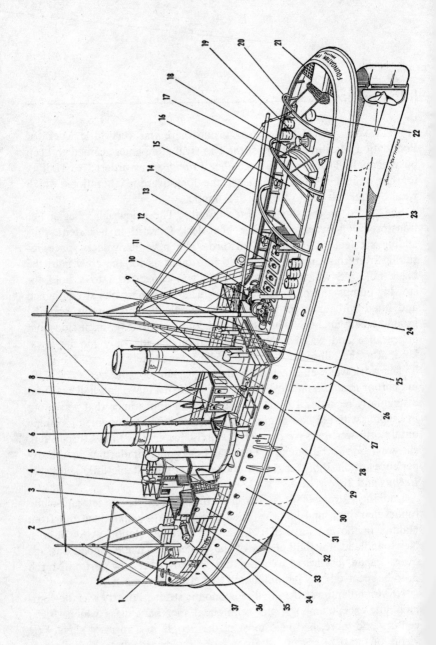

Key to *Franklin* Drawing

1. Anchor windlass
2. Forward cargo booms
3. Port wing of bridge
4. Pilot-house
   (Wheelhouse under)
5. Monkey island
6. Main companionway
   (port side)
7. Radio cabin
8. Direction finder loop
9. Coaling hatches
10. Steering chain housings
11. Towing winch with towing hook
12. Starboard alleyway
13. Engine room skylights
14. Engine room companionway
15. After derrick
16. Hatch (to salvage gear hold)
17. Dory
18. Ground-tackle anchor
19. Capstan
20. Towing bows
21. Grating over rudder quadrant
22. After peak scuttle
23. After-hold for salvage gear
24. Engine room
25. Port alleyway
26. Bunker
27. Stokehold
28. Depth sounder
29. Boiler room
30. Ash chute
31. Main deck cabins
32. Bunker
33. Master's cabin
34. Hatch to forward hold
35. Forward hold
36. Cargo winch
37. Crew's quarters

was nearly moribund. There was no new ship construction in those years, and so the yards were dependent on repair work to keep them going.

The people of St. John's had good reason to welcome *Franklin,* for they thought she might assist them by bringing crippled vessels to their shipyard. They streamed down to visit her with this thought in mind—but since Newfoundlanders were, and are, the finest seamen in the world, they stayed to stare because of something else.

They came to see her: old dory-men who had given their years to the Grand Banks; the young fishermen who took their little schooners laden with salt cod to Portugal and Spain each winter; the men of middle years who sailed the coasts of Labrador in search of cod, and who braved the ice for seals. They came and stood silent—for that is their way—and took her in. And out of the depths of a living knowledge of the sea and ships, they sensed her quality.

They gave her their unrestrained admiration then—and through the years which were to stretch ahead, they were to give her service that was as dedicated as only man's understanding love for a good ship can be.

But in the beginning she served them.

For generations the island's sealing vessels had put out from St. John's and from a score of lesser ports each spring, to seek the immense herds of seals that drift southward with the ice and bear their pups—the white-coats—on the shifting floes. For generations the annual seal hunt had brought the only notable cash income that many Newfoundlanders ever saw. In 1931, that year of black adversity, a successful hunt had become vital to the actual survival of many families.

Consequently the early spring of that hungry year saw every sizable vessel which could be kept afloat sail out to meet the ice. Many of those ships were so old and rotten that they would not have made safe coal-barges in a sheltered harbor. They were crowded to the gunwales, for in Newfoundland they still believe in sharing what they have, be it no more than an opportunity. Some of those ancient vessels carried more than two hundred people, in hulls of less than five hundred tons burthen. No man was left ashore who wished to come, and not many boys were left there either.

Early in March, when *Franklin* was making her way into St. John's, the sealing fleet was already far to the north; part of it bucking the ice in Belle Isle Strait, and the rest cruising the edge of the ice barrier off the great eastern bight that enfolds Notre Dame and White Bays. The seals were there—but well inside the ice—and they could only be reached by entering the pack. Desperation drove the searching ships into the ice, with the full knowledge that some of them might not emerge again.

On March 14 the sealer *Viking*, six hundred tons, with "about" two hundred and thirty men and boys aboard, found herself far in the vanguard of the fleet and trapped in thick pack ice a few miles off the island of St. Barbe.

Viking was the patriarch of the fleet. Built in Norway in 1881, she was a wooden ship designed for sail, but fitted with a primitive low-powered steam auxiliary engine. She had lived her whole life in the north, and it had been a hard and unremitting struggle that had aged her more than the years should have done. Half a century of arctic ice had weakened her, and the rot was deep in all her timbers.

Her skipper, Captain Abraham Kean, was well aware of her disabilities. As the ice shoved and heaved about his ship he could feel her deck beams begin to buckle. She had insufficient engine power with which to extricate herself, but there was one remaining weapon her people could use against the ice. In a small hold aft, under the officers' accommodations and alongside the engine room, was enough blasting powder to force a path to freedom. As the early winter dusk came down on March 15 Captain Kean ordered the bosun to break out the powder.

The bosun and four men made their way to where the powder was stored, carrying a number of small tin canisters which were to be filled, then fitted with fuses. Through the night they labored and towards dawn they had almost completed a sufficient supply of bombs with which to begin their task.

Ashore, on the bleak rocks of St. Barbe—or Horse Island, as it is known locally—the young man who operated the antiquated spark-gap radio which was the island's only communication with the outer world was working his set. His shanty, with its single tiny window facing west, was one of a dozen that clustered on the treeless rock, and that made up the whole of human settlement upon the island. Otis Bartlet seldom glanced through the clouded glass of his window, for there was nothing to be seen from it except the crumbling waste of ice that stretched twenty miles to the mainland shore.

It was dark enough so that his oil lamp was still in use when the interior of the shanty was suddenly and brilliantly illuminated from outside. Bartlet jumped to his feet and thrust his face against the windowpane, frightened and awe-struck by the intensity of the light which had come flooding in upon him. The light was gone almost immediately and he was still staring into darkness when the rock beneath his feet shook with a heavy tremor, and a great and terrifying sound came thundering across the ice.

At 9 A.M. the radio operator at Twillingate, some sixty miles away, heard the faint squeal of a carrier wave in his earphones, and then the stutter of Morse.

HORSE ISLAND TO TWILLINGATE HORSE ISLAND TO TWILLINGATE TERRIBLE EXPLOSION IN THE ICE THIS MORNING WRECKAGE OF BURN-ING STEAMER VISIBLE EIGHT MILES WEST PARTY FROM HERE TRYING TO GET ON THE ICE SURVIVORS SEEN TRYING TO WORK TO SHORE. . . .

That first message from Horse Island was relayed immediately to St. John's, the capital, and a few hours later was further amplified by Bartlet's key.

ICE IN BAD CONDITION HEAVY SEA AND WIND BLOWING OFFSHORE FIRST CROWD OF SURVIVORS MAY REACH ISLAND OTHERS HAVE LITTLE CHANCE SHIP BELIEVED TO BE VIKING OUT OF ST. JOHNS

As the tragic day drew down to darkness, there was one further message:

HAVE SOME SURVIVORS MORE THAN ONE HUNDRED MISSING AND TWENTY-FIVE KNOWN KILLED WE HAVE NO SUPPLIES FOOD OR MEDICAL NO CHANCE OF REACHING MAINLAND HELP MUST COME BY SEA

Help for the *Viking's* people was already on its way. At 2 P.M. that day *Foundation Franklin,* under emergency charter to the Newfoundland Government, had put out from St. John's carrying three doctors, five nurses, and a full cargo of food, blankets, and medical supplies. Two hours later she was followed by the government steamer *Sagona,* and by noon of the following day both ships were entering the slob ice outside the pack.

Nor were they alone. From Belle Isle Strait the sealers *Beothic, Ungava, Eagle, Neptune,* and *Sir William,* all of whom had found seal and had just begun to make their harvest, gave up their work, rounded Cape Bauld and began trying to enter the pack from the northward.

No one aboard any of these vessels knew more than the bare fact that there had been a frightful explosion near Horse Island. But they were familiar with disaster in the pack, for through the years more than two score sealing ships and close to a thousand men had been destroyed by the consuming ice. They guessed the truth: that in the early hours of dawn on March 16 something had touched off the powder in *Viking's* hold.

And they knew with certainty that those who had survived the blast and the flames which followed would die quickly on the ice unless help came.

From the south and from the north the rescuers drove into the pack—but the barrier might as well have been composed of adamantine rock. Onshore gales had rafted it so heavily that not even an ice-breaker could have broken past its outer ramparts. The sealers tried. They drove their greenheart-sheathed vessels against those ramparts until wood shrieked and splintered and steel plates buckled. The measure of how hard they tried is to be found in the fate of the *Sir William,* a wooden schooner of two hundred tons out of Port Union who, in this hour, took the ice with as little hesitation as if she had been sheathed in steel. She found a little lead, drove into it, and two hours later was a crushed and sinking wreck. Her men escaped to safety aboard the *Eagle,* but the *Sir William* died.

Nor could *Franklin* make any better progress. She was not built for ice and could not risk the bruising which *Sagona* later dared—though not even *Sagona* could get through. The two steamers lay six miles off the island, and through the ice "blink" on the horizon they could see a dark encrustation on the floes, and knew it for the burned bones of a ship, and the bodies of men.

On March 18 they were joined by the sealing vessels, which had worked right down the seaward boundary of the pack, unsuccessfully seeking a lead. There were now seven ships lying off the island, but unable to approach.

The news from Bartlet grew steadily worse. Dazed by the blast, and many of them badly burned, a hundred of *Viking's* people had straggled to the island after enduring an agonizing passage of the ice and endless hours of subzero gales. Most were in urgent need of medical attention—all were in need of warmth and food and clothing. The meager resources of the islanders had been exhausted in a single day. There was nothing left to give.

The men aboard the rescue vessels knew the frustrations of the damned; until they found their own solution. They put their dories on the ice, ran hauling lines out from them, and took to the pack like seals themselves. Plunging through slush-covered cracks, staggering in freezing clothes, they half-swam, half-crawled across the floes, dragging their boats, which were laden with supplies and with the doctors and the nurses.

It took six hours for each dory to make the passage in and no man can tell how it was done at all. The sealers rested for an hour or two ashore, and then—in darkness—began the return journey to the ships, hauling the most seriously injured men behind them in the boats.

Franklin stood by the ice edge to receive them, while *Sagona* cruised the pack to the south-west in search of survivors who might have gone adrift on the moving floes. She found three living men and seven corpses, and these were the last of the *Viking's* people who were ever found.

The moving bridge across the ice from the island to the ships was maintained until March 20 and by then a hundred and twenty-seven men had been brought out to *Franklin* and *Sagona*. There were no more to come. There was no more to do. The sealers went aboard their ships, and those frail vessels turned northward to seek the seals once more. Dead men were dead; but ashore in every port in Newfoundland were hungry people who were still alive. The sealers went back north, back to the bitter ice.

Franklin steamed south, and from the hour that she landed her cargo of survivors at St. John's she ceased to be a foreign vessel—now she belonged to the islanders—and they to her.

The Belgian Sisters: One

AS 1934 APPROACHED ITS END, the North Atlantic set the stage for an epic combat. It was to be an epic in two parts; and it concerned two sisters of the Belgian merchant fleet.

The first of the sisters was the *Emile Francqui*. She was one of a class of vessels built in the early thirties for the Belgian Maritime Company. They were big, good-looking ships, of six thousand tons, intended for the general carrying trade; but each had accommodations for twelve passengers as well.

The weather encountered by the *Emile Francqui* in the last days of December while she was bound across the Western Ocean for New York was atrociously bad. One particular gale which came to its full stature on December 22 sank seven trawlers and fishing schooners, and three of these went down with all hands. This same gale caught the *Francqui* three hundred and fifty miles south-east of Halifax, and when it had finished with her the big freighter was helpless in the troughs of a mounting sea with her rudder gone.

She did not transmit a general SOS, for her master knew that a sister ship, the *Henri Jaspar,* was somewhere near at hand eastward bound for Antwerp. *Francqui* was able to contact the *Jaspar,* who immediately steamed to her assistance; but the interchange between the two vessels was overheard by Lindsay McManus, *Franklin's* radio operator, who frequently stood listening watches, alert for just such messages, even when the tug was at her berth in Halifax.

McManus passed the information on to Captain Reginald Featherstone, Foundation Maritime's versatile salvage master, who acted on it with his usual aggressiveness. He radioed:

> POWERFUL OCEAN TUG FOUNDATION FRANKLIN OFFERS IMMEDIATE ASSISTANCE PLEASE ADVISE OF YOUR CONDITION

Francqui's reply was not encouraging.

> LOST RUDDER PROCEEDING HALIFAX ASSISTANCE STEAMER HENRI JASPAR STEERING FROM ASTERN STOP NO OTHER ASSISTANCE NEEDED

Another man might well have let the matter drop. Not Featherstone. Ten minutes on the telephone told him that *Francqui* was lightly laden and that she would therefore be almost unmanageable if a new gale sprang up. His own instincts told him that such a gale was almost certain at this season and that when it came, *Francqui* would need professional assistance. He ordered McManus to remain on listening watch and to relay to him every message which passed between the two big freighters far at sea.

McManus was kept busy. During the night of February 24 a succession of messages passed between the masters of the ships, most of them relating to the extreme difficulty they were having in keeping the connecting line intact. Despite their best efforts to prevent it, the line parted several times—and this in moderate weather.

Featherstone drew his own conclusions. At dawn he boarded *Franklin* and she put to sea. She was barely clear of the harbor when Featherstone dispatched a second signal:

> FOUNDATION FRANKLIN WILL MEET YOU TOMORROW MORNING AND ASSIST YOU INTO HARBOR

Nor was he the least bit disconcerted by the reply:

> WILL REQUIRE NO REPEAT NO TOWING BEFORE ANCHORING CHEBUCTO HEAD

Captain Degryse of the *Francqui* sounded very certain of himself, and well he might, for the weather on that day was positively tranquil. The gale had died out completely on the twenty-fifth and by the time *Franklin* came in sight of the casualty early the next morning, the sea was almost calm. Only the deep and ever-present ocean swell testified to the transience of this moment of peace.

When Featherstone came alongside the *Francqui* at 9 A.M., he found her making fair progress toward Halifax under her own power, with the *Henri Jaspar* on a line astern acting as a rudder. Nothing daunted by this brave sight, Featherstone signaled to Degryse:

SUGGEST YOU LET FRANKLIN TAKE HOLD OF YOU BEFORE MAKING COASTLINE STOP WITHOUT PREJUDICE SALVAGE CLAIMS OF HENRI JASPAR

It was a well-phrased signal, and a wise one; but Degryse, poor innocent, believing himself in no more danger from the sea, chose to ignore it.

Franklin now took station abeam of the casualty and jogged amiably along without further remark until noon, when McManus received the weather report from Chebucto Radio. It was what Featherstone had anticipated:

ALL SHIPS SOUTHEAST TO SOUTHWEST WINDS INCREASING TO GALES WITH SNOW TONIGHT TURNING TO SLEET TOMORROW

McManus was instructed to find out if Degryse had also heard the report. When the Belgian admitted that he had not, it was politely relayed to him, together with a supplementary report which was received half an hour later:

STORM SIGNAL NUMBER THREE INDICATING A HEAVY GALE FROM EASTERLY BEGINNING THIS EVENING ALL SHIPS SHOULD TAKE PRECAUTIONS

Degryse declined to comment on either of these messages, other than to thank McManus; so Featherstone needled him.

IN VIEW OF HEAVY GALE WARNINGS SUGGEST YOU DO UTMOST AND INCREASE YOUR SPEED OR LET US CONNECT UP BEFORE DARK

Again the message was acutely phrased. *Francqui* obviously did not dare increase her speed for that would endanger the line to *Jaspar*. The alternative, then, was to take *Franklin's* wire at once.

This signal had some effect. It precipitated a flurry of messages be-

tween *Francqui* and *Jaspar,* the gist of which was that *Jaspar* was unwilling to share the salvage with the tug and saw no reason why she
should. Degryse inclined to the same opinion, but he was nevertheless
becoming slightly uneasy about the prospects if he *should* be caught close
to the coast by an onshore gale. He sent Featherstone a casual request
for information as to how *Franklin* would connect, supposing that it
should be necessary.

Featherstone's reply was terse:

WILL SHOW YOU HOW

He had no further time to waste, for he was well aware that the need
to get a wire on *Francqui* was no longer simply a matter of obtaining
a salvage job—it was fast becoming a matter directly affecting the chances
of survival of the crippled ship. He knew that if the gale struck *Francqui*
as she approached the coast and if, as was quite possible, *Franklin* was
then unable to get a line aboard her due to wind and darkness, the rud-
derless freighter would be driven onto the rocks despite the best the
Jaspar could do to hold her off. The probable outcome of further delay
was all too obvious to Featherstone; but Degryse, who did not know the
coast, remained irresolute. Eventually, and it was then 3:30 P.M., he
tried to compromise with his unease by offering to take *Franklin's* wire
when they got abeam of Sambro Lightship, from which point the *Jaspar*
would not be able to assist in any case. Featherstone replied:

IF GALE BREAKS YOU WILL NOT WEATHER SAMBRO WITHOUT MORE
HELP FOR YOUR OWN SAFETY TAKE OUR WIRE NOW

Still Degryse shied away from the decision. It was not until the wind
abruptly began to freshen out of the east at 4:30 P.M. that he gave in
and radioed:

ACCEPT LLOYDS FORM NO CURE NO PAY* COME ALONGSIDE GIVE US
YOUR TOWLINE

Franklin was at his side almost before the message could be acknowledged. Sambro was then only twelve miles off, and the sky was already

* Lloyd's Open Form, or the L.O.F., as it is called in the trade, is essentially a contract between the master of a distressed ship and the people
who are prepared to render aid. Under its terms a would-be salvor agrees
that he will not claim so much as a penny if he fails to save the endangered
ship; while the ship's master, owners, and underwriters agree that—should the
ship be saved—they will be liable to pay a salvage award commensurate with
the value of the vessel and her cargo.

black and angry in the east. The ships were well to the south of the harbor fairway and it was clear that even with the best of luck they would have difficulty weathering the Sambro ledges before they could turn into sheltered waters. It was going to be a near thing.

The wire was put across to *Francqui* in record time. *Franklin* immediately began to work up speed and at 4:50 P.M. the tow was under weigh with *Franklin* ahead and *Jaspar* still clinging to the line astern. *Jaspar* did not hold on long. As the quick seas began to lurch in from the east the strain on her manila grew, and at 5:30 her line parted. She made no attempt to replace it. It would have been waste effort anyway, for that morning, in a flat calm, it had taken her three hours to float a line down to the *Francqui* by means of buoys. In any event *Jaspar* was now most anxious on her own account to claw away from that waiting coast. With a long farewell blast on her whistle she turned and headed out to sea.

Jaspar's haste was pardonable. By 6 P.M. the easterly wind had become a full gale, blowing force 8, and the seas were becoming particularly sharp and ugly, for the vessels were now well in over the shallow coastal banks. Driving rain and the onset of darkness obscured the fury of the grey waters and from *Franklin's* bridge only occasional blurred glimpses could be caught of *Francqui,* who was wallowing almost broadside-to at the end of the tow wire. *Franklin's* course was roughly northward, in an effort to compensate for the eastward drift of the big freighter toward the reefs, which were then less than five miles distant, and straight to leeward.

By 8 P.M., in an impenetrable darkness, the gale was howling at seventy miles an hour full upon the shore, and the men in *Franklin's* pilot-house could almost feel the unseen presence of the ill-omened Sisters Reef close on the port beam. With her great freeboard acting as a sail, *Francqui* was now being blown off nearly at right angles to *Franklin's* course, and the tug had to alter, and keep on altering, until her head was pointing almost out to sea again, in an effort to hold the Belgian clear of the thundering rocks.

Franklin was now laboring and straining terribly. The beam seas were breaking clean across her after deck and over the boat-deck too. Occasionally a giant in the pack rose up so high above her that it broke down her funnels and filled the stokehold with stinking steam. Nevertheless she was holding her own—and a little more. Yard by yard she was edging the casualty past the surging breakers of the Sisters.

The thoughts of the people aboard the tug were concentrated on the towing wire. It was a new one of inch and three-quarter steel and strong enough for almost any task, but it was being fearfully abused. The salvors knew that there was the gravest danger it would begin to chafe at *Francqui's* bows unless a perpetual watch was kept upon it, and unless it was kept smothered in grease. They knew that if a single strand let go, the wire would part; and if that happened *Francqui* would be doomed and so, in all likelihood, would everyone aboard her.

Featherstone could evaluate every risk he could foresee. He had complete faith in his own ship and in her gear. But he could not watch that wire where it rose out of the seas to grip the *Francqui's* bitts.

At 9:20 he radioed Degryse:

WATCH OUR TOWLINE CLOSE FOR CHAFING AT YOUR BOW

Degryse did not reply to this directly, instead he radioed:

WE REQUIRE MORE ASSISTANCE ARE THERE ANY MORE SALVAGE BOATS CLOSE BY

Featherstone smelled the scent of incipient panic in those words. He knew that it was vital to calm Degryse, so he dispatched a soothing, if not entirely accurate message in return:

WE ARE SLOWLY WORKING YOU TO WINDWARD OF CHEBUCTO HEAD AND TRYING TO AVOID TOO GREAT STRAIN ON WIRE STOP NO SALVAGE TUGS EXCEPT GOVERNMENT STEAMERS BUT WILL ASK THEIR ASSISTANCE

That single word, except, contained the subterfuge, for Featherstone was well aware that only one ship in Halifax, the *Lady Laurier,* could hope to live at all on such a night; and that her help, at best, must be limited to the attempt at saving life if *Franklin* sank or if, as a last resort, *Francqui's* people tried to abandon their ship before she struck.

Featherstone now sent off a signal to R. J. Nelson, manager of Halifax Shipyard, who was acting as *Franklin's* shore agent. Once again the message was most carefully worded, for Degryse would undoubtedly intercept it. It read:

HEAVY SOUTHEAST GALES REQUEST IMMEDIATE ASSISTANCE GOVERNMENT STEAMER STAND BY WE ARE STRAINING TOWLINE AND PUNISHING FRANKLIN OFF CHEBUCTO HEAD JASPAR BROKE LINE AND DEPARTED SEAWARD

Nelson, who had been Featherstone's employer in salvage work for

336 The Grey Seas Under

almost twenty years, was quick to read between the lines. He knew that the admission by Featherstone that his ship was being "punished" was tantamount to the admission by another man that she was in danger of going down. He moved swiftly. Within five minutes he had the government agent on the telephone with an urgent request that the *Lady Laurier* put out to sea at once.

The government man replied, with all due apologies, that he had not the authority to send the *Lady Laurier* to sea, and that he would require specific instructions from Ottawa to do so.

Nelson wasted no more time on this bureaucratic nonsense. He immediately telephoned the Belgian Consul at Halifax, and that dignitary called the Department of External Affairs in Ottawa. Half an hour later Nelson was informed that the *Lady Laurier* was getting up steam and would be ready to sail in two hours' time.

That was something accomplished, but not enough. Nelson got in touch with the local owners of the two big new harbor tugs, the *Banscot* and *Banshee,* and hired them. The tugs put out at once, but neither of them got beyond the harbor mouth. Their masters put back into shelter claiming, with justification, that it would have been suicide to attempt to go "outside."

Featherstone had not expected any aid to reach him and he had planned accordingly. Knowing that the tow wire might let go at any moment (and that it could not, in any circumstances, remain intact much longer), he also knew that he would only hasten this inevitable moment if he continued to try and haul the *Francqui* off the shore. The only chance, as Featherstone saw it, was to edge the crippled vessel in *toward* the coast so that, by easing the strain on the wire, and with the assistance of the gale, he might hope to get *Francqui* over good holding grounds before the wire parted. There was only one such patch of mud and clay bottom on that entire stretch of coast, and it lay somewhere ahead and close inshore. The rest was rock, upon which no anchor would have held in such a storm.

It was a calculated risk, but such a one as few men would have cared to take. By 10 P.M. the wind was gusting eighty miles an hour and *Franklin* was being continually swept from end to end. The rain had changed to a driven, bitter snow that mixed with the salt spray and froze over the deck and bridge. The shore remained invisible, but it was close . . . so close that Degryse could hear Bell Rock and Duncan Reef breaking close beneath his lee.

That fearsome sound drove him to transmit a frantic message begging Featherstone to haul him out to sea.

Featherstone ignored the message.

Then, at 10:30, Degryse could stand the tension no longer. His radio began to crackle out a general SOS.

STEAMER EMILE FRANCQUI TO ALL SHIPS . . . EMILE FRANCQUI TO ALL SHIPS . . . AM TWO MILES SOUTHEAST CHEBUCTO HEAD NEED IMMEDIATE ASSISTANCE AM DRIFTING ONTO SHORE. . . .

Featherstone listened to that call, but he gave no sign that it disturbed him, and he held *Franklin* to her course. He was utterly preoccupied with the problem of locating a patch of mud hidden under fifteen fathoms of rolling water, on a winter night when nothing could be seen of the world about him except salt spray and squalls of snow.

At 10:45 he turned his eyes from the inscrutable sea and glanced quickly at the chart; then he scribbled a message for the *Francqui* and a deck-hand braved the seas sweeping over the boat-deck to get it to Mc-Manus in his little radio shack.

MASTER EMILE FRANCQUI WE ARE PULLING HARD AND MAKING PROGRESS BUT IF WIRE PARTS DROP BOTH ANCHORS AND STEAM UP TO THEM YOU ARE NOW OVER GOOD HOLDING GROUND

Featherstone's confidence was not shared by anyone aboard the *Franklin*—and certainly not by Degryse. As one of *Franklin's* officers remembered it:

"If Featherstone knew where we was at just then, he was the only man in the whole damn world who did—and maybe they would have had to guess in Heaven, too!"

Ten minutes after that message was dispatched *Franklin* gave a sudden sickening leap as she breasted a huge sea. Without being told, every soul aboard knew that the wire had gone.

Although he must have believed his ship was doomed, Degryse never-theless obeyed instructions. He let go both anchors with a run and then, with his engines at half-ahead, steamed up to them. At the same time he dispatched a pathetic signal to Featherstone:

ARE YOU LEAVING ME

The reply came back instantly:

WE ARE STAYING WITH YOU NO MATTER WHAT AND WILL GET A NEW LINE ON YOU WHEN THE TIME IS RIGHT

Featherstone's decision to remain upon the scene seemed suicidal to some of his officers. One of them said as much, but he was silenced by half a dozen words which left him dumb.

Franklin was still afloat. She would remain that way. Thus—Featherstone. And more than this, she would do the impossible if need be and get a line on *Francqui* if that vessel began to drag her anchors. If *Francqui* held, then *Franklin* would stand by and wait for dawn and less desperate weather, to reconnect.

INFORM AT ONCE IF YOU BEGIN TO DRAG, radioed Featherstone, and then hove the *Franklin* to.

And now, in a frightful paroxysm, the gale rose to its climax. On shore the weather station clocked the gusts at up to one hundred miles an hour, and at sea the wind had become an element as tangible as the grey waters of the Atlantic. It bore down upon the two ships and bludgeoned them unmercifully and without respite until, at 11:30 P.M., its strength began to fail. That was the longest interval in time that most of *Franklin's* men had ever lived through—what it must have been to the passengers and crew of the *Emile Francqui* can be imagined only dimly.

As the wind began to falter Featherstone again asked *Francqui* how she was, and the reply came back:

WE ARE HOLDING FIRM

The crisis was over. Chebucto Radio came on the air to inform Featherstone that the heavy gale warning had now been changed to strong gales from the south-west—offshore. The wind was dropping fast before the change, as the eye of the storm passed overhead. Featherstone radioed Degryse:

YOU ARE SAFE NOW WE ARE READYING ANOTHER WIRE BUT STILL SHIPPING SEAS FORE AND AFT WILL GET LINE TO YOU AS SOON AS POSSIBLE

While his men were laboring in the alleyways to lay out a new wire, Featherstone ordered *Franklin* to be brought around out of the wind so she could run down toward the *Francqui*. The helmsman watched his chance, but as he spun the wheel hard-over, an unsuspected giant loomed out of the darkness and broke full on *Franklin's* starboard side, almost burying her beneath it. Gamely the little ship turned and came up to it— but slowly, slowly. And at that crucial instant the steering-chain, stretched by the abuse of the long struggle, slipped free of the rudder quadrant.

Featherstone himself leaped from the bridge to the foredeck and fought his way hand over hand along the weather rail to reach the anchor windlass. He knocked off the brake and the chain roared out, sending a stream of sparks into the wind. There was a dreadful waiting minute, and then the anchor caught, dragged a few hundred feet and caught again—*Franklin's* head came up out of the trough in answer, and she lay into wind and sea once more.

The *Lady Laurier* arrived soon afterwards, having been unable to make any headway until the wind began to drop. Now, at Featherstone's request, she hove-to nearby while the salvage men endeavored to restore their vessel's helm.

Diver Tom Nolan and his diving attendant, Alan Macdonald, volunteered to go aft and try to replace the chain while Featherstone and a fireman clung to the turnbuckles on either side amidships, ready to slacken and then tighten them again as was required.

Tom and his companion crawled across the after deck like a pair of seals on a wave-washed rock, for the deck space had become a part of the North Atlantic. When they reached the grating in the stern they found it to be so thickly coated in ice that there was only room for one man to crawl under it. Following on the change in wind, the temperature had plummeted far below freezing. Spray froze on the two men's faces until they were masked in ice.

Alan crawled under the grating while Tom braced himself and clung to his companion's legs. Inside the narrow space Alan struggled with his bare hands to get the heavy chain back where it belonged. The quadrant, with the full weight of the rudder behind it, swung murderously back and forth within inches of his head. For half an hour he lay there waiting his moment, until at last he managed to lever the chain back into place. A kick of Macdonald's foot told Nolan that the job was done, and a hoarse Newfoundland voice broke through the sound of wind and seas.

"Tighten them goddamn bottles—she's back on!"

At 2 A.M. on December 27 *Franklin* hauled up her anchor and once more was under weigh.

Despite querulous complaints from the *Lady Laurier,* who was not enjoying the buffeting of the devilish cross-sea which had risen with the new south-westerly gale, Featherstone was in no hurry now. *Francqui* was no longer in any danger, and he felt it was better to wait until the easterly seas had fallen off a little. So wait he did, through a succession of blinding snow squalls, until the daylight came and the westerly began to smooth the seas. Only then did *Franklin* put her wire aboard the casualty and, with the *Lady Laurier* astern to steer, she proceeded for Halifax.

So they came up the harbor that morning: three ice-encrusted vessels hard-done-by at the hands of man's oldest and most implacable adversary. And the little ship who led them blew her whistle as she came, so that the sound of it rolled back from the great citadel in the city's heart to tell the people of that port of victory.

The Belgian Sisters: Two _____

IN JANUARY OF 1935 *Franklin* had just refloated a small freighter from an island off Newfoundland when she was ordered back to Halifax, where the large and valuable passenger-freighter *Silveryew* had driven onto Mars Rock.

Franklin was preceded to the scene by Chadwick, chief executive of Foundation Maritime, who had come down posthaste from Montreal hoping to obtain an L.O.F. contract in *Franklin's* absence and hold it for her arrival; but he was a few hours too late. The Salvage Association representative had already advised *Silveryew's* master to sign a contract with a local tug-boat company.

Chadwick's appearance (he was accompanied by Irwin Power, captain of *Foundation Franklin*) was not welcomed. He and Power boarded the stricken ship to find themselves being pointedly ignored. Phlegmatically they adjourned to the dining saloon, where they were treated to a seven-course dinner, complete with wines, by a dejected steward, who explained sadly:

"The passengers have all gone ashore and the officers are all up on the bridge figuring how to get us off. Sandwiches was all they wanted—and me with the best dinner of the voyage and not a soul to eat it. Please, gentlemen, *do* have a little more."

He had not been completely deserted, however. One passenger had remained on the vessel. She was an elderly lady completing a world cruise. When the lifeboats were launched she had resolutely refused to enter them. She explained matter-of-factly that she would probably never again have the chance to be shipwrecked, and she had no intention of allowing herself to be deprived of that experience.

By the time *Franklin* arrived, after bulling her way through a pea-soup fog at full speed all the way from Newfoundland, the would-be salvors who had signed the L.O.F. had begun to realize that they had bitten off more than they could chew.

Featherstone now boarded the ship and began making one of his apparently perfunctory examinations. While he was about it, the rival salvors approached Chadwick and, with a lordly condescension that fooled no one, announced that they were prepared to hire some of *Franklin's* salvage gear. Apologetically Chadwick explained that he really could not risk his valuable equipment in the hands of amateurs. However, he added, *if* the rival salvors were prepared to include Foundation Maritime in the L.O.F. contract on the basis of equal pay for equal work, then something *might* be arranged.

The salvage representative, who was only concerned with freeing the ship before an onshore wind destroyed her, swung his weight behind Foundation Maritime and the opposition salvors were reluctantly forced to accept Chadwick's terms.

As for the ship—Featherstone took her off on the next high tide by pumping her forward tanks and then juggling water ballast in her other tanks while *Franklin* towed. He made it look so easy that his rivals probably felt rather sick. In any event they never again attempted to engage in salvage in competition with Foundation Maritime.

After the *Silveryew* there was a month of inactivity culminating in the second episode in the affair of the Belgian sisters.

It began on March 25 when the Canadian trawler *Kerlew,* homeward bound from the Grand Banks, encountered a small and sorry-looking tramp steamer wallowing in the swells several hundred miles from land and flying international distress signals.

Kerlew altered course to investigate. When she had closed to megaphone range she learned that the distressed ship was the *Longbird,* out of Bermuda, bound for New York and twelve days overdue (as well as being more than two hundred miles off course) as a result of leaking boiler tubes which had left her all but helpless in the grip of a series of spring gales.

Kerlew was unable to tow the casualty, but she radioed an SOS for *Longbird,* whose own radio was out of action. The message was picked up by the Department of Transport stations ashore and was relayed directly to the Royal Canadian Mounted Police Headquarters in Halifax. There is some mystery as to why Foundation Maritime—the legitimate commercial salvors on the coast—were not also notified. At any rate the

R.C.M.P. promptly dispatched their police-cutter *Preventer,* with orders to take *Longbird* in tow.

If anyone had hoped to keep Foundation in the dark the hope was a hollow one. Chadwick had always had a penchant for cloak-and-dagger work, and early in Foundation Maritime's history he had laid the groundwork for a system of unofficial "agents" who were paid to report all marine casualties to his headquarters. Combined with this he had also invented a complicated company code whose use was mandatory during salvage operations.

Preventer had hardly cast off her lines before Featherstone not only knew of her departure, but also knew where she was bound and why. He promptly telephoned *Longbird's* agents in New York, told them that their vessel was in distress, and offered to assist. He made no mention of *Preventer,* but then of course he did not know, officially, that she had sailed. *Longbird's* agents were duly grateful for the information about their missing ship and they authorized *Franklin* to go and get her under the L.O.F.

Like most professional salvors Featherstone regarded government vessels, which engaged in rescue work as a sort of part-time hobby, with intense dislike. Consequently he had few scruples when it came to protecting his company's interests from such "unfair" competition.

Under command of Captain Power *Franklin* sailed three hours behind *Preventer.* Once clear of the harbor, Power dispatched an innocuous-sounding message to the police vessel:

UNDERSTAND YOU ARE LOOKING FOR LONGBIRD PLEASE ADVISE AREA YOU INTEND TO SEARCH AND IF YOU LOCATE HER

To which *Preventer* replied suspiciously:

SEARCHING SOUTH OF GIVEN LOCATION WHAT ARE YOUR INTENTIONS

Power answered innocently:

ENDEAVORING TO LOCATE LONGBIRD PROVISION HIM AND GIVE AS-SISTANCE IF REQUIRED

Preventer made no reply to this, but no reply was needed. During the first transmission from the R.C.M.P. vessel, McManus had been operating his direction finder. Power now knew which way to go.

Both ships had then been at sea for some time and the wind, which had been light earlier in the day, was making up into a moderate westerly gale. *Preventer* was easing up as the seas grew heavier; but *Franklin* was driving so hard that she was taking water fore and aft. If it was possible, Power intended to reach the *Longbird* first.

His hopes were dashed at 5 P.M. when McManus intercepted a message from *Preventer* to her base in Halifax.

HAVE LOCATED LONGBIRD NOW IN TOW

It was a brief transmission, but not brief enough to elude McManus's vigilance on the DF set. He passed a bearing to Power, and *Franklin* altered to an interception course.

Power knew that once the connection had been made, *Longbird* would hang on to *Preventer* like grim death, for her master would have the choice of a free tow to port behind the cutter or an expensive tow behind *Franklin*. Therefore, in order to get the job, Power had to separate the two vessels. There was one circumstance that favored him: *Longbird* was virtually deaf without her radio, and this meant that *Preventer* was the key. Somehow she had to be persuaded to relinquish her prize.

Power opened his campaign:

GOOD WORK PREVENTER PLEASE ADVISE YOUR POSITION COURSE AND SPEED WILL MEET YOU AND TAKE OVER TOW

Preventer refused to bite. Her reply was immediate and unfriendly.

MY INSTRUCTIONS ARE TO TOW LONGBIRD IN TO HALIFAX

With the failure of his opening play, Power prepared to unlimber heavier artillery. Using the company code he radioed Featherstone a full report of the situation, suggesting that he take the matter up on a higher level.

Featherstone entered the fray with gusto. He telephoned R.C.M.P. Headquarters staff and, having first congratulated them on *Preventer's* work, he asked if they were aware that they were interfering with a commercial contract which had been made between Foundation Maritime and *Longbird's* agents. This was a bombshell. Interference with free commercial enterprise can cause a government no end of embarrassment, even when it is not an election year.

Featherstone rang off, and gave the bomb time to explode before he called again. "I've just heard from Captain Power," he explained, "that *Preventer* refuses to relinquish the tow except under direct orders from your office. Perhaps you could straighten this little matter out for us?"

It was 8 P.M. when Power came in sight of *Longbird*. At almost the same instant McManus reported to him that the cutter had received instructions from Halifax to hand over the tow.

Preventer's master took the reverse with good grace. He prepared to release *Longbird,* but it was immediately apparent that *Longbird* had no intention of being released. Her skipper had observed *Franklin's* arrival on the scene with indignation and dismay. To *Preventer's* repeated request that he cast off the cutter's line, he turned a blind eye and a deaf ear. But to *Franklin* he signaled, using his lamp:

I DO NOT WANT ANY TUG I AM IN GOOD SHAPE AND CAN GET TO PORT ON MY OWN IF NECESSARY GO AWAY

Shortly thereafter *Preventer's* master dispatched a somewhat plaintive message to Power:

HE WONT LET GO AND ITS MY LINE AND WORTH FIVE HUNDRED DOLLARS WHAT DO YOU THINK WE SHOULD DO

Power was ready for that one. In fact he had been debating whether or not to make a suggestion before he was asked for it. Now he signaled:

FOUNDATION MARITIME WILL MAKE GOOD ALL GEAR LOST OR DAM-AGED IN CONNECTION WITH THIS JOB

The official report does not detail the events that followed this transmission. It merely records that at 9:40 P.M. *Preventer's* line mysteriously carried away at her stern, and that she then swung off to starboard and took station half a mile away.

Power was close in under *Longbird's* quarter when the line "carried away" and he had his searchlight trained on *Longbird's* stern, for he had noted that this unhappy ship was turning over her propeller as if to demonstrate that she really *was* able to look after herself. Power was still watching closely when *Longbird* overran the broken Manila rope and wound it so firmly around her screw that it looked like a gigantic piece of knitting. The screw stopped dead. Power turned to his mate, John Pynn.

"Poor chap," he said sympathetically. "He's gone and got his propeller all fouled up."

Franklin now came in close and Power yelled: "Stand by to catch our heaving line!" Which brought a scurrilous reply, the gist of which was that *Longbird* did not need or want a tow and in fact wanted nothing from *Franklin* except some food. Come dawn, said *Longbird's* master, he would start up his engine and run for Halifax.

Power understood. *Longbird's* master knew that his propeller was inextricably fouled (though he did *not* know that Power knew it too).

He believed that if he could persuade Power to give up and go away, he could then signal to *Preventer,* who was still in visual range, give the excuse that *Franklin* had abandoned *Longbird* and ask the cutter for another tow.

Power remained impeccably polite, as was his habit. Despite the high seas he launched a dory and sent a load of food over to the casualty—and then he settled down to wait.

He was a patient man.

At 7 A.M. the following day *Longbird's* master knew that he was beaten. With an ill grace he took *Franklin's* wire at last, but he was determined to make things as difficult for Power as possible. Despite the fact that the L.O.F. contract called for "delivery to the nearest safe port," he insisted that he be towed all the way to New York.

Power was willing to humor him. "All right," he cried through his megaphone, "New York it is."

Franklin eased forward to take the strain, and then she swung slowly on course for Ambrose Lightship, five hundred miles away. Power sighed contentedly and went below to his cabin for a little rest.

Twenty minutes later he was disturbed by McManus, bearing an electrifying message which he had just intercepted.

It was an SOS from the steamer *Jean Jadot,* reporting herself disabled six hundred miles east of Halifax and asking urgently for aid.

"I could have kicked myself good and proper," says Power as he recalls that moment. "There I'd been working for a day and a night to get myself fast to a great, useless lump of iron, and now I was tight to her and couldn't get away. I knew the *Jadot.* She was a sister to the *Emile Francqui,* and about as valuable a merchant ship as you could find on the Atlantic in those years.

"I just had to get shed of the *Longbird* somehow. I almost wished she'd sink. Then I remembered that she still had no radio, and I got a kind of faint idea what to do. I had McManus call direct to her owners in New York. I told them I had their ship in tow for New York at the master's orders, but that with the head-sea and all, it was going to cost them three times as much as to take her into Halifax. I asked them if they concurred in the master's choice of port. Well, sir, they came booming back. 'Take her to Halifax,' they said, 'and be damned to what the master says.' "

Power had not underestimated the economical ways of a ship's owner.

When *Longbird's* captain noticed the sudden change of course he almost went berserk. Blowing his steam whistle and howling through his megaphone, he demanded to know what in the name of all the furies was going on. Power waited for the din to die down, then politely explained that they were proceeding to Halifax on the owners' orders.

And that was that.

With less than a hundred miles to go before he could be rid of *Longbird,* Power dispatched a message to the *Jean Jadot.*

POWERFUL OCEAN TUG FOUNDATION FRANKLIN SAILING TO YOUR ASSISTANCE

It was a little premature, but Power was never a man to let the grass, or the seaweed either, grow underneath his feet.

The *Jean Jadot* had put out from Antwerp on March 16, bound for New York with a cargo of general merchandise valued at a million and a half dollars. Her master, Captain Sadi Gonthier, was expecting a hard passage, for March is always a bad month on the North Atlantic. Accordingly, he had prepared for heavy weather and his vessel was as seaworthy as good seamen could make her. Gonthier was not particularly disturbed when he met head winds and heavy seas almost as soon as Bishop's Rock and Europe lay astern. He had only one worry and that concerned his vessel's rudder, for as *Emile Francqui* had shown a few months earlier and as he had already discovered for himself, the design of the rudder in all five of the sisters was defective. Gonthier took no chances; he ordered relieving tackle rigged to the steering gear on the first day out in order to ease the strain on it.

For the next eight days *Jean Jadot* fought the age-old battle of a merchantman against the sea. The weather was wild throughout that time and the ship labored heavily, on some days making no more than a hundred miles of westing. She met almost incessant head gales and a sea that at times almost stopped her in her tracks. Nevertheless she held doggedly to her course, and in the afternoon of March 25 the skies cleared long enough for Gonthier to get a sight and to confirm his position as forty-three degrees north, fifty-two degrees west—about three hundred miles south-east of Newfoundland. During that afternoon the wind began to abate and the seas dropped a little. *Jadot* worked her speed up to six knots, and her people began to relax from the long tension.

Their relief was premature. By 11 P.M. the sou'west wind had again risen to gale force, and at midnight of March 25 the *Jadot* suddenly refused to answer her helm and began to steam in a great arc to port.

Gonthier guessed what had happened, but all the same the bosun was lowered over the stern on the end of a long ladder. When he climbed up again—half drowned—it was to report that the sole piece appeared to have broken off and that the rudder itself was jammed immovably to port.

So the *Jadot* was crippled even as her sister had been crippled in these same waters in December of the previous year; but this time there was no assistance near at hand. At 4 A.M. on March 26 Gonthier sent off a general SOS.

Two ships replied. One was the *Audania,* a freighter outbound for Southampton and several hundred miles away. The other was the United States Coast Guard cutter *Mendota,* on ice patrol a hundred miles to the northward. *Mendota* radioed:

COMING TO YOUR ASSISTANCE WILL REACH YOUR POSITION LATE THIS AFTERNOON IF NOT HELD UP BY WEATHER

Mendota was as good as her word and at 3 P.M. she came over the horizon and bore down on the crippled freighter. *Mendota's* master was dismayed to see how large the *Jean Jadot* was, for the little Coast Guard ship was not designed for towing. Furthermore, *Mendota* had been on patrol for several days and she had none too much fuel oil left.

Nevertheless she was prepared to do what she could. In order to conserve fuel *Mendota's* master suggested that he put a line on *Jadot's* stern and act as a floating rudder, while *Jadot* used her own engines to drive her towards Halifax, which was the nearest port.

The attempt was made, but it proved futile. The jammed rudder caused the *Jadot* to carry such a heavy port helm that *Mendota* could not hold her on her course. At midnight the attempt was abandoned and *Mendota* cast off, circled *Jadot,* and put a towline on the cripple's bow. Now it became a straight contest of strength, with *Mendota* struggling to pull *Jadot* along the course for Halifax against the resistance of the jammed rudder and against a mounting headwind and a massive head sea.

Power had dispatched his message to the *Jadot* before he knew that *Mendota* was already at the scene. A code message from Featherstone informed him that they had been forestalled, but Featherstone also made it clear that he was not much worried about the eventual results. He did not think *Mendota* could complete the job, and he was ready to confirm Power's offer as soon as something was heard from Gonthier.

However, Gonthier was quite content with his free tow and so he ignored Power's message for a full day, during which time *Franklin* steamed into Halifax, cast off the *Longbird* as if she had been a leper, and hurried back to sea again. She was fifty miles offshore when Gonthier finally radioed:

> AM IN GOOD HANDS SUGGEST YOU MAKE OFFER TO TOW ME FROM HALIFAX TO NEW YORK ON DAILY RATE OF HIRE

If he had thought to discourage Foundation Maritime with this, he was mistaken. Featherstone immediately replied:

> THANK YOU FRANKLIN ALREADY EN ROUTE TO BRING YOU IN WILL ALSO OFFER TOW NEW YORK

To which Gonthier, realizing that he was faced with a tenacious type, responded abruptly:

> I DO NOT ASK YOU TO COME OUT AND I ACCEPT NO OBLIGATION

This merely elicited the suave response:

> WE ALWAYS ENDEAVOR TO ASSIST SHIPPING WILL BE ON HAND TO RENDER ASSISTANCE IF REQUIRED

It is possible that Featherstone's messages were not directed entirely to Gonthier's ears, for he well knew that *Mendota* would also be receiving them. Foundation's salvage master was a man of cunning. He was not at all surprised when, an hour after the dispatch of this final message from Halifax, *Mendota* contacted Gonthier to say:

> MY FUEL SUPPLY TOO LOW TO GET YOU IN STOP MAKE ARRANGE-MENTS FOR TUG TO TAKE YOU IN TOW AS SOON AS POSSIBLE

Now, unlike *Longbird's* master, Gonthier knew how to accept the inevitable. At 1 A.M. on March 28 he radioed *Franklin:*

> NOON GMT 400 MILES FROM HALIFAX STOP MENDOTA FUEL LOW WILL YOU AGREE LLOYDS OPEN FORM TOW US HALIFAX SAFE ANCHOR-AGE

In Halifax Featherstone grinned cheerfully, while aboard *Foundation Franklin* Captain Power ordered the mate to get the towing gear laid out on the after deck.

It was a fine day when *Franklin* came alongside the *Jean Jadot*. The wind was light, the sky was clear, and only the lifting seas reminded men that this was the ocean of great gales.

Power put his little ship in so close alongside the freighter that John Pynn was able to throw a heaving line onto the *Jadot's* forecastle. The line was followed by a bridle composed of two two-inch wires, each a hundred and fifty feet in length, that came together at a shackle which was connected to *Franklin's* towing wire some distance off the *Jadot's* bow. Gonthier and Power, with memories of the *Emile Francqui* incident fresh in both their minds, were anxious that the *Jadot* keep her anchor cables free—in case.

At midnight on March 28, some three hundred and fifty miles east-sou'east of Halifax, the tow began. After saluting the two ships and wishing them good luck, *Mendota* bore off toward that port to fill her empty bunkers.

For the rest of the night things went well. *Franklin* had to strain a little to control *Jadot's* constant tendency to sheer to port; but the weather was moderate and, to Gonthier at least, it looked as if the balance of the trip would be uneventful. Power was not so sanguine. He knew that there is no such thing as uneventful weather off those coasts.

His pessimism was confirmed shortly before noon on March 29 when the wind began to make up out of the sou'east—and make up fast and hard. By 1 P.M. it was gusting sixty miles an hour. The skies grew black and the seas, which had never relapsed into quiescence, were rising with new vigor. Snow flurries drove out of the low scudding clouds and *Franklin* settled her stern a little deeper, as if preparing herself for the struggle which she knew must come.

Gonthier's optimism had meanwhile turned to mounting apprehension. A glance at his chart showed him that Sable Island, that place of death for ships and men, lay only thirty miles to the nor'west, and a glance out at the driven smoke from his funnel showed him that the wind was slowly but steadily backing into the east—direct for Sable's sands. He knew that thirty miles of sea room—or twenty to the shoals which are as deadly as the isle itself—is no more than four or five hours' drift for a disabled vessel in a gale of wind.

Gonthier did not need a reminder from Power asking him to "watch the wire where it passes through your chocks." He was a good seaman, and he knew that the life of his ship depended on the slender wire stretching over his bows. Despite the mounting gale, and seas which were already breaking over *Jadot's* forecastle, two men went forward every half-hour to grease the towline and to see that it was sound.

Meanwhile *Franklin* had all but disappeared from Gonthier's view. Only occasionally, when she mounted to a crest and hung poised for an instant before plunging to the trough below, could he catch a glimpse of her. As the gale raged on, *Franklin* finally became invisible. Gonthier knew that she was there, half a mile ahead of him, only because the towing wire still had a strain upon it.

Franklin's people appreciated the danger of Sable even better than did Gonthier. Despite the fact that *Franklin's* stern, dragged down by the great strain upon the cable, was often completely submerged, men still went aft every few minutes to check the bulldog grips and to spread grease on the taffrail. For the rest, *Franklin's* crew clung to anything that would support them and hung on. She rolled until at times it seemed as if she would never come up again. Taking the gale full on her port beam she staggered under the impact of the seas until her decks ran white and the whole vessel looked like a half-awash reef.

Those were forty-eight desperate hours from midnight on the twenty-ninth until midnight on the thirty-first. As *Franklin* struggled to drag the *Jean Jadot* past waiting Sable, the wind kept shifting as if in league with the Graveyard sands, so that it always blew toward them. At dawn on March 31 Sable lay only sixteen miles to the nor'west and the offshore banks were not ten miles away.

At this crucial moment Gonthier discovered that the port leg of the towing bridle, which was receiving the lion's share of the strain due to *Jadot's* wild sheering to port, had chafed and was starting to strand. He radioed *Franklin*. Power immediately stopped his engines and let *Franklin* swing inert into the troughs so that the strain would come off the wire and give Gonthier's men a chance to haul the bridle in a little. It was a dangerous maneuver, but less dangerous than to risk losing the link between the two embattled ships, which, once lost, could hardly have been renewed in time to cheat the sands.

Jadot's crew worked against time to haul the bridle in so that a new section would bear on the chocks; but the big freighter was blowing fast to starboard and inexorably she began to drag the bight of the cable under *Franklin's* stern. There was nothing Power could do about it. If he started his engines in order to escape the trap, he knew he would part the stranded wire at *Jadot's* bow. If he remained stopped, there was every likelihood that the bight would sweep under his counter and foul his propeller blades. He kept the engines stopped. The wire came under, and they could hear it all through the little vessel as it rasped against the blades.

The moment the work aboard the *Jadot* was completed Power called Gonthier and asked him to start his vessel's engines and ease her forward in order to allow the bight to sink deep below *Franklin's* stern. It was uncertain how *Jadot* would react as she gained headway but, considering her jammed rudder, there was a possibility that she would come far enough up to port to let the cable sag. While both crews watched intently the possibility became a reality, and an hour after she had stopped her engines, *Franklin* again got under weigh. It was none too soon. Their drift had carried the two vessels three miles closer to the Sable shoals.

Franklin again took up her tow at full power and by 2 P.M. on the thirty-first she and her charge were in the clear. Then it was as if the sea gave up its efforts to take the *Jean Jadot*. The wind, which had swelled to a full northerly gale, began to fall light. *Jadot's* jammed rudder broke loose and sank, so that the ship was no longer being forced out almost abeam of the tug. Now she fell meekly in astern of *Franklin,* and through a moderating sea, came in toward the land. On the evening of April 1 the second of the two sisters entered Halifax harbor—her ordeal done.

The *Jean Jadot* and the *Emile Francqui* owed their lives to *Foundation Franklin*. Their owners, Cie Maritime Belge, were not hesitant in acknowledging the debt; but at the same time Foundation Maritime owed much to the two Belgian sisters.

The salvage awards on the two vessels were huge by comparison with most of those the company had received from earlier jobs. The account books showed such a well-blown credit balance that even the sceptics in the Montreal headquarters who had long whispered of Chadwick's folly were impressed.

Of even greater importance was the fact that these two remarkable exploits firmly established the company's reputation for offshore rescue work. By the late spring of 1935 a phrase had been born which was to recur time and time again in newspapers across Canada through the next decade.

Canadian Press. Halifax. Tonight the powerful tug Foundation Franklin steamed out of this port under forced draft on another rescue mission into the North Atlantic. . . .

Franklin had found her way, and she had also found the men whom she could trust: Irwin Power on her bridge; John Pynn as chief officer; tough little John Sommers, chief in the engine room; Reginald Poirier as second engineer; Lindsay McManus in the radio shack; and Tom Nolan wherever he was needed. They and the deck-hands and the black gang were men to gladden the heart of a Frobisher or a Drake. They and their vessel were as one—indomitable and able spirits all.

Dead Man's Rock

ALTHOUGH THE DEPRESSION was still being keenly felt in Canada's Maritime Provinces in 1935, at least one major company was still doing a good business. This was Dominion Steel and Coal Company—the colossus which overstrode much of Nova Scotia and which, to all intents and purposes, was the financial master of Cape Breton Island.

Dosco owned or controlled most of the coal mines in the province, and to get its coal to the buyers it was Dosco's policy to charter a fleet of ships each spring. Most of these vessels were from England, where there were far more bottoms than there was cargo to be carried in them and where vessels could consequently be chartered for a pittance.

One of these hard-driven ships was the *Berwindlea,* fifty-two hundred tons, out of Aberdeen. *Berwindlea* had crossed the Atlantic in the early spring of 1935, and through the summer and autumn she had been almost constantly at work hauling slack coal through the Gulf and up the St. Lawrence River. In mid-October she was free at last, for her charter had expired. She and her weary crew were ready to sail for home; but first she had a cargo of pulp to load at Dalhousie for delivery in England.

It was a clean cargo, and *Berwindlea's* people were in a good mood as she put out from Dalhousie on October 22. The lateness of the season and the prevalence of autumnal gales and heavy fog did not dismay them. They were homeward bound.

Berwindlea's master was in a hurry. His ship would only log seven or eight knots, and Aberdeen was a long way off. He wished to make the best time possible while he remained in the relatively sheltered waters of the Gulf, for he knew that the winter storms on the open sea would strive against his vessel for every mile she made.

As darkness fell on October 22 it brought with it a black, impenetrable pall of fog. *Berwindlea* drove into it and disappeared. Her navigation lights glowed feebly, each contained in a hemisphere of fog not ten feet in diameter. The mate upon the bridge could not see the foredeck of the ship, and members of the crew vanished from each other's ken before five paces intervened between them.

The night was calm, but cold. There was no sound except the rusty *blat* of *Berwindlea's* whistle as it tried to pierce the fog, but which was blanketed and absorbed almost as it left the whistle's throat.

The course line laid out on the chart in the wheelhouse began to waver. The little penciled crosses which represented *Berwindlea's* position became fewer and less firmly placed. Dead reckoning alone was an uncertain pilot on such a night.

At 3:50 A.M. the master, Captain Williams, stood at the chart table with the officer of the watch beside him. They stared intently at the last dead-reckoning position. It showed *Berwindlea* on course and ten miles south of the dangerous nest of islands called the Magdalens. Williams was uneasy. It was not much of an offing on such a night, and he was contemplating ordering the vessel's head to be brought a little more toward the south when, without any warning, *Berwindlea* went on.

Men who have spent their lives sailing the Gulf make no pretense of familiarity with the strange currents which flow through it. *Berwindlea's* people—strangers all—had no way of knowing in advance what the current had been doing to their ship that night. But now they knew what it had done.

Berwindlea took the ground with a great shudder and the sound of crumpling steel.

In the engine room the chief was already starting up the bilge pumps even before the frightful shuddering of the initial shock was over. The bosun, thrown to the deck by the impact, had already regained his feet and had begun to turn forward to sound the wells, even before the order to do so reached him from the bridge. The moment of confusion which is close to panic and which always seizes on a ship at such a time was short-lived. It was succeeded by a questioning silence broken only by occasional hails from the officers to the men who had gone forward. It was a period of fantastic tension, of hope struggling with the fear of what must soon be known.

The destruction of the ship began within ten minutes of the time she struck. The bosun's measurements showed water rising fast in number one and number two holds, and when the pumps not only failed to reduce the flooding but were powerless even to slow its rapid rise, it was obvious that not only the vessel's bottom, but her inner bottom too was ruptured.

Captain Williams listened grimly to the reports of his officers, then, at 4:15 A.M., he ordered Sparks to make his call. At 4:20 the international distress frequency woke to life.

At 9 A.M. Featherstone in Halifax received a telegram from one of his "intelligence sources":

SS BERWINDLEA REPORTED ASHORE DEAD MANS ROCK MAGDALEN
ISLANDS STOP BELIEVED FLOODED FORWARD BUT NO IMMEDIATE
DANGER PRESENT WEATHER STOP FULLY LADEN PULP

Featherstone considered the information for fifteen minutes. He knew
that this late in the season good weather in the Gulf could not be expected
to last for more than two or three days. He was familiar with Dead Man's
Rock and he knew that a ship on that exposed pinnacle would be
doomed by any gale which blew. There was no time for him to try to
make arrangements with the ship's agents. There was, perhaps, just
enough time to save the ship if *Franklin* sailed at once.

So *Franklin* sailed "under forced draft," as the papers would have it.
Once more Power was on her bridge; but Featherstone intended to proceed by train to Canso Gut and meet the *Franklin* there, for he wanted
to collect Drake, the local Salvage Association man, en route.

Franklin had thick fog and heavy weather all the way north, but she
picked up Featherstone and Drake at Mulgrave at 3 A.M. on October 24
and by 4 P.M. of that day she had reached Dead Man's Rock.

The islet is a forbidding sight at the best of times. The craggy peak of
a submerged mountain rising abruptly out of the waters, its area is only
a few acres. Its shores are so precipitous that there is only one spot where
boats may safely land; and this lies on the opposite side to the cliff where
Berwindlea had driven ashore. Men seldom visit Dead Man's Rock, but
on the north shore there is a tiny turf and stone shack where fishermen,
or shipwrecked sailors, may find some meager shelter.

The place has a hard reputation—as hard as its name; but neither its
reputation nor its name meant much to Featherstone. What counted in
his mind was the terribly hazardous position of any vessel ashore upon
it.

As *Franklin* came in Featherstone saw that the light north wind which
had been blowing all that morning had kicked up such a sea that, even
on the lee side of the rock where *Berwindlea* lay, a boat could not safely
be launched. What must inevitably happen in the event of a real gale
rising from the south, the east or west was brutally apparent.

As things stood Featherstone considered it too dangerous to attempt
a landing, so *Franklin* withdrew into the lee of Amherst Island for the
night. During those hours Featherstone was in radio contact with Williams, and he learned some of the details of the problem which he faced.

Berwindlea was flooded and tidal in number one and number two
tanks (open to the sea in these), while her forepeak tanks and most of

the remaining double bottom tanks were also flooded. Mercifully the engine room was still dry, but there was every prospect that it too would flood unless the weather moderated soon. On this score Featherstone and Power were not immediately worried. Knowing the signs by instinct they expected the northerly to fall light with darkness, and they hoped they would then have a period of a day, or perhaps two, before the wind came round through east to south and began to blow.

Featherstone and Power made their plan. Williams was ordered to flood his deep tanks in order to hold *Berwindlea* firmly on the rocks and prevent her from working. At dawn *Franklin* would come in, lay two sets of ground tackle off *Berwindlea's* stern, land an air compressor on her and, after blowing the forward tanks and pumping the after ones, would try to take her off with her own winches.

Impelled by the knowledge that time was against them, the salvors went to work at dawn with demoniac energy. Within five hours both sets of ground tackle had been laid out. Featherstone, Tom Nolan and Drake went aboard *Berwindlea* and supervised the reeving and setting-up of the purchases. Nolan's helper, Alan Macdonald, brought *Franklin's* little motorboat in through the surf with a two-ton air compressor balanced across the gunwales and safely delivered it aboard the wreck. Nolan went over the side to make an underwater examination and to begin patching, if this proved feasible. Having fully assessed the situation, Featherstone radioed an urgent request to Sydney for a small coastal vessel which could bring out stevedores and coal, and which could take off bulk pulp if jettisoning proved necessary. The coal was particularly needed since *Berwindlea's* bunkers were low—her master having intended to bunker at Sydney before setting out across the North Atlantic.

Everything was in readiness for the first attempt to refloat the big ship at evening high tide, when Featherstone made a shocking discovery.

During her summer season *Berwindlea* had been unloaded, not with her own deck gear, but with shore equipment. Consequently her engineers had removed certain vital valves from the deck winches in order to prevent corrosion—and these valves had never been replaced. No one had thought about the matter until late afternoon on October 25, when Featherstone called for steam on the winches in order to take the preliminary strain on the ground tackle.

When the discovery was made that the winches were useless, it was too late to search out the missing valves and install them in time to make use of that evening's tide. Nothing more could be done until the following day.

Meanwhile Power, aboard *Franklin* lying at anchor half a mile off-shore, had heard some disquieting news on the standard broadcast radio. A violent hurricane had cut a swath of destruction across Haiti on October 23, killing more than two thousand people. The track the hurricane was following had not yet been plotted with any certainty, but Power knew that it might well run north-east over the Maritimes—as Caribbean hurricanes so often do.

With this possibility in mind, Power watched with increasing apprehension as the afternoon waned and as the wind came out of the east, then switched freakishly to the south-west and began to rise. Power kept his fears to himself until 4:45 P.M., when he radioed Featherstone:

WIND AND SEA RISING FAST SUSPECT HURRICANE TRACK WILL COME THIS WAY SUGGEST YOU ABANDON BERWINDLEA AT ONCE

Featherstone was not infallible. He could make mistakes; and when he did they were monumental. He made one now.

Irritated by the affair of the winches and by the fact that he had been robbed of a quick success by such a trivial matter, he made up his mind to stay aboard *Berwindlea* and have another try at dawn. He did not think much of the hurricane scare. In his experience a south-west gale was not likely to last more than a few hours.

Whether or not they were influenced by Featherstone's example, the officers and crew of *Berwindlea* also elected to remain aboard their ship. Drake too decided to stay, while Nolan had no thought of leaving if Featherstone remained.

At 5:30 P.M. Alan Macdonald was told to return to *Franklin* with the motorboat. It was none too soon. While rounding *Berwindlea's* stern Macdonald was caught in the surf and his boat was nearly swamped. Damaged and leaking badly it barely managed to get him back to *Foundation Franklin's* side.

Contrary to Featherstone's expectations the gale did not slack off. Instead it mounted with a ferocity that was terrifying. At 9 P.M. *Franklin* began dragging both her anchors and was forced to heave them in and stand offshore into the teeth of a force 8 gale and a wild and savage sea. She rose to most of the big ones, but she took it green across her decks many times that night.

Clamped in the vise of the rocks, *Berwindlea* could do nothing but accept her punishment. By midnight she was being swept from end to end and spray was breaking high above her mastheads against the glistening rocks of the cliff face.

Berwindlea had her crew accommodations aft, while her bridge and officers' quarters were well forward of amidships. Her boats were aft as well and the only communication between the poop and the bridge was over the open decks.

By midnight this route had been closed. Black water was falling on the decks to a depth of six feet. The stanchions of her rails were smashed, and the rails themselves carried away. Her starboard boat was shattered in its chocks. Her hatches began to break under the ponderous impact of the seas and she began to flood in number three and number four holds.

Her crew were now besieged in their quarters aft and dared not open a door or port. Forward, in the bridge structure, the officers with Featherstone, Nolan and Drake were marooned in a more ugly position—close to the destroying rocks.

By midnight the ship had begun to work so much that the sound of her plates grinding and gnashing on the rocks rose clearly above the high-pitched scream of wind and the sonorous thunder of the breaking seas.

Franklin was now hove-to some miles offshore and barely able to hold her own. Emergency weather reports were coming in steadily from the government stations, and these were increasingly ominous. The hurricane had indeed tracked up the American seaboard, and the center of that whirlpool of tortured air was rapidly approaching the Maritimes. Already the distress frequency was crackling with calls and McManus was logging them between his attempts to keep in touch with *Berwindlea's* young operator.

At 3:30 A.M. on October 26 there was no answer to McManus's signals. He fought his way to the bridge to tell Power, and found the skipper peering shoreward through the driving murk with his night glasses. There was no need for Sparks's message. Power had seen the dim glow of *Berwindlea's* lights suddenly go out.

Aboard *Berwindlea* both the ground-tackle wires had parted under the strain imposed by that irresistible sea, and the ship had swung broadside, tearing her belly out as she was flung across the reefs. She heeled over and the seas flooded into her engine room; the lights flickered once and then went out. Within half an hour she was flooded in every compartment and her doom was sealed.

That she did not break up immediately was tribute to her Scottish builders. Any lesser ship must have quickly gone to pieces under the merciless assault of the mounting seas; yet *Berwindlea* hung on, a shell of a thing, her bottom gone and her side plates buckling until her deck was hogged like a boar's back. She was dead, but not yet destroyed.

The storm-wracked daylight hours of October 26 were an ordeal that drove one officer mad, and that led the crew to the panic act of attempting to launch the remaining boat. It was swept from them like a chip and only a miracle spared the men who launched it. They crawled back into their prison and hung on.

At dawn the radio operator managed to get his emergency power working, and communications with *Franklin* were restored. It was a desperately anxious Power who talked to Featherstone, but though he was immeasurably relieved to hear that the men aboard the wreck were still alive, Power was driven half-distracted by the fact that he could do nothing for them. Until the hurricane had passed it was all that he could do to keep *Franklin* afloat; any attempt to venture close to Dead Man's Rock would have been suicidal. Standing three miles offshore he could not see *Berwindlea* at all. He could only see a succession of gargantuan columns of white spray such as might mark the seas which break across a submerged reef in a great gale.

The news upon the distress frequency was as chilling as the spectacle before Power's eyes. The steamer *Vardulia,* the same ship which had rescued the crew of the *Aggersund* off Newfoundland in that memorable spring of 1932, had called for help from several hundred miles east of Halifax, and then had not been heard again. She had gone down and taken her crew of thirty-seven with her. Nor was she alone. The Nova Scotian three-masted schooner *Esthonia,* from Barbados to Shelburne, also died that day, although her crew of ten were saved.

As the number of distress calls mounted, Power's frustration increased. Several times he sailed *Franklin* dangerously close to the foam-sheathed rock, but each time he was forced away before he had come close enough even to see *Berwindlea* through the driven spume.

Aboard the doomed vessel there were two kinds of men. There were those who saw death at arm's length, and who were afraid of him. And there were those who could not see him, either because they lacked understanding of their plight, or because they were too preoccupied to notice. Featherstone and Nolan belonged to this latter group. With a cigar thrusting aggressively out of his heavy jaw, Featherstone still would not admit defeat. Plan after plan to save not just the men but the ship as well went through his mind, and the notes in his little pocket notebook grew numerous as plan after plan had to be abandoned.

Not until noon of October 26 would he accept the fact of *Berwindlea's* loss; and then he concentrated his efforts on how to save her people. He knew that no boat could live in the hell's brew about *Berwindlea,* and that it would be death to try to leave her until there was a lull. He made plans for the moment when she would go under. He began a long and reasoned discussion with the ship's officers as to the relative merits of rafts and boats versus ladders, as life-saving gear; and he was irritated when the distracted officers refused to listen with the proper degree of attention to the niceties of his arguments. Somewhat grumpily he left them to their fears and turned to the phlegmatic Nolan.

"Best way in the world to leave a wreck on a lee shore—a ladder. Hold you up fine as you go through the surf, then with any kind of luck you can use it to bridge the breakers so you don't get bashed to bits. After that you can use it to climb up the cliffs. You get a ladder ready, Tom."

Tom routed out a ladder, but not because he thought it would be needed. He was not much worried by their plight, for as a Newfoundlander born and bred he had long since learned never to worry in advance about what the sea might do to him. What bothered him at the moment was the problem of finding grub; and he was considerably disgruntled by the steward's failure to provide an adequate grub locker in the officers' saloon.

The day passed in different ways for different men. Some were silent and withdrawn as soldiers are before the battle which they suspect will be their last. Some were violent in their futile rage. Some concentrated all their effort in the attempt to achieve sufficient self-control to fool their fellows. The madman screamed insensate things at sea and wind.

The hurricane continued unabated all that day and into the next night. At 1:30 A.M. on October 27 *Berwindlea* began to go. She split amidships, separating the two little groups of men one from the other, and the bow section began to settle steadily as she broke up below the waterline.

The salvage men and the ship's officers were soon driven out of the saloon by the invading waters. They made their way to the bridge—and the waters followed until they were knee deep. For a time the thundering breakers drove over the bridge structure as if it were no more than a piece of flotsam, and then, temporarily content with the destruction they had wrought, they slowly began to lose their fury. At long last the gale began to ease.

It was now or never for the men aboard the wreck and at 2 A.M. *Franklin* radioed a general SOS on their behalf, which was picked up and immediately rebroadcast by the powerful government station on nearby Grindstone Island.

SS BERWINDLEA ASHORE DEAD MANS ISLAND URGENTLY NEEDS AS-
SISTANCE SHIP WITH LARGE LIFEBOATS

There was no immediate reply, for there were few ships left at sea that night. A few minutes after sending the SOS Featherstone, his mind as agile as ever, radioed Power with a suggestion of his own.

DO YOU THINK YOU COULD LAND SOME MEN AT THAT SHACK ON THE
LEE SIDE OF THE ISLAND AND CROSS THIS SIDE AND RIG LINES FOR A
BREECHES BUOY FROM THE CLIFF

To which Power replied:

DONT THINK POSSIBLE LAND BOAT NOW BUT WILL DO SO AT DAY-
LIGHT IF HUMANLY POSSIBLE

This message was interrupted by a call from a strange voice. It belonged to a rare bird, the Japanese freighter *England Maru,* who reported herself as being abreast of East Point, Prince Edward Island, and able and willing to come to *Berwindlea's* assistance.

Her message brought a surge of hope, for it was a voice from a world that the survivors on the wreck had all but despaired of knowing once again. With the Gulf swept almost clear of shipping by the hurricane they had come to think of themselves as utterly abandoned. So *England Maru's* message brought hope, though of a tenuous kind, for they knew she could not reach them until late the following morning—and there was every likelihood that *Berwindlea* would have vanished before then.

Featherstone put the feelings of all of them into this brief message to Power:

THANK JAP BUT WE ARE RELYING ON WHAT YOU CAN DO WITH
SHORE PARTY

Nothing can better tell the story of the next few hours than the radio log kept by McManus. It is vivid, for it is truth.

England Maru to *Berwindlea:* WE ARE PROCEEDING YOU FULL
SPEED BUT ONLY MAKE SIX KNOTS IN HEAVY SEA GOOD WISHES

Franklin to Grindstone Radio: DO YOU KNOW OR CAN YOU FIND
OUT FROM FISHERMEN IF MEN CAN WALK AROUND BEACH OF DEAD
MANS OR MUST THEY GO OVER TOP TO CROSS

Grindstone to *Franklin:* SORRY DONT KNOW AND CANT GET INFOR-
MATION ALL PHONES DOWN

Berwindlea to *Franklin:* WHERE ARE YOU MAKE ALL POSSIBLE SPEED

Franklin to *Berwindlea:* AM NOW ABEAM ISLAND COMING AROUND AND UP LEE SIDE

Franklin to *Berwindlea:* GETTING BOAT READY UNDER COMMAND DOBSON WHO WILL HAVE SIGNAL FLAGS TO TALK FROM BEACH HOW ARE YOU AND HOW IS SHIP IS SHE BREAKING UP FAST

Berwindlea to *Franklin:* GLAD NEWS FROM YOU WE ARE WELL ALL HOPE IS IN YOUR EFFORTS THIS SHIP IN BAD WAY BREAKING BACK BUCKLING AND BATHED IN GREAT SEAS EVERY FEW MOMENTS

England Maru to *Berwindlea* via Grindstone: 28 MILES FROM YOU PROCEEDING BEST

Franklin to *Berwindlea:* BOAT OVER WITH MEN MAKING FOR ISLAND

Berwindlea to *Franklin:* ARE THEY MAKING GOOD PROGRESS

Franklin to *Berwindlea:* BOAT BEING SWEPT INTO BREAKERS THEY ARE ON EDGE OF BREAKERS WILL BE SWAMPED THEY ARE MAKING BIG EFFORT TO PULL CLEAR [And five minutes later] BOAT ESCAPED BREAKERS IMPOSSIBLE FOR THEM TO LAND AND LIVE SEAS SWEEPING BROADSIDE ON BEACH

Berwindlea to *Franklin:* FEATHERSTONE SAYS COME BACK STAND BY TO WINDWARD OF US AND COOPERATE WITH JAP STEAMER THERE MAY BE SLIM CHANCE FOR BOAT TO ROUND OUR STERN AND LEE SIDE STOP THERE IS A ROCK ON SHIPS PORT SIDE AMIDSHIPS RIGHT AGAINST HER

Franklin to *Berwindlea:* HAVE YOU ANY BOATS LEFT AND CAN YOU LAUNCH THEM AND COME OUT

Berwindlea to *Franklin:* BOAT SMASHED BUT WILL TRY IT IF ALL ELSE FAILS

These messages cover only three hours in time; but that was a decade in the lives of those concerned.

Power's attempt to land a boat upon the north side of the island had been nobly prosecuted. Second Officer Dobson (who was to die a few years later as a destroyer commander in the war), with three deck-hands and two firemen—all volunteers—had put off from *Franklin* in a twelve-foot boat. During the launching a sea had swept the little craft so hard against *Franklin's* bulwarks that it was half stove-in before it took the water. Once afloat it was at the mercy of the great seas, for the hope that Dead Man's Rock could provide a lee in the face of the hurricane was a delusion. There were three miles to pull in order to reach the roaring shingle beach. Dobson and his men were exhausted before they reached the line of surf. Dobson himself knew that there was little possibility of his crew's surviving an attempt to enter the surf, yet he decided they should try. The lifeboat was immediately caught, spun end-for-end and almost swamped. Half-full and leaking badly, it was still two hundred yards from land. There remained only the hope that the boat's crew could save themselves. With the strength of desperation they pulled clear of the surf and then dropped over their oars in a state of near collapse as the wind carried their boat clear of the islet and out into the Gulf. *Franklin* bore down upon them, and was able to retrieve them by a near-miracle of seamanship on Power's part. The broken boat was left to drift away.

All this took place between dawn and 6 A.M. *Franklin* then fought her way back around the islet and stood by the *Berwindlea;* but she was now completely helpless to assist the shipwrecked men, for she had only the motorboat left and, apart from the hull damage it had sustained earlier, its engine would no longer run.

It was at this juncture that the distant smoke of the *England Maru* came into sight. Power and the Japanese master were in radio communication and by 9 A.M., when the freighter was close upon the scene, they had devised a plan. It was an incredibly risky one that could only succeed if *England Maru's* big boat could be so packed with oarsmen that they could defy the wind and surf.

With a quality of seamanship that could hardly be believed, the Japanese skipper, Captain Honja, maneuvered his big vessel (she was light and therefore doubly hard to handle) broadside to the islet and less than half a mile from *Berwindlea.*

Honja then launched his biggest boat, a thirty-footer, and manned it with twenty oarsmen. Despite the bitter cold of that October morning the Japanese sailors were naked to the waist. They took up the stroke and made for the waiting *Franklin,* who was hove-to in *England Maru's* lee, halfway between her and the wreck.

Chanting in unison and rowing like superhuman beings, the Japanese crew slipped under the shelter of *Franklin's* lee, while Power eased his tug inshore.

Two hundred yards off *Berwindlea, Franklin* stopped. Not even Power dared to take her farther in. Now the lifeboat was on its own. It did not hesitate but plunged straight into the breaking seas that rose as high as *Berwindlea's* foretop.

The boat shot under the wreck's stern, seeking her lee side, but found instead a pinnacle of rock thrust into *Berwindlea's* belly that made a cul-de-sac from which there could be no escape. Second Officer Anto cried one shrill order, and in the last instant the men reversed their stroke and the boat came out alive.

Anto now took the only alternative. He brought his fragile craft in against *Berwindlea's weather* side. Bosun Okabe leaped to the boat's gunwale to prevent her being crushed against the wreck and with his own body took the shock of impact. It smashed seven of his ribs and nearly killed him—but he saved the boat.

The people on *Berwindlea's* after-part swarmed over the rails as one man. They had not far to drop, for already the after deck of the dying ship was awash. The lifeboat leaped away on a receding sea and pulled for safety.

Leaving her cargo of half-frozen survivors on *Franklin's* deck, the Japanese boat went back again—this time right into the surf in an attempt to reach the little group marooned on *Berwindlea's* bridge. She reached them too, but just how she did it no man can tell. Featherstone, his cigar still in his mouth, was amongst the last to leave and he recalls that moment in strange fashion.

"It wasn't the sea and the gale that bothered me just then. It was the seals. There must have been a thousand of them hanging about the wreck, just waiting to see us drown. They kept popping their silly heads up and staring, as if we were some kind of circus for their special benefit."

He was most indignant about those seals.

He was indignant too about the loss of *Berwindlea,* but philosophical as well. The loss of the ship pointed his favorite moral.

"Salvage on these coasts is always a knife-edge proposition. One little thing goes wrong, and you've lost out. There are no second chances. The wind and water see to that."

The wind and water saw to *Berwindlea.* Within three days nothing remained of her except a frieze of flotsam on the beach of Dead Man's Rock.

EXTREME LICENSE

A Complete Novel

EXTREME
LICENSE

by Jerome Barry

EDITOR'S NOTE

Chester Baggott, wealthy New York car dealer and devoted husband, was something quite different on his own time. Behind the facade of respectability was a scheming backslapper, who cheated on his wife and twisted the law to suit his needs.

Getting a driver's license for his seventeen-year-old helper Joey Tripp was part of Baggott's latest plan—a plan that included murder.

But Chester Baggott had underestimated Joey—the car-crazy kid from Brooklyn, who had learned a lot about survival of the fittest.

Here, in its entirety, is an unusual new crime novel in which excessive worship of materialistic values rides on a fast thruway to multiple tragedy.

I Baggott

ONE

TO JOEY TRIPP, the garage of Baggott Service on West Fifty-sixth Street had always been a palace. Baggott owned two places—the other was the big, flashy salesroom over on Broadway near Columbus Circle—but the one that gave Joey a terrific charge was the service garage.

The main floor, where the customers drove their sleek new jobs in to be tuned up, looked as big as Radio City Music Hall. Colored placards and streamers listed the special combination offers—motor check, exhaust system, wheel alignment. Electric signals winked above the ranks of cars, racks of equipment, and counters where clerks talked into intercoms. Pervading everything was exciting noise, made up of engine roar and men's shouts, and the warning blasts of horns at the intersections of ramps.

Joey liked it especially in the evenings, when he walked up the ramps to one of the work floors—the third or fourth—and Tim Meagher or Pete Krawcik of the night crew would let him put on an old coverall and help by handing tools or holding the extension light.

"Ye've got softenin' o' the brain, lad," Tim would say, "workin' like a grease monkey for free. Ye've got hot-rod fever."

But Joey wasn't a hot rodder. He didn't love cars for themselves. He didn't want to strip down an old model and soup it up and go drag racing with other jaloppies full of kids. Young Tony Marchand, who lived with a brigade of other Marchands in a row of brick flats on Fifty-fourth Street, owned a jazzed-up Chevvy; his brother Phil was a motorcycle en-thusiast. Sometimes Joey went with them in the Chevvy in the evening, along with a few giggling girls. When Tony and Phil wanted to horse around with the girls, they'd let Joey drive, somewhere out on Long Island on lonely roads where no inquisitive cop would be likely to stop them and ask to look at the driving license Joey didn't have.

While Joey enjoyed the driving and the feel of quick young reflexes exercising perfect control over an obedient mechanism, none of Tony's affection for the old Chevvy reached into him. Only a new car—any new and expensive car—moved him to a hidden and almost painful ecstasy. Sometimes he walked past the other place, the display room near the

Circle, Baggott Motor Sales. There on the broad floor the demonstration cars stood about for passers-by to stare at from the sidewalk. But they were like gems in a jeweler's window, remote and untouchable. Joey preferred to be at Baggott Service, where any night among the noise and gas smells he could put his hand on the long, sweet smoothness of a fender, a lover palming a beloved breast.

It was not the car itself that he loved, but what it stood for. That was the Dream. He wanted to own one, and if not to own it, then to drive it, handle it, master it, solely because he wanted to be one of those who did such things—the men who had money, know-how, power, men who drove these jobs in and turned them over to the mechanics, with a careless authority that came from the ability to pay Baggott Service. Joey included among such men Mr. Baggott himself, who showed up here occasionally, even at night, and had the staff on their toes just at the sight of him.

On the night that Joey was to remember so well, he was helping Tim Meagher. It was close to nine o'clock when Mr. Baggott walked through, smoking a slender tan cigar as usual, wearing a light-gray suit that was spotless among the grease and oil. The quick, dark eyes in the square, handsome face touched Joey lightly in passing, as if they'd hardly seen him, and Joey kept very still, not wanting to be spotted as an intruder and ordered to get out and stay out. He breathed more easily when Mr. Baggott went down the ramp to Pete Krawcik's floor.

A little later Tim said, "Run along, lad. Ye're in me way, and annyhow ye need yer forty winks so's ye can hold down yer own job tomorra."

"Oh, that!" Joey said. The thought of the supermarket made him feel listless.

He shed the borrowed coveralls, stowed them in Tim's locker, and tramped moodily down the ramps and out upon Fifty-sixth Street. He turned down Ninth Avenue and walked a block and a half south. A long car passed him slowly, pulled in to the curb and stopped. He noted idly that it was a 1959 job, a green two-tone sedan with dealer's plates. He was almost past it when the door opened and a crisp, deep voice ordered, "Hop in, son."

Joey had learned not to obey a command like that without studying the situation. He had a country boy's quiet caution, overlaid with the sharp alertness that came of intervening years of street-gamin decisions whether to fight some gang of unfamiliar characters or do a smart job of running. He wasn't getting into a strange car unless it was with someone he knew or until he could figure what the angle was. Then he recognized the cigar. He said, "Yes, sir, Mr. Baggott," and scrambled in.

The big car eased silently away from the curb and made a right turn at the corner, heading west toward the river. Mr. Baggott said, "I've been watching you, Tripp."

Joey gulped. "I—I didn't mean to do anything wrong. I just wanted to——"

"You're big. Good shoulders. You look about twenty years. You strong?"

"Pretty strong."

Mr. Baggott chuckled. "Developed those shoulders lugging crates of groceries around to the customers. Like that sort of work?"

"Not much."

"Well. Maybe a likely young fellow like you can do better than being a flunky in a market. How much education have you got?"

"High school."

"What are you thinking of doing with yourself?"

"My grandmother wants me to take a civil service examination and work for the city as a clerk. She says it's steady."

Mr. Baggott flicked cigar ashes out the window and spat after them. "What do you think of that yourself?"

"It's a job where I'd work all my life for peanuts. I want to get somewhere."

"How?"

Joey remained silent. You couldn't start talking about the Dream just like that, whenever someone asked you a question. It was too big, too mixed up, inside, with a lot of important things.

"Go ahead," Mr. Baggott said. "How does a young fellow in your spot figure to get somewhere?"

"Well," Joey said cautiously, "there's two ways. First, you can be very bright and win scholarships and get training for a profession or something like that."

"That's what you figure on?"

"No, sir. I had pretty good marks, but nothing special."

"What's your other way of getting ahead, Tripp?"

"Well, I figure this is a country where you never know what can happen if you only keep the avenues open—sort of—I mean, if you don't settle down in a rut but kind of go where the opportunities are—or maybe look around for a break——"

There it was. Before he realized it he was wriggling around on the seat and letting everything come out about the Dream. Because it really had happened to other people. They'd been poor one minute, and then they'd discovered a new little kind of business or made an invention or struck oil or this new uranium thing. You could read about it in the magazines and newspapers all the time.

"How you take me back, Tripp," Mr. Baggott said. "I'm forty-one years old, but it seems only a few years ago that I was a young hand on my father's tomato farm in Maryland, trying to read the future just as you're doing now. We weren't poor trash, you understand. My dad operated a small cannery as well as the farm. But we weren't wealthy, and I worked at canner's wages in the summers to pay my way through college." He chuckled at the memory. "God, how I hated it! Even before Pearl Harbor I'd got me a job peddling automobiles. In the Army, I used to figure ways of building up to an agency of my own. A pipe dream. But I knew what I wanted, and it came true. Baggott Sales and Service. I've done all right."

Joey made a little murmur of assent.

"There's still another way to get ahead," Mr. Baggott went on, "but I hope you haven't even considered it. I used to see these smooth operators in the Army—black market and all that. It never paid in the long run. There are kids in your spot who think right away about the rackets. How's it with you? Are you going to be a sucker for that kind of short cut, or are you willing to make yours the honest way?"

Joey didn't have to stop to think about that one. The answer came up out of a deep, comforting conviction that he was on the right side and would always stay there. Oh, there were little things like driving Tony's car without a driver's license, but that was the sort of temporary dodging around annoying regulations that a good many kids took. In the big things, he knew there'd never be any doubt in his mind.

"The honest way," he said.

"Good. You won't be sorry. The smart operators were strictly second-grade stuff. Not even high-class non-com caliber. I watched some officers get mixed up in it—I was a captain myself—and I knew they were typing themselves as small-time chiselers; when the war was over, they'd find their level in civilian life as two-bit hustlers. You want to be something better than that, Tripp."

"Yes, sir."

"I like to see a young fellow show ambition, combined with sound character. I might use a man like that. You drive, don't you, Tripp?"

"Yes, sir."

"Can you keep your mouth shut? Obey orders to the letter?"

"Yes, sir."

"Want to work for me?"

"Driving?"

"You'd have to do some driving. Your job would be more important than that, though."

Joey swallowed his disappointment. "I haven't got a driver's license."

"Now that's an honest admission," Mr. Baggott said. "I'm glad you told me right out. I like a man who does things the straightforward way."

He drove the car up the narrow ramp and out on to the elevated highway that ran along past the docks. The *Queen Mary,* as big as a house, her white bridge bright in the floodlights, was nosed right up to the waterfront alongside the Cunard White Star pier. Joey looked back at her. Big people—powerful, rich people like Mr. Baggott—were going aboard her. And Joey Tripp had just missed his chance of taking the first step toward joining them someday. He ground a wet palm round and round on the knee of his gray work slacks. Maybe the chance might never come again.

He felt unsustained in this enormous city. He had returned to it only to find he felt alien here. The young people he knew, like the Marchands, were only a cool rain check to friendship, and Gram was only—Gram. For a moment Mr. Baggott had opened a door to something real, exciting, worth while; now it had slammed in Joey's face.

"As it happens," Mr. Baggott said, "I know you're only seventeen and you only finished high school last January. Of *course* you haven't a license."

"How did you know?"

"You were born in Brooklyn, weren't you, Tripp? Your people went to the Adirondacks when you were seven."

Joey knew by this that Mr. Baggott must have been asking Tim Meagher about him. He said, "My father had trouble with his lungs. He died up there on my uncle's farm near Lake Placid when I was twelve."

"Your mother?"

"She died the same year. Heart."

"Then you came back to the city to live with your grandmother."

"That's right."

On the distant black barrier of the Palisades, lighted signs winked on and off, laying a pattern of red and yellow sparkles on the gloom of the river.

"Tripp," Mr. Baggott said, "the man I want has to be able to go to work for me right now. This opportunity can't wait. There's a big future in it for someone. You see how it is?"

"Yes, sir," Joey said, numb with discouragement.

"But I believe in being broad-minded. Naturally I insist upon strict obedience. And also upon strict honesty. In the big things. But oftentimes we have to cut corners on the little things to achieve the greater good. You follow me?"

"Yes, sir."

"Maybe we could finagle that license business. I was just thinking of a way. What religion are you?"

"Catholic."

"Then you were baptized in Brooklyn. Where's the church?"

"Near Fort Greene. St. Gervase's."

"Okay," Mr. Baggott said. "I'll think about it."

North of Yonkers he left the parkway and took a road that ran up through Westchester. It was dark and deserted. He pulled up at the side.

"Take the wheel, Tripp."

Joey ran around eagerly and climbed in on the driver's side.

"Thirty-five miles an hour, Tripp. On the nose. This road is posted, and I don't want any cop stopping us."

Joey set the car into motion skillfully. He drove for mile after mile, intent but happily relaxed. Mr. Baggott sat beside him, silently watchful.

"Make a U-turn, Tripp. Fast!"

Joey braked, swung the car to the right-hand edge of the road, and then whipped the wheel around to the left. The tires squealed just enough to show that he was taking the turn at maximum safe speed. In one smooth arc the car completed the maneuver and headed south. He scanned the road quickly in search of a reason for the turn. He could see nothing.

"Okay," Mr. Baggott said. "I just wanted to test your reactions. And your ability to follow orders to the letter. I'll take over now . . . If I can get around this age angle, you'll have to take a driving test to get your license. Have you a friend with a car? Will he go with you?"

"I know a guy would do it for me."

"Good. Take tomorrow afternoon off from your job, Tripp. Be on the southwest corner of Fourteenth Street and Eighth at two o'clock."

"Yes, Mr. Baggott."

"One thing."

"Yes, sir."

"I'll be using you on private work. Very private. So keep this whole thing private. And that means from everybody. But everybody."

"You can depend on me," Joey said earnestly.

"I'll drop you off at the subway at Van Cortlandt Park."

When Joey reached his home block, the Chevvy was out in front of the house. Tony Marchand had the hood up, racing the engine and tinkering with the timing. One of the girls was watching him, doing a little dance step to keep her feet occupied.

Tony looked up as Joey stopped beside him. "Hi, Joey, boy."

Joey remembered his first days on this block. He'd taken his lumps. Every kid his size had tried to run him off the sidewalk. They'd called him the Apple-knocker. Or the Hay-baler. Or the Stump-jumper. One by one he'd had to lick them or get licked. Every few days he'd go back to Gram with a bloody nose or a split lip. Now he was one of them—and yet not one of them. He had learned to talk as they did, and he knew everybody along the block and what the score was—what apartments strange men went to at night and which of the elevator operators in the big building on the corner of the avenue were taking bets for the bookies. Joey knew those things, but he wasn't having any of them himself. They were offbeat. Joey was going to make his way legitimately, so that someday he could drive his own Caddy into Baggott Service and turn it over to Pete Krawcik for a tune up with a clear conscience. Of course, as Mr. Baggott had said tonight, you have to be broad-minded about little things, though.

He said, "Hi, Tony. She sounds good."

"I got to check the points again."

"Look. When I take my driving test, can I use this heap? Can you come with me, Tony?"

"When?"

"Soon. I'll let you know."

"You can't take no test. You're under the age. And there ain't no junior license in this city."

Joey said grandly, "It's going to be fixed. I know a man."

Tony straightened up and turned a pointed olive face under a shock of wavy black hair toward Joey. "Big wheel, huh?"

"I can't mention any names."

Tony whistled, half in admiration, half in derision. "Waddya know!"

The girl let her dancing feet sidle her up to Joey. "Take me out with you when you go for a drive?" She came to a halt with her hip resting against his. It was firmly cushioned and warm through the thin dress, but he got no charge out of it. She smelled of some perfume that was strong and probably cheap. She wasn't the kind he wanted—the kind who stepped into the big expensive jobs that Mr. Baggott sold, the kind that knew how to talk right and dress right. And smell right.

He said, "You or somebody else, baby."

Tony cut in sharply, "You're booked up solid, Laurie. With me. Remember?"

Laurie laughed. "Unless I get a better idea."

Tony said, "Unless you want a slap in the mouth."

Joey didn't care to be bothered with any more of that. He ran up the three pairs of stairs as if he had sponge rubber feet. Gram was still up, ironing some fresh curtains for the living-room windows. She had his couch opened out and made up for the night.

"Joey, you're late." She still had a Viennese accent, after all her years in America. It had persisted, like the timeless vigor that still drove her lean frame through endless little household tasks every day to keep the two rooms immaculate. She lived here on a pension. Joey's grandfather had been a metalworker in the Brooklyn navy yard.

"You want some cocoa, Joey?" she asked.

"Yeah, Gram. I'm hungry." He gave her a hug as he passed. "I'll hang a diamond pin on you yet, sweetie pie. As big as the Queen Mary's anchor."

"Diamonds? From the supermarket, maybe."

"I'm getting a real job soon."

"Sure. When are you taking the examination, Joey?"

"The driving test? How did you——? Oh, the civil service. Someday. Maybe. Or never."

"Joey, a steady position like that you ought to be glad——"

"A big opportunity, the man said. A future in it. That's what he said, Gram . . . All out for the Bunny Hop!" He grabbed her round the waist. "Right, right, left, left. Forward. Back. Hop, hop, hop!" He bounced her about until she was breathless and shaky from laughter.

TWO

WHEN HE DROPPED young Tripp, Chester Baggott drove back to the Cross County Parkway and turned off it at the big new shopping development at Central Park Avenue. He drove north through Yonkers to a group of garden apartments that was only one of a number of mushroom growths in what had recently been open land. He parked two blocks away from his destination (he left the car in a different spot every time he came here) and walked.

The entrances to the one-story buildings were set back from the street in little courts. Wrought-iron lanterns above the doors cast a discreet light upon the grass plots and narrow cement walks. Baggott made sure there was no one abroad in the court in front of the building where Crystal Day lived. He turned quickly into it and used a key to open the door of the apartment at the left of the entry.

She gave a little high-pitched cry of pleasure and came to meet him. "Chet, lover!"

He said, "Crys, darling."

One moment she was an uncoiling curve of beauty, in chartreuse satin lounging pajamas, rising from the armchair with as flowing a grace as the cigarette smoke that ascended in everchanging spirals from the ash tray on the low table beside her. The next second she was in his arms, pressing her body against his, digging her long nails into his neck and shoulders, fastening her mouth against his lips.

Chester Baggott wanted to pull away from her. Then the violence in his own body turned toward the violence in hers instead of against it, answering it uncontrollably. His lips rammed almost brutally against the warm red cushion of her mouth until he bruised them on the hardness of her teeth.

He remembered in a cool recess of the mind, even while his blood leaped in response to her, that it had been like this ever since the first evening. There had been a state convention of automobile dealers at the Statler Hotel, and after the meeting a group of them had gone out to meet some party girls and make a night of it. It was a familiar enough experience to Baggott—all but the girl with whom he was paired.

Her hair was a soft, glowing shade of red—he had learned since what it cost to keep it that color—and the same smoldering fire seemed to dwell in the gray-green eyes, the full mouth, the figure that was opulent yet elegant in its proportions. It was increased by an impression of strong restraint that might be fully abandoned at will.

She was young and new to this sort of thing. He had been suddenly seized with the belief that here was something that every man at some moment dreams of finding and seldom finds—the virgin-mistress, the harlot-maiden, the concubine who holds her inmost fire from a world of eager seekers, saving it for him alone to blow to a consuming blaze.

That first night he had done his best to see her restraint abandoned. He should have felt, he thought now, with his mouth hot against hers, something like the fascinated curiosity of a man under a cliff who sees that a stone may start an avalanche—and throws the stone. What, he wondered grimly, taking his lips from hers and murmuring, "Lover! lover!" before he closed his teeth not too gently on the lobe of her ear, does the man do about stopping the avalanche?

She whirled away from him and dropped to the ottoman of the armchair, curling her legs under her like a child. "Had a hard day, Daddy?"

"Dealers' convention all this week. There was a meeting tonight. I left early."

"Just like the one we met at last fall?"

"This was strictly business. Things are getting tough. Mind mixing me a drink, Crys?"

She sprang up. As she moved toward the kitchen, she looked back at him over one shoulder. "I want a car, Daddy."

"Darling, we've been all over that. Again and again. For weeks. Please face facts. The boom days in my business are over. After the war we weren't selling. We were accepting orders and raking in the money. It's different from now on."

Her smile showed a gleam of even white teeth. "A convertible, Daddy sweet."

He felt his collar tighten around his neck. Yet there was no need for genuine anger. He had made up his mind, after the last scene they'd had, just what he must do. But take it easy, Chet, son. Don't give in too quickly. Make her think she's forcing you to yield. And always—always there's the chance that you can sell her the idea of being sensible. You're a salesman, aren't you?

"You have a good grasp of reality, darling," he said persuasively. "You see things clearly. Now look at the matter from a common-sense—"

"I got to have it, Chet."

"Sometime, maybe. When the situation eases again."

"Now. When I go up to Saratoga for the races."

"We decided you wouldn't be able to go."

"I decided I would. I told you that. Over and over, honey."

"I was sure you were kidding."

"I never kid, sweet. And I got to have some cash. It won't be no fun if I can't put down a bet whenever I really like a horse. And look at him run. Instead of him being just a name in a scratch sheet."

He stood up and took her face between his hands. She smiled impudently at him. "Don't try to sweet-talk me out of it, Chet."

He could feel a throbbing in the fine white line of scar tissue that crossed his left palm. He remembered the German soldier who had come at him with a bayonet, the day after the enemy counterattacked near Bastogne. Baggott's automatic jammed. He threw the useless weapon at the man's face—pale, drawn, undernourished features, streaked with mud —and for an irrational fraction of time, as the German jerked his head up and away to dodge the missile, Baggott noted how pitifully scrawny the neck seemed above the ill-fitting uniform. In the same instant he turned the thrusting bayonet with a desperate clutch at the bare steel. It laid the palm of his left hand open, but he felt no immediate pain as he closed with his assailant in a desperate scuffle. They were up and down, this way and that, over and over in the mucky earth, and somehow Baggott got the lean head between his powerful hands and gave a twisting wrench.

Later he often recalled the curious sound as the neckbone broke and the man went limp and dead. Sometimes the memory gave him a touch of revulsion, but more often a disturbing consciousness of guilty-innocent power, of lawful meddling with the great forbidden mystery of life and death. He experienced it now, feeling Crystal Day's nectarine cheeks between his palms, realizing that only the graceful column of her throat was between him and security.

He moved his arms, and her head began to turn.

"Don't rush me, Daddy," she said. "I'll get you your drink right away."

He let his hands drop. Not now. Something completely unforeseen might happen to bring a knock at the door. The superintendent hunting a gas leak. A policeman investigating a report of a prowler. Any of a hundred unpredictable chances. And here he would be with the dead girl.

Dead she had to be. He had decided that weeks ago. The rest was unremittingly careful planning. The killing of the German soldier had been something licit, something he had been trained to do. The killing of Crystal Day would be the illicit act of an untrained amateur. All the more need for exquisite preparation and attention to detail.

The first and most important precaution at this moment was to act as if he still hoped he could out-argue her, to give in with the utmost reluctance to her demands, so that she would not suspect for a moment that in his eyes she was already lying lifeless and broken on the——

Crystal brought him the highball, moving across the white rug with a gay swing of glossy chartreuse thighs. After she handed it to him, she stood beside the chair, leaning a warm leg against his arm.

He drank half the glass in two gulps and said, "It costs plenty to run this apartment and keep you in clothes and spending money, Crys."

"And taxes are high," she agreed cheerfully, "and prices are terrible. I know . . . And Evelyn don't never have to find out a thing."

At the mention of his wife's name, Baggott set the glass down with a thump on the coaster Crystal had laid on the rug beside his chair.

"You don't care if you ruin me, do you?"

She stooped and kissed his temple. "I don't want to ruin you, Daddy. You're the most, just the way you are. I only want a convertible. So I can drive around when I go to Saratoga."

"No," he said.

She laughed. "When Evelyn finds out——"

He took hold of her wrist. "Don't call her Evelyn."

"You hurt when you squeeze so hard. But I like it, sort of. You're all man, Daddy . . . When are you going to let me have the convertible?"

"Forget it. And my wife isn't going to find out anything."

"No?" She sank to the rug beside the low table and picked up the telephone. "I told you the last time. I told you and told you, but you wouldn't believe me."

He said, "You'd be throwing away everything. All of this."

She nodded merrily. "That's right. So I would. But I could find someone else, lover. And I bet you couldn't find another rich wife to put you into the automobile business again."

"Don't be crazy, Crys. You know you haven't the slightest intention——"

She dialed, intoning aloud, "Y-O-seven-five-four-eight-two."

There was a pause. Chester Baggott leaned forward and got his weight balanced on the balls of his feet. The girl watched him, her gray-green eyes still merry and merciless. She held the receiver a little way from her ear to let him hear in the silence the faint rip-rip of the ringing signal. And the distant murmur of a voice.

"Mrs. Baggott?" Crystal said. "You don't know me, but you'll be interested in sump'm I got to tell you. My name——"

Baggott lurched from his chair and was on her in a long bound. She flinched not a bit, as if she knew his big hand would come down not on her but on the telephone, breaking the connection.

His face was almost against hers. She smiled into it, whispering, "When, lover?"

He let out a gust of breath that fanned her red mouth into laughing. "As soon as I get a turn-in that I think will suit you."

"Wonderful! You're a lamb!" She followed him to his chair, and when he threw himself into it moodily, she sank to her knees and swayed in front of him, turning so that her face was under his. She drew his head down, both arms around his neck. He kissed her sulkily.

She said, "I'll start taking driving lessons right away, Daddy. A miner's daughter in Scranton don't learn them things for free, like rich kids."

"You can't get a license in time for the Saratoga races. It takes a while. First, lessons at a driving school. Then you have to make an application. After that there's the driving test."

"I want that car at Saratoga."

"For God's sake, why?"

She sat on the rug at his feet. "I was a dirty little thing. Coal dust all over. My bare feet were always grimy." She pronounced it *grimmy*. "My dress wasn't clean even the minute it was washed and ironed. My sister wore it until it was too small for her and they give it to me, and the dirt was ground into it. One day I saw a newspaper laying on the street, and there was a picture in it. I got down on my hands and knees on the sidewalk and looked at it. Men and women in the grandstand at Saratoga. On the society page. Beautiful . . . you know—sharp clothes—you could tell they cost plenty money. And clean. Even in that filthy-dirty newspaper you could see they must be clean. I made up my mind I was going there someday and sit in that grandstand. It's a picture I got in my mind ever since."

She closed her eyes, and her face took on the lovely virginal look that he had seen on it that night of their first meeting. He realized how little he knew about her. Her name wasn't Crystal Day, of course. The smooth planes of her face below the wide cheekbones suggested Polish ancestry. Or perhaps her people had come from one of those little countries up on the edge of the Baltic that Russia has swallowed—Lithuania and the other two. Only in bits of reminiscence like this could he glimpse the bitter hard childhood she had escaped from.

"The picture in my mind is me," she said, "there at Saratoga. Not with anybody particular, you know. Just by myself. But I got on a beautiful dress that fits me and never belonged to nobody else. There's other women there, but nobody notices them. I go down to the windows and make a bet, and then I come back to my seat and I sit there and everybody looks at me. And when I go down and get in my car and drive off, they all turn and watch me as long as they can see me." She opened her eyes.

"This is my chance to make it come true. Maybe I wouldn't get any other chance."

Baggott said, "If you'd wait until next year——"

"Anything could happen between now and next year. I'm going to have it now. Then nobody can ever take it away from me . . . If I can't get the driving license in time, you'll have to do something about it."

"What do you mean, do something? What could I do?"

"Something." Her eyes moved slowly, smoothly to the telephone, and back to his face. "Don't you want to, sweet?"

"Well—maybe I could give you a driver to run the car up to Saratoga for you and stick around until you pass your test."

"You angel!" Rising, she caught his hand and drew him toward the bedroom.

In the midst of his most intense drive of physical desire, he had the feeling that even in this phase of their relationship her response outmatched his stimulus, that he was being harassed, overmastered, used . . . But he took grim satisfaction from the thought that he had maneuvered her into compelling him to make the arrangement that was the heart of his plan to expunge her as a living and deadly threat to his comfortable way of life.

It was two o'clock in the morning when he drove into the garage of his house in the North Broadway section of Yonkers. A side door led directly to the kitchen. He went through a short passage to the front hall and mounted the stairs.

Evelyn was in bed with a book. The reading lamp on the headboard threw a corona of light upon her dark hair and picked out the early strands of gray. She was only thirty-eight, but no dye job for Evelyn. She was, Baggott thought as he kissed her, the most uncompromisingly honest person he knew, yet never stuffy about it. A thoroughly admirable woman. He was fond of her, and he was sure that she loved him. Yet if she ever found out about Crystal, she would divorce him without undue recriminations, might even see a little rueful humor in her own heartbreak. And all hell wouldn't keep her from kicking him out of Baggott Sales and Service. She had put her own money into it shortly after they were married and had seen to it, as a matter of simple fair dealing, that the ownership was in her name.

He wondered what she would have to say about the strangely interrupted telephone call from a girl with an unfamiliar voice, though even while he prepared to show the appropriate mild lack of interest he knew that she would probably not even think of mentioning the incident to him. Women, from one or another of the many civic and charitable organizations she belonged to, were always on and off the telephone.

He took part in public affairs now and then himself, but only as a pipeline to new business. A year or two before, he had served on the citizen committee that pushed through a salary raise of $700 across the board for the underpaid policemen and firemen. That little effort had paid off in several leads for sales of new cars to prospects—not in Yonkers, for Baggott Sales didn't poach on the local dealer's territory, but across the city line in Manhattan.

Evelyn's civic activities, however, grew entirely out of her sense of rectitude and community spirit. She could understand his mingling of altruism and self-serving and be wryly amused by it without either condemning or condoning it. Her own motives were unmixed; she built up her ego by avoiding egotism.

She laid down the book and smiled up at him. "Droll doings at the meeting, I suppose?"

"You'd have died laughing. Everybody was in kinks over the funniest things. More new cars pushed onto the dealers than we can sell, especially the creampuff models—everybody's money tied up in a lotful of used cars —repossessions—customers shopping around to get us to up our trade-in allowances until the blood drips."

She chuckled. "Your poor head must ache. I'm sure mine would if I tried to understand it all. But that's your share of the load, Chet. Mine is to make a comfortable home for you. I do, don't I?"

He paused in the act of untying his tie to pat the toes that made a hillock in the bedspread. "Wonderfully comfortable, Ev."

He spoke sincerely. It was not dissatisfaction with her or his home that had led him to Crystal and this thin edge of disaster that he was walking along. It was some relentless unrest. It had driven him into being a competent soldier and a tough and able company commander. It had actuated him in his headlong courtship of Evelyn, the daughter of the rich Garners of Baltimore, a cut above the son of a well-off tomato farmer and canner from Reisterstown, even though that suitor had gone to Cornell to study agriculture. That dissatisfied compulsion had turned him from the thought of farming. In the summers, when he had worked in the cannery, he had revolted at the stink of sour tomato pulp from the clothes of the men who worked and slept in the same shirt and pants day after day. Even before the war he had switched over to selling automobiles. The exercise of his natural aggressive charm to dominate a prospect left him, for a few elated hours, with a sense of triumphant potency that was hardly matched by the lift of either liquor or sex. It gave him almost the feeling of power he had had in that second when the German's life had gone out in the shock of a snapped neck.

"How did your own meeting go?" he asked.

"All right. They want me to talk about the Garden Club on the radio."

"A big network?"

"The local station. I don't know whether I will."

"Why not?"

"The program's sponsored by an investment house. This girl that passes out daily household hints and marketing advice on the air has some local celebrity give a guest talk once a week. Every organization I'm in has had someone speak on that program. The day nursery and the hospital fund committee and the Ivy Ball. Now they want me to go on about the Garden Club."

"I promise to tune in. I'll be proud of you."

"People write in, and this investment house sends them folders. And suppose someone loses money investing and wants to know why I spoke on that program? I'd feel sort of morally responsible, Chet, as if I'd endorsed the bonds they bought. And if I feel that way, I don't think it would be honest of me to go on the air for them."

"You're being overscrupulous."

"I'm just trying to do what I think is right. Especially now that money's getting a little tighter and people can't afford to lose anything. I've heard you say business is slowing down."

"You'll hear me say it again." Let Crys go on the way she's been doing, and even Ev is going to realize there ought to be more money available than I can account for. And if she starts wondering—then what? If she once got the slightest idea of what's going on, she'd forget all about this Southern belle pitch of being amusingly helpless where business is concerned. She'd start digging like a terrier, looking for the honest—the very, very honest—facts. She wouldn't stop until she'd rooted everything out.

He tied the drawstring of his pajama pants, went to the bathroom, and brushed his teeth. Spitting out minty foam he called, "When are you going down to Washington for that convention of the women voters?"

"The end of next month. Chet, did you read in the *Herald Statesman* what Mayor Simmons said about . . ."

Her voice went on and on with quick enthusiasm, while he buttoned his pajama jacket, thinking, "The end of the month. That'll be just the time."

He turned out the lights, kissed her, and slipped into his own bed. She talked on for a while in the darkness, but he heard nothing of what she was saying. He lay flat on his back, and his brain was busy with a time schedule, carefully ticking off days and intervals.

That Tripp kid . . . He looks on me as a big operator. I thought of myself that way too. Baggott, head of a successful agency. Baggott, the heavy spender. Baggott, whose needs couldn't be taken care of by any one girl—Chet, son, do you know what? You're not the sort who gets dominated by a woman. You're the special sort who gets himself hag-ridden by *two* women.

His lips drew tight over his teeth in the blackness. That's funny. Laugh at it, boy. But *do* something about it, you bastard.

So much time from here to here at such a speed . . . She will . . . so if he . . . And then if I . . .

A professional gangster would know where to turn for a quick, un-complicated answer: a hired killer. But an honest businessman, with everything to lose, doesn't dare to lay himself open by approaching people like that. They'd bleed him. Far worse than Crys. So he thinks of an alibi, of devious methods, of devices that are darkly preposterous at the first notion but steadily grow brighter and more seductive under the intense, dizzying glow of secret thought.

Such and such a distance . . . this many hours to account for . . .

THREE

JOEY TRIPP WAS WAITING EAGERLY the next day at the appointed place. Mr. Baggott picked him up and drove to Brooklyn over the Manhattan Bridge. The river, gay with sun speckles under the jumble of piled-up skyscrapers, was like a flood of glass marbles spilled from the playboxes of a kindergarten of giants.

At Tillary Street, Mr. Baggott turned left off the Flatbush Avenue Extension. A block from St. Gervase's Church, he halted at the curb.

He said affably, "Tripp, I'm paying you a week's wages in advance. This is a tentative arrangement. If everything goes okay, your regular salary will be more than this." He took out his wallet and thumbed three twenty-dollar bills, a ten and a five from the sheaf it contained.

As Joey took the money he felt his face flush and his heart speed up. This was the first step up for him, the one he'd been sure was coming sometime—the first step toward becoming a man like Mr. Baggott himself, strong and knowing and able.

"Walk to the rectory," Mr. Baggott said. "When you're through, meet me here again. Now here's the program. Ask the priest for a baptismal certificate. Give him all the correct information about yourself. Right?"

"It'll show I'm only seventeen," Joey said.

"Naturally. But he'll have a pad of forms. He'll be writing out your certificate on the top one. If something happens to take him out of the room, be ready for the opportunity. Get a blank sheet from the pad, somehow. Slip it into your pocket. Okay?"

Joey looked out the car window. He didn't recognize the neighborhood any more. A seven-year-old had walked along here past unbroken ranks of low frame houses facing the street, their paint dingy and peeling from weathering and the city's fumes. Now twelve-story red brick cliffs sliced strange diagonals from the sky, and the curved walks and greenery of the housing project almost surrounded St. Gervase's spire. Between two of the buildings, high on the crest of the park behind them, the tower of the monument to the prison-ship martyrs of the American Revolution stood tall in the sunlight. Here below, where youngsters had played stickball, the street was deserted, and cries of children came from a playground glimpsed between trees.

The seven-year-old had been wearing a dark-blue suit. A white bow of silk was fluffy-tickling under his chin, and a white carnation smelled like pickled pears in his buttonhole. He joined his group in the basement of St. Gervase's, and two by two they marched up to First Communion behind the little girls in white veils. His hands felt queer in the white cotton gloves, and the cover of the prayer book, white celluloid deeply embossed with the Cross, tasted slick and chemical when he sucked a corner of it. Then he was bending his head fearfully and holding his breath while the gold curves of the chalice sparkled in the light of the candles as the priest raised the Blood of God——

He said, "Mr. Baggott, wouldn't that be illegal?"

Mr. Baggott threw his head back and laughed heartily. "Tripp, you kill me! I've often chatted with reputable businessmen. People who follow thoroughly ethical methods. They have a few drinks, and off the record they let down their hair. They'll tell you. Now they've made the grade they can *afford* to be ethical; but on the way up . . . why, they'll give you the details about the corners they cut and the little shenanigans they had to pull to get by. Strict ethics, Tripp, is a luxury like dollar cigars and Napoleon cognac; you enjoy it only after you've battled your way up to where you can relax and indulge yourself." He turned toward Joey decisively. "The question is, are you in a spot in your career where you can be nasty-nice about things? I don't think so, but I may be wrong. If so, you don't want the job I'm offering you. I won't think any the worse of you. Make up your own mind. Take it or leave it."

He held out his fingers and rubbed them together in the give-me-the-money gesture.

Joey's hand closed in a damp spasm on the seventy-five dollars in his pocket. "I'll take it," he said.

The priest hauled down a register from a row on the shelf beside the single stained-glass window of the small room off the dim entrance hall of the rectory. He ran a finger down a page, then along a line, and began to fill in the spaces on the top sheet of the pad of blank certificates. His face Joey remembered vaguely. It was middle-aged, thin and lined, beaded with sweat above a black cassock that looked cruelly hot on this summer day. His ball-point pen skipped a few letters over a spot where his hand had rested, and he muttered impatiently.

Glass crashed. Light bloomed suddenly brighter from the stained-glass window's burst pane. Something bounced off the table, skittered along the floor, came to rest against the baseboard. A stone.

"Jesus, Mary, and Joseph!" The priest sprang from his chair. "Those young hoodlums! Haven't they a playground to keep them out of devil-try?" He hurried to the entrance hall, the skirts of his cassock snapping fretfully at his heels.

Joey saw daylight fall in a broad bar across the hall and knew the priest had opened the street door to look for the stone-thrower. Joey rose to follow him. He was almost to the hallway when realization jerked his mouth open. *If something happens to take him out of the room, be ready* —He wheeled back, caught up the leaves of the pad, and tried to tear one out. Haste made him clumsy. The sheet ripped across the middle. He heard the street door slam. He got hold of a few sheets next to the cardboard backing of the pad, and tugged diagonally, more gently. They came away whole. One quick fold and they slid into his coat pocket. He had thrust the pad into place and was moving toward the door again when the priest entered.

"Those rascals! There wasn't one of them in sight—only a car disappearing around a corner. But they all drive cars now. Steal them, too . . . Where was I? Oh, yes." He picked up his pen again.

Joey said unsteadily, "Is there a charge for this, Father?"

"No. But it's customary to leave a little offering."

Joey fingered the money that Mr. Baggott had given him, but he didn't like to ask for change. He fumbled for a crumpled dollar bill of his own. He was in a hurry to get out of this place. From somewhere had come a faint drift of incense smell, and it was all mixed up in his memory with the taste of white celluloid and the feel of a silk bow under his chin and the scared sensation as he tilted his head back for the first time and thrust his tongue out of aching-wide jaws and saw the priest's fingers come near with the round white Bread that was so little and so terrible. . . .

Mr. Baggott smoothed out the blank baptismal certificate on a magazine across the steering wheel and drew a fountain pen from his pocket. He had parked on the service road of the Shore Parkway.

"Fill this in just as it is here, Tripp," he said, "except for the date of birth. We'll make you officially of age to get a driver's license." He chuckled. "I'm enjoying this. Haven't had so much fun since we used to hide behind the outhouse of the old folks' home—it was on the edge of a gully—and reach up and tickle their bottoms with a branch that had a bunch of burdocks tied on the end. One old girl nearly deafened the whole county, she squalled so loud. We never knew whether she thought it was a spider or a snake."

"The signature?" Joey asked.

"Sign the padre's name. But don't try to imitate his writing. You'd only be awkward about it. Make it good and free in your own handwriting. Nobody'll check up. They never do."

Joey hesitated.

"I have your first assignment all laid out for you," Mr. Baggott said casually. "It's pretty much in the nature of a test run. How well do you know the Taconic Parkway? Say, as far as Albany."

"I've been to Poughkeepsie."

"Think you could find your way to Saratoga?"

"Easy. From Albany you take Route 9. Wouldn't the Thruway be quicker?"

Mr. Baggott said quietly, "I thought you knew how to follow orders, Tripp."

"Yes, sir."

"The money I've given you is an advance against salary. It'll do you until you get your driving license, because without that you're no use to me. As soon as you get it, you can quit that crummy job at the supermarket and go to work for me full time."

He held out the pen. Joey took it. It was lucky that in his haste he'd torn more than one sheet out of the priest's pad. He spoiled two in his nervousness. Once he put his own name where his father's should have been, and then he wrote the correct year of his birth before Mr. Baggott could check him.

Finally he got a form filled in properly, and Mr. Baggott folded the spoiled sheets. "Not wise to throw these around where someone might just happen to pick them up, Tripp," he smiled. "Watch the trifles, I always say, and you won't have to worry about the big things." He tucked the marred sheets away in a long leather wallet that was plump with other papers.

He paused a moment and then drew from a compartment in the wallet a gold badge. "Local police department up home gave it to me. Honorary. I helped them get a salary raise . . . Nice?" He weighed the disk jovially in his palm.

Joey felt warm reassurance ease out along his tense muscles. If Mr. Baggott was like that with the police, what was there to worry about?

"When you get the license," Mr. Baggott said, "call me at Baggott Sales. Don't give your name. Just say it's personal business. And it is, boy. Remember, you'll be on a special mission." He gave Joey's shoulder a firm, confidential pressure. "I'll tell you when to meet me. I'll pick you up where I did today. Got it all straight?"

"Yes, sir."

"Good." Mr. Baggott's deep, crisp voice warmed a little. "I think we're going to get along fine, Tripp."

The day Joey went for his driving test, he took the afternoon off at the supermarket and stopped by the photoengraving shop where Tony Marchand worked.

Joey was wearing the new tan gabardine suit he'd bought out of the money Mr. Baggott had given him. He'd paid thirty-five dollars for it at Klein's on Union Square. He had to have enough left over to pay Tony the wages he'd lose for taking the half day off at the engraver's. It wasn't a bad-looking suit, but when the real money began to come in Joey planned to buy his clothes at a high-class men's store. Rogers and Peet, maybe.

Right now, though, with a new tan-bordered rayon handkerchief tucked in his breast pocket, he was conscious of looking like a broker alongside Tony in grubby work clothes. The job Tony had was just another flunky deal, hustling supplies around and wrapping and shipping the metal plates when the engravers had completed them.

In the bluish glow from the fluorescent tubes overhead, the place had an offbeat look that had always attracted Joey. Through a door to a side room, he could catch a glimpse of an enormous camera with a bellows that seemed to stretch out like a fat twelve-foot caterpillar, along a flat steel bed. And just beyond Tony's wrapping table, there was a metal box with a light under its ground-glass top, where an engraver bent over a color transparency, studying it. The glow coming upward through the transparency lighted his face weirdly as if he were an actor in a TV horror program. Another man passed by, and Joey saw that his hands were as red as blood from some fine powder that the engravers used when they were etching the plates.

Might be interesting work, and an engraver made good pay if you could ever get into the union. But it wasn't for Joey. He had it made already!—or practically—and without all the slavery and dirt.

He moved his shoulders comfortably inside the sleek gabardine. "Let's get this show on the road, Tony boy."

"Man," Tony said, his small dark face unimpressed, "you're too pretty to go and take a test in an old busted-down Chevvy. Where's your Thunderbird?"

"Coming up, buddy," Joey said confidently. "I got it on order. All but almost."

"Yeah. A month from some rainy Tuesday. You got your learner's permit? You can't take no test without one."

"I got it. I went down to Worth Street. They gave me the eye test then." Joey remembered his shiver of dread when he had presented the forged baptismal certificate, but the clerk had just made a note of it on the form and returned it to Joey without comment.

"How'd you get around the under-age angle?" Tony's little brown eyes inspected Joey sideways.

Joey shrugged. "My guy knows a guy." He held fast to the memory of the gold police badge. It was a symbol of ultimate righteousness, after a few necessary corners had been cut.

The test wasn't anything. They picked up the Chevvy in West Fifty-second Street—the Marchands moved it to a different spot every night to avoid parking tickets—and Tony drove it uptown to the side street where they lined up, and waited with other cars until a brown-uniformed examiner motioned Joey into the driver's seat, had him steer around the block, back, turn, and park. A few questions on rules of the road, and that was it.

A week later Joey telephoned Mr. Baggott at the sales office. The receptionist asked, "May I tell him who is calling, please?"

"Personal business."

After a little, Baggott's heavy voice said, "Yes?"

"I got it in the mail yesterday, Mr. Baggott. I mean, the li——"

"Okay."

Gram had handed the letter to Joey the night before as soon as he got home. She was twittering between joy and fear.

"It's from the gover'ment, Joey. Maybe it's like I always wanted, you got a civil service job. You maybe fooled your gra'ma and put in a application on the sly? You always fooling me, Joey . . . But then I think maybe it's a notice you got to go in the Army. No. You too young. They wouldn't make you go anyway on account you're big for your age?"

"No, Gram. It's a driving license. Now I'm going to get a real swell job. Secret mission. I'm going away for a little while."

"Where, Joey? How long?"

"I can't tell anyone, sugar. Only a few days, I guess."

She put a gnarled hand to her temple. "Well . . . I got to iron your shirts right away."

"Don't bother, Gram. The old ones are worn at the collar. I'll get whatever I need when I land up there."

Great old girl, he thought now, as he listened to Mr. Baggott's deep, pleased voice. "You're ready to go?"

"Any time."

"Three o'clock tomorrow."

At two the next afternoon Joey trundled a dollyload of cartons of frozen orange juice from the refrigerator truck at the side street entrance into the back of the store, ripped open the corrugated cardboard boxes and stowed the frosty cans in the display cases. Then he walked through the aisles, where women in wild-striped toreador pants and sun glasses bumped wire shopping carts with women in house dresses and floppy mules.

He found the assistant manager who handled personnel talking to the head of the meat department. Chops and steaks, wrapped in transparent polyethylene film and stacked in cartons, came rumbling down a slideway of metal rollers from the cutting room overhead.

Joey said, "I'm taking off now, Mr. Aaron, for the rest of the afternoon. I won't be back. I'll pick up my pay whenever I get a chance."

The assistant manager nodded. "Quitting?"

"That's right."

"Why?"

"Another job."

"What doing?"

"Just another job."

Aaron Whiteside said, "Hold it a minute, Joey." He was dressed in a neat gray flannel business suit, like the other bosses, and under a balding scalp that still held the remnants of a Florida tan his plump face wore its usual expression of hurried calm. "I've been keeping an eye on you. We're always watching for good workers, with a little extra on the ball. You know what I mean?"

"Sure," Joey said. In his joy he could have laughed.

"Well . . . when this store started up before World War II, it was just a specialty grocery—not too big—free deliveries—monthly credit to customers. I was popping sodas in the drugstore on the corner. A fresh punk out of high school, getting nowhere. You know what I mean?"

"Yeah," Joey said.

"I came in here, horsing crates around. I saw maybe a future. Take a good look, kid." He swiveled his thumb. Joey glanced at the long, crowded aisles, the vistas of tubes glowing overhead, the clerks and wrappers hustling at a dozen check-out counters.

"The store's come a long way," Mr. Aaron said. He glanced worriedly at his wrist watch. "Biggest in the city . . . That soda-jerking kid rode along with it. Never been sorry he did. There's still a lot more ahead for the store. Thought about riding with it? You know what I mean?"

"I know," Joey said. "I'll stop by for my money."

"You're calling the shots, boy . . . Let me know if you change your mind." Mr. Aaron turned away and followed his perpetual hurry down a canyon of canned goods.

Joey went down to Fourteenth and Eighth. A car just happened to pull out from a parking place at the curb as Mr. Baggott drove up, and he eased into the space and motioned Joey into the seat beside him.

"Tomorrow evening you drive to Saratoga, Tripp. These are your instructions. I expect you to follow them to the letter. At exactly seven you'll arrive at my house in Yonkers. No one will be at home. There'll be a red and cream convertible in front of the house. This is the key to it. You'll get into it and drive at once to Three Garden Crescent——"

Joey listened intently, breathing shallowly in concentration as he fixed each detail in his mind. When the briefing was over, he repeated the instructions almost word for word.

Mr. Baggott whacked Joey's shoulder in approbation. "Now for expenses. This'll hold you for the time being. I'll be in touch with you later."

Joey slipped the folded bills into his pocket without counting them. The outside one was a fifty. As he sidled out of the car into the rattle and drum-roar of traffic, he thought of Aaron Whiteside and the supermarket success story. This time Joey let himself laugh aloud. The noise of his merriment went unheard in the bellow of truck exhausts.

FOUR

CRYSTAL DAY GLANCED SIDEWAYS at the young man with the excited-looking crew cut above a serious young face. The warmth of the night had made him throw his tan gabardine coat on the deck behind the seat of the red convertible, and in the last bluish glow of the starlit evening, his light-colored rayon sport shirt showed off his good shoulders.

Crystal recrossed her shapely nylons and felt the bulge in one stocking top as her thighs sleeked together. An uncomfortable lump, but delicious. Cautious old Chet never gave her a check—always cash. When she reached Saratoga it would be safer to put it in a bank under her own name. In the meantime, if young Shoulders knew how much her left leg was worth, would he be more dangerous? Her glow of pussy-cat contentment made the thought absurd. "Less harmless" would be a better way to put it. He was a sweet sort of a kid, the way he answered all her remarks so carefully and politely. A different kind of an animal from the men you met on these after-the-convention-meeting-breaks-up parties.

"Joey," she said.

"Yes . . . yes'm."

"How fast can this thing go?"

"I don't know. Maybe ninety or a hundred."

"I want to see. Let it out. There's no one on the road ahead of us."

He shook his head.

She glanced back. "That's just a passenger car behind us. Not police."

"I can't."

"Why not?"

"Orders."

"Chet's?"

"Yes'm."

"He isn't here. Let's go."

"I'm sorry."

Crystal said, "Oh, shoot!" She hummed under her breath a little while and then said, "You know, Joey, I still can't figure out why you called for me so late."

"Well, it was Mr. Baggott's——"

"No, let me guess." She made a derisive little sound with the lips that he knew, without looking at them again, were deliciously curved. "Orders, schmorders . . . We won't get up there until midnight, and we'll have a fine time trying to find a room." She tapped his bare forearm with warm, light fingers. "I mean a room apiece, baby boy. Don't get ideas."

She took a deep breath of the placid night and wriggled her back and hips against the white leather upholstery, soft over foam rubber.

Her car! Hers! Whenever Chet sent her the bill of something-or-other or the registration or whatever it was that was necessary. But now at least she had the use of this powerful, obedient, red-metal-and-marsh-mallow monster. Pretty soon she would suggest they stop somewhere for a drink. She wasn't thirsty and had no need for a powder room yet. She merely wanted to work the thing on the dashboard that made the top go up and down. Her fingers yearned toward it. This was her toy. It was all the toys rolled together—all the lovely go-to-sleep dolls with red lace-trimmed clothes, all the red sleds with shiny steel runners, all the mini-ature red-flowered tea sets, the little stoves and refrigerators and sewing machines and playhouses that the dirty little girl in Scranton had longed for and never had.

She said, "When I get to drive it, I'll find out how fast it'll go. How much are we doing now?"

"Fifty."

"Do sixty."

"I can't."

"Fifty-five, please . . . Please."

The boy's face turned toward her, and in the subdued glow from the dash she saw the thing that she could always cause in males. The awareness. The red liquid going up in the glass tube. Only a little bit, as yet, with this fuzzy chick of a new-hatched man, but there were days ahead. Long, wonderful days.

Joey felt her sidle along the seat until she was close against him. The whirl of night air flowing over the onward rush of the car brought a whiff of scent to his nostrils. An arresting, insistent fragrance—but not coarse or cheap. This was the sort of girl he'd pictured himself driving with, in just such a car—beautiful, clean, expensive—both of them. But not his yet.

The headlights picked up the white shirt of a walker at the grass edge. A face turned back. A young face under close-cropped hair—half-hopeful. A lifted thumb waggled northward, then drooped as they passed. The headlights despised him and reached ahead for the arch of blackness where a concrete bridge crossed over the parkway.

Crystal thought, Young men everywhere—and isn't that a wonderful provision of nature? She moved her shoulder against the boy's arm.

"Joey, this interests me. As a special favor to me, will you slow down to forty? For just a little while?"

"Why?"

"Say it's just for kicks. Because I'd like you to do it for me."

The boy said uncomfortably, "Gee, Miss Day, I——"

"Crys to you, darling."

"I would—Crys—but I can't."

"Let me figure this out now. Did Chet tell you he wanted you to drive at a certain rate of speed all the way up the parkway?"

"Well—he doesn't want me to be picked up for speeding, just in case they check up on my li——"

"On what?"

"Nothing."

She said, "It could be that he wants to know exactly where you'll be at any given time." Her mind walked around the thought on soft paws, an alley kitten inspecting a strange trash can.

She leaned toward Joey, raising her voice a little as the sedan that had been behind them drew alongside and then a little ahead, with a rushing sound of airflow and tires. The black archway loomed up large to receive both cars. The abutment on each side of it shone bright white in headlight glare.

"Joey, let me get this. Chet told you to drive all the way on the parkway at exactly fifty—— *Joey! Aaaaah!*"

The sedan swung in on them. Clang of metal. Swerve to the right. Scream of brakes. No blackness ahead. That had veered to the left, as if the whole bridge had moved, leaving only the blazing white of concrete in front of them, brilliant in their headlights, every crack and stain as plain as——

No breath to scream. Strain back against the seat, the soft, foam-rubber seat. Try to shrink into it and escape. Don't let yourself pitch forward like this, face-first——

Light lost in light, bursting into light.

Darkness.

FIVE

THE HITCHHIKER BEGAN to run. Far down the parkway the red taillights of the two cars that had passed him, ignoring his pleading thumb, had reached the overpass. One car had swerved through it and vanished. The other had suddenly blacked out a long moment before the sound of the smashup came to Sid Keene's ears.

As he trotted along the edge of the concrete, two other cars passed him, but he didn't try to halt them. He wanted this to himself until he could see what was in it for him. Scraps of action played themselves out on the television screen of his mind. In each of them he came through at the end with some advantage . . . He would help somebody who was badly hurt in the wrecked car—somebody who would be grateful afterwards. "Take this little roll o' moolah, my young friend, on accounta you saved my——" Only people don't do like that; hell, they expect you to get 'em out of a jam for free . . . "Buddy, I'll give you ten bucks if you can get this crate started runnin' again for me. I gotta make Schodack before——" Nuts. Sid didn't know a thing about what made a car run or stop, and the way that heap sounded at this distance when it smacked the concrete, it was a job for a wrecker. He slowed to a walk. Anybody in that crate would be out like a——

Loot!

His feet quickened on the pavement. It was about time he got a break. Sixty-five cents in his pocket, and this time of night nobody'd stop to pick a guy up. He raised narrowed eyes to the sky, powdered with stars like sugar on a lunch-counter cruller, but he couldn't tell time by them. Down in the city you were lucky to see two, three of the biggest ones through the hazy pink smear overhead. They didn't make you feel the way these stars did, like a peewee marble lost in the gutter. He shivered a little. He hadn't dared go home for his coat, after it happened, and the night air sent coolness through his shirt.

"Wisht I was back down there," he muttered. But he knew he couldn't keep out of the way of the cops if he went back. And if he could, his old man would hear from Mittelsohn what he'd done and would beat the jeeziz out of him or turn him in. The whole neighborhood would know by now that he'd jumped Mittelsohn, the cleaner, on his way home with the day's take because his store had been busted into so often at night.

Sid Keene winced whenever he thought of what had happened then. He'd done it the right way; he'd waited in the parking lot, empty that late in the evening, and when Mittelsohn passed along the street, Sid leaped out and got him from behind with the correct mugger's grip, forearm around his throat, knee in the small of his back. But somehow the chunky little cleaner had twisted sideways and fought him off, backed away, yelling, "Sid Keene! . . . dirty gonof! Breakin' windows with stickball is one thing. But a holdup, I tell the cops!"

Sid still felt sick inside at the shame that had filled him. He'd loused up his first heist, like he'd loused up everything else. Nothing to do but run to the subway, take an express north to Van Cortlandt Park, and start to thumb his way. Three lifts had taken him this far.

If he could get to his uncle's place, he might be all right. His uncle hadn't any use for Sid's old man. Ran a roadside diner on Route 9, north of Red Hook. A guy could work there—wash dishes or wait on the counter —until he figured out an easier way to make a fast buck. An easier touch than that rugged old Mittelsohn character. Maybe he should make himself a zip gun.

Through the dim starlight he could see the car now, nuzzling the concrete at a drunken angle. Something seemed to stir by it, a shade of darkness in the dark.

SIX

THE IMPACT of car against car sent Chester Baggott's sedan into a skid. The crumpled-metal clang of fenders rammed together turned into a smashing impact as the heavier car shouldered the convertible off the road and into the abutment, and then in a wink of time that noise was muted in the roar of engine-sound that the tunnel wrapped around the sedan as it lurched and slewed under Baggott and went skidding crazily through the arched-over space and out into open night again.

He fought the wheel with desperate wet palms, gripping it so hard, when the car was under control again, that his arms ached to the elbow. He braked, letting out a great breath of relief. A few hundred feet along the parkway, he eased the car over the edge of the concrete onto the grass and cut the lights.

He sat still, letting the shakes have their way with him for a few moments. His heels chattered silently on the rubber floor mat, and his shoulders played snap-the-whip with his elbows. It had all been a thinly figured, far-fetched gamble, with his own life laid right on the line. He wanted to drive like a lunatic along the highway, shouting at the stars, "I did it! I'm shed of her! I'm in the clear!"

But he wasn't in the clear yet. There were other things to do. First, make sure. He fumbled around for the wrench he had laid on the seat beside him and found it at last on the floor where it had slid.

He backed along the grass almost to the archway and got out. A car passed him. Then another. He hung his head, to keep the headlights from showing his face, and hurried his pace. Fear trotted along with him. The boy might not be dead—the driver often gets it easier in a crash—and if some Good Samaritan happened to spot the wreck and stop—— He ran through the blackness of the tunnel toward the arc of dusky sky beyond. The sponge rubber soles of his sport shoes made a faint pad-pad-pad on the concrete. As he reached the open and slowed and stepped around the edge of the arch, his buttocks screwed tight in a spasm of anxiety.

The boy. Alive. Out on the grass. The glow from some sort of light in his hand silhouetted his broad white-shirted shoulders and short hair-cut.

Quick. Before another car comes. Three bounds across the silent turf. Wrench rising in sweaty grip through night air blowing cold against sweaty face and neck. Smash down on bone, light going out, wrench finding its way again and again under the starlight to its mark on the drooping, collapsing figure . . . wet. Not with sweat.

Working with desperate haste now, Baggott felt in the dark for the boy's arm, slid his fingers down to the pulse. He leaned into the car and groped for Crystal's wrist, with no more compunction than a mechanic checking a motor on an extra-rush job. As he stepped back, his elation returned, wildly, briefly.

Careful, though. He didn't want anything to be found that would connect the girl directly with him. She might have written some sort of memo or random note on a scrap of paper—you could never tell what a woman would do—one damning unpredictable flaw to wreck the whole structure. His cigarette lighter was in his hand—he didn't remember dropping the wrench and reaching for the lighter—but as its tiny flame leaped into life he saw a wider area of light grow around him, and he quenched the wick with a violent jerk of his wrist. His chin touched his shoulder, and his buttocks squeezed together again. A pair of headlights was slowing down and veering to the road edge.

Baggott plunged head and shoulders into the car, scrabbling wildly about with clawed fingers. Sweat stung in his eyes, dripped from his lower jaw. His nails raked the girl's body, scraped the seat cushion, tore themselves on the floor mat.

They hit a hunk of plump resilience, smooth, firm. Leather. A strap along one edge. He snatched it out of the car and ran. Light was glaring on him now, and he ducked low. A man's voice called, "Hey, there! You! Wait!"

Instinctively he went uphill toward the road that crossed over the parkway. He didn't need to reason consciously to realize that retracing his steps through the tunnel would invite the nosy Good Samaritan to step on the gas and overtake him. Panting, he skirted a clump of bushes on the slope, crossed the road at the top, and bounded downhill on the dark grass beyond, in great lurching strides toward his own car. Once in it, he kicked the motor into life and roared away. By the time he knew the Good Samaritan wasn't following him, he was doing eighty. He slowed abruptly. No sense in being picked up by the parkway police at this stage.

He turned off at the next crossroad and drove several miles before parking at the roadside. By the map light on the dash he examined Crystal Day's handbag. There was nothing in it but the usual feminine gear—

lipstick, cleansing tissues, and a mess of random trifles. Nothing written. He snapped the catch shut and after wiping the smooth leather clean of fingerprints with a piece of the cleansing tissue left the bag on the seat. No matter if the police found it. He wanted the two cars tied together in the official mind.

Getting out, he took a bottle of water from the trunk and washed his hands and arms. There was a change of clothing in a suitcase. He stripped to the skin and put on clean duplicates of everything he had been wearing. The garments had been ready in the suitcase for a week. Planning! Careful, intelligent planning!

The discarded clothing and shoes, with the bloodstains that were surely on them somewhere, went into the suitcase. He had a sheet of thick brown paper to wrap them in so that the lining wouldn't get even the slightest stain. When he had finished he wiped the steering wheel and front seat carefully with a dry cloth to erase any stains that might soil his fresh clothing.

He slipped behind the wheel then and drove along back roads toward Scarborough. It wouldn't do to take this car home. The right front fender beyond any doubt had traces of red paint on it from the convertible. He had read enough in the magazine articles about police work to know that the laboratory men could identify even a small trace of paint with their spectroscopes. And if he left the car at the repair shop on Fifty-sixth Street and asked Pete Krawcik for a quick body job, he might as well book a seat in that electric thing in the big prison at Ossining, a few miles to the north. Even if Pete didn't leak to someone, the police would be almost sure to snoop around and dig up the information.

On the outskirts of Scarborough he parked the car. He left the key in the ignition. Dangling from it was a chain loaded with keys for the same make of car. He'd been accumulating them quietly for the last month. He wiped the keys clear of fingerprints, but he didn't bother with anything else. It would seem strange if his prints weren't all over the car. He'd used it for weeks.

He walked along lonely streets, carrying the suitcase, his cocoanut straw hat low over his brows, his gray cord summer suit not worth a second glance to anyone who passed him, for you'd see a dozen like it in an hour's stroll anywhere. The sky had clouded, and the air smelled damp.

His schedule was working out well. He had only a brief wait on the station platform before the 9:17 came through. Slumping down in a seat, he took a newspaper from the suitcase, spread it out in front of him and read assiduously without grasping a word . . . keeping the sound of metal-clang and crash-into-concrete and wrench-on-bone from ever slipping into his mind and making his stomach turn the rest of the way over . . . thinking doggedly, Safe! . . . Safe! . . . Safe! but dreading what was just ahead, until after forty minutes the conductor wailed, "Yong-kaaahs," and Baggott walked unobtrusively through the station.

This was the ticklish moment—the one he had liked least of all to think about beforehand. Suppose someone who knew him and who had no business to be here at this hour of a summer evening except by some freak of fate——

He gripped the handle of the suitcase hard to keep from running. But his sidelong glances found no familiar face anywhere. No one bothered to look at him. And now he was out in the sanctuary of the night, headed home.

As he mounted the hill, he noticed that it had been raining heavily here. The gutters were flooded, and a drizzle was still falling, giving him an excuse to lower his head and hide his face. He was just another anonymous commuter, returning late. He had about two miles to walk. Once past Getty Square, he found the streets almost deserted. A block short of his house, he cut across a vacant lot. He knew every foot of the ground here. This spring, Evelyn's garden club had dug up nearly half of it, as in previous years, to raise flowers and fresh vegetables for the crippled children's home. He'd taken his turn with the other husbands, on Saturday mornings, weeding and cultivating the beds. It was raining hard now, and the grass flicked wetness against his socks and pants cuffs along the edge of a waist-high mass of darkness—that would be the white and purple phlox. He felt a wave of almost tearful tenderness wash over him.

Evelyn . . . a sweet girl. Now that all the danger was over and Crystal could no longer threaten, he'd be by-God good to Evelyn. A thank offering. A promise to the dark spirits who had taken care of him through what was after all a pretty crazy venture. But clever. When he thought of how many different ways there had been for it to go wrong, he stopped short for a moment and was hard put to keep from vomiting on the phlox.

He got going again and reached smooth lawn. Home ground. Here were Evelyn's own beds—the ones that she worked in, in faded blue denim slacks and a crimson halter and a big straw sun hat and grubby gardening gloves, after a Czech man-of-all-work came around and spaded the ground every year. And in the corner under the big willow tree—black fishnet against the rainy sky—this soft heap that he stubbed his toes into was the mulch pile. Organic gardening. That was one of Evelyn's little enthusiasms. She saved all the grass clippings and stalks and leaves and layered them on here with some sort of fertilizer——

A sweet girl. He would spend more time with her now, in quiet and peace. Damned if he hadn't earned it, after going through what no man ought to be forced to go through.

The pitchfork was right there, leaning against the shed. His hand found it, gripped the wet, smooth handle. Make a hollow here, in the soft, silent stuff. Then open the suitcase. Bury the bundle of clothing deep. Cover it with forkful after forkful of the mulch. It would be safe here until trash-burning. Then he could pick the clothes out of there and destroy them piece by piece in the bonfire of fallen willow limbs and other odds and ends unsuitable for the mulch.

He let himself indoors quickly, for he had left lights burning in the front of the house, and he didn't want anyone to glimpse him. He wasn't afraid Evelyn would be there to ask questions. She'd planned for a month to attend the convention in Washington, and she wouldn't be back until day after tomorrow.

He swung the valise to its place on a shelf in the hall closet, slipped on a raincoat over his wet suit, hung up his hat, grabbed an umbrella, and went out through the front door.

At the curb he paused, looked up and down the gleaming-wet street with elaborate uncertainty, walked down the block as far as the darkened Courtney house, returned, stood under the street lamp rubbing his jaw in a pantomime of perplexity, and then crossed under the tall arches of the elms and mounted the steps of the house opposite his own. Mrs. Denker always sat up late on summer evenings, watching the last stir of activity before the neighborhood went to sleep.

A small, reedy voice said from the shadows of the porch, "Good evening, Mr. Baggott."

"Good evening, Mrs. Denker. I hate to bother you. But something queer has happened."

The voice rose to a shrill piping. "Woo-oo! Hatt-eee! Light, please."

The dumpy Denker housekeeper and practical nurse, shapeless in a kitchen apron, appeared behind the screen door, silhouetted against a dim glow from the rear of the hall. An overhead bulb went on, revealing in the corner of the porch an elderly woman in a wheel chair. In spite of the warmth of the evening, a light blanket was spread over her legs, and a brushed-wool jacket, bluish-gray like her hair, covered her thin shoulders. When she spoke her hands lay dead in her lap, but her head and lips moved animatedly, and her small dark eyes were a living dance of curiosity.

"You said something queer happened, Mr. Baggott."

"Both my cars are gone."

"I saw one of them. A red convertible, parked right out in front there. The one your wife's been using for the last week."

Good, Baggott thought. He'd known the old girl would keep tabs. She was the Recording Angel of the block, as far as her vivid black eyes could reach.

"After Evelyn did some last-minute shopping in it this morning," he said, "I drove her to La Guardia in my own car. She took a plane to Washington."

"That women's league? Vote With Knowledge?"

"That's right. I came home from the office early in the afternoon, watched a ball game on TV, fell asleep on the couch, and woke up hungry just a little while ago. I started to go downtown to get a hamburger, and then I was going to put both cars away in the garage. As soon as I stepped out of the house I noticed Evelyn's convertible was gone."

"The red car?"

"Yes."

The dark old eyes sparkled happily. "Well, now. I can tell you what happened to it. About seven o'clock a young man walked up and got right into it and drove it off."

"A young man?"

"Tall. Broad shoulders. Short haircut. Wearing a tan suit. Had kind of a snub nose. Looked like Van Johnson, some. Last time I was to the movies—four, no, five years ago—I saw Van Johnson in——"

"Did he use a key?"

"That's right. He opened the door with a key and started the motor immediately. Didn't fool around or fumble. I thought sure he must be one of your men. Every once in a while somebody drives a car to your house or takes one away."

"I'm in the business, and the help keeps changing. But nobody was supposed to take this particular car away. And when I went down the street a little way to get my own car just now, it was gone too. I left it in front of the Courtney house."

Mrs. Denker's bright glance went rueful. "Oh, my. I can't see that far for the trees."

Baggott said, "Too bad." He had parked his car there for that very reason. The Courtneys were away for the summer, and there was a vacant lot opposite them. Early that evening no one could have seen Chester Baggott slip out of his house, take the back way through the Courtney driveway, get into the car and set out for a trip up the parkway that ended in a rendezvous at a concrete abutment.

"Anyway, I think you've turned up something, Mrs. Denker," he said. "There's a young hoodlum been hanging around my service garage in New York, and he answers to the description you just gave me. If he's the one, I owe you thanks for spotting him. You'd make a good investigator. You notice details."

"Oh, my lands! I'm just a nosy old woman, sitting here gawking at the neighbors."

"You've been a very great help to me," Chester Baggott said earnestly.

He patted her shoulder, all fluffy wool outside and thin bone within, and returned across the street to his own house. As soon as he had shed his waterproof and his wet suit coat, he telephoned the police.

"This is Chester Baggott. I want to report two of my cars stolen."

The desk man's voice warmed up. "How are you, Mr. Baggott? *Two* cars! We got to do something about that. What happened?"

Baggott repeated the story he had told Mrs. Denker. He liked the policeman's reaction. Undoubtedly it was a by-product of the gold honorary badge. When he hung up the telephone, he moved his shoulders vigorously inside the damp shirt, feeling the tension slacken and run out of him.

He strode into the living room, ready to sit down and relax. The crazy, walk-the-chalkline scheme couldn't have gone any better. Crystal was dead and no longer a threat to his whole pattern of life. The young punk, Tripp, was dead and identified by Mrs. Denker as the boy who had used stolen keys to run off with the car in which the two were killed. Not a link left behind to connect Chester Baggott in any other way with either of them.

Now jubilation could run unchecked through his body and mind. All the careful planning had paid off. In retrospect some of it seemed foolishly complicated. That business about getting the kid to forge his own baptismal certificate. Throwing a rock through the rectory window, so the punk could swipe a blank form. But it hadn't been silly. It had been only a well-reasoned precaution. The boy was a made-to-order tool—a gift of fate that might never be repeated; and suppose he'd been picked up on the way to the chosen spot, arrested for some trifling traffic-law violation. Without a license, he'd be through as a weapon against Crystal; with it, he'd get by to be used another day. The chance that such a thing would happen might be only one in a million, but it was those freak little things a man had to plan for and guard against.

And Baggott had planned. God, how he'd planned. And won! He started back toward the kitchen to mix himself a drink. He could afford to take one now. No more need to have every nerve unblurred and ready for—— Something moved, in the shadows of the dining room.

Every muscle in Baggott's body jerked. A cool and remote someone in the back compartment of his consciousness said, "Quiet down. If you leap like this at a noise, what will you do when the police begin to ask innocent questions, just for information?" while his hand darted out to the wall switch and snapped on the ceiling fixture.

At the sight of what stood on the other side of the shiny surface of the dining table, with its spray of yesterday's flowers in a glass bowl, he felt his heart lurch.

He said, "Lord God almighty."

SEVEN

JOEY KNEW he was still alive because his chest hurt him at every breath. For a few seconds he was content to remain still in the darkness, eyes closed, feeling the pain every time he sucked air, glad to know he was not dead.

After a little, he moved his fingers. His left hand was on something slender and smooth. That would be the steering wheel. He ran his palm along the cool arc of the plastic. It was bent down away from him in a curious, unnatural curve. He remembered bracing himself, arms stiff, shoulders jammed back in a desperate hope that by using all his frantic strength he could keep the crash of the car from hurling him through the windshield or crushing his chest. He remembered the smash and his head and body smacking into the wheel like the crack of a whip. His rigid arms must have bent the wheel into the odd sag that he felt now.

He moved his right hand. It rested on something smooth and curved but much larger around than the plastic. Softly firm. Faintly warm. His fingers moved further and touched cloth. Nylon?—sheer and tight over the delicately resilient column of——

The girl. His hand, as he snatched it away from her leg, struck the bulk of something wadded into her stocking top.

His head was clearing fast. As awareness came back, panic crept in with it. He had to do something quickly—— He wasn't sure what.

He reached across the still form beside him and fumbled for the door of the dash compartment. The shock of the pile-up had burst it open. Rummaging among a mess of maps and cleansing tissues, he gripped the cylinder of a flashlight. The beam struck the windshield, turning it into a spiderweb of fine white shatter-lines against the darkness of outer night. There, at the center of the radiating threads of fracture, this dark stain must be where the girl's head had——

He swallowed hard, feeling his stomach squirm. In spite of the chest pain he breathed deeply several times to gain control of himself, drawing in the scent of the shrubbery and freshly cut grass along the edge of the parkway and hearing the peeping of tree frogs shake the air as the pounding of his heart shook his body.

Light bloomed on the edges of the car, and he switched off the flash before two cars whipped by and disappeared into the cavern of the underpass. Night collapsed into blackness again. But he couldn't tell when a state police car, patrolling, would see this wreck and stop. Or some driver would pull up and try to help.

He flicked the flash on again. The girl was a tumble of wide-flung limbs. After the crash she had been tossed back from her impact with the windshield and had piled up limply sideways on the seat. Her head was twisted toward the right side of the car. He was thankful he couldn't see much of it. Her skirt had rucked up over her thighs. One leg stretched out in a graceful curve, the toe almost touching the purse that lay on the floor under the brake pedal. The other leg was curled up on the seat. Joey Tripp could see plainly, through the nylon, that the lump he had felt was a thick wad of folded bills tucked down into the stocking on the inside of the thigh.

One arm lay casually across her middle, under the hillock of her left breast. He took the wrist in his fingers. There was no flutter of a pulse. Even though he knew it was useless, he fought down squeamishness and bent over, thinking to press his ear against the thin dress just below the mound of the breast to listen for the faintest thud of life, but the posture brought his chest against her hipbone and sent agony through him. He coughed, and the spasm was a knife between his ribs. From the cloth near his face, a spicy, heavy perfume filled his lungs and conquered the clean smell of growing leaves.

He straightened up, mouth dry, face wet. His head hurt now, and his left hand felt queer. It was puffed to twice its normal size. He thought dully, When my head snapped down onto the wheel, my hand was there and acted as a bumper, or I'd have got a fractured skull.

At once he was angry with himself for thinking of anything so unimportant when he ought to be acting swiftly and decisively. He had to get to Mr. Baggott. Mr. Baggott would know what to do.

Right now Joey Tripp mustn't be found here with the dead girl. The police might check on his driving license, and if they ever found out, he was in a bad jam. He didn't know what they'd be able to hold him for. Vehicular homicide, anyway. And if they found out about the forgery of the baptismal certificate, he'd be in real trouble. Get going, Joey! Find Mr. Baggott!

He gripped the door handle and then released it again. What about the money? Anyone who stopped to examine the wreck could see that roll of bills at a glance. Joey reached for the edge of the dead girl's skirt, to pull it down and cover her thigh. But what about Mr. Baggott?

Sour in Joey's mouth, along with a salty stickiness, was the taste of knowledge that he hadn't let himself think about before now. Crystal Day, beautiful and gay like the red convertible, had been Mr. Baggott's floozy. The same sort as the girls that men went to visit in certain apartments of that building on the corner of the avenue.

The gutter wisdom of his city years turned the corners of Joey's mouth down. So what? You drive for the boss. He says take someone somewhere, you take her. It's a job. You get smashed up on that job when some dopey driver goofs, it's up to the boss to get you out of the jam. And it's up to you to look out for the boss's property.

Joey's fingers found the wad of bills in the darkness. He drew it from under the nylon, shivering when the elastic edge of the stocking slipped free and made a little spatting sound against the still flesh.

A squirt of light from the torch and a riffle of his thumb on the edges of the crisp paper showed him mostly fifties and twenties. He felt around under the brake pedal and retrieved her purse. There were two tens and a few smaller bills in it. He took them and dropped the purse to the floor.

The door opened stiffly when he twisted the handle. He stepped out on the grass and ran his hands gingerly over his chest. It was agonizingly sore. He wondered if any ribs were broken. He coughed and spat. His mouth tasted salty again. As he retrieved his jacket from the car, somewhere out of the darkness a little chuff-chuff-chuff grew louder. Feet on concrete. Someone hurrying in this direction on foot along the parkway.

Joey bent low and made for the dark mounded mass of bushes that showed against the high sky line of the overpass. When low branches scratched and plucked at him he crouched under them and watched. By starshine he could see the shape of the car against the light concrete of the abutment. A whitish blur moved toward it across the grass. A match scratched, glowed and went out. A moment later it was replaced by a sudden steady patch of light. The newcomer had found the flashlight on the seat where Joey had left it. Against its glow Joey could see a white-shirted figure leaning to peer into the car.

And then, in a haze of indistinct motion, another form rushed from somewhere, and there was a sound of blows, and the flashlight went out. One of those guys, Joey thought, was pounding the upholstery of the car for some crazy reason. And yet it didn't sound quite like that, but harder and sharper.

Down the parkway two bug eyes of light came around the curve, straightened out and threw their beams in this direction. As they drew nearer, they slowed down and angled over the edge of the grass, pointed straight this way. They picked up the form of a man in a darker shirt, leaning into the car now. Joey thought how wise he'd been to save Mr. Baggott's money.

There was something white lying on the grass. Must be the other guy. Maybe they'd fought over who'd get to rob the car, and one of them knocked the other cold.

Suddenly the man leaning into the car pulled himself out and ran up the slope, head low, right at the bushes where Joey was belly-to-earth. The sore ribs winced in fear of being trodden on, but Joey remained frozen-still. Flash of memory from his boyhood years on the farm at Lake Placid: a chick crouching like a stone in the dust while the hen cackled furious sounds that meant "Hawk! Hawk!"

Feet pounded past, leaves swished, and a backlash of twigs raked Joey's head. Some man was shouting, "You! Come back here! What goes on?"

Joey didn't want any more of it. Painfully he slid himself backward until the bushes hid the cars. Then he snaked his way uphill to the road that crossed over the parkway. He got to his feet, shielded by the stone wall, and followed the road until he could turn down the arc of the clover-leaf intersection that joined the southbound lane of the parkway. A row of poplars, dark spires against the sky, stood along the dividing strip and shut off any view of the wrecked convertible.

He didn't expect any of the cars that occasionally boomed past out of the archway to stop for him. Three of them swept by before the thing he was hoping for happened. A sedan came down the clover leaf from the side road and pulled up at the stop sign. A man was driving, alone.

Joey said, "I got to get to Yonkers, mister. It's an emergency. Mind giving me a lift?"

"Sure, climb in," the man said.

Joey settled back on the cushions and watched the parkway come flowing at him down the tunnel of light that the headlights made. It began to waver crazily. He fought off a weakness that started him swooping through cold space in long, wild spirals.

"What's your emergency, bub?" The driver was a stout man with a pleasant voice.

"I was hurrying home because I got word my father had a stroke. My old coop broke down, back there a ways. Water pump. I had to park on the grass and start thumbing." Joey coughed again, his ribs knifed him, and he wiped the salty taste off his lips with his handkerchief. It was the one with the tan border that he'd bought to go with the gabardine suit he was wearing. He remembered the lift it had given him when he bought it with the first money Mr. Baggott had given him. It was his start toward the big things.

As the driver droned on, in his bumbling, friendly way, about people he'd known who'd recovered from strokes and about his own high blood pressure and the different things doctors had told him to do for it, Joey closed his eyes and made occasional grunting noises, to ease his pain and to keep from having to answer.

He was roused by the slowing of the car.

"I'm going to pull in here at Kitchawan," the driver said. "A sandwich and a cup of coffee won't hurt us. It's been a long time since dinner."

Joey's legs shook as he walked across the hard surface of the parking lot. In the high-ceiled room he stared at the moose head mounted over the fireplace and ate mechanically.

"Don't take it hard, kid," the stout man said kindly. "You'll find everything's going to be all right when you get home."

Joey thought, I've got to make Mr. Baggott understand it wasn't my fault. I was making good with him. Big money. Clothes. Everything I'd been out to get. And honest and square, except for that thing about the driving license. It didn't make any never-mind to me what the girl was. I was just driving her someplace.

The stout man talked and talked and ordered more coffee, and the people eating at the tables put coins into gaudy boxes on the wall and punched plastic keys that made drooly music slop around in the air from the juke-box records until Joey gasped coffee up into his throat and swallowed it again and coughed and squeezed his arms against his aching chest, wanting to shout, "Can't we go? I've got to find Mr. Baggott!"

An hour must have crawled by before they were on the road. It was almost as long again before the stout man dropped Joey off on Broadway in Yonkers. Any corner, Joey said. Any corner at all.

The streets down there were wet from a shower, and rain began to fall again as he walked toward the house where he had picked up the red convertible earlier in the evening—so long ago. He was almost there when he had another spell of coughing. He spat into the gutter, and when he wiped his mouth with the tan-bordered handkerchief, he saw by the glow of a street light that the cloth was smeared red.

You may be hurt bad, Joey. Think fast. You *got* to. Orders are never to phone Mr. Baggott or come to his house to see him. But this is special. If you're careful——

He stopped in a little candy store on a corner, looked up Mr. Baggott's number, and dialed it. He waited in the muggy booth for minutes, listening to the ringing signal in the receiver. There was no answer.

He walked through the rain to a street corner from which he could see the house. Dim lights glowed behind the windows downstairs. Better wait here until Mr. Baggott came home. But then suppose there was someone with him. Joey wouldn't dare go up to the door and ring the bell. Mr. Baggott would blast him for disobeying orders, and things were bad enough as they were.

He waited in miserable indecision. The rain beat harder on his bare head, running cold down his neck and shoulders and his shivering chest, warmer when it began to slide inside his clothes and heat itself up along his skin. The trees weren't any shelter. They gathered the rain into big drops that landed on his scalp like buckshot.

I can stick it out until he comes, Joey thought, bowing his head like a bull caught in a blizzard. And then somehow the tree trunk he was leaning against moved away, and the earth wavered and wobbled, and he found himself on his hands and knees, up to his wrists in a puddle.

Panic shook him as he lurched to his feet. Faint here, and someone'd find him—call an ambulance—cops——

He stumbled off through the light-splashed darkness. His feet made squashy noises in his sodden shoes. Past the corner street lamp and down the side street he found an open space from which he could see the back of the house. The windows there were dark. He stood swaying for a while in the pounding rain before he set off, floundering and tripping, across the rough turf. For a while then he blundered across ridges of muddy earth. He fell once, and his hands landed on growing plants lined up along the crests. He knew he was crossing a vegetable garden.

At last he reached the house and moved along it, arms extended, until his fingers touched and closed on the wet metal railing of a set of back steps. He stumbled up them and tried the knob of the door. It turned. He lurched through the opening, closed the door behind him, and stood motionless, listening and sniffing for signs of human presence. Linoleum under his feet. A feeble glimmer on white enamel and suspended copper-ware.

A sudden chugging sound made his heart bounce. It was followed by a steady vibration that came up through the floor and set his legs shaking again. Only the refrigerator, kicking on after a rest period.

A faint smell of stale cigar butt came on the slow current of air that moved from the yellow rectangle of doorway into this dark kitchen. Some-one had smoked in this house, but not recently.

He plodded from the kitchen into a hallway that led to the front door. A ceiling globe shed a subdued radiance. He didn't want to be in the light. He slop-footed his way to a door and found himself in a room with a dining table, a sideboard, shelves of glassware and china, and some straight chairs, all dimly visible by the light of a lamp in the adjacent living room.

He didn't like to spoil any furniture with his sopping clothes. And he preferred to keep out of sight. There was a screen sort of thing—three panels hinged together—standing beside the sideboard. Bamboo or some-thing equally light. It moved easily when he took hold of it. He slumped to the floor behind its flimsy shelter, resting his hot forehead on his wet, drawn-up knees. Once in a while he coughed and used his handkerchief.

He was lapsing into semiconsciousness when the latch of the back door clicked and feet thumped through the hall. A man passed the door of the dining room so fast that Joey couldn't tell who he was and didn't dare to move. He waited to get a better glimpse of him.

Strangely enough, the man opened the front door, and his steps receded and died as the door closed. Joey couldn't figure why anyone would come in out of the rain by the back door and then go right out again by the front door. A long while passed, and Joey was so stiff and cramped that he was about to stretch himself when the front door opened, and almost immediately he heard the sound of dialing and then a voice talking over the telephone. With a qualified feeling of relief, he recognized the voice as Mr. Baggott's. He braced himself to start his explanation, expecting a stiff bawling-out at the best. As he straightened his stiffened joints and began to ease himself to his feet, his mind took in the gist of what Mr. Baggott was saying to the phone, and he remained crouched, listening incredulously.

Police . . . young hoodlum . . . Baggott had seen him loitering around the garage . . . had asked the mechanics about him . . . named Throop or Trapp or something like that . . . lived near the garage . . . probably stole car keys while he was hanging around the place . . . a neighbor across the street here had watched a boy who answered his description drive one car away early this evening . . . maybe one of a gang, because both cars were missing.

Joey stood shivering, feeling the darkened dining room swoop and dive around him. He knew he had to get away from here fast, but he was afraid to move for fear he would fall flat on the floor. Then there were footsteps, and the lights went on.

EIGHT

BAGGOTT'S MOUTH was dry. His right forearm remembered the feeling as the wrench, swung down on bone, had sent the shock back up through his wrist. His fingers remembered the splatter of wet from the burst skull.

But across the table this damnable boy leaned his hands on the polished wood to hold himself up; his head sagged from weakness, but the wet dark-blond hair was plastered to a skull that hadn't a mark on it.

Who was it I killed?

Baggott said, "I thought you'd be in Saratoga by now, Joey. What happened?"

He took a few steps around the table.

The boy circled away from him, still holding to the table edge. His eyes were wide in a paper-white face. His voice was a hoarse whisper. "It was you . . . in the other car. Rode me off . . . into the wall."

"What are you talking about, son?"

The boy frowned, blinked his glazed eyes, trying to think his way through. "You slugged some guy was looking into the car. Knocked him out."

"You're sick, Joey. You're delirious." Sweat was coming out on Baggott again. He felt a drop start from one armpit and tickle his ribs. He had to get his hands on this boy.

"Don't come any closer to me, Mr. Baggott," Joey said. "I'll yell. You just told the cops you were talking to a neighbor across the street a few minutes ago. So if I holler, someone'll hear me."

Baggott's foot halted in its stealthy motion. "You can't yell, Tripp. It'll bring the police. You'll be picked up. And I guess you realize by now you're in a bad position."

"Yeah . . . You put me in a bad position, Mr. Baggott. You piled me up in a wreck. That was you in the sedan that rode me off into the concrete wall. You tried to kill me."

Joey scowled, trying to concentrate. "Was it the girl? Did you have to get rid of her?"

Baggott ran a forefinger slowly along his wet upper lip. His mind was questing nimbly. Where do you hide a body, starting from scratch in your own living room? He's too big to put under the mulch pile. You can't drive him away somewhere and dump him. Both your cars are gone, remember? And you can't let his body lie around here while you go down to the salesroom and pick up another car. Somebody might just happen to come in and find him. A grave in the garden takes a lot of digging. People might see you at it. Under the concrete floor of the cellar? You haven't any cement to do the patching. But you could buy it; it's something any homeowner might need. And you can take all the time you need down there, digging and laying a new section of floor. Ev won't be back from the women voters thing for two days.

His thoughts must have showed in some tensing of the muscles, some gathering of force preparatory to his move, for the boy's dull eyes widened in alarm. "Keep away! I tell you I'll yell! Don't——"

Young Tripp tried to lurch toward the door that led to the kitchen, but Baggott's rubber-soled shoes made three planned strides around the table, gripping the hardwood boards surely. His hands smashed through the boy's feeble guard and had the young throat in their clutch, crushing the first exhalation of a scream.

He drove hard with hand grip on the neck and with hip against the boy's belly, pinning him to the wall, smothering his attempts to punch and claw and knee and kick. The pale young face close to Baggott's darkened to red, to purple; the eyes grew wide—blue marbles on white saucers; the tongue, a glistening crimson hunk of meat, came out of the agonized mouth, reaching for the air that couldn't pass the vise of Baggott's fingers; and the doorbell shrieked across the panting silence.

Baggott's reactions were instinctive—first, to relax his grip in panic, and then, to tighten it again, in a spasm of hope. Freeze! Whoever it is may go away! The boy's struggles are growing feebler. A minute more, and you can drag his body to the basement stairs, tip it down, shut the door on it and answer——

The bell trilled again. Twice. Something soft and solid—a fist?—thumped the frame of the screen door, and a voice said, "Police." It was a clear masculine voice, with the calm ring of authority.

Baggott's stomach muscles knotted. The boy sagged lifelessly, too big and too heavy to be held erect by the throat. As Baggott's fingers loosened, the inert body folded to the dining-room floor.

"Police, Mr. Baggott," the voice outside said again, deprecatingly but positively. It went on, evidently directing the words toward a companion somewhere. "May be something wrong. I guess I better go in."

Baggott strode through the living room to the foyer. A blue-clad young officer under the lighted porch lantern removed his cap. "Sergeant Lowery, Mr. Baggott. They put the call on the radio—about you getting both your cars stolen." He jerked a thumb toward the street, and Baggott saw that there was a police prowl car out there. "So we hopped it right over here. We wanted to give you some quick action. Naturally. Account of you went to bat for us on the salary raise."

Baggott was carrying on a silent feud with his own ribs. They wanted to heave in and out, sucking great noisy blasts of air. He fought them hard, making them draw it down deeply but silently. He answered the young policeman's friendly smile with a matching one. He said, "Well . . ." and waved a hand modestly, as if at a loss for words. He didn't dare to talk much, or he'd break into panting. And maybe this friendly young man was like other bright young cops you meet these days—eager to get ahead and alertly fond of asking why and how and where and who. He was tugging a notebook out of his pocket now.

"Can you let me have all the facts, Mr. Baggott? They got the license numbers over the phone from you, and it's on the teletype now. But most likely they'll find the cars abandoned somewhere."

"I guess it was just a kid prank," Baggott said.

"This young guy that Mrs. Denker saw drive your car away, now," the policeman said. "Can you give me some more dope on him?"

"I really don't know much about the boy." Except that he's lying dead on the dining-room floor. "I'd noticed him . . . hanging around the garage evenings . . . and I asked one of the night men . . . who he was . . . just a kid fooling around."

"Did you call the garage since it happened? They might know something that would help us or the Manhattan police to pick him up." The sergeant looked at Baggott expectantly, then let his gaze roam around the foyer with the chronically curious glance of the well-trained police officer. His eyes settled on the telephone on the hall table. "We might do it right now."

Anything to get rid of him quickly, Baggott thought. He dialed the garage number and said, "Mr. Baggott speaking. Give me Tim Meagher."

He pulled out the small bench from under the table, gestured toward it and handed the instrument to Sergeant Lowery. "You know better than I do what you want to ask him."

He tried to stand there, unconcerned, while the terse questions went on, punctuated by pauses and scribblings in the notebook that the sergeant had laid on the telephone table. After all, they'd never pick the boy up this way. The problem was back there on the other side of the dining-room wall.

Baggott's legs moved in spite of him. The turmoil in his middle compelled him. Not directly toward . . . it. That would be idiocy. But straight back to the kitchen. Snap on the light. Take a bottle of beer from the refrigerator. Excellent pretext. Hold it up to the sergeant's gaze, with an inviting lift of the eyebrows. Accept his smiling negative shake of the head with an understanding nod. Of course . . . not while on duty.

And then——

He walked slowly to the doorway that led from kitchen to dining room, with a random, half-formed purpose dawning over the horizon of his dread. Perhaps to lift the thing and shift it where it couldn't be seen readily. But mightn't there be some unavoidable noise? Maybe just move something in front of it. The screen! Light to lift. It would easily hide a body——

What body? The floor was bare.

With his diaphragm rebelling, Baggott walked back to the kitchen. Through the metal mesh door, a fresh wind blew in from the rain-washed darkness of the back garden.

He heard Sergeant Lowery say, "Well, if he should happen to come into the garage, detain him and get word to the police. We want him picked up for questioning."

For questioning. The words were like melted lead in Baggott's ears. He thanked Sergeant Lowery, saw him to the door, and watched him go down the steps toward the waiting prowl car—all in a sort of whirling daze. Then he went back to the living room, threw himself into a chair and fixed wide, vacant eyes on the ceiling.

This was it. This ripped it. The kid would spill his gizzard. It didn't matter how much the police believed what young Tripp would say. But Evelyn—— Once let her get her suspicions aroused by the mention of a kept woman, and that ironclad passion for honesty would start her delving until she satisfied herself she knew the truth, no matter where it led her.

Then get to the boy before the police do! . . . Yes? How? . . . You can't go running madly all over Yonkers and Manhattan, asking for the boy. Even if you could find him, you'd be leaving a trail a yard wide. Then if anything happened to him, the cops would wonder. They'd trace your movements.

Nothing. There was nothing for him to do now except go through the motions of innocence and wait, hour by hour—day by day, maybe—for the catastrophe to come and get him. Just wait like this, with his nerves screaming at him and his belly trying to wriggle up into his mouth, while the time grated by, a heart thump at a time.

He sat up suddenly, clenched his fists and began to pound them on his knees. *If I could get my hands on him again——*

He walked back to where the beer stood on the kitchen drain board, growing flat. He threw it into the sink, snatched a bottle of bourbon from the liquor cabinet, took a quick slug that burned his gullet and then mixed a highball with ice and soda.

He sat in the living room for a long while, sipping. He was turning the empty glass slowly round and round in his fingers when the thumping on the door came again. He let Sergeant Lowery in.

"They picked up the kid," the policeman said. "We just got word."

What do I do now? Baggott thought sourly. Hold out my hands for cuffs already? Do American cops warn you, "Anything you say may be used against you in evidence"?

"I saw your lights were still on," Sergeant Lowery said, "and I thought you'd like to know."

"Sure I'd like to know. Tell me all about it." And what do I do then? Give you a reward? Kiss your hand?

Baggott couldn't stop himself. He asked the question he didn't want to hear the answer to. "What did the boy have to say?"

"Not a word," Lowery answered. "He was dead. He piled the car up against a concrete embankment on the Taconic Parkway. Killed in the crash. The troopers got the report from a passing motorist and found him in the wreck with some girl. We got it just now on the teletype."

Baggott fought for self-control. Relief was a more disrupting shock than fear. "A girl?" He raised his brows. *You don't know about any girl, remember?* "These kids! I suppose she told you the usual story—out for a ride, and she didn't know it was a stolen car."

"She was killed, too. Smashed up—but good."

Baggott clicked his tongue. "Well, that's what these juvenile delinquents let themselves in for. Too bad, though. I'm sorry . . . Thanks for letting me know."

When the prowl car drove off again, Baggott turned back into the house after stepping to the porch to see Lowery go. His step was heavy. There was still nothing to jubilate about. This was only a reprieve.

Unless——

If he could only get to that boy before the police realized it wasn't Joey Tripp who had been killed.

NINE

IT HAD BEEN RAINING in New York, and the air was still filled with fine moisture. Joey stood at the gutter edge, feeling the drizzle tickle the side of his face. He was heading for home, because there wasn't anyplace else to go. In a daze of pain and shock, he had crept along the dining-room floor of Mr. Baggott's house and escaped through the kitchen, not daring to wait to find out what lucky chance had saved him from the roaring fog of unconsciousness that had been closing down on him. His throat was bruised and sore from Mr. Baggott's clutch.

He could remember only vaguely the details of his flight—the stumbling across wet earth to the street, the bus at Getty Square that took him to the city line. The climb up the long stairs to the subway train that trundled along an elevated structure for station after interminable station until it dived into the thundering underground.

But should he go home? Doubt was beginning to check the panic of his flight toward the only safety he knew. His uncertainty seemed to be mimicked by a neon sign over a bar and grill, washing by turns a flood of cheerful red and then a pall of sickly blue-green across the shiny wetness of the sidewalk. If he didn't go home, where could he go?

A hand took him by the arm and thrust him along the sidewalk. He tried to twist and run, but the big fist gripped him and shoved him staggering across the shimmering gridwork of fire and ice reflected in the rain-blackened pavement.

"Why'd ye come here, ye young *omadhaun?*"

"Tim!" Joey's voice emerged in a croak. Pain lanced his throat at the effort.

"Into the ginmill here, ye *gomeral,* before someone sees ye."

Tim Meagher hustled Joey into the grill and into a booth beyond the dimly lighted bar.

"A beer and a burger, Nildo," he said to the Puerto Rican waiter. "D'ye want annything, lad?"

Joey shook his head. When the waiter had gone, Tim leaned forward over the table and spoke in a rough, low voice. "Lucky I was out to get meself a bite to eat an' seen ye before they could grab ye . . . Why did ye do it, boy?"

Through the haze that was gathering before his eyes again—*am I bleeding to death inside?*—Joey blinked at the rugged Irish features, made grimmer by a half-healed scar along the jaw where a chain hoist had broken and ripped the mechanic's face a few weeks before.

"It wasn't my fault, Tim. He ran me off the——"

"Is it never a man's fault that he's a *gomeral?* That's what we call it in the ould country, boy. A thief."

"You got no right to call me——"

"Who gives a damn what ye call it? Hot rodder. Joy rider. Just a kid wid rocks in the skull, havin' a ball for himself. Good clane fun."

"Let me tell you how——"

Tim raked a set of broken, grease-darkened fingernails down Joey's sleeve, hushing him while Nildo clacked the glass of beer down on the crimson plastic surface of the table. While the waiter went for the hamburger, Tim said, "The boss put the cops on the phone to ask me about ye. They're lookin' for ye, Joey."

Joey coughed, felt for the handkerchief, changed his mind and reached for Tim's glass. A swallow of the cold, bitter-bubbly beer eased the pain in his throat.

"They don't have to look for me. I'll go to them and tell them how it happened. I can explain it." But he knew he wouldn't dare to.

"Musha! an' ye're the one can do it," Tim said darkly. "The way ye'd talk to me nights—about the things ye were goin' to do someday—ye'd talk a bird out of a hedge. Ye *gomeral!"*

"Don't call me a thief, Tim," Joey said. "Mr. Baggott let me have that car. He *ordered* me to take it."

Tim Meagher studied his beer as if it were cyanide. Without lifting his head, he raised his small eyes and peered at Joey through scraggly red brows. "So that's yer story . . . Ah, well, the worst they can do is send ye to reform school . . . Where's the car?"

Joey shivered. "Wrecked." He had to tell somebody. "Tim, there was a girl. She's dead. I can't go to the cops and explain how it happened. They wouldn't believe me."

Tim tapped a big, mutilated fingernail on the back of the boy's hand. "Hould yer tongue!" he said, deep in his chest.

After a little, he wiped the palm of a hand across his long upper lip. "I ought to turn ye in, but I fought the Black and Tans in Dublin when I was no older than ye are, an' I seen too many informers in me time. Go away from here, boy, before I lay hands on ye meself. I hope to Christ if I ever have a son o' me own he won't turn out like you. Get out o' me sight, ye murrderin' thief."

He was still sitting there, his heavy workman's shoulders slumped over the table, when Joey walked out of the bar into the rain.

Nowhere to go. The police might be looking for him at Gram's. They'd be looking for him everywhere. He coughed and tasted the blood in his mouth again. He didn't dare to see a doctor. The police might have an alarm out for anyone who acted as if he'd been injured in a car crash.

He shambled into the side street, but short of where he lived he turned in at an entrance fronted by three brownstone steps. He knew the street door was never locked. A narrow hallway, poorly lighted, painted a malarial yellow, led to the stairs. He climbed three flights, gasping, clinging to the iron railings but setting his feet down carefully, silently on the stone treads. As he turned to face another flight, he caught a murmur of voices and halted.

A girl said in an irate whisper, "But why can't you? You keep all the time telling me how much you love me."

A boy's unhappy mumble answered, "God, Laurie, I don't make that kind o' money."

"Dino gave Stella one. And Shirley has a steady that only last Valentine's day—look, it wasn't even her birthday or Christmas or anything——"

"Sweetie, if I had the chips——"

"Don't sweetie me, Tony Marchand. If I really mean so awful much to you I should think you would somehow or another find a method or a means——"

The boy's voice rose to an anguished bleat. "I can't *swing* it, baby!"

The girl's reply was airy. "So if you can't, maybe there's other people who——" Her voice changed abruptly. "Ssh! There's somebody——"

Joey rounded the landing below them. "Tony . . . Laurie . . . it's me."

The steps were hard against his knees, smooth against his palms, cool against his face.

They got him up the last half-flight, pulling and lifting.

"Don't let anybody know," he kept mumbling. "The cops . . ."

"What happened, Joey?" Tony asked.

"It was bad . . . bad . . ."

"The new job? The swell deal you took on?"

"I gotta have a place . . . to stay tonight . . ."

The girl whispered excitedly, "The cops, Joey? Are you in the rackets now? That's a sharp suit. It's all wet, but it's a nice——"

Tony said, "Quiet! . . . You go upstairs, Laurie. Go home. Go to bed. I'm going to take Joey in and put him on our couch."

"I'll help. Don't you try to make me go up home, Tony, or I'll start yelling."

Tony said a vile word between his teeth.

The girl giggled. "Anyway, he's hurt. I can help fix him up."

"I'll fix *you* up," Tony muttered, but he made no further remonstrance as she took Joey's other arm.

The threesome wavered down the hall to the door of the Marchand flat. Tony held Joey with one hand and fumbled a key out of his pocket with the other. The door opened on a living room that was dim in the glow of one amber bulb in a table lamp.

Joey, in his half-stupor, did not need to glance around at the familiar surroundings to know what was there—worn overstuffed chairs with not over-clean doilies on the backs and arms; a veneered table and desk, chipped and cigarette-scorched; a cheap record player on an iron stand that held albums of popular disks; and, in one corner, an incongruous luxury—an eleven-hundred-dollar color television set, bought on a weekly payment plan.

"Mom's door is closed," Tony whispered, "and Phil is working tonight, but don't make any noise."

Joey slumped to the couch. He wanted to fall back and let exhaustion have its way with him, but the girl's arm was around his neck.

"Wait, Joey. Where are you hurt? Once you get flat on your back, we can't get your clothes off so easy."

"I'll take care of that!" Tony said sharply.

"Oh, *you!* . . . Where are you hurt, Joey, sweetie?"

"My chest," Joey gasped.

"Hold him, Tony. Keep him sitting up. I'll slip his coat off . . . now his tie."

Joey felt the small warm hands at his neck, at his breasts, deftly undoing buttons. His arms were tugged this way and that. He had neither the will nor the strength to do anything about it. Cool air touched the bared skin of his chest and set him shivering.

"Lay down now, sweetie," the girl whispered, and he let himself go limp. His legs were lifted, and he felt his shoes being drawn off. His toes in the damp socks were immediately cold.

The girl's hands moved about his chest, pressing, stroking. He winced.

"That hurt, Joey? . . . Here, I'll kiss it and make it better."

Her face moved about his breast. Hair brushed his skin . . . tickle of trailing cobwebs . . .

The girl's head was yanked briskly away. Tony's furious whisper said, "You need a good belt in the mouth, Laurie! Let's get him fixed up quick, and you get out of here."

"We got to tape up his chest, Tony. Maybe he's got a cracked rib. Any wide adhesive in the bathroom?"

"No."

"The drugstore's closed . . . When the Red Knights gang beat up on Dino, the doctor taped his chest to keep the broken ribs from moving, so they wouldn't—— Got any wide cloth tape? Maybe we could tie him up with that."

"We got plenty o' *nothin'* in this dump," Tony said sullenly.

"Well, what could we use? . . . Oh, I know."

Joey heard little swishing sounds. Tony said, "Damn it all, Laurie——"

"Oh, pooh! . . . Joey's too groggy to look."

Joey opened his eyes. Laurie had stripped off her dress. It was thrown across a chair. She was pulling her slip off over her head. Her well-filled brassière and snug briefs, outlined against the lamp-glow, accentuated the youthful slimness of her bare midriff and legs.

"Here, Tony, honey—help me tear this into strips. We'll bind him up good."

Joey closed his eyes again and heard sounds like a giant snake's hissing, as the slip was ripped apart.

He lapsed into torpor then, letting them turn and haul him, feeling the tight support of the cloth most welcome around his rib cage. Before he could sink down into the blackness that was waiting for him, he heard the girl say, "Let's get his pants off now, so he can go bye-bye."

As the quick, small hands worked at his belt buckle, he remembered the money he had taken from the dead girl's stocking. It was in the wallet in his hip pocket. He struck at the hands, knocking them away.

As he did so, he heard Tony say, "Jeez, Laurie! stop that! You'll drive me nuts yet . . . Get out o' here and go home before I——"

"Get a blanket, then, and cover him and let him sleep that way. And I'll give you a nice big good-night kiss, only don't be such a big old fusser."

Joey heard a quick scuffle and the girl's avid little love-moans—her routine reaction whenever a boy kissed her, he knew—before he let himself go down into the darkness.

He was climbing a stairway that swayed. The steps were irregularly wide apart. Between them he could see that the ground was terrifyingly far below. The wood of the steps was rotten and badly nailed. It gave way as he scrambled frantically away from the horror that was following him. He dared not look back at it. Now the stairs were only a ladder, rocking drunkenly without support, leading up to a little ramshackle platform fastened loosely to the top. Beyond—nothing.

He turned, at last, to face what was behind him. With intense relief he saw that it was only Crystal Day, smiling her red-lipped smile.

"Why, Joey!" she said, reaching up to pat his foot. Her fingers were icy. "You had me wrong, sugar. You thought I was Baggott's floozy. Didn't you now?"

Joey said, "Well, Miss Day——"

"Call me Crys. I told you that, baby."

"I did think Mr. Baggott was keeping you, Crys. Wasn't he?"

"No, Joey. I was waiting for you. Didn't you know that?"

Joey wanted to believe her. He wanted to cling to the relief and the safety of that moment, but something was happening to Crystal Day's face. It was beautiful still—but changing—the lovely features wavering as if in green water——

And in that instant, the snake that she had become was writhing up the ladder rungs in pursuit of him, had thrown a coil around his throat, squeezing . . . squeezing . . .

He strove to cry out but could not, until the head of the thing, swooping and hissing, crossed before his eyes and he saw its face. It was no longer that of Crystal Day.

"Mr. Baggott . . . Mr. Baggott!" he cried, in dreadful recognition.

He tried to strike at it, as he awoke to cold-sweat consciousness, but the coils held him fast, turning only gradually into the folds of a cheap cotton blanket, stiffish and nubbly against his naked skin.

The face of Baggott was still there, close to his. He gasped and shrank from it. "Mr. Baggott!" he said again. "No! No——"

"What's wrong, Joey?" Mr. Baggott said, in Tony's voice, and Joey gulped air in a passion of reassurance, for it was only Tony after all, sitting beside the couch in a straight chair, bending solicitously over him.

"I got to get away, Tony."

"Where?"

"I don't know." There was nowhere for him to go, no one he knew to take him in. He might as well be still at the top of that nightmare ladder.

"Out o' the city?" Tony asked.

As if the answer had come, fully formed, straight out of the terror-dream, Joey knew exactly where he would go and what he would do.

"Yes. Out of the city." He struggled with the blanket. "Where's my shirt? . . . Tony, would you drive me to Grand Central? Right now?"

"Okay." Tony stood up and began running a finger tip round and round in a tear in the doily on a chair back. "What about your grandma?"

For the first time Joey thought of Gram's worry and anguish. His own pain and fear had been a tight little prison of the mind. He could remember bouncing her around in the Bunny Hop the night he told her, "I'll hang a diamond pin on you . . . as big as the Queen Mary's anchor." He could foresee the gesture of fright and worry—the twig-thin fingers going to the gray-fringed temple—when they came to question her about him.

He said, "I guess I'll have to write to her from wherever I go."

Tony's finger made another circuit of the ragged hole before he said, "And have the cops trace the letter by the postmark?"

"I can mail it from somewhere else."

"You may be on your back for days or weeks, boy. You got a fever. I felt your head. It's like a radiator."

"Tony, will you just tell Gram——?"

"You think she'd believe me? She knows how we cover up for each other when we get in a jam."

"What'll I do?"

"Write her a note. Just a short one. Tell her not to worry, you got to go away for a little while, but it's all right and you'll come back and clear everything up satisfactory. Look, we got some five-and-ten paper somewheres here in the desk, and I got a thirty-nine cent ball-point in my pocket. The cops couldn't trace 'em. And I'll hand the note to your grandma personally."

"Let's do it quick, then, Tony. I want to get away right now."

Joey's head reeled in a hot haze as he sat up, but by a protracted effort he forced the world to stop revolving. He couldn't afford to let it spin wildly for a while yet. Once he got to where he was going, it could whirl at its own crazy will.

He wrote the note at the desk and managed to get dressed somehow while Tony went downstairs and brought the old Chevvy from its overnight parking spot to the door. In the watery dawn light, Joey made a wavering dash across the sidewalk, ducking his head low, and stumbled into the car.

At Grand Central Terminal, there was plenty of space for the Chevvy at the curb that early in the morning. Tony went with Joey into the station and down the ramps to the Oyster Bar. At the counter, Tony had bacon and eggs. Joey tried to force down a few bites of toast, but only the coffee got past his throat. It revived him enough so that when he glanced up he was alert enough to notice the redness of Tony's eyes.

"You sat up all night?"

"Well—you might have been real sick, boy. I didn't know."

Joey felt a wave of emotion like the one he'd felt when Tony mentioned Gram. He reached out and squeezed Tony's wrist. "You're a real pal, Tone."

"Forget it, kid . . . Look, if we want to get you on that train——"

"Let's go."

All the way across the broad expanse of the main concourse, where an enormous blown-up photographic transparency of a mountain vacation scene filled one end of the great room with overpowering brilliance of colored light, Joey's shoulders shuddered with expectation of a clutch from a hand stronger and more fearsome than Tim Meagher's. But now he and Tony were past the gate, and the train stretched out there through the underground dimness in a dwindling vista of windows and doors, and the platform, reaching ahead to infinity, was the pathway to safety.

Tony saw Joey board the train and turned back. That evening he visited Gram and shook his head at her bewildered inquiries.

"The policemen been in asking about Joey. They won't tell me nothing, Tony. Did anything bad happen to him? Oh, my, it's awful. I wonder —Tony, what happened to him?"

He handed her the note. "He's all right. Don't show this to the cops or to anybody."

She peered through her spectacles at the single word of address on the envelope. "That's Joey's writing, all right. 'Grandma.' See, he makes the G always with the tail curled the wrong way, so I always tell him it looks like a Q. The children these days they don't learn how to write good, like when I was a girl."

By now she had thumbed the flap loose and read the brief note. She shook her head doubtfully. "He says he's going to be all right, but I don't know. I hope. I pray. Tony, if you hear anything, let me know. God bless you, Tony; you come here and try to make me feel a little better. You're a good, good boy."

"That's all right, Mrs. Tripp," Tony said awkwardly.

TEN

EVELYN BAGGOTT RELAXED, watching the long, graceful sweep of the cables flowing up to the top of the sun-brightened towers, gleaming against a gray-blue sky. The pendant curves dropped away again as the car mounted the slope of the Whitestone Bridge. In the edge of her field of vision, Chet's strong, able hands controlled the wheel with an efficient minimum of motion. He had driven to La Guardia to meet her plane.

Her contented gaze roved over the wide prospect. To the south, the toy building blocks of Manhattan were almost lost in distance and haze. Below, the blue-black waters led off toward the white specks of houses along the shores of the Sound. Ahead was the Hutchinson River Parkway and home.

She was always glad to come back to it and to Chet, as she was often glad to get away from both. The apparent contradiction was, she thought, part of what she liked to refer to as her "rebel blood." Actually, her ancestors had not been deeply involved in the War Between the States, although a few of her great-uncles had fought on one side or the other.

Nor was she herself at heart entirely a rebel. Her attitude toward life was a blend of reasonable revolt and strong conservatism.

What principles and traditions she chose to consider as authentic and binding she held to firmly. One didn't tell a lie without a tremendously compelling reason or a very minor one—to save a life, yes—or to avoid causing a moment's embarrassment to a stranger—but not to escape one's own personal culpability for a serious breach of conduct. And in matters financial, one accounted scrupulously for the last penny. Evelyn's household accounts were kept in a looseleaf notebook, with the same care she gave to rendering her yearly report as treasurer of the Garden Club.

In matters sexual she set a high value on loyalty, a low one on chastity. Once committed to a mate, one was steadfastly uninterested in extramural dalliance, although beforehand one might have experimented. That she and Chet had reached their mutual understanding through a premarital affair had never given her the slightest feeling of guilt at breaking a law on which she looked as an antiquated convention that had existed when there were no other means to prevent bastardy.

The bridge they were crossing now combined with the physical need she felt after days of separation from Chet to touch off a fleeting memory of the night they had returned across a bridge over the Susquehanna, when he was taking her home to Baltimore after a dance. They were not even engaged then, but when he had parked in a side road and taken her in his arms, the excitement left over from the contact of cheek and body in dancing had responded joyfully to his maleness. In the confines of the car the resultant mating had been a breathlessly awkward venture, marred by the buzzing of mosquitoes and a few distractingly vicious stings at the most intense moment. Later, in the comfort and well-practiced teamwork of the conjugal bed, they had often laughed at the comic aspects of that first coupling.

Warmed by the flash of memory, Evelyn knew that tonight at bedtime she would touch her ears and eyebrows and the hollow of her throat with Péché Gaillard (for users who had no French, the label on the ornate bottle gave the translation in fine type: Gallant Sin), and she knew as well that Chet without a spoken word of acknowledgment would respond to the invitation. It was one of Evelyn's perhaps irrational set of conventions that an attractive woman never invited a man to have relations with her; she granted her favors only in response to ardor. Like most wives, however, who have learned how to set the pace through subtle signals, she had made Péché Gaillard serve as her Pandarus. It was a distinctive fragrance, heavier and more exotic than the light floral scents she usually wore, and its implication was always unmistakable to Chet.

The car drew up before the house. The driveway to the garage was narrow, and usually Chet—or Evelyn, if she was driving—put the car away only at night. By day they preferred to find a spot under the shade of the maples that were spaced out along the block. As Chet lifted her bags from the trunk, Evelyn saw in the shadowed recess of the veranda across the street a pale oval of face, with two dark dots of observant eyes. She raised a hand in a friendly greeting.

"Mrs. Denker's on her tour of duty," she remarked. "If I need to get caught up on the neighborhood doings, I have only to drop by for a chat."

"She's a great old girl." Chet waved a warm salute at their chair-bound neighbor, then bent to his task again.

Evelyn was in the house before him, drawing off her short white gloves, touching her gray-brown hair into order before the hall mirror, with its ornately carved walnut frame—a period piece from the old house in Baltimore—and then stepping into the living room to cast a quick glance of homecoming and stock-taking at her abode.

Like every other good housewife, she was as quick to read and interpret the subtle signs of her own domain as an American Indian in one of Cooper's novels or an Australian native tracker. Light from an almost closed Venetian blind, slanting flatly along the surface of a table, bore to her sensitive eye the faint gray filming that confirmed her calendar-based knowledge that Mrs. Clark, the woman who came one day a week to give the house a thorough cleaning, had not been in during Evelyn's absence. She was due tomorrow.

"Who was your visitor, dear?" she asked, as her husband set down her bags in the hall.

"Visitor?"

Chet, she thought, should take care or he'd fall victim to an occupational disability—the businessman's caution and hesitation about committing himself. Lately he'd slipped into the habit of studying the simplest question for a few seconds before answering it. She must speak to him about it soon—very lightly and tactfully, of course.

"The cigarette butt in the ash tray on the hall table," she said. "Plain tip."

"Oh, yes . . . That was where the police sergeant sat while he was telephoning the night the cars were stolen."

Chet had told her about the theft as he drove her home, and she had accepted the occurrence as part of his workaday problem of dealing in automobiles. Other cars had been stolen before this, and naturally there was insurance coverage. She was more interested in the incident as it bore upon the wider question of juvenile delinquency. Combating crime among the youthful had been the subject of a panel on which she had sat during the Washington conclave. "We're going to have a full committee meeting devoted solely to that subject, in Tupper Lake in late August," she had told Chet. "I'm glad it's going to be somewhere cool. Washington would have been unbearable if it weren't for air conditioning."

She opened a window, then straightened the drapery she had disturbed, until it hung in its proper graceful folds. "Why did the sergeant go into the dining room?"

"He didn't." Again Chet temporized, like a dealer bargaining over the allowance on a turn-in. It was becoming a most amusing mannerism. "So far as I know."

"Then who moved the screen? You never touch it, darling."

"I know better, hon." He gave her a playfully affectionate slap on the bottom in deference to their standing joke about her meticulous house-keeping. The Compulsive Chatelaine was his tag for her at times when her insistence on neatness irritated him. He canted his head sideways to inspect the screen. "Looks in the same old place to me. Where'll we have dinner?"

"I don't like a screen to be exactly even with the edge of the door. That makes it seem too set, too planned. I always prefer it an inch or two—like so."

She took hold of the light framework, with its stylized Oriental design of mountain peak and willows in muted tints, and easily moved it a little to one side. Then she stooped and picked something from the floor, where it had been almost completely hidden beneath the sideboard.

"What on *earth* have you been up to, Chet?" She held the thing between a thumb tip and finger tip, touching as little of it as possible.

Chet said, with that maddening slowness, "A handkerchief."

"Obviously. But whose? And what's that stuff all over it? It's stuck in a wad."

He took it from her fastidious pinch and gave it a rough pressure of fingers. "It's dried. Not sticky. So it sure as hell isn't plum jam."

"Blood dries blackish. Could it be that?"

"I wouldn't know."

"That's not your handkerchief." She said it positively. She knew every item of clothing he owned and in what corner of what drawer or closet it belonged. "It has a tan border."

"Mice aren't using tan-bordered handkerchiefs this year. And anyway we haven't had mice for an elephant's age." He showed his white teeth briefly.

She appreciated his taking the light tone. It was part of the strong masculine protectiveness that the feminine part of her needed and depended upon. She appreciated equally the sober expression that came over his handsome face then as a token that she was adult enough to face a situation.

"Of course, Ev," he went on, "it could be that someone broke in. And cut his hand somehow. Or maybe he just walked in. We're not always careful about locking up, you know."

"I know . . . Do you suppose it has anything to do with that other thing—the stolen cars?"

"It could—or it couldn't. Coincidences happen all the time. Might be no connection at all."

The first moment of startled realization had passed, and Evelyn Baggott felt the rising of a slow tide of resentment against the violation of her home. This house was an extension of her own personality; for a stranger to come in here and push her screen aside was as intimate an indignity as the grab of a rough hand at a breast.

"Of course we'll have to find out the truth about this," she said firmly.

He thought that over for a few seconds, then nodded. "Naturally."

"What was the name of that police sergeant?"

"Lowery."

"Well? . . . Well, darling?"

He walked out to the hall and picked up the telephone.

ELEVEN

EVELYN LIKED the young policeman—the intelligent, homely features, the simple good manners with which he accepted her invitation to come into the living room and sit down, the air of quiet competence with which he took notes, like someone who not too long ago was making entries in a similar notebook in a college lecture room. If he did good work in catch-

ing the impudent invader of her home, she must remember to write a
letter of commendation to the police commissioner. It was only when
citizens showed an awareness of able work by a public servant that they
deserved to get such service.

"You're absolutely sure a stranger must have entered the house while
you were away?" Lowery asked.

"Are you married, Sergeant?" Evelyn countered.

"Yes." He glanced up at her questioningly.

"Ask your wife. If anyone moved a table lamp one inch, she'd know."

He smiled. "Guess you're right."

"Then there were the muddy footprints on the kitchen floor."

"They were pretty faint. Don't let anyone scrub that floor until we
see if the photographers can get a good shot of the prints . . . Of course,
they might have been left by Mr. Baggott."

Chet said slowly, "I wasn't—I didn't come in by the garden path when
it was muddy."

The sergeant riffled back a few pages through his notes and studied
them. "No, but you'd gone across the street to talk to Mrs. Denker and
get her story about seeing the thief who took your car. The streets were
still wet. And you walked back into the kitchen while I was phoning."

"You've a good memory!" Chet said admiringly. "An asset in police
work, I'd say."

Sergeant Lowery looked pleased. "There's the handkerchief, of course.
We can't get around that. The laboratory men will check it. I don't doubt
the stains are blood, but they'll type it and see what they can find out."

He closed the notebook. "Anything else disturbed? Drawers ransacked?"

Chet said quickly, "Say, they might have been, at that! I wouldn't
notice, if the thief had been careful. There wasn't anything of value to
take. Mrs. Baggott's furs and the good silver are in the bank vaults for
the summer." He took two long tan cigars from a humidor on the table
and extended one to Lowery, who slipped it into his breast pocket. "I
wouldn't want anyone to get that silver for the world. It's a heavy, ornate
pattern—Baltimore Rose, by Stieff. An heirloom of Mrs. Baggott's
family."

"Nothing was ransacked, Sergeant," Evelyn said. "I thought of that
and looked about upstairs. Nobody could possibly have put everything
back just as I had it arranged. My dresser drawers were exactly as I left
them. So were my husband's, except for the changes of shirts and underwear that he'd lifted off from where they were neatly stacked."

"Then no professional thief had been at them," the sergeant said. "Burglars don't ever try to put things back neatly. They dump the contents of a drawer in the middle of an open space and paw through the stuff . . . I'll make a guess at who was in your house, Mrs. Baggott. I think it was a boy called Joey Tripp."

He looked squarely at Chester Baggott as he said the last few words, and Evelyn automatically followed his glance. Chet had just bitten off the end of his cigar and had been about to take the morsel from his mouth with his thumb and forefinger and deposit it in an ash tray. No random spitting out of tobacco leavings in Evelyn Baggott's house. She had put her foot down on that long ago, genially but definitely.

Chet's mouth remained slightly open, tongue protruding, brownish fleck on the crimson-wet tip, fingers poised ready to pinch, like a startled lobster's claw. Then, instead, he wiped the tobacco away with the back of a wrist, swallowed hard and said, "Tripp . . . that's the boy who was hanging around the . . ." He glanced down at his wrist, saw the damp tobacco scrap clinging there, picked it off and put it carefully on the closed lid of the humidor. "You gave me a start, Lowery. I understood from what you said the other night that Tripp was killed in the crash."

"That's what we thought at the time. The bodies have been definitely identified since then. The girl called herself Crystal Day. Either of you know anybody by that name?" He glanced from Chet to Evelyn. They shook their heads. "Anyway, she had an apartment in Garden Crescent. She was a model, but nobody knows anything about her, what agency she worked for or anything. May have been hanging around with this gang of young hoods and living off them."

He leafed through his notebook again. "Now for the guy that got himself killed. He was identified by a social security card in his pocket as a Sidney Keene. He's a cheap little thug from New York City, down in the section they used to call Hell's Kitchen. He was running away from an attempted mugging charge."

Chester lit his cigar and took several thoughtful puffs. Evelyn waited for him to speak. This was a man-type affair, and she felt a comfortable confidence in his ability to handle it well, even though he had been obviously taken aback by Sergeant Lowery's revelation that some boy who was supposed to be dead was really alive.

Chet said, "Then it was just another youth-gang thing. Tripp, and this Keene and the girl—and maybe some others—out for a ball and maybe helping Keene get away from being arrested. Stole a couple of my cars and smacked one up. Have they found the other one yet—the sedan?"

"It was picked up in Scarborough, abandoned. Right front fender wrecked. Paint on it matches the paint on the red convertible."

Chet nodded. "That's it, then. Drag racing. And one of them lost control, sideswiped the other, piled up and killed himself and the girl. Well, what can you do about these crazy kids, anyway?"

"That's just the question the panel kept agonizing over," Evelyn said. "We didn't come up with any brilliant answer. And yet something has to be done." She remembered Miss Yarrington—bushy white hair almost as short as a man's crew cut, severe white shirtwaist over a bouffant, brightly patterned skirt, sharp gray eyes behind dark-rimmed trifocals—saying, "There's a world of psychology in a good leather strap applied to the bare buttocks." And little Mrs. Purcell, orange-haired and pudgy, bleating, "But the psychic trauma, Madge! Brutality has left scar tissue on too many young personalities."

Sergeant Lowery said, "It wasn't just a drag race and an accident. Keene was murdered."

Evelyn looked from one to the other of the two men. Their glances were locked. Lowery, she thought, was getting a quiet enjoyment out of showing Chet that in his own field an able policeman could stay a step ahead of an able businessman. Chet, she noted with the secret and affectionate amusement a wife reserves for her husband's less brilliant moments, didn't seem to like it.

"How do you figure that?" he asked.

"The doctor says the girl's injuries were caused by the crash of the car against the concrete arch of the overpass. She pitched head-first into the windshield. But Keene's weren't. He didn't have any damage to his chest from the wheel. Nor to his face or the front of his head. The injuries to his skull came from the back, and that's not normal when a car piles up head-on. Someone clobbered him from behind and knocked his brains out. With a heavy weapon that had hard edges. They found a wrench in the grass. Some of his hair was stuck to it."

Chet raised his brows, examined his cigar and licked a little loose bit of wrapper into place. "Fingerprints?"

"No good ones. Too smeary."

"Well . . . a fight among the members of the gang. Right?"

"Looks like it."

"Over what?"

"If they'd been in a stickup, over a split of the take. Or maybe over the girl. I'd say the girl."

Chet said, with a nod of deference to the policeman's knowledge, "I'm interested. How'd you figure that out?"

A touch of complacence crept into the sergeant's manner. "For one thing, there wasn't a stickup of any consequence in the vicinity that evening. In the second place, the Tripp kid had been helling around in new clothes, looking very sharp, for the last couple of weeks. The people at the supermarket where he used to work remember he was wearing a tan gabardine suit, with a tan-bordered handkerchief like this one sticking out of the breast pocket. When a kid suddenly starts spending money on clothes, it means crime or a girl—or both."

"And you think that's the handkerchief that I found here, in my dining room?" Evelyn said. "Why should the boy come here?"

Lowery frowned. "That's harder to figure. Suppose he wants to make a getaway after the murder. But he has no money. Logical thing to do is to start stealing other cars to switch to, staging a quick stickup whenever he runs short of money. But the blood on the handkerchief indicates he was hurt in the crash. Maybe he doesn't feel up to a program of running and robbing. So perhaps he'd cased this house before he and Keene stole your cars. He might know that Mrs. Baggott was away, and if he could come back and rob the place——" He shrugged. "We've put out the alarm for him, and when we pick him up we'll find out what his idea was in coming back to this house."

Chet said slowly, "I'd hate to think the kid was a murderer. I caught a glimpse of him once or twice when he was hanging around the garage. He seemed like a clean-cut boy."

"Sure." The sergeant's young features hardened. "Most of those teen-age killers do. At the supermarket they thought a lot of him. They had him tabbed for a promotion. But underneath, he was a bad egg."

"How do you know that?" Evelyn asked.

"We checked and found he had a driver's license. But he was under age. The grandmother told us he's only seventeen. We found out he got the license on a forged baptismal certificate."

Evelyn said, "This is becoming more and more interesting. How could a lad get away with that? Have you examined the certificate?"

"No. The license bureau down there in New York City records the data from the certificate and then returns it to the applicant. But when we contacted them, they checked with the parish priest at the church in Brooklyn where it was issued. He said the register shows that the boy's under-age, and he's sure the certificate he gave Tripp showed that to be so. He remembers because some gangsters drove by and pegged a rock through the window while the kid was there."

Evelyn said, "This is fascinating. Why should they do that?"

"To distract the padre's attention. Tripp could have swiped a blank from the pad of forms under cover of the excitement and then filled it in any way he wanted to. It goes to show he was a bad actor to start with."

Evelyn felt a tingling little stir of her "rebel blood." She held up a hand to check the sergeant's flow of speech. "Now, wait. It seems to me it's a long step from a prank like that to a vicious murder." She turned to her husband. "Why, my goodness, Chet! it sounds for all the world like a bit of rascality that you might have been mixed up in yourself."

Chester Baggott seemed to have trouble in finding the tray to receive the ash from his cigar tip. "Ev, I don't see how on earth you can figure——"

"Oh, I don't mean *now*. But whenever you're letting your hair down with Lou Ewell or Vic Savory or some of those other old cronies of yours from Reisterstown, you tell about tricks you played when you were kids that were just about as bad as this. You *did* break windows, and you *did* go joy-riding in other people's cars a few times. And there's that story you always tell about how you and Lou went down into the gully behind the outhouse of the old folks' home and reached up to tickle their bottoms with a bundle of burrs tied to the end of a branch——"

Chet's face softened sheepishly. "Well, that's what I've been saying. We don't *know* this Tripp boy committed the murder. It might have been someone else in the gang. Or a passing psychopath who came along after the accident. The Tripp youngster may have been just going through a haywire period of mischief before settling down. And the cars were insured. I don't feel vindictive toward him. He's probably punished enough right now by a realization of what a serious incident grew out of a bit of juvenile horseplay."

Evelyn turned to Sergeant Lowery. "You said the New York police got some information from the boy's grandmother. What about his father and mother?"

"He's an orphan."

"But there you are! The broken home. The usual pattern." She felt a glow of knowledge, remembering stout little Lily Purcell's tables of figures —the overwhelming preponderance of divorced and separated and deceased parents among the cases of delinquency. "What else do they know about this boy?"

Sergeant Lowery gave her a quick digest of the known facts—place of birth, cause of death of father and mother, shifting of residence out of the city and back again, schooling, work record.

She thought intently for a moment. Imperceptibly her attitude toward this boy she had never met had changed from one of indignation at his penetration of her home to one almost of fellow-feeling.

I had a junior license at his age, she thought, remembering her occasional eighty miles an hour on Route 40, *but if I hadn't, I might very well have broken a few rules to get around the situation. The letter of the law—I've never been impressed by it. If anyone had happened to throw a flashlight on Chet and me that night when we were in the back of the car, my dress up around my waist—it was all I had on except my shoes and I kicked those off—and wasn't the woven plastic of the seat cover scratchy against my bare skin—the biddies of Baltimore might very well have put me down in their black books as a depraved little tart not fit to ask to their dinners . . . But if I'd smashed up a car, I wouldn't have run away from the accident—I'd have faced the consequences; and when Mamma asked me point-blank one night what about Chet and me and what had been going on, I didn't flinch; I said, "Mamma, I've had sex relations with him, and I intend to marry him." But you take this boy, this Tripp youth. How could you sympathize with him when he had turned his back and run?*

She felt irrationally disappointed, as if this were someone she had known and trusted, who had betrayed the confidence. Lily Purcell had said intensely, "If we could only *know* what goes on in the heads and hearts of these children, we wouldn't just turn away in loathing and give up the thought of anything but a reformatory or a prison—which only damns them to irretrievable worthlessness. We could understand and help——"

Evelyn Baggott had heard the voices of Chet and Sergeant Lowery going on and on, but she had no notion of what they were saying. An idea had come to her, almost with the clear force of a revelation. It seemed to grow out of the odd feeling of identification she had somehow developed for this unknown Tripp boy—this minor rebel against convention who had fallen so badly afoul of law and circumstance.

She said abruptly, "Why, I know why that boy came back here, Chet . . . It wasn't to steal anything. It was to talk to you."

He tamped the fire out of his cigar in the tray, pressing down so hard that the butt end burst into brown rags of tobacco. "That beats me, Ev. How on earth did you come up with that notion?"

"Well, if he's really at bottom a decent boy—and there's some evidence he is—and he found himself in a desperate jam that grew out of a bit of lawless mischief that a lot of kids think is just fun—joy-riding in somebody else's car, I mean—he might very well have wanted to try to clear himself a little, even if it was only in his own estimation, by coming straight to you and saying, 'Mr. Baggott, this is what I did, and I'm sorry if it got out of hand and caused all this extra distress to you. I just meant to borrow the cars and bring them back. I want you to know. It helps me feel better to make a clean breast of it. Now tell me what to do next to settle the score for what I've done.' You see, maybe the other two weren't dead then. Or he may not have known it. That's it! After the sideswipe, he was injured and dazed, and he didn't stop to see what had happened to them, or didn't realize they were badly smashed up. The sedan was found in Scarborough, so he probably just drove there in a sort of mental fog, abandoned the car there, and came straight down here, hitchhiking or by train, because he was afraid he'd be picked up in the damaged car. He came here to see you and make his amends."

She saw the suppressed amusement in both the male faces, but she still refused to smile apologetically.

Chet said, "No comment," and chuckled.

The sergeant passed a veiling hand across his mouth. "So why didn't he speak to Mr. Baggott, if he came here to do just that?"

Evelyn pressed her fingers to her temples. "Because when he slipped in the back door he overheard my husband talking on the telephone, denouncing him to the police as the probable thief in very antagonistic terms. The boy saw at once that his idea was a bad one under the circumstances, so he panicked and stole out again, unobserved, after accidentally dropping his handkerchief."

Chet said, "Nice going, Ev. It's as good a theory as any. And maybe it's true. The kid should be here now to hear you sticking up for him. He wouldn't run; he'd settle right down and expect to be treated to a hot dog and a bottle of soda pop . . . Lowery, let's level on this. What are the chances he'll be caught?"

The sergeant closed and pocketed his notebook. "To you especially, Mr. Baggott . . . well, I wouldn't give you a line of hooey about all the forces of law being mobilized, from the local detectives right on up to J. Edgar Hoover himself. This isn't a big case. The girl was a nobody. Sid Keene was a small-time no-good. Cars get stolen every day. Young hoods get into fights and skull each other. We've got wanted notices out on Tripp, but the only real chance we have of catching up with him is to have some informant latch on to who he is and turn him in. That's the way ninety-nine out of a hundred fugitives are caught, anyway. Matter of fact, he's probably playing it safe, holed up in a furnished room somewhere in New York City. He'd be safer there than anywhere else."

Chet rose and held out a hand to the policeman in dismissal. "It's a matter of no great importance to me. As I said, I don't feel vindictive. I'd like to see him caught and punished for whatever he's done, but I won't bleed if he isn't. He'll get his comeuppance somewhere, somehow . . . And give my thanks to the boys at headquarters for clearing up the thing so promptly."

Later that night, home again after a drive over to Bronxville for dinner at the Birch Brook Inn, Evelyn lay at ease under a single sheet in her twin bed, listening to the barely audible hum of the air conditioner in the window. Soap and water, followed by cold cream, had removed the last traces of Péché Gaillard from brows and ears and throat. No matter—that signal-scent had conveyed its message, and now she extended arms and legs wide under the cool percale, delightfully relaxed after the ecstatic submission that was also somehow a violent affirmation. Her thoughts were freed for the comfortable randomness that comes before sleep.

She could not know that at the moment of climax Chet had almost shouted at her, "For God's sake, take that stink off your face!" and very nearly had leaped from the bed in revulsion. Neither could she know that Crystal Day had once rubbed a nose against his cheek and murmured, "Your wife doused herself with Péché Gaillard before you kissed her this evening, didn't she?" The acuteness of perception for apparently irrelevant trifles that women showed never ceased to baffle him. "That's expensive smellum, isn't it?" Crystal had continued. "I want you to buy me a big flagon of it, precious. *This* big." She had insisted upon it. She had worn it the last night he lay with her, before the—accident. That was the way he tried to think of it. But the smell of that particular perfume did uncomfortable things to him now.

Evelyn stretched and settled herself in the bed. There were some special tasks of house-cleaning she would call on Mrs. Clark to do tomorrow—wiping up the floors of the clothes closets and washing the Meissen china that hadn't been used since wintertime and was showing faint traces of dust that had seeped through the chinks of the glazed cupboard doors. But perhaps some tasks might better be left for late August; Mrs. Clark could attend to them during the time that Evelyn would be away at the conference in Tupper Lake. She thought of Lily Purcell, whose carroty hair would never quite stay in a well-behaved wave and who always wore black in an effort to minimize the dumpiness of her figure, but whose rather amusing exterior hid a wonderfully humanitarian spirit and a sharp, forceful mind. It would be interesting to find out what Lily thought of this juvenile case—the Tripp boy—that had been so dramatically and tragically propelled into the very heart of Evelyn Baggott's home. Really, she would say to Lily, it's only when an incident like that comes *home* to one, in every sense of the word, that one realizes the magnitude and importance——

She stirred abruptly, struck by another of those feelings of sudden truth. Listening for Chet's breathing, she could not hear the longer, deeper inhalations that would mean he was falling asleep, as he usually did promptly after he had visited her twin bed.

"Asleep?" she whispered, so gently that the faint sibilance would not disturb him unless he was wide awake.

He answered immediately. "No."

She said in full voice, "Chet, if you knew where that boy had run away to, would you tell the police?"

There was that long hesitation (really, she thought, it's getting to be a sort of psychic block with Chet, whenever you ask him a question—maybe he should see an analyst) before he answered, "What else could a person do? Civic responsibility and all that. I thought you were hell-bent on that pitch."

"Well, yes. But perhaps sometimes getting to understand the deep-seated causes for individual action—well, that might be the best way to promote the general good."

Chet yawned. "Excuse it, please, hon. Sleepy . . . What's this all about, anyway?"

"I know where that boy ran away to."

The springs creaked, and in the dim reflection from the stripings of light cast on the ceiling through the Venetian blinds by the street lamp, she could see him raise himself on one elbow.

"Do you honest-to-God know? Or is this just a wild hunch?"

"I'm reasonably sure."

"Oh." He subsided with a little amused grunt. "Where'd he scram to? According to Mrs. Evelyn Sherlock Baggott?"

"I'm not going to tell you. You said you'd put the police right onto him. I'm going to talk to him myself first."

"Is that so! . . . When?"

"When I get around to it . . . Good night, darling." She reached across the space between the beds and patted his arm. It always gave her a refreshing sense of competence and independence to run a little project of her own, in half-defiance of Chet—knowing, of course, that in a pinch, if she tired of it, she could throw up her hands, plead the ineptness at practical affairs of a Southern lady and find Chet, cheerfully grumbling, ready to clear up the loose ends.

It was seldom, however, that her pride let her take that easy way out, and now—as coming sleep sent her thoughts into a vague tangle—she was determined to think seriously about carrying out her hastily announced plan of searching for the Tripp boy. There were several weeks in which to make up her mind, before she went up to the mountains for the panel conference. She would have a good talk with Lily Purcell first; Lily had sound judgment and could advise her. And if Lily's analysis of the available facts about the Tripp boy was at all like her own—well, it was a drive of only a couple of hours from Tupper Lake to where she thought she might pick up a lead to the whereabouts of——

At this point, the Meissen china got mixed somehow into the muted crash of harmlessly colliding cars, and she was asleep.

II Joey

TWELVE

THE DOOR OF THE ROOM was open to let the air sweep through to the little sleeping porch, but the girl knocked on the jamb and paused briefly before she came in.

Joey lifted his head from the pillow. He had been lying there looking through the tracery of leaves toward the distant mountains, thinking.

He'd been thinking, Elephants and parrots . . . they live a long time . . . and an article I read said there's a kind of big turtle in some islands down off the coast of South America . . . what's the name? . . . lives to be hundreds of years old. I'm older than any of them. A few days ago I was a kid. I thought I knew this and that. I didn't. Now I do. I'm old. Old. Old.

It wasn't his body that felt ancient. That was growing strong again. It was the inside of him that had suddenly learned the loneliness of manhood.

He watched the girl cross the room and come out into the sunlight that was tempered by the wire mesh of the screens that covered the sides of the sleeping porch. Gay little leaf shadows came through the screening and danced over her features and the green plaid gingham of her dress. Her face, like her bare arms, was lightly tanned and had a faint nutmeg dusting of freckles on the honey-colored skin. Her brown hair was tied back in a pony tail from features so smooth that he knew she could be no older than he.

In one hand she had a small pad, in the other a pencil. She held them poised, but instead of taking his order for dinner at once, she gave him a quick scrutiny. Her eyes, large and set wide apart in a rather slender face, were the smoky gray-blue of the hills. In repose her features were pensive, almost moody.

"How are you today?" she asked. It sounded like a routine question.

"Galápagos," Joey said.

She wrinkled her forehead.

"Turtles," he explained. "I just remembered their name."

"Why?" Her voice was low in pitch, pleasant in quality.

"That's what I feel like."

She considered his reply, touching the butt end of the pencil to her firm young chin. "Hard-shelled?"

"Well, yes. That, too."

"Doesn't everybody have to be, sometimes?"

"You found that out?"

Her gray eyes examined him coolly, then lowered themselves without embarrassment to her pad. "Nurse won't be in to give you a bed bath this afternoon. Dr. Lytton says you're to go to the bathroom yourself for a shower. In a day or two you can get dressed."

Joey sat up straight in bed and stretched his arms wide. The sleeves of the new pajamas rode up his forearms, and the cool mountain air stroked his skin like soothing fingers. The pain was gone from his chest. "I hate to have you running around waiting on me, Miss McTaggart. I've never been used to anything like this."

She smiled, and at once her face was transfigured. It seemed to Joey, taken off guard for a moment, that this wouldn't be a girl who ever did things by halves. Her full lips widened instantly to a generous showing of teeth, and her eyes were alive with light. But a second later she was serious again, the competent young manager of a cottage sanatorium.

"It's my business to make you comfortable."

The bitter knowledge he had had thrust on him in the last few days moved in on Joey again like a salt tide, drowning out any feelings of friendliness or ease. So if she did things for him, it was because she was in the business. She made money out of running this place for sick folks. People behaved as they did for reasons like that. Profit for themselves. Selfish ends. They'd smash your brains out against a concrete wall or choke the eyeballs out of you. There wasn't a one of them you could trust, except maybe one of your own blood, like simple-hearted old Gram, or maybe a close pal, like Tony Marchand. And in that moment even Gram was so far away he could hardly call up her features; and he realized how little he really knew of the inside of Tony's life. This cheerful sunshine, slanting across the figured white counterpane, was a thin patina on top of a deep, bleak aloneness. Maturity was a sifting weight of sand pouring down over his spirit from the four corners of this sunny, smiling world of his boyhood—a knowledge that kid dreams were over and that all the grimy evil he had thought was just the other side of life was its real, pervading substance. That was what growing up meant —facing the knowledge that this was all there was, and in the middle of it you had nobody to look to but yourself, naked and alone.

The girl said crisply, "We have pot roast for dinner today. Or you may have a lamb chop, Mr. Josephson."

Joey still had to be careful to resist the temptation to look around for "Mr. Josephson," whenever anyone used the name. Here, to these people, he was Arthur Josephson.

There were many things to get used to besides his own new name. Dinner was at noon, supper at six. When you were well enough to go to the bathroom, you performed your morning face-wash at a time stated on the schedule thumbtacked to the outside of the bathroom door, and you had just a quarter of an hour before clearing out to let some other patient in.

"Pot roast'll do," he said.

Before all this happened he would have had the impulse to add, Sit down and talk to me for a while.

She looked like the kind of girl who would understand a man's problems and maybe have a word of sensible counsel to give, although she was probably too young and inexperienced to know much about the sort of people he'd just been mixed up with. A few days ago he'd have thought that if someone like her listened as a fellow talked out whatever he happened to have on his mind——

Yes, and turn him in if she could make a dollar by it, the bitter new wisdom warned him. It's her business to get something out of you, boy. Money for your board and lodging; a reward, if there's any offered for your arrest; a smile from the local police or the state trooper who puts the cuffs on you. Whatever else she can squeeze out of it.

Her pencil made a swift jotting on the pad, and she turned to go, the plaid cotton of her dress swaying to the rhythm of her lithe motions. She paused to say, over her shoulder, "Dr. Lytton says you're well enough to have visitors now."

"I don't know anyone here. I don't expect anyone."

"I mean the other patients in the house."

"Oh."

"Aren't you interested?"

"No . . . Maybe." Better act like a normal person, he reminded himself. Be lonesome and bored. Don't rouse suspicion.

"I'll bring a few of your neighbors in later and introduce them." She added, "It's a favor to them as well as to you, you know. Life can be dull for them."

Joey lay back on the pillow. The breeze off the mountains, redolent with pine, whispered through the screen, "Home again . . . home again," just as it had when he got off the train that first afternoon after the blurred nightmare of the train trip.

In his seat he had dozed feverishly whenever the train settled into its jiggling progress and had waked to pain and alarm whenever it jolted to a stop at little mountain stations labeled with names like Thendara and Old Forge and Raquette Lake. Before the train reached Snowden he had gone to the men's room and in the privacy of the toilet stripped to the waist and used his penknife to slash away the torn slip with which Laurie had bound up his ribs. His breathing hurt worse now, but such a wrapping wouldn't fit in with the story he was forming in his mind.

It was late afternoon when he descended from the coach at Snowden and walked across the roofed platform dizzily to the row of three or four taxis lined up waiting for customers on the sunny concrete. He sucked in deep breaths of the piny air, feeling a wonderful sense of homecoming, an urge to run, to scamper away from all the fear and doubt as a bare-legged kid had run in helter-skelter happiness through the shin-whipping grass with a dog from the house down the road—what was his name?—black and white, with a dustbrush tail and fly-swatter ears—only there was no grass on this hot pavement, and the taxis and the station were part of a giant merry-go-round that had just started up without music. He grabbed a door handle and listened to his voice booming inside the bass drum that someone had somehow put around his head. "Get me to a doctor, please. I'm very sick."

Someone said, "Kid, you look like you ain't in such good shape. Maybe I better take you somewheres you can get right into bed. They'll call the doctor and take care o' you. Okay?"

"Okay," Joey whispered.

The town was all hills. You could see the big ones whenever you rolled your head sideways against the back of the seat and opened your sweat-wet eyelids and glanced along the vista of a street. The mountains were tall in the sky, blue-black in shadow or red-purple with sunset light. The little hills were all over the village. The taxi went up one street and down another like a carnival car on a roller-coaster.

Then the driver had his arm around Joey's waist and was helping him up a walk and some wooden steps to a veranda and pushing a bell button at a screen door. A girl with big serious gray eyes stood in the doorway in the midst of a swarm of black spots that were forming in the air out of nowhere and circling and growing larger. She said things in a quiet, low voice. Something about a room and porch and perhaps you'll be needing nursing care.

"Audrey or Katherine . . . it could be either," Joey said distinctly and felt annoyed when the girl answered coolly, "I'm Sandra McTaggart." She should have understood that he was referring to the Hepburn type of face—slender and sensitive, like hers. But it was too much trouble to explain, and he let the black spots blow up as big as balloons because it was easier than trying to fight them and keep them small, and when they had all flowed together into one big blackness he was at peace . . .

There were some mixed-up fragments of memory after that, which he never was able to sort out clearly. The first really lucid interval began with lying on his stomach, his face turned sideways on the squashy pillow and his rear cold and hurting. His pajama pants were pulled down, and a needle was being withdrawn. A nurse in starched white pulled up the pants and helped him to turn over.

A dapper little gray-haired man was putting away the needle. He said, "How did this happen anyway, Mr. Josephson?"

Joey had the story all ready. He'd planned everything in his intervals of wakefulness on that nightmare train ride, even this new name. Josephson—he had chosen that because there was a bare possibility that somehow he might let the name "Joey" slip out. If so, he could always say that his nickname came from his last name, just as anyone named Stephenson is called Steve.

Joey knew somehow that the gray-haired man was Dr. Lytton and had been here before.

"I was on the station at Poughkeepsie when the train pulled in." It came off his tongue haltingly, like something he'd memorized not too thoroughly for an English recitation in high school. "I must have stepped out without looking, to cross the platform and get aboard, because one of those motor baggage trucks was rolling along past, and it banged into me and knocked me down."

The doctor clicked his bag shut. "Didn't you report it? You might get a settlement from the railroad company."

"I didn't think I was hurt. You don't feel it at first."

"That's true. Numb. Maybe a little shocked."

"I didn't want to miss my train. So I jumped up and ran and got aboard. It was only when I began to spit blood I knew there was something wrong . . . What happened inside there, Doctor? Anything busted?"

"The X-rays showed no broken ribs. The blow on your chest had ruptured a small blood vessel, and you were headed for a nice little bout of pneumonia." The doctor added casually, "How come you landed here in Snowden, son?"

Joey was ready with the answer to that one, too. As he reeled it off, he turned his head and saw that the girl who had admitted him on his arrival was in the room too. Her cool gray eyes watched him as he squeezed the edge of the sheet tightly to keep his thoughts straight as he lied.

"I thought I'd spend the rest of the summer working in one of the resort hotels—at Placid or Saranac Inn. I didn't like the job I had, driving a delivery truck for a paint company in Poughkeepsie, so when my vacation came along I quit. But when I was on the train and knew my chest was hurt, I thought I'd better get off at Snowden, because it's famous for treating lung cases. And whenever you spit blood, you think of TB."

"You haven't any TB. And as to Snowden's being famous for treating the disease, son," Dr. Lytton added drily, "it was—but no more."

"How come?" A faint alarm stirred in Joey. Now that he'd succeeded in running to cover, was the cover going thin on him? "The way I've always heard it, Snowden is full of people getting their health back. The town has a lot of houses like this, and every house is full of people with lung trouble, taking the cure."

Why, that was Joey's whole idea. He had remembered—from the times when he had driven into Snowden on his uncle's farm wagon, piled high with fresh vegetables—that the long verandas were lined with patients, lying in cushioned Adirondack recliners, taking the mountain air that would slowly heal their sick chests. Here, in this crowd of health-seekers, one more blood-spitting young man would be lost like a grain of sand on a beach, unnoticed, unsuspected, for as long as he chose to stay. Anywhere else a newcomer would have to explain himself, submit to scrutiny. But here—he was safely hidden in a mob . . . wasn't he?

The doctor chuckled and turned to the girl. "How many cottages are still open in town, Sandy?"

Her low-pitched voice was a little rueful. "Three. The Mountain Vista closed last week. They're going to convert to tourists."

Dr. Lytton said, "It's the new anti-TB drugs, son. Streptomycin and isoniazid and PAS. Patients don't have to come to the mountains and go on bed rest for months and years any more. They undergo ambulant treatment at home, for the most part. Snowden's through as a cure town. A few years more and it's going to be just another resort village for summer vacationers and winter sportsmen . . . Well, you don't need to worry about that, boy. There's nothing wrong with you but the fag-end of a bump in the bosom. Two weeks rest and you can go on your way re-joicing."

Joey suddenly felt as cold and naked as his behind had been when the needle was in it.

The nurse was no longer here on the sleeping porch. The doctor de-parted now with Sandra McTaggart, but he turned back for a moment and took Joey's chin in a firm grasp and tilted his head back.

He said quietly, "Where'd you get those bruises that were on your throat when you came here, boy?"

Joey had foreseen that question. His answer was pat. "At the paint shop, I was horsing around with one of the guys—another driver. We got to wrestling. He grabbed me by the neck to make me break a wrist-lock I had on him."

He met the doctor's steady gaze defiantly.

"So many different things can happen to the young," the doctor said. "It's a bewildering time of life, isn't it, son?"

He went out without waiting for a response. As soon as the hall door of the room closed behind him, Joey flung back the blankets and swung his legs out of bed. The boards of the sleeping porch floor were chill against his bare soles. As he tried to take a step, giddiness seized him, and his hips slumped back against the mattress on the high iron bed-stead. Breathing heavily, he looked down at himself. The pajamas—broadcloth with a wide striping of red, gray and white—were ones he had never seen before. The slippers beside the bed were equally strange. He shoved his toes into them. An increasingly panicky urgency was driv-ing him.

Another try at walking got him across the porch and into the room. Two upholstered chairs and a couch. A small table. Framed prints against flowered wallpaper. A chest of drawers!

He yanked the top drawer open, staggering with the effort. It was clean, lined with fresh shelf paper—and empty. A second and a third yielded the same result. He swung around, panting. A white-painted door, the twin of the one leading into the hall, was beside the dresser. He twisted the knob and yanked. In the spacious interior was nothing except clothing on hangers—just what he'd had on his back when he arrived.

He rammed his hands into pocket after pocket of the tan gabardine coat. There wasn't a thing in them. He dragged the trousers off the wire hanger through which they were neatly folded. One side pocket, a rear pocket—his fingers clutched smooth leather. He opened the billfold and fingered the money—the bills Mr. Baggott had given him as advance on his salary before trying to kill him. It might support him for two weeks —no more than that. One last grope, and in the left side pocket his fingers closed on the thick flat packet he was seeking—the folded bills he had taken from Crystal Day's stocking.

Before relief could pour its soothing tide the length of his body, a knock on the door startled him. He retreated to the bed before calling, "Come in."

He slipped the money under one hip and pulled the counterpane up to his chest as Sandra McTaggart emerged from the room to the sleeping porch.

"How do you feel now, Mr. Josephson?"

"Wobbly . . . Where did those come from?" He plucked the cloth of the pajamas and pointed to the slippers beside the bed. "I arrived here with nothing."

She wrinkled her brow. "I told you I was going to order them sent up from Ackroyd's—that's the men's clothing store. You said go ahead."

"I don't remember that."

"You were running a high fever."

"Did you pay for them?"

"No. They'll send you a bill. If you want a razor and stuff like that, let me know and I'll telephone one of the drugstores. They'll deliver it and put it on a charge account for you."

He could feel the little lump that Crystal Day's money—his now—made under his thigh. "Did I ask you how much my room and board would be?"

"Yes. I told you fifty a week, with nursing extra whenever you needed it." He saw the shadow of worry on her young face. "Have you the——" She hesitated and rephrased the question more delicately. "Is that satisfactory?"

Joey thought, You land here without any luggage, so right away she asks if you have the ready money. "I can pay you a week in advance right now," he said sharply. "Do you want it?"

Pink washed slowly up her throat, above the checked gingham, and into her cheeks among the sprinkling of freckles. "You may, anytime, if you wish." She started to turn away but paused and said, "Did I ask you for it when you arrived here?"

Joey felt his own face grow hot. "No . . . You just took me in and took care of me . . . Look. Would you mind coming over here and giving me a good sock in the snoot?"

The girl's smile suddenly flashed. "Not until you're in shape to fight back, Mr. Josephson . . . I'll close your door, so no one will disturb you during rest hour."

As soon as he was alone, Joey snatched the bills from under him and counted them. They amounted to a little more than five hundred dollars. They could buy him some two months in the comparative security of this hideaway. When the money was gone, what would he do?

The passing days, though they brought him no answer to that question, saw him gain strength. On the morning when Sandra McTaggart announced she was going to introduce some of his housemates, he was dubious about strangers, yet relieved at a break in the monotony.

It was not yet noon when a knock came at his door. He expected a group to march in. Only the girl came through the room—but as she emerged into the sunlight of the porch he saw that it wasn't the girl. It was a woman. Her molasses-taffy hair rose in smooth curves to a crown of orderly curls; her face, softly handsome rather than beautiful, was freshly lipsticked and penciled; the belt of a silky crimson negligee accentuated the fullness of her breasts.

"Neighborly call," she said. "Sandy says you're ready for visitors. I'm Jane Cumberland. And you're Arthur Josephson, aren't you? Hello." She had the assured, unaggressive manner of a woman who is used to getting everything she wants without any difficulty.

Joey said, "Hello . . . You—you want to sit down?" He glanced around, but there wasn't a chair on the little porch.

"Oh, don't bother, dear," Jane Cumberland said. "We're free and easy around here. I'll sit on the bed."

With a practiced swing of the hips she lifted herself to the lower edge of the counterpane and sat there, crossing her legs. The skirts of the negligee fell apart. Through the filmy nightgown beneath it, one leg, long and shapely, was visible to well above the knee. Joey looked quickly away. It reminded him of Crystal Day's leg.

"Have a cigarette?" she asked.

"Not just now, thanks."

His visitor drew from a pocket a black-and-gold enameled case with attached lighter. The movements made the negligee open wide at the throat. The nightgown beneath was cut deep into the cleavage. She made some modest little adjusting gestures that left the panorama unchanged.

"What was Dr. Lytton's report?" she asked and then laughed. "My dear, you'll learn all the conversational clichés in no time. That's one of them. Dozens of times a year. 'How was your last report?' Lordy me, the number of times I've heard that and asked it!"

"He said there's nothing much wrong," Joey answered cautiously.

"Oh, I know, I know. That's what they tell everyone at first. To keep your courage up. It's what they told me. Eight weary years ago." She sighed and lighted a cigarette.

"I don't know how long I'll be here," Joey said. Where could he go if he had to leave, with people asking questions and wanting to see a social security card before they'd give him a job?

"It's nice to be able to say that, honey. Keep right on thinking it. I do so wish I could get away from this town. But it's just my fate to be stuck here."

Joey was content to let her talk about herself instead of asking any more questions about him. "Dr. Lytton says people can cure at home now, with these new drugs. Couldn't you do that?"

"Those who are lucky can. But me—! INH makes my fingers and toes go numb. And PAS raises holy Nellie with my poor tummy. I can't take either of them. And without one or the other, strep is no good; your bugs develop resistance to it. So I have to keep battling it out on the same old slow-going line—rest, rest, and more rest. It gets to be pretty tiresome as the years go by."

"I'm sorry," Joey mumbled.

She patted the long elevation his shin made in the counterpane. "Don't fret yourself about my fate, dear. I accept it . . . I hear your dinner coming now. When you're up and around, drop in on me down the hall and take some of the curse off the tedium."

She slid gracefully from the high bed as a heavy-set, brown-faced girl bore a loaded tray through the door and set it on a wheeled stand.

"Your dinner's in your room already, Mrs. Cumberland. Want I should bring it in here?" The broad coppery face crinkled into a grin that seemed to be always ready, just beneath the surface. "He's nice-looking, ain't he?"

"Maybe some other time Mr. Josephson will feel like having company, Elizabeth," Jane Cumberland said carelessly. "In the meantime, try to keep your Iroquois stoicism from bursting out all over the place." She disappeared with a rhythmic undulation of silky crimson hips.

Elizabeth chuckled and winked at Joey as she trundled the stand into position across the bed and lifted the aluminum domed covers from the plates. As the savory smell of the pot roast touched Joey's nostrils, he realized that he was hollow-hungry. He reached eagerly for knife and fork.

Elizabeth stood beaming down at him, big hands on broad aproned hips. "I hear you come from Poughkeepsie. My husband's got a brother works in Poughkeepsie."

Joey's throat closed against the bit of meat he had taken. He thought, There'll always be somebody from Poughkeepsie. No matter where I go, wherever I say I come from, there'll always be somebody with a close relative just around the corner from there.

The wisdom of his new maturity stirred in him. He had escaped from Jane Cumberland's questions when she got to talking about herself. Those were the tactics. Do the questioning.

He said, "Are you from Poughkeepsie, Elizabeth?"

"No. Do you know the Nelson House, on——"

"Where *are* you from?"

"Around here. Do you——"

"Born here?"

"I was born on the Indian reservation." She had a cackle of laughter ready for the blank look he gave her. "Me Lizzie-bet. Me good Indian. Ugg . . . Say, why do people think Indians say, 'Ugg'? I'm an Indian, and I never say it. Never heard any of my people say it, either."

Joey forked a bit of potato. "One time we read a story about Indians. In high school, this was. The teacher said that writers have different ways of putting down the grunting sound that everybody makes sometimes in conversation. Sometimes they write it ee-aitch or you-aitch or aitch-you-aitch. He said the people who wrote about Indians got into the habit of writing it you-jee-aitch."

"Then it's not pronounced 'ugg'?"

"No. It's just a grunt."

"I'll have to tell Pete. He often wonders about that. He's my husband. He's coming back from Peru."

Joey chewed the potato. "Is he a Peruvian?"

Elizabeth let out a gurgle of mirth. "He's an Indian like me. He's a high steel worker. Been working on a bridge down there. It's his first job at it, and he makes good money now. He's going to be working on a big new building in New York this winter. I'll quit pretty soon and go down there to join him. We're going to live on— You know Brooklyn?"

"I've been there."

"We're going to live on Pacific Street. My cousin and her husband got a big apartment there we can share. You know Pacific Street?"

Joey nodded.

"There's a whole colony of Indians there. Mohawks mostly. High steel men and their families. Indians are the best high steel workers in the world. They're not afraid of height. Did you know that?"

Joey's mouth was full of pot roast. He shook his head and grunted a negative. *Nnnh-nnh.*"

Elizabeth showed twenty-odd teeth and a wall-to-wall carpeting of pink tongue. "You *said* it! Right then you said it! You-jee-aitch. Pronounced——" She made a sound like an aquarium seal asking for a fish. "Right?"

Joey said, "Uh-huh."

"Ugg-*ugg*," Elizabeth said. "Pronounced like two belches." She went out gurgling. Joey heard her say in the hall, "Finished already, Mr. Finnegan?"

A moment later a tall, bony man in a bathrobe ambled out upon the porch. He said, "Hi," and set his rear unceremoniously on the counterpane where Jane Cumberland had sat. His lean skull looked famished for hair, his large, pale eyes ravenous for information.

He took a sprig of raw spinach out of one of his bathrobe pockets, looked at it unenthusiastically, and began to munch it.

"Read about this diet in a magazine," he said suddenly. "Personally, I think it's a fiasco, but I have an open mind. Give anything a try, I say . . . How are things in Poughkeepsie?"

"Do you come from there?" Joey countered.

"God, no. You going to be with us long?"

"I don't know. Is that maid really an Indian?"

"Hell, yes." Finnegan swallowed, retrieved a package of dates from another pocket and pulled one loose. "Silly damn combination, raw spinach and dates, but this fellow said it gives you a combination of minerals . . . What did you expect an Indian to be like? Poker-faced and speechless? Some of them clown around and chatter worse than we do . . . How'd you come to break down?"

Finnegan's intent gaze fastened itself on Joey's face.

"What I'm concerned about," Joey said, "is how long I'll be here. I was talking to Mrs. Cumberland. She says she's been here eight years. That's a long time."

Finnegan's mouth puckered around another date. After a while he said contemptuously, "I've been here twenty-two years . . . She could have gone home five years ago."

"She says she couldn't take the new drugs."

Finnegan's mouth went down farther at the corners. "She couldn't give up her boy friend. Now his company's made him go back home—they were paying his way up here—so Janey's looking the field over. Only it ain't much of a field any more. Boy! I can remember the day when this was a cosmopolitan little burg. Lots of fun going on, over and under the surface. Wherever you'd look . . . How'd you happen to come here?"

"Is she a widow?"

"Ha! Got a husband's crazy about her. Has a good job with a chemical company. Drives up regular to visit her. You'll see him in a few days. Always wanting her to go down home to Rochester. But she likes it here. No responsibilities. Perpetual vacation. Lives her own life. You couldn't pry her loose from this setup. I've seen more than one case like that . . . Did you come here on your own or did your company send you?"

"Are there companies that do that?"

"There were. Some of 'em used to maintain their own cottage sanatoriums up here. Mine did. All closed now—all of them. Even the big Snowden san is closed, and that was known all over the world . . . Do you work for a——"

"You mean your company's kept you up here for twenty-two years?" Joey interrupted. He had the hang of the thing now—get your questions in first and fast—but the strain of fending off these lonely, curious people was telling on him. The remnants of his weakness made sweat prickle out on his forehead and the backs of his hands.

"Thank God there was a pension and disability plan that I came under," Finnegan said. "I'm rated totally and permanently disabled under it . . . What was the outfit you worked for in Pough——"

"Do you mean you've got to stay here for the rest of your life?" Joey was beginning to feel too desperate to be considerate of the man's feelings.

Finnegan pried another date loose. "I could go somewheres else and get along on my allowance, but why? What few friends I've got left are here. The good days of this town are over, but what else have I got? A game of bridge; a chat in the Ski Room at the hotel . . . You didn't tell me what it was that you were doing before you came up here."

The girl's quiet, firm voice said, "Rest hour, Mr. Finnegan."

Sandra McTaggart had come through the room on silent rubber soles and was standing in the doorway of the sleeping porch. Finnegan marched obediently past her. She gave Joey a quick glance of inspection as she wheeled the stand aside. "Elizabeth will take your tray away in a few moments. Was everything all right?"

"Super," Joey said.

THIRTEEN

FOR A FEW DAYS after Dr. Lytton allowed him to get dressed and go downstairs, he rested in a beach chair on the lawn. One morning he walked down the hill to the center of town. In Ackroyd's he bought some necessary clothes—slacks, shirts, underwear. He also picked out a small, cheap suitcase to use in case he had to get out of this town in a hurry. "Deliver them to McTaggart's," he told the clerk, and added, "Where's the public library?"

The man pointed. "Just beyond the Square, on the other side of the street."

The neat building of light-colored sandstone was set back behind a small lawn. The librarian, a plump, gray-haired woman, nodded when Joey asked if she had a file of *The New York Times*. At a table he spread out the broad, bound sheaf and began turning the pages.

The issue of the day following the incident contained no item concerning it. Joey thought, It happened at night, so there wouldn't be time for it to make the morning paper.

He turned to the following issue. Even that one, he was beginning to believe, might not carry the story. After all, an automobile accident—a girl killed—it happened all the time; it was hardly real news. If he could just hide out in this town for a little while longer, the whole thing might be forgotten.

A small headline on an interior page caught his eye. "Police Call Crash Death Murder." As he glanced at the story beneath, hardly expecting it to have any bearing, his own name leaped to his eye with the force of a physical blow.

"Joseph Tripp, seventeen, of"—his glance leaped past the address—"is alleged to have been seen by a neighbor in the act of driving away the stolen car. The girl, according to the medical examiner, died of injuries sustained in the crash, but Keene's death resulted from several blows on the head with a heavy instrument such as a tire iron or a wrench. The police believe the killing may have resulted from a quarrel between the youths following the death of the girl in the wrecked car. Tripp is being sought for questioning."

It all came back to Joey in a wild rush of memories . . . lying on the grass and hearing the sound of blows, then the shout from the passer-by, the flight of the killer . . . and, later, Mr. Baggott's amazed horror at seeing Joey.

He killed that other fellow . . . a stranger . . . somebody who just happened to come along . . . but he thought he was killing me. And now they've got it figured out that the poor guy was with me and that I'm the murderer.

He walked up the hill slowly, his mouth and throat dry.

Each day he felt strength returning to his body, but at night—and when he was alone on his porch in the afternoon hour of quiet rest that was part of the routine of the house—he felt overborne with dread of the future.

Weeks slid uneventfully by. Dr. Lytton dismissed him. "Go anywhere, boy. Do anything."

"I'll finish out a nice long vacation here."

"That's your own concern, son. You're well now. Exercise, build yourself up—and get out of this town. Don't get illness on your mind. You're not ill."

Joey said, "Yes, sir . . . It's just—I'm in no hurry. That's all."

Passing days brought him no respite from his fear of the day when he would have to leave his haven. Yet there were times when the natural resilience of youth had the best of it and he could, for a few moments, push apprehension aside.

One morning, as he toweled himself in the bathroom, a knock on the door startled him into silence and he realized he had been humming loudly. He put on his pajama top hastily, gathered up his toilet things and went out.

Jane Cumberland, towel slung over one shoulder, toothbrush and dentifrice tube in one hand, reached up and pinched the lobe of one of his ears as he passed her.

"You ran over your scheduled time, butch," she said, without malice, "but you're guilty of a worse crime than that."

He halted abruptly. Once Gram had tried to get used to a pressure cooker some door-to-door salesman had pressured her into buying. She took the lid off too soon, and the pot behaved like a volcano. Whenever Joey heard some words now, they caused a similar disruptive release of emotion. Just the sight of one of them in reading or the sound of it when someone was talking about something innocuous would make the always-underlying anxiety boil up into his consciousness in a scalding rush. "Crime" was one of them.

He said, "What do you mean?" and fought his Adam's apple down into place.

"No one has a legal right to be so happy this early in the day," she said. "A result of youth, honey child. It's an insult to a sour old witch like me. I can't think of a more exasperating form of juvenile delinquency."

Her smile was easy and good-humored. She must have been up for a while; her hair was carefully combed into its coronal of taffy curls, and her new-looking negligee of a crisp white cloth in a tiny waffle weave was sparkling fresh.

He said, relieved, "Don't call yourself names. You look real cool, Mrs.——"

"Jane."

"Okay. Jane."

"What do your friends call you?"

"Joey," he said, without thinking, and was immediately thankful for his forethought. "On account of Josephson."

"Of course. Have your dinner in my room today. Will do?"

"All right."

He went back to his porch, pulled out the stand, set a straight chair in front of it, and waited for the Indian maid to bring his breakfast tray up. When it arrived, Sandy was carrying it. He jumped up.

"Where's Elizabeth?"

"She took off to join her husband. I've been trying for days to get a replacement lined up. No go."

"You're carrying all the trays today?"

"There's no one else." She turned to leave.

"Who'll make the beds?"

"I will." Her slender figure was gone in a few lithe strides.

After breakfast he went for a walk, up one tree-lined street and down another. House after house, with its tiers of screened sleeping porches above neglected lawns, was closed and lifeless. From childhood glimpses, he could remember them peopled with health-seekers. Now they made Snowden seem like a ghost town. From the high ground at the end of St. Cloud Street, he could look across the roofs of the village to the hill-top where the buildings of the famous Snowden san peeped through the trees. Deserted, now. Waiting for some unguessed future. Like himself.

He walked back to the house. Instead of lounging on the lawn he went up to Finnegan's room. It was as bare of any attempt at individuality as a wall tent. Finnegan, in pajamas, was lying on the bed reading the Adirondack Enterprise and munching what looked like the stalk end of a head of raw cabbage. He gulped and said, "Vitamin C and minerals. The Roman doctors knew cabbage had germ-killing powers. Galen recommended it as a poultice on wounds."

Joey said, "How come a kid like Sandy is running this joint? How many patients here altogether?"

Finnegan laid down his paper and tapped his fingers on it, one by one. "Ten. When her mother was alive the family had a good setup. They've got a farm over toward Waubeek. The old man works it—potatoes for a cash crop and a garden where he grows a lot of the vegetables we eat. Mrs. McTaggart ran the cottage san here."

"Sounds like a nice deal," Joey said. "They must have made a potful. Must still be making it."

Finnegan produced a little buzzing sound with pursed lips. "Five hundred a week sounds like a good take when you say it fast. Over twenty-five thousand a year, gross. But you got to feed patients well all the year round. Plenty of good meat you got to buy at the butcher's. And you got to heat the house. It's a long, hard winter up here, boy—nine months of it. I've seen week after week of forty below. The houseful of patients you had all summer dwindles down to two or three, but you got to keep the whole shack warm, and that furnace eats up the tons of coal."

"I see," Joey said. "Every winter they have to plow under the profits they make in summer."

"All told, they just make a living. And even that won't last many years more. The McTaggarts figured on putting Sandy through college. She wants to be a nurse. But the mother died last year, and old Mac has been having his troubles with a bad back—a slipped lumbar disk. Sandy's got to try to ramrod this place along by herself. Too much for a kid, if you ask me."

"She has to carry the trays and make the beds today," Joey said. "Elizabeth is gone."

"I know. I told Sandy—I said, 'Look here, honey, just close this place up. It's only a matter of time anyway. If you don't, you'll have a breakdown yourself.' Was I right, Josephson? Or was I right?"

"I don't know," Joey said. He suddenly felt as naked as when they had pulled the clothes off his butt to shoot him with the hypodermic. The shelter he had found was about to be snatched away.

He walked downstairs, turned back along the entry hall, and opened the door that led to the kitchen. Mrs. Wennergren, the cook, in a calico dress and a blue-checked apron, was stirring steaming pots of food on the range. Sandy was working at a metal-covered table as long as an interurban bus. She had drawn the trays from a tall rack that stood against the wall. A neatly lettered card under each space in the rack identified the patient to whom the tray was assigned. Now the trays were lined up on the table, and she had just finished setting them with napkins and silver.

"Some of us are up and around, Sandy," Joey said. "We could come down to the dining room. Save you some trouble."

She smiled, with a quick shake of her head. "It would make us double work." Her deft movements continued as she talked. "We used to do that and charge extra for trays sent up. But we learned it was easier to give trays to everyone."

He saw the momentary sag of her shoulders as she turned to study the individual diet cards that were tacked to a piece of corkboard against the wall near the range. Mrs. Wennergren was ladling out the vaporous food now.

"You've been making beds all morning, haven't you?" he asked Sandy.

"Please run along."

He stepped past her and shifted the glasses on a tray. "This way, the water and milk are like the supports of a bridge. We can put another tray on top—like so—and I can carry both of them at once."

She cried in protest, "We *can't* have that! You're a patient!"

"I'm a convalescent. Dr. Lytton says I'm to have exercise. This is it."

He shouldered her aside and carried the double-decked pair of trays toward the rear stairway. It felt good to have the old power in his back and arm and leg muscles as he took the ascent two steps at a time. Compared with his job in the supermarket, this was light calisthenics.

He carried the rest of the trays up, two at a time, meeting in the course of his rounds a few top-floor patients—bed cases—he had never visited before. On his last trip he took up his own tray and Mrs. Cumberland's. On her porch, after setting them down on a small table she had cleared, he sat opposite her.

"Have you given up your amateur status and gone professional, Joey?" she asked. "Are you the new tray-boy for keeps? Working for your board?"

"It's an idea. Right now, though, I'm just a volunteer helper-outer. For the emergency. It's my exercise."

"Think of *that,* now. I suppose pretty soon you'll be giving all of us our back rubs. Just for the exercise."

"No. Just for kicks," Joey said, and they both laughed.

It was easy to joke with Jane Cumberland. She was a relaxed sort of person. Since the first talk they'd had, she had seemed to accept him as one of the more amusing features of a placid existence, which gave her whatever she asked for without demanding much of anything from her in return. Her room, Joey observed whenever he passed through it on the way to or from the sleeping porch, was graced with a good many touches of luxury—an orchid silk puff on the day bed; a pair of tall silver candlesticks on the dresser, against the occasional nights when a thunderstorm caused an electric power failure; a rackful of women's and fashion magazines; an array of expensive-looking toilet articles and perfume bottles in front of her make-up mirror; a huge spherical vase of bubbly glass that was always filled with fresh flowers.

"I suppose this means you'll soon be well enough to be leaving us," she said.

"I'm in no hurry. It's a good vacation."

"I'll be sorry to see you go, Joey. It's a lonesome existence."

"Finnegan says your husband's coming up next weekend. You must be glad."

"I must be. You're so right. But he's not coming this weekend. He said he couldn't make it . . . Do you know what you've just done to me, Joey?"

"Why, no, Mrs.——"

"Jane."

"What have I done to you, Jane?"

"You've made all the little muscles in my shoulders and neck get as tight as—— Even my scalp feels like an electric guitar."

"Because I mentioned your husband?"

She took a hot roll from beneath its aluminum cover and pinched off a piece with delicate viciousness. "He'll be at me and at me and at me to go back to Rochester. God!" She made so unexpectedly horrible a face that Joey choked on his coffee, and both of them went into belly-knotting laughter.

It suddenly occurred to him that she was just the sort of woman Crystal Day had wanted to be—the sort that Joey had thought once of knowing, but only as a vague and unconvincing wish. Yet here he was, sitting and eating and chatting with her—with a more-than-pretty, sophisticated, easy-mannered woman who had the good things of life and a careless facility in using them.

He said, "Does Dr. Lytton say you oughtn't to go home to Rochester?"

She spread her slender, silver-nailed hands. "He's a defeatist. Snowden's all washed up—that's his creed. But it's the only place where I've been able to stay reasonably well, Joey. Isn't that a good reason for me not to risk any change?"

"I wouldn't know."

She reached out and took his chin in her warm fingers. "You evaded my eyes. Don't tell me you're against me too. Look straight at me. Nobody knows anything about you, Joey, so I've decided you're a mysterious visitor from another planet, with the gifts of extra-sensory perception—hindsight, foresight and sidewayssight. Tell me honestly, my fine young space-gypsy, don't you agree that it isn't worth the risk for me to go back where I broke down, when I'm so well and so secure in mind here? Wouldn't it be unwise for me to jeopardize all that?"

Joey's mind fizzed with the excitement of it—her confiding in him, the touch of her fingers on his face, the whimsicality in her eyes. He tried to look mock-oracular as he blurted out a joking remark without holding it in quarantine for the momentary inspection that might have saved him. "And could be your boy friend would come back here and find you gone."

Her nails dug into his chin painfully and released it. She tore another piece from the roll, then threw it on her plate.

"What have you done—signed on as apprentice to Finnegan? He's been the town's worst gossip for years, the old biddy."

"I didn't mean——"

"You may go now."

"I—I guess that was a stupid thing to——"

"It was. You have trays to carry down. You'd better get started."

"I'm sorry, Jane."

"Mrs. Cumberland to you, laddie. Tell the cook not to send up any dessert. And close the door as you go."

Joey said, "You're the one that's calling the signals."

He stacked the trays, balanced them shoulder-high on one palm, marched out, and pulled the door closed with a thump.

As he turned, he was chest to chest with Finnegan. The man's mouth was down at the corners as usual, but this time in a gloating smile. His cheeks twitched with enjoyment, and his eyes were narrowed and moist.

"She threw you out, bud . . . eh? You're not her speed, Josephson. Her boy friend had two Mexican divorces and an MG car. Where did you think *you'd* rate?"

Finnegan's hand gripped Joey's upper arm. The thin fingers dug in as if they were trying to pierce to the bone.

Joey suddenly recognized the expression on Finnegan's face. He'd seen it many a time on the face of a wino, squatting on the curb with a buddy, reaching for the shared fifth of Sneaky Pete and glancing up to see some strange man walk furtively into the house near the corner of the avenue with one of the girls who lived there. Contempt, mixed with wet-lipped envy, would slacken the wino's mouth before he put the bottle to it again. Finnegan wasn't even a wino—just a watcher and listener.

Joey felt grown-up in this moment—older and stronger and more of a man than the elderly, sickly lecher whose fingers tried to hurt him. He said without anger, "I don't like to be pawed. Not by another guy, Finnegan."

Something in his tone made the bony hand drop hastily away.

"Don't get sore, kid."

"I'm not a kid any more," Joey said.

He carried the trays for the rest of that week. The second evening, he left the house with the vague purpose of going down to the Square, perhaps to the library to read. He hadn't taken out a card to withdraw books, for fear the librarian might ask for personal information. Sandy came out into the hallway, dressed in a white blouse and a skirt of flowered cotton print that swung from her slim hips like a bell.

"Going downstreet?" Joey asked.

"There's a fine afterglow. I'm going up to the railing to look at it."

He walked with her to the iron fence that ran across the dead end of the street at the brow of a steep declivity. Below, the roofs of the village were purple-gray in shadow. Beyond, on the opposite hill, the buildings of the abandoned Snowden san were silhouetted against the violet swell of Mount St. Cloud on the horizon. Above, bright orange clouds caught the last rays of the sunken sun. It was all so delightful that it made Joey's lurking inner misery twist around among his viscera worse than usual.

The girl stood and watched the loveliness of the evening, her face still and tranquil. Joey glanced sideways at her now and then. She wasn't as beautiful as Jane Cumberland. She wasn't even strikingly pretty, as Crystal in her flashy way had been. The slender, wiry body was not, like theirs, an instant invitation to male excitement. Even the brilliance of the smile that lighted her face at times with sudden unexpected gaiety was probably, he thought, no more than the chance formation of her strikingly white teeth rather than a glimpse of any inner radiance.

"Why don't you get out of this?" he said suddenly.

"Out of what?"

"All this flunky work you're doing. You're smart enough to run this house; you're smart enough to get a job in an office in some bigger town. You'd make decent money and you wouldn't have to break your back whenever a maid walks out."

"Before my mother died I thought of getting away from Snowden. It's pretty deadly to be young in this town now."

"No playmates?"

"There aren't many boys. They go away to college or technical schools. Mostly they don't ever come back. And the few who still come here, for their health, like you——" She made a little gesture of dismissal with one slender hand.

He felt an irrational resentment. "What's wrong with us?"

"Nothing. You come and you go. So do the leaves on the trees."

"If a guy got to like you, if he told you so, if he said, 'When things get straightened out, I'll come back——'"

Her low laugh stopped him. "But they do. They *all* do. They all say it, I mean. But they never come back. Never."

"If a guy——"

"Never," she repeated, and there was a quiet finality in her voice that was years older than the girl herself, an autumn sadness that came of a childhood of watching her elders hope and stop hoping.

He said, "So you wanted to get away. And do what?"

"I have a cousin who's a Navy nurse. She's flown to Iceland. And to Saigon." The smile glowed. "Think of it, Joey!"

"Then why *don't* you cut loose from here and go for something like that?"

Sandy said quietly, "I'm needed."

"How?"

"I can't turn my patients out. There's nowhere else in town now for them to go."

"You don't owe them anything." He didn't know why he was taking this line with her. Certainly he didn't want to see his temporary hideaway vanish. Perhaps his own inner anguish was testing itself against her strange youthful poise.

"I took on the job of making them comfortable. I like to see a job through. A person has to have some standards."

Joey said, "You sound like a character out of one of those movies about an old aristocratic Southern family. Magnolias and fine old traditions. And stuff."

Her clear gray eyes studied him without rancor. "Do you know where John Brown's body is?"

"Sure. I read about it in the library one day last week. A few miles over that way at North Elba. He had a farm in the Adirondacks, and they buried him here after he was hanged."

"My father's only a little mountain farmer. With a bad back. But his great-grandfather was one of John Brown's supporters. Nearly died for it. Just as a matter of principle. He came from New England stock. A McTaggart was whipped at a cart tail for saying Roger Williams ought to be allowed to preach his own opinions. So you think I have no right to any traditions, to any code of conduct."

Joey had met Mr. McTaggart. Sandy's father came in from the farm with vegetables a few times a week, and on Sundays he spent the day in Snowden, eating one of Mrs. Wennergren's chicken dinners with Sandy in her sitting room at the rear of the house. He was a lean, sunburned man with keen gray eyes and a habit of massaging the curve of his spine with his knuckles.

Joey thought about this country character as an oracle on the ways of the world and didn't feel impressed.

"You'll learn," he said bitterly.

"Maybe I did learn."

"Where, for instance."

"School, for instance."

"What one?"

"Sacred Heart."

"Nuns!" Joey said. "A lot they know about life. It's tough and dirty, Sandy. I can tell you that."

"They didn't see fit to teach us about toughness and dirt."

"What else is there to learn? Arithmetic and reading and writing you can use once in a while. But toughness and dirt you got to face all the time."

"Did I mention standards?"

"You certainly did."

"They taught us those. Once you have them, you can face pretty nearly anything. At least, you know what to do."

"So the other guy throws the standards on the muck pile and tries to beat your brains out. With a wrench. When he misses, he tries to choke you. With his bare hands. Standards! Yeah."

She waited, her eyes as still as the evening.

He clenched his teeth so hard his jaws hurt all the way up into his temples. Nice going, boy. You almost spilled it to her that time. Maybe it's all she was waiting for. Suppose her standards call for her to run right down to the town hall, where the chief of police has his office in the basement.

"Let's go," he said. He turned his back on the dimming west and walked, not looking back to see if she would follow.

After that, every evening, he fell into step with her when she went for a stroll, up to the railing or down to the shore of the lake that was only a wide stretch in the little river that ran through town. But their talk now was always on the safe level of chitchat about the day's minor happenings, punctuated by long silences that were without constraint. It was the girl's unobtrusive self-command, Joey decided, that kept him from being uneasy when they walked for long minutes without exchanging a word. She seemed so sure of everything that he began to feel resentment at the contrast with his own inner anxiety at the threat of the future.

Friday morning a new maid came to make up the beds and clean the rooms and carry the trays. Without his thrice-daily chore, Joey felt lost and restless.

Finnegan, cradling a brown paper bag in his arms, found him sitting on the veranda railing before supper, swinging his legs.

"Bananas and milk is the perfect combination of foods, fella says in an article I read. I'll give it a try for a week." Finnegan let Joey have a dour grin. "How does it feel not to be slaving for free, sucker?"

"Okay," Joey said.

"I thought you told me you weren't a kid any longer. She really wrapped you up in a neat paper bundle, baby boy. Fly paper, I mean. You were just the little pigeon that Tom Sawyer finagled into whitewashing the fence. Hey?"

"Tell it your way," Joey said.

Finnegan set his bag of bananas on the flooring and sprawled in a long upholstered chair on the veranda, puffing from the climb up the hill. Whenever Joey's glance came anywhere near him, he began to cackle to himself.

Joey went upstairs to get away from him. He decided suddenly that he wasn't going to walk with Sandy that evening. When the new maid— a middle-aged woman with thick glasses and a chronic expression of dissatisfaction—took away the tray after he had eaten alone, he lay on the bed with his hands under his head, looking at the grain of the wainscotted porch ceiling. He had turned on the small table radio he had bought to ease his lonesomeness, but he didn't listen to the dull thumping of the rock-a-billy record that was being played on the local station.

What do I do? After my money gives out and I have to leave here, I'm on the run. Try for a job, and they ask questions. No good. So steal a car and stick up gas stations (where can I get a gun?) and stay on the run until they catch up. They will. Brother, they will.

There was a knock on the door. He knew who it was. Her and her standards.

"I don't feel like walking," he called loudly.

The door opened. "I don't feel like it either. I feel like screaming."

The voice wasn't Sandy's. Jane Cumberland came through the shadows of the room into the light of the table lamp that stood beside the little radio. Her blond hair still swept upward in pulled-taffy neatness to the crowning froth of curls. She didn't look like the screaming type.

She slipped gracefully to her perch at the foot of the bed. "You're a stubborn man, Joey."

He didn't answer.

"Oh, damn you, anyway," she said cheerfully. "All week you've been stalking in and out of my room with the trays as if someone had put a broomstick up you from stern to stem. And now that Old Goody Grumbleguts has taken over, I don't catch a glimpse of you all day."

Joey kept his eyes on the ceiling. "You told me to get out and——"

"'Told you told you told you.' What an utterly illogical argument to use with a woman. It makes my scalp feel twice as tight just to listen to you. Anyway, you wouldn't know the first thing of how to go about it. You wouldn't know how to begin."

Joey raised his head from the pillow. She was wearing the crimson negligee again. The lamplight made curves of silky gleam along it. "Begin what?"

"You talked about it, but I'm sure it was only talk. I don't suppose you ever gave one in your life."

"Gave what?"

"A back rub."

Joey thought about the Marchands. They seemed to be farther away than Egypt. "My particular pal was a hot rodder. Had a souped-up Chevvy. But his brother was a motorcycle nut. He'd spend a whole weekend with a gang of put-put boys like himself. They'd go hundreds of miles. Sunday nights I always had a standing date to give Phil a rub-down. He said if it wasn't for that he'd have been too stiffened up Monday morning to make it to the shop."

"I know how he felt. The thought of going back to Rochester makes me stiffen up worse than a million miles of bouncing on a motor bike."

"He'd take a hot soak in the tub," Joey said, "and then I'd go over him with wintergreen oil. Easy at first, because he'd yelp when I dug into the kinky spots too hard, but when I got the circulation going good, I'd really work on his muscles, one at a time." He lifted his hands and looked at them. "I've got pretty strong fingers."

Jane Cumberland looked mildly horrified. "Good God! Winter-green . . . What a despicable reek! Couldn't you use something less re-volting, like——"

"Rubbing alcohol? Sure, sometimes I——"

"That smells almost as contemptible. Toilet water was what I started to say."

"On Phil? He wouldn't want to smell like a he-Lucy."

"I wasn't thinking of your Phil. I was——"

"Why, once we were fresh out of wintergreen and alcohol and all, and I tried giving him the rubdown without anything. Nearly took the skin off him. So he said he'd heard of using talcum powder. And anyway, when you're shooting pool they always have a can of talcum near the cue rack, so if your hands get sweaty and the cue sticks, you make your fingers slick and slippy with the powder. So I tried it on Phil's back, and it was okay for lubrication and not as sloppy as the other gook, but even so he griped because it made him smell too pretty."

"I repeat: I didn't mean your Phil, Joey lamb," Jane Cumberland said patiently. "I meant me."

"Oh," Joey said.

He thought, When you're on the run, between gas-station stickups, you might as well have something to remember before they catch up with you.

He walked to the door of the room with her.

"Later on, after everyone's turned in," she said.

"Okay, Jane." Joey opened the door for her.

Finnegan was standing in the doorway of his room, directly across, peeling a banana. In red-and-green-striped pajamas, he looked like a large doll made of a shriveled watermelon and long sections of a par-ticularly gaudy Maypole.

"They may be good for you," he said discontentedly, "but so doggone many of 'em makes you feel bloated."

"Save that one for an eye-opener in the morning then, butch," Jane Cumberland said. "If you eat it for a nightcap now, it may keep you awake."

"They're better than spinach in one way," Finnegan said. "They make you belch sweeter."

He disappeared into his room.

Jane walked toward her own, two doors down the hall, near the head of the staircase. She gave Joey a quick smile over a crimson shoulder. Her lips formed the words, "Be seeing you!"

FOURTEEN

THE LAST SCUFFINGS of slippered feet along the hall, to and from the bathroom, died down and ceased. Joey had taken his bath earlier and sprawled, waiting, on his bed. The evening was unusually warm, and he didn't bother to put on anything over his pajamas.

He got up now and tiptoed to his door. The house was perfectly still, but someone was smoking somewhere. The scent of cigarette came through the chink of the door the moment he opened it a crack. He paused, looking into the dimly lighted hall and listening. A lonesome bell tolled in the distance; at the railroad station, they were making up the night train.

He was about to push the door wide enough to slip out when he saw a red spark glow and fade. It seemed as bright as a small tail light, for it was framed in the slit of blackness where Finnegan's door was slightly ajar.

Joey went back to his porch and lay down. Finnegan—the watcher and listener—the wino whose Sneaky Pete was other people's emotions—was sitting in the dark, smoking and waiting to see what would happen.

The stinking peeper, Joey thought. He must have been listening outside my door when we made the date.

Joey suddenly drove a fist into the door jamb, as if it personified Finnegan and Mr. Baggott and his own naive credulity and all else that had brought him to crouch in this insecure hiding place. The pain in his knuckles was nothing. He whispered, "God damn him! I can wait him out. There's a long night ahead."

Twice he barefooted it to the door. Each time the spark or the tobacco whiff told him Finnegan was still on duty. The third time he could sense nothing. He went back to the bed and turned the radio on, whisper-soft, so that he could keep track of time. Half an hour for good measure, to make sure Finnegan would doze off.

At the end of the achingly long period he had set himself, he snapped off the radio and eased his way into the hall. He took short, slow strides toward Jane's room, wary of any creaking floorboards.

The knob turned noiselessly under his firm, cautious grip. He slipped through and closed the door gently. The room was dark, but some sort of low night light was burning on the sleeping porch. Jane was rising from a long chair on which she had been lying.

"Joey?" she whispered.

"Yes."

A fist was banging against his ribs, from the inside, fast and heavy. She was wearing a short nightgown that came only to the top of her thighs. It startled him for a moment until he remembered the girl he had watched a few times across the apartment house court at home, earlier this summer, when he got up to go to the supermarket and she was still asleep with her blinds raised all the way to get more air and her bare legs asprawl. He'd been curious until she rolled over in her sleep and he saw that she was wearing a tiny pair of briefs under the gown.

Jane turned and slipped into the bed next to the screened windows. There was a smooth swirl of naked limbs, and then she had pulled the sheet over her to her waist.

Joey stood above her. He glanced at the screens; they were opaque now, for the dim light misted this side of them and there was blackness beyond.

Jane smiled. "Nothing out there but trees and a view of Mount St. Cloud. Haven't you ever noticed?"

"I guess I was too busy noticing you."

"Now you're my nice space-gypsy again." She patted the side of the bed and he settled down on one haunch. She stretched an arm to the bedside table and handed him a cylindrical container.

"Let's use this. You said it wasn't so sloppy."

As he took the can of bath powder in his hands, she turned quickly over upon her face, at the same time drawing up the short gown until it was just a necklet of sheer cloth.

"Help me off with this, darling."

He drew it over her head and over her extended arms and tossed the wisp of fabric toward the long chair. Jane rested a cheek on the wrists she had crossed on the pillow. She crinkled the corner of one eye at him. "We'll see how good a masseur you are."

He dusted the powder along her back. The scent came up to his nostrils strongly—a sort of two-toned odor, spicy on top with a sultry underlayer. The talc made the warm skin satin-smooth under his finger tips as he began at the nape of her neck, gently at first, then pressing more deeply.

"Oh, good!" Her voice was a mere murmur. "That's—mmm!—so relaxing."

His kneading hands went out along her shoulders and upper arms. His fingers followed the slender valleys beside her spine as far as her waist, digging in with little rotary squeezes at each rib-joining. Now and then she gave a little murmur of approbation.

He rested his palms on her back, bearing down, and smoothed the flesh outward and upward from the loins over the shoulderblades. The added weight made her nearer breast, half visible beneath the curve of her rib cage, swell outward in delicate plumpness at each stroke.

"Lower down, darling," she said. "The small of my back has been aching with tension."

He shifted his hip, wiping his forehead with the back of a hand. His face was damp. The smell of the powder was all over his paws. He took a deep, shaky breath, and when he tried to get a firm support with his outer foot again, to brace him in his side-saddle position on the bed, he found his knee had developed a pronounced tremor too.

"You're doing beautifully, Joey."

"Thanks."

"Now the legs."

"I'll have to pull the sheet down."

"That's all right."

"And you'll have to take your pants off."

She made a small sound of merriment. "I haven't any pants on, dear."

Her thighs were round, warm, tapering, twin columns of resilience. His hands grasped them, kneading, and she let out a little chuckling sigh and began to turn over. The tree branches outside the screen leaped into visibility as headlights wheeled through them; a car's tires squealed on the asphalt of the street; and suddenly the scent of the talc that was rising into Joey's face was the sickly rich redolence that had choked him as he pressed an ear toward a silent heart; and the round swell of living, moving flesh was the still-warm, cushiony thigh that had pressed motionless against his fingers as he felt for the wad of bills along the dead girl's leg. Stab of car beams—shriek of rubber—crash against concrete—dead flesh under your hands—someone wants to kill you—run, Joey—breath is agony in your crushed chest—your stomach is lurching—run, boy, run—run——

His shins sent the long chair sliding across the porch floor; his hips rocked a table in the dark room; he yanked the door open and charged through into a leaning, listening shape that bulked black against the dim light of the hallway.

Finnegan yelped, "God . . ." at an angle of forty-five degrees, continued with ". . . almighty!" as his slippered feet clattered down the first half-dozen steps of the staircase like a boy rattling a stick along a picket fence, and then crashed the rest of the way with a wordless yell.

Joey turned toward his own room. Maybe the man had been too startled to recognize—— Even as he realized the futility of that thought, he heard Finnegan's enraged clamor from below.

"Josephson, you whoremaster! You knocked me downstairs! You broke my back! Come down and help me!"

Joey's fists squeezed until his bruised knuckles were darts of pain. He wanted to get hold of Finnegan's skinny neck and clamp down on it with a Baggott grip, until the peeper had to hush his yapping.

As he marched down the stairs, the lights went on in the hall below. He took Finnegan by an arm and hauled him to his feet. The man groaned, rubbing the small of his back.

"What do you expect, listening at door jambs?" Joey demanded harshly. He hated himself for his moment of panic.

"That's the kind word you have for me," Finnegan gasped. "A fall like that could start up my bad lung and——"

"Then pull in your neck."

"Young delinquent!—giving a bad name to the house—in bed with a woman old enough to be your——"

Sandy McTaggart's voice, low and controlled, said, "Quiet, Mr. Finnegan. I'll handle this."

She had struggled into a seersucker robe in a hurry, for it was clutched round her haphazardly, showing most of the legs of her rumpled blue pajamas. Her hand was dropping away from the wall switch.

"You'd better do some fast handling, then." Finnegan's teeth were chattering with shock and fury. "You'll be losing all your decent guests if you let Josephson and the Cumberland woman go on shacking up together every night after everyone else is——"

"Hush!" In two strides she had him by the other arm, shaking him. She looked back over her shoulder, and Joey turned in the same direction and saw just inside the front door a middle-sized man in a gray suit.

The newcomer had a round face beneath thinning hair brushed back in orderly striping over a pink scalp. His light-colored eyes were rounded now, and his lips, as well, made a small circle with a little black hole in the middle, as if he were about to whistle or complain about the heat.

After a moment he said, "Sorry to get you up so late, Sandy."

"It's no bother, Mr. Cumberland."

Finnegan said, "No *bother*. My God in——"

He ended with a yelp as Joey twisted his arm.

Cumberland went on in a thin, low voice. "I found out today that I could make it after all. There was time to get here before evening if I stepped on it, so I just jumped in the car and took off without wasting time phoning. But I got hung up with a leaking master cylinder."

He walked toward the stairs. The three stood aside for him. Silence was painful when the shuffle of their slippers ceased. He put his foot on the first step and turned toward Joey.

"Say one word, boy, and I'll beat the hell out of you."

Suddenly his round chin was shaking. He stamped up the stairs, fast. Finnegan followed him slowly, muttering.

Joey said, "Sandy, I want to ex——"

She turned swiftly away toward the living room. Her own quarters lay beyond. For a moment he could see her outlined against a table where some of the patients had left a partly assembled jigsaw puzzle they had been working on all evening. Then her hand hit the wall switch and she was gone into darkness.

He ran after her, racked by the need for her to know the truth of the matter, and made a guesswork grab in the dimness. His hand found a twisting shoulder, tried to grasp it, slipped down inside a fold of cloth, clutched a rounded softness that must be——

As he snatched his fingers from her breast, something exploded against his face. A fury of blows rocked his head from side to side. One landed flat with a deafening *whump* against one ear, and the eardrum sent a jet of agony through his skull. For all her slenderness, the girl had an amazing wiry strength, multiplied by her fury. He reached out at random, trying to catch one of the flailing arms. Something rock-hard and round—

her forehead?—banged him in the nose from straight ahead. He gasped with shock and pain. A second later something hard and pointed—an elbow?—whacked into the nose from the side.

He lurched back. "Sandy——!"

Her whisper was sharp as an icicle. "You think you can paw every female in the house. Get out!"

"Give me a chance to tell you——"

"I'll give you until tomorrow morning to pack. I want your room then."

His eyes were too full of the water of pain from his twice-battered nose to see anything stir in the dimness, but he sensed the movement of her going. He lunged after her, to detain her and make her listen, but the cool flatness of wood slammed against his finger tips, and a bolt snicked home. Warm wet was tickling his upper lip, and he knew that his nose was bleeding.

He made his way across the dark living room toward the faint glow that came down the stairs from the upper hall. At the top of the steps he had to pass the door of Jane Cumberland's room. It was ajar.

"Now! Right now!" That would be the round-faced husband. "So it's the middle of the night. You can do other things in the middle of the night, you can pack up in the middle of the night . . . Because I goddam well *say* you will. Or else I'll throw your things in a heap into the car and throw you in after them."

Joey could hear the murmur of Jane's voice. Then the husband again: "The doctor says you can get along anywhere. Pack! . . . I've been a patsy long enough, keeping you on a perpetual vacation while you were taking on God knows how many fancy men. I'm fed up. Pack!"

Joey went on out of hearing. He lay on his bed a while. His nose had stopped bleeding, but he couldn't get to sleep. He could feel rather than hear the stir of the awakened household all around him. After a while he dressed. He took the fiber-and-plastic suitcase down from the closet shelf, threw his few belongings into it and went softly down the stairs and through the dark lower hall.

When he emerged upon the veranda, the rays of the street lamp, striking through a gap in the tree-gloom, dazzled him for a moment. He sat on one of the cushioned reclining chairs and tried to think. The night train had left long ago, and there weren't any buses until morning. The Snowden Inn didn't take lung patients, and he was straight from a cure cottage. There was a smaller hotel on Spruce Street——

A voice from the chair beside him said, "I didn't tell you you had to get out in the middle of the night."

"I couldn't sleep."

"Neither could I."

"You have standards," he said bitterly. "You're poised. The nuns fixed you up so you know what to do under any circumstances. You shouldn't have any trouble sleeping."

She didn't say anything to that.

"You didn't give a hoot about finding out my side of it," Joey went on. "You and Finnegan figured it all out in a flash."

There was a rustle as she stood up into the dappled lamp-shine, and he saw that she had put on a dress.

She said, "We'll keep the patients awake, talking here. Come."

He walked beside her to the upper end of the street. They sat on the cold wooden slats of a bench beside the crunching path and looked across the roofs that slumbered below, to where the distant deserted Snowden Sanatorium was a jag-toothed jawbone biting on the star-salted sky.

A cool wind blew in from the mountains and tossed a strand of her hair across his face. It smelled freshly washed and sweet, and suddenly the immense and lonely beauty of the night rejected and humiliated him.

"I tried to grow up," he said, "but I guess I didn't make it. I hadn't any call to snarl at you, as if you'd got me wrong."

She said in her accustomed voice, so quiet and controlled for one so young, "I might have asked you for your side of it."

"All I could have told you was a lie. Or else the truth—that I'd have liked to get into bed with her and wasn't man enough to go through with it. But her husband is taking her home anyway because of it. Right away. He's making her pack now."

"I know."

"So there'll be a scandal in your house, and I was the cause. I'll always be ashamed of it. You can remember that."

After a while she said, "I'll be honest, too. I have to ask for your room, because of the scandal. If it weren't for that . . . I'm not naive, Joey. I've known that some patients get lonesome and desperate and turn to one another for comfort and—— Being around a cottage san all my life, I've known about things like that since I was old enough to know why men and women go to bed together. I can understand it, even sympathize with it in a way—but I can't let it go on in my house."

"You don't have to explain," Joey said. "I made things harder for you. I wish I hadn't."

"Joey! You're crying." Her fingers were hesitant and comforting on his. That lightest of touches tore him wide open.

He said, truthfully and indignantly, "I'm *not* crying! You gave me a bloody nose back there when you beat up on me. It's started in again. That's why I sound like a head cold." He clutched her fingers, to keep them from withdrawing, and went on savagely, "I didn't even particularly want her. I guess I was just doing it to sort of hit back at all of them, because they've got me on the run, and then at the last I turned chicken and didn't take her. Do you know why? When you hear, you'll want to belt me in the face again for having the gall to sit here with you. It was because—this is funny—it was because her powder had a smell that was a little like the stuff the girl was wearing."

"What girl?"

"The girl I killed."

He heard her breath make a sharp in-going sound, but her fingers weren't snatched away from his.

After a while she said, "Do you want to tell me about it?"

"Yes," he said.

When he had finished with the telling and the silence closed in tight around them again, he found his forehead was down on the back of the hand he clasped in his. Her other hand touched his hair.

"When you said you killed her, I thought for a second you meant you'd murdered her."

"I might as well have. She's dead because I was stupid."

She said, "You've got yourself into a fix."

He was glad she hadn't said anything pitying or tried to tell him it was somebody else's fault.

"I've got to get myself out of it," he said.

"You know what you ought to do."

"Sure. And I'm not going to do it. They'll send me to the chair if I give myself up. Nobody'll believe I didn't kill that Keene, whoever he is."

"Are you a Catholic, Joey?"

"I was brought up to be one. Last few years, though, Gram had a hard time getting me to go to Mass."

"Have you thought of going to Sacred Heart, to confession?"

"The priest would only tell me I should turn myself in. And I don't intend to."

"How do you know? He might not."

"When he heard how I stole the blank certificates from that other priest in Brooklyn, he'd work me over."

"He'd tell you what you *ought* to do. The rest is up to you."

"Then I'm doing all right on my own. I *know* what I ought to do."

"But what *will* you do?"

He didn't say, "Start swiping cars and sticking up gas stations." He knew now that he had turned his back on that. And he definitely couldn't stay on in Sandy's house, even if she broke with principle and offered to let him. He wouldn't, he decided, feel the same toward her if she did. It would somehow spoil the notion of her that he had built up.

Where was he to go, how should he get money to live by? The future was blacker and chillier than this midnight perch that was his for only a few swift minutes.

He said suddenly, "Why did you wallop me so hard? You could have just told me to get out. I would have. Without a bloody nose to take along."

There was an uncharacteristic hesitation in her answer. "I—I thought you were attempting to paw——"

"Do you sock every guy who touches you?"

She tried to draw her hand away. "Coming down, straight from her, and— Never mind."

"It made that much difference to you!" Joey tenderly ran the fingers of his free hand over his sore nose. "Well—it did, didn't it? Didn't it, Sandy? . . . I never had the nerve to think you— Hey!"

He straightened up, shivering with the night chill and a sudden new realization. "I know! I know what I'll do. I won't run. And I won't give myself up. I'll play it smart. But smart!"

She didn't pull away from the arm that went around her shoulders, but she didn't lean to him. "What's this smart thing you're going to do?"

"I won't tell you till I get it set. Maybe you wouldn't like it. No, I guess you won't, but I'm going to do it anyway."

"Joey, are you sure——"

"What's 'sure'? I've got to fight my way out of this thing. My *own* way. I've got to take things as they come."

"The dirty, ugly things."

"That's right."

"In a dirty, ugly way. Is that it, Joey? Is that how it's going to be?"

"Don't ask anything about it yet. If I start answering questions, you'll wiggle it out of me. And then maybe you'll—— I won't tell you. Leave it to me."

"I'll have to," she said.

The wind off the mountains whistled in the pines. Sandy, too, was shivering now.

FIFTEEN

THE BOOKKEEPER brought in the monthly report, and Chester Baggott spread it on his desk and prepared to look through the figures.

The wavy glass in the upper part of the partition transmitted whimsically distorted shapes from the sales floor, where the demonstration cars, even longer and more bizarre in color and design than last year's models, stood about like fragments from the prophetic dream of a sedan-chair maker to the court of Louis XIV.

Baggott was definitely on the up-swing today. First thing you know, he thought, they'll be bringing out a line with decorative panels on the doors. They've gone about as far as they can with fishtails and multiple lights and interior trim. Next they'll be tickling the women's itch for décor by painting the jobs like the English coronation coach. Or an old-time music box. Shepherdesses and cupids. Watteau and Fragonard. Strictly custom jobs for the rich bitches who've graduated from the Cadillac and Lincoln set and don't care for foreign sports cars. Conspicuously expensive fol-de-rol.

He chuckled.

Every week that passed meant that much less probability that the Tripp boy would be turned up anywhere. After all, there must be lots of people who walked away and got themselves permanently lost, built new lives, were never identified with their old personalities. Sergeant Lowery had as much as said that there was a good chance the youngster would never be found.

If a year passed without repercussions, or even six months—hell, make it three months—Chester Baggott would breathe freely and put the whole thing behind him.

He applied himself to the figures in the report. The accounting system that the automobile company imposed upon its agencies was a complicated one, but Baggott's attention skipped past all that and centered on the one item of the profit-and-loss sheet that was of prime importance to him—the ledger account entitled "Entertaining and Promotion."

It was into this account that he had had to load most of the expenses of keeping Crystal Day. There had been a sharp decrease—a most comfortable and reassuring one—since the "accident," as he was able to think of it more and more readily now. The sick-making crash-and-crunch sounds seldom filled him now with wild remembered startle whenever a door slammed or a motor backfired. With the passing of months to come, there would be little or no reason for even Evelyn, in the unlikely event that she ever saw these figures, to go back to the point where heavy "entertainment" expenses would arouse curiosity or doubt.

The clothes he had worn the night of the accident were no longer a worry. The first night after Evelyn had left for the conference at Tupper Lake, Baggott disinterred them from the mulch pile and brought them indoors. The cloth he scissored into small bits and flushed down the bathroom toilet, little by little. The buttons and other parts heavy enough to sink and remain in the S-shaped trap of the plumbing he strewed at widespaced intervals along the roads on a night ride through a distant part of Westchester. That disposed of the only bit of physical evidence to connect him with the death of Sid Keene.

A public address system was playing music out on the display floor—soothing lilts from the good musical plays, with lots of violins and wood winds—luxury music—money-to-spend music. Not the cheap jump-and-stomp stuff, with crackpot arrangements that mated piccolos and tubas in the endless repetition of some inane little fragment of tunelessness.

Baggott was humming along with the music—"You'd look at me . . . and I would see . . . the smile you're smiling now"—when a girl swung through the door in a little waltz step. She was holding a small sheaf of mail outstretched in one hand; the other lifted her full skirt so that it wheeled wide with the swing of her hips.

She let out a little "Oh!" of chagrin and froze in place like Lot's wife, the skirt wrapping itself about her with a climbing swirl that exhibited a handsome height of nylon leg before it fell into demure perpendicularity.

"I thought you were over at the garage, Chester."

Baggott liked everyone in the office to use his given name. It made for a friendly sales atmosphere, he always said, and anyway it was part of modern business practice. Like almost everybody else in his circle of acquaintance, he was on a first-name basis with many persons he knew only as voices over the telephone. Wouldn't recognize them if he ran into them on the street or at a cocktail party, unless they were introduced.

He said, "Glad I'm not at the garage this very second, Lois. I'd have missed an unexpected little treat."

She gave him a pleased sidelong smile, let her eyes cling to his the few extra seconds that a woman uses for a signal of interest. As definite in its way as Evelyn's Péché Gaillard. Close-curling light-brown hair. Excellent legs. A straight, easy carriage. Not a smashing redheaded beauty, like Crystal, but good-looking. Really good-looking, with all the smooth finish of fine breeding. Vassar graduate. A little apartment by herself on a side street off Sutton Place. Didn't team up with other girls. That was good . . . He'd known a few men she'd gone out with. Steadily, sometimes. But always very discreetly. Very.

It was something to think about. Not immediately, of course. Lord, no! not with that other thing hardly past the jitters point yet. But when the good old antibiotic of Time the Healer had had a chance——

Lois Beviere laid the letters on his desk. "The afternoon mail just came in . . . You've been tense lately, Chester. I think you need to relax more."

"Maybe you're right."

He glanced up, and again her eyes dwelt on his those few important seconds before dropping to the letters.

"Any plans?"

"No." He was about to add, as an obvious countermove in this little game, "Any ideas?"—but he checked himself in time. No rush, Chet, old boy. Pace yourself intelligently. "I'm figuring, as a matter of fact, on a few weeks in Bermuda with Evelyn this winter. We can rent a cottage on the beach, near Hamilton."

"You haven't taken any time off this summer at all."

"No, but Ev's been away now and then. She's up at Tupper Lake now, doing her bit for the sociological health of the country."

"It's lovely terrain up there."

"I wish I were able to join her. But no can do right now. I'll have to settle for the Bermuda deal." He chuckled. "You know something? I used to do quite a bit of duck shooting, Lois. We always had bird dogs, when I was a boy down in Reisterstown. There was a retriever called Romany Rye that was practically human. He used to—— Hell, if I get started on that, I'll prattle all afternoon. What I meant to say was, every spring I get out the old twelve-gauge and oil it up, check the ammunition and if it's too old I get fresh stock, and when the returns are all in, where do I go for vacation? To some summer resort with Ev. Oh, well . . . Anything interesting in the mail?"

"Not very. I opened all the letters but this one. It's marked 'Private.' So many things in life have that warning posted on them. Haven't they?"

"Until someone takes the sign down," he said.

They exchanged brief, knowledgeable smiles. She left the office, moving with graceful, assured ease.

He picked up the unopened envelope. It was addressed in longhand. The word PRIVATE in the lower lefthand corner was thrice underlined. Briefly he examined the postmark—Amsterdam, N.Y.—and then used the onyx paper knife from the desk set Evelyn had given him on some half-forgotten birthday. The note on the single sheet of cheap paper was handwritten too.

Mr. Baggott;

It's on account of you I got to go into hiding. I do not want to be caught by the police, but if I am caught by them it will be necessary for me to tell them everything. How you told me what to do. How you fixed it so that those two people got killed. How you made it look like I was the one.

I am willing to keep my mouth shut, but I got to have a few dollars to live on so I will not have to do anything to get me in wrong with the police but can just stay out of sight some place and out of trouble.

Five thousand dollars will take care of me for quiet a while. I will keep my mouth shut and that is it's price. If you are willing to pay it, put an add in the *N. Y. Times* every day for the next week, saying exactly like this:

GUARANTEED LIKE NEW. Demonstration models. At substantial savings, Baggott Motor Sales.

When I see this add, I will let you know how to get the money to me. If I do not see it in the paper, I will write letters to the D.A. and your wife and the Pres. of the automobile company telling them the truth and they should investagate your whole life, particurally with respect to the girl, and they would only find out who was the one was to blame for the killing of them two inocent people.

Joseph Tripp

Baggott took the paper knife of onyx plastic firmly in both hands and broke it in half. He laid the fragments carefully side by side on the green blotter pad that partly covered the plate glass that topped his desk. He gazed unseeingly at the shadow play of wriggly figures in the translucent partition—salesmen and customers swimming by like fish in a murky aquarium.

There were words that went with the music the public address system was playing now. *"The Lord above gave man an arm of iron——"*

If I could get my hands on him again.

"With a little bit of luck . . . someone else will do the blooming work."
No. You have to do it yourself to get it done right.
"The Lord above made man to help his neighbor—" *
If I could *only* get my hands on him.
Make ready to pay it. What else can you do? Dig it up somehow—out of Entertaining and Promotion or wherever else you can scrabble it up. Throw it down the rat hole. But that's a chasm you can never level over. Many a man has gone down to hell, trying to fill the Grand Canyon of a blackmailer's demands. There'll be another five thousand, then ten, then more . . . and more . . .

And you may not even be sure who's getting it. For that matter, who wrote this note? You don't even know that. And there's no way for you to find out.

He reached out a stiff-fingered hand to sweep the pieces of paper knife into the waste basket. It stopped in mid-motion, changed direction, went into his coat pocket and came out with the long, flat wallet. Behind memoranda on prospects, notes on luncheon and office engagements, and a sheaf of dog-eared miscellany, he came on them, folded down and tucked unobtrusively into a corner—the two baptismal certificate forms young Tripp had spoiled before he completed his successful forgery.

At least one fortunate break, Baggott thought. Instead of destroying them, he had kept them, moved by an obscure idea that perhaps they might, in some unforeseen contingency, be a threat to hold over the boy, to scare him into line, if necessary. It hadn't worked out that way, but they were now unexpectedly useful.

He laid the two spoiled certificates beside the note, ran his gaze back and forth, comparing, letter by letter. It didn't need the trained eye of an examiner of questioned documents to see that the handwriting on all three sheets was the same. The capital G with the tail looped the wrong way—the circles for dots over the i's—there were dozens of similarities. The formation of every letter in the note was unmistakably authentic.

He plucked the pen from the onyx holder and wrote on his memorandum pad. Then he folded the certificates and the note and stored them away in the wallet. He spoke under his breath. "You think you have me over a barrel, Tripp. So you have. And I'll bury you in that barrel yet, boy."

He raised a clenched fist, ready to bang it down hard on the glass

---

* *Four lines from WITH A LITTLE BIT OF LUCK. Copyright © 1956 by Alan Jay Lerner and Frederick Loewe. Chappell & Co. Inc. New York, N.Y., Publisher and Owner of allied rights throughout the world.*

surface, but he took a deep breath, lowered the hand gently, and pressed a buzzer button twice. When Lois came in he tore the note from the memo pad. "Insert this in the *Times,* please. Every day next week."

She glanced at it. "Don't you think we ought to go into more detail? List some of the stufferoo on the de luxe models—automatic windows, electronic dimmers—little tidbits of bait? All at a great reduction, et ceterah-rah?"

"Let's try it this way for once, Lois. It's just a tiny morsel of bait. But I think someone will bite."

The door closed behind the gracile swing of her hips, and she was just another wavy shape in the aquarium.

SIXTEEN

JOEY GOT DOWN from the bus with his suitcase, light in his hand. All he had added to his meager belongings were two pairs of work pants and a couple of denim shirts.

He walked up a dirt road between two groves of blue spruce that stood straight and still, like an attentive audience for the gay hillside beyond, where beech and birch were glowing with the first golden tints of the coming performance of autumn. The sun, still warm, was slanting lower to the south each day.

Around a turn he came on the low farm building he was looking for. Past it, in a hay field, a horse rake stood unused. The hay was drying in neatly spaced piles. The horses had been unhitched; he could glimpse them tossing their heads to shake off the flies under a shed beside the barn. In the distance, through a stake-and-rider fence, Joey could glimpse half a dozen black-and-white cows, with a few calves, grazing in the shade of a clump of half-scarlet maples.

Will McTaggart was swinging a scythe along the edge of the hay field, where uneven ground made any mechanical cutter useless. As he stopped and watched Joey approach, he pressed one hand to his back.

Joey said, "Hi, Mr. McTaggart."

"Let's see now. I remember you. You're young Josephson. Staying at the house. Came with a message from Sandy for me? Couldn't she phone?"

"She didn't know I was heading this way."

The bright gray eyes in the leather-brown face glanced at the suitcase. "You got well and you're off for home?"

"No, sir. I thought I might work for you."

The leather went into folds of amusement. "Those are city clothes you're wearing, young fella."

"I've got dungarees with me."

"Any experience on a farm?"

"Yes, sir."

"What doing? Who'd you work for?"

"I was just a kid, but I helped with the chores at my uncle's place, over toward Placid. I can milk a cow. And I can drive a truck——" He gulped. "I mean, I know how to drive. I haven't got a license yet." The spurious license was tucked away in a zippered pocket in the lining of the suitcase. Perhaps he ought to destroy it. He certainly wouldn't dare to use it.

"Why should you want to work here, Josephson? To get your health back before you go down to the city?"

"That's right," Joey said. And then he pressed his lips firmly together for a second. "No, sir. That's not all of it. I'm not going to lie to you. I'm hiding out."

Will McTaggart moved his shoulders stiffly, rested the scythe against a fence post and massaged the small of his back with both hands. He gave a little grunt of pain. "Hiding out from what? Are you a criminal, at your age? You're a big fella, but you can't be much more'n twenty."

"I give you my word," Joey said, "I didn't do anything terribly bad. But there's somebody wants to have me get the blame for something real bad. I need a place to stay until I can think of a way to clear myself."

"Why didn't you stay right on at the house? Sandy runs it every bit as good as her mother used to. You could have stayed there and not told anybody anything." The keen gray eyes measured Joey.

"I meant to. I got in a foul-up."

"What kind?"

"I was in the room of a married lady yesterday evening, and someone raised a fuss, as if I was doing something wrong, and he got the house upset. Sandy said I'd have to leave. So I thought if you'd let me help out——"

"Josephson, it looks to me like you've got a habit of getting into trouble and then coming up with excuses."

"But nothing had happened! I was on my way *out* of her room when he"——

"You better run along and try elsewhere, young fella. I haven't any place for you."

—"he had his ear to the door, and I came out and bumped him and he went ass over head down the stairs, screeching. The damn old woman!"

"Who're you talking about, anyway?"

"That Finnegan!" Joey shouted. "If he hadn't been shoving his snout into the keyhole——"

He choked it off, unprepared for the lusty whoop that came out of Will McTaggart.

"Finnegan! Well, by dad! I'd have liked to been there and seen it. That old needle-nose had spread more gossip around the village than any half-dozen sewing-circle ladies with double-jointed tongues. So you dumped him down the stairs on his rump, eh? Isn't that an awful thing!" Merriment rumbled in his chest.

Joey began eagerly, "So you see it wasn't——"

"I can't keep you here, Josephson, but I'm going to send you on your way with a pat on the back for spilling Finnegan on his brisket."

Joey tried again. "When they were after John Brown to hang him, your great-grandfather didn't turn his back on him, just because people said he was a criminal."

Will McTaggart looked thoughtful. "What you got into trouble about, Josephson—was it trying to help your country or your fellow-man?"

"Well . . . no."

"Did that snippy daughter o' mine put you up to dragging old Johnny Brown into this rickumstance? Trying to work on family pride and sympathy?"

Joey met McTaggart's sharp, unsmiling gaze. "No, sir. She didn't even know I intended to come here. I didn't tell her, because I didn't think she'd approve. She has," Joey added glumly, "standards."

"Well, yes," McTaggart agreed. "So did her ma. A good thing, too . . . Come to think of it, I got 'em myself. For instance, I couldn't let you stay here without you have a social security card. Got one?"

"No," Joey said quickly, and as quickly corrected himself. "Yes, I have, but I don't want to use it. I thought if you'd just let me help around for bed and board, I wouldn't ask for any pay."

"Probably wouldn't be worth any. But here's where standards come in. I can't profit by your offer to work free. Know why? The regulations say I got to report the fair value of any lodging or meals given in payment for services, just as if it was money wages. And I got to pay toward your social security on that basis. I wouldn't try to get around that."

Joey said, "Then let me pay you just a little for my keep. For a short while, anyway. I'll help you all I can, just for the sake of something to do, to stop me from going off my——"

"I wouldn't take advantage of you like that. Anyway, you couldn't be of any help to me. Sorry, boy. Good luck on your travels."

Will McTaggart took hold of the scythe and walked away. Joey heard the breath of anguish go into the man and saw him shudder.

"Shouldn't ha' stopped to gabble. That disk o' mine stiffens up."

Joey caught up with him. He saw that McTaggart's shirt was black with sweat, under the arms and all across the back, and now the water of suffering was suddenly in pendant drops on the man's chin.

Joey shed his coat, tossed it upon the suitcase, stepped around Mc-Taggart, and grabbed the scythe handle.

"Let go o' that," the older man snapped. "Dad burn it! you wouldn't know the first thing——" His voice gave a little bounce of agony, and his grip involuntarily slackened.

Joey had the scythe now. He reached for the whetstone that protruded from a rear pocket of McTaggart's khaki pants.

Many a time, using a crooked bough and a piece of stick, he had mimicked with a child's accurate apery the whetting of a scythe blade, as he had seen his uncle perform it. Now he found the motions returning without conscious effort at remembering. The stone sang along the steel edge, one side and then the other, over and over. He thrust the stone into his own back pocket, grasped the scythe handles, and took his stance.

A man shouldn't try to force it, his uncle had said, proud like any other worker to exhibit the skills of his task. Let the weight of the scythe do the job and guide it with the swing of your body as you step forward in the proper rhythm.

Joey tried it tentatively. Swish. Good. Then—no, don't press, remember? Another step and let your arms and shoulders go easily, with the implement swinging freely like a pendulum. There. And another step. Again. Swing and recovery. Swing and return.

The play of muscles was like music along his young body.

When he reached the corner of the fence, he shouldered the scythe and walked back. "How's that?"

McTaggart groaned. "Give me your shoulder to lean on, boy. I got to get to bed where I can lay flat. That damn back is throwed out again."

Joey helped him hobble to the house. In the simply furnished, neat living room, with its dark oak table and its gay hooked rugs spread on the wide floor boards, McTaggart sagged to the couch and stretched out with a series of groans at every stage of the operation.

"Call Dr. Vanderpoel. He'll strap me up so I can get around somehow. Dad burn it, I can't afford to be laid up."

Joey looked up the number in the telephone book and made the call. Then he went out and got his suitcase. In the kitchen he changed to work clothes, peeked into the refrigerator and took a quick glance around, down in the basement. Then he went out, retrieved the scythe from where he had hung it in the fork of a tree, and went to work again on the grass along the field edge.

He quit and went into the house when a car trailed a dust plume up the dirt road.

"The doctor's coming. He'll tell you to rest that back."

"Flapdoodle! How can I take a rest when there's——"

"I'll look after the horses and milk the cows. I'm not much of a cook, but I can fry some bacon. Or get a steak out of the freezer. You've got potatoes down cellar, and I'll pick some wax beans out of the garden as I go by."

"For somebody who ain't going to be around here long, you're taking over in high style," Will McTaggart said.

Joey set his feet solidly on the flat circle of a hooked rug. "You need me. I'm staying until you don't."

The bald, ruddy-faced, burly doctor let the screen door slam behind him. Without a word he began to poke around in McTaggart's anatomy, making resentful sounds in his throat. "I told you to go easy," he said finally.

"I got my work," McTaggart said, "and I got to do it."

"Huh . . . you won't. Not for a couple of weeks anyway."

"I *can't* lay around——"

The doctor stood up abruptly. "I want you shifted to where you can be taken care of properly. I want you in your daughter's house, where you'll be looked after and where you'll be handy for me to give you treatments. You're to have traction——"

"Fiddle-faddle. A man's got to do what he's got to——"

Dr. Vanderpoel let out a bull's roar that set the chimes in the grandfather's clock jangling faintly.

"Quiet! . . . Look here, Will McTaggart, you sog-brained old recalcitrant—do you want to have to have an operation that'll fuse your vertebrae and leave you with a poker spine for the rest of your life? . . . so you'll have to turn and bend all in one piece? . . . like the little plastic farmer that sits on the seat of a child's toy tractor?"

"Well," McTaggart said meekly, "if you put it that way, Doc." He seemed to find a great relief in being forced at last to give up.

Dr. Vanderpoel turned to Joey. "Pack some nightgear and a toothbrush for him. I'm taking him with me in the car right now. I can't trust the old renegade. He might have a change of heart."

"Tell me what has to be done right away around the place here, Mr. McTaggart," Joey said. "I'll make out somehow, and on Saturday afternoon I'll go into the village on the bus and we can talk over everything and lay out the work that's ahead. You can give me detailed directions then."

"You'll make a mess of things, Josephson," Will McTaggart groaned. "Bound to . . . Just don't ruin the place any more than you have to."

Joey helped the doctor get McTaggart into the car. Will put a hand on Joey's shoulder for a moment.

"I'll thank you later on, bub . . . When I find out what I've got to thank you for," he added wryly.

The car backed around and dragged a new dust plume after it into the distance between the blue spruce groves.

Joey stood still for a while, taking deep breaths of the evening. The copper ball of the sun was nibbled at by the dark teeth of trees under an amethyst west. To the east, the green mountain slopes had turned a burgundy red in the low, warm slant of light. A cow bawled in the meadow, and a pair of crows flapped by overhead like hoarse-voiced black butterflies.

"Is this where I belong?"

A jumble of visions flickered through Joey's mind. Some were preposterous—too silly to accept or remember—but some were——

Will this be it? A new thing to start and go on from? Removed entirely from that kid who used to think he could——

A man now. A man named Josephson.

SEVENTEEN

TONY MARCHAND took his time with the set of engravings he was packing to ship to an electrotyper. One by one the rest of them left—the engravers and the two girls in the office—and he was alone.

He turned on the light under the glass surface of the box where the engravers examined the colored transparencies. From his coat, hung in one of a row of steel lockers, he took a manila envelope and fingered through its contents. There were newspaper clippings in it—every reference he'd been able to find in his assiduous reading of all the morning and evening papers for weeks after the night he had bent over Joey Tripp, listening to his partly coherent mutterings and outcries.

He left the clippings and took out of the envelope a sheet of notepaper. This he spread flat on the illuminated surface. It was the original of the note that Joey had written to his grandmother the morning he left town. The one that Tony Marchand had passed along to her had been a careful tracing of that original.

He laid a clean sheet of paper over the note. The light came up through both pieces, showing plainly the writing on the under one. He began tracing a letter or a group of letters at a time, shifting the upper sheet about so that Joey's authentic fist would lie beneath the proper spot.

> Baggott;
> If you followed the instructions in my second letter, you have now got the money in old bills, nothing larger than a ten and not in consecutave numbers. And not marked in any way. Also tied up in a strong package of wrapping paper. Now I will tell you what to do with this package.

He stopped and began tapping the butt end of the pen against the margin of ground glass.

Laurie . . . If this deal went through all right, he could buy her the things she wanted. And in return she would—— His flesh felt the warmth rising through it, almost as if she were actually there, letting her body press against his, making the little moaning love-sounds or else giggling softly against his lips as she slipped a hand inside his shirt and did mischievous little plucking things with her fingernails until he was so crazy that he was ready to—— She would push him away then. "If you want me so much—Dino gave Stella one for her birthday. Don't you think I'm as nice as Stella?"

One of these nights she wouldn't push him away. He'd show her he could give her things. She wouldn't have to needle him by making up to other guys, like she made a fuss over Joey Tripp when it looked like Joey was going to be in the money.

Tony scrubbed the knuckles of his right hand against his chin, almost as if he were measuring himself for a punch . . . Joey . . . It wasn't as if he was actually double-crossing a friend, when he did this to Joey. Matter of fact, Joey was in so deep that this wouldn't really matter—like a splash of water on a guy that's drowned already. And in a way it was doing something for Joey he wouldn't be able to do for himself—making the Baggott character pay for what he'd done.

Tony scrubbed harder with the knuckles. He wished he knew more details about just what had happened, so he could make these notes more convincing. From what he'd heard of Joey's mumblings, in his tortured sleep that night, and from a careful reading of the newspaper clippings, he had a good idea of what had happened. But only a general idea. If he had more details——

The door from the main stairway of the building banged open. Tony gripped the sheets of notepaper, ready to whip them out of sight, but he didn't need to. It was Phil.

The other Marchand was wearing the chino pants and the black leather jacket that were his favorite garb on or off his motorcycle. He was small and dark, like Tony, and he had a habit of letting his head loll back and looking at the world through hooded eyes. At times it made him seem coldly wise—at others, almost moronic. He let his limber body flow jointlessly onto a stool, leaned back, and spread his arms wide along the edge of the wrapping table.

"Where you want me to mail this one from, Tone? Jesus Herman Christ, not from Amsterdam again. I can't make a special run up there. I got to get some sleep tonight."

"No, anywhere over in Jersey this time." Tony bent over the glowing paper again. "I'll finish this in a little while."

"Jersey. Okay. Boy, was I stiff in the back after that other run. Amsterdam was just a quick stopover to mail your letter. We went all through the Finger Lakes that weekend. I was wishing I had Joey to give me a good rubdown when we got back." Phil hung a cigarette in one corner of his mouth. "What's the pitch, Tone? Who's this guy Baggott? What are you getting out of it?"

Tony painstakingly traced letters and words, speaking each word aloud as he finished writing it.

Be at your own house on Saturday night between seven and a quarter after. I will call you on long distance and tell you where to drive your car and what to do with the package.

He said to his brother then, "I'll call him from a booth somewheres. He won't know if it's long distance or not. You got to follow him on your poop-poop thing and make sure nobody is trailing along behind him to watch us or grab us. I'll drive the Chevvy to the spot ahead of time and give him the signal where to make the drop."

Phil lowered his eyelids and let smoke trickle gently out of his mouth. It crawled up each side of his nose in lazy, milky little spirals.

"Shakedown, huh, Tone? How much you taking this guy for?"

"That's my worry. You should only worry about how much you get out of it."

"So how much I got to worry about?"

"This time, a thousand bucks. Next time, more."

"Jesus Quincy Christ," Phil said.

Tony tapped the fountain pen against his front teeth. He thought, I could put something in about don't try to trap me or knock me off because I left a note to be opened in case of my death. But Baggott would spot that for a phony. Joey is on the lam from a murder rap. He wouldn't leave no "open only in case of my death" notes with nobody. That's like hanging out a neon sign: "Please Investigate Me. I'm Hot."

Tony worked briefly on an envelope—tracing, sealing, stamping.

"Okay, Phil boy. Mail it somewheres in Jersey."

EIGHTEEN

ON SATURDAY MORNING Joey attended to his chores. He milked the cows and turned them out to pasture and threw some feed to the chickens. After he cooked and ate a breakfast of oatmeal, bacon and eggs, and coffee, he hitched up the horses, forked the last of the raked-up hay onto the cart, drove to the barn, and pitched the load up into the hay mow.

He ate a lunch that was a duplicate of breakfast, washed his dishes in the sink, bathed in the bathroom tub, shaved, put on his one good suit, and took the bus to the village.

The main street was well lined with diagonally parked cars. This was the day of the week when farmers and their womenfolk from all around the neighboring mountain country came into Snowden. During the afternoon they would visit the stores along Main Street, buying clothes, supplies, hardware. In the evening they would crowd the movie house, where a special Saturday night program always included an adventure serial and a Western.

Joey walked on, unheeding, until the crowded sidewalks were behind him and he was climbing the hill toward the house at the top of Mount St. Cloud Street. The maples were all scarlet and tangerine now, and in the shadows the wind laid a tang along the skin like a dash of menthol.

He thought of going up the side drive to the kitchen door, but something of the lonely responsibility of his last few days stiffened his neck. He marched up the front steps and saw Finnegan sprawled in an Adirondack recliner. In the chair beside him, a woman in a smart-looking tweed coat was taking her ease.

Finnegan said to his companion, without giving Joey a second glance, "Some people have more brass than the knocker on the front door."

Joey didn't even hesitate. What can you do to a surly old peek-and-talk semi-invalid? Straight through the front door and the hall and into the kitchen he strode. Mrs. Wennergren and the maid whom Jane Cumberland had christened Old Goodie Grumbleguts were finishing the cleanup after the midday dinner.

Sandy turned from putting the last of the trays into the tall rack and saw him.

"So that's what you had in mind, Joey."

Her freckle-dusted face was enigmatic. She walked past him into the front hall. He followed her.

"If you swing on me again," he said, "no bloody nose this time. I'm set for you. I'll duck."

Suddenly the big smile lighted all her face. "No wonder you didn't tell me beforehand you were intending to move in on my father. I'd have forbidden it."

Joey said, "So——?"

"So you'd have tried it anyway and been turned away. You were, you know—if it hadn't been that his bad back went worse . . . How are things going, out there?"

"Good. I think so, anyhow. I got all the jobs done that had to be done right away."

Her eyes met his steadily. "Either you're growing up fast, Joey—or else your luck has turned . . . Let's go upstairs. Dad's in the room you used to have."

As he moved to follow her, Joey could see through the window of the living room that the woman on the front porch had risen and was coming toward the front door.

"Who is she?"

"Her name is Miss Garner. She has Mrs. Cumberland's room." One of her eyebrows went up a little.

Joey said, "Yeah. And I should only keep out of there . . . Look, Sandy. About that night." He fumbled for words.

"You were chicken. That's what you think . . . Joey, I have news for you. Your father and mother, before they died, then your grandmother afterward—whether you know it or not, they gave you standards. That's what made you run that night." Her warm, strong little hand touched his arm. "You're not tough and smart. You're one of us. You're one of the soft-headed traditionkeepers."

He shook his head. "I swiped those blanks from the priest. That did it. That made me one of *them*. The crooks. The killers."

"But you're not."

"Try to sell that idea to somebody, once I'm caught."

He waited for her to argue with him, to convince him.

The screen door from the front porch opened, and Miss Garner came in. She said, "I haven't met Mr. Josephson, Sandy."

As the girl spoke brief words of introduction, Joey glanced casually at the woman. She was not as old as he had thought when he had passed her on the way in. Her face was younger than her graying hair. Early middle age, say. A pleasant, easygoing expression, in spite of her interested, seeking eyes. At any rate, not the sort you'd expect to be a troublemaker—unless you remembered Jane Cumberland.

"Mr. Finnegan says you made a quick recovery," she said.

Joey nodded.

"I understand you know the country around Snowden very well."

"Pretty well," Joey said cautiously. "When I felt better I took long walks."

"Do you know anything about the famous sanatorium? The one that's been closed?"

"I've walked through the grounds. And I've read about it." He didn't say, When I was a kid, I rambled over every square foot of it.

"I'd like someone to show me around there. I'd really like to know those buildings before they're torn down—the little red house where Dr. Knowland started the first rest cure long ago, the other cottages, the famous lab."

"I guess you could find somebody to take you there."

"How would we go? Walk?"

"There's a short cut, down by Sullen Pond and up Maple Hill, but it's tough going for anybody who's here for the cure."

"I'm not here for the cure. I've been very busy, and it has me worn down. I wanted a good rest, and a friend of mine told me this was a wonderful place for it. I hate walking, just the same. We'll go in my car."

"That would be the best thing," Joey said, turning away to follow Sandy. She had already mounted the stairs.

"When can you make it? This afternoon?"

"Not me," Joey said quickly. "I've got chores to do in a little while, back out there on the farm I'm looking after. Sorry. Somebody else——"

"I'd expect to make it worth your while."

"That isn't it. If I could do you a little favor like that I wouldn't charge for it."

"Some other time?"

"I wouldn't be able to."

Miss Garner's smile was gentle and unruffled. "Tomorrow's Sunday. Surely you could spare me an hour or two."

"No. Honestly I couldn't." He started up the stairs. "I'm sorry."

She called after him, very softly. "Joey . . . Joey Tripp."

He came to an abrupt halt on the third step. The sound of his real name, spoken hardly above a whisper, was like an explosion in his ears.

III Evelyn

NINETEEN

"IN THE FIRST PLACE," Madge Yarrington said, "you haven't the slightest assurance you can find this young tough—nothing but a wild hunch. In the second place, even if you could find him, it's a wild-goose chase. You couldn't do a thing for or about him—except to hand him over to the police. And you could save yourself trouble by just telling them now about your hunch or your feminine intuition or whatever you want to call it."

Evelyn smiled. It amused her to see how Madge's manner was affected by her day's choice of clothing—or was it vice versa? The chill of this early morning in the mountains would be followed by the warmth of noon sun, and Madge had appeared for breakfast in a mannishly cut suit of black Italian silk, relieved from complete severity only by a frilly white jabot. The suit, undoubtedly tailor-made to Madge's precise instructions, looked incongruously masculine beside Lily Purcell's shapeless chemise dress, which made Lily look, Evelyn thought, as if she were always getting ready to sit down. Even after she had already sat down.

When Evelyn answered, the latent Southern-belle in her manner intensified in an automatic reaction against Madge's manfulness.

"I've thought the same thing, often, in the last several weeks. I've been just about ready to forget it, more than once."

"I would if I were you," Lily said. Her pudgy fingers wielded knife and fork. The sausage on her plate burst its crisp brown skin and sent up a mouth-watering aroma to join the bouquet that wheat cakes and coffee made with the tang of pine needles swept through the windows by the breeze off the lake.

"You wouldn't recognize him even if you found him," Madge said. "It's just plain silly for you to try to play F.B.I.-ette." She gave a basso rumble of laughter at her own verbal whimsy.

"Not *entirely* silly, darling." Evelyn's slight drawl lengthened itself perceptibly. "Shortly after I got this idea—bright or not though it may be—I looked up the boy's grandmother. That seemed a logical step."

"No parents?" Lily wagged her plump little jowls sympathetically.

"Squalid surroundings, I suppose. The old story. Rebellion against love-lessness and unbelonging and dirt and——"

"The grandmother is a dear old Viennese lady," Evelyn said. "It's just a little apartment, but she keeps it as neat as a handkerchief box. She's bewildered by the whole thing. The boy's home life was a good one. I got her to believe that I wanted to help him. She gave me a snapshot. I'll know him if I see him."

"You'd know a needle if you saw it," Madge said, "but how find it in the haystack? And what's the good, if it's rusted beyond use when you do find it?"

"But *is* it?"

"I made my opinion very clear at the final session last night, I think. Everyone's quite mad to believe we can salvage rotten apples. Once these young hoodlums have gone wrong we're crazy to count on saving them by lenience and understanding. Then the others run wild, because they're old enough to have a cynical realization that they can get away with murder—yes, murder!—and not be punished. Let the police use repressive measures at that point. And let society use exemplary punishment. I say your little thug deserves——"

"Madge! Please!" Lily swallowed a morsel of sausage hastily and waved small, sausagelike fingers in remonstrance. "I maintain that you're mis-taken about that, as I explained fully in my formal report. But I agree with you about Evelyn's self-appointed mission. These aren't matters for individual haphazard crusades. We need organization—studies by com-petent investigators, handling of cases by trained field workers. You *know* that, Evelyn."

Evelyn Baggott looked from one to the other. They've made up my mind for me, she thought. Until now I hadn't really formed a definite intention; I was just playing with the idea. But they've persuaded me what to do.

Madge had taken off her glasses after examining the menu. She let them drop, suspended by a broad black grosgrain ribbon that ran around the back of her neck, another touch that made her look pontifical, magisterial, gentlemanly. And Lily, pouring syrup generously over her wheat cakes, seemed as vaguely sweet as her dress—the amorphous dress that when she stood up gave no indication of which way she was pointed. Yet she spoke with the calm assurance of a high priestess who alone has all the answers to the sacred mysteries and the words of oracles.

"Oh, my boiling rebel blood," Evelyn said silently to herself, taking the last sip of her coffee.

Then there were good-bys and engagements for future meetings, and under a climbing sun she was driving east on Route 3 in the light-blue hardtop with which Chet had replaced the smashed red convertible. At times the forest closed in on both sides, making the road a cathedral aisle between giant green pews; at times on her left hand the view suddenly broadened out over Middle Saranac Lake and Lower Saranac Lake, with waves sharp and close and regular, like the teeth of a blue-steel file, and the distant low mountains knife-clear against the tall, transparent wall of sky.

A curve and a steep descent brought her suddenly down into the main street of Snowden an hour before noon. She had to circle the business district twice before she found a parking place, for shoppers were trooping in and out of the principal stores, The Snowden Hotel, a tall building that looked fairly modern, stood across the street, its lowest story a row of specialty shops. A logical spot, she thought, in which to begin her quest.

In the coffee shop—the Ski Room, walled with photomurals of winter sports scenes—she ordered tea and cinnamon toast. When the waitress laid the check on the table, Evelyn detained her.

"I have a young friend who came up here early this summer. He was ill. I'd like to look him up, but I haven't his address. Is there any directory of cottage sanatoriums?"

Immediately she began to feel as ridiculous as Madge Yarrington had tried to make her seem. *Even if the boy came here—even if I was right about that—he's probably long gone by now. And he wouldn't leave any forwarding address convenient for an amateur snooper like me. I'll just ask a few questions to relieve my meddling soul, and then I'll head for home, more or less contented.*

The girl shook her head and smiled. "Used to be an information bureau for health-seekers, and people would have a whole lot of houses to choose from. But now there ain't no use for no information bureau. Only a couple, three houses left in town that take sick folks."

"Do you know who they are?"

"Try Haddon's, on Catalpa Street. Number seventeen."

Halfway up the slope of Catalpa Street, Evelyn came on a young man in a faded blue denim shirt wrestling a hand lawn mower along the steep grassy bank that edged a high, level lawn.

"I'm looking for Haddon's," she said.

"I'm Ken Haddon. If you want a room, better see my mother. She's up there." He nodded toward the tall yellow house beyond the lawn.

"You might help me. I'm looking for a young friend. He's been ill.

Is he staying here?" She produced the snapshot of Joey Tripp from her purse.

"What's his name?"

"He might have changed it. He was in a little trouble."

Ken Haddon narrowed his eyes at the photograph and shook his head. "I've been here all summer. Home from college. He might be here in town and I wouldn't see him."

"Where else could I try?"

"Well, I don't— Oh, I'll tell you. Why don't you look up Ben Finnegan?"

"Is he young? About seventeen or eighteen but tall for his——"

"No, no. This is an old-timer around town. He's lived in our house sometimes—moves around when he gets discontented and fed up. He knows everybody, all the gossip, who comes and goes, what everyone does. Try him—if he doesn't know this friend of yours, nobody does."

"Where will I find Mr. Finnegan?"

"At McTaggart's, on Mount St. Cloud Street—if he hasn't had a hassle with somebody overnight and walked out in a huff." Ken Haddon gave his lawn mower a jocular shove.

TWENTY

AT SEVEN O'CLOCK that fine Saturday evening, Chester Baggott sat in his living room, waiting. He was sipping the second rye-and-soda of the two he had decided to allow himself.

What lay ahead of him would call for quick thinking and quick acting. He couldn't afford to let himself be muddled. In a way, he welcomed the fierce tension of these final minutes. It was better than a long drawn-out torment of not knowing. During the last few weeks, he had found that the up-beat hours of optimism alternated with times of morbid dread, when all the likelihood of final revelation weighed down upon his spirit unbearably.

Tonight let it be finished. He drained the last of the glass and wondered if he hadn't better set the quota at three drinks.

The trill of the telephone jerked him out of the chair and into the hall as if he'd been a mail sack snatched by the hook of a fast train.

Play it cagy, he reminded himself. Be surly but compliant. Let this kid think he's got you by the——

"Hello," he said gruffly into the instrument.

"Hi, darling."

"Ev!" He gulped air and rubbed the sudden aching stiffness at the base of his skull with his free hand. He didn't know whether to be relieved or angry at this interruption. "How are all the social welfare gals up there at Tupper?"

"All finished with our doings. I'm over at Snowden now. Chet, be proud of me!"

"I always am, honey. You're Mrs. Public Spirit herself. Say, right now I'm waiting for an important call, sweetie, so——"

"Not as important as this one, Chet."

"Well, I have a date coming up with a chap——"

"So have I. Guess who?"

"I wouldn't know. So if you'd hang up, I could call you back——"

"Chet, it's with Joey Tripp."

He shook his head, as if to clear it after being dazed by a solid punch on the chin. "With——? What was that?"

The gay triumph in her voice was discernible even in the thin sounds in the receiver. *"Now* you'll have to admit that I'm a good deductress. Is that a legitimate word? Anyway, I've heard of a 'seductress,' so why shouldn't 'deductress' be valid?"

"Are you sure it's Tripp?"

"You'll have to let me tell it my way, darling. To start at the beginning, I tried to figure out where that boy would run to. I thought about his early history—loss of parents and so on—and I decided what he wanted most was what Lily Purcell told us about—a feeling of security, of belonging. Well, then the blood on his handkerchief showed he was hurt—and it all clicked. When his father was ill, they'd gone to the mountains, full of hope. His childhood there, I understand from his grandmother, was a happy one. So he'd naturally think of returning there to be cared for. How am I doing so far?"

"Not bad." Baggott ran his tongue over his lips. "You still had a lot of ground to cover."

"When I drove over here from Tupper, armed with a photograph of Joey I'd got from his grandmother— What did you say, dear?"

"Nothing. I just cleared my throat."

"Well, I asked around, and I was directed to look up a character named Finnegan, who's supposed to be a regular old village bulletin board in pants. He turned out to be the local combination of Walter Winchell, Mrs. Grundy, and a tape recorder."

"And he knew the boy?"

"He recognized the photo at once. Of course he doesn't know it's Joey Tripp. He said some nasty things about him, but then he's the sort who hasn't a good word to say about anyone. I'll form my own opinion when I talk to the lad."

"What's he doing? What name is he traveling under?"

There was a brief pause before Evelyn said, "Chet, you told me you weren't vindictive."

Baggott's fingers closed on the telephone until they ached. "I'm not."

"So will you promise me not to say a word to Sergeant Lowery or anybody else about this until I've had a chance to talk to the boy?"

"I promise."

"Well, then . . . I'm to see him tomorrow morning."

"Where?"

"He and I are going to drive over to the abandoned san. The famous Snowden one, you know. The ostensible reason is so that he can show me the historic features of the place. That's what the people here at the house are supposed to think."

Baggott said slowly, "I'm against that."

"But, darling——"

"The boy is a killer. Keep away from him."

"I doubt he's a killer, Chet. From what I can see of him and from what I've heard by a little judicious questioning of these people, he's behaved very well, on the whole, except for one rather harmless escapade. And he's well liked."

"What escapade?"

"Some silly, lonesome married woman made a pass at the youngster. I can understand how it was. He's rather an attractive lad, and I suppose the patients marooned up here get pretty desperate——"

"You'd better watch it, Ev. Suppose you were alone with him, and he——"

"Don't be a fussbudget, dear! It wouldn't do him any good to harm me. It would only make things worse for him. I'll have a good talk with him tomorrow and let you know what I find out."

Baggott nodded in automatic agreement. Good God! *will* she let me know if that boy starts talking!

His voice was hoarse from the dryness of his throat. "Chances are the kid won't show. He's probably running again already. He'll disappear overnight."

"I doubt it. He knows if he did I'd be convinced of his guilt and I'd report at once that I'd seen him. He can't get out of these mountains on foot, and if he starts stealing cars again, they'll catch him very quickly. Anyway, I'm convinced he trusts me, because I could have turned him in already if I were going to. He'll keep his date tomorrow."

Baggott massaged the back of his neck again. He thought, Lucky you didn't take that third drink, man. You might have made yourself even stupider than you are. Come to! Act!

"How have I done so far?" Evelyn demanded.

"All I can say is, you're nothing short of pretty fair."

"Don't be so fulsome, Chet darling. You know I'm not really as wonderful as all *that*."

Half of his mind took him through the rest of the chat, with its routine little family witticisms. The other half was realizing . . . arranging . . . planning.

When Evelyn hung up, he glanced at his watch. There were five minutes left of the quarter-hour during which the note had said Tripp would call. Either the boy would go through with the extortion attempt in spite of Evelyn's discovery, hoping to make a fast getaway, or else he would lay off for the present and change his plans, hoping to keep her quiet and continue the blackmailing demands more safely later on. Or else he would try to clear himself by revealing everything to her tomorrow.

Baggott walked the living-room floor for five minutes. The telephone remained silent.

Snowden, eh? The letters had had postmarks from widely separated points. But that was easy enough for the boy to manage. Enclose each in a letter to someone. "Please mail this for me." Even so, it would leave a trail, of sorts, back to Snowden, if the police had ever got on the track.

Ev's discovery short-circuited all of that. If the telephone didn't ring, Baggott knew what he had to do. So give it five more minutes, to be absolutely certain.

He used the five minutes to get the twelve-gauge, double-barreled shotgun from the back of the closet. There was no need for more than the quickest checking. As he had told Lois Beviere, he had gone over it thoroughly in the spring, cleaning, oiling, making sure the shells were not too old.

He gave a last glance at his watch. This was it, then. The boy was playing it safe, staying pat until he could see Ev tomorrow. Would she win his confidence? Would he spill the whole thing to her, more eager to clear himself than to sell out for the dubious chance of blackmail?

A topcoat was justified; the evening had a bit of chill in it outdoors. He held the gun tight against one side of his body under the cover of the coat as he walked to his car in the dusk. He was pleased to see that Mrs. Denker had been driven indoors by the cool weather. There was no one to see him drive away.

Tony Marchand gave an impatient cluck with his dry tongue as the busy signal stuttered in his ear again. He hung up, heard the dime tinkle down through the machine, took it out of the coin release receptacle and laid it on the ledge of the booth where he had lined up three nickles in case the call went overtime. In a few minutes he tried again.

Still busy. That made about eight times. Tony glanced at his cheap Swiss wrist watch and checked it against the electric clock over the back bar of the soda fountain. The drugstore was one he'd never been in before, about two miles from Baggott's house. Except for that quick glance at the clock through the narrow glass of the closed folding door of the booth, he kept his face averted. No sense in letting anyone have too long a look at him, sitting there and sitting there, poking his dime into the hole over and over again with sweaty fingers.

What call could be holding Baggott up that long? Tony realized he was jiggling a foot as if it had been hitched to one of those electrical machines in a fun park. He tried to keep it quiet and couldn't. Even if somebody had called Baggott on business—but who would, at this time of a Saturday night? And even a business talk—would it take so *damn* long?

Tracing the call!

The words leaped into Tony's consciousness as if someone had spoken them aloud directly into his face. He'd been figuring it was perfectly safe. He knew nobody can trace one quick call on a dial phone. But suppose you knew somebody at the telephone company. Somebody who was in cahoots with you. Suppose they said, "Just leave your phone off the cradle, Baggott. Then this dopey guy will think you're talking on a long business call or something. He'll keep calling up, over and over again, and that'll give us plenty of time to get a fix on him. As soon as we find out where that call is coming from, you can go right down there and——"

Was it possible to do that? Tony didn't know. But if it *was* possible, and Baggott *did* know somebody who could do it, and if—and if—— He was out of the booth as fast as he could whack the door aside. Never mind stopping to grab at the row of coins. To hell with them. He'd called and called—how many times?—a dozen? Plenty enough for them to be outside now, maybe, waiting for him—ready to blast him or grab him and shove him into a car——

He was running. Wildly. Bumping against people who moped along the aisles of the drugstore to look at the counter displays, bolting past the smell of toast and bacon and coffee, where a white-capped soda man stared across the row of stools at his panicky flight. Out into the evening and sprinting down the street to his old Chevvy and into it and away, gasping with relief.

After a while he got control of himself and drove by a circuitous route to the street where Baggott lived. He cruised slowly the length of it, but there was no sign of a lurking motorcycle or of Phil.

When he got home, everyone was out. He sat and looked sullenly at television, turning the sound low and paying no attention to what was happening on the silly little screen. His mother came in from shopping with his unmarried sister, Lina.

"Where's Phil, dear?" his mother asked.

"On another motorbike run with the guys."

"Where to?"

"He didn't tell me."

"Oh, my . . . I wish he'd settle down and stop that crazy running around. And you too, Tone. If you'd just find some *nice* girl——"

"Okay, Mom. *Okay.*" He knew what she meant. Anyone but Laurie. *Love-moan against his lips. Hands——*

His mother went to bed. He sat watching the light-and-dark flicker of the screen, unendingly, uncomprehendingly. Now and then he went to the door of the apartment, opened it softly and listened. There was only silence, along the hallways and on the stairs, except for the dull hum of night-sound that in a big city is never stilled. Each time, he went back and resumed his vigil. Chill crept into the room.

The telephone rang.

The voice in the earpiece shrilled at him. "Jesus Clarence, Tone! how far do I follow this guy? To the North Pole?"

"What happened?"

"Long Island, you said. Long Island my asbestos fire suit."

"That's where I was going to tell him to go, Phil. Along the Grand Central and out the Jericho Turnpike, like I told you, until I gave him the signal for the drop. But I couldn't get him on the phone. Where are you now?"

"In Lake George! I'm quitting. I ain't gonna follow this guy all the way upstate and into Canada. He's on the lam."

"Why'd you go that far? Didn't I——?"

"You told me stay on his tail. So I stood on his tail. How'd I know he wasn't going to Long Island by way of somewheres else? By way of Montreal, looks like."

"Phil, did he make you?"

"No, no, no. On the Thruway, whenever there was a long stretch without an interchange, I went way to hell out of sight ahead of him. I didn't stick right behind him so he'd get suspicious. I'm not dumb!"

"All right, bud. Come on home. I got to study this out. We'll get him lined up, and next time we'll put it over right."

He hung up on Phil's griping. Next time. If Baggott was really headed for Canada, there'd never be a next time.

When he opened the door again and listened, he heard low voices drifting down the stairs from the floor above—male chuckles and a lighter voice—Laurie's. And a scuffling. And, low and throaty, the little love-moan.

He rested his wrist against the jamb and put his face against it. He sank his teeth in his own flesh, but it didn't hurt enough to give him any comfort.

TWENTY-ONE

FAR OFF WERE the blue swells of the mountain peaks; nearer, the pine-clad hills. Cobblestone, its shoulders mottled with scarlet and russet foliage, hid half the town.

Right here, under the toes of their shoes almost, rock fell sheer for a hundred feet. Leaning on the slender rail that was strung on wooden posts along the lip of the cliff, they could look straight down at the water of Sullen Pond.

"What do they call this spot, Joey?" Evelyn Baggott asked.

"Inspiration Point."

"I'd have thought they'd show more imagination—or inspiration. In other things they did so wonderfully well."

She was watching the boy's face whenever she could do so without embarrassing him. No sign of evil in it, she thought; but of course physiognomy's an exploded science. It's only by deeds that you can tell what a human being is. Yet the boy talks and acts like a normal, decent person. No sneakiness. No snarling resentment. He's worried, of course, because he doesn't know yet who I am or what I want.

He broke the silence, uncertainly. "People used to park here to look at the view." He jerked a thumb toward her car, standing a few yards away on the level expanse of blacktop between cliff lip and rising grassy ground. "The san staff, though, used to put their cars in a garage up there by the administration building. Would you like to go through the offices? They're not locked up, but there isn't much left to look at. Just an empty building."

She shook her head, smiling, and turned toward the lovely sweep of distant mountains. "I really didn't come here to see the san, Joey. I wanted to talk to you where we'd be sure no one would interrupt. Let's begin at the beginning: your parents died up here in this part of country, both within a year. What did it do to you? How did you feel about that?"

She tried to make her voice winning. Let us dig for the truth together, child, she tried to make the tone of it say. Truth is a wonderful thing— and interesting, too. Now if we can only get hold of a little piece of it and begin hauling it out of its hole—— A droll thought occurred to her. She had once seen a mother robin showing its offspring how to listen with cocked head for the sound of an earthworm burrowing, then drive hard with sharp beak to draw out the resistant strand of living provender. She banished the thought at once as amusing but trivial and unworthy. After all, this boy's social salvation was a serious matter. Always assuming, of course, that he was *not* a criminal.

"You were lonely, naturally," she said. "Lost. Resentful, perhaps. Weren't you, Joey?"

He ran his fingers—strong, square-tipped, competent fingers, she noticed—along the wooden rail, to and fro.

"Who are you?" he said.

"Does it matter?"

"Yes. You're going to try to get me to talk."

"I am. For your own good."

There was vinegar in the boy's voice. "I finally met a few people I'd believe that about. Not many."

"Not me?"

"I don't know you."

"Won't you trust me?"

"No."

"Who do you think I am?"

"Yesterday I thought maybe you were a policewoman."

"Today?"

"You talk more like a social service worker."

"I'm not either of those."

He rested his elbows on the wooden rail, looking gloomily down the face of the cliff. "It doesn't matter much. What are you going to do? Turn me in?"

"No . . . The important thing is, what are *you* going to do, Joey?"

"I thought a lot about it overnight, since you spoke to me. Before that I'd been thinking maybe I'd try to stay lost up here. Start a new life doing what I'm doing now. On a farm . . . It wouldn't work."

"Why not?"

"What would I ever get to be but a hired man? I wouldn't have any land. Nothing but a pair of hands. Anybody could replace me. This morning Mr. McTaggart told me there's a relative of his coming over from Burlington to work his farm while he's laid up. So he won't need me any more. And it wouldn't matter if I went somewhere else. Always I'd be waiting for somebody to find out about me. Like you."

"Then what *will* you do, Joey?"

"I've been thinking about it most of the night. I'm going to turn myself in. I'll get it finished off, one way or the other."

"Have you mentioned that decision to anyone else yet?"

"No."

I must tell Lily Purcell! she thought. He *did* talk. I was with this boy—this young man—at the moment when he burst the chrysalis and turned from a pupa—is that the right biological term?—into an adult organism. Psychologically, that is. Most rewarding. Worth all the trouble I took to come over here and look him up. And won't Chet and that able Sergeant Lowery be properly chagrined! I'll have to be very considerate of their feelings and not show the *least* little sign of triumph, of course.

She said gently, "I'm going to ask you, just this once for all time, Joey: did you kill that other boy—that Sid Keene?"

He answered promptly. "No. I never met him, alive or dead."

"Then I'll do all I can to help you clear yourself, if you'll tell me the straight of it."

He moved his shoulders slightly. "It's going to take some doing to clear me."

She said, "I'm so glad you've made your decision to do it this way, Joey. So very glad. Do you know why? . . . It's because my name isn't really Miss Garner. Or rather, that's my maiden name. I'm Evelyn Baggott. Mrs. Chester Baggott."

She enjoyed the bewilderment in his eyes as the crew-cut head came sharply up and turned toward her. She had known she would surprise him—had waited with a tickle of expectant enjoyment for the moment when he would learn she was the wife of the man whose car he had taken for his youthful fling that had ended so disastrously—but she had no idea that the impact would be so overpowering. His eyes grew wider until white showed all around the irises. His teeth were bared in an animal snarl. His hands came up, the strong fingers hooked.

Good God! she thought. Chet was right! What a horrible mistake I've made! This *is* a killer. And I'm alone with him! What incredible folly——

The boy was coming at her with a tigerish bound. In the moment that she realized he wasn't looking at her at all but past her at someone else, that he was brushing by her in his flight, a familiar voice said harshly, "Hold it, Tripp. Try to run and these slugs'll rip your belly out."

"Chet!" she gasped. "Oh, thank God! I'm so glad that I phoned you last night."

She went straight to him with a kiss of love and gratitude, noticing the shotgun and relieved to have its comforting protection. As she lifted her lips to his, she was already phrasing in her mind the words of honest admission. You were right, darling—and this is your territory now. I'm just a confused ex-rebel, quite willing to let a man of action apply conventional and forceful methods to the situation—for this once, anyway.

The kiss never reached his mouth. He shouldered past her, penning the boy between himself and the railing, moving in on him fast.

The boy stood straight, his face a mask of doom, waiting. He said rapidly, "Mrs. Baggott, he's going to kill me, like he killed the others. Crys was his floozy——"

Chet's roar drowned his voice. "Keep your mouth shut!"

The boy made a sudden dash to one side, but Chet was ready for him—closed in, darted the barrel of the shotgun at the boy's face as though it had a bayonet on it, and when his hands went up to catch it, swung the butt of the gun under and up at his groin.

The boy's reflexes were young and fast, or he may have expected the move. He brought a knee up to guard himself, turning a little. The gun-butt struck the side of the knee with a dull whacking sound.

Evelyn winced, remembering the day she had played field hockey on the college team and a brawny girl had larruped her in that vulnerable spot with a wildly swung stick. She could still remember the crippling agony.

The boy tried to run, but the leg crumpled under him and he went down. Chet swung the gun again. The impact of wooden stock against skull was sharper, clearer.

"Chet, don't *kill* him!" Of course the boy had been lying, desperately trying by a last foolish accusation to shift the blame to someone else for what he had done.

She saw that Chet had stooped and was using one hand in powerful lifts to turn the boy's body over and over, like a roll of loose carpeting, toward the railing and beneath it to the edge of the cliff.

Even as she ran toward him she felt what some fleeting, truth-seeking instant of awareness told her was a morbid gratification—a pleasure in the realization that her man had gone berserk at the threat to her safety, had flamed into the rage that sends a lynching mob of the best citizens to execute a man who has harmed a decent woman.

She caught his arm. "Chet! Darling! Leave him to the law."

He tried to thrust her away, but her moment of shock and humility had passed now. It would be strange indeed if the habit of years deserted her in this crisis. She must be the wiser one again—the keeper of the larger truths.

She held tight to him, lifting, pulling him back from the brink where the boy's body lay.

He straightened up slowly and turned toward her, and she saw his eyes more clearly. They were reddened and sunken and— The only word that came to her mind was, "Alien."

Why, he's in shock, she thought. And no wonder, poor dear. Talk to him. Get him back to himself.

"How did you come up, Chet?"

"Drove."

"I didn't see your car as we came in here. Did you just arrive in the very nick of time?"

"I put it in the garage up there. Out of sight."

"When?"

"Early this morning."

She noticed how dead his voice sounded. He was tired, naturally, from the long drive. Without sleep. And filled with worry for her.

"But why didn't you come to the house, dear? I told you where I was staying. Then all of this would have been avoided. We'd have——"

Her voice dwindled and stopped. He had taken a step toward her, shifting the shotgun so that now he held it in both hands, balanced across his body, as he had held it before whipping the butt against the defenseless young——

"No!" she said.

She stood quite still, and the calm, detached part of her mind was acutely aware of the wide peace of the morning—the Sabbath hush on the hills and trees as the wind died down for a moment—all as restfully quiescent as the body of the boy on the edge of the cliff.

She said, driven mercilessly by the need to know the truth, "Chester, what was that girl to you—the one who was found dead in your car?"

When he spoke, his voice was low and hoarse, and he seemed to be talking in answer to his own thoughts. "They'll find his body down there. Smashed up from the fall. They'll say he jumped. They'll say he realized that he was in a hopeless spot."

She shook her head wonderingly. "But, Chet . . . you know that I'll have to tell them what really——"

He took another small step toward her, setting his feet solidly on the blacktop, hunching his shoulders. And she knew.

There was no need, there was no time, to pick it out in detail—the certainty that whoever found the bodies would say the boy had killed her and then in despair had killed himself by jumping. All of it—whole and horrible—was clear in her mind in one glimpse, like a single glance across to the far mountains—as if the landscape of her life, hers and Chet's, was revealed by a sudden shaft of light as a painting of mad, satanic shapes, the lunatic daubings of some depraved——

Was it shock or pride or wild rebellion that kept her from running and screaming, or was it the knowledge that he was so much faster and stronger than she that flight was an undignified folly?

And then the time for a choice, conscious or instinctive, was past. The gun-stock was flashing toward the side of her head, so fast that her eyes could report it to her brain, but the brain could not tell her what to do, her muscles could not stir, her lids could not even blink before the darkness hit her.

TWENTY-TWO

HE CAME BACK to agony. His head was a ball of pain. His leg sent spasms of torment the length of his side. The roughness against his face was a minor misery. Paving of some sort. Blacktop.

Memory revived. Mustn't move. He didn't need to remember the chickens crouching when the hen made the sound that said, "Hawk!" He lay motionless, waiting to know what came next, waiting for the gun-butt on his head again.

He could see the gun now. Baggott had it in his hands. He was talking to his wife. Something about somebody being found at the bottom of the cliff. "They'll say he jumped." Who?

Me!

Joey very gently pushed up with his hands. His back hit the railing. He edged forward, tried to get his legs under him. Evelyn Baggott's car was only a few yards away. But the pain almost made him sick. His left knee was useless. He sank on his belly again.

Then he saw Baggott swing the gun, and there was a sound like a butcher slapping a lamb chop with the flat of his cleaver, and the woman went down.

Baggott turned and walked toward Joey, paralleling the railing. No use to play chicken-in-the-dust now. No use to try to hop away on one leg. Just wait. That's all you can do.

What do you think of when you're falling a hundred feet? Maybe you won't know. Maybe he'll knock your brains out first, to be certain.

Baggott's feet were almost to him when the girl's voice called, "Joey!"

Baggott halted and turned, looking back. Sandra came over the grassy rise on a little path between the clumps of beech trees. It was a path that wound down steeply to Sullen Pond and so by a short cut to the village.

Joey opened his mouth to shout, "Sandy, go back! Run!" He closed it again.

Worse than useless. He had learned how ruthlessly quick Baggott could be. She wouldn't get a hundred feet down the path before being overtaken. And Baggott couldn't let her live to tell that she had seen him here.

Sandy said, "Why, you're not—— I'm sorry. I expected to find a friend of mine here."

Joey knew then that she hadn't seen him yet, hadn't had time to notice Evelyn Baggott's inert form, hidden from her by the car. He saw Baggott lean negligently against the railing, heard him say, "I may be able to tell you where he is. Give me an idea what he looks like. Come on down here."

She made her way down to the blacktop, slender and young and straight, the pony tail bobbing gently to the spring of her step.

The reviving breeze whipped across the flat area, whirling a scurry of yellow beech leaves before it, sending a rustle through all the trees.

Joey's dry mouth formed words of thanks. The wind noises covered the sound he made as he used his elbows and his one good leg to snake himself to the side of the car.

Baggott's attention was fixed on Sandy. He was intent on talking her nearer, getting her within reach of his big hands. And she was coming. Beneath the car, between the wheels, Joey could see her slim legs draw closer.

The door of the car was open. Evelyn Baggott hadn't slammed it when she got out. The car was pointed directly at the spot where Baggott stood, waiting for Sandy to reach him. Joey's mind worked with desperate speed, measuring distances and times. He could try to haul himself awkwardly into the car, get seated somehow, start it, back and turn—all of this with a loaded shotgun a few yards away.

But he was acting ahead of thought. He had his left hand on the steering post, pulling himself up just enough to reach the key in the ignition lock with his right hand. He twisted it, felt the engine catch softly. He grabbed the shift lever, swung it from the parking to the drive position, and then whipped his hand down to the accelerator pedal, pressing with all his strength.

Engine roar and scream of rubber against the blacktop—wild lurch forward—his left hand still gripping the steering post, his right jammed down on the pedal, for the few long seconds that he dared hold on.

Then he let go and sprawled on the blacktop, whirling and scraping along its harshness, seeing the door flap almost closed like the wing of a hawk folded back against the bird's body as it launches into a murderous dive.

He saw and heard the car crash into the railing where Baggott stood, and then he saw Baggott.

Baggott—only a few feet away, standing erect.

The man had heard the car sounds in time. He had spun and side-stepped. Only a foot or two. But enough.

Joey, glimpsing him in the clear, as the hood and fender of the car smashed through the railing just alongside him, could taste dust and blood in his mouth and the bitterer savor of failure. Looking up from the ground, almost at the man's feet, Joey could see plainly on his face the ugly grimace of alarm, realization, and rage.

What happened next he always remembered afterward as if it all had been in the slowest of slow motion, although it took only the time of a single breath.

The door waved out like an opened wing as the impact with the railing checked the forward speed of the car a little. Casually, as a hand would flap at an annoying insect, it swept wide, caught Baggott across the middle, and carried him on through the space where the bumper and hood had smashed an opening.

In the next moment, car and man were gone. A long, diminishing shriek disturbed the rustle of the beech leaves. The crash of metal that came up from below, seconds later, seemed like an afterthought.

Sandy was on her knees beside him. "Joey, are you hurt?"

He shook his head. "Not too bad . . . He tried to kill me."

She pointed at the still form, plainly visible on the blacktop now that the car was gone.

"What——"

"His wife. He killed her. Because she found out."

She held his head tight against her breast. He could feel her shaking. "It's dreadful . . . But this clears *you,* Joey. Thank God for that."

He didn't say anything. He let her, let both of them, have that moment. Then he moved a little and found he could work his leg after a fashion. He stood up, using the support she eagerly gave him.

"How did you get here, Sandy?"

"Finnegan. He always has to talk. He hinted and then he came out with it. About the picture she showed him. So I knew she was someone who knew who you really are, and I hurried up here to warn you about her if it wasn't too late. But now you're all right!"

He had to tell her. "I'm not in the clear, Sandy."

"Why not? Of course you are. This proves he was the one——" She checked herself.

"It proves that maybe I killed both him and her when they caught me."

"But I can tell the police that I——"

"What can you tell them? They'd say you're my sweetheart and you'd say anything to get me off. And just what *did* you see? You saw her lying there, and you saw me knock him over the cliff."

She held tight to him for a while. "There must be some way." For the first time since he had known her, he saw tears in her eyes. "Joey, there *has* to be some way."

He pressed his cheek against hers. "One of us better go down and get the police."

She disengaged herself from his arms and went to where Evelyn Baggott was lying. She bent and took hold of the lax wrist. At the touch the woman jerked her arm away.

Sandy's cry of joy rose thin and clear above the gusty bustle of the tree branches. "Joey! She's alive!"

TWENTY-THREE

FRIDAY WAS A TOUGH DAY at the supermarket. People came from all over that section of the city to put in a week's orders. The cartons of groceries, checked through and paid for, were trundled out the side entrance on big wheeled frames built of pipe lengths, to stand at the curb while the white-aproned boys loaded them into the panel trucks for delivery.

Joey made it a point to get there early, before the really rugged afternoon rush would make a madhouse of the place. He found Aaron Whiteside, frowning, in a huddle with Nick Pappas, who drove one of the trucks.

Aaron wore the air of efficient desperation that was characteristic of him on Fridays. The coat of his neat gray flannels was off, and the rolled-up sleeves of his clean white shirt had come half unrolled already.

He gave Joey an irascible up-and-down glance. "I suppose you'll want your job back, Tripp. No jail sentence?"

"They didn't press any charges."

"Did they give you a citation?"

"No. But they were glad to crack the case."

"How's your head feel? For size, I mean."

Joey looked at him steadily. "I'll be content with a little peaceful hard labor."

"You've come to the wrong shop," Aaron Whiteside said. "Hard labor, yes. Peace, no. Not on a day like this. And get one thing straight. We've had guys come in here with records worse than yours. Not so splashy—no front pages—but real bad. And they made good."

Nick Pappas said, "Look, Aaron. Harry and two other guys out with flu, and I got to keep that heap moving."

"You heard the man, Joey," Aaron Whiteside said. "You know the ropes. Get the lead out of your pants and take charge here. There's some new guys to help you and you'll have to show them what to do . . . Coming. Coming!" He trotted into the delivery entrance, pressing the heel of one hand to his forehead.

Joey went in and hung his coat in a locker. Suddenly it was the window of a day coach, and he was looking through it and seeing her standing on the platform, slim and straight as one of the pine trees of her mountains, watching his train pull out with him and the detective aboard—the one who was taking him down here to the city for the hearing.

The gay smile wasn't on her face—only the still, serious look. He knew what she was thinking. *They say they'll come back for you, but they never do. Never . . . Never.*

And she was facing it steadily and bravely, in full awareness, knowing that was how it was going to be.

She's smart, Joey thought. Wise. I mean, she's got real wisdom. More than I'll ever have, after all I've been through. She's got the courage to face the truth. And intelligence.

And baby! how wrong she is.